THE MEMOIR OF

Lieutenant Dumont,

1715-1747

Sauvage a la chasse

THE MEMOIR OF

Lieutenant Dumont,

1715-1747

A SOJOURNER IN THE FRENCH ATLANTIC

Jean-François-Benjamin Dumont de Montigny

TRANSLATED BY *Gordon M. Sayre*

EDITED BY *Gordon M. Sayre and Carla Zecher*

Published for the
Omohundro Institute of Early American History and Culture,
Williamsburg, Virginia, by the
University of North Carolina Press, Chapel Hill

The Omohundro Institute of Early American History and Culture is sponsored jointly by the College of William and Mary and the Colonial Williamsburg Foundation. On November 15, 1996, the Institute adopted the present name in honor of a bequest from Malvern H. Omohundro, Jr.

The Memoir of Lieutenant Dumont has received subventions both from the general publications fund of the Newberry Library, Chicago, and from the University of Oregon Humanities Center.

Library of Congress Cataloging-in-Publication Data
Dumont de Montigny.
[Regards sur le monde atlantique, 1715–1747. English]
The memoir of lieutenant Dumont, 1715–1747 : a sojourner in the French Atlantic / Jean-François-Benjamin Dumont de Montigny ; translated by Gordon M. Sayre ; edited by Gordon M. Sayre and Carla Zecher.
p. cm.
Includes bibliographical references and index.
ISBN 978-0-8078-3722-1 (cloth : alk. paper)
1. French—North America—History. 2. France—Colonies—America—History. 3. North America—History—Colonial period, ca. 1600–1775.
I. Sayre, Gordon M. (Gordon Mitchell), 1964– II. Zecher, Carla, 1959–
III. Omohundro Institute of Early American History & Culture. IV. Title.
E18.82.D8613 2012
973.2—dc23

2012016643

The paper in this book meets the guidelines for permanence and durability of the Committee on Production Guidelines for Book Longevity of the Council on Library Resources. The University of North Carolina Press has been a member of the Green Press Initiative since 2003.

16 15 14 13 12   5 4 3 2 1

ACKNOWLEDGMENTS

The project of editing and translating Dumont de Montigny's memoir has continued for almost a decade and has involved a team of friends and colleagues who have all shared, in smaller or larger parts, the excitement of rediscovering not just a document but a life from the eighteenth-century French Atlantic.

Preparation of this translation was supported by a Collaborative Research grant from the National Endowment for the Humanities. Any views, findings, conclusions, or recommendations expressed in this publication do not necessarily reflect those of the National Endowment for the Humanities.

A separate NEH grant supported preparation of the French edition, published in 2008 by Les éditions du Septentrion of Quebec. Shannon Lee Dawdy, of the University of Chicago, was the third member of the editorial team for the French edition, and her expertise in New Orleans history and archaeology, as well as her contributions to the introduction and notes, were invaluable. We also wish to thank historian and publisher Denis Vaugeois and editor-in-chief Gilles Herman at Septentrion.

Other colleagues in Quebec, Thomas Wien and Stéphanie Charland of the Université de Montréal and Catherine Desbarats and Allan Greer of McGill University, provided valuable assistance with research on aspects of Dumont's time in Canada.

At the Newberry Library in Chicago, James Grossman provided guidance for the project in numerous ways, Karen Christianson assisted with editing, and Emily Kelley drew the maps of Dumont's travels. Chicago-area scholars also pitched in, notably Lydia Cochrane and Ellen McClure, who reviewed drafts of the translation, and Lisa Meyerowitz, who assisted with editing.

Many colleagues working on colonial Louisiana history and archaeology took an interest in Dumont and contributed expertise and hospitality. These include Jim Barnett and Smoky Joe Frank of Natchez and Vincas Steponaitis of the University of North Carolina, who has conducted many seasons of archaeology there. Jordan Kellman and Carl Brasseaux of the University of Louisiana at Lafayette hosted a talk about Dumont's narrative there and a visit to the Atchafalaya Basin. George Milne shared some of his work on the Natchez Indians. Erin Greenwald of the Historic New Orleans Collection shared some of her valuable research connected with her translation of the manuscript by Marc-Antoine Caillot, a contemporary of Dumont's, which will appear shortly after this volume.

Colleagues in France who contributed to the project include historians Gilles Havard and Gilles-Antoine Langlois and archivists Roseline Claerr and Yoann Brault, who found documents connected with Dumont's family and career. Brigitte Nicolas assisted with the archives in Lorient. A special thanks to Arnaud Balvay for generous help with research on Dumont and Natchez.

At the University of Oregon, Emily Thomas provided research assistance, and Fabienne Moore helped with the translation. James Walker of Eugene shared his comprehensive knowledge of early American cartography. A large part of the translation was carried out during a sabbatical leave from the University of Oregon in 2007–2008.

At the Omohundro Institute, we would like to thank editors Nadine Zimmerli and Fredrika J. Teute, manuscript reviewers Catherine Desbarats and Andreas Motsch, as well as research fellow Alexandre Dubé and copy-editor Kathy Burdette.

CONTENTS

LIST OF ILLUSTRATIONS

ABBREVIATIONS AND SHORT TITLES

ADM—Archives départementales du Morbihan, Hennebont

ANF—Archives nationales de France, Paris

   AC, C13A—Archives des colonies, Correspondance générale—
   Louisiane

ANOM—Archives nationales d'outre-mer, Aix-en-Provence

   DFC—Dépôt des fortifications des colonies

BNF—Bibliothèque nationale de France

FFL—Carl A. Brasseaux, *France's Forgotten Legion: A CD-ROM
Publication: Service Records of French Military and Administrative
Personnel Stationed in the Mississippi Valley and Gulf Coast Region,
1699–1769* (Baton Rouge, La., 2000).

FFLa—Glenn R. Conrad, ed., *The First Families of Louisiana*, 2 vols.
(Baton Rouge, La., 1970).

HJEFL—Jean-Baptiste Bénard de la Harpe, *The Historical Journal of the
Establishment of the French in Louisiana*, ed. Glenn R. Conrad, trans.
Joan Cain and Virginia Koenig (Lafayette, La., 1971)[1]

Histoire de la Louisiane—Antoine-Simon Le Page du Pratz, *Histoire de
la Louisiane: Contenant la découverte de ce vaste pays; sa description
géographique; un voyage dans les terres; l'histoire naturelle, les mœurs
coûtumes et religion des naturels, avec leurs origines . . .* , 3 vols. (Paris,
1758).

1. This book is a translation of *Journal historique de l'établissement des Français à la
Louisiane* (New Orleans, 1831), which lists no author. Conrad explains in a note at the start
of the text that both Marcel Giraud and Marc de Villiers du Terrage believed this book to be
the work, not of Bénard de la Harpe, who is referred to in the third person in the text, but
of a royal geographer, Chevalier Jean de Beaurain. See *HLF*, III, 399, and Villiers du Terrage, *Histoire de la fondation de la Nouvelle Orléans, 1717-1722* (Paris, 1917), 24. Mildred
Mott Wedel, however, explains that although one of three manuscript copies of the text,
held at the Library of Congress, bears the name of Jean de Beaurain, the other two, at the
American Philosophical Society, Philadelphia, and the U.S. National Archives, Washington,
D.C., do not. She attributes the text to Bénard de la Harpe. See Wedel, "J.-B. Bénard, Sieur
de la Harpe: Visitor to the Wichitas in 1719," *Great Plains Journal*, X, no. 2 (Spring 1971),
37–70 n. 16.

HLF—Marcel Giraud, *Histoire de la Louisiane française/A History of French Louisiana,* 5 vols.[2]

HNAI—Raymond Fogelson, ed., *Handbook of North American Indians,* XIV, *Southeast* (Washington, D.C., 2004).

JR—Reuben Gold Thwaites, ed., *The Jesuit Relations and Allied Documents: Travels and Explorations of the Jesuit Missionaries in New France, 1610–1791; The Original French, Latin, and Italian Texts, with English Translations and Notes,* 73 vols. (Cleveland, 1896–1901).

LHQ—*Louisiana Historical Quarterly,* vols. I–XL (New Orleans, 1917–1957).

Margry—Pierre Margry, ed., *Découvertes et établissements des Français dans l'ouest et le sud de l'Amérique septentrionale (1614–1754): Mémoires et documents originaux . . . ,* 6 vols. (Paris, 1875–1886).

Mémoires historiques—Jean-François-Benjamin Dumont de Montigny and Jean-Baptiste Le Mascrier, *Mémoires historiques sur la Louisiane: Contenant ce qui y est arrivé de plus mémorable depuis l'année 1687 jusqu'à présent . . . ,* 2 vols. (Paris, 1753).

MPA—Dunbar Rowland, A. G. Sanders, and Patricia K. Galloway, eds. and trans., *Mississippi Provincial Archives, 1729–1740: French Dominion,* 5 vols. (1927–1984).

"Poème"—Dumont de Montigny, "Etablissement de la province de la Louisiane, poème composée de 1728 à 1742 par Dumont de Montigny," ed. Marc de Villiers du Terrage, *Journal de la société des Américanistes de Paris,* N.S., XXIII (1931), 273–440.

SHD—Service historique de la défense, ministère de la Défense française, locations at Château de Vincennes, Lorient.

---

2. Volume I, *The Reign of Louis XIV, 1698–1715,* is cited in the English translation by Joseph C. Lambert (Baton Rouge, La., 1974). Volume II, *Years of Transition, 1715–1717,* and volume V, *The Company of the Indies, 1723–1731,* are cited in the English translations by Brian Pearce (Baton Rouge, La., 1974, 1993). Volume III, *L'époque de John Law, 1717–1720* and volume IV, *La Louisiane après le système de Law, 1721–1723,* have not been translated and are cited in the original French (Paris, 1966, 1974).

THE MEMOIR OF

Lieutenant Dumont,

1715-1747

INTRODUCTION

In the opening lines of his manuscript memoir, Jean-François-Benjamin Dumont de Montigny addressed the patron to whom he had dedicated the manuscript and for whom he had carefully penned its 443 pages: "I have written it as clearly as I could, so as to conceal nothing from you, Monseigneur, of the events that took place in that distant land," the French colony of Louisiana. Dumont then compared himself to a fictional character: "All I can say to Your Excellency is that it is a French Robinson Crusoe who comes to throw himself at your feet and to make a complete confession of his life, from 1715 until this year, 1747." Dumont's real life as a colonial officer matched Crusoe's tale for its pathos and misadventures, but unlike Crusoe, Dumont did not live alone, and the setting for his tale was no imaginary island but the ports and ships, forts, towns, and backcountry of a vast French Atlantic world that touched four continents and countless islands. Dumont crossed the Atlantic six times between Quebec, Louisiana, Saint-Domingue, and the colonial entrepôts of western France, along the military and commercial circuits that traced the first French empire onto the globe. Yet his tale has remained little known until now, when his autobiographical memoir is published in English for the first time.

In the last two decades, many historians have focused on the Atlantic world as a geographical and ideological framework for understanding the transnational and maritime forces of the early modern period, and few primary sources portray the French Atlantic in such grand scale and rich detail as this eighteenth-century manuscript memoir.[1] However, Dumont did not

1. Quotation from original manuscript [2]. Atlantic world studies have spawned new journals, textbooks, and doctoral programs in history and inspired literary scholars to break down the institutional divisions between English and American literature. Despite foundational work by Jacques Godechot and Pierre Chaunu, however, the movement has been weaker in France than in Britain and the United States. See Cécile Vidal, "La nouvelle histoire atlantique en France: Ignorance, réticence, et reconnaissance tardive," *Nuevo Mundo / Mundos Nuevos* (Sept. 24, 2008), at nuevomundo.revues.org/42513. A related article in English is Vidal, "The Reluctance of French Historians to Address Atlantic History," *Southern Quarterly*, XLIII, no. 4 (Summer 2006), 153–189. Several of the most prominent studies of the French Atlantic world have been written in English by Canadian and U.S. historians, such as Kenneth J. Banks, *Chasing Empire across the Sea: Communications and the State in the French Atlantic, 1713–1763* (Montreal, 2002); and James Pritchard, *In Search of Empire: The French in the Americas, 1670–1730* (Cambridge, 2004). Early studies include Jacques

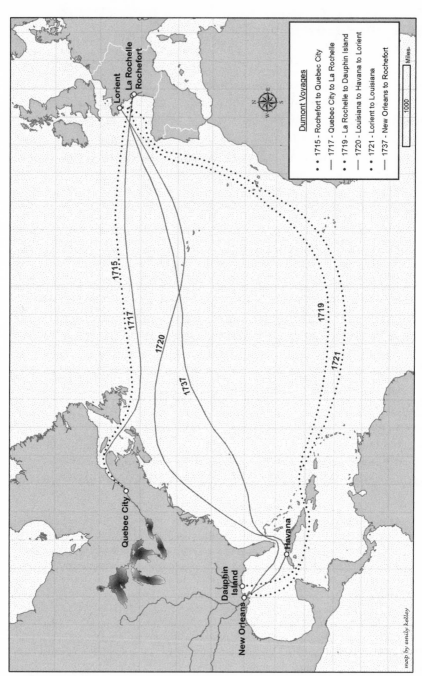

Map 1. Dumont Voyages: Atlantic. Drawn by Emily Kelley

Dumont Voyages

- 1715 - Rochefort to Quebec City
- 1717 - Quebec City to La Rochelle
- 1719 - La Rochelle to Dauphin Island
- 1720 - Louisiana to Havana to Lorient
- 1721 - Lorient to Louisiana
- 1737 - New Orleans to Rochefort

1000 Miles

map by emily kelley

describe a coordinated system of imperial power so much as lament the weaknesses and lost opportunities of the French colony in Louisiana, as well as document the many forms of resistance to metropolitan control— soldiers who deserted the ranks, native Americans who rose up against the French, and officials who embezzled supplies and smuggled trade goods. The memoir acquires such a transatlantic scope because Dumont did not remain in America but returned to France, and his account of his subsequent ten years in Brittany tells us not only what life was like for a returning colonial but also about the very important role that Lorient—founded as the main port of French East Indies trade in 1666—played in a ragged-edged but rapidly expanding Atlantic network that also extended into the Indian Ocean. As an aging, weather-beaten officer, Dumont looked back across the Atlantic toward America and wrote of honor in the face of misfortune, indulgence amid penury, and abundance reduced suddenly to desperation.[2]

Dumont's father, Jacques-François Dumont, had been a lawyer in the Paris *parlement,* or high court, and four of Dumont's five older brothers achieved the same status.[3] In 1715, family connections to Louis-Claude Le Blanc, who was serving on the council of war during the regency of Philippe d'Orléans, secured for the eighteen-year-old Dumont his first commission in the colonial military, and he sailed from Rochefort for a two-year stint in Quebec.[4] When he returned to France in 1719, enthusiasm for the colony of Louisiana was at its highest point, and Le Blanc and Charles-Louis-

---

Léon Godechot, *Histoire de l'Atlantique* (Paris, 1947); Pierre Chaunu, *L'Amérique et les Amériques* (Paris, 1964); Pierre Chaunu and Huguette Chaunu, *Séville et l'Amérique aux XVIe et XVIIe siècles* (Paris, 1977). Among the textbooks that have responded to the need for courses on the theme are Alison Games and Adam Rothman, eds., *Major Problems in Atlantic History: Documents and Essays* (Boston, 2008); Jorge Cañizares-Esguerra and Erik R. Seeman, eds., *The Atlantic in Global History, 1500–2000* (Englewood Cliffs, N.J., 2006); Douglas R. Egerton et al., *The Atlantic World* (Wheeling, Ill., 2007).

2. For Dumont's life in Brittany, see Chapters 8–10, below.

3. The *parlement de Paris* was the supreme court of appeals in ancien régime France. Lawyers who had been admitted to argue cases were *avocats au parlement,* whether at Paris or one of twelve other parlements throughout France. For more on Dumont's brothers, see the section on the Dumont family, below.

4. See original manuscript [5]. Upon the death of Louis XIV in 1715, the dauphin, his great-grandson Louis XV, was just five years old, and thus the king's power was conferred upon the regent Philippe, duc d'Orléans. During the regency, the ministers, or secretaries of state in charge of the various branches of royal administration, were replaced by councils of state, a system referred to as the *polysynodie,* which lasted until 1718. Claude Le Blanc was part of the council of war in 1718–1723 and then *secrétaire d'état à la guerre,* or minister of war, in 1718–1723 and 1726–1728. See Pritchard, *In Search of Empire,* 233, 239.

Auguste Fouquet de Belle-Isle joined as investment partners in a land grant, called a concession, in that colony. From them, Dumont received new commissions as a lieutenant and an engineer, with the assignment to develop forts and plantations on these concessions. After Le Blanc's death in 1728, Dumont continued to benefit from the protection and sponsorship of Belle-Isle through the entire period he narrates in the manuscript, and Dumont dedicated and addressed his manuscript memoir to Belle-Isle, the most important of several patrons who sustained his career in the French military. In offering his memoir to Belle-Isle, Dumont hoped to obtain a post in the French military bureaucracy or a pension to support himself in retirement, as he was then fifty-one years old. However, there is no evidence that Dumont ever received any such reward. Instead, he eventually obtained a post with the Company of the Indies, as a Company director had promised him when he returned to Paris in 1738—only to withdraw the promise when he learned that Dumont's brother had represented a plaintiff in a suit against the Company. Nonetheless, Dumont finally resumed his rank as a lieutenant in the *troupes de la marine* under the Compagnie des Indes and, in 1754, sailed from Lorient for the French colonies in the Indian Ocean and India.[5]

The humility Dumont expresses in the dedicatory epistle to Belle-Isle was not merely conventional, for, in retrospect, Dumont regarded his life as "a tapestry of miseries and dangers," and indeed his miseries were manifold: he was attacked by Indians, got lost in the coastal swamps, was afflicted with malaria and scurvy, survived quarantine on a pestilential ship, nearly drowned in the Mississippi River, and saw his home and belongings destroyed by fire. In a Louisiana colony where a large proportion of European migrants died of illness, starvation, or attacks by hostile natives, Dumont survived, but he did not prosper.[6] Though he fought in several battles, he

5. The name Fouquet de Belle-Isle is widely known for Charles-Louis-Auguste's grandfather, Nicolas Fouquet (1615–1680), who became fabulously wealthy as a superintendant of finances early in the reign of Louis XIV. He was later accused of corruption by Jean-Baptiste Colbert, the king's closest advisor, and stripped of his post in 1661. Charles-Louis-Auguste might have been sympathetic to appeals from junior officers such as Dumont, judging from his *Instruction du maréchal de Belle-Isle sur les devoirs du chef militaire* (Paris, 1869), translated as *The Will of the Marshal de Belle-Isle: To His Son on the Duties of a Military Commander* (n.p., 1980). Writing to his son, who was then a colonel, he advises, "Remember that many of your subordinates have earned more than you the right to command a regiment. Many have a more ancient and illustrious family than yours. The only thing they have lacked in not having been placed over you is a little wealth or good luck" (11). For the meeting with Company of the Indies director Fulvy, see below, original manuscript [282].

6. Quotation from original manuscript [5]. It is difficult to determine the death rate in the

did not rise through the military ranks. Dumont's family connections gave him a sense of invulnerability that often emboldened him to defy his commanding officers, and although his patrons did prevent him from being dishonorably discharged from the military, they could not protect him entirely from the wrath of the superiors he antagonized.

Dumont's tales of survival resemble those of Defoe's fictional narrators such as Crusoe, and his penchant for dark humor anticipates that of another Mississippi boatman, Mark Twain, yet the basic historical facts Dumont supplies about events and individuals in eighteenth-century Louisiana, Quebec, and Brittany are almost always corroborated in other documentary sources. His manuscript memoir therefore offers a counterpoint to the exaggerated promotional tracts that lured emigrants and investors to the colonies, and the fantastical novels and travel narratives that portrayed Europeans easily dominating native populations.[7]

Dumont was aware of the popularity of contemporary colonial histories and novels of travel and adventure and wrote in a lively, first-person voice that combines autobiography, colonial report, and natural history and ethnography. But he stuck close to the ground and to his own sensory experience. He told of his hunting exploits and his favorite pastimes of drawing and gardening. He wrote of insects and storms, of the taste of bear grease, of paddling against the Mississippi current and way finding through the swamps and forests. He described not only local plants and animals but also the recipes colonists used in folk remedies and in their daily repasts; not only the traditional Green Corn celebration of the Natchez Indians but the role of French guests in the wild parties that followed it; not only the major leaders and events of the day (such as Governor Bienville and the Natchez revolt of 1729) but palpable character portraits and scandalous scuttlebutt, which he put forth as his own explanations of what he perceived as colonial Louisiana's many troubles. By creating a narrative with himself

---

colony at a time when immigration was heavy and when the conditions endured by African slaves and European migrants on crowded vessels was often the cause of death for immigrants shortly after their landfall. Paul Lachance reviews demographic evidence and asserts, "It is quite possible that both the white and black populations continued to fall from a high point reached around 1730." See Lachance, "The Growth of the Free and Slave Populations of French Colonial Louisiana," in Bradley G. Bond, ed., *French Colonial Louisiana and the Atlantic World* (Baton Rouge, La., 2005), 223. For more on the population of French Louisiana, see below, note 35.

7. For several of the promotional texts about Louisiana, translated into English, see May Rush Gwin Waggoner, ed. and trans., *Le Plus Beau Païs du Monde: Completing the Picture of Proprietary Louisiana, 1699–1722* (Lafayette, La., 2005).

as a sympathetic protagonist, Dumont tried to persuade readers to accept his judgments about the colonial leaders who, he maintained, had treated him unjustly.

Dumont went unrecognized in his day, and he has not yet received the recognition he merits for his contributions to the francophone literature of North America.[8] Six years after completing his manuscript memoir in 1747, Dumont collaborated with editor and coauthor Jean-Baptiste Le Mascrier to produce a two-volume history of the French colony in the Mississippi valley titled *Mémoires historiques sur la Louisiane*. After publication in 1753, the book was never reprinted, and it has never been translated in its entirety into English, but historians and anthropologists have long consulted it as an important source for information on eighteenth-century Louisiana.[9] Unfortunately, most of these scholars did not know of the existence of

8. Scholarly studies of Louisiana literary history, beginning with Alcée Fortier's *Louisiana Studies: Literature, Customs and Dialects, History and Education* (New Orleans, 1894), have often excluded eighteenth-century texts by limiting the field to works published in Louisiana, even though the first printing house in the colony, started by Denis Braud, opened only in 1764. Germain Joseph Bienvenu opens the field to authors (like Dumont) who lived in and wrote about Louisiana, even if they returned to France to publish their writings. See Bienvenu, "The Beginnings of Louisiana Literature," in John Rowe, ed., *Louisiana Culture from the Colonial Era to Katrina* (Baton Rouge, La., 2008), 25–48. In *Anthologie: Littérature française de la Louisiane* (Bedford, N.H., 1981), 1, editors Mathé Allain and Barry Jean Ancelet assert, "The French literature of Louisiana was born at the same time as the colony," and include very brief excerpts from La Salle, d'Iberville, and Le Page du Pratz. John R. Carpenter's *Histoire de la littérature française sur la Louisiane de 1673 jusqu'à 1766* (Paris, 1966) is the most thorough study but considers the works primarily in the context of French literature of the period. See also Bienvenu, "Another America, Another Literature: Narratives from Louisiana's Colonial Experience" (Ph.D. diss., Louisiana State University, 1995).

9. The full title (cited on the abbreviations page, above) of the *Mémoires historiques* translates as "Historical Memoirs on Louisiana: Containing the Most Memorable Things That Have Happened There since the Year 1687 until the Present. . . ." The work was dedicated to Etienne de Silhouette, who had been appointed royal commissioner for American affairs in 1752. In the mid-nineteenth century, B. F. French translated the first forty-one chapters of the second volume of the *Mémoires historiques* into English, omitting the lengthy final chapter: "History of Louisiana: Translated from the Historical Memoirs of M. Dumont," in French, ed., *Historical Collections of Louisiana; Embracing Many Rare and Valuable Documents* . . . , 5 vols. (New York, 1846–1853), V, 1–125. As part of the Works Progress Administration's Survey of Federal Archives in Louisiana, Olivia Blanchard translated the first volume as "Historical Memoir on Louisiana," Survey of Federal Archives in Louisiana, 1937–1938, Howard Tilton Library, Louisiana State University. In this typescript publication, now very rare, the author's name was given incorrectly as *Louis* François Benjamin rather than Jean. Because Dumont's full name did not appear in the *Mémoires historiques*, some nineteenth-century scholars and some library catalogues erroneously attributed the book to Georges Marie Butel-Dumont (1725–1788), author of two major books on the history and

the manuscript memoir, which consists of 443 pages of text and 23 water-color maps and drawings all in the author's hand, and is conserved at the Newberry Library in Chicago.[10] The title suggests that the published book was based on Dumont's manuscript memoir, but although some passages appear in the *Mémoires*, the vast majority of the manuscript memoir is distinct from the published work. The printed version suppressed Dumont's eyewitness narrative persona, sanitized his irascible character and personal politics, omitted large sections of his narrative, and added some material written by other authors. The continuous narrative of the manuscript memoir was broken up and reorganized into sections treating the natural history and geography of Louisiana, the ethnography of its native peoples, and the history of the French colony. Moreover, the book treats only the years spent in Louisiana, whereas the manuscript memoir also tells of his stay in Quebec from 1715 to 1717 and of his life after he returned to France in 1737. This is the first English translation of the manuscript—published in French by Septentrion of Quebec in 2008—and, as such, is the first opportunity for anglophones to read this significant text of colonial American literature.[11]

DUMONT'S CAREER AS A WRITER

An obscure and impoverished man living in a remote, coastal garrison town in France, Dumont nonetheless created a substantial legacy of writings, and

commerce of the English colonies. Perhaps the best access to the *Mémoires historiques* for English-language readers is John R. Swanton, *Indian Tribes of the Lower Mississippi Valley and Adjacent Coast of the Gulf of Mexico* (1911; rpt. New York, 1998). Swanton's ethnography contains dozens of lengthy excerpts translated from Dumont and Jean-Baptiste Le Mascrier's book. Historians who have used the *Mémoires historiques* as a source for studies of the colony include Charles Etienne Arthur Gayarré, *Histoire de la Louisiane*, 2 vols. (New Orleans, 1846–1847), translated as Gayarré, *History of Louisiana*, 4 vols. (New York, 1854–1866); Pierre Heinrich, *La Louisiane sous la Compagnie des Indes, 1717–1731* (Paris, 1908); Emile Lauvrière, *Histoire de la Louisiane française, 1673–1939* (Baton Rouge, La., 1940); Régine Hubert-Robert, *L'histoire merveilleuse de la Louisiane française: Chronique des XVIIe et XVIIIe siècles et de la cession aux États-Unis* (New York, 1941); and Bernard Lugan, *Histoire de la Louisiane française, 1682–1804* (Paris, 1994). None of these authors consulted the manuscript memoir.

10. "Mémoire de L—— D——, officier ingénieur . . . ," VAULT Ayer MS 257, Newberry Library, Chicago. Among the historians who did read the manuscript in the mid-twentieth century are Jean Delanglez and Marcel Giraud. See Delanglez, "A Louisiana Poet-Historian: Dumont *dit* Montigny," *Mid-America*, XIX (1937), 31–49; Giraud, *Histoire de la Louisiane française*, 5 vols. (Paris, 1953–1974).

11. The French edition is Dumont de Montigny, *Regards sur le monde atlantique, 1715–1747*, ed. Carla Zecher, Gordon M. Sayre, and Shannon Lee Dawdy (Sillery, Quebec, 2008).

his 1747 manuscript memoir stands alongside several previous and subsequent literary efforts. Many of his texts, maps, and drawings have survived in archives, and from them it is possible to piece together the outlines of his career as a writer in several genres, from his years in the colonies to the publication in Paris of the *Mémoires historiques* in 1753.

Dumont began his literary efforts with poetry. He brags in his manuscript memoir about entertaining others with his verses and songs, or "chansonnettes," at the best tables in Quebec during his stay there in 1715 to 1717. Later, the reason he found himself in prison in Port-Louis in 1747, with time on his hands to compose and copy out his long memoir, was because "someone" had angered the local governor by composing satirical verses about him. Dumont is evasive as to his probable responsibility, noting simply that in the region many people, "including at least one woman, the wife of a council member," liked to participate in this activity. Roughly five years before composing his prose memoir, Dumont had written a long poem about Louisiana in four cantos comprising more than four thousand lines of alexandrine couplets. Dumont might have begun it while still living in Louisiana, but since the poem describes the Chickasaw wars that took place as late as 1740, he must have completed it only after his return to France. According to neoclassical aesthetics, a successful epic poem would dignify the checkered history of French colonization in Louisiana and make its author a noble spirit possessed of a national purpose. Dumont singled out Etienne Périer, who was governor of Louisiana from 1726 to 1732 and who had bestowed several favors on him, as the hero of the epic, lauding him with epithets including "Caesar" and "Solomon."[12]

There are two extant copies of the poem. One, likely written in 1744, is dedicated to Marc-Pierre de Voyer de Paulmy, comte d'Argenson (1696–1764), another of Dumont's protectors, who was minister of war beginning in 1742. It bears the title "Verse poem on the establishment of the province of Louisiana, known by the name of Mississippi, with all that occurred there from 1716 to 1741; the massacre of the French at the Natchez post, the customs of the Indians, their dances, their religions, and finally all that concerns the land in general." Dumont did not have a natural gift for verse. Antoine-René de Voyer de Paulmy d'Argenson, nephew of the dedicatee and founder of the Bibliothèque de l'Arsenal in Paris—which still holds the manuscript today—wrote at the bottom of the first page that the verses were

12. Quotations from original manuscript [22, 348]. On the political value of epic poetry in imperial settings, see David Quint, *Epic and Empire: Politics and Generic Form from Virgil to Milton* (Princeton, N.J., 1993), 1–17.

"execrable," even though "remarkable things" were recounted therein. Ultimately, the poem reads more as a mock epic than an epic; the battles it narrates were often losses for the French, and the commanders often timorous or incompetent.[13]

A second copy of the poem has been held in the Library of Congress in Washington, D.C., since the late nineteenth century and is probably the earlier of the two poem manuscripts. It bears no title and has never been published. On its first leaf is a fold-out map of the "province of Louisiana," drawn by Dumont in pen and ink, and on the back of the map, he drew a rough coat of arms, a preliminary version of a more refined one that appears on the recto of the next leaf, above the dedicatory epistle. Although the frame of the second coat of arms is identical to the first, the inner portion is different and does not match Belle-Isle's, d'Argenson's, or two other coats of arms Dumont drew on surviving maps. Under the second coat of arms, he wrote one name, then crossed it out and wrote a second name over it. Unfortunately, neither name is readable. Dumont evidently prepared this fair copy of his poem with the aim of presenting it to a patron yet could not find any suitable candidate—or had not decided who would be the most advantageous dedicatee.[14]

13. BNF, Arsenal, MS 3459. The original French title is "Poème en vers touchant l'établissement de la province de la Loüisianne conniiee sous le nom du Missisipy avec tout ce qui sy est passé de depuis 1716 jusqu'à 1741: Le massacre des François au poste des Natchez, les mœurs des sauvages, leurs dances, leurs religions, enfin ce qui concerne le pays en le géneral." The younger d'Argenson's assessment is cited by Marc de Villiers du Terrage, "Avant-propos," in "Poème," 275.

14. MSS 22,923, Library of Congress. The dating of this manuscript to 1736 in the Library of Congress catalog is inaccurate, erroneously based on the appearance of this date in a marginal note on page 155. That note refers to a historical event described in the poem at that point and not to the date of completion of the poem itself. We know that the extant draft cannot be earlier than 1742, because a watermark of that date is visible on the last leaf of the manuscript, which is blank. An allegory of Fortune appears in a heraldic cartouche on the first page. It is unlikely that this represents another coat of arms, for the two families who used that image at the time would have had nothing to offer to Dumont, who was hoping for a pension or other recompense for his years of service. In fact, the design is fanciful enough to support a hypothesis that Dumont was trying to create a sort of decorative emblem for his manuscript rather than draw the coat of arms of a particular individual. In any case, in order to present the manuscript to someone, he would have had to rework this first page to add the name of a dedicatee. The wheel of fortune is a recurrent theme in Dumont's writing, including the dedicatory epistle of his prose memoir. Notes made by a Library of Congress bibliographer in 1897 indicate that he or she believed the manuscript to be dedicated to the *garde des sceaux,* or keeper of the seals. This unknown librarian might have known of the second poem manuscript and might have been confusing that manuscript's dedicatee with

Comparison of the two poem manuscripts reveals that the Arsenal version contains a more extended text, particularly in the latter part of the first canto, which deals with the 1729 Natchez Massacre and its aftermath. This suggests that the Arsenal version was written later and that Dumont saw a need to expand upon what he then felt was the most dramatic and historically important part of the work. The inclusion of seventeen hand-colored maps and drawings in the Arsenal manuscript, in comparison with the single map found in the Library of Congress manuscript, also supports this hypothesis. The first map is dated 1744. Perhaps Dumont sent the manuscript to d'Argenson to thank him for the two commissions he had received from this minister, one dated October 11, 1742, and the other at the end of February 1743. Unfortunately, in the manuscript memoir, he does not mention his work on the poem.[15]

Marc de Villiers du Terrage edited and published the Arsenal manuscript of the poem in 1931 in the *Journal de la société des Américanistes*. In his introduction, he reviewed what was known about Dumont de Montigny at the time. He was clearly unaware of the existence of the Library of Congress poem and the Newberry prose manuscripts; he wrote, for instance, that the date of Dumont de Montigny's birth is unknown, whereas Dumont himself provides that information in the prose memoir. When the Works Progress Administration sponsored a published translation of Dumont's poem by Henri Delville de Sinclair, Sinclair worked from the Villiers du Terrage edition, for he was also unaware of the Library of Congress manuscript of the work.[16]

Dumont's decision, in the mid-1740s, to rewrite his poem in prose allowed him to elaborate on events in the colonies, provide long, descriptive passages, and foreground his own experience in a way he could not in the epic poem, which focused upon scenes of battlefield valor appropriate to the genre. As he commented in the opening lines of the dedication to Belle-Isle, "Rhymed works can only give . . . a crude portrayal of events,

---

his father, Marc-René de Voyer de Paulmy, marquis d'Argenson (1652–1721), who held that post from 1718 to 1720.

15. For the two commissions, see below, original manuscript [300–301].

16. See "Poème." Villiers du Terrage was a prolific writer on the history of French Louisiana. His other publications include *Histoire de la fondation de la Nouvelle-Orléans, 1717–1722* (Paris, 1917), and *La découverte du Missouri et l'histoire du Fort d'Orléans, 1673–1728* (Paris, 1925). For Dumont's birth date of July 31, 1696, see below, original manuscript [166]. The translation is Marc de Villiers du Terrage, *Settlement of the Province of Louisiana; or, Poèmes* [sic] *en Vers by Dumont de Montigny*, trans. Henri Delville de Sinclair (Baton Rouge, La., 1940).

unworthy of Your Excellency. I believe therefore it is my debt, and my duty, to send it to you now in prose." Indeed, the prose memoir includes many precise and verifiable details: names of dozens of individuals, dates of embarkation, names of ships, even times of day, dating back to 1716. Although he does not mention it, Dumont probably kept a journal during his transatlantic voyages and during at least part of his residence in America. He states that he drafted reports for the Company of the Indies and that, near the end of his stay in Louisiana, he acquired a reputation as an author of legal briefs. As outlined below in the section devoted to Dumont's maps and drawings, there is also evidence that he began drafting maps while he was still in Louisiana and saw this work as another means by which he could advance his career and make his expertise valuable to those in positions of influence.[17]

DUMONT, LE MASCRIER, AND LE PAGE DU PRATZ

Because the manuscript memoir survived, Dumont likely did present it to his patron, Belle-Isle, who either took a personal interest in it or passed it along to an associate. Someone read it carefully and was interested enough to add a title page, a preface, a list of Indian nations, and an index, texts that are included with the manuscript but are not in Dumont's own handwriting.[18] Dumont might have waited in Port-Louis during 1748 and 1749 for Belle-Isle to give him a pension or a better post, but we know that he moved to Paris in 1750 or 1751. In a 1753 treatise on North American geography, based on an address delivered to the French Academy of Sciences on August 9, 1752, the French royal cartographer Philippe Buache wrote, "The Sieur Dumont, who has been in Paris for nearly two years now after spending more than twenty years in Louisiana . . . wrote to me last year a long letter on the subject of my Map of New Discoveries, and of the route one must take to reach the Sea of the West from Louisiana." The letter, dated August 15, 1750, is extant, but in it Dumont makes no reference to whether he was then residing in Paris or Brittany or to how he had become acquainted with Buache. Belle-Isle or his associate might have provided Dumont with an introduction to Le Mascrier, to the cartographer Philippe Buache and / or to the printer C. J. B. Bauche, and encouraged Dumont to

17. Quotation from original manuscript [1]. For the first legal brief, see original manuscript [198].
18. See the "Editorial Methods and Description of the Dumont de Montigny Manuscript Memoir," below, and the translations of these paratexts in the appendix.

prepare a publication about Louisiana. At this time, the competition between the French and British imperial ambitions in North America, left unresolved by the Treaty of Aix-la-Chapelle in 1748, rendered the Mississippi valley a region of great geopolitical significance, as indeed it proved to be during the Seven Years' War, which erupted in North America in 1754.[19]

In September 1751, the first of twelve installments of a "Mémoire sur la Louisiane" appeared in the *Journal œconomique*, a new periodical of commerce and science. The author was Antoine-Simon Le Page du Pratz, and the series continued through February 1753. These publications provided the basis for Le Page's *Histoire de la Louisiane*, published in three volumes in 1758. During the same span in which Le Page's contributions appeared, the *Journal œconomique* also published four much shorter articles by Dumont: "Pottery of the Peoples of Louisiana" in the November 1752 issue and three others in April of that year. "The Technique of Tanning, Treating, and Softening Skins, as Used by the Native People of Louisiana" and "Method for Taking from Pine Wood a Greater Quantity of Resin Than Is Ordinarily Made" were, like the pottery essay, expanded versions of passages in the manuscript memoir. "Method for Making Sea Salt Quickly and at Low Cost" was distinct and based upon his experience both in Brittany and in Louisiana.[20] Although there is no reference to Le Page du Pratz in the manuscript, Dumont must have known him both in Natchez and New Orleans. Le Page had also emigrated to Louisiana during the boom years and was employed by another major concessionnaire, Marc-Antoine Hubert. In 1720, Le Page moved to Natchez with a Chitimacha woman who

19. Philippe Buache, *Considérations geographiques et physiques sur les nouvelles découvertes au nord de la Grande Mer* . . . (Paris, 1753), 36–37. The letter Buache refers to is preserved in the Beinecke Library at Yale University. Among the provisions of the Treaty of Aix-la-Chapelle was to return to France the fort at Louisbourg, which had been taken by the British during the war. The French had tried and failed to recapture it in 1746, an expedition Dumont refers to indirectly; see below, original manuscript [325].

20. "Maniere de passer, tanner, et teindre les peaux, usitée par les peuples naturels de la Louisiane," *Journal œconomique* (April 1752), 109–116; "Poterie des peuples de la Louisiane, par M. D. M.," ibid. (November 1752), 133–135. For the manuscript source for the techniques of tanning hides, see below, original manuscript [358–360]; on the technique for making tar and pitch, see original manuscript [416–417]; and on the Indian methods of pottery, see original manuscript [373]. Le Page's accounts of Indian life in the *Histoire de la Louisiane* have distinguished him as an important source for modern ethnohistory. Patricia Galloway writes: "Archaeologists and ethnohistorians have nearly deified the author for his apparently sympathetic and insightful portrayals—of the Natchez Indians most of all." See "Rhetoric of Difference: Le Page du Pratz on African Slave Management in Eighteenth-Century Louisiana," *French Colonial History*, III (2003), 1. The manuscript memoir and poems establish Dumont as an equally careful observer of native life.

had contacts among the Natchez Indians and probably became his wife *à la façon du pays*. When he arrived, he negotiated the acquisition of the Saint Catherines concession for Hubert and bought his own land directly from the Natchez. He moved back to New Orleans in 1728, where he took the job of managing a large plantation on the west (right) bank of the river owned by the Company of the Indies. In 1731, this became the king's concession after the colony reverted to crown control.[21]

A holograph manuscript held at the Chicago History Museum and dated June 1721 reveals that Le Page had aspired to write a book about the colony ever since his first years in Louisiana. It consists of a sixteen-page outline listing the key resources of the region, names and locations of rivers, native villages, and French outposts, as well as notes on published works about the Mississippi valley. Le Page returned to France in 1734 but disappeared from the historical record until 1750, the date of a short document in the archives of correspondence with Louisiana in which Le Page seeks investors to lend him thirty thousand livres of capital for a new expedition to Louisiana, to exploit a mine of rock crystal he found there. In that same year, Dumont's letter to Buache proposes that Dumont lead an expedition to the same region, the Arkansas and Missouri River valleys, not primarily in search of mineral wealth but to confirm the geographical theories of Buache and his associates.[22]

Neither man returned to Louisiana, but these two previously unknown documents demonstrate that both were in Paris between 1750 and 1752, and both were promoting their expertise for exploring and exploiting the remote regions of the Louisiana colony. There is evidence that the two exchanged drafts of their writings and drew upon reminiscences of informants living in France who had also been at Natchez in the 1720s and 1730s.[23] Whatever

21. *Histoire de la Louisiane*, I, 125–128; Le Page du Pratz manuscripts, 1720–1724, Chicago History Museum.

22. ANF, AC, Correspondance générale, C13A, XXXIV, fol. 386 bis. Le Page wrote that he had a connection to the ministry of the marine through the minister's mother; the minister in 1749–1750 was Antoine-Louis Rouillé. Rouillé succeeded Jean-Frédéric Phélypeaux, who had held the job from 1723–1749. It seems likely that both Le Page and Dumont believed they had a renewed chance to find favor under the new leader.

23. The two men must have exchanged drafts of their work, because excerpts from Le Page du Pratz's writings that Dumont printed in the *Mémoires historiques* differ from the versions that appeared in the *Journal œconomique*. See the account of the origin of the American Indians in [Antoine-Simon Le Page du Pratz], "Suite du Mémoire sur la Louisiane," *Journal œconomique* (August 1752), 142–156, and in *Mémoires historiques*, I, 117–130; the story of the journey of Moncacht-apé in *Journal œconomique* (August 1752), 159–168, and (September 1752), 145–160; and *Mémoires historiques*, II, 246–254, where Dumont says Le Page

the extent of the two men's friendship or collaboration, it appears that when Dumont saw Le Page's work emerging in a respected journal, he decided to rush his own work into print so as not to cede the field to a rival.[24] Dumont and Le Mascrier must have worked on their book during 1752 as they read successive installments of Le Page's work in the *Journal œconomique*. The chapters of the *Mémoires historiques* follow the same loose thematic sequence that Le Page followed in the twelve journal articles.[25]

Jean-Baptiste Le Mascrier, the editor who transformed Dumont's account into the *Mémoires historiques,* was born in Caen in 1697 and entered the Jesuit order in 1717 but left it in 1729. Starting around 1735, he published a number of lengthy works of history, geography, and ethnography and contributed to encyclopedic compilations, such as the 1741 Paris edition of Jean-Frédéric Bernard's *Cérémonies et coutumes religieuses de tous les peuples du monde* ("Ceremonies and Religious Customs of All the Peoples of the World"), a text best known for its engravings by Bernard Picart. Le Mascrier therefore was well qualified to produce the *Mémoires historiques* by transforming Dumont's autobiographical memoir into a book with the encyclopedic scope and Enlightenment objectivity that readers in the 1750s expected. Five years later, Le Page du Pratz published a larger, three-volume history covering much of the same material but embellished with lengthy

---

sent him the story in manuscript. For more on how their published texts reveal their contentious relationship, see Gordon M. Sayre, "Natchez Ethnohistory Revisited: New Manuscript Sources from Le Page du Pratz and Dumont de Montigny," *Louisiana History,* L (2009), 407–436. Le Page refers to Gonichon, a draftsman to the engineer Broutin and known for his own map of Louisiana (British Library Maps, K.Top.122.91) as living in Paris and possessing firsthand knowledge of the Natchez Indians; see *Histoire de la Louisiane,* I, xii.

24. In 1750, the only comprehensive published history of French Louisiana was found in the Jesuit François-Xavier de Charlevoix's *Histoire et description generale de la Nouvelle France: Avec le journal historique d'un voyage fait par ordre du roi dans l'Amérique septentrionale,* 3 vols. (Paris, 1744). Charlevoix had traveled from Quebec through the Great Lakes and down the Mississippi from 1720 to 1722 and published a journal of his voyage as well as a two-volume history of all the French colonies in North America. Given the twenty-year lag before publication, the work must have seemed out of date to Dumont, Le Page, and their peers. Charlevoix's travel narrative has been edited and republished as *Journal d'un voyage fait par ordre du roi dans l'Amérique septentrionale,* ed. Pierre Berthiaume, 2 vols. (Montreal, 1994). The portions of Charlevoix's work that concern Louisiana have been republished from eighteenth-century translations in Charles E. O'Neill, ed., *Charlevoix's Louisiana: Selections from the* History *and the* Journal (Baton Rouge, La., 1977).

25. The *Mémoires historiques* begins with the climate, plants, and animals of Louisiana, which Le Page covered in his first five installments through March 1752. In volume I, chapter 17, the *Mémoires historiques* shifts to ethnography of the Indians, which is also what Le Page published in the fifth, sixth, seventh, and part of the eighth installments down to August 1752.

heroic speeches by Natchez Indian leaders as well as sensational adventures by himself and others.[26]

For two and half centuries, Dumont's writings have sat in libraries and archives, and scholars have been unable to put them all together. Only now can one read and compare all of his works: the *Mémoires historiques*, this manuscript memoir, his epic poem, and the extant maps and letters. Only now can readers appreciate Dumont's many literary, rhetorical, and cartographic efforts and come to know the proud, resourceful, stubborn, but not always admirable man who created these writings. Following the publication of the *Mémoires historiques* in 1753, Lieutenant Dumont began another adventure as he embarked along with his wife for the French colony of Mauritius, known at the time as Ile-de-France. In 1755, he moved on to Pondicherry, a French trading post in southern India, and he died in India in 1760.

Given the transatlantic setting of his life and work, Dumont's manuscript memoir must be understood in the context of both French and North American history and literature. A title page atop the manuscript, written by another hand, reads "Mémoire de L . . . D . . . ," which has inspired the title for this English translation. Today, the word "memoir" in English and in English-language publishing has become widely used and roughly synonymous with "autobiography." The latter word was coined in the early nineteenth century and entered French only after that, whereas *mémoire* has a long history in French as the term for an eyewitness narrative not only of the writer's own life but also of historical events and important personages, "an intermediate form between history and autobiography." The classical canon of French mémoires is grounded in the seventeenth-century Court of the Sun King, Louis XIV, who wrote his own mémoires. Politicians and courtiers including Anne Marie Louise d'Orléans, duchesse de Montpensier, Paul de Gondi, cardinal de Retz, and Louis de Rouvoy, duc de Saint-Simon wrote some of the most celebrated mémoires. The mémoirist defended his or her actions in service to the king and Court and often promised a secret or revelatory insight that could correct or refute official histories. Many less wealthy and less well-connected men and women also wrote mémoires in

26. Jean-Frédéric Bernard, *Cérémonies et coutumes religieuses de tous les peuples du monde*, 9 vols. (Amsterdam, 1728–1743). This work is the subject of Lynn Hunt, Margaret C. Jacob, and Wijnand Mijnhart, *The Book That Changed Europe: Picart and Bernard's Religious Ceremonies of the World* (Cambridge, Mass., 2010); see 264–269 for the changes to the text made for the 1741 edition by Le Mascrier and Antoine Banier. Other titles of Le Mascrier's include *Histoire de la dernière révolution des Indes orientales* (Paris, 1757), published by Veuve Delaguette, one of the publishers of Le Page du Pratz's book.

seventeenth- and eighteenth-century France, and some of these texts remain in manuscript or have been published only recently, such as that of the itinerant glazier Jacques-Louis Ménétra. In mémoires by obscure individuals, it is often impossible to establish the veracity or even the existence of the narrator, and hence in French the word often appeared in the titles of what scholars now consider to be early novels. To further muddy the waters, the word *mémoire* was also used in the titles of political tracts, policy statements, legal briefs, and reports from the colonies such the one by Le Page du Pratz.[27]

Dumont can therefore be associated with many of the historical and intellectual currents of mid-eighteenth-century France, although he never directly participated in the salons and academies for which this period is famous. His published book contributed toward the Enlightenment "republic of letters," notably by his quasi-scientific interest in plants, animals, and climates of distant lands, whereas, in his manuscript writings, he tried to benefit from the relationships of aristocratic patronage that were common among the courtiers of Louis XV and among some of the leading Enlightenment thinkers.[28] In his relationships to his protectors and commanders,

27. On the manuscript title page, see "Description of the Dumont de Montigny Manuscript Memoir" and "Translator's Note," below. On the seventeenth-century French genre of *mémoire*, see Frédéric Charbonneau, *Les silences de l'histoire: Les mémoires français du XVIIe siècle* (Quebec City, 2000), esp. 3. See also Frédéric Briot, *Usage du monde, usage de soi: Enquête sur les mémorialistes d'ancien régime* (Paris, 1994); Christian Jouhard et al., eds., *Histoire, littérature, témoignage: Ecrire les malheurs du temps* (Paris, 2009). Because historiography has changed since the eighteenth century, the corpus of mémoires has come to be read less as alternative history and more often as a source for mainstream historians. See, for example, [Claude-Bernard] Petitot, Alexandre Petitot, and L.-J.-N. Monmerqué, eds., *Collection des mémoires relatifs à l'histoire de France* (Paris, 1819–1829). It consists of fifty-two volumes in the first series, down to the early seventeenth century, and seventy-eight volumes in the second series, continuing to 1763. Jacques Ménétra's memoir has been translated as *Journal of My Life*, ed. Daniel Roche, trans. Arthur Goldhammer (New York, 1986). For examples of other reports from Louisiana entitled "mémoire," see Paul W. Mapp, *The Elusive West and the Contest for Empire, 1713–1763* (Chapel Hill, N.C., 2011), 151.

28. The period 1747 to 1753, when Dumont wrote his memoir and then, along with Le Mascrier, the *Mémoires historiques*, saw the publication of a wave of important Enlightenment texts including Montesquieu's *De l'esprit des lois*, Rousseau's *Discours sur les sciences et les arts*, Diderot's *Lettre sur les aveugles*, and La Mettrie's *L'homme machine*. On the republic of letters, see Dena Goodman's influential *Republic of Letters: A Cultural History of the French Enlightenment* (Ithaca, N.Y., 1994); Elizabeth Heckendorn Cook, *Epistolary Bodies: Gender and Genre in the Eighteenth-Century Republic of Letters* (Stanford, Calif., 1996); and Anne Goldgar, *Impolite Learning: Conduct and Community in the Republic of Letters, 1680–1750* (New Haven, Conn., 1995). On political patronage in this period, see Sara E. Chap-

Dumont veered between flattering men who might recognize and reward his lengthy service to the crown and exposing men he saw as the ancien régime's unjust or self-interested agents, a rhetorical strategy common to many other mémoirists. Although his own behavior was hardly above reproach, he claimed to defend France's national interest. His narrative portrays a colonial Louisiana guided by improvisation and survival, the underside of the grandiose imperial designs described in many letters and reports from its officials. As Shannon Lee Dawdy has written, "The 'founders' of Louisiana came from a culture of military privateers and *coureurs de bois* whose livelihoods depended upon the violation of imperial law." Louisiana officers and traders "skimmed profits from the Indian trade; used the king's ships to conduct their own business; 'redistributed' goods from the Company [of the Indies] and military stores at exorbitant prices"; and engaged in other behaviors Dawdy characterizes as "rogue colonialism."[29] Dumont saw himself as a victim of profiteering and favoritism in Louisiana, and in addressing his powerful protectors in the 1740s—at a time when wars with England for control of colonial North America loomed on the horizon—Dumont exhorted French leaders to clean house and restore the promise of the colony. Louisiana held the potential for rich indigo, tobacco, and rice plantations, and Dumont includes detailed instructions for indigo processing as well as for growing grapes and gathering oysters. But he also knew that some forts that had been drawn on maps had not, in fact, been built, that corruption had often held back efforts to build them, and that several expeditions against hostile native nations had been disastrous failures from the French point of view. Dumont's partial and skeptical history of the colony demands a review of the longer historical context into which he arrived in 1719.[30]

man, *Private Ambition and Political Alliances: The Phélypeaux de Pontchartrain Family and Louis XIV's Government, 1650–1715* (Rochester, N.Y., 2004).

29. Many of the official letters and reports are collected and translated in *MPA*. Volume III is devoted to the papers of Bienville. Quotation from Shannon Lee Dawdy, *Building the Devil's Empire: French Colonial New Orleans* (Chicago, 2008), 234. Dumont's most direct experience of such smuggling and profiteering comes when he sets sail on the *Profond*, ostensibly for France, only to return to New Biloxi after nearly six weeks at sea (original manuscript [169–173]). The cargo of "many ingots of silver taken from the mines of Illinois" had more likely been mined in Mexico or Peru and smuggled or pirated from a Spanish ship, and the voyage to France was apparently aborted by M. Delorme so as to remove the ship's pesky passengers, then circumvent tariffs and embargoes and extract a personal profit.

30. On indigo and grapes, see below, original manuscript [409–414]; on oysters, see [252]; on mythical fortifications, see Dawdy, *Building the Devil's Empire*, 86–89.

French interest in the Mississippi valley began when Louis Jolliet and Father Jacques Marquette descended the great river in 1673, as far as the Quapaw (or Kappa) Indian nation near the confluence with the Arkansas River. But when Jolliet returned to France, he was denied his request for a trade monopoly in the region, since Louis XIV's key minister Jean-Baptiste Colbert saw little need to exploit it as long as the Saint Lawrence valley was still so thinly settled. Robert Cavelier de la Salle then stepped in. In 1674, he allied with the governor of New France, Louis de Buade, comte de Frontenac, to obtain command over the fort at the east end of Lake Ontario, then returned to France to secure letters of nobility for himself and his family as well as a mandate to explore toward the west and south. In 1681 and 1682, his expedition retraced Jolliet and Marquette's path and finally reached the Mississippi's mouth. A fort at that location, La Salle and others recognized, might control much of the continent's resources, including precious minerals the French expected to find in an area they imagined as bordering Spanish New Mexico. When La Salle and his supporters in Paris—the abbés Claude Bernou and Eusèbe Renaudot—presented the results of the expedition, they represented the mouth of the Mississippi as located much farther west on the Gulf of Mexico than it actually is and possibly confused its outlet with that of the Rio Grande. So when La Salle sailed again from France during 1684 and 1685 and into the Gulf of Mexico, he landed on Matagorda Bay in modern Texas. After months of uncertainty, he set out to travel overland in search of the Mississippi, but along the way he was murdered by his own men. La Salle's failed venture aroused an anxious response from New Spain, which sent several expeditions to locate La Salle's settlement and apprehend its survivors.[31]

---

31. On La Salle and the geography of the Mississippi valley, see Mathé Allain, *"Not Worth a Straw": French Colonial Policy and the Early Years of Louisiana* (Lafayette, La., 1988), 32–45; and Dale Miquelon, "Les Pontchartrain se penchent sur leurs cartes de l'Amérique: Les cartes et l'impérialisme, 1690–1712," *Revue d'histoire de l'Amérique française*, LIX (2005), 53–71. The best account of La Salle's last voyage is that by Henri Joutel, one of the men who witnessed the murder of his commander, then continued a trek from Matagorda Bay to the Mississippi River, and from there returned to Canada and France; see *Journal historique du dernier voyage que feu M. de La Salle fit dans le Golfe du Mexique . . .* (Paris, 1713). A translation that collates the 1713 publication with manuscript versions is William C. Foster, ed., *The La Salle Expedition to Texas: The Journal of Henri Joutel, 1684–1687*, trans. Johanna S. Warren (Austin, Tex., 1998). In the manuscript memoir, Dumont does not describe this early history of Louisiana, but the introduction to *Mémoires historiques* compares Dumont to Joutel. The opening lines suggest to the reader that the book be "seen as a con-

In the 1690s, Louis Phélypeaux de Pontchartrain, the minister of the marine, reversed the policy of Colbert (who had died in 1683) and conceived a plan to control the Mississippi valley and thus surround the English colonies in North America with a chain of posts stretching from Quebec through Michilimackinac and the Illinois country. Products from the Mississippi valley would become part of a French Atlantic trade network including Saint-Domingue and the French colonies in the Antilles. The Louisiana colony was finally founded in 1699, when the Canadian Pierre Le Moyne d'Iberville, renowned for his exploits battling the English in Hudson Bay and Acadia, arrived on the Gulf Coast with an expedition from France. His timing was perfect: in May, he and his men repelled an expedition of English and French Protestants led by Daniel Coxe, sending them fleeing from a spot still known as the Détour des Anglois, or English Turn. D'Iberville envisioned wealth from mines and from Spanish galleons acquired either through trade or outright piracy. Initial posts were established at Biloxi, at Mobile, and on Dauphin Island, at first called Massacre Island after a large ossuary d'Iberville's men found there.[32]

---

tinuation of the journal published by the Sieur Joutel in 1713" (iii) and insist, "The author [Dumont] writes nothing in these memoirs that he has not been witness to and is certain of, during twenty-two years' stay in this land, in service to France his country" (ix). For studies of La Salle's last expedition, see Robert S. Weddle, ed., *LaSalle, the Mississippi, and the Gulf: Three Primary Documents* (College Station, Tex., 1987), and Weddle, *The Wreck of the Belle, the Ruin of La Salle* (College Station, Tex., 2001). Interest in La Salle's last expedition was revived by the discovery and excavation of his ship the *Belle* in Matagorda Bay in 1995.

32. See Margry, V; Gilles Havard and Cécile Vidal, *Histoire de l'Amérique française*, 2d ed. (Paris, 2006), 120–126; and John C. Rule, "Jérôme Phélypeaux, Comte de Pontchartrain, and the Establishment of Louisiana, 1696–1715," in John Francis McDermott, ed., *Frenchmen and French Ways in the Mississippi Valley* (Urbana, Ill., 1969), 179–198. Jérôme Phélypeaux was the son of Louis Phélypeaux and held the same office as his father from 1699 to 1715, as well as the title of comte de Pontchartrain. On the Coxe expedition, see Bertrand Van Ruymbeke, "'A Dominion of True Believers Not a Republic for Heretics': French Colonial Religious Policy and the Settlement of Early Louisiana, 1699–1730," in Bond, ed., *French Colonial Louisiana and the Atlantic World*, 83–94. On the larger geopolitics of colonial Louisiana, Jerah Johnson explains how, before the War of the Spanish Succession, it was clear that "the decrepit old Charles II of Spain was going to die without a son to succeed him. Both Louis XIV and the Hapsburg emperor had laid claim to the throne for their families. If the Spanish inheritance then went to a French prince, France would be in a position to protect it [Louisiana] from English westward aggression; or, if it went to a Hapsburg prince, France herself would be in a position to attack Mexico." See Johnson, "Colonial New Orleans: A Fragment of the Eighteenth-Century French Ethos," in Joseph Logsdon and Arnold R. Hirsch, eds., *Creole New Orleans: Race and Americanization* (Baton Rouge, La., 1992), 28–29. On d'Iberville's expedition, see Richebourg Gaillard McWilliams, ed. and trans., *Iberville's Gulf Journals* (Tuscaloosa, Ala., 1981). On the life of d'Iberville, see Bernard Pothier, "Pierre Le Moyne

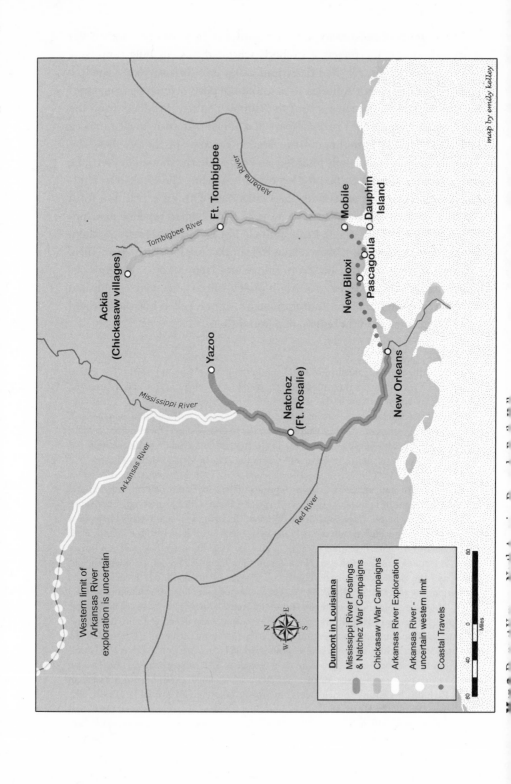

map by emily kelley

Louisiana developed slowly during the first fifteen years. To speed things up, in 1712 the crown granted the colony's trade rights to Antoine Crozat, one of France's richest financiers. In the Treaty of Utrecht in 1713, settling the War of the Spanish Succession, France ceded Newfoundland and Acadia to Great Britain, and thereafter the control of the Mississippi valley seemed vital to securing the French colonies in Canada and the Caribbean. For Crozat, however, the profits from Louisiana were minor compared to selling slaves and amassing Spanish silver from ports in the Gulf of Mexico and Caribbean. He abandoned the monopoly four years later, and it was granted to the newly founded Compagnie d'occident, or Company of the West, controlled by the soon-to-be infamous Scottish financier John Law. By 1719, Law had merged the Louisiana venture with the Company of the Indies, which held a monopoly on all French colonial trade. During a brief period, the value of shares in Law's company rose quickly, in a speculative mania fueled by promises that the land and resources of the Mississippi (as Louisiana was also called) would return huge profits. Law and many of his investors sent ships full of men and supplies to develop their concessions.[33]

This was the state of the colony when Dumont arrived in 1719. At that time, New Orleans, the future capital, had scarcely been surveyed. The convoy he arrived with immediately set off to attack the Spanish fort at Pensacola, which had been taken by the French in May (after France had declared war against Spain in Europe, in the War of the Quadruple Alliance) and then retaken by the Spanish in August. These attacks ended a period of peaceful coexistence during which the two outposts had exchanged food and supplies in spite of imperial rivalry and policies prohibiting intercolonial trade.[34] Between 1717 and 1723, the colonial population of Louisiana increased from around six hundred to a peak of as much as five thousand. Most of these people landed at the site of modern Biloxi, Mississippi, where, as Dumont recounts, the masses of migrants struggled to feed themselves,

d'Iberville et d'Ardillières," Dictionary of Canadian Biography, www.biographi.ca; and Nellis M. Crouse, *Lemoyne d'Iberville: Soldier of New France* (Ithaca, N.Y., 1954).

33. On Antoine Crozat and his monopoly, see Guy Chaussinand-Nogaret, *Gens de finance au XVIIIe siècle* (Paris, 1993), 29–42.

34. On early New Orleans, see Villiers du Terrage, *Histoire de la fondation de la Nouvelle-Orléans;* Edna B. Freiburg and John Churchill Chase, *Bayou St. John in Colonial New Orleans, 1699–1803* (New Orleans, 1980). On the battles for Pensacola, see Jack D. L. Holmes, "Dauphin Island in the Franco-Spanish War, 1719–22," in McDermott, ed., *Frenchmen and French Ways*, 103–125, esp. 105; and Stanley Faye, "The Contest for Pensacola Bay and Other Gulf Ports, 1698–1722, Part II," *Florida Historical Quarterly*, XXIV, 302–328.

build shelters, and construct the boats and pirogues that might carry them to their concessions.[35]

One of the largest investments in the land sold by Law's company came from a partnership formed by Dumont's patrons Belle-Isle and Le Blanc, along with two other prominent men, financier Gérard-Michel de la Jonchère and military commander Claude-François Bidal, marquis d'Asfeld. They purchased four separate concessions, and Dumont's commission for his second voyage to Louisiana assigned him to a military company organized by this partnership to oversee the development of their lands. In the manuscript memoir and its illustrations, Dumont reminds Belle-Isle that it was he who drew the plans for the fort at Yazoo, one of the four concessions, in 1721. The manuscript also includes maps showing the houses, fields, fences, and slave quarters of the concession at Chaouachas, downstream of New Orleans, as well as the Terre Blanche concession at Natchez. Dumont's efforts to claim credit for the development of his patrons' holdings in Louisiana are largely wistful and anachronistic, however. In the summer and autumn of 1720, while Dumont was in Lorient preparing to return to Louisiana for the second time, Law's "Mississippi Bubble" collapsed. Many of the investors who had begun to develop their concessions lost their shirts in the financial debacle and were unable or unwilling to continue transporting men and supplies to the colony. To the French public, which had been reading hyperbolic promotional tracts extolling the bountiful climate and resources of the colony (primarily in the periodical *Le Nouveau Mercure*), "Louisiana" now aroused images of fraud, criminality, or, at best, false promises. Dumont makes no direct reference in the manuscript memoir to the financial crash, but he must have known about it, and he soon shared in the setbacks the colony experienced in the 1720s. The trans-

35. See Lachance, "Growth of the Free and Slave Populations," in Bond, ed., *French Colonial Louisiana and the Atlantic World*, 204–243. Lachance cites a 1708 census that counted 339 residents and censuses of various settlements in 1721–1723 that counted 2,849: 1,716 whites, 950 Africans, and 183 Indian slaves. Lachance believes, however, that these censuses missed many African slaves and also some criminal transportees. On the effects of the rapid migration, see Dawdy, *Building the Devil's Empire*, 144–158; and Jennifer M. Spear, *Race, Sex, and Social Order in Early New Orleans* (Baltimore, 2009), 45. On Biloxi, see below, original manuscript [95], where Dumont mentions the camps of five concessions. A map of Biloxi in the Service historique de la Défense, département Marine, receuil 68, no. 70 (formerly in Bibliothèque de la Service hydrographique, 4044C–58), drawn in 1720 and variously attributed to Ignace-François Broutin or Valentin Devin, shows encampments of eight concessions owned by Le Blanc, Law, Danceny, Mezières, Kolly, Dumanoir, Diron, and Dartagnan. See Samuel Wilson, Jr., "Ignace François Broutin," in McDermott, ed., *Frenchmen and French Ways*, 231–294, esp. 235.

atlantic disinvestment from Louisiana stretched over several years. The Yazoo post where Dumont had lived during the first half of 1722 was virtually abandoned in 1723 and then completely destroyed in 1729, when the Natchez and their allies rose up and attacked the French forts and concessions in the area. The Chaouachas concession no longer belonged to Belle-Isle and his associates when Dumont wrote the manuscript memoir, having been sold in 1738. Dumont's narrative voice of the 1740s tries both to recapture the optimism surrounding Louisiana at the time he had arrived and to criticize the men whose errors led to financial losses and military defeats.[36]

In addition to French soldiers and officers such as Dumont, the hastily gathered colonial settlements of Louisiana included Canadian fur traders, African slaves, German peasants, and exiled French convicts. Canadians followed the route Jolliet and Marquette had pioneered to the Illinois colony, established in the 1680s, and then on down the Mississippi. Africans began arriving in 1719 from French slavers' posts in Juda (Ouidah) in present-day Benin and in Cabinda, Angola. Nearly two thousand Africans landed in Louisiana during the next two years, but the trade ground to a halt for several years following the collapse of Law's scheme. German emigrants, primarily from the Rhineland-Palatinate, fled religious conflicts and land expropriations to come to Louisiana just as many of their compatriots were going to Pennsylvania, but often they found only more misery on their journeys. A pestilence struck the crowded cargo of German peasants and other migrants on the *Charente*, a ship in which Dumont tried to make his second voyage to Louisiana. The malady killed hundreds and, after Dumont had endured a quarantine in the harbor and gone ashore in Lorient, afflicted him with a life-threatening fever and delirium. The involuntary colonists grew in number after a ban on forced emigration, imposed by Louis XIV, was lifted in 1717. Those sent to the colony included salt smugglers and petty criminals who had had their penal sentences commuted to exile, as well as victims of *lettres de cachet*, a legal instrument often used by families against relatives whose behavior threatened to dishonor the family name. Dumont

---

36. On Law and the collapse of the Mississippi Bubble, see *HLF*, III, 1–150; Edgar Faure, *La banqueroute de Law, 17 Juillet 1720* (Paris, 1977); and Arthur H. Cole, "The Great Mirror of Folly *(Het Groote Tafereel der Dwaasheid):* An Economic-Bibliographical Study," Kress Library of Business and Economics, *Publications*, VI (Boston, 1949). On the colony's reputation in France, see Carl A. Brasseaux, "The Image of Louisiana and the Failure of Voluntary French Emigration, 1683–1731," in Glenn R. Conrad, ed., *The French Experience in Louisiana* (Lafayette, La., 1995), 153–162. On Chaouachas, see Heloise H. Cruzat, ed. and trans., "Documents concerning Sale of Chaouachas Plantation in Louisiana, 1737–38," *LHQ*, VIII (1925), 589–646.

was assigned to guard some of these involuntary colonists in 1719 as they waited to embark, held in the Tour Saint-Nicolas at the entrance to the harbor of La Rochelle:

There were five hundred prisoners, of whom three hundred were deserters who had been granted freedom by the king if they passed over to the New World. The two hundred others were younger sons of families whose parents, so as to be rid of them, were sending them out to make their fortune, so to speak. Doubtless I was numbered among them, although honored with an officer's commission.

It is uncertain whether, by sending him across the Atlantic, Dumont's family was trying to get rid of him or to offer him a path to wealth and success (or both). Either way, he did not make a fortune in Louisiana, and his narrative portrays his experiences as a series of accidents and adventures guided by fate or by the whims of despotic or incompetent leaders, an outlook that resembled that of the picaresque heroes of early modern novels.[37]

DUMONT, THE PICARO

Dumont created, in his manuscript memoir, a text that can be read as a report on the French colony in Louisiana and his service to it or as an autobiographical novel. Indeed, his style and point of view, notably the lively

---

37. Detailed figures for the numbers of slaves are in Gwendolyn Midlo Hall, *Africans in Colonial Louisiana: The Development of Afro-Creole Culture in the Eighteenth Century* (Baton Rouge, La., 1992), 60–64. On German emigrants, see Reinhart Kondert, *The Germans of Colonial Louisiana, 1720–1803* (Stuttgart, 1990); Alice D. Forsyth and Earlene L. Zeringue, *German "Pest Ships," 1720–1721* (New Orleans, 1969); Marcel Giraud, "German Emigration," in Conrad, ed., *French Experience in Louisiana*, 136–147, which is a translation of *HLF*, IV, 154–167. Giraud casts doubt upon Dumont's account of the voyage of the *Charente*, however, in part because Dumont overstated the capacity of the vessel. See below, original manuscript [93]. Quotation from original manuscript [36–37]. On forced emigration to Louisiana, see Glenn R. Conrad, "Emigration Forcée: A French Attempt to Populate Louisiana, 1716–1720," in Conrad, ed., *French Experience in Louisiana*, 125–135; James D. Hardy, Jr., "The Transportation of Convicts to Colonial Louisiana," ibid., 115–124. Among the best-known emigrants were young women, some of them accused of prostitution or petty crimes in France, who were sent to the colonies to provide wives to male settlers. They were called *filles du roi* in Canada and *filles de la cassette* in Louisiana. Their notoriety in genealogy and folklore is out of proportion to their true numbers. See Josianne Paul, *Exilés au nom du roi: Les fils de famille et les faux-sauniers en Nouvelle-France, 1723–1749* (Sillery, Quebec, 2008). On the lettres de cachet, see Arlette Farge and Michel Foucault, *Le désordre des familles: Lettres de cachet des Archives de la Bastille* (Paris, 1982).

dialogue and dramatic battle scenes, reflect the rising popularity of novels of travel and adventure in the mid-eighteenth century. Dumont makes several allusions to the Bible and shows off his education with a few Latin quotations from Virgil and allusions to the *Iliad,* but the only reference to contemporary literature is to *Robinson Crusoe,* which was published in 1719, the year he departed for Louisiana. Dumont must have read the novel, in a French translation that first appeared in 1720.

From the perspective of literary history, Dumont's closest connection to Defoe lies in their common use of the picaresque genre, a loosely structured, first-person narrative of adventure and comic misadventure set in a realistically amoral world filled with dangers, both natural and human. Dumont's memoir casts him as the hero of a first-person, picaresque narrative such as the enormously successful *Gil Blas* by Alain-René Le Sage, which appeared in three parts in 1715, 1723, and 1735. Le Sage had translated into French the popular Spanish picaresques *Histoire de Guzmán de Alfarache,* first published in two parts in 1599 and 1604 by Mateo Alemán, and the anonymous *Estebanillo González,* first published in 1646.[38] But whereas those and most other sixteenth- and seventeenth-century picaros were young men of low status, bereft of family support, who engaged in comic or bawdy adventures, Gil Blas, like Dumont, is a character of more genteel origins who, by the end of the novel, achieves (or hopes to achieve) a measure of wealth and social status. Le Sage had set much of the action of another of his picaresque novels in Canada, and in 1738, Claude Lebeau, himself a lawyer at the Paris parlement who had been exiled to the American colonies by his

38. Among Defoe's many works, *Moll Flanders* is the novel most often cited as a picaresque. See Ian Watt's important study, *The Rise of the Novel: Studies in Defoe, Richardson, and Fielding* (Berkeley, Calif., 1962), 94–96. Moll Flanders travels back and forth between England and its colonies of Virginia and Maryland. For a colonial picaresque autobiography in English contemporary with Dumont's, see Susan E. Klepp and Billy G. Smith, eds., *The Infortunate: The Voyage and Adventures of William Moraley, an Indentured Servant,* 2d ed. (1743; University Park, Pa., 2005). For a history of the picaresque that encompasses works in all three languages, see Claudio Guillen, *The Anatomies of Roguery: A Comparative Study in the Origins and the Nature of Picaresque Literature* (New York, 1987). Alain-René Le Sage's translations were *Histoire de Guzman d'Alfarache* (1740) and *Histoire d'Estévanille González, surnommé le garçon de bonne humeur* (1734), which was not so much a translation as an adaptation. The full Spanish title of the latter is *La vida y hechos de Estebanillo González, hombre de buen humor, compuesta por él mismo.* These two works, together with the anonymous *La vida de Lazarillo de Tormes, y de sus fortunas y aduersidades* (1554), are considered among the most important of the Spanish picaresques. Tobias Smollett published an English translation of *Gil Blas* in 1748, as well as his semiautobiographical picaresque novel *Roderick Random.*

father, published an account of his voyage to Canada transformed into a bawdy and fantastical novel. It is doubtful that Dumont read Lebeau, but he might have been familiar with the Abbé Prévost's tremendously popular *L'histoire du chevalier des Grieux et de Manon Lescaut* (1731), the tale of a man who follows his promiscuous lover to New Orleans after they are both disinherited and she is arrested and exiled to the colony.[39]

Part of the fascination with the story of Manon Lescaut and the chevalier des Grieux was the idea that an aristocratic man would abandon wealth and family status for the love of a woman who had already sold her favors to other men, and that he would voluntarily sail to New Orleans, which, by the time the novel was published, bore a reputation for criminal behavior and a malodorous climate. Dumont recognized that he had been shipped off to the colony by his family and appears to acknowledge the sensational nature of his writing by employing a literary device commonly used in eighteenth-century novels and memoirs, factual or fictional, that presented themselves as exposés of the lives of the powerful. Dumont conceals his own name throughout the text, as well as the names of several other men, including his friend Jean Roussin ("the bourgeois") and his rivals the "chevalier de St. M——" and the "Sieur de C——," whose stories resemble that of the chevalier des Grieux. The names most frequently suppressed, however, are those of two hostile commanding officers: his commander in Port-Louis at the time he was writing, Simon de la Vergne de Villeneuve, who is referred to by his title, the *major de la place,* and the longtime governor of Louisiana Jean-Baptiste Le Moyne de Bienville (although Dumont slips up and writes the name at two points). When Dumont replaced the letters "i-e-n-v-i-l-l-e" with eight dots, he offered readers the pleasure of unmasking Bienville's identity and sharing Dumont's sentiments toward him.[40]

39. Claude Lebeau, *Avantures du Sr. C. Le Beau, avocat en parlement; ou, Voyage curieux et nouveau parmi les sauvages de l'Amérique septentrionale* (Amsterdam, 1738); Alain René Lesage, *Les avantures de Monsieur Robert Chevalier, dit de Beauchêne, capitaine de flibustiers dans la Nouvelle-France* (Paris, 1732). On Lebeau's novel, see Andréanne Vallée, "Edition critique des Avantures du Sieur Claude Le Beau . . ." (Ph.D. diss., University of Ottawa, 2008). An English translation of Prévost's novel is *The Story of the Chevalier des Grieux and Manon Lescaut,* trans. Angela Scholar (Oxford, 2004). For discussion of the novel in the context of the history of French Louisiana, see Mathé Allain, "Manon Lescaut et Ses Consoeurs: Women in the Early French Period, 1700–1731," in James J. Cooke, ed., *Proceedings of the Fifth Meeting of the French Colonial Historical Society* (Lanham, Md., 1980), 18–26; and Dawdy, *Building the Devil's Empire,* 46–49.

40. The name Grieux was that of a real man who had fought in the battles of Pensacola in 1719 and might have been known to Dumont. On concealed names, see Robert Darnton, *The Forbidden Best Sellers of Pre-Revolutionary France* (New York, 1995), 6–8, 91. In fact,

Although Dumont's family might have shipped him off to the colonies, he nonetheless absorbed from his father and brothers an interest in the law, and his manuscript memoir points to the intersection between popular literature and legal writing. Historian Sarah Maza has explored the impact of the *mémoires judiciaires* (briefs by lawyers defending the actions of their clients) and the *remontrances* (opinions by judges on the parlements, criticizing actions by the royal administration) that were published or distributed for free in France from the 1750s to the 1780s, in an effort to influence public opinion. The Louisiana colony permitted no professional lawyers, but Dumont began writing briefs in the late 1720s on behalf of individuals who had been called before the Superior Council of Louisiana in New Orleans. His first effort was his defense of his landlord, Jean Roussin, who had been cheated in the purchase of a heifer. The governor at the time, Etienne Périer, ruled in favor of Roussin, and Dumont was able to continue his legal writing when he settled in New Orleans in the 1730s. He admits that the councillors did not appreciate his legal interventions and that, even after he had been forbidden to appear in the council, he continued to draft dossiers that his clients then recopied. So long as neither Dumont nor his handwriting appeared in the council chamber, he could not be accused of disobedience.

Not only did Dumont engage in legal writing on behalf of others—his entire memoir functions as an appeal to justice. A self-styled whistle-blower, Dumont appeals to his patron Belle-Isle to correct "the injustice, the treason, the corruption, and the massive expenditures that have been made and are still being made" in Louisiana. During the late 1740s, there was little chance that Belle-Isle would or could take action to correct these wrongs, but Dumont's rhetorical strategy nonetheless invoked France's national interest and geopolitical imperatives in the interest of demanding a small reward for himself. Many other French colonials penned similar appeals, which also resemble the genre of the colonial Spanish *relación de méritos y servicios*, a narrative of the experience of an individual subject who appeals directly to the king or to a powerful minister for redress against corrupt colonial leaders and reward for loyal, if controversial, service in the colonies. Roberto González Echevarría has identified the relación as contributing to the development of the Spanish picaresque and thus the modern European novel: "Narrative, both fictional and historical, thus issued from the forms and constraints of legal writing . . . the *picaro*, the chronicler,

---

Manon Lescaut was one of the novels that used these masked, initialized names. Bienville's name is first concealed at original manuscript [50] and is spelled out at [247, 429–430].

and in a sense the whole new world, seek enfranchisement and a validation of their existence through the writing of their stories." Although most such texts remained unpublished, the well-known narrative by Álvar Núñez Cabeza de Vaca of his eight-year odyssey around the Gulf of Mexico, for example, was a relación addressed to Charles V, explaining and justifying his conduct following the disastrous expedition of Pánfilo de Narváez in 1528.[41]

Among the published corpus of French American colonial literature, a counterpoint to Dumont's manuscript memoir is the *Nouveaux voyages . . . dans l'Amérique septentrionale* by another half-pay lieutenant gone AWOL, Louis-Armand de Lom d'Arce, baron de Lahontan. Lahontan served ten years in Canada, from 1683 to 1693, until he fled from a hostile commanding officer in Plaisance, Newfoundland, and found refuge in Portugal, Spain, England, and Holland. His work is a pointed critique of Jesuit missionaries and French policies in Canada. Dumont, like Lahontan, devoted portions of his text to a voyage of exploration into the interior of the continent and to the region's natural history and the ethnography of its native peoples. Also like Lahontan, Dumont had a wry sense of humor, was highly critical of some colonial leaders, and showed little interest in the state-sponsored missionary efforts to convert the Indians to Catholicism.[42]

41. Dumont, original manuscript [442]. Ralph Bauer characterizes the relación genre "by its positionality and directionality not only in social space but also in geographic space: it moves 'upward' in social space at the same time it moves 'inward' in geographic space from imperial periphery to center." Dumont's periphery would be Louisiana and then Brittany, and the center, of course, was the Court and ministries in Paris. See Bauer, *The Cultural Geography of Colonial American Literatures: Empire, Travel, Modernity* (Cambridge, 2003), 36. See also Roberto González Echevarría, *Myth and Archive: A Theory of Latin American Narrative* (Cambridge, 1990), 45–46. As González Echevarría put it in an earlier essay, "Many of the adventures and misadventures, by people who were marginal to society, found their way to legal or quasi-legal documents in which lives large and small were told in search of acquittal or social advancement." See "The Life and Adventures of Cipion: Cervantes and the Picaresque," *Diacritics*, X (1980), 20–21. For more on *La relacíon que dio Alvar Nuñez Cabeza de Vaca . . .* (Zamora, 1542), see Rolena Adorno and Patrick Charles Pautz, "Introduction," in Adorno and Pautz, eds., *The Narrative of Cabeza de Vaca* (Lincoln, Neb., 2003), 24–28.

42. Louis-Armand de Lom d'Arce, baron de Lahontan, *Nouveaux voyages de Mr. le baron de Lahontan, dans l'Amerique septentrionale*, in Réal Ouellet and Alain Beaulieu, eds., *Œuvres completes*, 2 vols. (Montreal, 1990), I, 241–786. An English translation is *New Voyages to North-America*, 2 vols. (London, 1703). Lahontan's literary aspirations aimed at neo-classical forms of satire and the edifying dialogues of François Fénelon, not the eighteenth-century novel, which of course had not yet developed. On Lahontan and Fénelon, see Anthony Pagden, "The Savage Critic: Some European Images of the Primitive," *Yearbook of English Studies*, XIII (1983), 32–45. On the form of colonial histories and travel texts, see Gordon M. Sayre, *"Les Sauvages Américains": Representations of Native Americans in French and English Colonial Literature* (Chapel Hill, N.C., 1997), 79–129.

Dumont justified his conduct toward his superior officers not only by claim-ing to expose their corruption but also by referring to a code of honor. He tried to uphold the image of an *honnête homme,* a man of integrity. In seventeenth-century France, the honnête homme was promoted as an ideal for dignified behavior among courtiers, noblemen, and the rising bourgeoi-sie. Dumont would have become aware of these ideals as a young man in Paris, where his family fit into the third group, and in his memoir, he sought to show Belle-Isle that he had behaved with honor in Louisiana. A major part of the drama of his narrative is his ongoing struggle with Bienville, called by some historians the "Father of Louisiana," who served as governor of the colony for four separate periods between 1701 and 1743. Bienville was born in Canada into a family of adventurers and soldiers, and he arrived in Louisiana as a teenager with the expedition of his older brother d'Iberville. Their father, Charles Le Moyne de Longueuil et de Châteauguay, though the son of an innkeeper in France, had lifted himself and his sons into the colony's elite through military valor and the acquisition of seigneurial titles on newly granted Canadian land. The Le Moyne legacy rose to even greater heights in the newer colony along the Mississippi.[43]

Dumont's fate as a marginal figure in the colony's power structure was sealed when, after his first disembarkation in Louisiana, Bienville undertook a review of the troops by calling out the name of each officer and demanding an account of his genealogy. In principle, only a man of noble parentage, or whose father had been an officer, could receive an officer's commission in the French military. Dumont himself met neither criterion, and in practice, some commoners did rise into the officers' ranks, either by deception or by valor and merit. But Dumont felt offended by Bienville, whose family had no aristocratic lineage in France. In a subsequent encounter, when Bien-ville inquired whether Dumont had met, during his recent stay in Quebec,

43. See Nicolas Faret, *L'honneste homme; ou, L'art de plaire à la court* (Paris, 1630), and the posthumously published *De la vraïe honnêteté* of Antoine Gombaud, chevalier de Méré (1607–1684). On the value of honor in eighteenth-century France, see Arlette Farge, "The Honor and Secrecy of Families," trans. Arthur Goldhammer, in Roger Chartier, ed., *A His-tory of Private Life,* III, *Passions of the Renaissance* (Cambridge, Mass., 1989), 571–607. On Canada's seigneurial system, see Louise Dechêne, *Habitants and Merchants in Seventeenth-Century Montreal* (Montreal, 1992); Allan Greer, *The People of New France* (Toronto, 1997), 37–40. On the Le Moyne clan, see Nellis Maynard Crouse, *Lemoyne d'Iberville: Soldier of New France* (Ithaca, N.Y., 1954); and Heinrich, *La Louisiane sous la Compagnie des Indes,* 285–289.

a man named "le M——" ("Le Moyne" or another family surname), Dumont answered yes, but added: "He is a drunkard and a person unworthy of the society of honest men." Bienville then stood up and toasted Dumont before a table of officers, sarcastically thanking Dumont for attributing such good qualities to Bienville's uncle. These two confrontations reflected the attitudes of some Frenchmen toward Canadians in positions of power in New Orleans, colored by a belief that, in the words of the Capuchin priest Father Raphaël, the creoles had been "brought up, so to speak, among savages, and know little of the customs and mode of government of the kingdom." Thus the French officers used manners, dress, lineage, and perhaps even linguistic marks to denigrate the Canadians, who themselves looked down upon the French as unskilled and cowardly in military matters and ridiculously inept at economic survival in the New World.[44]

Dumont's sense of honor emerged not only in defense of a Eurocentric prejudice. It reflected a widespread belief in France of the value of personal and family honor for all but the lowest strata of society. Parents who sent their disgraced children to prison or to the colonies by means of lettres de cachet were acting in defense of family reputation. A sexually compromised woman or a cuckolded man could bring dishonor to a household regardless of its social status. The judicial records of colonial Louisiana, as in France and elsewhere, include many actions for slander and insult. The common colonial soldiers and sailors, though they ranked among the lowest of free people, shared this sense of honor. However, they tended to exchange insults more freely and creatively than their superiors, and without resorting to violence. For them, reputation could be a joking matter, at least to a point. Such was not the case for gentlemen.[45]

---

44. Original manuscript [64]; "Lettre de Père Raphaël," Mar. 12, 1726, ANF, AC, Correspondance générale, C13A, X, 41. On the nobility of officers, see Jay M. Smith, *The Culture of Merit: Nobility, Royal Service, and the Making of Absolute Monarchy in France, 1600–1789* (Ann Arbor, Mich., 1996), 213–225. Historian Jean Delanglez observed, "There was in France an unwritten law according to which no native French officer should be the subordinate of a Canadian" (Delanglez, ed. and trans., "The Journal of Pierre Vitry, S.J.," *Mid-America*, XXVIII [1946], 27). On the conflict between Jesuit and Capuchin priests and between priests and military officials, see Charles E. O'Neill, *Church and State in French Colonial Louisiana: Policy and Politics to 1732* (New Haven, Conn., 1966). On tensions between *criollos* and *peninsulares* in New Spain, see David Brading, *The First America: The Spanish Monarchy, Creole Patriots, and the Liberal State* (Cambridge, 1991), 293–300. The word "creole" has acquired specific signification in Louisiana, but in general it refers to those of European descent who are born in America.

45. See Peter N. Moogk, "'Thieving Buggers' and 'Stupid Sluts': Insults and Popular Culture in New France," *William and Mary Quarterly*, 3d Ser., XXXVI (1979), 524–547;

When he arrived for the second time in Louisiana, Dumont impulsively went back to Bienville, and when the governor refused to look him in the eye or speak to him, Dumont provoked him by drawing a black cross on the door of Bienville's chambers, proclaiming that only when the cross turned white would he come again to pay his respects. The governor's response was to demote Dumont and deny him any food or pay. Upon being thrown in jail, Dumont claims, he quickly became the "king of the prison" by virtue of the consideration shown him by the jailer in giving him a mattress. During his several incarcerations, both in New Orleans and in Natchez, Dumont benefited from a sense of solidarity among soldiers and lower-ranking officers who supported his rebellious acts and helped him to escape punishment.

The "insubordination" of the troops was a frequent lament of Louisiana governors, and Dumont reveals something of the anarchic spirit of pirates and buccaneers among colonial soldiers and sailors. The Caribbean in the 1720s was the heyday of piracy, and Dumont shows how not only pirates but also imperial navies practiced disguise, deception, and mercenary self-interest. During his first voyage to Louisiana, his vessel made two encounters in the Gulf of Mexico with ships that were English yet were first seen flying Spanish colors, replacing the flags with English colors only once they determined that the other fleet was French. If no ship could be trusted to declare itself honestly by flying its national flag, then in effect every ship was, at first sighting, assumed to be a pirate ship. In addition, since naval ships were manned in part by impressed sailors and mercenaries, mutineers and turncoats were common. In the battles for Pensacola in 1719, French troops captured by the Spanish quickly switched allegiance so as to save their skins or better their future prospects. The distinction between pirates and navies became even more blurred inasmuch as top officials such as d'Iberville were engaged in smuggling. Dumont maintained his loyalty to France, which, of course, was another matter of honor, but the tensions within the fragile social hierarchy of the French colonies are everywhere visible in his manuscript memoir.[46]

---

and Dawdy, *Building the Devil's Empire*, 172–174, upon which this discussion is based. For biographical studies of Bienville, see Philomena Hauck, *Bienville, Father of Louisiana* (Lafayette, La., 1998), and Charles E. O'Neill, "Jean-Baptiste Le Moyne de Bienville," Dictionary of Canadian Biography, www.biographi.ca.

46. On mutinies and piracy in New France, see Allan Greer, "Mutiny at Louisbourg, December 1744," *Histoire Sociale/Social History*, XX (1977), 305–336; and in the Caribbean, Peter Linebaugh and Marcus Rediker, *The Many-Headed Hydra: Sailors, Slaves, Com-*

Dumont's rebelliousness was not simply the result of a general bad attitude toward authority. When it served him, and when he thought a higher-ranking individual merited his praise and loyalty as an honnête homme, he could be quite obsequious as well as politically astute. In 1723, when the ministers in Paris sent a royal commissioner named Jacques de la Chaise to reform governance in Louisiana, Dumont immediately sought him out and explained his dispute against Bienville. The timing was right, as La Chaise had been sent to the colony to investigate charges of malfeasance, including smuggling and profiteering, which eventually resulted in Bienville's recall to France. After meeting Dumont, La Chaise described him in a report to the director of the Company of the Indies as "all naked like a poor wretch [because] M. de Bienville refused him not only provisions but also shoes and stockings. . . . This young man aroused pity in everybody." He ordered that Dumont be paid four months' back wages. La Chaise saw Dumont's plight as emblematic of Bienville's abuses of power. The enmity between Bienville and Dumont was so strong that Bienville's reinstatement as governor in 1733, in the aftermath of the Natchez revolt, might have influenced Dumont's decision to return to France. Still, the years 1730 to 1735 were a period of relative peace in Dumont's life, about which he writes little in the memoir. In April 1730, during Périer's administration, he successfully petitioned the Louisiana Superior Council to evict a tenant who had failed to pay rent on his house in New Orleans. After he left Natchez in 1729, Dumont no longer held a military commission, and in the early 1730s, he fathered two children, as well as raised step-children, with his wife, Marie (née Marie Baron). In a census of 1731, "le Sieur Montigny" is listed among the *habitants* living along the Mississippi, with a wife, two children, and three black slaves, two adults and one infant. Only later, after he and his family returned to France, did Dumont again become embroiled in conflicts with his superior officers over honors and prerogatives he felt he was due.[47]

---

moners, and the Hidden History of the Revolutionary Atlantic (Boston, 2000), 143–173. On the flying of false flags, see below, original manuscript [48, 54]. On smuggling, see the essays in Franklin W. Knight and Peggy K. Liss, *Atlantic Port Cities: Economy, Culture, and Society in the Atlantic World, 1650–1850* (Knoxville, Tenn., 1991), esp. Anne Pérotin-Dumon, "Cabotage, Contraband, and Corsairs: The Port Cities of Guadeloupe and Their Inhabitants, 1650–1800," 58–86.

47. Jacques de la Chaise to the directors of the Company of the Indies, Mar. 8, 1724, *MPA*, II, 337–338; "Petition of Dumont Demontigny," Apr. 7, 1730, Superior Council of Louisiana, *Proceedings*, Louisiana State Museum, no. 1730040602 (part of the page is cut off; see abstract in *LHQ*, IV [1921], 518–520); Charles R. Maduell, Jr., ed. and trans., *The Census Tables for the French Colony of Louisiana from 1699 through 1732* (Baltimore, 1972), 114. The two

Dumont's critical military history is consistent with his stated goal of providing, in the manuscript memoir, a "reflection, touching upon the building of colonies and the choice of officers." His dedicatee, Belle-Isle, might have been particularly interested in his account of the English attack on Brittany in October 1746, for this was part of the larger War of the Austrian Succession, in which Belle-Isle was a prominent general. Dumont claims to have been a key advisor to the commandant at Port-Louis, Deschamps, and to have therefore had a unique perspective on the 1746 invasion. Although the French successfully defended the towns of Lorient and Port-Louis, their victory owed less to their own valor than to the incompetence of the besiegers. Dumont writes that the narrative of these events as included in his manuscript memoir is an expanded version of a report he sent to Belle-Isle at the latter's request immediately after the battle and that he was disciplined by his superiors for sending it.[48]

Given that Dumont was a military man, proud of his status as an officer, it should come as no surprise that a large portion of his manuscript memoir is devoted to narratives of warfare, in Louisiana, in France, and on the Atlantic and Caribbean waters. In his epic poem, Dumont chose to focus three of the four cantos on battles: the work begins with the battles for Pensacola in 1719, followed in the latter part of the first canto by the Natchez Massacre of 1729 and subsequent French retaliations; then cantos 2 and 3 portray the expeditions led by Bienville against the Chickasaw Indians in 1736 and 1739 to 1740. In rewriting the poem as a prose memoir, Dumont retained the narratives of all these battles, even though doing so introduced gaps into his first-person, eyewitness perspective. The account of the Pensacola War includes events that took place before Dumont arrived in Louisiana on September 1, 1719, and the 1739 to 1740 Chickasaw expedition took place after he had returned to France. It is not certain whose testimony or which written narratives Dumont relied upon for the latter section, but it is obvious why he included it: it represented Bienville's final misstep and professional collapse. Having failed to subdue the Chickasaws in 1736, the governor expended huge sums of money bringing troops from France and transporting them up the Mississippi as far as present-day Memphis, only to retreat without ever striking a serious blow against the Chickasaws. Bien-

---

children might have been two surviving offspring of Marie and Jean Roussin or one of Roussin's children and the newborn Marie-Anne-Françoise Dumont.

48. Quotation from original manuscript [5], and report on the invasion of Brittany [328].

ville's military failure led to his being recalled to France, which for Dumont represented a moral vindication and made a fine denouement to his memoir's polemic against the governor.[49]

Dumont's skeptical attitude, resistance to authority, and instinct for self-preservation seem to have made him ill suited for battlefield leadership, and he never boasts of his bravery under fire or of the courage of his commanders (apart from the hyperbolic epithets given to Périer). He expresses loyalty to some of his immediate commanders—such as Deschamps, Drouot de Valdeterre, and Louis-Pierre Le Blond de la Tour—and hostility toward others, including his captain, Graves, and the major de la place Simon de la Vergne de Villeneuve, but only on a couple of occasions does he write of his own leadership of detachments of soldiers. He was discharged from his commission in 1730, did not fight in the sieges against the Natchez in 1730 and 1731, and in the 1736 expedition against the Chickasaws, he served as part of the civilian militia. Dumont writes of most battles from the perspective of a common soldier. He is always conscious of the fear and suffering of the enlisted men (if not of enemy Indians) and eager to memorialize the deaths of men who suffered from the poor leadership of Bienville or the Natchez post commander Chepart. Some of the most powerful scenes in his manuscript are when he witnesses the gruesome deaths of his comrades in arms—such as La Sceine, Grondel, and the unnamed Swiss soldier who tried to save the life of the latter—even though he often mixes in a sense of farce.[50]

The remaining battles related in the manuscript memoir are those with the Natchez Indians, a complex, mostly agricultural society living in the area around the city that bears their name in present-day Mississippi. The Natchez were likely the direct descendants of the pre-Columbian peoples who had built the enormous temple platform known as Emerald Mound, the second largest such earthwork in the United States. The French saw

49. On the Chickasaw wars, see two articles by Michel Foret: "War or Peace? Louisiana, the Choctaws, and the Chickasaws, 1733–1735," and "The Failure of Administration: The Chickasaw Campaign of 1739–40," both in Conrad, ed., *French Experience in Louisiana*, 296–312, 313–321. Studies of Indian relations and conflicts in Louisiana include Patricia Galloway, *Practicing Ethnohistory: Mining Archives, Hearing Testimony, Constructing Narrative* (Lincoln, Neb., 2006); and Kathleen DuVal, "Interconnectedness and Diversity in 'French Louisiana,'" in Gregory A. Waselkov, Peter H. Wood, and Tom Hatley, eds., *Powhatan's Mantle: Indians in the Colonial Southeast*, rev. ed. (Lincoln, Neb., 2006), 133–162.

50. On the relationship between the French colonial military and civilian militias, see Louise Dechêne, *Le peuple, l'état, et la guerre au Canada sous le régime français* (Montreal, 2008), 139–145, 225–231. For scenes of the deaths of comrades, see below, original manuscript [62] and [264–265, 272]. For the 1723 expedition, see original manuscript [150–158].

great potential for tobacco and indigo cultivation in the fertile soil at Natchez and, in 1716, established Fort Rosalie on a high bluff above the river. The soldiers and farmers known as *habitants* were soon living in intimate proximity to the Natchez, who continued to live on their farms and to gather in their ceremonial centers, including temple mounds and mortuary collections that have become the focus of several modern archaeological expeditions. Some Natchez people labored as hunters or field hands for the French, and a few even became wives to Frenchmen. Still, skirmishes took place between the French and the Natchez in 1722 and 1723, set off by disputes over livestock and trade. Dumont was sent to attack the Natchez in October 1723 and wrote of how peace was restored owing to the influence of Serpent Piqué, a Natchez "Sun" and war chief who became a heroic figure as portrayed in the *Mémoires historiques* and also in Le Page du Pratz's *Histoire de la Louisiane*. A close relationship to the Natchez appears to have lulled the French into believing that their alliances with native peoples were based upon more than the gifts of trade goods and military alliances at which Bienville and other leaders seemed (for a time) to be so skilled. By the 1740s, when Dumont was writing his poem and manuscript memoir, the Chickasaw wars appeared to have been embarrassing setbacks, but it was the struggle with the Natchez that emerged as the turning point in the history of French Louisiana. When Dumont and Le Mascrier compiled the *Mémoires historiques,* the portion of the text devoted to the Natchez Massacre was expanded, whereas the pages of text and level of detail devoted to accounts of other battles was reduced compared to the manuscript memoir.[51]

In the revolt of November 29, 1729, the Natchez killed 230 to 240

---

51. On Natchez archaeology and ethnohistory, see Robert Neitzel, *Archeology of the Fatherland Site: The Grand Village of the Natchez* (New York, 1965); Ian K. Brown, "An Archaeological Study of Culture Contact and Change in the Natchez Bluffs Region," in Patricia K. Galloway, ed., *La Salle and His Legacy: Frenchmen and Indians in the Lower Mississippi Valley* (Jackson, Miss., 1982); Karl G. Lorenz, "A Re-examination of Natchez Sociopolitical Complexity: A View from the Grand Village and Beyond," *Southeastern Archaeology,* XVI, no. 2 (Winter 1997), 97–112; and Vincas P. Steponaitis, ed., *The Natchez District in the Old, Old South* (Chapel Hill, N.C., 1998). DuVal has observed of the French colony, "Because they wanted a colony to rival the Spanish and English and because they sought to rule Louisiana despite lacking a large army, they had to pay attention to Indian priorities," and "in reality, the French had little power, and the Mississippi valley remained largely an Indian-defined and Indian-controlled place through the end of the eighteenth century" ("Interconnectedness and Diversity in 'French Louisiana,'" in Waselkov, Wood, and Hatley, eds., *Powhatan's Mantle,* 133–134). See also Khalil Saadani, "Gift Exchange between the French and Native Americans in Louisiana," in Bond, ed., *French Colonial Louisiana and the Atlantic World,* 43–64.

Frenchmen in and around Fort Rosalie, including the commander Chepart (whose first name is unknown and whose family name was spelled variously, such as "Etcheparre"). Dumont, Le Page, and other observers blamed Chepart for provoking the attack. The Natchez spared the lives of women, children, and African slaves, numbering several hundred captives. The French under Governor Périer tried to strike back and in February 1730 besieged the Natchez inside two forts the latter had built near the site of their Grand village on the banks of Saint Catherine Creek. Dumont claims that in 1728 he had been ordered to help the Indians design and build one of these forts, even though he foresaw the danger of such assistance. The siege went poorly for the French, who relied upon the help of their Choctaw allies. When the Choctaws liberated some captives, they turned to the French and demanded ransom payments. Most of the Natchez, along with many of the African slaves who had joined them, escaped the fort and fled to refuge among other natives, including the Chickasaws. It was partly to attempt to punish these refugee Natchez that Bienville, restored to his post as governor in 1733, pursued the two failed campaigns against the Chickasaws.[52]

DUMONT, ETHNOGRAPHER

Writing the history of the Natchez uprising posed several challenges for Dumont. He could not produce the kind of eyewitness battle narratives he wrote elsewhere in the manuscript memoir, for he did not participate in the 1730 siege of the Natchez or the retaliations that followed the Indians' surprise attack on the French. (Likewise, he had not participated in a 1722 expedition against the Natchez, which is excluded from the text.) Although the *Mémoires historiques* state that he had left Natchez the day before the revolt, in fact, he had departed ten months earlier. He relied on eyewitness information from women who had been held captive by the Natchez following the revolt, notably his wife, Marie Baron Roussin. Marie had lived at Natchez for longer than he had, had been his landlady during his service at the post in 1727 and 1728, and her first husband, Jean Roussin, was killed by the Natchez. She and her children had been held by a female chief who retained high status in the matrilineal political system of the tribe. Marie

---

52. For Dumont's design of the fort, see below, original manuscript [194]. On the revolt, see Arnaud Balvay, *La révolte des Natchez* (Paris, 2008); James F. Barnett, Jr., *The Natchez Indians: A History to 1735* (Jackson, Miss., 2007), 101–135; and the list of victims compiled by Father Philibert, the priest assigned to Natchez, in *MPA*, I, 122–166.

might have spoken Mobilien, the trade jargon of the Mississippi valley, and also some Natchez, so she was able to learn information that no living Frenchman would have known: how the Natchez had planned and executed their devastating attack. This information was even more important to the epic poem and the *Mémoires historiques,* in which the narrative of the planning is more elaborate and romanticized than in the manuscript memoir.[53]

Dumont's ethnography of the Natchez near the end of the manuscript contributes new insights not only for understanding that nation but also for understanding the rhetoric and epistemology of French colonial ethnographies in general. In the *Mémoires historiques,* the Natchez feast of the Green Corn (which Dumont calls the "tonne de valeur," after the tun, or silo, where the corn was stored) is described from a generalized perspective, as if it proceeded in exactly the same way every summer. The manuscript memoir, on the other hand, tells which Frenchmen were invited along with Dumont to participate in it and what role they played in the ceremonies. It also allows inference about which two summers Dumont took part. And, whereas colonial ethnographies often claim to provide a total account of indigenous customs, the manuscript focuses on the crafts of tanning and pottery, which were performed mostly by women. Hence it gives an idea of the daily labors and exchanges between French settlers and the Natchez, the elements of a "frontier exchange economy" that enabled French colonizers and their slaves to survive when imports from France were scarce and expensive and French settlers were still learning agriculture in an unfamiliar climate and soil. Dumont, at one point, was ordered to go from Natchez to the Arkansas River to buy corn from the Indians, and later, after being stopped at Pointe Coupée, he reported on the profitable trading of a settler there. These exchanges also included sexual liaisons, which the manuscript acknowledges more openly than the published book does. Finally, in the manuscript memoir, Dumont does not express the kind of distance from or disdain for indigenous spiritual practices that both pious Catholics and rationalist Enlightenment authors conveyed in their colonial ethnographies. The Jesuit Joseph-François Lafitau, in his voluminous ethnography

53. See *Mémoires historiques,* II, 134–138, 154; "Poème," 323–324. In those texts, as in Le Page du Pratz's *Histoire de la Louisiane,* III, 230–251, the Natchez attempt to coordinate a surprise attack with allied nations by distributing a bundle of token sticks represented the number of days until the attack. The plan goes awry when a woman or young child steals a few of the sticks. See Gordon M. Sayre, *The Indian Chief as Tragic Hero: Native Resistance and the Literatures of America, from Moctezuma to Tecumseh* (Chapel Hill, N.C., 2005), 232–248.

of the Iroquoian peoples in New France, analyzed their religious practices as vestiges of ancient beliefs of peoples in Asia and the Holy Lands; Recollet Chrestien LeClercq saw among the Mikmaq clues that they had received the revelation of Christianity. Conversely, Lahontan had portrayed the sexual and spiritual beliefs of the Hurons as a form of rational deism. By contrast, Dumont does not attempt to theorize native religion but suggests that, for some Frenchmen, including himself, their shamanist prophetic techniques were legitimate and even powerful. When a ship from France is late arriving in Quebec, Dumont recounts how a native woman explained the causes of the delay. When a drought afflicts the Yazoo area, a shaman of that tribe does a successful rain dance. Dumont did not distinguish between European and native beliefs as a matter of science versus superstition; he was most of all concerned, as in his own unconventional medical cures, with what proved effective.[54]

DUMONT, CARTOGRAPHER AND ARTIST

At times in his life when he enjoyed periods of calm leisure, such as in Quebec in 1717, Yazoo from 1721 to 1722, and La Rochelle during his layover in 1718, Dumont occupied himself by drawing and painting. His extant maps and sketches, including the twenty-three watercolors that accompany the manuscript memoir, not only illustrate and corroborate his autobiography; they constitute a worthy source in their own right for research on French Louisiana. Dumont's techniques as a cartographer were crude compared to some of his contemporaries in the colony, such as the engineers and draftsmen Valentin Devin, Adrien Pauger, Jean-Paul Le Sueur, the Broutins (Ignace-François and his son Ignace), and Louis-Pierre Le Blond de la Tour. Mapmaking was an integral part of training for colonial officers and engi-

54. On dating the new corn ceremony, see Sayre, "Natchez Ethnohistory Revisited," *Louisiana History*, L (2009), 428–430. For other accounts of the ceremony, see *Mémoires historiques*, I, 195–209, and *Histoire de la Louisiane*, II, 363–381. Daniel H. Usner, Jr., *Indians, Settlers, and Slaves in a Frontier Exchange Economy: The Lower Mississippi Valley before 1783* (Chapel Hill, N.C., 1992), 16–43, describes frontier exchange with many references to Dumont's published book. For trade on the frontier, see below, original manuscript [160, 189]. For native spiritual practices, see Joseph-François Lafitau, *The Customs of the American Indians Compared with the Customs of Primitive Times*, ed. and trans. William N. Fenton and Elizabeth Moore (Toronto, 1974); Louis-Armand de Lom d'Arce, baron de Lahontan, *New Voyages to North-America, Part 3: Dialogues between the Author and a General of the Savages* (London, 1703); Chrestien Le Clercq, *New Relation of Gaspesia with the Customs and Religion of the Gaspesian Indians* (Toronto, 1910); original manuscript [24–25; 127–128].

neers and particularly important in the colonial context. More than thirty maps were made of New Orleans alone during the French colonial period.[55]

The simplicity and roughness of Dumont's maps arise in part from being drawn from memory after he returned to France. They were not drawn to scale using the skills of a surveyor. Similarly, his drawings of ethnographic and natural history subjects are not up to the standards of later scientific travelers and naturalists. Nonetheless, his efforts were self-motivated and based on firsthand observations, and they count among a small, extant corpus of such illustrations from French colonial Louisiana. Only the portfolio of fourteen drawings by Alexandre de Batz and the recently rediscovered images by Marc-Antoine Caillot are comparable, if distinguished by greater artistic talent.[56]

Although he likes to present himself in the manuscript memoir as an engineer and artist, Dumont does not appear to have received training in France to acquire such skills. He was only nineteen years old when sent to Quebec and had served in the army a short time, so his limited abilities can largely be attributed to a lack of experience. When given a part-time commission as an engineer, he was probably expected to receive this training in the field, but owing to his fraught relationships with superiors, he never got very far in his formal education. Nevertheless, he certainly engaged in drawing and mapmaking while in the colonies. Because of several mishaps, such as an overturned canoe and the burning of his house below New Orleans, only a sample of his work survives in the archives, and he most likely drew those maps after his return to France. At least one map by Dumont was drawn on-site in Louisiana, however. A map of Pascagoula, now at the Bibliothèque nationale de France, bears an annotation by a clerk or conservator explaining that on the back of the map appears a manuscript note, indicating that the map was sent to Paris along with a letter by La Chaise dated October 30, 1726.[57]

55. The best access to these maps and dozens of others is the website maintained by Vincas C. Steponaitis of the University of North Carolina, Chapel Hill, at http://rla.unc.edu./natchez/. See also Dawdy, *Building the Devil's Empire*, 63–98; and Samuel Wilson, Jean M. Farnsworth, and Ann M. Masson, eds., *The Architecture of Colonial Louisiana: The Collected Essays of Samuel Wilson, Jr.* (Lafayette, La., 1987).

56. The de Batz drawings are held by the Peabody Museum of Archaeology and Ethnology at Harvard University. The Caillot manuscript is held by The Historic New Orleans Collection: "Relation du voyage de la Louisiane ou Nouvelle France fait par le Sr. Caillot en l'année 1730," acc. no. 2005.11.

57. "Carte de la riviere de Pascagoula, où l'on voit la situation des isles, lacs, et terrain des habitans," BNF, Ge–DD 2987 (8818B). Because conservators have added a linen backing to the map, it is not possible to confirm the presence of this note.

On his first voyage to Louisiana, Dumont had a commission as an engineer under chief engineer Perrier (not to be confused with Governor Périer). On his second voyage, he was assigned to Le Blond de la Tour, who at the time commanded the engineers' brigade in the colony. The job of engineer was a highly respected one in the French military, and Dumont, ever sensitive to matters of rank and status, seems to have aspired to a promotion. Drawing maps of colonies, forts, and battlefield engagements was a way to accomplish this, as well as increase the value of his manuscript memoir. He writes that, when he returned to Paris and visited Gérard-Michel de la Jonchère, a partner of Belle-Isle, he drew a map of one of the plantations the two had owned at Chaouachas. Another of Dumont's maps of Louisiana, held today at the Bibliothèque nationale, is catalogued as having been drawn in 1737, the year Dumont returned from Louisiana, and owned by M. le maréchal de Coëtlogon, a relative of Dumont's commander in Brittany. When assigned the task of designing a fort on the concession at Yazoo, Dumont writes, "I outlined a fort with four bastions, after the style of M. de Vauban." Sébastien Le Prestre, Seigneur de Vauban (1633–1707), the famous military architect of the ancien régime, is credited with establishing the proud tradition of French military engineering, and his clever geometric designs for virtually impenetrable fortresses were a key to French military success during the reign of Louis XIV. Vauban was also responsible for the expansion and professionalization of the engineer class within the French army. Training for draftsmen and engineers included hand-copying Vauban's extensive oeuvre of designs, which then became a reference source in the field. Dumont's sketches are not of the quality of a true military architect, and in any case, there was neither the time nor the resources to build a Yazoo fort up to the standards of Vauban's famous designs in France.[58]

Dumont's sketches of such posts and forts are not entirely concerned with military strategy and are not consistent in their techniques. Some of his maps function like storyboards, with a sequence of events represented at various places in the image and letters in the legend serving as a key to the narrative (see, for example, Figure 11, depicting the army at Chickasaw, and Figure 12, of the battle near Polduc in Brittany). The same technique

58. Original manuscript [114]; "Carte de la province de la Loüisiane autrefois le Mississipy," BNF, Cartes et plans, SHM Portefeuille, 138 bis, no. 29; Bernard Pujo, *Vauban* (Paris, 1991); F. J. Hebbert, *Soldier of France: Sebastien LePrestre de Vauban, 1633–1707* (New York, 1990). Dumont, in the mid-1740s, lived and worked in the Citadel de Port-Louis in Brittany, which, although not designed by Vauban, had been modified in the mid-1600s in a manner consistent with his principles.

was used by Ignace-François Broutin and other engineers who documented the battlefield tactics used by the French in besieging the Natchez Indians in 1730 and 1731. On other maps, Dumont's cartographic style is a mixture of elevation and plan that may be unfamiliar to modern eyes but was also used around the same time in Giuseppe Vasi's engravings of Rome, printed in his popular tourist guides to the city. In Figure 6, Dumont drew the Yazoo fort with its four bastions and adjacent parterre garden in plan view, but the houses of the concession's workers are depicted in elevation views, as are the nearby hills and ravine of canes. The scale is wildly inconsistent, with the canes and what appears to be an animal hiding among them drawn on a much larger scale than the houses or the river at the bottom of the frame. Dumont's illustrations of his sponsors' concessions at Terre Blanche (Figure 9) and Chaouachas (Figure 13) and the sketch of his property near New Orleans (Figure 8) are not so much cartographic guides as portraits of colonial plantations intended to show off the owners' wealth or to demonstrate improvements made in the wilds of Louisiana. The same is true of his maps of New Orleans, which show exactly which lots were built up when he lived there in the 1730s.[59]

Some of the extant maps in Paris archives allow glimpses into Dumont's life beyond what he relates in his manuscript memoir. The Delisle collection at the Archives nationales in Paris contains six little-known sketch maps that Dumont supplied to the royal cartographers, Philippe Buache and Joseph-Nicolas Delisle, who were always eager to get firsthand information that could enhance their maps of the Americas. Dumont's six sketches most likely date from the period 1748 to 1752. Buache and the Delisles were committed to the existence of a river route westward across North America, emerging in a large bay the French cartographers called the "Sea of the West" *(mer de l'ouest)*. In his letter to Buache of August 15, 1750, Dumont offered to lead an expedition to find this route, and on his map of the Arkansas River, he wrote that, from the westernmost point of his travels with Bénard de la Harpe in 1722, the Spanish colony of Santa Fe was "at a distance estimated as 10–12 leagues," or barely more than fifty kilometers. Likewise, in the *Mémoires historiques,* he claimed the expedition had followed the Arkansas upstream "to within a few days' journey of Santa Fé." His sketch map of Arkansas might have been less serious cartography than an effort to flatter the royal cartographers.[60]

59. On Vasi, see James T. Tice and James G. Harper, *Giuseppe Vasi's Rome: Lasting Impressions from the Age of the Grand Tour* (Eugene, Ore., 2010).

60. *Mémoires historiques,* II, 282. On Buache and Delisle's methods of gathering carto-

Four of the twenty-three illustrations to the manuscript memoir, as well as five of the sixteen in the manuscript poem, are drawings of plants, animals, birds, and fish. In 1747, the year Dumont was writing his memoir, there had yet been few botanical explorers of North America, although the Louisiana colonist and memoirist Vallette de Laudun did write of scientific matters, and Mark Catesby published his *Natural History of Carolina, Florida, and the Bahama Islands* in that year.[61] In 1735, Carl Linnaeus had published his *Systema Naturæ* and thereafter began to attract students, sending them off to colonial corners of the world to collect specimens and record observations. In France, the influence of Georges-Louis Leclerc, comte de Buffon, as steward of the Royal Gardens was already being felt, although the first volume of his *Histoire naturelle, générale, et particulière* was not published until 1749. Dumont's observations reflected a fashionable interest in describing the natural world, but it would be unreasonable to expect him to adhere to the taxonomic standards of the scientific vanguard, Linnaeus and Buffon. His description of sharks and porpoises in the first chapter, for example, is filled with folk mythology.

In the manuscript, Dumont's goal was, not to classify taxonomically or anatomically the species he drew, but to document their behaviors using direct observation. In this respect, his drawings of alligators laying eggs and of the Indians' methods for tracking animals are observant and informative (Figures 22 and 14). In drawing and describing the natives' method of using a deerskin disguise to approach and shoot deer, Dumont is relying upon his eyewitness experience, not a library of exotic images frequently invoked by colonial writers (such as the oft-copied John White drawings and de Bry engravings). The final section of the manuscript, in which these topical illustrations are embedded, adopts the ethnographic mode common in colonial history texts. Some of Dumont's images and descriptions depict aspects of native life discussed by few others, such as the square frame used to torture captives, and various types of musical instruments. In their immediacy and naive honesty, the manuscript memoir's illustrations offer significant ethnographic and environmental information about the indigenous peoples of

graphic knowledge, see Nelson-Martin Dawson, *L'atelier Delisle: L'Amérique du Nord sur la table à dessein* (Quebec, 2000), 102–108. The six maps are in ANF, collection Delisle, 6 JJ 75, and the map of the Arkansas River is entitled "Cours de la rivierre des Arcansas ou Zotaoüis dans laquelle a eté le Sr. de la Harpe a la decouverte d'un rocher demeraudes en 1722, et la ditte R. relevée par le Sr. Dumont Demontigny lieutent de la Compagnie des Indes et des concessions du Marechal duc de Belleisle, etablie au yazoux."

61. Vallette de Laudun, *Journal d'un voyage à la Louisiane, fait en 1720* (Paris, 1768).

the New World, but, even more important, they show how a common soldier might have viewed them.[62]

In addition to the obvious pleasure Dumont took in the pastimes of drawing, writing, and storytelling, he also applied himself to agricultural pursuits with enjoyment and pride, even as his marginal economic existence in the colony and later in Brittany necessitated this skill. He boasts of his expertise and of the beauty and bounty of his produce. In New Orleans in the 1720s and 1730s, most food eaten by French colonists came from local Indians, and Dumont's contributions to the market would have been welcome. His descriptions of Louisianans' seasonal diet and cuisine, particularly in the last section of the manuscript—the chapter entitled "Natural History" in this translation—are an unusually detailed and valuable source for historians and anthropologists. As Dawdy has revealed, French Louisianans quickly learned foodways from local native peoples: unfamiliar game such as opossum and buffalo, numerous fishes, and plants, including corn but also *plaquemine* (persimmon), and flour made from a species of cane. Louisianans both devised new recipes for new ingredients and sought out substitutes for familiar dishes, such as when Dumont gathered wild sorrel for a salad and dressed it with bear grease and his homemade oak syrup vinegar.[63]

Dumont's agricultural career, in his garden in New Orleans (illustrated in Figure 21) and as a gardener in the fort at Port-Louis, was undertaken as a practicality but may also reflect the growing interest in gardening that comprised part of the French Enlightenment. During Dumont's lifetime, many new, high-profile gardens were designed and created in Paris, and a plethora of writings about agriculture appeared. The interest in gardening within Enlightenment intellectual circles spanned from the purely aesthetic "folly" gardens, as a form of baroque aestheticized nature, to agronomical and scientific interests in biology and efficient production. Dumont's gardening is proudly focused on food self-sufficiency but also clearly satisfied his own aesthetic and sensual pleasures. Compare his writing on gardening to that of his Louisiana rival, Le Page du Pratz, who experimented with dif-

62. Among the engravings in de Bry's *Florida* (Frankfurt, 1591), based on now-lost drawings by Jacques Le Moyne de Morgues, is one of native Americans hunting deer by using a deerskin disguise. See the reproduction in Stephen Lorant, *The New World: The First Pictures of America* (New York, 1946), 85.

63. On the New Orleans food market, see Daniel H. Usner, Jr., "American Indians in Colonial New Orleans," in Waselkov, Wood, and Hatley, eds., *Powhatan's Mantle*, 163–186; Shannon Lee Dawdy, "'A Wild Taste': Food and Colonialism in Eighteenth-Century Louisiana," *Ethnohistory*, LVII (2010), 389–414. For the salad dressing, see original manuscript [160].

ferent strains of tobacco and other plants with the purpose of developing an efficient cash crop. Le Page du Pratz's agricultural writing is matter-of-fact and scientific rather than personal in tone, perhaps reflecting the fact that he directed slaves in this activity rather than worked at it himself.[64]

CONCLUSION

The combination of autobiography and colonial history in Dumont's manuscript memoir, with its touches of picaresque and ethnography, is a unique gift to students of both history and literature and a remarkable portrait of the French Atlantic world. Although earlier French American travel accounts like Samuel de Champlain's provide a sense of the movements possible through navigation, from the Isthmus of Panama to the Saint Lawrence seaway, they offer little about what life was like for Champlain the explorer, who, among his many adventures, saw twenty out of twenty-eight colonists perish in one winter. And whereas other writers might report on life in the colonies with some detail, as did Dumont's rival Le Page du Pratz, the authors' own roles in the events of history and their individual personalities often become obscured by a dispassionate, impersonal language of history and natural history.[65]

Writing more than a travel account or a colonial history, Dumont takes us along on his life's journey through a Louisiana that suffered periodic food shortages, Indian wars, and a high degree of lawlessness. Like Dumont's cartography, the colonial endeavor was more of an improvised affair than a planned and surveyed blueprint. Dumont prayed with nuns on shipboard to be saved from tempests, planted corn and tobacco in the muddy Louisiana soil, suffered scurvy and tropical fevers, and walked delirious and barefoot across the icy streets of Quebec. He married and raised children in frontier

64. Although Dumont also owned slaves in Louisiana, he writes that he rented them out to earn cash and appears to have tended his New Orleans garden himself. His aptitude for farming was fortunate, since, like most early Louisiana colonists, he hailed from France's cities and, as Johnson has observed, "not a single one of more than three hundred troops sent to Louisiana before 1720 listed farming as his former occupation" ("Colonial New Orleans," in Logsdon and Hirsch, eds., *Creole New Orleans*, 32). On gardening in eighteenth-century France, see Elizabeth Hyde, *Cultivated Power: Flowers, Culture, and Politics in the Reign of Louis XIV* (Philadelphia, 2005); Gilles-Antoine Langlois, *Folies, tivolis, et attractions: Les premiers parcs de loisirs parisiens* (Paris, 1991); and Dawdy, *Building the Devil's Empire*, 83–84.

65. Portions of this final section, and the preceding one, were written by Shannon Lee Dawdy. On Champlain and his impersonal style of writing, see David Hackett Fischer, *Champlain's Dream* (New York, 2008), 4.

New Orleans. He fought Indians and ate bear fat. These experiences, sensual and quotidian, are as important to understanding the French Atlantic world as his narratives of battles and exposés of crooked and inept officials. Dumont's view comes neither from the top nor exactly from below. The very fact of his literacy sets him apart from the true underclass. His is a view from the middle of the Atlantic world—indeed, from the very thick of it.

CHRONOLOGY OF THE LIFE OF DUMONT
AND EVENTS IN HIS MEMOIR

1696 July 31—Jean-François-Benjamin Dumont de Montigny born in
      Paris
1698 Spanish establish a fort at Pensacola
1699 French colony founded in Louisiana by Pierre Le Moyne
      d'Iberville, with Fort Maurepas at Biloxi
      Jean-Baptiste Le Moyne de Bienville repels English and Huguenot
      explorers at English Turn on the Mississippi
1700 D'Iberville and Bienville return on second expedition and sail up
      the Mississippi as far as Natchez. Bienville also explores the Red
      River, and Pierre Le Sueur begins a voyage along the Mississippi
      River nearly to its source
1702 Bienville establishes Fort Louis at Mobile and is appointed
      governor of colony
1706 D'Iberville dies at Havana
1710 Bienville moves the capital of the colony from Dauphin Island to
      Mobile
1712 September—Antoine Crozat, a wealthy financier with interests in
      Saint-Domingue and Guinea, is granted a monopoly on trade
      in Louisiana in exchange for commitments to populate and
      develop the colony
1713 March—Treaty of Utrecht brings an end to the War of the Spanish
      Succession; France cedes claims in Hudson's Bay to Britain
      Lamothe Cadillac replaces Bienville as governor of Louisiana
1714 Dumont enters military service as a cadet and is posted to Verdun
      in northeastern France
      Jacques Barbazon de Pailloux builds a trading post at Natchez
1715 Dumont is sent to Rochefort and enlisted in the *gardes de la
      marine*
      July 21–Sept. 12—Dumont sails to Quebec in the *Victoire*
      Sept. 1—Louis XIV dies; the regent, Philippe d'Orléans, rules
      France in place of the five-year-old Louis XV until 1722
1716 Dumont, ill with scurvy, convalesces in Quebec hospital
      Fort Rosalie founded at Natchez

March—Jean-Michel de l'Epinay is appointed as governor of Louisiana and arrives a year later to replace Lamothe Cadillac

November—Marc-Antoine Hubert replaces Jean-Baptiste Dubois Duclos as *commissaire ordonnateur* of Louisiana

1717 Crozat gives up his monopoly concession on trade in Louisiana; it is granted to John Law

Nov. 12—Dumont sails from Quebec for La Rochelle in the *Cheval Marin*

1718 Dumont's father, Jacques Dumont, dies in Paris sometime before March 11

Dumont spends the year at La Rochelle

The Compagnie de l'Occident is created and given monopoly of the Louisiana colony

New Orleans is surveyed and designated as the site of Louisiana's future capital city

War of the Quadruple Alliance in Europe sets off battles between France and Spain in the colonies

1719 Dumont receives commission as sublieutenant in the troops of the Company of the Indies, guards emigrant prisoners at La Rochelle, then sails for Louisiana on May 21 in the *Marie*

Aug. 31—Dumont arrives at Dauphin Island amid battles with Spanish forces at Pensacola, which is twice captured by the French in May and September

1720 May—Dumont sails for Lorient, via Havana, in the *Mutine*

August to October—John Law's financial scheme collapses in the Mississippi Bubble

October to November—Dumont assigned as a half-pay lieutenant to the citadel at Port-Louis, Brittany, then receives commission as lieutenant for the Company of the Indies in Louisiana

1721 January—Dumont sets sail in the *Charente*, which returns to port stricken with pestilence

March—Dumont sails from Lorient to Louisiana in either the *Portefaix* or the *Saône*

November—Dumont assigned to post at new fort at Yazoo

1722 February to April—Dumont participates in exploration of the Arkansas River, led by Bénard de la Harpe

September—Hurricane badly damages the new settlement of New Orleans

October—Dumont imprisoned in New Orleans

November—Pensacola is at last returned to Spanish control, more than two years after the Treaty of the Hague ended the War of the Quadruple Alliance in Europe

September to October—Skirmishes with Natchez Indians begin with death of Pierre Guenot de Tréfontaine

1723 April—Royal commissioners La Chaise and Saunoy arrive in New Orleans and support Dumont in his dispute with Bienville; La Chaise serves as commissaire ordonnateur following Saunoy's death

October to November—Dumont participates in military expedition against the Natchez

1724 A specially revised Code Noir is promulgated for Louisiana

April—Louis XV orders Bienville to return to France

July—Dumont departs Yazoo and descends the Mississippi River to New Orleans

August—Dumont sails for France on the *Profond* but returns to New Biloxi Oct. 31

November—Dumont moves to Pascagoula and works at the concession of Delagarde

1725 April 1—The *Bellone,* on which Bienville and Etienne Véniard de Bourgmont were to sail to France, sinks while at anchor off of Dauphin Island

June 11—The Superior Council of Louisiana grants Dumont one year's salary

June to August—Bienville returns to France on the *Gironde*

1726 August 9—Etienne Périer is appointed to replace Bienville as governor of Louisiana

Ignace-François Broutin replaces Claude-Charles Dutisné as commandant at Natchez; Dumont travels upstream to Natchez, where he serves under Broutin

1727 March—Périer arrives to take the post of governor

February—The first party of Ursuline nuns sails from Lorient for New Orleans with mission of opening a hospital and school

1728 February—Chepart replaces François-Louis de Merveilleux as commandant at Natchez

October to December—Dumont held in irons by Chepart

1729 Jan. 7—Dumont flees Natchez and descends the Mississippi to New Orleans

June 3—Dumont receives land grant and advance on his salary from Governor Périer

November 29—Natchez Indians attack Fort Rosalie and kill 240
French

1730   January–February—Siege of the Natchez led by Jean-Paul Le
Sueur

April 19—Dumont marries Marie Baron Roussin, widow of Jean
Roussin, in New Orleans

June—Conspiracy for a slave revolt in New Orleans is unraveled
and suppressed

1731   Etienne Gatien Salmon is appointed commissaire ordonnateur

January–February—Expedition against the Natchez refugees at
Natchitoches

June 1—Louisiana monopoly is withdrawn from the Company of
the Indies; the colony reverts to crown control

November 28—Marie-Françoise, daughter of Dumont and Marie
Baron, baptized in New Orleans

1732   September—Dumont's house along the Mississippi, below New
Orleans, is destroyed by fire

December—Bienville returns to Louisiana and resumes post as
governor

1733   January 2—Jean-François, son of Dumont and Marie Baron,
baptized in New Orleans

1734   The Dumont family resides in New Orleans on Dauphin Street

1736   February—Dumont joins militia for expedition against the
Chickasaw Indians

May—French troops and militia attack Ackia, a Chickasaw town in
eastern Mississippi

1737   June 12—Dumont and family sail from New Orleans for Rochefort
in the *Somme*

August–September—Dumont family travels to Le Mesnil-Thomas
and Verneuil-sur-Avre to visit Marie's relatives

1738   Dumont resides in Paris, then, in May, is posted to Port-Louis

1739   Dumont serves as lieutenant in the citadel at Port-Louis

September—Bienville begins a second expedition against the
Chickasaw Indians; Fort Assumption built

1740   April—French make peace with the Chickasaws, destroy forts
they had built near site of Memphis, and retreat down the
Mississippi

1741   Dumont begins dispute with major de la place at Port-Louis

October—Dumont again travels to Paris, visits Gérard-Michel
de la Jonchère

1742   Dumont returns to Port-Louis, obtains appointment as captain of the gates, completes manuscript of epic poem about Louisiana

1743   Bienville retires, and marquis de Vaudreuil replaces him as governor of Louisiana

1744   The Arsenal manuscript of Dumont's epic poem is completed and dedicated to comte d'Argenson

1746   September–October—English expedition invades Brittany and attempts to capture Lorient

1747   March to May—Dumont's son Jean-François sails from Lorient on the *Philibert* and is captured and held prisoner in England

Jul. 21–Nov. 24—Dumont imprisoned in Port-Louis, completes his prose memoir

1750   August—Dumont writes to Philippe Buache concerning exploration of the Arkansas River and likely location of the mer de l'ouest

1751   Dumont presumably resides in Paris as he writes and publishes articles in the *Journal œconomique;* maps preserved in the Delisle collection at the Archives nationales are likely also from this period

1753   C. J. B. Bauche publishes *Mémoires historiques sur la Louisiane*

1754   March 31—Company of the Indies ship the *Paix* is armed at Lorient; Dumont embarks as a passenger along with his wife, Marie; he holds rank of lieutenant

August 20—Dumont and wife disembark at Ile de France, or Mauritius, after stopovers at Gorée, Senegal, and Madagascar

1755   June 12–Aug. 2—Dumont and his wife sail from Mauritius to Pondicherry, India, aboard the Company of the Indies vessel the *Bourbon*

1758   Antoine-Simon Le Page du Pratz's *Histoire de la Louisiane* published

1760   Dumont dies in India

THE DUMONT FAMILY

The author of the memoir presented in this volume might more accurately be known as "François-Benjamin Dumont," but we cannot alter the fact that library catalogs and biographical dictionaries have long referred to him as "Jean-François-Benjamin Dumont de Montigny." In eighteenth-century sources, his given and family names appear in several forms, and such polymorphism was common in that era.

To begin with the surname, we do not know why the youngest son of Jacques-François Dumont and Françoise Delamare chose to call himself Dumont de Montigny and not simply Dumont, as did all other members of his family except one niece, Louise-Madeleine Dumont de Montigny. The historian Jean Delanglez, in his 1937 article entitled "A Louisiana Poet-Historian: Dumont *dit* Montigny" (where "dit," literally "called," is equivalent to the English acronym "aka"), asserted of our author: "It seems he changed his nickname, *dit*, into a title of nobility. Self-ennobling was not uncommon in colonial Louisiana." Some Louisiana colonists did assume titles that they had not brought with them from distant France, but Delanglez was unjust in his accusation. On the list of passengers of the *Marie* in 1719, our author is already inscribed as "Dumont de Montygny," and, once in the colony, he appeared in official documents as "Dumont Demontigny," "Demontigny," "Demonsigny," or simply "Dumont."[1]

The form of his given name was also variable. Our author signs the dedication to this memoir "F. Dumont" and within its pages tells the reader that he celebrated the feast of Saint François as his name day. On the inventory of his father's estate, he is identified as "François-Benjamin." The use

---

1. "Inventory upon the Death of Marie-Anne de Lutel, Widow of Jean-Baptiste Dumont, Mother of Louise-Madeleine Dumont de Montigny," May 8, 1782, ANF, Minutier central, LX, 440; Jean Delanglez, "A Louisiana Poet-Historian: Dumont *dit* Montigny," *Mid-America*, XIX (1937), 31–49, esp. 32; Albert Laplace Dart, trad., "Ship Lists of Passengers Leaving France for Louisiana, 1718–1724," *LHQ*, XV (1932), 453–467, esp. 455 (the original document is in ANOM, COL, G1 464, no. 13); "Petition of Dumont Demontigny," Apr. 7, 1730, and "Petition of Demontigny," May 1737, both in Superior Council of Louisiana, *Proceedings*, Louisiana State Museum, nos. 1730040602, 1737050404, transcribed in *LHQ*, IV (1921), 518–520, V (1922), 399. Dumont signed these petitions as the name appears in these titles. On names and social hierarchies of colonial New Orleans, see Shannon Lee Dawdy, *Building the Devil's Empire: French Colonial New Orleans* (Chicago, 2008), 160–173.

of "Benjamin" is probably explained by the fact that he was the youngest of the brothers in his family. In Louisiana, on the day of his marriage, he called himself "François-Benjamin." In Brittany, where he wrote the memoir, he was recorded as "François-Benjamin" when he served as captain of the gates in Port-Louis in 1746–1747, as "Jean-Baptiste-François" by the pen of a bailiff at the seneschal court in Hennebont on November 3, 1747, and as "Jean-Baptiste-François" on the register that records the death of his daughter in Port-Louis in 1759. Certain specialists have deduced from the "L—— D——" on the title page of the memoir that his given name was Louis, but the *L* more likely stands for "Lieutenant," and hence the title for this translation.[2]

That Dumont could set down his life and times in both an epic poem and a prose memoir was a consequence of his education and literacy, as well as his family's connections to influential men such as the duc de Belle-Isle and the comte d'Argenson. Dumont's paternal grandfather was identified simply as a "bourgeois de Paris" at the time of his father's marriage in 1673. His mother came from a family of more elevated social standing. Her father was a prosecutor in the Paris parlement, and at her marriage to Dumont's father, she was attended by witnesses of high social standing and of the nobility; her family provided a substantial income for the couple.[3] They had seven children: six boys and one girl (the youngest). Among Dumont's five older brothers, three were lawyers, one was a priest, and one both a lawyer and a priest. If the young François-Benjamin was destined to become the black sheep of the family, his brother Pierre-Jean-Baptiste was its pride, first a lawyer in the parlement and then, beginning in 1719, in the *conseil du roi*, or King's Council.

When his father died in the winter of 1718, Dumont had just returned from his voyage to Quebec and was in La Rochelle, awaiting further orders. At the time, the Dumont family was living in a rented house in Paris on the rue des Poitevins, in the parish of Saint-André-des-Arts. Five of the seven children were present for the inventorying of their father's possessions on

2. Earl C. Woods and Charles E. Nolan, eds., *Sacramental Records of the Roman Catholic Church of the Archdiocese of New Orleans*, I, *1718–1750* (New Orleans, 1987), 12; Henri-François Buffet, *Vie et société au Port-Louis des origines à Napoléon III* (Rennes, 1972), 33; ADM, B 2660, fol. 2v (Registre des dépôts de sentences rendues au siège de la sénéchaussée d'Hennebont); ADM, 4 e 181/2, fol. 376 bis. (Municipal Archives of Port-Louis, register of baptisms, marriages, and burials for the years 1748–1779).

3. Marriage contract of Jacques-François Dumont and Françoise Delamare, Jan. 22, 1673, ANF, Minutier central, XLIV, 46.

March 11, 1718. The eldest son was already deceased; the youngest son, our author, did not attend. The Dumont home was well furnished, and several *rentes* contracted by the father assured a steady revenue. This inheritance presumably allowed Pierre to purchase his office in the council the following year, which, in turn, must have enabled him to secure the Louisiana commissions for his youngest brother. François-Benjamin only learned of his father's death in winter 1719 as he was preparing to embark for Louisiana, and even allowing for the fact that news often traveled slowly in ancien régime France, this delay confirms the general impression given in the memoir that Dumont was somewhat estranged from his family. On the first page of the inventory of his father's possessions, where the Dumont children are all identified, his name does not appear in the body of the document but was added in the margin, as if the family only remembered to tell the notary of his existence as an afterthought. Nonetheless, the memoir and the archives suggest that Dumont's brothers and his patrons continued to pull strings for Dumont throughout his years of colonial service.[4]

Dumont's memoir records a tumultuous life and a gradual decline in social status from the urbane gentility of his parents to the humble status of a market gardener in Louisiana and a low-ranking officer in the citadel at Port-Louis. On his initial voyage to Quebec, Dumont enjoyed the privilege of the captain's mess and had enough money in his pocket to pay the sailors an *amende* to avoid being drenched and humiliated in the carnivalesque "Baptism of the Line." During his sojourn in Quebec, he was excused from his military duties for a bad case of scurvy and spent most of the time convalescing in the *hôtel dieu* under the gentle care of nuns. But by the time he was writing the memoir, Dumont was struggling to claim the prerogatives that went with his post as captain of the gates, begging for a promotion, and scrambling to pay the rent and support his family. Dumont repeatedly sought backing from influential men such as d'Argenson, Belle-Isle, the marquis de Vaudreuil, Gérard-Michel de la Jonchère, and Dumont's own brother Pierre-Jean-Baptiste Dumont. One wonders that Pierre was not able to provide more assistance for his brother in the mid-to-late 1740s, when the memoir paints such a bleak financial picture for François-Benjamin. The inventory drawn up after Pierre's death in 1755, for his apartment on the rue des Fossés-Montmartre in the parish of Saint-Eustache, points to a very comfortable lifestyle. In one *cabinet* were four maps representing Europe, France, Paris, and Italy. The silver was valued

4. Inventory after the death of Jacques-François Dumont, Mar. 11, 1718, ibid., XLVI, 227.

at more than two thousand livres. There were 756 books in the library, including many volumes on law, but also works by writers such as Plutarch, Horace, Rabelais, and Molière. Nonetheless, Pierre must have been carrying large debts, for the widow and children renounced the succession, and all was sold at auction. This may account for Dumont's repeated pleas to such officials as d'Argenson and Belle-Isle for assistance in the 1740s. His brother might not have been able (or perhaps was unwilling) to help him out financially. There is no definitive evidence, but it seems likely that before Pierre Dumont's death, he and his youngest brother had become estranged.[5]

Still, a man in his fifties might not ask or expect to receive help from his brother, and in Louisiana, Dumont de Montigny had begun a family of his own. His wife, Marie Baron, was born around 1700 in Le Mesnil-Thomas, now a tiny farming village in the *département* of Eure-et-Loir, just southwest of Paris. She had arrived in Louisiana in 1719 or 1720, disembarking at Biloxi from the *Mutine*, among other women recorded on a list of women sent from Paris "by orders of the King." The reason for which Marie was forced to emigrate is not specified; whether as a prostitute, vagabond, criminal, or through a lettre de cachet is impossible to know. Louisiana had a reputation for welcoming women exiled for such debaucheries, but according to historian Vaughan Baker, these female *forçats* represented only one-fifth of all the women who emigrated from France to Louisiana during the period of John Law's scheme. In 1722, the church registries recorded the death of a daughter, Marie-Louise Baron, for whom the identity and age of the father are not specified, which suggests that the infant was illegitimate. Shortly afterward, Marie Baron married the habitant Jean Roussin. They appear on a census at Natchez in 1722 and again along with two children in 1726. Jean Roussin and his elder son, also named Jean, were killed in the uprising of the Natchez Indians in 1729, as Dumont tells us and as is confirmed in the list of victims prepared by Father Philibert.[6]

Dumont married the widow Marie in New Orleans on April 19, 1730. Considering how scarce French women were at the time in the colony (the gender ratio among Europeans was at best 1:5, even in denser settlements

5. Annual tables of burials for the years 1709–1775, Archives municipales de Lorient, GG 86; inventory after the death of Pierre-Jean-Baptiste Dumont, following which is recorded the renunciations of the succession by his wife and children, Apr. 18, 1755, ANF, Minutier central, LVIII, 380. T 202: Procès-verbal of the sale of the books and furnishings of the estate of Pierre-Jean-Baptiste Dumont.

6. *FFLa*, I, 28, II, 80; Vaughan B. Baker, "Cherchez les Femmes: Some Glimpses of Women in Early Eighteenth-Century Louisiana," *Louisiana History*, XXXI (1990), 21–37.

like New Orleans), Dumont married as well as he could for his station. Together, they raised Jean Roussin's second son, Jean-Charles, until he died on July 28, 1733, aged six years. In between, the couple had two children of their own, Marie-Anne-Françoise, born in 1731, and Jean-François, born in 1733. During this period, Marie participated in the founding of a lay confraternity of women associated with the Ursuline religious order in New Orleans, a group that also included the wives of some of the colony's elite planters and officials. Marie-Anne-Françoise eventually married Bernard Pesron, a bourgeois of Port-Louis, in that town in 1748. She died there in 1759, at the age of twenty-eight. As for Jean-François, the memoir indicates that he was to set sail early in 1748 on the *Hercule*. He does not appear on the list of passengers for that ship, which sailed in January, but is listed as an ensign on the roll for the *Auguste*, which was armed on February 15. The note next to his name, however, indicates that he stayed ashore in Port-Louis when the ship departed. Jean-François Dumont next appears in the archives as an ensign aboard the *Achille* on December 11, 1749, when that ship was armed at Lorient. The *Achille* sailed to Gorée in Senegal, to the Cape of Good Hope, to India and Mauritius, but Jean-François is reported as having deserted on September 23, 1750, to be replaced in his rank by the son of Etienne Lobry, the ship's captain.[7]

Evidently, neither the memoir presented to Belle-Isle nor the book published in Paris succeeded in winning Dumont a pension or a leadership post in Louisiana, but in 1753, he did resume service for the Company of the Indies. As he neared sixty years of age, he followed his son to the East Indies, where the latter might have remained in a civilian capacity after his desertion. On March 30, 1754, Dumont *père* and his wife embarked on a Company of the Indies ship, the *Paix*, with the privilege of the captain's mess but with Dumont again at the rank of lieutenant. Another ship's roll, for the *Bourbon*, shows the couple sailing from Mauritius to Pondicherry

---

7. Woods and Nolan, *Sacramental Records*, I, 91, 230; *FFLa*, II, 80; Charles R. Maduell, Jr., ed. and trans., *The Census Tables for the French Colony of Louisiana from 1699 through 1732* (Baltimore, 1972), 29; Emily Clark, "'By All the Conduct of Their Lives': A Laywomen's Confraternity in New Orleans, 1730–1744," *William and Mary Quarterly*, 3d Ser., LIV (1997), 769–794; see also Clark, *Masterless Mistresses: The New Orleans Ursulines and the Development of a New World Society, 1727–1834* (Chapel Hill, N.C., 2007), 76–82; Register of baptisms, marriages, and burials for the years 1748–1779, Municipal Archives of Port-Louis, ADM, 4 e 181/2, fol. 8, and fol. 376; "Les armements au long cours de la deuxième Compagnie des Indes (1713–1773)," nos. 1483, 1573, SHD, Lorient; see also below, original manuscript [352]; "Rôle de l'Auguste, 1748–1749," "Rôle de l'Achille, 1749–1752," both in ANOM, 2P, 33–I.12, 34–II.4.

between June and August of 1755. He survived the English attack on Pondi-cherry in 1758 during the Seven Years' War and died in India in 1760. He left behind an estate of 6,486 livres, a considerable fortune compared to his previous standard of living in Louisiana and Port-Louis.[8]

8. "Rôle de la Paix, 1754–1755," "Rôle du Bourbon, 1754–1757," both in ANOM, 2P, 37–II.5, 38–I.10; Philippe Haudrère, *La Compagnie française des Indes au XVIIIe siècle (1719–1795)*, 2 vols. (Paris, 1989), II, 1381.

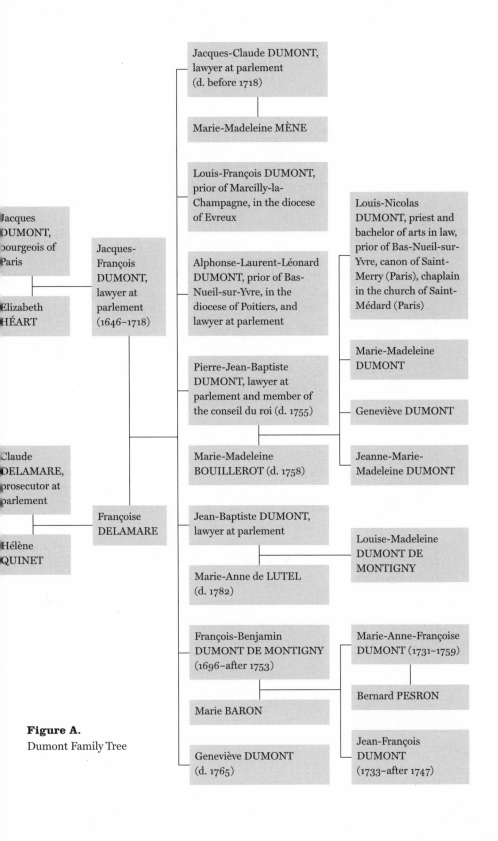

Figure A.
Dumont Family Tree

Epitre

Monseigneur

Quoique le Poeme que j'ay pris la liberté
de vous envoyer, renferme dans quelques endroits
des particularités de plusieures années D'observations
que j'ay faites de la loüisianne, Cependant, Comme les
sortes d'ouvrages rimés, ne sont propres qu'à donner
simplement une idée simple, et embarassante, a Vostre
grandeur. j'ay cru, qu'il etoit de Mon devoir et de
ma reconnoissance, de Vous l'envoyer en prose, il est
plus etendu et je l'ai rendu plus intelligible que je l'ay

Figure B. Facsimile of the first page of the memoir,
with coat of arms of the duc de Belle-Isle

EDITORIAL METHODS AND DESCRIPTION
OF THE DUMONT DE MONTIGNY MANUSCRIPT
MEMOIR

The Dumont de Montigny memoir (VAULT Ayer MS 257) came to the Newberry Library, Chicago, as part of the book and manuscript collection of the Illinois businessman Edward E. Ayer (1841–1927), who amassed a large fortune in the second half of the nineteenth century as a supplier of wooden ties for the westward expansion of the railroads. Ayer began collecting in the mid-1860s, buying predominantly from dealers and at auctions. His particular interest was primary source material relating to contact between Europeans and the indigenous peoples of North and South America, the Philippines, and Hawaii. Ayer was an early trustee of the Newberry, and he gradually donated his entire book and manuscript collection to the library during the early years of the twentieth century. There is no mention of the Dumont manuscript in Ayer's collection correspondence, but this is not surprising, because after 1885, he traveled widely and made many purchases in person, leaving no written record.

At some point before Ayer's acquisition of the manuscript, it was in the possession of Francis Baring (1800–1869), 3rd Baron Ashburton (as of 1864), whose bookplate appears inside the front cover. This member of the distinguished Baring banking family was involved, to some extent, in both business and politics, but his volatile personality proved a liability in the first and his hesitant speech a drawback in the second. In 1832, he married Hortense Eugénie Claire Maret, daughter of the duke of Bassano, one of the ministers of Napoleon I, and from then on, he spent much of his time at his home in Paris, on the Place Vendôme.[1] Ownership of a French manuscript is therefore quite logical, and the Louisiana content of the Dumont memoir might even have carried a particular symbolic meaning, since the House of Baring had handled the financing of the Louisiana Purchase in 1803–1804.[2]

The manuscript measures twenty-seven centimeters and consists of 229 folios. The body of the manuscript, which begins on the fourth leaf, is a fair

1. On the Baring family, see Philip Ziegler, *The Sixth Great Power: A History of One of the Greatest of All Banking Families, the House of Barings, 1762–1929* (New York, 1988).
2. See Ralph W. Hidy, *The House of Baring in American Trade and Finance: English Merchant Bankers at Work, 1763–1861* (Cambridge, Mass., 1949), 33–35.

copy in Dumont's hand. The leaves have writing on both sides, on paper of a consistent weight and hue but bearing a number of different watermarks. They are lightly ruled to create four margins, and Dumont numbered them himself, beginning with page 1 and continuing to page 443, although there are several errors in his pagination. The duc de Belle-Isle's coat of arms appears in pen and ink at the top of page 1, followed by a dedicatory epistle addressed to the duc on pages 1 to 4. Pages 5 to 443 contain the memoir itself. Pages 429 to 432 are written on a leaf of stamped paper from Brittany, folded in half, which perhaps had become mixed in with the other paper Dumont was using. He simply wrote around the stamp, which appears at the top of page 429.

At some point in the late eighteenth or nineteenth century, most likely before Ayer acquired it, the manuscript was trimmed, the edges were marbled, and the book was either bound for the first time or rebound. As a result, some marginal notes and portions of notes were cut off. By the mid-twentieth century, the binding was falling apart. The manuscript was then rebound, without further trimming or edge decoration, by Gérard Charrière, a Swiss artist-bookbinder who worked at the Newberry from 1965 to 1968. Charrière's binding is in brown leather, with gilt-ruled borders and gold-stamped corner *fleurons,* raised bands on the spine, and gold-stamped spine ornaments and title. Charrière reinserted the Francis Baring bookplate.

The manuscript originally contained twenty-three plates, hand drawn and colored by Dumont himself. Two maps (numbers 1 and 7) had already been removed before Charrière's rebinding of the manuscript and were housed in a separate portfolio. In 1993, Newberry conservators noted that some of the remaining images were torn and split down the folds, and they decided to remove all of them. The pages were treated, mended, encapsulated, interleaved, and bound in a post binding. In the manuscript, there are paper stubs, still bound in place, where the illustrations were removed. In this edition, footnotes indicate the pages at which the maps and illustrations were bound.

The first three leaves of the manuscript present a title page and preface, whereas the last two provide a list of Indian tribes said to be known to Dumont and an index to the memoir in which topics are listed alphabetically; with each entry is given a page reference. These paratextual documents are not in Dumont's handwriting but in another eighteenth-century hand. The list of Indian tribes appears on the recto of the final leaf in the body of the manuscript, which Dumont had left blank. The leaves used for the title page, preface, and index are added, on a paper of a more bluish hue. The four paratextual documents appear to have been prepared with the intention of framing the memoir in such a way as to make it interesting and useful to a potential publisher. For this translation, we have put the paratextual documents in an appendix.

It is difficult to guess at Dumont's possible intentions to publish the work that he had dedicated to his protector Belle-Isle. The manuscript itself bears no printer's marks. Once a decision was made to publish it, the printer would have suggested or required substantial revisions of the kind the memoir eventually received in order to be transformed into the *Mémoires historiques sur la Louisiane* (Paris, 1753). The anonymous eighteenth-century hand may be that of the Abbé Le Mascrier, editor of the *Mémoires historiques*. Since there are no known examples of Le Mascrier's handwriting, this must remain a hypothesis, but it seems noteworthy that the material found in the introductory pages inserted before chapter one of the *Mémoires historiques* appears to be a combination and expansion of two excerpts from the manuscript: the short description of Quebec provided by Dumont and the section in the anonymous preface that names the different European colonies in the Americas.[3] This suggests that Le Mascrier drafted the preface himself or, at least, that he had it in hand when preparing the *Mémoires historiques*. The first-person style of the preface raises the possibility that Dumont participated in the drafting of that document, and some of the rough statistics in the list of Indian tribes ("peu nombreux," and so on) could have been provided by Dumont himself.

Whoever prepared the paratextual documents, these—along with the manuscript itself—were soon set aside, as the *Mémoires historiques* project began to evolve into something quite different from the original memoir. The preface in the printed version, emphasizing the exploration of the lower Mississippi valley by Robert Cavalier de la Salle, is entirely different from the one added to the manuscript, and although the *Mémoires historiques* does contain a list of Indian tribes, it is not identical to the one found in the manuscript (each list includes some names not found in the other).[4] Likewise, the topics referenced in the manuscript index do not correspond to those taken up in the various chapters of the book. Indeed, once the decision was made to abridge the memoir by cutting the sections on Quebec and Brittany, some topics included in the manuscript index became irrelevant.

3. *Mémoires historiques*, I, 2–3.
4. Ibid., 134–135.

It is nonetheless a fascinating historical document, offering insight into the subject areas deemed important at the time.

EDITORIAL METHODS

The edition of the memoir published by Les éditions du Septentrion in November 2008 is the copy text for this English translation. In the French edition, we divided the memoir into twelve chapters, using several large divisions made by Dumont himself and adding others. The same chapter divisions are used in this English edition. The chapters delineate Dumont's transatlantic voyages as well as the ethnography and natural history sections. We have indicated the original pagination in brackets.

Dumont uses paragraphing in some sections but not in others. Where he does use it, we have retained it. In the other sections, we introduce it in order to render the text easier for modern readers. He appears to have worked from a variety of preexisting documents in drafting the memoir: a journal, correspondence, reports written for the Company of the Indies and for individual sponsors, his epic poem, and so on.

The index notes found in the margins of the manuscript, all in Dumont's hand, orient the reader by providing dates, place-names, and brief indications of topics covered. In the French edition, these are reproduced at the bottom of each page, above the footnotes, using asterisks. In this translation, they appear among the footnotes, but always identified as "Index note."

The text is a fair copy and very clean. We silently corrected a handful of copying errors: the repetition of a word, the inversion of two words, and misspellings of a few simple words spelled correctly everywhere else. We did not reproduce crossed-out words, of which there are very few.

We applied current usage for punctuation and capitalization. Dumont relies heavily on commas and uses relatively little capitalization.

In the Septentrion edition, we preserved Dumont's original spelling, for it shows how he heard the French language. However, we did correct his usage of some very short, common words that sound almost identical, by replacing, for example, *se* with *ce*, *s'en* with *sans*, *d'en* with *dans*, *s'y* with *si*, and *l'a quelle* with *laquelle*. We united locutions such as *en fin, lors que,* and *se approchant (s'approchant)*, and we resolved common abbreviations, such as *octobre* for *8bre*, *cependant* for *cependa*, and *nullement* for *nullemt*. We also modernized the use of French accents, in which Dumont himself was inconsistent, but we retained nearly all the archaic forms of the verb *avoir,* such as *eut, eust, ust, ut, eût,* and *ût,* while adding or suppressing the accents that reflect the grammatical mood, subjective or indicative. In the translation, these corrections will, of course, be invisible.

When a word is illegible in the manuscript, we so indicate in the translation by leaving an underlined blank. When we were able to reconstruct a word, we placed the reconstruction in brackets. Occasionally we also added a clarifying word between brackets, or replaced a pronoun with the proper name to which it refers, to facilitate reading.

TRANSLATOR'S NOTE

In composing his memoir, Dumont de Montigny maintained an elevated tone appropriate to the dignity of his patrons; at the same time, he had to represent the language of soldiers, sailors, and native Americans as well as narrate the moments of terror and scenes of violence he had experienced both in America and in France. This range of discourses is comparable to that found in many French and English novels and travel narratives of the eighteenth century, particularly those written in epistolary form, where the putative addressee is a man or woman of high status and genteel sensibilities.[1] In translating Dumont's prose memoir to make it accessible to a modern anglophone audience, I have tried to match the sense of decorum appropriate to a text written for one of the most important men in France; to be accurate with respect to the vocabularies of navigation, natural history, and military affairs that were part of Dumont's expertise; and to preserve the suspense and immediacy that were perhaps his greatest talents as a writer.

The copy text for the translation is *Regards sur le monde atlantique, 1715–1747,* the French-language edition of Dumont's memoir published by Septentrion of Quebec City in 2008 and edited by Carla Zecher, Shannon Lee Dawdy, and myself. The editorial methods of that volume are explained in the note above. In the translation, I have further modernized and standardized the text, particularly with respect to the use of proper nouns. Rather than follow Dumont's variations in the spelling of personal and place-names, I have standardized them according to the most familiar or frequently used spelling. In the biographical dictionary at the end of this edition, entries for more than 150 individuals Dumont named in his memoir are alphabetized according to this spelling, but each entry also lists many of the alternate spellings that appear in the original manuscript. The forms

---

1. Notable examples in the literature of French North America include Charlevoix's *Histoire et description générale de la Nouvelle France, avec le Journal historique d'un voyage fait par ordre du roi dans l'Amérique septentrionnale* (Paris, 1744), and Louis-Armand de Lom d'Arce, baron de Lahontan's *Nouveaux voyages de Mr. le baron de Lahontan, dans l'Amerique septentrionale* (The Hague, 1703), both discussed in the Introduction. In both cases, however, the text was not likely composed in the form of actual letters to the addressee. See Pierre Berthiaume, "Introduction," in Charlevoix, *Journal d'un voyage fait par ordre du roi dans l'Amérique septentrionale,* ed. Berthiaume (Montreal, 1994), 47–49.

of address that often precede these names employ the abbreviations that Dumont frequently used: "M." for "Monsieur," "Mgr." for "Monseigneur," "Sr." for "Sieur," and "Mssrs." for "Messieurs." With respect to place-names, I have rendered them according to modern usage, such as Cabo San Antonio, Cuba, for Dumont's "Cap Saint Antoine" and Bayou Saint John, in New Orleans, for Dumont's "Bayou Saint Jean."

The title of this translation differs from the title of the French edition. A title page to the manuscript, one of the paratexts described in the note on Newberry Library Ayer Manuscript 257, reads (in translation): "Memoir of L—— D——, Engineering Officer, Containing the Events That Have Occurred in Louisiana from 1715 to the Present, as well as Remarks on the Manners, Customs, and Strengths of Various Native Peoples in North America, and Its Productions."[2] This title page is written in a different hand from the text of the memoir but might have been a proposed title for a published version or possibly the work of an owner of the manuscript or private librarian. In its length and style, it resembles book titles of the time, and some phrases resemble the title of Dumont and Jean-Baptiste Le Mascrier's book published in 1753 by Bauche of Paris, which translates in full as "Historical Memoirs on Louisiana: Containing the Most Memorable Things That Have Happened There since the Year 1687 until the Present, with the Establishment of the French Colony in That Province of North America under the Direction of the Company of the Indies; the Climate, Nature, and Products of the Land, the Origin and Religion of the Indians Who Inhabit It, Their Manners and Customs, etc. Composed upon the Memoirs of Mr. Dumont by M. L. L. M. the Text Embellished with Maps and Figures." The title added to the manuscript conceals the name of the memoirist, just as, in his text, Dumont avoided writing his own name and concealed the names of several individuals. "L. D." are initials, I believe, for "Lieutenant Dumont," much as, in the 1753 book's title, the editor Le Mascrier is referred to by the initials for "Monsieur l'abbé Le Mascrier." So, for this translation, I have chosen the title *The Memoir of Lieutenant Dumont.*

Because Dumont was sent to Quebec and Louisiana as a military officer and was highly sensitive to the perceived injustices perpetrated by his superior officers and to matters of status in general, his narrative is filled with the language of military ranks. Between 1683 and 1755, nearly all military forces sent from France to the North American colonies belonged to the *compagnies franches de la marine,* a branch of the navy created by Louis XIV's powerful minister Jean-Baptiste Colbert to advance France's im-

2. See below, Appendix 1.

perial ambitions. These troupes de la marine should not be confused with the gardes de la marine, a training corps for sons of the privileged such as Dumont himself, who writes at the beginning of his memoir that he was assigned from Verdun to the gardes de la marine in Rochefort. I have generally translated *marine* as "marines" to reflect the fact that, in the colonies, these troops fought primarily on land, and Dumont himself had only a rudimentary knowledge of navigation and did not serve as an officer on the ships in which he sailed to and from the colonies. The colonial marines were organized into companies commanded by a captain and consisting of, at most, fifty soldiers; other officers included one lieutenant, an ensign, and a second ensign, as well as noncommissioned officers, namely two sergeants and three corporals.[3] Many of these words for military ranks also exist in English, even though their place in the hierarchy of the U.S., Canadian, and British militaries may be different; I have used an English equivalent in the translation, with the exception of a few terms described here.

To begin at the top, the command of the Louisiana colony was split between two offices. The *gouverneur,* or *commandant général,* the position held by Jean-Baptiste Le Moyne de Bienville and by Etienne Périer during the period when Dumont was there, was the supreme commander of the military. In the absence of any civilian police force, the military was in charge of maintaining order as well as defending forts and dealing with Indian affairs. In New France and other French colonies (as well as in the French provinces), the governor shared authority with an intendant, but in Louisiana, the top civil and administrative official was, instead, the commissaire ordonnateur. There is no satisfactory English term for this post. The commissaire ordonnateur was responsible for budgets and supplies as well as chairing the Superior Council of Louisiana in New Orleans, which, as the lone deliberative body, was both court and legislature for the colony. Because, as Dumont makes clear, supplies were costly and scarce, the power of the commissaire ordonnateur and the warehouse keepers, or *gardes magasins,* who answered to him was considerable. Tension between the governor and the commissaire ordonnateur contributed to the dysfunc-

---

3. See below, original manuscript [99], where Dumont lists the composition of a typical military company. During the period from 1717 until 1731, when the Louisiana colony was granted to the Company of the Indies, this company was empowered to commission officers in its service. For clarity, I have used "Company" with a upper-case *C* to refer to the Company of the Indies and "company" in other instances. On the organization of the French Navy in the eighteenth century, see James Pritchard, *Louis XV's Navy, 1748–1762: A Study of Organization and Administration* (Kingston, Ont., 1987), 60–65.

tional leadership of French Louisiana, although Dumont emphasizes the specific personalities rather than the structural problems. Another title that defies translation is the major de la place. As Marcel Giraud explains, "A *major* was an officer appointed to take charge of all the material needs of the soldiers—pay, food, clothing, equipment, accommodation, and so on—but who was more than a quartermaster . . . he might be given the command of a small town or fortress, in which case he was known as a *major de place*."[4] The major de place (or, as Dumont puts it, major de la place) at the citadel town of Port-Louis, Brittany, whose name was Simon La Vergne de Villeneuve, became Dumont's key enemy at the time he composed the memoir. A final untranslated military title is *anspessade*, a noncommissioned rank roughly equivalent to a corporal in the modern U.S. system.

As Shannon Dawdy, Jennifer Spear, and Cécile Vidal have explained, in French colonial Louisiana, terms and systems of racial identity were quite different from what they would become two centuries later, and the classifications of freedom and unfreedom were more significant than those of race.[5] The term *esclave*, or slave, could refer to one of the Africans brought by French slave traders from west Africa, to an American Indian held by a French slaveowner, or to a native or European or African captive taken by the Indians in a raid such as the Natchez uprising of 1729. The unfree among the Indians included the *loués*, a Natchez term that was part of the complex caste system of that tribe. The unfree among the French included indentured servants condemned to labor, for a term of seven or ten years or longer, because of crimes or vagrancy in France; and *forçats*, laborers who were involuntarily shipped to the colony. Dumont used these terms as well as signifiers for racial or cultural identity, such as *nègre*, which I have translated as "negro," and *sauvage*, which I render as "Indian." Rather than *tribu*, a word generally used in classical or biblical contexts in the eighteenth century, Dumont more often used *nation* to refer to the Choctaws, Natchez, Chickasaws, and other native American peoples, and I have used the word "nation" rather than "tribe" in English.

In ancien régime France, as in preindustrial Europe generally, units of length, volume, or weight often differed widely by region. The French

---

4. *HLF*, V, 399.

5. Dawdy, *Building the Devil's Empire*, 182–183, 228–232; Jennifer M. Spear, *Race, Sex, and Social Order in Early New Orleans* (Baltimore, 2009), 52–78; Cécile Vidal, "Caribbean Louisiana: Church, *Métissage*, and the Language of Race in the Mississippi Colony during the French Period (1699–1769)," unpublished MS, forthcoming in Vidal, ed., *Louisiana: Crossroads of the Atlantic World*.

league, or *lieu,* might extend between four and seven kilometers. Other terms are much more confusing. According to the scholar of early modern measurements Ronald Zupko, the measure of capacity called a *quart* could refer to an amount of wine equivalent to less than a modern liter or to an amount of grain as large as sixty-one liters.[6] Where Dumont wrote of a quart, *tonne,* or *lieu* in Louisiana, his usage cannot be linked to his native Paris or to another region of France, and so when he uses the word *quart,* it is necessary to judge the actual quantity based on context, such as the type of vessel referred to. Dumont's measurements often reflect his experience as an officer in the marines and his six transatlantic voyages. For example, he uses the term *brasse,* which translates as "fathom" (a measure of the depth of water equivalent to six feet), in land-based as well as in maritime contexts. More important, most of the grain, flour, wine, water, and gunpowder he writes of would have been transported on shipboard in barrels of various sizes, and he refers to such barrels by a host of different French words.

I have used English terms such as "foot" for *pied,* "ell" for *aulne,* "bushel" for *manne,* "league" for *lieu,* and "quart" for *quart* in such cases where the translation is clear but the exact length or volume is vague. The establishment of the metric system following the French Revolution was intended to promote commerce and rational efficiency by standardizing measurement. It would be anachronistic to use the metric system to translate Dumont's terms in his narrative, but I do use the metric in the notes and apparatus rather than impose the United States's system of miles, feet, and yards.

The unit of currency in Louisiana and in France during this period was the livre, which was subdivided into twenty sous, each twelve deniers. These units and proportions were similar to the British pound, shilling, and pence. Dumont also occasionally refers to the ecu, a coin worth six livres. Paper money in these denominations was issued beginning in 1701, but John Law's investment scheme led to hyperinflation and a collapse of the paper currency in 1720. New money, backed by gold and silver, was issued starting in 1726. The economy of colonial Louisiana suffered from the collapse of Law's scheme, as well as from protectionist monopolies, a shortage of currency, and inconsistent supplies of staple goods, all of which

---

6. Ronald Edward Zupko, *French Weights and Measures before the Revolution: A Dictionary of Provincial and Local Units* (Bloomington, Ind., 1978), 147–149. See also John J. McCusker, *Essays on the Economic History of the Atlantic World* (1997; rpt. London, 2005), chap. 4; David Hackett Fischer, *Champlain's Dream* (New York, 2008), app. N, "Champlain's Weights and Measures," 627–631. Fischer, however, is too exact in many of these measurements, stating, for instance, that a *pot* was equal to 2.2648 liters.

drove up prices and forced residents to rely on subsistence farming, hunting and gathering, and a barter economy. Hence I believe there is little point in stating an equivalent value of the livre or sou in modern dollars. Because Dumont frequently describes his economic predicaments and his efforts to collect his unpaid salary, readers will quickly get a sense of the value of money in his world.[7]

A historical manuscript is an artifact of the language of its time, and scholars of the French language have examined both how the Quebecois preserved many forms of seventeenth-century French and how Louisiana French evolved out of a blending of French, African, Spanish, and other elements. There are a few places where Dumont used words that were new to the French language of his day and that became characteristic Louisiana vocabulary later, and I have called attention to these in the notes.

Gordon M. Sayre
Eugene, Oregon
May 2011

---

7. Dumont discusses Louisiana money and markets in Chapter 12, original manuscript [405–406]. A useful resource for Louisiana prices are the tables in Daniel H. Usner, Jr., *Indians, Settlers, and Slaves in a Frontier Exchange Economy: The Lower Mississippi Valley before 1783* (Chapel Hill, N.C., 1992), 208–209, 262–272.

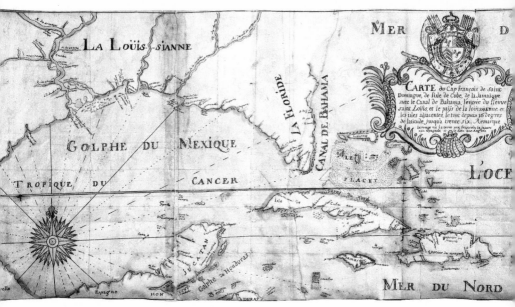

Figure 1. *Map of Cap François (Gulf of Mexico)*. VAULT oversize Ayer MS 257, map no. 1. Courtesy The Newberry Library, Chicago

[1] EPISTLE

Monseigneur,

Although the poem I have taken the liberty of sending to you includes, in some places, detailed observations from the many years I spent in Louisiana, nonetheless such rhymed works can only give a crude portrayal, unworthy of Your Excellency. I believe, therefore, it is my debt, and my duty, to send it to you now in prose. Here it is more extended, and I have written it as clearly as I [2] could, so as to conceal nothing from you, Monseigneur, of the events that took place in that distant land, where Your Excellency and associates had as many as four well-established concessions. You will also see the pains and travails that I have suffered. All I can say to Your Excellency is that it is a French Robinson Crusoe who comes to throw himself at your feet and to make a complete confession of his life from 1715 until this year, 1747.

You shall also see, Monseigneur, that we are dealing with a land capable of supporting a colony most flourishing and rewarding for the crown, if only it were guided and governed with care and justice, as the Romans did in ancient times. Instead, it has yielded, up until now, only difficulties and losses for our nation. This I can assure you, having been an eyewitness during twenty-one years and having experienced the same pains and injustices that the greater part of those who commanded and ruled there imposed upon all the subjects and colonists, in spite of my scrupulously performing all of my duties. This you shall see, Your Excellency, if you take the trouble to read this relation and memoir.

This is why, Monseigneur, to bring it all into the light of day, I have rewritten my poem in prose, corrected and augmented. You will here learn of the manners and customs of the Indians, of their religions, their dances, and their ways of making war with one another. And of the land, you will see here its quality and its climates, the riches and potential that could be [3] exploited for the advantage of His Majesty. Here, Your Excellency will see that this colony, well governed, could be the equal of Peru and the other neighboring colonies of the Spaniards and the English. I pledge above all to speak only the truth, even at the risk of my life.

Monseigneur, I hope this memoir may relieve you from your troubles, that you will recognize the effect, however small, of my humble recognition for the goodness that you have seen fit to bestow upon me. Because, without the protection of Your Illustrious Excellency, where would I be? It is only you, Monseigneur, who sustains me, and in the hope of being under the wing of your protection, I rest in peace there, although assailed from all sides by a furious enemy who is set upon destroying me and who has raised powers against me, even though I don't deserve it. What consoles me is that I have nothing, and I can cry out like the sage, "Omnia mea mecum porto."[1] It is true that I have waited long and that the zeal I have for His Majesty's service, in which I pride myself on never having fallen short, gives me grounds to hope that the day may come when I will enjoy peace and the fruits of my labors and pains. But alas, the wheel of fortune must bring the high down low again. This may be, but even if the wheel remains in this position, I do not mind, provided that it keeps me in Your Excellency's protection [4]. Guard me there, and receive these memoirs graciously, as a token of my efforts to earn your attention and the support of Your Excellency, to whom I have the honor to be, with the most profound respect and a humble submission,

Monseigneur,
Most humbly yours,
F. Dumont

1. "All that is mine I carry with me."

Chapter One

VOYAGE TO QUEBEC;
RETURN TO LA ROCHELLE

1714-1719

[5] When a man has begun to enjoy the leisure of old age, it is appropriate to recall his wayward youth so as to make honorable amends through an honest return to God, his creator. I have felt all too strongly His helping hand amid the trials of my life, which has been nothing but a tapestry of miseries and dangers, [not] to give thanks unto Him.[1] It is with this aim that I write these memoirs, in which certain individuals up to the rank of minister will find matter for reflection, touching upon the building of colonies and the choice of officers. My main goal is to provide a clear and straightforward idea of Louisiana—to describe the manners and customs of its inhabitants, its commerce, and the events that have taken place there up to the present, interlacing with this my voyages, my labors, and my sufferings during twenty-one years there and in the vast surrounding lands. But before turning to that project, I must say a few words about my first voyage, departing from France and destined for Canada.

I will therefore say that although my dear father spared nothing to make me pursue my education rather than follow the example of my brothers—who, like our father, donned the robes of the law and the clergy—I, the youngest, followed my stars and took up arms as a cadet in the Auxerre regiment, then posted at the citadel of Verdun. But I had not been there a year when my father arranged with M. Le Blanc, who was then minister, to have me assigned overseas. I was sent an order to leave the regiment and report to Rochefort to enter the marines. I arrived at that town with a special recommendation to M. de la Galissonnière, governor of the place, and was also recommended to [6] M. de Bégon, the intendant. I was received by these men with great courtesy, and the next day, they enrolled me in the ranks of the marines. At the end of five months in that unit, continuing the studies in mathematics for which I had a strong inclination, I received an order to embark on a royal frigate named the *Victoire* for my first campaign at sea. The ship was to sail to Quebec, capital city of Canada, to carry there

1. Dumont omitted the word "ne pas," or "not," in this negative sentence construction.

a considerable sum of French coinage so as to supposedly replace the paper money that was then in use in that land. Another royal frigate, named the Astrée, was to go with us, but for reasons known at Court, the Victoire was ordered to depart first by itself.[2]

After having gone aboard, paid my tribute of seasickness, and counted my shirts (as the sailors say), the wind turning favorable we set sail on July 21, putting ourselves under God's wing for our voyage.[3] We must have numbered at least 640 on board. With good winds and good weather, nothing out of the ordinary occurred on our voyage, and as we hoped to reach the bank of Newfoundland soon, we made preparations for the baptism of those who had not yet passed through there.[4] This is a ceremony that the sailors never fail to perform on first-time passengers, as much to entertain themselves as for the profits they derive from those who do not wish to be dunked. I will describe this ceremony elsewhere, for our captain forbade its performance here after the ship was rolled onto its starboard side by a wave and 52 persons were maimed. They burned themselves with the hot broth that spilled out of their mess kits. Since the captain [7] had prohibited the baptism, to appease his crew, he ordered them to be given a double dram for that day, both at dinner and supper. This is why I was not able to go through the ceremony of my baptism, which surely would have taken place and would have cost me the last coins that remained in my pocket.

Finally, we arrived at the bank, so famous and profitable to those who keep Lent or observe meatless days on account of the excellent cod that is caught there. We had scarcely arrived when we had to rescue a fishing boat that, having broken all three of its masts, had also lost its cannons, powder,

2. The *gardes de la marine* was a corps of naval officers–in-training founded by Jean-Baptiste Colbert in 1670 and made up of young gentlemen and sons of privilege such as Dumont. In his service in Louisiana, Dumont served in the *compagnies franches de la marine*, a separate, larger corps of marines who provided nearly all the forces for New France and Louisiana from 1683 to 1755. Both were administered under the secretary of state for the marine. See Arnaud Balvay, *L'epée et la plume: Amérindiens et soldats des troupes de la marine en Louisiane et au Pays d'en Haut (1683-1763)* (Quebec City, 2006), 38; and James S. Pritchard, *Louis XV's Navy, 1748-1762: A Study of Organization and Administration* (Kingston, Ont., 1987), 57–65. There were two men, father and son, named Michel Bégon. The father was intendant of the port city of Rochefort until his death on March 31, 1710, four years before this account. The son, known as Michel Bégon de la Picardière, was intendant of New France from 1712 to 1726 and is mentioned below, original manuscript [10].

3. Dumont wrote an index note in the margin, "1716," which he then crossed out and corrected to "1715."

4. Dumont here refers to the Grand Banks, an important fishing ground southeast of Newfoundland.

balls, even its compass and binnacle. Two pirate ships had stolen all these things and had beaten up the captain and his mate. We gave them supplies to repair the mast and all that they needed. They told us there were three pirate ships that had learned of our cargo and our route and had boasted that they would either take us or die. Given this news, we continued on our route, watching carefully for those who sought us. The next morning, we found them, and without giving a description of our combat here, let it be said that one of them was blown up, one sent to the bottom, and the third taken. But as 190 of our ship's company were either killed or injured and as we now had no enemies, our captain judged it prudent to put in at Sainte-Anne on Cape Breton. We arrived there on August 21.[5]

On the eve of Saint Louis's Day, we hanged all the pirates, ninety-one in number, reserving for the captain alone a crueler form of execution, as you will see below. We stayed [8] a week in this place to recover, take on stores, and repair parts of our ship that had been damaged by the pirates, after which we put out to sea again to go to our destination. But after just twenty-four hours, those who had been injured in the combat as well as those who had been burned, as I said above, were attacked by scurvy, the dangerous yet common illness of the sea. You cannot escape death from it unless you have the good fortune to reach land, where you can regain your health more easily than on shipboard. It may well be said that the very desire to reach land causes this illness. I was not exempt from it myself; it began attacking me on my right leg, where a cyst or boil had taken hold.[6]

Once we were out of sight of land, the trial of the pirate captain was held, and he was condemned to be hoisted from the end of the mizzen yard by a rope, with a board attached to it that passes in between the criminal's legs so that he rides it as if astride a horse. His arms and body are tied to the rope, which runs through a pulley at the end of the yardarm and down to the bridge so that the criminal can be hoisted up to the yard, then let go, and from his own weight, he falls into the sea. As he falls in between two cannons, they are fired with a shot of powder. This is what is called "keel-hauling." This [9] naval punishment is performed seven or eight times, although, for this pirate captain, our men did not have to raise and lower the rope—only to leave him dangling six or seven feet above the water. Each time the ship rolled and pitched to port, he fell into the sea, and when it rolled back to starboard, he found himself lifted out of the water and would have slammed helplessly into the side of the ship if he had not taken the pre-

5. Saint Ann's Bay, on the east side of Cape Breton Island (Ile Royale to the French).
6. August 24 is the saint's day for Saint Louis of France.

caution to push off with his feet. He was made to sit on the rail of the ship for all his meals and remained hanging for six days, but between the sixth and seventh, in the dark of night, he was bitten in half by a flesh-eating fish called a shark.[7] One might say, by the very name of this fish *[requin]*, that it would be a requiem to whomever it catches.

A peculiar thing about this wolf of the sea is that it has no eyes and cannot see at all.[8] It has two little fish attached, one on each side of its gills, who guide it and serve as pilot. What is more, this fish never opens its mouth when it is swimming on its belly, because to eat, it has to turn upside down. And to take them on board a ship, you have to use a large harpoon or an iron hook held by a strong chain. You put a piece of lard or beef at the end, and when the shark has swallowed the bait and is hooked, you can lift it on deck. All of its strength is then only in its tail, which can break a person's leg, for I have seen one that, with its tail, broke the leg of a cow. As soon as the tip of its tail is cut off, a few drops of blood fall out, and it is quickly dead. There are some sailors who [10] have eaten its flesh, but it is said that this causes hemorrhaging, and captains generally forbid serving it. The brain of this aquatic animal is like a gruel; you can hardly pick it up. But if exposed to the sun, it becomes as hard as a stone, and I was even told by one of our surgeons that it is very good for pregnant women.[9]

Finally, we arrived in the city of Quebec on September 12. I will not bother to describe this city, capital of Canada; I will only say that it is well built and well fortified, with governor's and intendant's buildings and a *hôtel dieu* administered by the good and charitable Sisters of the Order of Saint Augustine, and that there is a very beautiful citadel and a bishopric. It was M. l'abbé de Saint-Vallier who was then bishop, M. the marquis de Vaudreuil, governor, and the brother of M. Bégon was the intendant. As I was ill with scurvy and was in the marines, M. de la Corne, Knight of the Order of Saint Louis and major general, took me under his wing from the moment I stepped off our ship onto land. I was sent to the hôtel dieu and given a bed, whereas all the other scorbutics from our ship were placed in the citadel in the open air and slept on beds of straw on the stone floors of the rooms in that fortress. I had scarcely been in that place a day when I had the pleasure of meeting a nun, a well-born young lady from Paris, whom I recognized, as she did me, from our childhood. It was the daughter of M. du Plessis, who

7. Index note: "Death of the pirate."
8. Index note: "Description of the shark."
9. Dumont is repeating folk beliefs of his time regarding sharks. The lampreys who often attach themselves to sharks do not guide the sharks' swimming.

had come to Quebec as treasurer and had died there. This nun was called Mother Saint Joseph. She had [11] with her in the same convent a companion sister named Mother of the Infant Jesus, who had preferred to follow the fine example of her sister in taking religious vows rather than accept the hand of marriage offered to her by M. de Cavagnial, son of M. le marquis de Vaudreuil. Hence these two young women and charitable sisters did me a service that I will never forget, as did M. de la Corne, a man filled with generosity and virtue.[10]

I have said that they did me a great service during the two years I was in this city, because I was often stricken with illness. It was not from scurvy, however, for I was perfectly cured of that, in the manner that is used to expel the disease from those who are attacked with it. Here is how they are treated.[11] A big hole is dug in the ground to the height of a man measured from the feet to the neck. The earth is sifted through a wooden screen and the stones taken out, and then the scorbutic is placed in the hole standing up and buried there, and he sweats in large drops. Some have the strength to stay there longer than others. The surgeon keeps a finger on the temple of the patient, and when he deems fit, the man is removed from the trench by the means of a board that, when taken away, allows the dirt to fall back into the hole. The patient is covered with warm blankets and carried to bed, where, with good broths and teas and careful treatment, he will find himself perfectly cured. I went through this remedy myself and I felt much better, so that after two major illnesses in a row, one of scurvy and one of dropsy, I became convalescent [12], but with much sorrow in my heart, finding myself in a land I never would have imagined living in. The two royal frigates, the *Victoire* and the *Astrée*, had left on October 16 to return to France and sail out of a river that freezes over nearly every winter.

What consoled me little by little were the ongoing favors of our major general, who, during my illness, did me the honor of visiting and helping me

10. The Royal and Military Order of Saint Louis was founded by Louis XIV in 1693 and constituted a noble status within the French military with three separate grades: the *chevalier*, the *commandeur*, and the *grande-croix*. Each rank came with a pension, and membership was an honor to which many Louisiana officers aspired. Dumont spelled the name "Cavagnolle" and added the index note: "Presently governor of Louisiana." In 1747, when Dumont was writing his memoir, the governor of Louisiana was Pierre de Rigaud, marquis de Vaudreuil de Cavagnial, a son of Philippe de Rigaud de Vaudreuil, governor of Quebec in 1716. The hôtel dieu of Quebec was founded by the Hospitalières, an Augustinian order of nuns, in 1639 and is the oldest hospital in North America. The oldest surviving buildings now house a museum of medical history, and adjacent structures are part of the hospital system of the Université du Québec.

11. Index note: "Remedy for curing scurvy."

with the comforts that a patient always needs, as much to restore his appetite as his good humor. When I was perfectly cured, he made me a cadet in the artillery company. I never did serve in it, however, because I was still of a very delicate constitution. My service was accounted for and my meals and board paid for by the company. I stayed with the good sisters, where I had a room. I had good food and clean linens, my chest having been brought to me by the captain of our frigate. I passed my time in drawing, embroidering altar cloths, and designing blocks for pious inscriptions to be stamped in gold or silver letters, for there were no printers in Quebec. And although every month there was a review of the troops, I was counted as present, even though absent, by the authority of our major.

Toward the month of October of the same year, four soldiers from Montreal, which is a city sixty leagues from the capital, joined together to find a way to make more than eighty thousand livres in counterfeit card money.[12] Among the four was the son of a famous engraver, who made the dies for printing the money. Another was a skilled scribe who counterfeited on the cards not only the writing of the treasurer but also the seal of M. le marquis de Vaudreuil and that of M. Bégon, so well that, when the false bills were shown to those men during the inquiry, they admitted they could not believe the seals were not authentic, except that, in [13] the treasurer's, five letters were slightly different. What is more, to print the cards with the die, they had included in their conspiracy a drummer who beat on his drum while they were striking the engraving onto the cards. And since they had made a large number of them, they had brought in the sergeant major, who, when he went to collect the pay for the whole garrison, exchanged the real cards that he received for the counterfeits, which were then distributed to the soldiers and others.

This clever scheme lasted for no more than two months, for men who are not accustomed to being rich and opulent find that money is hard to manage. You have to find a way to spend your wealth and make it known that "That which comes by the drum returns by the flute," as the proverb says. Such was truly the case, for it was nothing but feasts for them, parties that enriched those who supplied them, dances and sumptuous diversions, and what is more, they had no qualms about lighting their pipes with hundred-

---

12. Index note, partly illegible, presumably reads "1716." Since the 1680s, the intendants of New France had addressed the shortage of hard currency in the colonies by issuing "card money," sometimes consisting of modified playing cards. André Lachance has found in the archives sixty-four defendants accused of counterfeiting this currency in the French colonial period; see Lachance, *Crimes et criminels en Nouvelle-France* (Montreal, 1984), 68.

livre notes. All this led them to be watched closely, and one day, when the four of them had withdrawn to amuse themselves and the drummer was beating his instrument (for it was the time of day when they printed the money), a detachment of soldiers broke into the room. The four men were seized and searched, and the dies, so well made and so fatal, were found, as well as more than four thousand livres of freshly made cards. They were placed [14] in separate cells, and the very next day, their interrogation and trial began. But after the drummer, the sergeant, and the engraver had been examined and the scribe was led in, he challenged the authority of the judge, saying that he had been his schoolmaster and could not be judged by his student and thus must be remanded to the Superior Council of Quebec. The prisoner had, in fact, taught writing and arithmetic to the judge.[13]

As it was winter when this affair took place in Montreal, and the river was frozen over and all the country was covered with snow, it was no small matter to transport these men sixty leagues. Nonetheless, they had to be brought, and this was done across the ice in carriages fitted with iron runners and propelled by iron rods. There were three men in each carriage, two prisoners bound and garrotted together and a driver in the front of the sleigh who guided it along. Besides this, there was a large detachment of armed soldiers on ice skates. They thus arrived in another town called Trois-Rivières, which is thirty leagues from both Quebec and Montreal. From this town, they were led to the capital overland in carriages drawn by horses fitted with shoes for the ice. As soon as they arrived, they were put in prison, all four together. The prison is next door to the intendant's building.

They were interrogated the next day, convicted, and confessed to their crime. But because in that country cruelty is rarely seen and charity is in fashion, as much toward prisoners as toward the poor and [15] especially toward criminals, a means was found to slip the prisoners a meat pie in which they found files suitable for cutting their chains, and having accomplished this, they called out, asking to speak to the jailer. The jailer's husband was a clerk in the office of the intendant, and it was his wife, with a servant, who managed and oversaw the prisons. When they asked to speak to her, she suspected nothing and came with a lantern, opened the cell, and entered. She was immediately seized. They put a gag in her mouth, grabbed the two pistols that she always carried, and shut her up in the same cell after

13. The four counterfeiters were Jean-Baptiste Leclerc, Henry Jarran, Antoine Fruitier, and Louis Ducatelle. The interrogations and trial records are found in the Archives nationales du Québec à Montréal, Juridiction de Montréal, côte TL4, S1, D2061. Available at www.banq.qc.ca, "Pistard" collection, accessed July 15, 2010.

tying her hands behind her back. They went to the kitchen and did the same to the servant, then opened the doors of the cells to release the prisoners. As the four went out the back door, they all started shouting, "Fire! Fire in the hospital!"

This building, half a league outside of Quebec, housed the poor, the insane, and the aged and infirm. On this cry of "Fire!" the alarm was sounded. Smoke was, in fact, seen in the neighborhood, and everyone, believing it a real fire, rushed in that direction while the prisoners ran off, splitting into two groups. One group fled into the church of the hôtel dieu and from there passed on to a safe place; the other took refuge with the Jesuits. In this way, they saved themselves from the gallows the next day. The search for them was fruitless. They finally had [16] the good fortune, all four of them, to return to France by embarking on cod fishing vessels that carried them to the bank of Newfoundland, and from there, they transferred to other ships that took them to France.

There also occurred in the capital an instance of the justice of God toward an assassin. In this case, no one attempted to save him, and here is the story. It was around October 10 of the same year. A letter of recommendation to M. le marquis de Vaudreuil arrived on one of the royal frigates on behalf of a young man who was a soldier in the troops of the garrison, along with a bill of exchange for nine hundred livres. The governor summoned the young man, who was a soldier in the company of M. de Cavagnial. He spoke to him, asked him about his family, and having inquired with his sergeants and commanding officers about his conduct, which was good, he encountered no difficulties in the way of his obtaining this sum in silver. But as this soldier strongly disliked that country, he decided to desert and go over to the side of the English, believing that this would be an easy thing to do and that they were not far away. This is why he shared his plans with a sailor, the only son of a master butcher, who had signed on as a crewman on a merchant vessel that had put in to Quebec for the winter. They were both staying in the same woman's boardinghouse. This is why the soldier told the crewman that he might be receiving twelve hundred livres in silver and that if he wanted to come with him to the English, he would pay all of his expenses. The sailor consented to the plan, and, having packed up some provisions, the two left one fine morning, crossing over in a boat they found to the Ile d'Orléans, about a league's distance [17] from the town. Once there, they entered the house of a *habitant* and asked him for a large meal, for which they paid handsomely. After this, they asked to borrow a bark canoe to cross the Saint Lawrence to the mainland on the other side, saying that they were going hunting and that they would come back for another meal on the return trip. The habitant, who was pleased to have been so generously paid in French coin and hoping to get more of it toward evening, readily lent them his canoe. They got in, crossed the river, stepped ashore, tied the boat to a tree, and walked into the forest. Along the way, the sailor cut a log into a kind of club and told his companion that it was to defend himself against wild beasts and Indians.

After walking a league and a half into the depths of the forest, guided by a compass, toward the lands of the English, the sailor stopped suddenly to relieve himself. The soldier continued slowly along. Then the devil tempted the sailor, who succumbed to the evil thoughts that this enemy suggested to him. Having started out again and caught up to his companion, he unleashed a horrible blow to the back of the soldier's head with the club that he was carrying. The soldier was stunned and fell facedown onto the ground. When he turned onto his back and tried to draw his sword, the sailor smashed in his head with another blow. Pulling out his butcher's knife, he then slashed his poor victim seven times; having thus murdered him, he took off the soldier's cloak and jacket, which he filled with stones and threw into a deep lake nearby. But because the soldier's shirt was trimmed with magnificent [18] fine lace, the sailor kept that, as well as his breeches, his money, his silk stockings, and his fine hatband. After that, he dug a big hole in the middle of piles of dry leaves fallen from the trees and buried the body there, covering it with leaves. He also took the precaution of gathering up the leaves that had been stained with the soldier's blood and burning them. In a word, he believed he had safely gotten away with the blow he had just struck amid the immense forests, frequented only by wild animals and Indians. After a short rest, he made a bundle of all he had stolen and retraced his steps to the canoe tied up on the bank, as I said above. We shall see that such sins are always an abomination in the sight of God, as was that of Cain against his brother Abel long ago. There are no witnesses; he is alone in his crime; who could find out? Yes, he is well hidden from men, but an angry and vengeful God will discover him, and indeed, this is how it happened.

Back in the canoe, he returned to the house of the habitant, who, not seeing the sailor's companion with him, asked what he had done with him. He replied, with a wild-eyed look, that they had found another canoe on the bank opposite Quebec and that the soldier had passed over in it, whereas he had retraced his steps specifically to return the first canoe to the habitant so that on another occasion he might lend it to him again. Then the sailor asked for something to eat, but while eating supper, he trembled, his eyes were filled with rage and fury, and he looked around him at every sound he heard. Everyone in the house who saw him in this state fled the dwelling, and when he had finished eating and [19] wanted to pay, there was no one left to speak to. So, putting an ecu on the table, he took advantage of the opportunity and returned to Quebec. He went back aboard his ship, put all his loot in his sea chest, and from there returned to his landlady's house.

Five or six days passed, and no one said anything, but the hour of divine vengeance was yet to come. It would not wait much longer, because the landlady, not seeing her boarder, asked the sergeant of the company where this soldier was, whether something had happened to him, or whether he was in prison or at the hôtel dieu.

The sergeant replied to her, "Is he not at your place?"

No, truly, having made inquiries, they did not find him there, nor was there any news of him. The rumor circulated that he had drowned. Finally, the miserable sailor was his own betrayer: since he had given the laundress his dirty linen, including the shirt stained with blood and pierced with five holes, she recognized it as belonging to the soldier. She took it the next day to M. de Cavagnial and told him it was that sailor, naming him and his ship, that he had given it to her for washing, and that the soldier had clearly been murdered. M. de Cavagnial took the name of the sailor and that of the landlady where he was staying, and after putting on his coat and hat, he went to the house of that woman. He knocked at the door, and someone called to him, "Come in," not imagining that it was a person of his rank. He went in and passed through the room of the sailor, who was at that moment in front of the fire, putting on his shoes. The captain, in coming upon him, gave him a look that struck like a thunderbolt. The sailor jumped out the [20] window, one foot bare and one shod, and fled to his ship. M. de Cavagnial had him followed by some soldiers. They searched and found him hiding between two barrels, more dead than alive. He was bound and carried off to a cell, and his sea chest was seized. That afternoon, they interrogated him, and upon opening the chest, they found the soldier's breeches, stockings, hat ribbon, and even his money.

The next day, they interrogated him again. He admitted his crime, for it was not easy to deny it, the knife used to commit the bloody butchery having been found on his person. As soon as he had admitted his crime, they took him by canoe to the scene of the murder. M. de Cavagnial went along like a hunter, with dogs who went straight to the spot and who indicated the place where the cadaver was with their paws. The soldier was dug up; his face was as fresh as if he were still alive, and his blood was as red as when his body was still warm. He was carried to the town in the same canoe and buried in magnificent fashion, and the sailor was condemned to be broken on the wheel the next morning. All the laborers and carters quickly left their homes for fear of being asked to gather and carry the wood to build the scaffold. It was necessary to order a detachment of soldiers to carry it, and the condemned did not leave the prison until about five o'clock in the evening.

On October 31, justice determined that he be strangled before being broken on the wheel. So, when he was carried up on the gallows, which was erected in the market square facing the church of Notre Dame des Victoires in the Lower Town of Quebec, and attached to the wheel, the executioner, who was not very experienced at his craft, tried to strangle him first with a sort of tourniquet. But when, after hoisting the man onto the wheel, [21] he started to give it the first turn, believing there was no life left in the victim, the latter let out dreadful screams. When the spectators heard this, they cried out against the executioner, but he was not bothered and said that if anyone among them knew the craft better than he did, he had only to come up and finish the job in his place. The business was therefore brought to a conclusion, but not without great difficulty, because it was his first execution, and he had been appointed executioner only because no one else had been found who would accept the post. It had been decreed that the criminal would be exposed on the wheel for three days, but as he was a sailor, others of his kind came during the night and seized the sentinel who was guarding the body. They blindfolded and gagged him, unloaded his gun with a ramrod, and untied the body, which they put in a sack with some cannonballs and threw into the river. When the sentry's relief arrived, he was untied, and as it was All Saints' Day, no one took the trouble to find out who had mocked the sentinel and the law. This was the wretched end of a man who tried to hide the fact that he had murdered his brother. How just are God's judgments, for nothing can be hidden from His sight.[14]

Toward the middle of January, around three o'clock in the afternoon, some houses in the Lower Town caught fire.[15] The alarm was sounded; habitants, bourgeois, soldiers, and even the Recollets tried to help put it out. The fire was very violent. They feared that it might even damage the bishop's residence, which was built above, on a high hill. But by a prompt response, the fire was extinguished, and it consumed only half of the house where it broke out. I wanted to help [22] as the others did. With this intention, I leave the hôtel dieu and come down the hill toward the Lower Town. I was not used to walking on the ice, and I fell down repeatedly, so many times that the fingers of both hands froze. I climbed halfway back up the hill and

14. No reference to this crime could be found in the judgments and deliberations of the Superior Council of Quebec for 1716. It is likely that a military tribunal tried the criminal.

15. Index note: "1717."

reached the house of the innkeeper, La France. Going inside, I went up to the stove to warm myself. The master of the house no sooner saw me than he gave me a rude slap on the cheek and asked whether I wanted to lose my fingers. At another time, I would have hit back, but how could I, if I could not use my hands? After giving me an example of his short temper, he gave me another of his charity, for he went out to fetch a bucket of water frozen over. He breaks the ice and has me put my hands in the water up to the wrists. In the space of a quarter hour, life returns to my fingers, but this was not without great pain. Eventually, I was perfectly cured. I thanked him kindly and I returned to my room, vowing to myself that in such winter weather the entire town could go up in flames, but I would not go out.[16]

I continued to pass my time in drawing and in studying artillery under the Reverend Father LeBrun, a Jesuit. On the first of May in this same year, which was the name day of M. the marquis de Vaudreuil because his name was Philippe, I had the honor of winning the cannon-shooting prize, which consisted of a complete cannoneer's uniform, a hat and six shirts, and ten ecus of local currency, which gave me the reputation of master cannoneer. I was welcomed wherever I went, and even the best houses offered me the honor of their tables. I entertained them by verses that I wrote or by some little song, but the desire I had to see my homeland again caused me much [23] sadness and sorrow.[17]

I have forgotten to say that it was only for winning another shooting prize that M. de Vaudreuil gave me a reward. By custom, the prize was contested three times each year, but after I won it the first time, there was a bet between the governor and the major general that if I were given two more cannonballs to fire, I could not equal my first score. But when I aimed and fired, I put the first in the same spot, and on a second try, I again hit the bull's-eye. With these three shots, I won the prize, which was awarded to me in the home of the governor, and I received from M. de la Corne a present of a silver sword.[18]

At the end of that month, I suffered an inflammation in my chest with an

16. The house of this innkeeper, Jacques Joignier, nicknamed "La France," was located in the Upper Town on the rue de Buade; see Louis Beaudet, ed., *Recensement de la ville de Québec pour 1716* (Quebec, 1887), 15–16.

17. At this time, May 1 was Saint Philip's Day; later, it was moved to May 3.

18. Vaudreuil was ill when he returned to Quebec in October 1716 after two years in France and spent several months in the hôtel dieu, where Dumont was also staying. It seems likely that the two became acquainted there. See Yves F. Zoltvany, *Philippe de Rigaud de Vaudreuil: Governor of New France, 1703–1725* (Toronto, 1974), 156.

abscess. Anyone else would have been done for, but I was destined for further dangers and infirmities in this life. My doctors and the good sisters of the convent gave up on me, and the prayers for the dying were read at the foot of my bed. At this moment, an officer of a merchant ship who had arrived two days earlier from France came to the hôtel dieu to bring some letters addressed to me. He found me in this extremity, at death's door. When he came up to my bed and presented them to me, it caused me to shudder from head to toe. The officer took out his snuffbox; it was Spanish tobacco. I lifted my arm out of the bed, and I took a large, two-fingered pinch of the powder and carried it straight to my nose. One part of it went to my head; the other fell down my throat and sent me into horrible contortions. Everyone thought I was dying, but in exciting myself to vomit, [24] I expelled the abscess, and this, little by little, led me to recover, so that after two weeks, I had enough strength to go on board the ship, where the officer received me kindly and put into my hands the sum of two hundred livres in French specie. The letters from France were from my family. They informed me that I was about to receive, by the royal vessel that was to arrive this year, my commission as an officer.

The more the warmth returned to the land, the more my health returned with it. Generally, it was toward the month of June that the fruits of the earth took on their healthy appearance, but this year, the land was covered with locusts who devoured in an instant all the crops or grass in every place where they were found. It was a veritable plague of God. M. l'abbé de Saint-Vallier, our bishop, ordered a novena of prayers with the exposition of the sacrament and nine days of fasting. At the end of six days, there were processions as during rogation days, and God granted the prayers of his humble servants; when the ninth day arrived, the insects disappeared, and we found piles of dead carcasses, as if they had been burned to a crisp. This allowed the grasses, grains, and vegetables to spring up as was their wont.

After September 8 had passed without any sign of the arrival of the royal vessel, no one could imagine why it would be so late, and the authorities had recourse to an Indian woman who knew how to juggle, that is to say, knew the art of divination.[19] After performing all her mysteries, she said to M. the governor that the royal ship would not come to anchor in the port, that another ship might well arrive, but that, rather than bring us abundance, it

---

19. Dumont uses the word *jongler*, which, in addition to the common signification "to juggle," was commonly used for native American shamans or medicine men and women, *jongleurs*.

would cause us sadness and want. Things turned out just as she had said, because a ship [25] named the *Eléphant* sailed from Rochefort, and it had the finest weather in the world for coming to this capital. But just as it arrived at the entrance to the Saint Lawrence River, the weather changed all of a sudden, and the wind became contrary. At least six weeks it [the ship] waited, hoping that any moment the wind might change, but no. Winter was coming on, and the stores on the ship began to run out. The ship was obliged to double back. Thus the first part of the diviner's prediction was already fulfilled.

And here we see the remainder: You have to realize that at Cape Breton, there was not only a shortage of food but of drink, and the soldiers, tired of their duties and of not having enough to eat, revolted against their officers. Having seized a merchant ship that was in the harbor, they boarded it, nearly all of them with fewer supplies than they needed, and forcing the captain and crew to do their bidding, they set sail for Quebec, where they felt sure they could find something to live on. Finally, after bad weather and good, they arrived at last in the capital, not bringing us abundance but as the harbingers of famine and want. They looked like absolute skeletons when they arrived. The order went out to the bakers and other shopkeepers of the town to close their shops, and so these poor men were dying of hunger. As they were being led to the hôtel dieu, if they saw a garden open and in it spied some cabbages, they devoured them like beasts of burden. At the end, it is enough to say that out of the 590 who were on the ship, only 100, if that, survived. Thus one sees that all of science cannot explain everything, and that an Indian woman who does not know A from B nonetheless knows the art of astrology and in such situations knows how to prophesy or divine exactly what will happen.

[26] Toward the end of August, when I still had not seen the royal vessel, I raised the issue with the major, who had promised me that I could return to France if I wished, as well as with the religious sisters and even M. l'abbé de Saint-Vallier. I finally persuaded them to obtain M. de Vaudreuil's permission for my return voyage, although in the sailors' mess rather than at the captain's table. There were two merchant vessels that were ready to depart, one called the *Cheval Marin,* commanded by M. David, and the other the *Providence,* commanded by M. Gaillard. It was on the first that I was to travel. The good sisters gave me three chests: one filled with needlework done in porcupine quills and in gold and silver and some fine linen, another that contained my clothing and linens, and the last one had some food and drink for my voyage. After taking leave from my dear protector M. de la Corne and thanking the good sisters, I embarked. On November 12,

after saluting the town with nine cannon shots, we set sail, the two ships in convoy.[20]

A bet was made between the captains of the two ships that the one who arrived in France before the other would be the winner. When we were off Cape Maillard, it was quite late, and the wind was not the most favorable, so we put in behind the cape in the lee of the wind and anchored. The *Providence,* or rather the captain of that ship, wishing to gain the lead, passed us by as if mocking us and fired a three-gun salute, which we answered. She had no sooner doubled the cape than the wind as well as the tide came full around on her bow such that she was pulled into the maelstrom, a swirl of water that [27] measures two leagues in circumference. When the *Providence* entered it, she would have lost all men and cargo had not her shallop and her canoe been still in train, that is, towed behind, in addition to a lifeboat. All hands in these three boats, by force of oars, pulled the ship toward land between Quebec and Beauport, where it ran aground and leaned over on its side. As for us, we spent the night at anchor and were safe, though we were frustrated in thinking that our captain would lose the bet, for we imagined that the *Providence* would arrive before us at La Rochelle, where we were supposed to land. This goes to show that a true salt's wisdom is not found in every head, for M. David, our captain, before dropping the anchor, had said that the wind was likely to pull us into the maelstrom.

The next morning, there came a favorable wind, and as the sea, or rather the tide, was rising, we weighed anchor and set sail. After doubling the cape and making two good leagues, we saw a ship along the coast and many people on the shore. At first, we believed that it must be the king's ship, but upon approaching, we recognized our companion. Our captain, using his bullhorn, cried out to M. Gaillard that the bet between the two ships was off and graciously consoled him on his misfortune. Not being able to help them, we continued on our way.

I had, as I said, the mess for my meals and the bridge of the ship for my table, but we had no sooner left the Saint Lawrence River and gained the open sea than our captain, to whom I must have been recommended, had me dine for the rest of the voyage at his table. And in place of a swinging hammock, he gave me a bunk [28] in the officers' quarters, the warmest

20. The deliberations of the Council of the Marine for February 3, 1717, approved a request from Governor Vaudreuil for a leave to be granted to "le Sr. de Montigny" to return to France (ANF, AC, C11A, XXXVII, 57). However, because the document mentions wounds rather than illness, it is likely that the officer referred to was Captain Jacques Testard de Montigny.

place on the ship. Our sails filled with good wind, we happily passed the banks of Newfoundland without any ice or verglas, and in short, we looked forward to happy days and nights in our homeland. But a fair morning quickly turns into a stormy afternoon, and a squall was waiting for us. On December 3 came upon us a hailstorm with hailstones that struck the ship so hard they cut the rigging and left bruises on the sailors' heads. But this lasted no more than a half hour. Then, on the ninth or tenth of the same month, it was only by the grace of heaven and the favor of the star of the sea, the Holy Virgin Mary, that we did not succumb to another storm that struck us, and this is what happened.

At about eight o'clock in the evening, prayers had been said, and half the crew went below to sleep until the next watch (the watches were four hours below and four hours on deck). Around nine or ten o'clock in the evening, while the first watch was above and I was asleep in the officers' quarters, I awoke with a start from the noise I heard as the mainmast fell. I had actually slept through the collapse of the mizzenmast. I threw myself under my bunk. The tiller was moving with a horrible force, as we had lost control of it. The first mate, as he was trying no doubt to give orders for some maneuvers, suddenly had his knees crushed against the capstan by the barrel of a cannon that had escaped from its carriage and broken the hinges that held it in place. Eleven sailors working to take in the mainsail were carried overboard as a wave washed over the deck. In a word, it was a dire situation. It was nighttime, and Saint [29] Elmo's fire was twice visible on the ship. This is a kind of little flame that appears during storms, similar to the will-o'-the-wisps that are seen in the country after a deluge of rain.

We thought ourselves lost. Our ship was spinning uncontrollably, as we were unable to get a hand on the tiller, which is a long beam attached to the rudder. When this wind first hit us, the sailor who was steering—the helmsman, as he is called—was either asleep at the wheel or else was not prepared, for he was pushed over by the tiller, and when another tried to grab it as it swept in a semicircle at amazing speed, he had his arm broken. There were only cries and lamentations, and all were deaf to orders. "Alas, must we be so close to port," said one, for by this time we were near the coast of Les Landes at Gendron; "must we perish without hope of saving anyone?"[21]

One man longed to see his wife, another his children and parents, and nearly all were certain of death; we confessed our sins out loud, for we had no chaplain. (It is rare to have one in merchant vessels, unless it is in a ship

21. Landes is a region in southwest France, south of Bordeaux. "Gendron" may refer to Girons, today the coastal town of Saint Girons-Plage.

of the Company of the Indies.) The livestock were crushed by the fallen masts, and all were in danger of perishing. But then, all in one voice made a vow to the Queen of the Seas, of Earth and Heaven, and we even threw sacred relics into the maw of the furious deep.[22] And as soon as this vow was spoken, the benevolent Mother, the refuge of fishermen and the home port of navigators, heard the humble and fervent prayers of her servants, and she chose the youngest of [30] the cabin boys to save all the rest.

I have already mentioned that we could not get control of the helm to steer. This young sailor grabbed hold of a short, thick block of wood and slipped nimbly up to the binnacle, the small, three-chambered box in the middle of which is a large lamp that illuminates the marine compass by which one keeps on course. When the tiller had swung over to the port side, the cadet dropped the block into the hole on the starboard side, with the result that the tiller could move only in a quarter circle, and it was easy to secure it with ropes that, when passed through pulleys, allowed us to begin to steer the vessel and bring it slowly around to windward. In less than a half hour, the sea, which was so furious, had begun to calm; from the rude, wild tempest that she had been before, she became gentle, and the weather turned as fair as could be.

We took up a collection to fulfill the vow, and each gave according to his means. A nun who was traveling with us had been on the gallery of the ship and was carried overboard by a wave in the midst of all the mayhem and the cries and lamentations that everyone was making. But as she told it afterward, when she made a vow of renunciation and committed herself to the Holy Virgin, another mountain of water washed her back onto the poop deck in the stern of the ship, where she lay in such a pitiable condition that she could not move, and when the calm came following the storm, she was found [31] between two chicken coops more dead than alive, as much from fear as from the cold that had taken hold of her. Help was immediately provided.

Then, a moment later, we had to try to rig a new mast, for day was dawning. We did the best we could and then continued our voyage. The second day after the storm, the mate died. After chanting vespers for the dead, we threw his body into the sea.

22. Index note: "Vows made." Catholic mariners and passengers who had survived a storm at sea or had enjoyed a successful voyage through dangerous seas or warfare frequently would commission an ex-voto painting. Several are extant in Quebec today. See Pierre Berthiaume and Émile Lizé, *Foi et légendes: La peinture votive au Québec, 1666–1945* (Montreal, 1991).

The night of the twelfth of December, we arrived at the Ile d'Aix, but even as we arrived, we faced new perils. The weather was very overcast, and for more than ten days, we had not been able to take readings. We navigated by dead reckoning, and though we believed we were still far from port, the ship began to scrape bottom. We cut the cables securing the anchor, and when it fell, it pulled out only a short lead of chain. There was no more than a foot of water under the ship's keel! Not knowing where we were and fearing that we were in danger, M. David, our captain, ordered a cannon to be fired. This was about two hours after midnight. The cannon was loaded with a ball that passed over the walls of the city, through a house, and fell into the rue du Pérot, for this was La Rochelle. But we knew nothing of this at the time, and we actually imagined that we were off Belle-Isle-en-Mer. After the cannon was fired, a great length of cable was paid out, as if for a deepwater anchorage. At the end of this cable, another anchor was made fast, the first was raised up, and the second was lowered so that we could put the vessel to rest without fear.[23]

The next morning, as light dispelled darkness and objects [32] began to be visible, we recognized that we were in the roadstead off La Rochelle and that it was on Pointe des Minimes that we had thought we might run aground. Toward ten o'clock, a shallop came to our side, bringing an order to go speak to M. de Chamilly, then the governor of the town, on the subject of the cannonball that we had fired. But our captain wrote to the governor and informed him that, as he and his crew had made a vow, they could come ashore only to carry it out at the foot of the altar. In fact, no one went ashore, and we spent five days in the roadstead to allow time for a painter to make a devotional image representing the storm we had weathered, above which was written in gold letters, *Votum equi marinis*—"vow of the *Cheval Marin*." On one side of the painting was our ship, half submerged beneath the seas, its masts splintered this way and that, the men swimming and trying to stay above the waves and get back on deck. On the right side was the Virgin—holding her Son and, with her right hand, commanding the sea to calm itself—and seamen, who appeared as supplicants, some with hands joined in prayer and others with arms outstretched, imploring the Queen of the Heavens and the Mother of Goodness.[24]

23. The tiny Ile d'Aix lies fifteen kilometers south of La Rochelle. The rue du Pérot is known today as rue Saint-Jean du Pérot, and in the 1720s, this street was fewer than one hundred meters from the water, parallel to the city walls, whereas today, it is farther inland. The larger island of Belle-Isle is located two hundred kilometers to the northwest.

24. The Pointe des Minimes lies just south of La Rochelle's harbor.

The sixth day after our arrival in the roadstead, all the crew of the ship—captain, pilots, officers, seamen, passengers, sailors, cook, and cabin boys—all embarked on two shallops. We numbered fifty-two persons altogether. We arrived at the chains of this grand, beautiful city, and without stepping ashore, we waited for the procession of the Holy Carmelite Fathers from the rue du Pérot [33] to come fetch us to take us to their church, where the vow was to be solemnized. When the monks came to the chains, only then did we step out of the shallops, and we divided into two columns: one of seamen in shirts and bare feet, although there was snow on the ground, walking one by one, each holding a candle; the other of us passengers, nine in number, including the lady.[25] We were each led by a white ribbon tied around our wrists held by a pauper of the town, who led us like slaves, followed by M. David, our captain, carrying in his arms an image of the Virgin in relief. In the middle of this procession, the painting, which was very large and represented the subject of our vow, was carried as our standard. Alongside it were four men, who carried on their shoulders an immense and magnificent loaf of consecrated bread. Then followed the monks and the officiant, and chanting the litanies of the Holy Virgin, we very slowly proceeded to the church.[26]

This was the order of the procession, and as you might imagine, there was no shortage of spectators, such that when we reached the church, guards were necessary to prevent people from entering, much as they might want to.[27] A High Mass was sung, a second collection was made, the consecrated bread was presented, and just before completion of the service and giving of the benediction, the painting was raised next to the altar on the Bible side, and after the Mass was completed, we sang the *Te Deum*. Only then, having satisfied our vows and paid our conductors, did we return on board to relieve the eight men who had been left there [34] to guard the ship in our absence. Our captain gave us a beautiful dinner to say farewell. I promised to go see him if I stayed for some days in La Rochelle.

When we had to go our separate ways, I thanked him for the generosity that he had shown me, and just as I was ready to go ashore once and for all, I was surprised to see the agents of the customhouse, who ordered me

25. Index note: "Order of the procession."
26. The narrow entrance to the harbor at La Rochelle was closed by a chain to prevent entry by unauthorized vessels. The Eglise des Carmes, or Eglise Saint-Jean, was built 1671–1676 in the rue Royale des Carmes, known today as the rue de la Monnaie, a continuation of the rue Saint-Jean du Pérot.
27. Index note: "Fulfillment of the vow."

to open my chests, which I was obliged to do in spite of all my best excuses. But as soon as I opened the one that had the embroidery of porcupine quills, the chief of the group said to me that this was contraband and that I would have to come with him. So I got into his boat, but as we made our way over the water, I recognized him as having been a clerk in my father's office. I addressed him by name, and he recognized me, and instead of taking me to the customhouse, he took me instead to his lodgings in the rue du Pérot near the sign of the Three Green Oaks, where we shared a table, bedroom, and company. He was very helpful to me in finding people who were interested in these kinds of needlework, and I was able to get at least seven hundred livres for them. This friend disappeared one day without saying a word to anyone, and I have heard no news of him since.

I counted on hearing some news from my father around Christmas, for I had written to him. I waited at my landlady's house for his orders until I finally decided to set out for Paris, as I had not received any letters in the month since I had disembarked. On January 18, while at the dinner table, I saw a man enter, of a respectable age and bearing. He asked to speak to me. After I greeted him and introduced myself, he put in my hands a letter from my father, which directed me to stay at La Rochelle until I had fresh orders from him, at the home of this man (who was M. de Goezeau, treasurer for the navy) [35] in the rue des Prestres.[28] So I left my landlady, whom the treasurer was kind enough to pay for my room and board, and I went with him. He was a widower and had just one son, who was then in Paris, and as he had built a superb house in this quarter of the city, he said that I must come take all of my meals with him, and he set me up in a furnished room in the home of a schoolmaster and tinsmith at the end of the street. Although back in France, I did not lose my taste for drawing and used it to pass my time agreeably. I went for walks, and I went every day for dinner and supper at the treasurer's, who liked me and gave me an allowance each month for my little expenses. There was a flower garden at his house, where, in his leisure time, he took pleasure in gardening, and I helped him.

Around carnival time in that year, M. de Chamilly, governor of that city, ran a lottery in which tickets were one ecu. I bought ten of them and had the good fortune to win two prizes—one of 700 livres and the other of 220 livres—which led me to think of M. de la Corne, my protector at Quebec, and of the good sisters. I thought it my duty to send them some present to remember me by via M. David, the captain of our *Cheval Marin*, who was

28. Today, the rue Alcide d'Orbigny. I am grateful to Didier Begel for locating this address.

preparing to return to those lands in another vessel. After giving him the present of a silver snuffbox, I gave him to deliver to M. de la Corne a gold watch that cost me 350 livres, along with one of those knives with the beautiful silver [36] inlay. And for the sisters, I sent silver and gold thread, silk in all sorts of colors, marbled and gold-embossed paper, and yarn, with paints and paintbrushes. Altogether, this cost me 1,060 livres.

Nothing happened to me in the course of that year at La Rochelle that merits being written here, but in the month of February, I received from my family a commission in the Company of the Indies, which was beginning to establish itself in the Mississippi country, now known as Louisiana.[29] This commission was as a second lieutenant at fifty livres per month, with the captain's table on the ship during the passage across the ocean.[30] In addition to this commission, I had one as second engineer at twenty-five livres per month, to serve under the Sr. Perrier, who was supposed to be in that country in the capacity of engineer. I had no sooner received these two commissions than I had several outfits of clothing made suitable for that country; I bought linens, had shirts made, some embroidered and others plain, and equipped myself with three flagons of liquor and provisions for the voyage. With my uniform, I reported for duty to M. de l'Estobec, who was the Company's first director in that city. He received me well, as I had been recommended by M. Diron d'Artaguiette, the Company's director at Paris.

M. de l'Estobec charged me, by an order written in his hand, to oversee some prisoners who were being held in a large tower in the walls of La Rochelle, facing the sea. It is called the Tour Saint-Nicolas. There were five hundred prisoners, of whom three hundred were deserters who had been granted freedom by the king [37] if they passed over to the New World. The two hundred others were younger sons of families whose parents, so as to be rid of them, were sending them out to make their fortune, so to speak. Doubtless I was numbered among them, although honored with an officer's commission. I had responsibility for fetching supplies for these captives. Every five days, I went to give them their money; they were allotted ten sous per day. At the base of this tower lived a guard with his family, who made them their soup and furnished them with bread and whatever was necessary. They were separated into several chambers and slept on straw. Guards patrolled there to prevent disorder. From time to time, small groups of prisoners in turn were given permission to take a little fresh air on a wide,

29. Index note: "1719."

30. To take meals with the captain's mess was a privilege on board a ship, especially given the scarce and poor quality of food for crew and passengers on transatlantic voyages.

spacious platform at the top of the tower. In spite of its height, six of the prisoners threw themselves into the water below the shorter tower during a high tide. They must have been good swimmers, because they thus found the secret for gaining their liberty. We were not able to catch any of them.[31]

After six months in my capacity as petty merchant to the prisoners, I found myself relieved by several officers, who came from all over to take passage for the Mississippi and serve in the companies of troops that were being sent there. Among them were two captains, one of whom was named the Sieur de Valdeterre, a lively man [38] and experienced in the service of the king. But against all reason, he was responsible for an incident that occurred here. One day, this captain wished to take the opportunity to inspect all the chambers of prisoners, and so we went together to the tower. When we arrived, I stayed below to pay the guard what he was due. The captain, accompanied by a sergeant, ascended, with his sword at his side. After visiting several chambers and hearing the complaints of the prisoners, he entered one in which the lead prisoner of the group came straight up to him in order to demand or try to obtain some favor. When he was denied, the prisoner immediately laid his left hand on the captain's stomach and with his right hand drew out the sword. Jumping back, he said, "Monsieur, you are disarmed, and if you advance one step, the blade that should have defended you shall wound you instead!"

To this, the captain, who on another occasion might only have mocked and belittled the man, instead became enraged, either out of the shame of finding himself disarmed or because he was angry at the prospect of having to yield. He ordered the prisoner to give his sword to the sergeant, who stood by with four armed soldiers. The prisoner's reply, according to what the sergeant told me, was that the king had armed Valdeterre with his power and authority and that, since he had allowed himself to be disarmed, the weapon could not be restored unless the captain produced an order bearing the king's own seal. He then flourished the sword like a sabre. The captain, defying all prudence [39] and caution, ordered one of the armed soldiers to fire, which he did immediately, and the prisoner fell, stone dead.

From where I was, down below, I no sooner heard the gunshot than I ran up the stairs of the tower four steps at a time and came to the scene just after it happened. I saw the chamber in an uproar, with cries of, "Killed, killed!"

31. Two towers still guard the narrow entrance to the old harbor of La Rochelle, the Tour de la Chaîne on the west side and the taller Tour Saint-Nicolas on the east.

I pushed back the crowd and, standing in front of the rebels, addressed them: "So, my friends, if it is me whom you want to see, here I am."

As soon as they saw me, they said, "No, no, not you, dear officer."

When the furor had died down, I asked them what had happened, and they told the story. I gave them a little lecture explaining how the dead man had been wrong to disobey, and their anger gradually subsided. To give them more reason to calm down, I asked for twelve jugs of wine to be brought. There were forty-two of them in the chamber at the time. I had the dead body of that miserable man carried away and buried. The captain was at fault, but because the prisoners were soon to depart, no one pressed the issue on behalf of the dead man, and eventually it was forgotten.

There were, anchored offshore, two ships of the Company of the Indies that had been loaded up and were waiting only for a favorable wind to set sail for the Mississippi, that distant land said to be filled with gold and silver. It was, or was supposed to be, another Peru, and our fortunes were all but assured, a rosy promise and a false one, as you shall see. As for these two ships, one was the *Union,* of thirty-six cannon, commanded by M. de la Mansillière.[32] The other was a flute captained by M. Japy, an old salt [40] of the sea who in his many voyages had always been a scourge to pirates, having captured many of their vessels. At last, since the ships were ready and the order to depart given, the prisoners were brought from the tower two by two, their arms tied behind their backs. Thus they were marched down to the Tour de la Chaîne by armed soldiers and put into boats to take them out to the ships—half in the *Union* and the other half in the *Marie*—where they were kept in irons until out of sight of land. Although our company of troops was on board, we officers remained ashore for more than twelve days. It was during this time that I learned that my dear father had died and that it was one of my brothers who had acted on my behalf and obtained my commissions through the agency of the Minister Le Blanc and his friends.[33]

32. A database created by the SHD, Lorient, "Voyages à longs cours des navires de la Compagnie des Indes," no. 19, confirms that the *Union* (commanded by M. de la Mansillière) was armed at Saint-Malo for a voyage to Louisiana on March 2, 1719, but there is no entry indicating if or when it stopped over in La Rochelle before crossing the Atlantic.

33. Jacques-François Dumont died during the winter of 1718; the inventory of his estate was filed on March 11 (ANF, Minutier central, LVI, fol. 227). That our author was not promptly informed of the death suggests his disfavor in the family. Likely it was the fourth eldest of the six Dumont sons, Pierre-Jean-Baptiste, who secured the military commissions for his youngest brother.

Finally, on May 21—the officers as well as I having sent our chests and flagons to be stowed—we came on board to set sail. Before leaving La Rochelle, I thanked M. Goezeau for being like a father to me. He embraced me and wished me a good voyage, advising me to make my fortune. So I embarked on my second sea voyage, giving myself over to God to go where He should command me to go. I have so often been reminded that it is He who preserves, governs, and orders all things, and that without Him, alas, man would be a worthless creature; but also that by the grace that He gives us, man rises above all the other beings He has created. All this shall be shown in the remainder of these memoirs, if my reader sees fit to continue, for his satisfaction and his pleasure.

Chapter Two

VOYAGE TO LOUISIANA;
RETURN TO LORIENT

MAY 1719-MARCH 1721

[41] At eight in the morning on the twenty-sixth of May,[1] after firing a seven-gun salute to the city, the *Union* and the *Marie* together set sail for the New World that was then called the Mississippi. I was in the latter ship, commanded by Sr. Japy, along with twelve other officers, of whom M. de Valdeterre was our captain.[2] We had on board 250 deserters, who were released from irons as soon as we had lost sight of land, as well as 112 enlisted men, without counting the men of the ship's crew. Everything was governed as usual in such vessels, which is to say that the men were assigned to stations, the watches were set, with half to be on deck while the others slept, and the mess was served in groups of seven men. We sailed in the best weather one could ask for, easily rounded Cape Finisterre, and soon after, we saw the Canary Islands, which we passed on our left-hand side; after that, we had behind us the trade winds *[alizés]*, so called because they blow always from the same direction. All we had to fear now was a calm, since that entails the consumption of supplies whether one is moving or not.

We arrived at the Tropic of Cancer, where ordinarily a baptism is given to all those who have never before passed under that line. It should be known that this ceremony is practiced in three places: at the banks of Newfoundland, under the line of the tropics, and at the equator, with the distinction, however, that when one has crossed the equator, even if only on a single voyage, one is exempt from the other two baptisms. But if you have passed the two others, you still must undergo a third baptism at the equator. Because I was exempted from the first baptism at the bank of Newfoundland, as I [42] explained above, I must here fulfill my promise and satisfy my reader

---

1. Index note: "Second voyage."
2. "Les armements au long cours de la deuxième Compagnie des Indes (1713–1773)," no. 24, SHD, Lorient, confirms that the *Marie*, commanded by Elie Jaspie, was armed at La Rochelle on May 15, 1719, and bound for Louisiana.

with an account of the ceremonies that are performed on those who are baptized.[3]

Two or three days before arriving at these places, the navigators alert those who have already been baptized to prepare all that is necessary for the festival, for their greater amusement. On the leeward deck is a large tub filled with water, which is used on these occasions as the baptismal font. The canteens are filled from it. On the tub is placed a plank as a seat for the adults who must receive their baptism. Finally, on the day when the line is reached, as soon as Mass has been said (assuming there is a priest) and dinner is finished, a cry is heard from the mainmast, the complaints of an ancient and venerable god, known by the name of the Bonhomme Tropique. His cries are accompanied by those of his retinue, played on whatever instruments are available on the ship. If there are none, they pound on mess bowls or wooden boards, on kettles or pans, whatever can be found to make music to announce his arrival. A moment later, you see this god appear, or rather, a sailor disguised as a venerable old man. He wears a large beard made of white oakum and is festooned with patchwork clothing of many colors, a big hump on his back, a feathered bonnet, and stockings, one pinned up, the other loose. He is, in a word, an appealing, agreeable, and horrible man, seated on the shoulders of four of his slaves, who with difficulty help him climb down from their shoulders along the shrouds. This descent is accompanied by the laughs and cries of the sailors and all the rest of the crew. The venerable god holds in his hand a trident, like a god of the sea, a prince of the Court of Neptune, who no doubt conferred this office

3. The custom of shipboard baptisms seems to have begun in the sixteenth century and is still practiced today. It is a carnivalesque occasion that allows common sailors to briefly gain authority over their captain and passengers of a higher social status. The earliest published account is of a Norman French ship from 1529; after 1725, English accounts become more numerous than French. The mythical deity was commonly called Neptune in English and *le Bonhomme Tropique* or *le Bonhomme de la Ligne* in French. Dumont's account is longer and more detailed than most excerpts collected by Henning Henningsen in his study of the literature, *Crossing the Equator: Sailors' Baptism and Other Initiation Rites* (Copenhagen, 1961). Other notable French examples from this period include the manuscript narrative by Marc-Antoine Caillot of his voyage to Louisiana, "Relation du voyage de la Louisiane, ou Nouvelle France, fait par le Sr. Caillot en l'année 1730," MS, 38–46, The Historic New Orleans Collection; the anonymous manuscript "Lettres Canadiennes," MS, I, 64–67, Toronto Public Library; [Vallette de Laudun], *Journal d'un voyage a la Louisiane, fait en 1720* (Paris, 1768), 35–38; and Claude Lebeau, *Avantures du Sr. C. Le Beau, avocat en Parlement; ou, Voyage curieux et nouveau, parmi les sauvages de l'Amérique septentrionale . . .* , 2 vols. (Amsterdam, 1738), I, 34–42.

upon him, and with it certain rights that have not yet been revealed to the knowledge of mortals.

When he has arrived on the bridge, he acknowledges his [43] previous children and embraces them, asking for news of the lands that they have seen and traveled through since they last left him and whether they have any complaints to bring against those in their companies who might have broken the promises made at their baptisms. After this, he asks for the number of adults or catechumens who are to receive baptism. The larger the number, the happier he appears and the more he jumps for joy. As soon as he is given the catalog of names, he takes a position next to the baptismal font, otherwise known as a tub, and he appoints his officers and officiants, then calls out, one after another, the names on the list. The first one named is, as you might expect, the one from whom the god of the tropic hopes or expects to get the most money. The one named comes forward and salutes the god of the tropic and takes a seat on the plank over the tub. Right away, he is presented with the collection plate and puts one or more ecus on it. The custom here is the opposite of the ceremonies followed in a church, for whereas there, the more one gives, the more attention he receives, here, one furnishes more but receives less. For, once the offering is given, the god of the tropic simply pours a little water over the wrist of the one being baptized and makes him swear to do the same to all those who pass these lines and have not yet been received as he has; to never make a cuckold of another sailor; in short, to hold to these rules as do all his subjects.

Once those who give much have been dealt with in this manner, only then are summoned those who are destined to be the subjects of amusement. When these are called, they are asked to take the same vows, and each is given the name of an island, just like those who paid. They are asked, as they sit upon the plank placed over the barrel, [44] whether they have ever known any seamen who told them what is done on this occasion, to which they reply yes or no. Then the plank is pulled back, and with a little push, the victim falls butt-first into the tub. From then on, it's a free-for-all; from the top of the masts, from the lifeboats and the shrouds, from everywhere on the ship come torrents of water, on his clothes, his face and head, everywhere that he can be hit. Those among the baptized who have their wits about them grab a flask or a bucket and throw water back in the faces of those who are soaking them. Rather than blows of the fist or words, it is water that serves as the weapon, both offensive and defensive. Since the climate is warm, it becomes a big bath.

A new ship or shallop or dinghy that has never before passed through these places is also baptized, and in this case, it is the captain in command who makes the offering, large or small. If he is a miser and does not give enough, the sailors perform a similar ceremony, and especially if they are quarreling and waging battle, they will go cut off the nose of the figurehead, which is carved on the bow of the ship, or cut a piece off of the bow of the shallop or dinghy. This is the cost of the avarice of the captain. No captain wishes to take the risk of acquiring such a public, visible renown. After these operations, the Bonhomme Tropique, by his divine and immortal powers, suddenly disappears, or at least he is never seen climbing back up the path by which he came.

We went along under full sail during the ceremony, which lasted until nightfall. But thereafter, we encountered a calm, during which some went over the side of the vessel to swim or bathe and others went fishing, taking in some excellent fish known as dorados. These fish, like bonitos, prey upon [45] the smaller flying fish that are found in flocks like starlings. They fly up and stay in the air as long as their wings stay wet, so that when they launch themselves to maximum height, some twenty or twenty-five feet above the surface of the water, it sometimes happens that they get caught in the shrouds or even fall on the deck of the ship, more than a hundred at a time. They are no larger than the sardines that one sees in Brittany and are excellent to eat. Porpoises are also caught sometimes, which are the real pigs of the sea, as they have lard just like those on land. They have no feet, however, and their grease reduces to oil. You also see in the shrouds the birds known as boobies, since they show no fear and allow themselves to be captured by hand, watching intently the person who climbs up to take them. They are good to eat. When you approach land, you see many kinds of birds, either in flocks or separately.

I return to our voyage. After a passage of six weeks, owing to the calms that delayed us, we espied La Grange Rocher, so called because of the resemblance it bears to one. It is not far from Cap François. After approaching a little closer to shore, we fired a cannon to call out the coastal pilot to bring us through the entrance of the port. The entrance is difficult here because there are sandbanks and rocks. Once the pilot had come on board, he guided our ships with the greatest of skill, and we anchored in the roadstead next to three royal vessels that were there at the time. The first was the *Hercule*, commanded by M. de Champmeslin; the second was the *Mars*, under M. de Roquefeuille; and the third was commanded by M. ————.[4] We had

4. Dumont left a blank space here, as if intending to fill in the name later. By contrast, when he wished to conceal a name, he wrote the first letter followed by a series of dots or

no sooner anchored than we both—that is, the *Marie* and the *Union*—fired an eleven-gun salute [46] to the standard borne by the *Hercule,* which replied to us with nine cannon shots. Since we were putting into this island to take in water and stores, the officers went ashore to walk about. We took lodging at an inn in that town. Because, at the time, we were at war with Spain, we delivered an order to M. de Champmeslin to escort us with his squadron to the Mississippi so that, if the Spaniards gave us trouble, he could help us. So the three royal vessels, together with our two, took in stores in order to complete our voyage.[5]

While this work was being done, we were able to amuse ourselves in Cap François. I had from M. de Goezeau a letter of exchange for six hundred livres drawn upon Sr. Jarland. Two days after coming ashore, I went to the home of this gentleman, who received me graciously and insisted that, during my stay here, I should not lodge nor dine anywhere but in his home, an offer I could not refuse. Thus I found myself free from care and from the expenses that my comrades were running up in profusion. Among them, there was no end of meals, dances, amusements, rendezvous, liquor, gaming; nothing was lacking in this place for those who had money. As for me, where I was lodged, I was being fed like a pig in a pen, as the saying goes. Because the weather was exceedingly hot, I slept after supper in a finely made cotton hammock, hanging in a room with a black slave woman or man who constantly cooled me with a fan.

It is not necessary to provide a description of Cap François, since so many others have written of it, so I shall say only that it is a land of cockaigne, especially for the newly arrived. I passed the time either by taking walks or drawing, and [47] one day, when I wanted to draw a view or perspective of the harbor and the ships that were there, I made the acquaintance of a young man who was a fine sketch artist and who was traveling from France to the Mississippi under a *lettre de petit cachet.* His name was the Sr. de C——. Two negroes went with us to carry our provisions up to a tall mountain that lies behind the town of Cap François, and when we had climbed up and reached the plateau atop the mountain, we settled down to eat. A short

---

asterisks. The third ship was, in fact, the *Triton,* commanded by M. de Vienne. The three royal vessels, together with the *Venus,* commanded by de Vieuxchampe, are listed in "Estat des vaisseaux et galeres du roy armez pendant l'année 1719," BNF, MSS fr. 2549, 86–87, as departing from Brest on March 22, 1719, and returning on January 12, 1720.

5. The peninsula Dumont refers to as "La Grange Rocher," or "the Stone Barn," is situated about fifty kilometers east of Cap-Haïtien in what is now the Dominican Republic; see also *Histoire de la Louisiane,* I, 27. Dumont refers to the colonial theater of the War of the Quadruple Alliance (1718–1720).

time after, walking over close to the edge of the slope to get a better view of the port and the town, we were surprised to see only a thick layer of clouds. We heard claps of thunder below us while, up where we were, we enjoyed beautiful clear skies. But as night was approaching, we were obliged to retrace our steps without making any sketches, and as we walked down the mountain, we realized that there had been a rainstorm in Cap François that we had escaped, thanks to our elevation.[6]

Finally, after three weeks had gone by, the royal ships being ready and ours as well, everyone went back on board. All of our deserters were transferred to the three royal vessels so as to augment their crews. Only those of the *Union* remained on board the same ship, and we, the officers of the *Marie*, would have also been transferred to the *Union* if we had not preferred our captain's table to the mess that M. de Champmeslin had ordered for us. What is more, our ship, the *Marie*, was chosen to be the exploding decoy in case of combat. Everything was set, I had my six hundred livres, and we set sail, all five vessels, to go to the New World.

Having rounded the Cape of Saint-Domingue, avoided the Mouchoir Carré and the Jardins de la Reine, and sailed along [48] the coast of Cuba, controlled by the Spanish, our convoy was under the latitude of Grand Cayman. As the *Mars* made better headway than the other four ships, she was in the vanguard and on the lookout when, one fine morning, she raised a red flag, making known by that sign that she had spied a fleet of ships. She luffed up into the wind to let us come alongside, and we learned that there were forty-one sails up ahead. Since we believed that these were Spanish ships, we proceeded toward them with the intention of engaging in combat. We were fully prepared for this, but after we had come closer to them and raised our French colors to declare ourselves, all the ships of the fleet lowered the Spanish colors they had been flying and raised English ones instead, after which they saluted our French colors with several cannon shots, each in turn. Then their ship's commander had his launch lowered and boarded M. de Champmeslin's ship; he told him that he was en route from Jamaica (an island controlled by the English) to the Bahamas Channel in a convoy, so as to be better prepared to resist if the Spaniards should attack. We passed a couple of days sailing with them, after which they took their route and we continued ours.[7]

6. It is possible that the young man in question is Jean-Baptiste de Chavannes, sent to Louisiana for killing a man in a scuffle. See *HLF*, IV, 365; Shannon Lee Dawdy, *Building the Devil's Empire: French Colonial New Orleans* (Chicago, 2008), 168–169, 172. On the lettres de cachet as a means of exile to the colonies, see Introduction, above.

7. Dumont refers to the Mouchoir Bank, or Diana Bank, a shoal of reefs just east of the

The third day, that is, the day after we parted from the English fleet, the *Mars*, still in the van, spied a two-masted bilander. Seeing us approaching under French colors, it raised the Spanish flag and declared itself. When the *Mars* saluted with several cannon shots, the captain of the bilander appeared to be luffing up to come alongside the *Mars* but then sheeted in again and began to flee. We all five fired upon it, and we continued to give chase from eight in the morning until three in the afternoon. Finally, the ship had to give up, but before doing so, she lowered [49] the Spanish flag and raised that of England, surrendering herself under those colors. The bilander approached M. de Champmeslin's ship, and when the captain came on board, he declared himself to be of that nation and showed his commission, saying to M. de Champmeslin that he had not been able to keep pace with the forty-one ships that had departed Jamaica en route to the Bahamas. Our fleet commander gave him a very strong reprimand for his maneuvers and was even on the verge of having him keelhauled, but instead pardoned him, and he went on his way, and we continued ours. We soon spied the bluffs of Cabo San Antonio, after which we altered course toward Dauphin Island, formerly known as Massacre Island, the site of the French settlement that was then suffering great difficulties, as I shall soon explain. First, my reader should know that, after a furious gale, with angry and high seas, we were happy to see that island. Before I describe it, however, let us leave behind for a moment our five ships and speak of other matters.[8]

In the year 1718, war being declared between ourselves and the Spanish,[9] the commandant at Dauphin Island did not want to wait until the Span-

---

Turks Islands, Bahamas. The route of Dumont's convoy from Cap-Haïtien was through the Windward Passage and along the south coast of Cuba. The Jardins de la Reine are a string of islands to the south of Cuba and northeast of the Cayman Islands. Such deception in self-identification using ship flags was common, especially during war or among smugglers and pirates. See Dawdy, *Building the Devil's Empire*, 117–129.

8. For "keelhauling," see above, original manuscript [8–9]. The best account in English of the battles for Pensacola is Jack D. L. Holmes, "Dauphin Island in the Franco-Spanish War, 1719–22," in John Francis McDermott, ed., *Frenchmen and French Ways in the Mississippi Valley* (Urbana, Ill., 1969), 103–125. Holmes had access to an account of the battle from the Spanish perspective: "Relación de la sorprese hecha por los franceses de la Movila al Casillo de San Carlos y Punta de Sugüenza y su resauración por las armas de S.M. el día 7 de agosto 1719," a copy of a pamphlet printed in Mexico, found in the Archivo del ministerio de asuntos exteriores, Madrid, XIX, MS no. 56. See also the account of the Pensacola war in *Mémoires historiques*, II, 9–28.

9. Index note: "1718." War was declared by France, Britain, and Austria against Spain in December 1718 and by France against the Spanish colonies in January 1719, but the news did not reach the colony until April. See Holmes, "Dauphin Island in the Franco-Spanish War," in McDermott, ed., *Frenchmen and French Ways in the Mississippi Valley*, 112.

iards came and attacked first. So, having chosen fifty of the best men that he had at that time, together with some Canadians, he set out at midday, with a favorable wind, in two large boats. Reaching Santa Rosa Island toward dusk, without being detected by the soldier on watch, our men seized him and had no difficulty in also overpowering the detachment there that constituted a small advance guard, composed of soldiers asleep on their cots. This was accomplished without firing a single shot and without spilling any blood. These men's weapons were [50] seized, and all fourteen of them were bound. Our soldiers then dressed themselves in the Spaniards' uniforms, and when, at four o'clock, the next watch (consisting of an equal number of Spaniards) came to relieve the guard on the island, they, too, were taken as the others had been. The Frenchmen embarked in the same boat that had brought the guards and crossed over to the large fort, where they entered as if Spaniards, seized the guards, the magazines, and the fort, and took the governor and everyone in the fort prisoner in the name of the king. But because the Sr. de B—— was worried that French ships would not arrive soon enough and thus feared a shortage of food, he dispatched a French officer to take all the prisoners to Havana, a city located on the Spanish island of Cuba, and return them to their homeland. He named the Sr. de Richebourg captain of this detachment of fifty soldiers. The Spaniards were put on board the ship in irons, except for a few officers who were granted freedom of movement, and when the ship was provisioned with food, water, and wood, and the wind was favorable, it set sail.[10] While they were en route to the island of Cuba, the Sr. de Chateaugué—brother of M. d'Iberville, the former well-known captain of Mexico—was named captain and commandant of Pensacola and provided with a garrison of seventy soldiers, with three sergeants, a drummer, three captains, two lieutenants, and two

10. By "B——," Dumont refers to Jean-Baptiste Le Moyne de Bienville, who at this time was commandant general of Louisiana during its administration by the Company of the Indies. On Dumont's practice of concealing names, see Introduction, above. The expedition to take Pensacola set out on May 12–13 and involved the *Comte de Toulouse*, commanded by Jean-Gaston, chevalier des Grieux; the *Maréchal de Villars*, commanded by Joseph Lemoyne de Serigny; and the *Philippe*, commanded by Captain Dilhourse, or Dehourse, as well as several smaller boats. The previous year, Chateaugué had briefly established a Fort Crèvecoeur on Saint Joseph's Bay to the east of Pensacola. The prisoner exchange was stipulated by the articles of surrender. Other sources indicate the prisoners were carried on the *Maréchal de Villars* and the *Comte de Toulouse*, commanded by the chevalier des Grieux and Jérémie de Meschin, or Mechin, not by Richebourg. See *HLF*, III, 301; Holmes, "Dauphin Island in the Franco-Spanish War," in McDermott, ed., *Frenchmen and French Ways in the Mississippi Valley*, 114; and "Voyages de longs cours de la deuxième Compagnie des Indes," nos. 38, 39, SHD, Lorient.

ensigns. The Sr. de B—— returned to Dauphin Island in glory, having won such a victory without losing a single man.[11]

Let us return to the French ship that was carrying the Spaniards to Havana. No sooner had it put the prisoners ashore than the Sr. de Richebourg was himself taken captive, his ship seized, and his men put in prison. They had to sleep on straw, were given very little food, and as a consequence were reduced to the most abject misery. What is more, the same Spanish soldiers who had been so well treated when prisoners of ours now came to their [51] cell to insult these men, offering the choice of either deserting the flag of France and making friends with the Spanish or, if they did not wish to take up arms, to be set free so long as they settled there on the island. These propositions enticed the poor prisoners; some of them took the first option, others the second.

The governor who ruled this town for the Spanish king did not sit with his arms crossed, however; he resolved to have his revenge. To this end, he outfitted the same French vessel, as well as another, with soldiers and crew and all that was necessary for both sustenance and combat. When the two ships were ready, they set sail, and after three days at sea came in sight of Pensacola. The French one was the first to enter into the roadstead of the port. The sentinel cried out to it:

"From whence hails this ship?"
"From France," was the reply.
"Who is the commander?"
"De Richebourg."

And so, believing that it was a French ship returning from Havana, the sentinel allowed it to enter the port, which it attacked and seized. The second ship entered not long after. The flag of France was lowered, and that of Spain replaced it, and the Sr. de Chateaugué was summoned to surrender.

But the French commander rejected this summons and vowed to defy the enemy with what few men he had. Even before the battle was over, he immediately dispatched a messenger to Massacre Island to ask the commandant for reinforcements. But since he himself was shorthanded, he was not

11. Dumont may mean to be ironic here in referring to d'Iberville, the most famous of the Le Moyne family of adventurers, as "cet ancien et fameux capitaine du Mexique." D'Iberville had died at Havana in 1706, and his widow and estate were, for nearly thirty years after his death, burdened by lawsuits accusing him of embezzlement and smuggling with the Spanish colonies, including Mexico. See Dawdy, *Building the Devil's Empire*, 115.

able to satisfy this request. The third day after the attack and defense began, in the dark of night, forty-three soldiers of the French garrison scaled the walls of the fort, which was composed of four bastions. These [52] deserters turned against us, such that the Sr. de Chateaugué, in the desperate straits in which he found himself, with just twenty-seven soldiers, was forced to capitulate[12] and surrender Pensacola, with the honor of marching out with drums beating and torch lit. This was carried out the following day.[13]

But no sooner was he outside the fort than his men were taken prisoner and conveyed over to Santa Rosa Island and imprisoned there. As for the Sr. de Chateaugué, he was sent to Havana. From there, three ships were sent to Pensacola with a large force of troops. They fortified the fort to make it better capable of defending itself and to protect the entrance to the harbor, even though this entrance was a very difficult passage with sand banks on both sides and no more than twenty-two feet of water above the bar. For this purpose, they built a new fort on Santa Rosa Island, on the point next to the entrance to the harbor. When I say "they built," I mean that they ordered the work done by our French prisoners, who labored as slaves and beasts of burden, and they gave them nothing to eat other than rancid cassava bread. Cassava is a species of root plant of which the juice is a dangerous poison; at least, that is what I've heard, never having seen it myself. In a word, these prisoners had neither rest nor sustenance.

No sooner had they—the Spaniards, I mean—fortified these two places than they resolved to take Dauphin Island from the French. To this end, they sent a two-masted boat named the *Grand Diable,* carrying six small cannons, four-pounders, to make an attack on this island, where, ever since the retaking of Pensacola, the men were armed and on the watch. The Spaniards came and presented themselves. There was, in the roadstead, a ship that had come from France, named the *Philippe.* [53] Given its small crew, it was in danger of being boarded by the enemy, and so it was holed up in a

12. Index note is partly illegible, but concludes, "by the Spaniards."

13. The Spanish arrived to recapture Pensacola on August 6, 1719. Primary accounts of the battle include *HJEFL,* 79–89; Antoine François Laval, *Voyage de la Louisiane, fait par ordre du roy en l'année mil sept cent vingt* (Paris, 1728); Charles Le Gac, *Immigration and War, Louisiana: 1718–1721; From the Memoir of Charles Le Gac,* trans. Glenn R. Conrad (Lafayette, La., 1970); Jean-Baptiste Le Moyne de Bienville to council, *MPA,* III, 269–275; [Marc-Antoine Hubert], "Narrative of the Events after the Spaniards Recaptured Pensacola," *MPA,* III, 242–254. The sources differ on how many French soldiers defected to the Spanish side during the attack. See also Holmes, "Dauphin Island in the Franco-Spanish War," in McDermott, ed., *Frenchmen and French Ways in the Mississippi Valley,* 114–115, which identifies the last of these as Hubert's narrative.

tight anchorage close to shore, secured by multiple anchors. Its captain had turned the ship into a battery, mounting all the cannons on the side facing the enemy, and with these cannons now and then really battered the attackers. The greater part of the French inhabitants of Dauphin Island, fearing that the island might be captured and that they would lose with it all of their wealth and possessions, carried them over from the other side of the island onto the mainland, to the land of a man named Miragouin, believing that they would be more secure there than on the island, since they imagined that the Spanish would soon arrive. But because of their firm resolution and vigorous defense, the enemy never did risk a full-scale invasion. The Spaniards contented themselves with simply making a bluster of activity, going from one side to the other but never advancing nor winning any ground. They no doubt did find the settlement of the Sr. Miragouin, approached it, and even attacked it. But whether they pillaged it or not, either way, the inhabitants of Dauphin Island never could reclaim the things that had belonged to them. After the Spanish had landed at the settlement of this habitant, they returned to Pensacola. They did not stay there long, however, but came back two days after, with another armed bilander, and by this caused a second alarm among the French of the island.[14]

It was at this moment that our squadron of five ships appeared, four of them displaying Spanish colors. I leave it to my reader to imagine how the hearts of the poor islanders were pounding when they saw us, as they had no reason to doubt that we were Spanish ships. Their fears must have seemed all the more confirmed since [54] the flute the *Marie*, which they easily recognized, was flying its French flags at half-mast as if it had been captured en route, and, because it was not as fast as the royal vessels, the *Mars* was towing it. Eventually, however, the *Mars* dropped the towline to go cut off the Spanish bilander, which was trying to escape toward Pensacola. The *Mars* was not able to catch up because it drew more water than the Spanish boat, and the latter was able to escape along the shoreline. I wonder how our French brothers on shore could not have believed that we were a Spanish squadron, since they saw seven Spaniards leave the *Grand Diable* in a shallop to come on board the *Hercule*, believing that the latter belonged to the king of Spain, their master. These men had no sooner come

14. On Dauphin Island's successful defense in August 1719, see Holmes, "Dauphin Island in the Franco-Spanish War," in McDermott, ed., *Frenchmen and French Ways in the Mississippi Valley*, 117–121; and Le Gac, *Immigration and War*, trans. Conrad, 15, 28–30. The "Spanish" did sack Miragouin's plantation on August 13–14, but when Indian allies captured eighteen of the attackers, they turned out to be renegade Frenchmen, wrote Le Gac.

on board than they became the first prisoners taken in this battle. During this time, the *Grand Diable* as well as another bilander arrived at Pensacola and brought joy to the hearts of the habitants and soldiers there by assuring their governor that Dauphin Island would soon be captured, because they had five large ships of their nation offshore, ready to attack.

Around five o'clock in the afternoon, we sailed into the anchorage, about one league off the island, and lowered the Spanish flags that we were carrying to raise those of France in their place and declare ourselves. This restored calm to the hearts of those who previously had been in grave fear. We sent ashore the shallop of the *Hercule* with an officer of that ———[15] carrying papers and orders to the French commandant. The next morning, all the other officers disembarked, myself included, and all the passengers and all the soldiers who were assigned to this land went ashore. We officers went to pay our respects to the commandant of this island, who, after dinner, having sounded the report for a roll call of all the troops and habitants, recognized each of us according to his rank as an [55][16] officer and the tenure of his commission. I was named as a second lieutenant in the company of M. de Valdeterre, and in addition to this post, I had one as a second engineer under M. Perrier. I was, however, all alone in this second capacity, because this senior engineer had died during the passage from Cap François to this island.

Massacre Island was so named because, when the French came to settle there during the time of the Sr. Crozat, they found several ossuaries and even skulls in great quantities, which led them to give it the name "Massacre." But since then, it has been given the name "Dauphin." It is no greater than two leagues in width and six or seven leagues long. It lies with its width north and south and its two ends at the east and west. Along the latter axis lies Pensacola and its Spanish fort, which is seven or eight leagues distant. Ships arrive on the sea side, which is the Gulf of Mexico, and this shore is covered with fine, white sand. Houses line the shore, although they are little more than cabins built of pine wood. The island is covered only with these sorts of trees, and so the houses are covered with cypress bark, which is stripped off in season. Aside from the homes of the habitants, the island

15. A hole in the manuscript obliterates a word in this sentence. Also, an index note, partly cut off, reads "——— August ——— 1719." The fear of the French on Dauphin Island when they saw ships flying Spanish colors is confirmed by Hubert, "Narrative of the Events after the Spaniards Recaptured Pensacola," *MPA*, III, 254.

16. Figure 2, "Massacre Island (Dauphin Island)," was originally located at this spot in the manuscript.

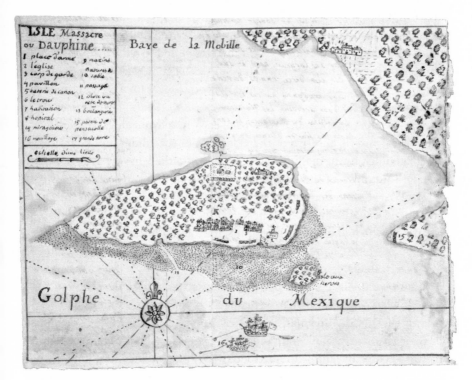

Figure 2. *Massacre Island (Dauphin Island).* VAULT oversize Ayer
MS 257, map no. 2. Courtesy The Newberry Library, Chicago

also has several storehouses, some for wines and spirits, others for grains
and for the necessities of life, and still others for dry goods. Each storehouse
has its manager.[17]

On the eastern point of the island, a grand mast was planted in a deep
hole in the sand, which served as a pole for a flag, which was raised and
lowered when the occasion called for it. A small house sat not far from the
flagpole, which served as a church, and a long league farther inland was a
hospital for the sick. The soil of this island is not the most excellent [56] for
crops because it is more sand than dirt, and it is only with great toil and care
that one can grow a few salad greens in it. And although the island is surrounded by the ocean, one can dig a hole in the sand just six feet from the

17. The journals of d'Iberville and André Pénicaut confirm this origin for the name "Ile
Massacre." See Margry, IV, 147; and Pénicaut, *Fleur de Lys and Calumet: Being the Pénicaut
Narrative of French Adventure in Louisiana,* ed. and trans. Richebourg Gaillard McWilliams
(Tuscaloosa, Ala., 1988), 11.

shore and find fresh water, very good for drinking. This was the first establishment of the French.[18] Just a week after we arrived there, our detachment of officers and soldiers embarked in the *Union* and in the *Philippe,* which had been removed from its anchorage in the basin, to sail to Pensacola to rescue our men from their misery and make ourselves for a second time the masters of Pensacola.

The seventh of September, we set sail early in the morning. We were five: three royal vessels and two of the Company of the Indies, not counting a small bilander. It was in this last boat that I embarked, having been ordered to take soundings of the entrance to Pensacola Bay and to mark it with buoys. We set off under full sail and in fine weather. There was on the *Hercule* an old Canadian who knew perfectly the entrance to the Spanish roadstead and who had distinguished himself by guiding through the entrance the ship of M. de Champmeslin, which drew twenty-one feet and nineteen inches of water.[19]

When we finally came into view of Pensacola, still under sail and flying French colors, the Spaniards, realizing that their expectations had been frustrated, sounded the alarm and took up arms. There were seven ships in their roadstead. The commandant of Dauphin Island under the Company had come by land with his troops and a few Indian allies. Finally, the *Mars,* which was the best-sailing vessel, was in the van, followed closely by the *Marie,* on which I was, which was taking the soundings and placing the buoys. The *Mars* sailed first [57][20] into the bay, sailing upwind, flying only its topgallant sails. Not a single man was visible on board the ship, save the captain, who was walking on the poop deck. The fort on Santa Rosa Island unleashed heavy fire upon his ship and upon ours. The *Triton,* the *Union,* and the *Philippe* were next to enter the bay, and the *Hercule* was the last. When the ships had anchored, the cannonballs began to fly from them as well as from the seven enemy vessels and Fort Santa Rosa. As for the fort on the mainland side, no sooner had the commander there spied our ground troops, which were augmented by more than one hundred Indian warriors of the Sr. de Saint Denis (a cousin of the Sr. d'Iberville and M. de Chateaugué), than the Spanish commandant, after firing just one cannonball, lowered the flag and surrendered.[21]

18. The Dauphin Island post had been established by d'Iberville in 1699.

19. This Canadian was named Grimeau, according to *Mémoires historiques,* II, 22. See also original manuscript [73], below.

20. Figure 3, "Plan of Pensacola," was originally located at this spot in the manuscript.

21. Index note: "Surrender of Pensacola."

Figure 3. *Plan of Pensacola.* VAULT oversize Ayer MS 257, map no. 3.
Courtesy The Newberry Library, Chicago

But it was quite a different story in the roadstead. The Spanish ships defended themselves bravely, as did the smaller fort, and a cannonball fired by one of the enemy vessels at the *Hercule* carried away two and a half feet of the main yard of our squadron's chief vessel. At this, the Spaniards all began crying out, "Long live Philip the Fifth!"[22]

There was among them a smaller ship named the *Neptune.* The commanding officers withdrew in their shallop and dinghy, as did the crew on board one of the larger vessels. But before abandoning the ship, they attempted to set fire to it and blow it up by means of a fuse leading to the Sainte-Barbe, the place where a ship's powder is stored. They lit this fuse

22. The commander of the Spanish fleet was Admiral Don Alfonso Carrascosa de la Torre, and the commandant of the Pensacola forts was Governor Matamoros de la Isla, who was reluctant to believe that France and Spain had, in fact, declared war on one another. See Holmes, "Dauphin Island in the Franco-Spanish War," in McDermott, ed., *Frenchmen and French Ways in the Mississippi Valley,* 122–124; Charles E. O'Neill, ed., *Charlevoix's Louisiana: Selections from the* History *and the* Journal (Baton Rouge, La., 1977), 53–58; Le Gac, *Immigration and War,* trans. Conrad, 34–38.

just before they disembarked. Then our eighteen prisoners, no longer hearing any noise coming from the crew of the ship, broke out of confinement and came on deck. They saw the poop deck catching fire but were able to save themselves by [58] putting it out just in time. If another inch of wood had burned, the fire would have reached the powder. It was not without great effort, but by their vigilance and strong presence of mind, they extinguished the fire and then lowered the Spanish flag to raise the French one in its place.

There was, among these prisoners, a second lieutenant named the Sr. Carpeau de Montigny, who resolved to come on board the *Hercule* to seek safety in the French fleet and to inform those on board what had happened on the *Neptune*. But how could he do this without any dinghy or other boat? He sat astride a beam that was in the water alongside him, and with a paddle—a type of oar—he managed, in spite of the gunshots fired at him, to reach the *Hercule* and present himself to M. de Champmeslin, who promised to take care of him.[23] Our fleet commander, seeing that the enemy had cut off the end of his ship's main yard, quickly ordered that four thirty-six-inch cannons be aimed at the enemy vessels to dismast them, and this was immediately carried out. In the first volley, three of their masts were hit, and the Spaniards no sooner heard the report of these four huge guns than their hearts began to quiver and they hid below decks, shouting at the top of their lungs, "Strike the colors, strike them!" But no one had the courage or strength to do it. Finally, I have to say, it was the French prisoners who had to carry out the maneuver.

Although the seven ships and the large fort had surrendered, the smaller fort located, as I have already indicated, on the point of Santa Rosa Island continued to fight. The commandant there, after another good hour of fighting, finally surrendered in turn, only because of loss of men and lack of powder. He thus became the third to come on board [59] the *Hercule*, where he presented his sword to M. de Champmeslin and said to him, in French spoken with the accent of the Spanish nation: "I surrender, for lack of powder. I was deemed worthy of defending the fort that I give up to you, and I have done my duty there. No man can be expected to do the impossible, and thus I hand over my weapons to you as my conqueror," and he held out his sword. But our fleet commander returned it to him, saying that the French did not intend any insult to men or officers such as him. Champmeslin even embraced him and added that, if all the Spaniards had been like him, he did

23. The French word *pagaille*, or paddle, was new to the language at the time Dumont was writing, so he provides a gloss.

not know whether the victory would have been on our side. This officer was henceforth held and considered as a man worthy of laurels, even in defeat. But the man who commanded the larger fort at Pensacola was not held in the same regard. When he came on board to see M. de Champmeslin, he was treated to insults, even by the soldiers, and sent to join the prisoners on board the *Mars*, which goes to show that courage in war is always respected and cowardice condemned.[24]

After the surrender of the smaller fort, all the Spaniards were taken prisoner and distributed among the three royal ships, and our Frenchmen who had been enslaved regained their freedom. But our deserters, the forty of them who were recaptured, were put in irons. M. de Champmeslin went ashore to join M. de B——, the commandant of Dauphin Island. They made an inspection of the storehouses and an inventory of all the goods, of which one part was loaded onto the royal vessels and the remainder onto the two belonging to the Company of the Indies. [60] As with the goods taken from the Spanish, these were used to support the settlement of the new colony. After the division and lading of the goods (wine and flour, spirits and other merchandise, as I just explained) was complete, the next day a council of war was called on the subject of the forty deserters. They were made to draw straws, and twenty were hanged from the end of the yardarm of the mainmast of the ship, *Hercule*. The other twenty were condemned to serve in the capacity of forced labor for the span of ten years. Such is the fate of men who betray their homeland.[25]

Following the conclusion of all these expeditions, we spied a large pinnace in the gulf coming under full sail toward the mouth of Pensacola Bay. By this time, all our vessels had their sails and flags hoisted for drying; they were put away at the first sight of this ship, and only the Spanish colors were left flying. The pinnace, or rather its commander, had no doubt that all these ships were of his own nation and so sailed proudly into the port. He anchored there and fired a five-cannon salute. A moment later, the *Grand Diable*, which was now a prize of ours, began to pull up alongside and, firing guns into the air, called for surrender, all the while shouting, "Long live the king of France!"

24. On the recapture of Pensacola in September, see Bienville to the council, *MPA*, III, 269–275; and *HJEFL*, 86–88.

25. Bienville reported in a letter dated Oct. 20, 1719: "In the Spanish vessels that . . . Champmeslin captured there were thirty-seven of our deserting French soldiers who were brought before a naval court martial and twelve of whom were condemned to be hanged and the others to serve as convicts" (*MPA*, III, 274); see also Le Gac, *Immigration and War*, trans. Conrad, 38.

Alas, imagine his surprise in finding himself captured like a fox or, rather, like a bell caster who sees his molten metal flow away without completing his project. He had no option but to surrender, but he threw into the sea, through the latrines, the packets of letters that he had on board. They were spotted by one of our soldiers, who dove into the water three times and with great difficulty recovered them. They were enclosed in a lead box. As soon as they had been recovered and brought on board the *Grand Diable,* the soldier set out in a dinghy to bring them [61] to M. de Champmeslin, who, to reward him, had him promoted to sergeant from the common soldier that he was before.[26]

The box was opened, and in it were found several letters addressed to various persons. Among them was one from the governor of Havana, who wrote in the name of the king, his master, to the commandant of Pensacola. It was phrased in these terms: that the king, their master, having no doubt that his friends and subjects had taken the country of the French and the Frenchmen prisoners, wished to have it known that, to avoid a shortage of provisions, it would be necessary to send all the French to slavery in the mines. In this ship, there was also a generous gift of liquors and fine foods that the governor of Havana was sending to the governor of Pensacola but that went, instead, to his conqueror. I was ordered, as an engineer, to make a map of Pensacola and its surroundings. I did so and presented it to M. de Champmeslin, who, pleased with my work, made me a present of a fine silver sword.

It so happened that, two or three days after the capture of this place, the commandant of Dauphin Island wished to give a luncheon in honor of M. de Champmeslin, who had come ashore from his ship. And because he did not have much food, when our French cook of the colony walked out to the square in front of the fort and saw a sergeant taking out of the oven a large and excellent meat pie, he asked him for it. The sergeant sold it to him for several quarts of eau-de-vie. It was placed on the table and was perfectly seasoned. When it was presented to M. de Champmeslin, he found it superb, just to his taste, as did I and the other officers. We tasted some of the Spanish wine. Toward the end of the meal, many of the French soldiers were [62] heard howling and barking. An officer, hearing this noise, asked them why they were carrying on like that, but just one of the men in the group spoke up: "Alas, sir, you have eaten our dog, why would you not expect us to

26. Bienville wrote that the *Grand Diable* arrived on September 12 and that "in it were found letters from the viceroy [royal lieutenant] of Mexico" (*MPA,* III, 274).

complain?" and he showed the officer the head of this animal, the skin, and the four paws. And so, instead of the goat that we thought we were eating, it was dog. M. de Champmeslin learned of this and said jokingly that the dogs of that land were worth as much as the deer in France.

I forgot to say that in the battle, which lasted a good five hours, we had only a single man killed, named La Sceine, by a lead ball that had been cut into halves and attached by a thin brass wire. You load one into the gun just like a whole ball, but when it comes out, the two parts separate by almost half a foot, and it was one of these that took off this man's head.

We demolished the forts both on Santa Rosa Island and at Pensacola. Of all the buildings, only three houses were preserved: one for the Sr. Carpeau de Montigny, the officer who had the preferment from M. de Champmeslin; another for the soldiers; and the third for the guards. This garrison consisted of twenty-four soldiers, a sergeant, and this officer. M. de Champmeslin, after giving his orders and putting the prisoners that he wanted on board his ship and the rest on the other ships, returned to France, having won the fort from the enemy and earned his laurels.

As for us (by which I mean the group of men who were supposed to establish this new colony), we returned to Dauphin Island, where we each went about our duties according to our ranks. However, in the middle of October in this year of 1719, M. de Valdeterre, my captain, was chosen to go begin work on a new [63] settlement that would serve as a trading post and accommodate the people who were being sent from France, because the first settlement was not at all suitable for building permanent, desirable housing. Even women and girls were being sent from France and the soldiers were disputing who should have them as wives, to the point that, one day, two soldiers, fighting over which should have a certain one, were brought before the commandant, who, to settle the matter, put the decision to chance. He had them each throw the dice, and a soldier named Dusablon won the mount and her saddle.[27]

At last, the Sr. de Valdeterre embarked in a ship with fifty-two soldiers, nearly all of them Germans but strong and robust, to go establish himself at Old Biloxi. They nearly perished on the way over when they ran aground, or rather the ship did, on a sand bank, where they were forced to free themselves by throwing the cannons into the sea, along with their carriages.

27. On the character of French women sent to Louisiana, see Vaughan B. Baker, "Cherchez les Femmes: Some Glimpses of Women in Early Eighteenth-Century Louisiana," *Louisiana History*, XXXI (1990), 21–37. See also original manuscript [75], below.

This led afterward to great troubles for this captain; it even brought on the hatred of the commandant of the territory, who said that this officer had chosen to save his own chest rather than the property of the Company. They finally were lucky enough to get out of this difficulty and make it to Ship Island and from there in canoes and shallops to New Biloxi, where at that time there was only a single Canadian who had established himself. His name was Deslos.[28]

As for me, I was still staying on Dauphin Island, where I was already beginning to get bored. Then, one day, I was serving as officer of the guard, and the custom was for the man who had this duty to dine at the residence of the commandant. As we were having dessert, he said to me that he had heard I had been at Quebec. I told him yes, I had. He questioned me about one person and another, and I replied frankly. Finally, he asked me whether I had not been sent there for a period of thirty-six months.[29] I was a bit shocked, but since this was my superior officer, what could I do? I let it pass [64] silently, but he went on the offensive again, asking me whether I had not known a man named Le M——. I replied that yes, I had known him, but that it was neither a great pleasure nor honor for me.

"And why not?" he said.

"Because he is a drunkard and a person unworthy of the society of honest men."

At this, he asked that the glasses be refilled and, addressing himself to all those at the table, of whom M. de Valdeterre was one, he said to them: "Gentlemen, listen to me," and looking straight at me, he said to me, "Sir, I am much obliged for the good qualities that you have ascribed to my relative."

In fact, I learned afterward that it was his uncle. But I was not one to eat my bread in secret. I called for more wine, and with a nod of the head toward those at the table, I said to the commandant that I begged his pardon if I had spoken ill of this person, that I had not known it was his kinsman, and that, from the manner in which he had asked me for news of him, I had understood that the man had been his valet. At this, I excused myself, and I was never again able to earn his favor no matter what I did.[30]

28. New Biloxi, near the site of modern Biloxi, Mississippi, was not formally established until two years later. The settlement that Dumont works with Valdeterre to build in the passage that follows is Old Biloxi, near modern Ocean Springs, Mississippi. See Dumont's maps of "Old Biloxi" and "New Biloxi," Figures 4 and 5.

29. The insult implies that Dumont was a *forçat*, or forced emigrant, sent to serve a sentence of that length.

30. The coded name "Le M——" appears to refer to "Le Moyne," the name of Bienville's

I have forgotten to say that, after we had returned from Pensacola, one day when we were passing in revue before the commandant, he wanted to know who were the parents, the mothers and fathers, of the officers. He had his secretary next to him, who was writing down what each man said. But I was offended by this maneuver, and as I was young, I imagined that there might be some malice behind it. Given that I was an officer with a commission that the Company of the Indies had awarded to me, it was no business of his who I was or upon whom I was dependent. So when he came to question me about my father, I replied that he was a farmer.

"What, a tax farmer?"

"No," I said to him, "a farm laborer."

He believed me at the time, so much so that, by [65] the same vessels that had brought us over, he wrote a letter back to the Company asking why they were sending into this country the sons of farm laborers to be commanders in the service, no doubt referring to me by name. I don't know what was sent to him in reply, but six months passed, and when we were again at review, he said to me in front of all my comrades:

"Did you not say to me, Monsieur, that your father was a plowman?"

"Yes," I said.

"He is not, however, and I know it."

I replied to this that there were plowmen and plowmen and that mine worked upon paper for his soil, with a pen for his plow and fingers for his draft animals. This brought a big laugh from everyone else, but as for him, I don't know what he thought of it. I could nonetheless easily say it or guess at it, but I will leave it to the reader to judge by what follows.[31]

No sooner had M. de Valdeterre reported to the commandant that he had come ashore with his men at Old Biloxi and that they were encamped in a small tent city than I received the order to go in a small canoe to find a place to locate a second settlement, this one on the mainland. I was given six soldiers and food for a week, and we all embarked with what seemed like a good wind, setting sail from this little island, from the side by the hospital, which is to say, the opposite end from the settlement. As we departed, we skirted a tiny islet named Death's Head Island, and after this, we

family. The "uncle" is perhaps an error on Dumont's part, because Charles Le Moyne, Bienville's father, did not have any brothers in Canada, but Bienville was one of eleven sons.

31. Dumont's analogy between writing lines on paper and plowing a field repeats a literary topos, a famous Latin riddle that describes the plowing of the field and seeks as the answer "being a writer." That Bienville missed the allusion contributes to Dumont's intended insult of his commander as an uneducated American creole. Thanks to Andreas Motsch for pointing out this allusion.

entered Mobile Bay, which we quickly crossed.[32] Nine leagues farther along the coast, we arrived at an uninhabited and uncultivated part of the mainland. The wind failed us all of a sudden, and we had to put ashore and set up camp. Since we were not yet experts in these sorts of voyages, we found ourselves much embarrassed; we had forgotten to bring any fresh water with us. We looked everywhere, but we could not find any. We had eau-de-vie for our drink. But how to cook [66] the meat? We dug pits a short distance from the sea, for we believed it would be as it is on Dauphin Island, but although each man worked as hard as he could, it was all in vain. The water was always brackish, and we were obliged to make use of it even though the meat itself was already salted.

I have neglected to mention that, at Dauphin Island, the bread was distributed to all the men once every five days, unless one received only flour, which was distributed every fortnight. Wine or eau-de-vie and salted meat were also distributed on this schedule, all according to the orders of the Sr. Le Gac, who acted as the *commissaire ordonnateur.* There was another who was also a commissaire: M. de Saint Hubert.[33] There was never any coin circulating publicly, although sometimes an individual might have some. We received the wages corresponding to our appointments once a month, not in cash, but as food or merchandise given to us from the storehouse. The bills of credit written up by commanders, officers, and warehouse keepers or people who had wages or commissions were the legal tender that circulated among the community. There was plenty of need for this, because the smallest things—a salad of lettuce or some chicory—brought a high price, as did fresh meat, which some individuals acquired from the Indians and sold on their own account.

As for us, new travelers in this New World, after we had dined as best we could on our meat thus prepared, we went to sleep under a *berre,* which is a cloth at least fifteen yards in length that one uses to cover a bed made from tree boughs, folding it so as to surround one's bedroll. Without this precaution, it is impossible to sleep, and one would suffer greatly from the annoyance and bites of the many insects, such as the midges, gnats, [67]

32. Death's Head Island appears on Dumont's manuscript sketch map of "Dauphin Island first settlement of the Company of the Indies in 1716" (ANF, Cartes et plans, 6 JJ 75, collection Delisle, pièce 242).

33. In fact, Charles Le Gac was director for the Company of the Indies, and Marc-Antoine Hubert was commissaire ordonnateur at this time. Dumont erroneously adds "Saint" to the latter's name.

mosquitoes, and deer flies. This precaution is necessary for every traveler, and the cloth must completely cover your bed, because if there is even a tiny little hole, the bugs will find a way to get in, and just one is enough to prevent you from sleeping.[34]

We took this precaution and passed the night peacefully, as tired people will. At the first light of day, the wind was still against us, so I took two soldiers with me, and we set off to go hunting. We had scarcely gone a quarter of a league when we found a small, marshy lake filled with game: geese, ducks, teals, and grouse. With three shots, we brought down such a large quantity that we could not carry them all back to our pirogue, and we had to make two trips. This manna from heaven brought us great pleasure, because after plucking the birds, we put them on a spit to roast, and the juice from them seemed to relieve our thirst. We were forced to stay in this place for five days, and, the wind finally becoming a little more favorable, we left to continue our route along the coast, as far as we could follow it. Along the way, we killed more game, for winter is a time of plenty for all sorts of game, and even a blind man could kill them by the dozens so long as someone told him when they were within range. ———— it was the first time that any of us had been to this place. It seemed strange to see so much land without any houses. We had been ———— that we would find some. Each time we passed a point of land where a river flowed in, we took the water up in our hands and drank it, we were so thirsty; but it was always salty.[35]

Finally, at about eleven in the morning, we saw a wide expanse of water between two points of land. It was, at last, the river [68] that we had been seeking for so long. We stopped our boat to drink our fill of this liquor that, for us, was like the nectar of the gods. This river is known by the name of River of the Pascagoulas, after an Indian nation that is friendly with us. Entering this river, we saw on the right-hand side a fine plantation that belonged to the Sr. de la Pointe, a Canadian who, in the time of M. de Crozat, had come to establish himself there. His house has two stories, not to mention the granary, courtyard, kitchen, storage barns, corrals, numerous livestock, and slaves; the latter were Indians at that time, but some time after, he had Africans. This habitant received my detachment and me very well.

---

34. The term *berre* (also spelled "ber," "baire," or "bar") developed in Louisiana French. See John Francis McDermott, *A Glossary of Mississippi Valley French, 1673–1850* (St. Louis, Mo., 1941), 18, 22.

35. Here and on the reverse of the manuscript page, a few words are obscured by an old water stain.

He is widowed but has for company two rather good-looking daughters and two sons. I stayed there for two days to recover from the fatigues that I had undergone.[36]

The third day, after breakfast, we left and crossed the river, two leagues in breadth at that point, to go dine with another habitant named Graveline, a Canadian who was also among the first settlers there and who also showed great courtesy toward us. He did not have such handsome buildings as the Sr. de la Pointe, but this did not prevent him, as I learned on my own and from others later, from being much more wealthy. He had only one daughter and one son, whom he had ———— from his slaves. After dinner there, he provided us with an Indian slave to lead us to Old Biloxi by water. We left the plantation at about two in the afternoon, and ———— seven in the evening, we arrived at the spot where M. de Valdeterre had already begun clearing, that is to say, cutting down the big and small trees, the bushes and weeds. He was delighted to see me, all the more so since he saw that I was coming to help him. I shared his table along with the Sr. Saint Denis, who had retreated here with his natural daughter to escape the hatred and [69] bile that our commandant bore toward him, as I will explain in what follows.[37]

Our captain [Valdeterre] was a very experienced officer. His table was like a military academy: ordinances were read out, each made suggestions or requests as he judged appropriate, and then he delivered the oracle's voice, as it were. We had no chaplain at this place. Every day, evening and morning, a drumbeat was sounded as a call to prayer, which took place under a tent. Before this ritual, each man was called out by name. If he was found absent and he had no good reason to excuse himself, he was deprived of his dram, which consisted of a quarter-pint of eau-de-vie, and if a man missed the roll several times, he was put in irons. It was like a monastery.[38] The men numbered sixty-two, including the captain and myself, and we worked for the span of five weeks at clearing, cutting, and chopping trees, some of which were made into palisades and others from which we took

36. On this concession, see original manuscript [180]; and Jay Higginbotham, "The Chaumont Concession: A French Plantation on the Pascagoula," in Glenn R. Conrad, ed., *The French Experience in Louisiana* (Lafayette, La., 1995), 578–584.

37. Dumont refers to his account of Saint Denis's exploits in the final twenty pages of the memoir; see original manuscript [429], below. "Plan of Old Fort Biloxi," Figure 4, was bound opposite this page in the original manuscript.

38. By contemporary French military practice, official orders and communiqués were read out loud at table, a custom similar to the reading of Bible passages during meals in monasteries.

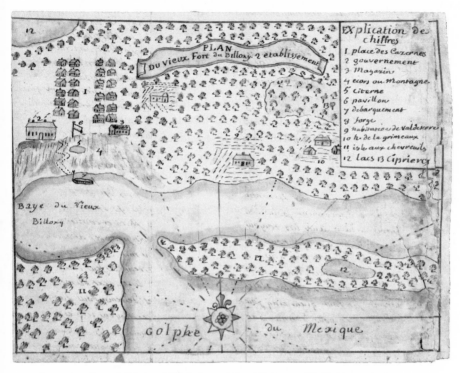

Figure 4. *Plan of Old Fort Biloxi, Second Establishment.* VAULT oversize
Ayer MS 257, map no. 4. Courtesy The Newberry Library, Chicago

bark for roofs. It reached the point where the whole place was covered with
sticks and canes. Close to the edge of the water was our encampment, where
some slept under tents and others in the open air, their beds always made
and covered with a berre. We carried to this spot all the wood fit for building
and the bark, where it was all stacked up. We set fire to the dry canebrakes
in several places, which, in turn, set fire to the branches and wood that remained on the ground. The fire, this devouring element, in just five days reduced all to ashes, and by this means, we were provided with an open space
large enough to lay out, as I did in my map, barracks for up to thirty-two
soldiers—sixteen on each side—and at either end a pavilion for the officers,
the storehouse, guardhouse, commandant's quarters, and the bakehouse.
All this being designed and surveyed, we turned to the task of carrying the
wood [70] that had been stacked up by the seashore and began to erect the
houses and to cover them. M. de Valdeterre kept an eye on everything as was
necessary and encouraged his men. He was beloved by his soldiers, workers,
and, if I may say so, even by the Indians, who brought him great quanti-

ties of buffalo, bear, geese, turkeys, and oil in deerskin bags, for his support and that of his workers. He paid them generously, and you might say that, although there was no butcher's shop established there, the workers always had, in addition to their rations of bread and salt meat, fresh meat that he had distributed to them.

At Christmastime, work was halted. I wanted to go hunting by myself in the woods, or rather, in the immense forests; the motive for this hunt was a wager with a young man who was a cadet in the company of M. de Valdeterre, who had invited him to share his table. He was from a very good family and a good hunter. We set a wager for an embroidered Spanish hat, to go to whichever of the two of us brought back the most game, and we each departed full of hope to be the winner.[39] He went in one direction and I in the other. Thus I went off into the woods, where I soon found myself among lakes filled with water that I had to walk around, although this does not discourage a hunter who wants to win. I killed on this first chase three pieces of game: a parrot, a squirrel, and a goose. I felt quite proud of myself. I kept going even though I was a little tired and worn out, not being used to this exercise. I sat down near a small ravine, and lying there on the grass, I fell asleep. That was perhaps an hour after midday, and I did not awake until about six in the evening; the sun was very low. I scarcely had time to pick up my gun when I heard from behind the ravine the sound of an animal grazing. I slid into a nearby ditch and, removing the fowling shot that was in my gun, put in a ball instead. I squinted to try to make out my target and perceived a deer [71] fifteen paces away from me. I leveled it in my sights and fired. It leaped, and then, raising up its little tail, it ran off through the trees and canes and brush. As I had no doubt that it was hit and that it could not go far, I determined to follow it wherever it went, and sure enough, I found it. I would have liked to carry it back, but it proved impossible for me to even move it. All I could do was cut out a shoulder, flesh and skin together. I covered up the rest of the deer with branches. Eight paces away from this spot was a large pile of dry and rotten brush, and I set fire to it so that at least I would be able to find my treasure again. After this, wanting to return

---

39. A cadet by the name of Sr. François Soyez, serving under Valdeterre, is on the ship list for the *Marie*. See Albert Laplace Dart, "Ship Lists of Passengers Leaving France for Louisiana, 1718–1724," *LHQ*, XV (1932), 455. The Spanish tricorne hat is described as having lace of the *point d'Espagne* style, a decorative border made with gold and silver filaments. These were produced in France and exported to Spain and Latin America. See Santina M. Levey, *Lace: A History* (London, 1983), 123.

to the settlement and seeing a light in the sky ahead of me, I believed it was the setting sun and that it was in that direction I needed to go.

I walked for more than two hours, unable to see well and without ever realizing that I had been mistaken in my reasoning, because it was the moon that was rising rather than the sun setting, as I had believed. I needed to return the way I had come, but by a different path, since there was no easy route through these forests. From time to time, I stopped and listened. Finally, I heard a sound, as if someone were hammering on an anvil. Since about a quarter of a league away from the old fort there was a smithy, and since the master, who was called Requiem, might well be at work there, I imagined at that moment that it was him, and I started yelling at the top of my lungs, in the forest in the middle of the night, "Requiem, Requiem!" From time to time, I fired shots from my gun. But there was no response save the echo amid the trees. At last, weary of this routine, my throat sore, I started walking again, hoping to find my fire and my treasure, where [72] I planned to stop and rest.

I had hardly gone sixty paces when I once again heard a hammering sound alongside me. I wondered what this might be, and I saw that it was a bird that we call the woodpecker. It is very well named, because this bird, which is rather large, lives entirely on ants that it finds in the rotting trees. It pounds on them with its beak and, after making a hole, it slides in its tongue, which is quite long, and the ants feel the moisture of the tongue and attach themselves to it and thus meet their end, for the bird, pulling them back into its beak, swallows them for his nourishment. As soon as I saw this bird by the light of the moon, I fired at it. It cost me more than nine shots from my gun, but in spite of that, I was happy to finally have it. I put it alongside the other birds attached to my belt and began walking again, sometimes able to see clearly by the moonlight, at other times, not at all. I was very surprised to find myself forced to pass through a cypress swamp, which is like a large marsh covered with water one or two feet deep. I walked through it but found myself so weakened, either by fear or by fatigue, that when I found a spot of dry land at the base of a large cypress, I sat down, putting my gun beside me, and fell asleep, even though my feet were in the water. I don't know whether I slept that way for a long time, but at the first light of day, I awakened, and seeing nothing around me but an expanse of water and no way to get across it, I regained land at the closest point I could reach and returned into the forest, moving now in the direction of the settlement. I had gone no more than a half of a league when I found my fire, and there, although I had no bread, I made a fine meal of my parrot, [73] which I cooked on the embers with its legs tucked under. After having thus regained some strength and dried out my shoes and stockings, I added some more dry wood to my fire and set out again to try at least to use the daylight to get myself out of this wilderness.

After much searching, I finally had the good fortune to find a small stream in which the water was very clear and which I found tasted very good. Because it had a current, I followed it along all its meanders, and it led me out of the woods near the sea, in a place known as Belle Fontaine, which is only a good three quarters of a league from the settlement of Old Biloxi. As soon as I saw the sea, joy and strength returned to me, and as I reached the vicinity of our post, I saw a house at some distance. It was that of a habitant named Grimeau, the widow of the man who had guided the vessel the *Hercule* into the port of Pensacola, as I have written above.[40] She had only one young son whom she was raising, and her settlement, or farm, rather, was fairly successful, with livestock, slaves, Indians, etc. As I was looking at the house and trying to figure out how to get to it without going the long away around, as would have been necessary to reach it, I saw that by crossing through a wooded area I would be able to make a shortcut. I did this, but as soon as I entered there, I heard a sow who was leading her seven piglets, fairly large and plump ones. Without knowing whether she belonged to someone or not, I shot and killed her. She was rather fat for a nursing mother. I left her behind, and as I walked on, I broke branches so as to be able to retrace the path to the place.

I arrived at last at the house. I had heard, as I was approaching, three [74] cannon shots fired from our post. I thought this must mean that the commanders were arriving from Dauphin Island. I did not let this stop me and arrived at the home of this habitant at around ten o'clock in the morning. She received me well and said that M. de Valdeterre had just left her house. She had someone run after him. He was, as she told me, very worried about me, and when I asked her about the three cannon shots, she said, "They are for you, so that if you had lost your way, you would be able to return toward the sound."

She offered me some broth, which I took, but as soon as I swallowed it, I was seized with a fever—either from the fatigue that I had endured or perhaps from the joy that I felt in finding myself freed from my labyrinth— and I began shaking violently and had to lie down. This did not prevent me, however, from telling her that I had just shot a sow, at a certain place nearby that I described. The woman, who had lost a sow about a year earlier, sent

40. See original manuscript [56].

two of her slaves, who brought it back in a pirogue, with the seven piglets, who would not leave their mother. She proved to be a fat one and was salted.

M. de Valdeterre came back to the house. He seemed delighted to see me, as he had been worrying that I might have had an accident. As he had come by canoe, before returning to the settlement, he sent some of his men to Belle Fontaine, and they went to look for my treasure, that is to say, for the remainder of my deer. When they had returned, we embarked, M. de Valdeterre and I, and proceeded to Old Biloxi. Victory was mine in the wager, and I collected the prize. My fever lasted for four days, but the emetic that I took loosened its hold on me. This is the remedy most often used in this land, for even the least [75] illnesses, and it has a very good effect.

After the lodgings, barracks, storehouses, and all the buildings were constructed, we built a nice cistern on the slope of a hill facing the wharf, to capture fresh water from a small trickle that flowed from above it. M. de Valdeterre, who stopped at nothing to make the place strong and stable, had made soundings and found a channel by which even large ships might sail up to the settlement. The port was good, with a safe anchorage sheltered from the winds. He had even marked the channel with buoys. But by the machinations of his enemies, the next morning, these buoys were found to be stolen or moved. It seems that he was too capable, and as competence sometimes proves annoying, he was harrassed to the point that he resolved to return to France.

Around this time, there arrived at Dauphin Island two ships of the Company of the Indies, laden not only with supplies for the territory but also with sixty girls who had been sent to this country to satisfy at least some of the poor men who saw among them very few women and with the goal that the French might thus multiply in this land. They had no sooner disembarked from the ships at Dauphin Island than they were put onto boats and carried over near our settlement to an island called Ship Island, where they lodged under tents.

It was at this time that M. de Valdeterre left the post that he had established to return to Dauphin Island and get ready to sail for France. The fact that he was close to me was enough that, being detested by the commandant, I was feeling some of the sparks of this fire, which led me to decide to return to France also, and having asked for [76] leave to do so, I was granted it. There were five ships in the roadstead at Dauphin Island, two of the Company, namely the *Mutine*, commanded by M. de Martonne, and the *Deux Frères*, under the Sr. Feret. The three others were royal vessels, under the command of M. de Saugeon, who had come to patrol these waters to see whether the Spaniards might be so brazen as to come disturb us. Not having found any, they were planning to return all five together, and as they were now ready, M. de Valdeterre and myself and two other officers bade farewell to our friends and embarked on the *Mutine*. But before doing so, I made a request to the commandant for a certificate of my service and my conduct, having done my duty to the best of my ability. He did not refuse me this and furnished it to me with all that befits an officer who has performed well, even adding that, if I wanted to return, I would be of use in the country. I had it signed by M. de Sérigny, captain in chief, and by M. Hubert, commissaire. Thus equipped, I set sail in the month of May, leaving behind a new settlement that we had built for all the people who needed to leave Dauphin Island and come over to establish themselves on the mainland, which they soon did.[41]

As for us, the five ships, we floated into the realm of Neptune with a favorable wind. In a few days, we passed Cabo San Antonio, which forms the point of the island of Cuba. When we were off Havana, we came close to shore and furled our sails—in other words, we hovered offshore while showing Spanish colors. We stayed for three days. On the fourth day, we spied off Matanzas, twelve leagues from the capital, a ship carrying [77] the Spanish flag, and as we believed it was of that nation, we put the wind in our sails and chased after it. No sooner did it see our ships than it raised its anchor and set all its canvas to gain the channel.[42] We followed it closely and, with our best efforts, were able to surround it. When it saw that we were flying the French flag, it lowered its Spanish colors, raised those of England, and declared itself. Being halted, it put its shallop into the water, and the captain came on board to speak with M. de Saugeon. He said that he had no choice but to flee when he believed we were Spaniards, for he had much to fear from them, since he had been one of two ships but was now all alone, as his companion was towing a Spanish ship that they had captured together. Because his ship had been damaged a little in the combat, he had been forced to hove to off Matanzas for repairs, and when he saw us and believed we were Spaniards, he had presumed that we were coming to capture him. But since he was English, we left him to go where he pleased, and we continued on our voyage. We had no sooner reached the latitude of the Azores when, during the night, our companion, the *Deux Frères*, commanded by the Sr. Feret, took a different route to avoid a bank of shoals, as did another of the royal vessels.

41. "Les armements au long cours de la deuxième Compagnie des Indes," nos. 94, 110, confirms the names of the captains of these two vessels, the *Mutine* and the *Deux Frères*, and records that the latter was armed at La Rochelle on July 22, 1720.

42. Dumont refers to the Nicholas Channel between Cuba and the Great Bahama Bank.

Forty-six days after our departure from Dauphin Island, we arrived safely inside the Ile de Groix, which is a good two and a half leagues off Port-Louis. The day following our arrival in the harbor, there came on board M. de Saint Martin, the second director of the Company, who issued an order from the king that all the passengers and others—sailors, officers, whoever was in the ship—must deliver to him all the letters that we had carried out of the country we were coming from so that they could be inspected to see whether they were suitable to be [78] forwarded. All this was to see whether we were speaking ill of the country. M. de Valdeterre had a lot of letters, and as for me, I had several, too. We were all quite surprised at such an order; each man obeyed. When I say "each," I mean the sailors, the cabin boys, the carpenters, and others. But when I heard this news, the thought occurred to me that I might well make myself exempt from this order. I descended to the officers' bunks, opened my chest, took my letters and those of M. de Valdeterre and even his journals. I made these into two large packets, and I wrapped them up and addressed them to "Mgr. Le Blanc, minister of war," etc. I put the two packets back in my chest and calmly returned on deck with a perfectly straight face.

A moment later, M. de Saint Martin asked me whether I did not also have some bundles of letters. I replied to him that yes, I did, but that I had to deliver them with my own hands and get a receipt. This was enough to provoke him, and he asked me for the key to my chest. An argument ensued. Finally, I had the chest brought to the bridge; in front of everyone, I opened it, and holding the two packets, I said to him,

"Monsieur, in my surrendering these to you, give me not only a receipt but also the weight of the packages, so that I can inform Mgr. Le Blanc, my sponsor."

He looked at me and said, "You are a protégé of the minister?"

"Yes, Monsieur," I replied.

"Ah, in your case, you can keep your packages. Letters to such persons are exempt."

So it was that, with a little sleight of hand, I saved not only four or five letters that I had but also more than eighty belonging to M. de Valdeterre and others.

The day before our arrival in the Ile de Groix roadstead, we had parted ways with the two royal vessels, which were returning to their home port at Brest. The coastal pilot having come on board, we entered the [79] channel and passed the forts of the citadel of Port-Louis, Saint Catherine's, the monastery of the Recollet Reverend Fathers (which we left to our right), and the Isle Saint Michel (on our left) to come to anchor in the port of

Lorient.[43] There were three ships at the same anchorage preparing to go to Louisiana, to bring enough people to establish the colony and build permanent settlements on the land grants that the Company had awarded to the owners of concessions. There were many people in the town of Lorient who were embarking for different concessions. There was one group known as the Le Blancs after Mgr. Le Blanc, the owner of the concession in partnership with Mgrs. Belle-Isle, d'Asfeld, and M. de la Jonchère. There were also others, such as the Germans (of whom M. Law was the leader) and the Mssrs. Mezières, Kolly, Dumanoir, and Diron, all of whom were owners of concessions. There were also four engineers appointed by the king for the country, among them one named Le Blond de la Tour, who was going over in the capacity of royal lieutenant and brigade commander of the engineers as well as of Mgr. Le Blanc's concessions (I say "concessions," plural, because they were going to establish four of them).

We all disembarked at Lorient, which was at that time only a small, unfortified post that scarcely deserved to be called a town, having only a few houses scattered here and there. M. Rigby was the director there for the Company. He was an Englishman close to M. Law. We all found lodgings, that is to say, Mssrs. de Valdeterre and Bourgmont and myself, with a widow named Le Sourd, who rented rooms.[44] She had grown daughters who were rather presentable for Breton girls. We paid seventy-five livres a month in silver, so specified because there were, at that time in France, only banknotes, and though the [80] ecu was valued at twelve livres, ecus rarely appeared in circulation. I had brought with me 118 piastres of Saint-Domingue, which seemed to me like a small fortune.

I spent just nine or ten days recovering from the rigors of the ocean voyage before, finding myself now in the land of my birth, I wrote to inform my brother of my arrival. By that time, another ship had arrived from Louisiana, ten days after ours, and had brought over M. de Sérigny, to whom I

43. Before the construction of lighthouses, mariners often navigated into port using the bells of Saint Catherine's, which lay just behind the ramparts of the city of Port-Louis, as a guide. See Claude Nières, ed., *Histoire de Lorient* (Toulouse, 1988), 10.

44. Etienne Véniard de Bourgmont, the celebrated explorer of the Missouri River, had sailed from New Orleans for France on the *Duc de Noailles* on June 4, 1720, along with his son, born to a Missouri Indian woman. It is significant that Dumont met Bourgmont at this time because Dumont drew a manuscript map of the lower Missouri River, which must have been based on Bourgmont's manuscript maps. See "Plan du cours de la rivière de Missoury avec le fort d'Orleans etablis par les francois ou M. de Bourgmont ch. m. de st. Louis," Miss. 2, Archives de la ministère des affaires étrangers, Paris. The original has been lost since 1948, but a copy is in the Louis C. Karpinsky Map Collection, Newberry Library, Chicago.

went to pay my respects. He did not stay for long at Lorient and left for Paris. I waited patiently for instructions from my family. But I will leave it to you to imagine what they thought of me. My brother had only obtained for me the post of second lieutenant and second engineer so that I might advance myself and make my fortune in this new land.[45] I had barely arrived and gotten seasoned there when I turn up back in France. And to do what? I did not know myself, except that I could not make myself comfortable anywhere. My destiny to travel, to run from here to there, precluded any stability. In a word, I would honestly say of myself that I knew not why I had come back, unless it was to accompany my beloved Captain de Valdeterre, who did not stay even two weeks at Lorient before he took leave of me, embraced me, and went off to Paris. I have heard nothing about him nor had any news from him since we parted. I passed my time in Lorient amusing myself by hosting dances after supper. We amused ourselves well, in an honorable fashion, because the Breton women love to dance, like women everywhere. Such was my routine, to the point that I even decided to get married.

M. de Sérigny had no sooner arrived in Paris than he went to pay his respects to Mgr. Le Blanc, who had in his hands the catalog of officers who had come back to France from Louisiana, in which was a list of good and bad [81] officers. On the list was M. de Valdeterre, captain, as having been demoted, and I was named as deserving of demotion, too. This was, of course, not flattering to me, but the esteemed and impartial minister, not fully trusting what he had in his hands (even though it was signed by the commandant of this New World) without first hearing my defense of my cause, was so kind as to write to M. Rigby, the director for the Company at Lorient, asking him to find out why I had returned to France and whether I had been demoted. As I was setting out one morning to see to my business, I saw a young man, who asked to speak to me. I approached and introduced myself, and he told me that M. Rigby was asking for me and wished to speak with me. I followed this request. He was confined to his bed by gout. He questioned me and finally said, "So, you have been demoted, or deserved to be."[46]

I was quite surprised at such a declaration and could not restrain my-

45. Dumont probably refers to his brother Pierre-Jean-Baptiste Dumont.
46. Claude Le Blanc did indeed write to Rigby asking why Dumont had returned to France so soon; see ANF, Archives de la ministère de la guerre, corr. 2569, no. 551, cited in Nancy M. Surrey, *Calendar of Manuscripts in Paris Archives and Libraries Relating to the History of the Mississippi Valley to 1803*, 2 vols. (Washington, D.C., 1926), I, 353.

self from saying that, if this was an age in which those who performed their duties well could be punished and demoted, then I was indeed running the risk of being so treated. Then he informed me that the commandant of Louisiana had so informed the minister. By this, I saw clearly that he wanted to pay me back for my excessive frankness. But in order to win my case, I made use of my certificate, which I showed to him, signed by the commandant, and when M. Rigby had seen and read it, he could not help but remark to me, in French spoken with an Englishman's accent, "Me see well that what black in land from where you come is white here, and what white here becomes black over there."

Then he had a letter to the minister written for me, consisting of just four words: *Vide Domine, judica me* (which means, "Look, my Lord, and judge me"). With it, he enclosed the certificate, so good [82] and so fortunate for me.[47]

When Mgr. Le Blanc received this, M. de Serigny had presented himself to pay his respects to His Excellency and to report that he was returning from Louisiana. The minister soon inquired about me. This commandant and captain replied that I had been a very good subject of the king, that I showed much promise, that I was intelligent, and that I understood well how to build fortifications. The grand and illustrious minister showed him in the catalog my name with the notation next to it, which bore the seal of the commandant and was countersigned by him, as was my certificate, except that the list of officers and notations was lacking the signature of M. Hubert. M. de Serigny was quite surprised and said to His Excellency that this was perhaps the work of the commandant's secretary, who might have borne a grudge toward me. Mgr. Le Blanc replied that he saw perfectly what was going on and that I would return to Louisiana. I had said to M. Rigby that my intention was to go to Paris, but he forbade me from going until I had received orders from the minister. He sent his secretary with me to go back to my landlady's house, where he told her that she was to supply me with everything I asked for, that the director would pay all my expenses and, as security, would pay a deposit for me. This was enough to begin to set me apart from the other lodgers. For me, it was nothing but dances, parties, meals, and treats, and all for the glory of a pretty little shepherdess to whom I had declared myself servant and shepherd and who, because of my gifts, was looked upon by all the others as the luckiest and their queen. Additionally, I received from the great minister a generous letter of credit.

47. This is a paraphrase of Lamentations 3:59.

I soon came to be known in Lorient as the chevalier Le Blanc, and when I was addressed by this title, I [83] responded to it.

There is no such thing as love without some danger or some rival to be conquered by one partner or the other. It so happened that there was a young man of good family who was called the chevalier de Saint M——, who wanted, as the saying goes, to cut the grass from under my feet. And to accomplish this, he spread a rumor that I was nothing but an opportunist who had neither hearth nor home of his own. Wishing, no doubt, to learn whether what he said was true or not, he obtained a letter from the post office addressed to me and countersigned by the minister. He must have read it, and two days later, he brought it to me sealed with a new seal. I asked him how much I owed him for the postage, and he said, "Seven sous," which I paid him. We were at the dinner table at the time, and I invited him to sit down, but he declined and took his leave. I sent for the postmaster, who lived not far from the home of the widow Le Sourd, our landlady. When he arrived, I asked him whether there not been a letter for me that day in the mail. It was a Sunday. He said no, but on Friday there had been one, and he had given it to the chevalier to give to me. I asked him, in front of all the company, whether there had been postage due on it.

"No, no, monsieur, I did not collect any; those letters are postpaid."

I showed him the letter, and he said to me that it had been unsealed and read. Everyone had something to say about this affair; there was much discussion of it. As for me, after dinner, I took the liberty of writing to His Excellency the minister, explaining to him that in the absence of his seal, I had not even opened the letter, because I had reason to believe that it had been [84] intercepted by a young man, whom I named. The letter was from my brother, who enjoyed access to and the patronage of the minister and was rewarded with such favors. Finally, this young chevalier spread so many lies and slanders about me that I resolved to go find him one night and challenge him. I found him, and we began fighting. He wounded me first, but I soon had my revenge, and, having made a wound that we both found sufficient, we retired, and from enemies we soon became the best friends in the world.

My brother, judging, no doubt, that a longer stay in France might only bring about my complete destruction, wanted to avoid that outcome, and so, one day as I was finishing up breakfast at my lodging with a friend and leaving the room to go out into the street, I saw a large crowd following five men on horseback. Four were archers, and the fifth, their brigade commander. They were asking where the widow Le Sourd lived, and when they mentioned my name, the crowd pointed to me. Some of the people, upon hearing my name, were saying to one another, "What has he done?" imagining that they were coming to arrest me. No sooner had I reached the doorway into the street when the brigadier asked me whether it was in this house that a certain sieur lived, speaking my name. They did not know my face, and so if I had been afraid, I would have responded differently and, as they entered the house, would have immediately run away. But I replied that it was I.

They dismounted and entered the room, closing the door behind them. The brigadier put into my hands a packet of letters from the illustrious Le Blanc. He also showed me his orders to [85] seize the postmaster as well as the young chevalier, who had become, as I have said, my best friend. I asked for some breakfast for these men, talked with them of the news from Paris and of my family. In a word, I gave them the best welcome that I could. After breakfast, the brigadier, along with his four archers, went to see the commandant of Lorient to take hold of their prey. I rushed out as fast as I could and went to warn my friend to go into hiding for a while. I lent him three louis and helped him to escape. After sending him off, I returned to my landlady's. Along the way, everyone I met asked me what these gentlemen were searching for, who they were after, and whether I was going to leave with them, but I replied that I did not know anything more than they did. The brigadier and his men wasted no time in returning to the widow's house, and their next move informed the public of what they were up to, for the gentlemen went to the post office, seized the postmaster, and put him in prison, where he was well guarded. They also went to the home of the chevalier, but the bird had flown the coop. People told them that he had left for Paris. They did not believe this and stayed for six days in Lorient looking for him, but it was in vain. Annoyed at not finding him, they departed, the five of them leading the postmaster in handcuffs. This event made me even better known in the town; everyone was aware of it, and I no longer had to go to the post office to know whether I had a letter. The whole town down to the youngest children knew it, [86] and when I was out in the street, I heard, "M. le chevalier Le Blanc, there is a letter for you!" When I went to the post office, I was sure to find one, except that, when it was given to me, I had to open it in the office and sign a receipt on the envelope.

In the packet that the brigadier had given me, there was a letter from the minister, who urged me to watch my conduct and informed me that I would enjoy his protection if I did my duty. There was another from my brother, who advised me in the same manner and who promised to help me with everything. With these two letters, I received a commission as a half-pay lieutenant attached to the citadel at Port-Louis, where I was to report for duty in February, and a letter of credit for my room and board in this town at Sr. Doré's (an innkeeper in the rue de la Pointe), under the sign of the Three Pigeons. I was to have twenty livres per month. M. Debarete was the royal lieutenant in command of the town and the citadel of Lorient and its dependencies and functioned as governor. The Sr. de la Garde was the major or quartermaster of these two places. There was also a half-pay captain assigned to this post named the Sr. Grondel, who came from the regiment of Alsace, and two brothers who, like me, were half-pay lieutenants. We made up the cadre of officers assigned to the regiment of the royal marines at this garrison, where M. de Villeneuve, a half-pay captain in one of these companies, was also stationed.[48]

Six weeks after receiving this assignment as a half-pay lieutenant, I received new commissions, one as a lieutenant for the Company of the Indies in Louisiana at the rate of sixty livres per month and another as a half-pay lieutenant assigned to the companies of troops organized by the minister and his partners to develop their concessions in this new land. At the same time, I received an order from the [87] king granting permission for me to leave my garrison at Port-Louis to go serve the Company of the Indies and ensuring that, in my absence, I would not be regarded as deserting the service of His Majesty and would not lose the rank that I held in the infantry companies. This persuaded me to prepare to return to the land from which I'd just come. And, in fact, I had another order directly from Mgr. Le Blanc not to be subject to any orders from the commandant of that land and to take orders only from M. Le Blond de la Tour, royal officer and commander of the engineers' brigade, so that I should be thus protected from a man who held a grudge against me.

The ship was ready, and it was time to embark. Oh, the tears that were shed by many women, above all by my shepherdess! I had to obey, and so, after bidding farewell to my friends and loading aboard my chests, flagons, and a small amount of trade goods as allowed by the director of the Company—which I had purchased at my own expense and my own whim—I embarked in the ship called the *Charente*, in which there was a large contingent of Germans who were being sent over to Louisiana for the conces-

48. These new commissions, secured through the influence of his brother and of Le Blanc, are at a rank and pay somewhat higher than the post he held for the first voyage to Louisiana. A *lieutenant réformé* (the term for Dumont's position) was paid half the normal salary and was not expected to perform all his duties. Officers in the colonial navy, or *marine*, were retained on this status when they were ashore in France.

sion of M. Law.[49] We weighed anchor in the roadstead of Lorient, which was beginning to be constructed at that time, and we passed by the base of the citadel of Port-Louis and proceeded with a favorable wind to the anchorage off the Ile de Groix. We stayed at this anchorage two days, after which we set sail on our voyage with every indication of good weather. But alas, the watery element is feared because it is unpredictable, and we had barely reached Cape Finisterre when the winds turned against us and we could [88] not get round it. We were there for nearly three weeks. A contagious illness struck the German passengers on board, then spread to the sailors and, from them, to the officers. The first group as well as the second quickly fell stone-cold dead, and the women who were pregnant went into premature labor and lost their own lives at the same moment as those of their poor, innocent offspring. This illness, or rather this pestilential air, struck the strongest as well as the weakest, and some sailors who were climbing up the ropes into the rigging found themselves seized by it so suddenly that they fell helplessly and lifelessly into the sea.

We were to be greatly pitied in this sad state. We were forced to reverse course and return to the Ile de Groix, and having learned that both Lorient and Port-Louis had put us under quarantine, we had to throw the dead into the sea. By the end, of the nearly 700 on board when we departed, there remained only 109, and we looked like walking corpses, although I managed to remain healthy on the ship, aiding and caring for those persons who had the good fortune to survive this time together. Finally, our quarantine finished, we entered the port of Lorient. I considered myself lucky to have escaped this illness, but upon setting my foot ashore at the wharf of this town, with the intention of returning to the house of the widow Le Sourd, my landlady, I fell to my knees and then flat on the ground, with a terrible shivering and a high fever. The master cannoneer on board had the charity to bring two men with a stretcher, and placing me on it, he [89] had me carried to his home in a house at the outskirts of Lorient, on the road to Kerentrech. I don't know if a pure spirit of friendship toward me inspired him in this or if it was also my merchandise, and he was hoping that if I died he would be my heir, but whether it was one or the other, I was laid down in a clean room and on a good bed.[50]

---

49. The *Charente* was armed on Jan. 19, 1721 ("Les armements au long cours de la deuxième Compagnie des Indes," no. 55). Dumont appears on the list of officers as "Jean Frde. Montigny Lieut à 150," or 150 livres per month's salary for two months' voyage (SHD, Lorient, 1P244, barre 22). Thanks to Roseline Claerr for archival research in Lorient.

50. Historian Marcel Giraud expresses doubt about the veracity of Dumont's account.

This was toward the middle of March of the year 1721. For eleven days, I suffered brain seizures and severe fevers. At the end of this time, the former ended, but not the latter, which burned like an eternal flame. I was told that I should be bled, but I strongly opposed this. The thirteenth day of my illness, toward evening, the rector of Lorient came to visit me, heard my confession, and promised to come back and administer the holy viaticum the next morning. He kept his word and, after saying morning Mass, came with a large company to my room, which had been cleaned and prepared for holy visits of the sort. After performing the usual ceremonies, he made a brief exhortation, and he was preparing to give me the sacred offering for the journey to eternity when a seizure hit me again with full force, and he saw no need to continue. He returned to the church and planned to come back to give me the sacrament of extreme unction. In the meantime, a woman was to watch over me.

This seizure lasted five days, and on the night between the fifth and sixth, I woke up feeling like a new man, although hungry as a wolf. I got up from my bed, and looking around my room, I saw a woman sleeping on a couch and a candle burned down to a stub. I dragged myself [90] to the table and swallowed everything on it—broth, gelatin, medicine, sugar, jam—and feeling my way, I opened the door, went down the stairs, which I had not yet seen or even known about, and, following a narrow hallway, found a door. I opened it and entered into a room. A voice made itself heard, saying to me, "Who is there?"

I replied, "The devil."

At this response, she must have been afraid. I opened the window facing the street and climbed onto the sill. I slipped outside and set off stomping through the mud, snow, and ice in my bare feet and nightshirt, down the street, across a stream, and on toward the first houses of Kerentrech, where I began pounding on the door like a blind man, as the proverb says. The poor folks who were there opened it and found me in this state. They at first believed that some highwaymen had robbed me of my clothes. They took me into their home. I could not speak a single word, so much had the cold overcome me. They put me in bed under covers and didn't stop at that; they warmed me with towels that they placed on the soles of my feet, along my

---

Ships of this size generally carried only 300 persons, not the 700 that Dumont claims, and the ship might have returned to port, not because of the illness, but because it was not seaworthy. See *HLF*, IV, 160; for an English translation, see Giraud, "German Emigration," in Conrad, ed., *French Experience in Louisiana*, 139. Kerentrech was then a village just north of Lorient, now the neighborhood near the SNCF train station.

sides, and even on my stomach. Little by little, warmth returned to me, and I lapsed into a deep sleep, whether from fatigue or from the warmth that I was feeling.

Let us return, for a moment, to the woman who was serving as my nurse. As soon as she woke up, she lit the candle and went to my bedside. I leave you to judge her surprise when she saw me missing. She looked under the bed; she searched all the corners of the room. What a predicament [91] for her. Where did she think I was? I ask you, for she was sure she had not fallen asleep. Finally, not finding her patient, she went downstairs and asked the mistress of the house whether she had seen or heard me.

"No," she said, "but I am only now recovering from my fright."

And she described how, during the night, she had heard her door open and close, and when she asked, "Who is there?" a voice replied, "The devil."

The news passed on to the neighbors and then spread quickly throughout the town that the angel of darkness had spirited me away. Each one retold the story differently. As for me, I was then at the home of these poor peasants, where I slept very soundly, for they were so kind as not to speak to one another nor even cough. Finally, however, I woke up, and because I had called out the name of the landlady at whose house in Lorient I believed I was, some people from this village went to her place and asked her whether she might not be able to tell them about a young man who was at their house, ill. The landlady once again told the story of what had happened overnight, and she sent to inform M. Rigby of the difficulty it presented for her to have me carried back to her house. The director was so kind as to send his cart for me, with a good bed in it, and they brought me back to my room, where, by virtue of medicines, strong broth, and visits from the Company doctors, I was brought through this crisis.

[92] Little by little, the seizures relented, and my high fever changed to a mild fever, which no longer prevented me from eating and sleeping. The latter continued for some time. I looked like a picture of the walking dead; my bones showed through my skin like a real skeleton, and if, in this state, I had stood atop the towers of Notre Dame in Paris and a wind had come up like those that blow in the islands (known as hurricanes) and I had thrown myself from the top of the towers, in less than a minute I would have been carried through the air more than a league, just like a feather. This is how you should imagine my weight. All the same, I felt good, although I walked only with the support of a cane. At last, I no longer had need for the rhetoric of Hippocrates, nor for the visits from his successors and followers.

Chapter Three

SECOND VOYAGE TO LOUISIANA;
SETTLEMENT OF THE COLONY
MARCH 1721–SEPTEMBER 1722

And so my life was preserved, by the grace of God, for He wished for me to stand as a true example of the errant voyager, traveling from country to country. For, as anyone who has come through such an illness can well attest, it lurks nearby, and he cannot go far without its catching him. He [God] preserved my life, I say, to return me once again to the Mississippi country. For I had no sooner begun to recover after the fever had left me than a vessel named the *Portefaix*, commanded by M. Dufour, was ready to depart for the colony. I was asked on behalf of M. Rigby whether I wanted to sail in it. I accepted the offer and had my [93] chests and merchandise put aboard the ship. After having once again satisfied all those to whom I might owe money out of the funds of the director of the Company, and thanked them, and having said farewell to my friends and girlfriends and received their good wishes for my voyage, I went aboard this ship, where, again, there were more than three hundred Germans. We set sail, but the ship had barely passed Belle-Isle when I began to suffer seasickness as if I had never been to sea before. But once again, this functioned as an inoculation and the best medicine than any doctor could have given me, because since then, I have never again suffered any illness as severe as that which I had just endured during my involuntary layover in Lorient.[1]

By the grace of the Master of Destiny, our ship, the *Portefaix*, escaped any

1. The *Portefaix* was a flute of 250 to 300 tons, completed in May 1720 in Hamburg. Dumont is not on the register of the *Portefaix*, dated February 1721, but he is listed as one of five "Lieut. réformées" on another ship, the *Saône*, commanded by Captain Frottin; however, on the list of passengers for the *Saône*, the date is left blank in front of the year "1721." Another source reveals that the *Saône* was armed on January 21, 1721 ("Les armements au long cours de la deuxième Compagnie des Indes [1713–1773]," no. 156, SHD, Lorient). Dumont likely switched from the *Saône* to the *Portefaix*, which was armed on February 22 (ibid., no. 161), but the register for the *Saône*, having been drawn up some time in advance of departure, was not changed. See also Alice D. Forsyth and Earlene L. Zeringue, *German "Pest Ships,"* *1720–1721* (New Orleans, 1969). The island of Belle-Isle, not to be confused with the name of Dumont's protector, is located in the Atlantic about fifty kilometers south of Port-Louis.

sort of pestilence or contagion. It had better luck than the *Charente,* which you might say had been cursed. For, after the pestiferous illness I've described, which had penetrated its timbers, after the ship had been cleaned out and reloaded and had departed on another voyage, it had barely passed the fort of Port-Louis when it wrecked on the Mouton rocks and there found its end—a great loss for the Company. Our ship, however, did not have this bad aura and was fortunate to pass easily around Cape Finisterre, and in eighteen days, we arrived at Cap François. I did not want to go ashore there for fear of becoming ill from the bad air. I wrote to M. Jarland, who came to see me on board and was graciously received by [94] M. Dufour, our captain. This merchant of Cap François [Jarland], being unable to persuade me to come ashore to his house, did nonetheless send us, by his negro slaves, some of the local delicacies.[2]

After sixteen days of respite and recovery in this place, and after taking on water and supplies, we raised our sails again and left the port of Cap François, after firing a seven-gun salute. We set a course to take us to the Isla de Pinos and, from there, to Cabo Corrientes. We tried to round Cabo San Antonio but were held up there for two weeks by calms, a result of sailing too close to the island of Cuba, which doubtless blocked our wind. There was there a small corsair that, hoping to capture a larger prize than the small boat it already held, came out to engage us. But she paid dearly for her courage and curiosity. The one cannonball that we fired at her hit its mark and forced her to abruptly reverse course and flee for the nearest port on the coast.

Once the wind changed and came up behind us, we passed the Cayman Islands.[3] We had no sighting of Jamaica, the island belonging to the English that is sometimes seen along this route, and we soon spied Cabo San Antonio. As we were trying to round it, we received a violent gust of wind that shredded half our sails and came close to turning the ship on its side, which would have left us all drinking from the same cup, as they say. Luckily, this wind lasted for only a half hour, [95] and then, when it shifted from a headwind to a tailwind, we set new sails and were able to profit from

2. Dumont might have confused his dates here. It is 6,250 km from Cape Finisterre to Cap-Haïtien, and the *Portefaix* departed on March 7, 1721, and arrived on June 4; see *HLF,* IV, 160; *HJEFL,* 122. We know that Dumont arrived in Louisiana before September 5, as he is included on a list of officers drawn up on that date; see *FFLa,* I, 152. The *Charente* was wrecked on April 28, 1722; see "Les armements au long cours de la deuxième Compagnie des Indes," no. 171. The Mouton Rocks are located some 20 km south of the town of Concarneau on the coast of Brittany.

3. The ship must have drifted a good distance to the southeast during the calms.

it. We reached Ship Island in just three days, where we anchored in the roadstead that was then located three leagues from the French settlement, the headquarters at Old Biloxi that I had had the honor to build under the orders of M. de Valdeterre. But the concessionaires who had left France in the month of August of the previous year had already arrived and had established themselves at New Biloxi, also known as Fort Saint Louis, and their houses were strung out all along the coast. There were several of these. One was that of the minister, the illustrious, just, and virtuous Le Blanc, and his partners, namely Mgr. Fouquet [de Belle-Isle], *duc et maréchal* de France, the late Mgr. d'Asfeld, and M. de la Jonchère, treasurer of the Royal and Military Order of Saint Louis. This concession was the best laid out, both in respect to the land it had been granted and for the number of persons attached to it. Next to it followed the concessions of Mssrs. Law, Mezières, Kolly, Diron d'Artaguiette, and Dumanoir. We arrived just in time, for all of them, from the highest born to the lowest, were beginning to suffer from shortages, in particular of bread, and we brought them great relief. The commandant of this New World was now stationed at Old Biloxi and presided there, and M. Le Blond de la Tour, royal lieutenant, chevalier de Saint Louis, chief of the engineers' brigade, and director general of the concessions of the minister, commanded at New Biloxi.[4]

At two in the [96] afternoon on the day following our arrival in this port, the officers among the ship's passengers, eight of us, set off from the ship in a shallop with our trunks and wine chests. There was also a priest with us, a chaplain attached to one of the concessions of Mgr. Le Blanc. For the moment, we enjoyed a calm sea, and so it was the power of the oars of the seamen on board that had to carry us to the mainland of New Biloxi. But as we were about to arrive at that settlement, there came up a sudden blast of wind from the west so furious that, with the tide ebbing at the same time, it drove us back out into the open sea, in spite of all the effort we could put to the oars. It threw us, I say, beyond the passage used by ships, and what was worse, the night was so black that we could scarcely make out the far end of our shallop. One could see only by the lightning, which struck repeatedly, accompanied by furious rolls of thunder. At the same time, the waves,

---

4. On the conditions at Biloxi, see Introduction, above; *HLF*, IV, 120–153; and Vallette de Laudun, *Journal d'un voyage à la Louisiane, fait en 1720* (Paris, 1768), 238. See also Dumont's map of New Biloxi (Figure 5). As part of his effort to flatter his dedicatee, Belle-Isle, Dumont here refers to him with the title "maréchal," which he did not obtain until some twenty years later. Dumont also enunciates the honor of Le Blanc and La Jonchère, perhaps in defensive reaction to a 1724 scandal in which they landed in the Bastille for embezzling funds appropriated for the War of the Spanish Succession; see *HLF*, IV, 117.

swollen and angry, promised us nothing but shipwreck and inevitable death. There came to me at this moment a memory of Jonah the prophet in his boat, and I said to myself that it was heaven, angry at me, that decreed the loss of this shallop, which, being only a small craft, did not carry many souls. And if I had had as much faith as that blessed prophet possessed, I would have cried out to the captain to throw me overboard. But having it not, I joined my prayers to those of all the others in the shallop, singing litanies to the Blessed Virgin that were led by the chaplain.[5]

We were pounded again and again by [97] mountains of water hitting the side of our shallop and seeming to want to sink it in the sea. The man at the tiller, who was among the best helmsmen of these craft, steered around them but could not guarantee his boat against every accident, with the result that, from each wave, some water got in, and we had to bail it out as quickly as possible. So each put his hand to the task and, paying no heed to the braids on our caps, whether silver or gold, we used them as buckets or pots to throw out the water. The chaplain made a vow to the Queen of the Sea. Our shallop was tossed about by the fury of the waves but still maintained its steerage, going along under sail, for we needed to fly one sail on the mast so that we could keep headway and steerage. But we were not able to follow any course and veered to one side and the other.

Finally, however, the storm ceased, the clouds lifted, the sun appeared overhead, and in the light, what did we see? No land in any direction. We were in the open sea. We look for the compass in the chest of the shallop, we orient ourselves and pull to the west toward shore. After a good hour and a half, we saw land. We run in as close as we can, cast the anchor, and, stepping through water up to our knees, we were on land.[6] It was a desert island that we call Cat Island because it is full of them. These are wild cats, quite good to eat.[7] We started a fire, dried ourselves out, and with a bit of sea biscuit that the [98] sailors had had the foresight to store inside their canteens, we made a meal, with two shots of eau-de-vie in place of wine. After this fine supper, we went to bed around the fire, on the sand and the grass, awaiting daylight. Our sleep was not the best, being that we were awakened every moment by mosquitoes and midges, which were much worse, much

5. See Jonah 1:12–15. Jonah disobeyed God's orders to go to Nineveh and believed a storm was sent as punishment. The two chaplains for the Le Blanc / Belle-Isle concession were Nicolas Darquevaux, who died in 1722, and Jean-Claude Juif (*HLF*, IV, 265). On Juif, see below, original manuscript [127].

6. In this passage and several others where Dumont narrates the action of storms and battles, he shifts into the present tense to provide a sense of immediacy for his readers.

7. In Louisiana French, *chat sauvage* is the term for raccoon *(Procyon lotor)*.

more carnivorous here than the kind that exist in certain places in France and are called *cousins*. The daylight we so eagerly anticipated finally appeared. We waited until the sun came up before we embarked, and before doing that, we took another dram, which is a shot of eau-de-vie. There were seventeen of us. While we were fortifying our stomachs in this manner, we heard seven cannon shots. We set sail again in a favorable wind, putting up two sails in the shallop, and steered in the direction from which we had heard the shots.

After an hour, we passed through the ship channel, leaving our own ship to starboard and, taking advantage of the strong wind, arrived at New Biloxi at about half past eight. We learned that there had been another boat lost, but all hands had been saved. So it was that I arrived for the second time in this new land, where I remained for eighteen consecutive years, years that brought me many troubles and travails, as my reader will see if he deigns to read the remainder of these memoirs. But he will learn also that, with patience, together with the assistance God renders to man, he can surmount all and will have occasion to give thanks unto heaven for such favors and goodness.[8]

[99] And so it was that, for the second time, I arrived in this New World, where surely the commandant of the country would never have believed I would return. When we had gone ashore at New Biloxi, I went to pay my respects to the man to whom I had been recommended by my generous and gracious minister, that is, M. Le Blond de la Tour, and to whom I had the honor of delivering letters as well as the orders pertaining to myself. He received me graciously, promised me his protection, and asked me to stay to dinner. Afterward, he had me placed in the first company of troops that the worthy minister was outfitting in this country to look after his future concessions, for his lands, or rather, his tracts of wilderness, had not yet been assigned nor surveyed. In addition to the post of lieutenant, I was appointed adjutant major.

There were, at that time, two companies of soldiers, one commanded by the Sr. de Graves and the other by the Sr. Bizard. Each company consisted of fifty men-at-arms, not including the two sergeants, two corporals, two *anspessades*, and two drummers, as well as lieutenant and sublieutenant, making six officers for each company. In addition to these two companies, there were two others of laborers and craftsmen, a hundred men in each, which also had sergeants, but they received orders from the captains and

8. Dumont lived for sixteen consecutive years in Louisiana, from this point in 1721 until 1737. He counts eighteen years from his first arrival on September 1, 1719.

military officers. Among these artisans were some who had wives and children. Thus there were enough people to establish handsome and spacious concessions. There was a director, M. de la Tour, and under him a deputy director, as well as persons who served in the capacity of warehouse keepers, and two chaplains, who carried all that was necessary for divine service. You may well assume that we had generous supplies, trade goods, and eau-de-vie. I took my meals at the concession's mess, along with the other officers who dined with the deputy director.[9]

I had scarcely taken my place when, on the second day after my arrival, I asked [100] our royal lieutenant M. de la Tour for permission to go pay a visit to the commandant of the colony. He said that he did not recommend it, but once I explained to him that by not going I should only attract the commandant's wrath and that by paying my respects to him I could not be held to blame, he finally consented. I had a strong desire to go to Old Biloxi to see how it had grown since my departure. I took a pirogue with some soldiers to paddle it, and with myself steering, we made our way over to that place. But imagine my surprise in finding it all in ruins from an accident that had happened there not long earlier. A sergeant named Louis Colet, nicknamed "Joly Coeur," who had drunk his fill and lost his senses, took a burning brand to light his pipe, lay down on his bunk, and after lighting the pipe, carelessly threw the ember onto the floor of the room. It rolled up against one of the posts of the cabin, and as the wind fanned it, the fire caught one post and then spread to another. The devouring element reached the roof, and the sparks flew through the air and set fire to other cabins. Those who were inside them, such as the sergeant himself, were lucky to save themselves. It was night. The guard cried, "Fire!" and the general alarm was sounded, but when the men tried to put out the fire by throwing water on it, it only sprung up again, for this pinewood is full of resin; it is from this wood that pitch and tar are derived. In spite of their best efforts, eleven houses, or rather cabins, were reduced to ashes. This, therefore, was the first sight that appeared to my eyes.[10]

9. This structure was typical for companies of the marines in Louisiana and other colonies. See *FFL*, 7; Arnaud Balvay, *L'epée et la plume: Amérindiens et soldats des troupes de la marine en Louisiane et au Pays d'en Haut (1683–1763)* (Quebec, 2006), 38. *Anspessade* was a noncommissioned rank below corporal; the etymology of the word suggests a cavalryman who had broken his lance and subsequently fought among the infantry.

10. For other accounts of this fire and the soldier who set it, see *Mémoires historiques*, II, 40; and Charles Le Gac, *Immigration and War, Louisiana: 1718–1721; From the Memoir of Charles Le Gac*, trans. Glenn R. Conrad (Lafayette, La., 1970), 55.

After taking in this scene all around me, I went to the governor's residence. I found the commandant pacing across the room. [101] I made a deep bow to him and inquired after his health, but he did not reply at all and pretended not to recognize me or even see me. He was meeting with an officer from the troops of the Company of the Indies, a captain who had been promoted from lieutenant in a regiment of the royal marines. His name was the Sr. de Blanc. The commandant and he, having taken several turns around the room, exited by another door and left me alone, master of the field. I saw that M. de la Tour had given me good advice in telling me not to come there, but it was too late now, and I was stung to the quick by my reception. I mulled it over for a while, and then, as I knew every corner of the place, having surveyed and designed it myself, I went into the kitchen to find a large piece of burnt firewood, and, returning to the room I had left, set about drawing on a door a large cross, three feet high with arms three inches wide. I have no doubt that the commandant, as well as the captain, were watching what I was doing, because the latter, returning alone to the room and never having met me before, walked straight up to me and, addressing me by my name, said:

"Monsieur, what are you doing here?"

I answered that I was making a cross, as he could very well see for himself.

"And for what purpose?" he said.

I replied, "So that when it has faded to white, only then will I walk through this door." I told him to say to his general that, in coming to see him, I believed that I was performing my duties, but that I now realized I was mistaken, that he did not deserve my visit, and I now knew that he did not know how to conduct himself and did not deserve the respect of honest men. I did not wait for a reply to this but walked out on the spot, not knowing what might follow.

When I arrived at our [102] settlement, I returned to my room to wait for whatever consequences might arrive. I did not have to wait long. Fewer than four hours had passed after my arrival in my room when the Sr. Andriot, a lieutenant in the troops of the Company, who also served as adjutant, came to New Biloxi. As soon as he stepped ashore, he came to find me, and after the usual preliminaries, he ordered me arrested on behalf of the commandant. Expressing myself with all courtesy, I told him I was very sorry for him that he had been assigned a duty that I would surely never comply with and that I was not going to respond to any orders from his general. He withdrew and went back to deliver my reply. As for me, I went to the lodgings of our director and royal lieutenant and told him what had happened and what was now happening. "I was afraid it would come to this," he said, "but nonetheless, I will try to take care of it."

The next day, the commandant himself came to New Biloxi with the intention of removing me from my command over my troops. No sooner had he entered the lodgings of his lieutenant than, complaining of me, he told the lieutenant that he had ordered my arrest, was shocked that I was not there, intended to make an example of me, and [that the lieutenant must] go sound an alarm. But then M. de la Tour showed him the orders from Mgr. Le Blanc, the minister. He regained his calm, but nonetheless our director, perhaps wondering if I was in fact mutinous, sent M. de Graves, my captain, to order me detained, perhaps also to give the commandant some satisfaction. His order, I obeyed promptly. The commandant of the colony [103] stayed and dined at M. de la Tour's lodgings, and as soon as he left to return to his residence, I was set free from confinement, and so I was detained for his satisfaction only about five hours.[11]

A few days later, everything was organized for our concession. Captain Bizard was detached with his company of soldiers and one of laborers to go establish a post in the name of our minister, 150 leagues upstream from the mouth of the river, at a place called Yazoo. There was, at that time, a detachment of fifteen French soldiers at this place, commanded by a lieutenant of the Company named M. de la Boulaye, and a square fort made of stakes, without gun ports, which was really more of a park than a fort. Thus M. Bizard would be the first to arrive with a detachment at this post that the Company had granted to the minister. Our company was to be the only one to remain at New Biloxi, with one of the companies of laborers and a chaplain.

It was scarcely two months after the *Portefaix* had arrived in this place when food began to run short. The soldiers of the Company had to go to the Indian villages, both the Biloxis and the Pascagoulas. These inhabitants of the forest received them very well, furnishing them with supplies of corn, which they cooked for them along with plenty of deer or buffalo meat or, if meat was not available, with bear grease. As for the rest of us, we remained in our barracks, with our soldiers reduced to beans and peas with a little salt meat, but no bread and very little eau-de-vie. And why was this? It was because our provisions had been lent to the Company of the Indies.[12]

---

11. Other Louisiana directors of the Company of the Indies, Deverger and Delorme, also wrote to Bienville in the summer of 1721 asking for help in countering the insubordination of certain officers; see *MPA*, III, 309–311.

12. The worst period was the autumn of 1721, but the famine began earlier. In January

One day, as I was out hunting, I rested at [104]¹³ a farm that the commandant of the colony had established across from the old fort at the point of the neck of land on which Fort Louis, or New Biloxi, was built. I knew the caretaker there, and I was smoking my pipe. He was married, and he invited me to stay for dinner with him and his family. I did not have to be asked twice, given the state we were then in. I dined there on an excellent soup and meat with excellent bread. While eating, I saw at the foot of his bed eight barrels of flour, which were hidden under a carpet. I didn't say a word at the time, but after I had thanked this man and taken leave of him to return to the concession, I went straight to M. de la Tour and told him what I had seen and found. The royal lieutenant ordered me to go with a detachment of fifteen men and a sergeant and seize what I had found, so as to help the concession and its troops. I took only seven of the barrels, leaving one to the caretaker, which would be enough for him to feed his household for more than four months. I did not do him any injustice in this, since they — the flour barrels, that is — belonged to the commandant, who was storing them there to sell to the highest bidder. We carried them in the pirogue to our settlement, and as soon as they were unloaded and placed in the storehouse, they were distributed in equal portions to the barracks of the soldiers along with advice to make it last. As for myself, I had 120 pounds for my share, and the other officers got only 60 pounds. It was like manna from heaven for all of us, for without it, we were on the verge of dying from hunger, because during this shortage, each man was forced to seek after his own food. I had a soldier who worked for me as a valet, and although I was his master, we lived [105] like two comrades. He possessed the skill of capturing fowl without letting them squawk, and even pigeons, as well as ducks and turkeys, and so with our flour, some lard, and some peas and beans, we always had enough to sustain us.

We had not yet run out of these supplies when a ship named the *Venus*,

---

1721, there were 1,249 people at New Biloxi, and 880 more arrived during that winter. In some camps at Biloxi, half the people died before they were able to reach their concessions. See Jean-Baptiste Le Moyne de Bienville to Philippe d'Orléans, *MPA*, III, 307–308; Le Gac, *Immigration and War*, trans. Conrad, 65; *HLF*, IV, 126, 134; Bernard Diron d'Artaguiette, "Journal of Diron Dartaguiette," in Newton D. Mereness, ed. and trans., *Travels in the American Colonies* (New York, 1916), 19; and Daniel H. Usner, Jr., *Indians, Settlers, and Slaves in a Frontier Exchange Economy: The Lower Mississippi Valley before 1783* (Chapel Hill, N.C., 1992), 31–43. To add to the climate of despair, the *Portefaix* brought news of the collapse of the Mississippi Bubble and the flight of John Law; see *HJEFL*, 122–123.

13. Figure 5, Dumont's map of "Fort Saint Louis; or, New Biloxi, Third Establishment," was originally located at this spot in the manuscript.

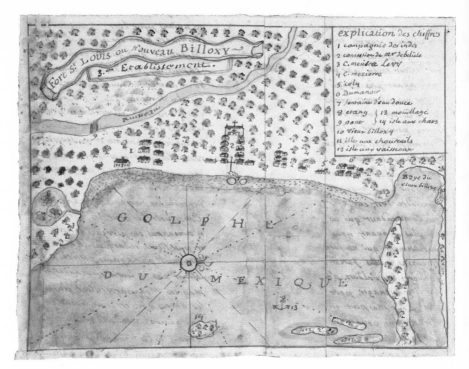

Figure 5. *Fort Saint Louis; or, New Biloxi, Third Establishment.* VAULT oversize Ayer MS 257, map no. 5. Courtesy The Newberry Library, Chicago

commanded by M. de la Mansillière, arrived along with another named the *Duc de Noailles* and brought us relief. The troops of the Company, as well as their officers, were immediately summoned from the Indian villages to return to their garrisons. The commandant general, seeing that Fort Louis was even more crowded than Old Biloxi and that the fire had destroyed many of the cabins there, decided not to rebuild them but ordered the engineers to move over to our side and to lay out a third settlement for the Company. The workers were all set to task and quickly built the settlement, and the commandant and all his staff then abandoned the old fort, just as they had done a year and a half earlier when they had left Dauphin Island. This new settlement was located at the head of the row of those of the concessions. The Spanish had, by this time, made peace with us. Pensacola had been returned to them, and they had set about rebuilding everything there. The troops of the Company performed their duties at their post, and we at ours.[14]

14. Jean de Beaurain concurs that the *Venus* arrived on July 15, having been armed at Port-Louis on April 2; see *HJEFL,* 253–254; "Les armements au long cours de la deuxième

I have forgotten to say that, some months before my arrival in that land for the second time, there had come a ship loaded with negroes, who were sold at very low prices because they were offered to those who could feed them. The Company reserved the largest number for itself, and during the shortage of food, these poor people, as well as many of the Germans and even some of the French, died of hunger. The Company of the Indies, or rather those who were in charge of [106] it at Fort Saint Louis, had a bridge built over a small stream, made from wooden planks and beams, to make it possible to take lumber for construction from the forests into the settlements; and although this bridge was not a large one and did not require much for its construction, it was charged to those in France at a very high price befitting a major project.[15]

As the commandant of this New World was now at New Biloxi, with M. de la Tour, who was his lieutenant, they appeared outwardly to be friends, and they conspired with one another to do whatever was necessary to make me lose favor in the eyes of the minister. Sure enough, soon they were writing to denounce me, a man who thought only of doing my duty to the best of my abilities. But they were not able to keep their actions secret, and I was alerted by the brother of the royal lieutenant himself, who was a friend of mine and who worked for his brother as his secretary. He had followed him [de la Tour] over in this capacity and had shared the table with his [de la Tour's] entourage, and although the Sr. de la Tour was chief of the engineers' brigade as well as royal lieutenant and director of the concessions of the minister, his brother was only a simple engraver. As the brother did not know the language of heraldry, I taught it to him, and it was in recognition of this favor that he informed me of the evil turn that they were doing me. I was in a difficult position. This was my superior and the man to whom I had been recommended, and moreover, it had appeared as though he liked me and was protecting me. I asked myself, Should I write against him? I thought that this would be a bad thing to do. Nonetheless, I took that

---

Compagnie des Indes," no. 166. On the abandonment of Old Biloxi, see "Minutes of the Council of Commerce of Louisiana," *MPA*, III, 298–302. The new site was closer to the roadstead at Ship Island, the land less swampy, and the water better. The king had ordered the surrender of Pensacola to the Spanish on August 20, 1721, and Bienville received the order in April of 1722; see Bienville to the Council of the Marine, *MPA*, III, 319–322.

15. Two ships, the *Duc de Maine* and the *Afriquain*, arrived in March 1721 from Ouidah, in present-day Benin. The first carried 349 Africans; the second, 182. See Gwendolyn Midlo Hall, *Africans in Colonial Louisiana: The Development of Afro-Creole Culture in the Eighteenth Century* (Baton Rouge, La., 1992), 63–64. This bridge is shown as no. 9 on Dumont's map of New Biloxi, Figure 5.

course and informed the minister of the intrigues of this officer with regard to the supplies for his concession. You will see in what follows what good this did me.[16]

When the Company of the Indies recognized that there would soon come another famine even worse than the first or that a pestilence might strike this place, so badly crowded and built literally upon sand, they chose the best course of action, which was to grant all the lands demanded by the concessionaires [107] and to give them contracts in proper form. This way, each could work for his own benefit and after his own fashion, and any surplus that might remain from those lands could help those who were lacking. In times of hardship, one might well say that the settlement of these land grants in the New World was like the Tower of Babel or the confusion of human languages, because the Germans were establishing the concession of M. Law at the Arkansas River, two hundred leagues from the mouth of the river called Barbancha, or Mississippi, by the Indians and the Saint Louis River by the French. The others dispersed here and there, some near, some far from the seat of the commandant. At this same time, M. de la Tour was ordered to go to the Saint Louis River to look for a suitable site to lay out a town that might serve as the capital of this country.[17]

So, having been provided with five boats filled with provisions and cargo for our concessions, we departed in the month of November, and we traveled across Lake Pontchartrain, later known as Saint Louis, to a small river that in this country is called a bayou.[18] We entered it and rowed upstream for two leagues to a portage, where there were some sheds that served as a depot. At that time, there were only three habitants living in this place. On the right bank of the river as one went upstream was a Canadian called Joseph Girardy, with his wife and children and Indian slaves; and on the left of the bayou was the Sr. Lavigne, who also had a family and a fine farm,

16. It appears that Le Blond de la Tour had two brothers who came with him to Louisiana, one known as the chevalier Le Blond and the other as Boispinel de Latour. The three came over together on the *Dromadaire* in 1720. See *FFLa*, I, 73. It is probably the younger brother, Boispinel, who is referred to in this passage.

17. Historians have disputed Dumont's assertion here and below that German emigrants settled at Law's Arkansas concession. See Morris S. Arnold, "The Myth of John Law's German Colony on the Arkansas," *Louisiana History*, XXXI (1990), 83–88. When Dumont refers to the Saint Louis River, it is the Mississippi. On names for the Mississippi River, see below, original manuscript [185, 353]; *Mémoires historiques*, I, 3; and *Histoire de la Louisiane*, I, 141, for the spelling "Balbancha."

18. Index note: "1721."

and the Sr. François Dugué, who was a bachelor. It was at his place that we landed. We slept there, and he received us very well.[19]

[108] There were several sheds within a hundred paces of his dwelling, as I've said, where the supplies brought from New Biloxi were covered and stored, ready for the new settlement that was planned to be built one league away from the Bayou Saint John, on the Saint Louis River. It was on this river that we now had to travel, going upstream to get to Yazoo, where the company of the Sr. Bizard already was. To reach this river on a well prepared trail with carts to carry all our cargo through the forests and brush might have been a simple matter, a pleasure, even. But no, we found upturned trees blocking the path, which our soldiers had to cut up and remove, and then a small ravine that was swollen with rainwater that had flooded the area and made the ground muddy and the trail very bad. It was no small matter to transport the supplies and the equipment for the troops. We had even more trouble in transporting our five boats, which, as soon as we got to the post known by the name of New Orleans, were put into the water of the beautiful Saint Louis River. All this required only a few days, after which we reloaded our boats once again, embarked the soldiers in them, and left behind this little outpost, where there were then only four or five houses all separated from one another, belonging to various habitants.[20]

Our five boats getting under way with the officers divided up among them, we reached Le Petit Desert, three leagues from the place we had just left. At this site, there was a large storehouse belonging to our concession. All the officers ate together and each [109] sergeant with the soldiers and workers of each boat. Never had there been seen on this river so many boats in a convoy so well equipped as ours. After resting at Le Petit Desert for three days and loading up with wine, eau-de-vie, and other goods to supply the post we were headed for, we left early in the morning. Our soldiers were rowing, and we had in each boat a helmsman who steered it. The boat in which M. de Graves was riding, as captain and commander in chief, went always in the lead and flew the French flag on its stern. The others followed him as best and as closely as they could. Every day, we departed at day-

19. See the entries for these three pioneer households on the Bayou Saint John listed in the 1722 census in Louisiana Historical Society, *Publications*, V (New Orleans, 1911), 91; and Dumont's Figure 7, as well as his map of "Le Grand Bayou," ANF, Cartes et plans, 6 JJ 75, collection Delisle, pièce 252.

20. This settlement is New Orleans, founded in 1718 but badly damaged by a hurricane on September 11, 1722. Le Blond de la Tour was assigned to redesign the town.

break, and at about eight o'clock in the morning, we pulled up alongside one another and took time out to light a pipe and eat breakfast, after which each man was issued a dram of eau-de-vie. After that, we continued on our way until noontime, when we went ashore for dinner, which was already prepared, our having had the foresight to cook it the previous evening after supper. As soon as we had eaten, we resumed our voyage going upstream under the power of oars, since only rarely could we use the sails, given the height of the trees that blocked the wind and given that, although the wind might be behind you for a half league or so, when you come around a point, it suddenly is found blowing in your face.[21]

So, when one can make five or six leagues between morning and night-fall, it is a good pace, given the rapid current in this river. And when the sun is about to disappear below the horizon, we stop the boats in the most convenient place to sleep. Some go into the forest in search of firewood to heat the kettle, others set up their berres, others pitch the tent for the commandant, and still others try to kill something to sate their appetites. When the kettle is ready, each eats from his own dish, and then after sharing a pipe, we go to bed. While [110] the majority are sleeping, the guns are stacked up together, and there is always a guard on duty, not only to look after the boats and the guns but also to get the kettle boiling for the next morning. We additionally set sentinels on the edge of the camp in case of an enemy surprise. During every voyage, this routine is followed, although some proceed differently from others, as will be seen below. But in any case, it all is at the will of the commander.

We finally arrived at Baton Rouge, which was then beginning to be settled by M. Diron d'Artaguiette's concession. It was not yet as well established as I have seen it since then, but already one house, or rather cabin, had been built. The same day that we arrived in this place, it happened that one of our boat captains had stolen a barrel with more than twelve pots of eau-de-vie in it and was constantly drunk. He was discovered as he went to tap the barrel again, and being [that he was] thus caught in the act, when we arrived at the concession and went ashore, a council of war was summoned. He was dismissed from his command, reduced to the rank of sailor, and condemned to a whipping. He was attached to a large tree, with his shoul-

21. "Le Petit Desert" was located a few kilometers upstream from New Orleans on the eastern shore. The November 1721 census indicated that there were one man, five women, seven domestics, and nine slaves living there. See Charles R. Maduell, Jr., ed. and trans., *The Census Tables for the French Colony of Louisiana from 1699 through 1732* (Baltimore, 1972), 22.

ders bare, and each soldier in turn gave him a lash on the back. He was not treated lightly, given that his theft had reduced the supply of eau-de-vie for the soldiers, who, angry at this thief, left on him the marks of their thirst.[22]

The day after our arrival in this place was a rest day. There was an officer named the Sr. Petit de Livilliers, from Quebec, a lieutenant in our squadron, who, along with three soldiers and a habitant of the concession, set out through the forest to reach the prairie. As soon as they arrived there, they saw a herd of buffalo, bulls, and cows, which, when they got wind of the hunters, began to run away. Still, they did not move so [111] quickly but that two were left behind, to the delight of our hunters. The five men could not carry even one entire carcass between them. Each loaded up and returned to our camp to inform us of their success. A detachment of soldiers was sent out to fetch the rest of this excellent provision, for ever since our departure from New Orleans, we had lived on lard and salt beef. Hence this fresh meat gave us great pleasure. It was portioned out to every dish in the company, though you need have no doubt that we reserved the best bits for ourselves.

After two days in this place, on the third, at the first light of day, we all embarked again and continued on our route upstream. It was then that we had the pleasure of killing some bears that were swimming across the river. A boat would break off to pursue them, shoot them, and then pull them on board. One day in particular, the boat commanded by M. Petit de Livilliers (who was a very good shot), having spotted one of these animals crossing over, set out to catch up to it by the power of their arms. The officer, who was standing in the bow, shot at it. But because of the movement of the boat, he only hit the animal in the ear, which caused the bear, who was surprised by this blow, to turn and come back toward the boat rather than continue swimming toward land. Having grabbed the boat with its large, handlike paws, it climbed in. All the soldiers who were rowing were seized with such fear that they threw themselves under their seats. There was not a single one among them who did not prefer to be suffocated by the body of his comrade rather than be left on top of him. But the animal, having climbed on board, rather than express rage and anger, only looked around to one side and the other, and then, walking over the backs of the men, passed by the boathouse and threw himself into the water. But at the sound of the splash, the guns were taken up again, and he did not make it far before he paid dearly for his good nature, [112] for he was killed and brought dead on board the same

22. Diron d'Artaguiette's concession was located on the site of the modern city of Baton Rouge. In 1722, it was home to thirty Europeans, twenty Africans, and two Indian slaves. See the census reprinted in Louisiana Historical Society, *Publications*, V, 96.

boat that he had just passed across alive. We passed a place called Pointe Coupée, where there was not yet the French settlement that has since been established. It is fifty leagues from New Orleans and halfway to Natchez. Forty leagues beyond this point, we stopped and slept in a village of friendly Indians about whom I will have more to say elsewhere. A league and a half beyond this village, on the left of the river as one goes upstream, is the confluence of the river named the Red River.[23]

Finally, we arrived at Natchez, a post established some time earlier and guarded by a fort of pilings built by the Company of the Indies. The Sr. Berneval was the captain and commandant there. There was a company of soldiers assigned to the post, along with a lieutenant named M. de Cazeneuve, who had a farm, although he was not married, and a second lieutenant named Massé, who had a wife and child. Within a league of this fort, there were two concessions. One was called Terre Blanche. It was managed by the Clairacs, who hoped to grow a lot of tobacco there. The other concession had been established one league away by the Sr. Hubert, commissaire ordonnateur, who had given it the name of Saint Catherine, the baptismal name of his wife. But by that time, it was owned by M. Kolly, who lived in Paris in the rue Neuve Saint-Eustache, had purchased it from M. Hubert, and was having it managed by a man named Guenot.[24] Around French Natchez, right in between these two concessions, in fact, was a large Indian village that went by the name of the Grand village. Outside the French fort, there were some habitants who had settled here and there, separated from one another, and married in the presence of witnesses, for lack of a chaplain

23. Pointe Coupée was the site of two concessions, one owned by Mezières and the other called Sainte Reine, but they were abandoned again in the 1720s. It was resettled by surgeon and militia leader Jean-Baptiste de Laye (*HLF*, IV, 242–244, V, 179, 396). The Indian village belonged to the Tunicas; see original manuscript [187].

24. The fort and settlement at Natchez had been founded in 1716; see James F. Barnett, Jr., *The Natchez Indians: A History to 1735* (Jackson, Miss., 2007), 57–67; and "Mémoire de M. de Richebourg, sur la première guerre des Natchez," in John R. Swanton, *Indian Tribes of the Lower Mississippi Valley and Adjacent Coast of the Gulf of Mexico* (Washington, D.C., 1911), 196–204. The concession called White Earth in English was located on the southeast side of present-day Natchez, Mississippi, on the site of the now-closed International Paper mill. First belonging to the Company of the Indies, it came under the Le Blanc / Belle-Isle partnership in 1721, when it was home to thirty-one men, seven women, and five children; see "Journal of Diron Dartaguiette," in Mereness, ed. and trans., *Travels in the American Colonies*, 46; and *HLF*, IV, 266. John Law and other concessionaires transported farmers from the town of Clairac, near Bordeaux, a center for French tobacco production since 1556. The other large Natchez concession was Saint Catherines, located north of Terre Blanche, along what is still known as Saint Catherine Creek. Le Page du Pratz had negotiated the purchase of its lands from the Indians in 1718; see *Histoire de la Louisiane*, I, 127.

or missionary. Our chaplain said Mass in a house and performed marriage ceremonies for those who had not received them.[25]

We stayed here only three days, after which we resumed our journey on the waters [113] of the river. We still had forty leagues to go to reach our destination. Everyone was eager to get there soon. During this stage from Natchez to Yazoo, we killed passenger pigeons, and I mean a lot of passenger pigeons, because with a single gunshot, we killed thirty or more. Only in certain years do these birds come in such huge multitudes, and then one could say that they are so thick, they foul the air.

As we were finally nearing our goal, that is, as we approached Yazoo, an accident struck our convoy. The boat carrying the barrels of powder, in which a man named Pascal was the captain, was rowing along, and he must not have seen a cypress stump that was just below the water. The boat's bottom was punctured, a plank separating from the keel. Immediately, the water began flowing in, and it would certainly have sunk if another boat following it had not quickly come to its aid. This second boat having given a signal, others arrived, and the powder was removed from the boat that was at risk of sinking and put into the others. Only three of the barrels got wet. It was very cold, as it was the month of December, and we built a fire on shore to warm up the soldiers who had been forced to plunge into the water.[26]

The Sr. de Graves, captain commandant, who was a very strict man, called to the helmsman, and although he had not been the cause of the misfortune that occurred to his boat, an accident quite common among all voyagers, upon hearing he was being summoned and fearing a whipping like the one at Baton Rouge, he ran off into the woods and did not reappear for as long as we were there. We tried to call to him, crying out that he had nothing to fear, but all in vain, and we finally had to leave some pieces of [114] biscuit for him and continue on our way. We had no sooner gained the

25. The Grand village was the seat of a tribal confederation of eight or nine Natchez villages. By the 1720s, however, political unity was fractured, as some villages (Grigra, aka "Gris"; Pomme, or "Apple"; Jenzenaques, aka "Noyers") had begun to trade with English traders from the Carolinas, whereas others remained close to the French (Grand; Farine, or "Flour"; Tioux). See Karl G. Lorenz, "A Re-examination of Natchez Sociopolitical Complexity: A View from the Grand Village and Beyond," *Southeastern Archaeology*, XVI, no. 2 (Winter 1997), 97–112. Today, the site of the Grand village is preserved as a historic site by the Mississippi Department of Archives and History. The absence of any priest at Natchez in the 1720s was the focus of complaints by Father Raphaël after a visit in 1726; see "Lettre de Père Raphael," ANF, AC, Correspondance générale, C13A, X, 47–52.

26. A "Pascal, boat captain" appears in the census of 1722 (Louisiana Historical Society, *Publications*, V, 89); see also Shannon Lee Dawdy, *Building the Devil's Empire: French Colonial New Orleans* (Chicago, 2008), 100.

middle of the river, crossing over to the other side, than we saw the helmsman return to his boat, which had been left there on the bank, and take stock of his craft.

Finally, on the day after this accident, we left the waters of the Saint Louis River and entered into the Yazoo River, and after ascending it for three leagues, we arrived at the concession where we were supposed to find two companies, one of laborers and one of soldiers commanded by M. Bizard. But whether from unhealthy air or water, more than half of them were already dead, including their commandant. We disembarked and unloaded everything in our boats into the storehouses.[27]

So I found myself stationed at my post, where it seemed that I ought to be able to enjoy some tranquillity in performing my duties as an officer. But no, I was not born for such happiness, as you will soon see. We had scarcely a week of rest after our arrival on the first of the year, when M. de Graves ordered every soldier, as well as every laborer, to each provide him with ten posts from the tree called acacia—a yellow, very hard wood, which does not rot when placed in the earth.[28] On the contrary, even when it has been cut square, if there remains a small bit of bark somewhere on the log, it will sprout a branch and take root in the ground. And it was me whom he ordered, because I was knowledgeable in fortification, to lay out the fort in which we, our troops, our belongings, and those of the concession, would all be protected from attack by enemy Indians. I obeyed his orders. I outlined a fort with four bastions, after the style of M. de Vauban. Each side of the polygon was 180 feet [115] in length. Once I had traced it, the foundation was dug, and when the palings had been furnished and sharpened on their top ends, they were erected. Each one was twelve feet in length, and three and a half feet of this was sunk into the ground. In each of the bastions, there were two gunports where cannons would be set up on their carriages. Once the palings were in place all around, to support the palisades, we attached behind them—that is, on the inside of the fort—beams of cypress at least five inches wide, secured by a long, thick nail that was pounded in from the outside. On the inner side of the fort, there was a parapet four feet wide and two and a half feet high, so that one might fire over the top of the

27. The census of 1722 indicates that Yazoo was Le Blanc's principal concession and was home to 140 workers, soldiers, women, and children; see Louisiana Historical Society, *Publications*, V, 95. Located about twenty kilometers upstream from the confluence of the Yazoo and Mississippi, near modern Vicksburg, it was soon abandoned and in 1729 had only about fifteen European residents.

28. An index note, partly illegible, reads "22," which must indicate the year 1722. Acacia is not native to the region. Dumont likely refers to a type of locust tree.

palisade if necessary. We also built a guardhouse next to the main entry, barracks, quarters for the officers, and a residence for the captain commandant, as well as four large storehouses and a room for the warehouse keeper. There were two gates in this fort, as well as a moat twelve feet wide all around it, which necessitated also building a drawbridge.[29]

No sooner had I finished designing all that I have just described when, on the second of February, there arrived at the fort the Sr. de la Harpe, captain commandant, who had received orders from the Company of the Indies to go discover, or rather to look for, a large topaz rock that some flatterers had told them would be found along the river named for the Zotoouis, or Arkansas, Indians who live some sixty leagues away from our concession. He also had orders to survey this river and to make an accurate journal of his travels and what he found there. He would not have had to [116] come to the post where we were to get to where he was sent, and in fact, it was quite a distance out of the direct route that he had been told to follow up the river. But he needed a surveyor and was unable to recruit one in New Orleans, where the engineers did not deign to leave a city that was just being established and were taking on airs, believing themselves to be kings. So I was chosen for this job, and I received an order from M. de la Tour to leave my garrison and go on this voyage of discovery, helping the Sr. de la Harpe to make the map that was demanded of him.[30]

Thus I was obliged to undertake another voyage. This did not please M. de Graves, our commandant. He liked me, since I had helped him a lot with the new fort. Nonetheless, he had to obey, and so, after bidding farewell to him and to my comrades—packing the linens and clothing needed for travel into an unknown land where I had never been and taking papers, pencils, pens, ink, my box of mathematical instruments, and a compass, which I charged to my account at our concession's warehouse—I embarked in the pirogue of M. Dufresne, who was going up to the Arkansas to be-

29. Sébastien Le Prestre, Seigneur de Vauban (1633–1707), was a model for young French engineers such as Dumont, and Dumont's plan for the fort at Yazoo, shown in Figure 6, follows Vauban's principles. Diron d'Artaguiette confirms that, when he visited on February 1, 1723, there was a fort with "four bastions surrounded by a little moat about six feet wide and three feet deep"; see "Journal of Diron Dartaguiette," in Mereness, ed. and trans., *Travels in the American Colonies*, 51.

30. Jean-Baptiste Bénard de la Harpe had ascended the Mississippi beyond the confluence of the Arkansas River in order to reach the Yazoo River. The Arkansas Indians were called, in other texts, the Soutouis, Soutéhouy, or Zautoouye (see also below, original manuscript [119].) One of the haughty New Orleans engineers referred to is undoubtedly Adrien Pauger.

come director of the concession of M. Law settled by the Germans. We all departed together, twenty-two people, that is, all going (or so they hoped) to make a quick fortune by taking possession of a topaz rock. How easily greed can motivate our actions, and how easily we will believe in the frauds and flattering imaginings that may be [117] proposed to us.[31]

What purpose would it serve to bore my reader with the narrative of this journey? All I will say is that, after a great deal of toil and trouble—of nights sleeping on the ground, in parched, frozen, snowy, or muddy weather— we found nothing. At the end of three and half months of travel by water and 142 leagues by land, through magnificent prairies and immense forests that lined the river (in which there were trees of all species, such as pears, prunes, persimmons, pecans, and even lilacs, not to mention the trees used by carpenters, cabinet makers, etc.), we found some rocks and mountains of very great height, of magnificent stone, some even resembling marble, plus some mines of slate. There were lands covered with thyme, wild thyme, tarragon, chervil, and chamomile, all herbs suitable for treating wounds. In a word, the country is very attractive for settlement, for all that one needs most can be found without too much trouble if one only has a little patience.

One hundred twenty-two leagues from the mouth of this river, on the right as you face upstream, there is a small creek, broad but shallow, in which the water is very clear. Take one yard square of blue or red limbourg

31. In his published book, Dumont refers to himself as a "Geometer" (*Mémoires histo-riques*, II, 70). He did later draw a map of the Arkansas River for the royal cartographers Delisle and Buache, but other maps of Bénard de la Harpe's explorations are more polished, especially the "Carte nouvelle de la partie Ouest de la province de la Louisiane sur les ob-servations et découvertes du Sieur Benard de la Harpe . . . dressé par le Sr. de Beauvilliers" (BNF, Cartes et plans, Ge C 5115). One of John Law's concessions was near the mouth of the Arkansas, and another, smaller one was operated by Lieutenant La Boulaye, a former co-soldier at Yazoo with Dumont; see Louisiana Historical Society, *Publications*, V, 96. The "topaz" found on the banks of the Arkansas River at the site of modern Little Rock was called the *"rocher françois,"* according to Beaurain, whose narrative recounts that La Harpe and Dumont arrived there on April 9, 1722. La Harpe compared it to marble, whereas Dumont referred to an "emerald rock" (*Mémoires historiques*, II, 69; "Extrait des journaux de Bénard de la Harpe," Margry, VI, 374). Le Page du Pratz used the same term, although he mocked the efforts of the expedition. Probably referring to Dumont, Le Page wrote: "La Harpe took with him a man who called himself an engineer with the aim of removing this rock by cutting it into pieces. To ensure their success, this self-styled engineer invented a machine" (*Histoire de la Louisiane*, I, 310). Today, Arkansas is known for its high-quality quartz as well as small deposits of diamonds, but it appears the expedition found only the former. See also "Extrait des journaux de Bénard de la Harpe," Margry VI, 364, 374. Margry's transcriptions are often faulty; the original is available as "Navigation faite sur la rivière des Zautoouye," BNF, MSS fr. 1074–1075, 139–159.

cloth, making it into a square dipping net; attach to the middle of it a stone weighing at least a pound and a half. Put this cloth in the river, where the water is no more than one foot deep. Leave it there for twenty-four hours, then take it out and leave it to dry in the sun, remove the stone, and strike it in the middle with your finger. You will collect at least one eggshell's worth of powdered gold. I have performed this experiment myself, and it demonstrates that, between the source of this little creek and that point, its waters must somewhere pass through a deposit [118] of gold. What is more, about a league's distance from this creek, in the middle of the main stem of the Arkansas River, is a bubbling spring that pushes up four inches above the surface level and from which the emerging water is salty, even though this place must be at least 360 leagues from the sea. One could easily produce salt from this, which also suggests that not far away there are some salt deposits or a mine of salt crystal, because if it were far away from this spot, the water would doubtless be only slightly brackish instead of being strongly salty. So I say again, the country there is very beautiful and rich, filled with wild animals such as deer, buffalo, bears, tigers, turkey, and game of all kinds. This did not surprise me and should not surprise my reader, because only rarely did the Indians come from so far away to look for game there.[32]

That is what we saw and examined in our discoveries, which were only achieved with great effort. We ascended this river for 375 leagues, though the route spanned a net difference in latitude of only 120 leagues. As we were unable to find enough water to float our boats, we were forced to travel by land for 142 leagues. When food began to run out and discontent was mounting among the detachment, we were forced to return to our pirogues and retrace our path down the river, toward the French forts among the Arkansas Indians, without being able to find the topaz rock, which did not exist—or, if it did, existed only in the minds of some dreamer, who nonetheless had convinced the directors of the Company of the Indies. These gentle-

32. Dumont here mocks Bénard de la Harpe for seeking a chimerical mountain of topaz but nonetheless promotes gold mining, perhaps based on rumors of early Spanish discoveries in the Ouachita Mountains, which the French imagined to be close to New Mexico. In the *Mémoires historiques,* he and Jean-Baptiste Le Mascrier wrote: "I have no doubt that there are mines of gold in his country, since we discovered a little stream in whose waters rolled little flakes of gold" (II, 71). In a 1750 letter to Philippe Buache, on the other hand, Dumont promised no gold and wrote that he and Bénard de la Harpe had explored "a beautiful country of mountains which ought to be more esteemed than gold." See Jean-François-Benjamin Dumont de Montigny to Philippe Buache, Aug. 15, 1750, D–897, S–97, Beinecke Rare Book and Manuscript Library, Yale University, New Haven, Conn. The reference to "tigers" here presumably refers to cougars.

men had sent along with us a sort of map showing the place where this precious rock was supposed to be. I don't know if it had been made a long time earlier, but the river we traveled on [119] was nothing like the map we had been sent, and they should now know the truth from the map and the journal that I have had the honor of making for them.[33]

Before leaving the Arkansas, let us say a few things about the Indians of this place. They bear the same name as the river. After leaving the Saint Louis River to enter this one, eight leagues upstream, you find their village on the left. It is very large, spacious and spread out, and there are at least 1,500 men who are capable of bearing arms, not counting many youths. Their houses are simply huts made of mud and grass pounded together and dried. They have a temple where they keep their god. But the following anecdote will show whether they are brave. They are superstitious, and when we first stopped in their village, during our voyage of discovery up the river, there was a gunshot fired in the night that set everyone on alert. The women at once believed that they were being taken as slaves and the men killed or captured. They had all lost their wits and did not know what they were doing. Our commander, the Sr. de la Harpe, however, spoke to them so well through our interpreter that he reassured them a little, and, after he asked them for thirty volunteers, I was chosen to lead them with ten of our soldiers, and we set out toward the place from which the shot was heard. We found one of their men, who had shot a large bear, on which he was working to remove the fat. The village was relieved.

The day after this panic, there came another, aroused by a crow. It is rare

33. Bénard de la Harpe's maps of the Arkansas do not show any "rock of topaz," but the "Carte nouvelle de la partie Ouest" does show "Villages of the Padoukas Noirs from whom the Spaniards take gold by caravans to the Tiguas, around this mountain." In his narratives, La Harpe did not claim to have found gold along the Arkansas River. According to Mildred Mott Wedel, he did write a letter to the duc de Choiseul in 1763 that cited Dumont's claim in the *Mémoires historiques* about possible gold mines but minimized its significance; see Wedel, "J.-B. Bénard, Sieur de la Harpe: Visitor to the Wichitas in 1719," *Great Plains Journal*, X (1971), 69 n. 93. In his letter to Buache, Dumont claimed that the map he and La Harpe had been provided with during the expedition had been acquired from a Spanish expedition from New Mexico attacked by Missouri Indians in the Villasur Massacre of 1720. The discrepancy between the two accounts seems to have been motivated by Dumont's desire to entice Buache and Delisle to support him in plans for another expedition to the region, to look for the mythical inland sea known as the *mer de l'ouest*, which the cartographers stubbornly believed in. See Lucie Lagarde, "Le passage du Nord-Ouest et la mer de l'Ouest dans la cartographie française du 18e siècle, contribution à l'étude de l'oeuvre des Delisle et Buache," *Imago mundi*, XLI (1989), 19–43; and Paul W. Mapp, *The Elusive West and the Contest for Empire, 1713-1763* (Chapel Hill, N.C., 2011), 203–223.

to see these animals [120] in this country, and when they do occasionally appear around the villages, the Arkansas believe that the bird foretells a war and their defeat, following, no doubt, these words from the famous Virgil: *Sœpe sinistra cava, predixit abilice cornix.*[34] One, in fact, did appear on a dead branch of a very tall tree near some of the huts of their village. When the animal began to caw, nothing more was needed to drive the villagers mad. Women, girls, elders, and little boys abandon their houses, cry out, and flee as fast as they can toward their temple, doubtless to go beseech their god to assist them. But the most alert villagers arm themselves, some with guns, some with other weapons, and the strongest and bravest of all take the calumet and walk in lockstep toward the animal to make a peace offering to it. For their notion is that, when they offer the calumet to the bird, it puts him to sleep and gives them time to prepare so that they can get within range for the best marksman among them to fire. If he misses, they believe that they will soon be attacked and will be so unlucky as to be taken by their enemies, but if he kills the bird, they believe they will be the victors. As they were arranging their marching rhythm, one of our soldiers, who noticed how the Indians were afraid of the crow but was not aware of their logic, no sooner saw the crow that was causing such havoc than he fired and brought it down from the top of the tree, dead. The Indians, seeing this, came and gave the calumet to the soldier. This shot brought him at least two hundred livres worth of presents.

[121] Half a league above this Indian village, on the right bank of the river as you face upstream, there was a post of the Company of the Indies. The detachment of soldiers there was the same one commanded by the Sr. de la Boulaye; he had been ordered to come up here, leaving behind the land and the post at Yazoo, where he had been stationed previously, to be replaced by our concessions.[35] This officer was only a lieutenant, with twelve men and a sergeant making up the entire garrison. Is not that a risky way to open up new lands? A good league from that post, deep in the woods, we found M. Law's concession, made up entirely of Germans. I helped them, during the week that we stayed there, to beautify it by drawing improved designs for their houses. M. Dufresne was there as the director. Although this con-

---

34. Virgil, *Eclogues* 9.15. The line should read: "Ante sinistra cava monuisset ab ilice cornix," or "Had not a raven from the hollow ilex [oak] on my left forewarned me." It cites an episode when farmers' land was seized and given to the veteran soldiers of Octavius (later Augustus) and Marc Antony. A raven warns the shepherd that he is about to be dispossessed, as the crow is warning the Arkansas. The translation is from J. W. Mackail, ed., *Virgil's Works: Aeneid, Eclogues, Georgics* (New York, 1950), 288.

35. See above, original manuscript [103].

cession was well established, it did not remain there more than a year and a half, because once M. Law, its owner, had fled from France, his concessions fell apart, and the Germans abandoned it to come downriver and settle some ten leagues above the capital, New Orleans.[36]

So finally I was led back to the Yazoo concession, which I found had not expanded much during my absence. The officers' quarters were not yet completed, and I took only a few days of rest before M. de Graves set me to work, because the new fort only had lodgings for the soldiers and officers—that is, for the garrison. I had to design the lodgings for the workers, situated a musket's shot away from the fort, under the protection of the four cannons that were set up on the two flanks of the bastion overlooking them. All this was done in five weeks. Because the water that we were drinking was infused with nitrates and might [122][37] cause illnesses, I advised the Sr. de Graves to allow me to look for a better source of water. I had a lot of trouble finding one, but I nonetheless succeeded in doing so. I had three reservoirs built. The first was under lock and key; it was for us, the staff officers. The second was for the troops and the workers, and the third served as a washtub accessible by a door in the curtain wall behind the commandant's house. I had a large and spacious garden put in, of which I was the master gardener. At last everything was completed, the flagpole set up next to the main gate of the fort, the troops settled in their barracks as well as the workers in their houses, and the workshops of the carpenters, locksmiths, [and] blacksmiths were all done. Two sergeants of the troops had built houses for themselves three musket shots removed from the fort, and in spite of warnings that had been made to them about how an accident might occur, they insisted on their plan, and they lived there. The misfortune warned of arrived all too soon for the one who was farthest from the fort.

It was a sergeant named Riter, who lived with his wife and a son about thirteen or fourteen years of age. The day before Pentecost, he was sleeping in his bed with his wife, and his son was in his bed, when, at two o'clock in the morning, a party of Indians of the Chickasaw nation came into the sergeant's house through a door that was latched only with a strip of cloth. They entered quite easily, as you might imagine, and slipped quietly into

36. Bertrand Dufresne had arrived in Arkansas before Dumont. On this concession, see "Extrait des journaux de Bénard de la Harpe," Margry, VI, 364; and Morris S. Arnold, "The Myth of John Law's German Colony on the Arkansas," *Louisiana History*, XXXI (1990), 83–88. Arnold pointedly refutes Dumont's account here and in *Mémoires historiques*, II, 67–71.

37. Figure 6, "Plan of the Fort at Yazoo," was originally located at this spot in the manuscript. It shows the three reservoirs Dumont built.

Figure 6. *Plan of the Fort at Yazoo, Concession of M. Le Duc de Belle-Isle and His Partners, Destroyed in 1729.* VAULT oversize Ayer MS 257, map no. 6. Courtesy The Newberry Library, Chicago

the room. The man of the house woke up, however, and asked, "Who goes there?" But there was no reply. He had a stack of loaded guns between his bed and the wall. There was only one of them that was not loaded, but unfortunately he grabbed that one, so when he pulled the trigger, [123] nothing happened. He repeated this three or four times, but the Indians, seeing that he was doing it only to try to scare them, sprang upon him, pulled him out of bed, and, after dragging him into the middle of the room, gave him a blow on the back with a tomahawk shaped like a fleur-de-lis. This type is made like a bayonet that has been hafted onto a wooden handle like a hatchet. The blow penetrated right through his chest. They were not content with this; they also took his scalp and left him for dead. They then set about ransacking the house. Others had seized his wife and taken her away toward a ravine filled with canes.[38]

38. This tomahawk weapon matches the one in Figure 19 on the right, labeled with numeral 2. For other accounts of this episode, see *Mémoires historiques,* II, 85–90; and *Histoire de la Louisiane,* II, 272–290.

During all this tumult, his son, who was asleep in his bed, awoke and got up, wearing only his nightshirt. He tried to escape toward the fort, calling for help. As he was running, some Indians left the group and ran after him, firing several arrows, one of which struck him in the left wrist and passed through it, causing the young man to fall to the ground. Immediately, the Indians jump on him and, while trying to cut his throat, only cut through his skin and then cut off patches of his scalp. During this cruel and painful operation, the young man did not cry out, which saved his life. After the Indians had dealt with the father and son, they ran to help their comrades, who called out to them because the sergeant's wife, leaving the bed, had grabbed hold of a kitchen knife (the kind called a lard slicer, or, in that country, a logger's knife) and had concealed it by tucking it up the sleeve of her nightgown. When she saw that she was alone in the ravine and guarded by only two Indians, she pulled out the knife and stabbed at the one who was on her left, but so skillfully that she laid him out [124] stone dead, and then, withdrawing the knife, she lunged for the other. She was not so successful at this second blow, as she only hit the left shoulder over the breast. The Indian, finding himself wounded, called for help. The other Indians came and quickly put an end to the days of this courageous heroine, who preferred to risk her life and meet her death than to see herself vanquished and led away as a slave to these barbarians, where her honor would have been at risk.

All this did not happen silently, however, and the Sr. Desnoyers, the second sergeant, who lived just below the house where this tragic drama was unfolding, heard a strange noise and was awakened by it. He jumps out of his bed, takes a loaded gun, leaves his house, and fires a shot into the air, which sounded an alert to the fort. A detachment of thirty armed men is immediately ordered to leave the fort and seek out the noise. On the way, they encounter the young man in his sad state and lead him back to the guard-house under the care of the surgeon. However, the gunshot that had given the signal to the fort had also given the Indians a signal to flee, and each of them grabbed his loot and escaped.

When our detachment arrived at the house of this poor sergeant, what tragic spectacle did they find? A man lying in a pool of his own blood, shirtless and naked, with no hair on his head and no skin, either, as it was all stripped off, in such a state as we had never before seen. When they touched him, they saw that he was still breathing, and he was put on a litter and in this manner taken back to the fort, to the place where his son was. The latter, seeing that everyone was busily attending to his father, could not help but say, in all innocence, to the Sr. Baldic, the surgeon, "Alas, my father is old and cannot [125] survive this, but me, I am young, and there is more hope for me, so save me first."

The Sr. de Graves, our commandant, had a special stone, the color of flesh and about as large as a walnut. He did not want to allow the surgeon to probe the wound nor even to put any metal instrument in it. Instead, he had some water heated, and when it was warm, he put this stone into it, which in an instant turned the water the same color. He had them wash the wounds with it, as well as the heads of the two poor victims, and then poured the water into the wound in the body of the father, and at the end of a week, the wounds had closed up and were completely healed.

During these operations, our detachment was pursuing the enemies, but although it searched hard for them, it did not find them and was forced to return to the fort soaked like ducks, having been caught along the way in a furious rain squall (although, at our fort, we hadn't noticed any storm). On the way back, as they passed close to the house where all this had happened, our soldiers found the woman, who had been killed by an arrow, and an Indian next to her, both of them without their scalps. Our detachment brought back some loot, such as a kettle, pillows, brass plates, etc., that the Indians had dropped as they ran. They also saw the blazes engraved on trees and learned from these that it was the Chickasaws who were making war on us. I will explain in its place what these blazes mean.[39] We had then at our fort an Indian from the Illinois nation, located some four hundred leagues from here. This man was living with us and was working as a hunter, and, seeing that our soldiers had not done anything, he asked for a little powder and some balls from the Sr. de l'Estivant de la Perrière, chevalier of Saint Lazarre, who was the supply officer for our concession. [126] When he obtained these, he left all alone to go in pursuit and only returned two days later, bringing with him the scalps of three Chickasaws he had killed during his outing. He avenged our losses all by himself. The three that he killed were the one who had been wounded by the woman and the two who were accompanying and guiding him.

Our two patients were getting better and better. At the end of two weeks, there came a party of fifteen Chickasaw men to offer the calumet to the Sr. de Graves, with some pelts as gifts. This officer, who like many others was looking only to add to his account and his profit, welcomed with pleasure this ceremony, which I will describe among the customs of the Indians. He thus made peace with our enemies, who, being inside our fort, were sitting ducks for us to exact our revenge. The soldiers and even the officers badly

39. See below, original manuscript [380].

wanted this vengeance, so long as it was offered at such a cheap rate. But no, the Chickasaws received only our compliments and promised that they would be our brothers and friends. Such were the orders we had to obey from our commandant, who showed them the two people whom their warriors had, so to speak, martyrized. But either because the poor sergeant was infuriated by seeing the butchers of himself and his wife before his eyes or because his anger reopened his inner wounds, this visit caused a high fever, and he died two days later. Only the son survived, and through the influence of the illustrious masters he was serving, by virtue of being on their concession, he gained admission to the royal Hôtel des Invalides.[40]

After this fatal catastrophe, we were obliged to maintain a higher state of alert. We performed our duties precisely, but whether from the fatigue that I had undergone in the voyage of exploration [127] or whether it was simply that the air of the country caught up with me, I fell ill with a tertiary fever, which consumed and wracked my entire body.[41]

Summer in that country came on so dry that year that we believed the damage would be such that we would not be able to harvest a single grain, neither of corn, which I refer to as Turkish wheat, nor of beans, tobacco, etc. As for the French wheat, although it grows well, as do grapes, flax, and hemp, we could not cultivate them because of orders forbidding it from the Company of the Indies. You might ask me why; it is in the interests of commerce. We had then at that post just a single chaplain, named M. l'abbé Juif, a worthy priest who had already served in the armies of the king of France. We were supposed to have another, who had come from France to this place with me, but like the greater part of that first detachment (along with its commander, the Sr. Bizard), he had died and gone on the voyage to the afterlife. They certainly needed a chaplain there, and the younger was called to go with them, whether this was his wish or not. This elderly, virtuous, and worthy priest, M. Juif, seeing how the drought persisted and was threatening his flock, called for forty hours of prayers in the chapel, with the exposition of the Holy Sacrament, to implore heaven for relief, to move God to pity and ask Him for water. But God was deaf to our prayers and did not answer them. So the Sr. de Graves had recourse, like a second Saul, to find in the art of demons and hell what he could not obtain from heaven. That

---

40. See below, original manuscript [365], on the calumet ceremony. No doubt the influence of Claude Le Blanc helped the young Riter be admitted to the old soldiers' home in Paris.

41. Most likely malaria; although yet rare in North America, it was widespread in the Caribbean and Europe.

king, having gone to the house of a woman who dabbled in divination, asked to see [128] King Samuel, and so on. In the like manner, our commandant asked to see the chief of the Indians called the Yazoos, who were then our friends, as they had ceded their lands to the French.[42]

When the chief arrived, our chief asked him, through our interpreter, if he could bring him water. He promised some, and sure enough, on the next day, it fell in abundance and continued for two days. The shaman was paid generously in merchandise belonging to the concession. This rain having thus fallen by the order of the Sr. de Graves so swelled up his pride and presumption that he could not refrain from saying that he had done more by himself than all the priests put together.[43] Ultimately, the commandant became a hypochondriac. He forbade the Sr. Baldic, the military surgeon, from giving out any medicines whatsoever without his permission, as if believing that the entire apothecary of the concession, which was well furnished with everything, would not be sufficient to meet his own needs. The soldiers and workers, rather than being credited in money, were paid with merchandise that the men then traded to the Indians for food, such as corn, oil, beans, meat, etc. The Sr. de Graves thus found the secret to enriching himself. He raised the prices of trade goods so high that the soldier or worker was forced to pay three sous for one ball of lead for his gun. For a yard of limbourg, a blue or red cloth that usually sells for sixteen livres in that country, he forced them to pay as much as forty, forty-five, or fifty livres a yard and likewise with other goods.

It was at this same time that I fell ill, and I could not obtain from the hands of the surgeon any sort of medicine. I would have benefited greatly from a dose of emetic, but it was impossible to obtain any help from the Sr. de Graves. The Sr. de l'Estivant de la Perrière needed some of the same medicine, but the commandant refused it to him also. So, one evening, [129] I decided to try chopping up some tobacco and making an infusion of it over

42. What Dumont calls "Turkish wheat" refers to maize. Because the Company of the Indies had been granted a monopoly, soldiers were prohibited from trading with the Indians or the colonists. The allusion to 1 Samuel 28 equates the commander with Saul, who sought out a woman diviner at Endor to raise the spirit of the deceased King Samuel to advise him. Saul's anxious fear of the Philistines and his reliance on a pagan soothsayer confirms his unworthiness as a military commander, and he soon commits suicide. In Dumont's allegory, Graves has just shown his cowardice by accepting the calumet from the Chickasaws, and he no doubt was one of the corrupt officers whom Dumont sought to expose in his memoir.

43. In the version of this story in *Mémoires historiques*, I, 169–175, in a chapter entitled "Des alexis, ou jongleurs," Dumont used the Choctaw words *alexi* and *jongleur*, or "juggler," but here, he uses *devin*, commonly translated as "soothsayer" or "seer." I have chosen to translate it as "shaman," which is better suited to native American practices.

the hot embers in my room, and early the next morning, I drank a large glass of it, which I thought would be my undoing, bringing about violent vomiting and purging of the stomach. I believed that this affair would lead me to the place from which one cannot return. As soon as the Sr. de Graves knew the state that I was in, he imagined that the Sr. Baldic, against his orders, had given me the emetic, and he ordered him arrested. But I had my cup taken to the commandant and made him see the tobacco in it. For a brief moment, this calmed him down, which is to say that he let the surgeon go. But he threatened him with prison and to expel him from the colony if he gave out even the smallest dose of medicine without his permission.

This sort of medicine that I had taken left me worse off than ever. The fever that I had had was tertiary; it now became quaternary. It was at this same time that the Sr. Desnoyers, one of the sergeants among our troops—who had a wife and a child and who had gone down to New Orleans—came back up to our post and brought me a letter from my family and one from the minister, by which I saw the effect of my writing to denounce M. Le Blond de la Tour, who had done the same thing against me, as I said before.[44] The illustrious and fair-minded minister declared to me that he did not want to try to get to the bottom of the question of who was right, me or the Sr. de la Tour, but that we had complained a lot about one another. This letter that the minister had been so good as to send me had been intercepted and read by the royal lieutenant, which later caused me [130] much trouble, as I will explain later in this relation.

The Sr. de l'Estivant de la Perrière, who, as I've said, was ill, wanted to go down to the capital for a change of atmosphere. I asked the Sr. de Graves to allow me to use this occasion to go there myself. He granted it, and we embarked in a small boat filled with the belongings of the Sr. Poulain, the interpreter, and thus left this post.[45] Drifting down the Yazoo, we before long reached the Saint Louis River, which by its rapid current carried us to Natchez after just twenty-four hours on the water. From the fort at Yazoo to the one at Natchez is a good forty leagues. We stayed at Natchez for two days, at the end of which we embarked again and continued on our way until we were opposite Pointe Coupée, which is the halfway point from Natchez to the capital. We saw a large boat that was pulled up next to the shore. We approached it, as much to see what it was as to learn some news.

44. See above, original manuscript [106]. Dumont placed an asterisk next to Le Blond de la Tour's name and two more in the margin.

45. On Figure 6, and on his "Carte du fort Rozalie des Natchez françois," ANF, Cartes et plans, N III, no. 1² (Louisiane), Dumont identifies the house of the interpreter Poulain.

In going aboard, we learned that this boat was going up to the Illinois and was a party commanded by the Sr. de Tonty, who was a lieutenant. As soon as our pirogue was tied up alongside that boat, the Srs. de la Perrière and Poulain went on shore, but as for me, I stayed in the pirogue, trembling with fever. The Sr. de Tonty, knowing that I was there, came to the water's edge and beseeched me to get out, saying to better persuade me that there was a big fire on shore and that I could warm up there. So I stood up from where I was sitting in the pirogue, and while trying to climb on board their boat so as to reach land, I put my foot on the gunwale of our pirogue and a hand on the side of the boat, and then as the pirogue moved away, I was so weak that I let go with my hands [131] and fell headfirst between the two boats into the river. I had no idea where I was in this aquatic empire—I couldn't even say whether there are castles and trees down there—but I can say that it is a miracle I survived. Being naturally curious but not knowing how to swim, I drifted along, drinking more water than I was thirsty for.

I had no sooner fallen than the Sr. de Tonty, having moved quickly to empty out part of our pirogue, ordered some men into it to try to recover me if I appeared above water. But it was a fisherman's line, some sixty or sixty-five fathoms long, which had been thrown into the river to catch some fish, that my hands found instead. As I was drifting downstream, I had evidently floated into it and pulled it with me, as a fish does when he has struck and swallowed the hook. The soldier who was then on the bank believed that it was a catfish. He gave the line a strong jerk, as one does to try to set the hook, and then feeling that he had caught something, he was sure he had a catfish. But he pulled up only a whiskered person. It was in this manner that I was retrieved from the empire of the fish.

Once I was on land, they lifted and hung me head downwards to make me spit up the water. I had lost my wits, and they changed my linen and clothing without my being able to help them, just as one changes a baby. Then they tried setting me by the fire, where, after I swallowed a good cup of eau-de-vie followed immediately by one of strong broth, my warmth returned to me little by little. And as it is said that a good fright makes fevers go away, it truly did leave me that [132] day and did not return until the third day after. Because of my accident, we slept there that night, in the same camp as that party.

The next morning, we said farewell to the Sr. de Tonty. All his men embarked in their boat and we in our pirogue, and we took leave of each other, he to go upstream and we to descend. The fourth day of traveling brought us to New Orleans, now capital of all the country. It quite rightly carries this name, given its beauties: attractive and well-made buildings, made all of brick or half timber and half brick. The streets are laid out perfectly straight, along which each habitant is in possession of a lot twenty yards wide and forty deep. Each island or block is one hundred yards square. All the lots are enclosed by pilings sunk in the earth and pointed at the top, arranged and secured in a straight line. The houses are covered with shingles or with flat tiles. The streets are twenty-eight feet wide, reduced, however, to eighteen feet because all around the palisades that enclose the properties, there is a three-foot-wide walk that serves as a parapet, and around this parapet there is a drainage ditch, or little moat, two feet in width and at least eighteen inches deep.[46]

Next to the city, along the riverfront, a strong levee of earth has been built, as wide as the streets, to protect the city from being flooded by the waters of the river, which rises every year beginning on the twenty-fifth of March (Annunciation Day) up until the twenty-fourth of June, when it starts to subside. And it must be understood that, when [133][47] it is in flood, it rises above its bed by about three and a half feet and thus above the surrounding land, and it would flood the city if not for this earthen levee that has been built to prevent such a flood. Behind the levee, there is a large moat to receive the water that, when it is full, flows through one ditch and then another in the gutters of the streets, which carry it off behind the city into the cypress woods.[48]

The Place d'Armes is very handsome and spacious, ringed by large, square posts with rails running between them. Facing this square is the parish church run by the Very Reverend Capuchin Fathers. This church is built in the shape of a cross; at the top of the cross is the main altar, and the two arms of the cross are two chapels. It is finished with brick, although the roof of the nave is superbly done in wood. To one side of the church, on the right of the entrance, is the monastery of the Reverend Fathers. To the left is the town prison, and on the other side of the prison is the guardhouse for the soldiers. Moreover, on either side of the square are barracks for the troops, faced in brick, three stories tall, not including the attics. Behind these on the right, as you enter the square, are the warehouses, and on the left is the residence of the intendant, in which the council chambers are also

46. The dimensions of the New Orleans lots and squares are accurate; see also *Mémoires historiques*, II, 47–48.

47. Figure 7, the "Plan of New Orleans," was located at this spot in the original manuscript.

48. The annual floods of the Mississippi were much greater before the systems of locks and dams were built in the twentieth century.

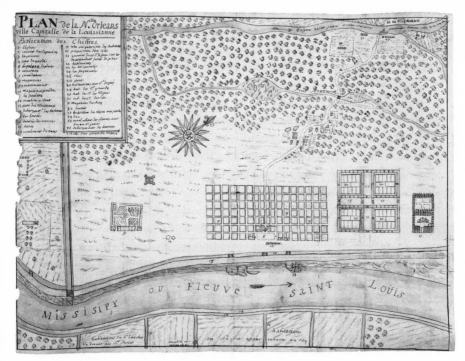

Figure 7. *Plan of New Orleans, Capital City of Louisiana.* VAULT oversize
Ayer MS 257, map no. 7. Courtesy The Newberry Library, Chicago

located. In a word, one can say that it is a city well laid out, well built, but
not at all fortified, as I will have occasion to mention later. The land, which
is lower than the waters of the river, is suitable for growing rice, which is a
species of grain from which, in that land, they even make bread. This plant
grows in the water, and it is only below the level of the river that it can be
[134] made to grow. The levee serves as a marketplace where the habitants
go to sell their wares; the market is held in front of the intendant's residence.[49]

It was, therefore, to this town that I came to try to regain my health. I
found lodgings with the Sr. Blancheron, who was a wigmaker. I was very ill
and approaching the end when, seeing that all the medicines and remedies

49. The Place d'Armes today is Jackson Square. The Company of the Indies granted religious authority over the city to the Capuchin Friars, but the Jesuits vied for control due
to their older mission of Indian conversion in the colonies. See Charles Edwards O'Neill,
Church and State in French Colonial Louisiana: Policy and Politics to 1732 (New Haven,
Conn., 1966), 137–144.

that I was taking were only making me weaker and weaker, I stopped taking them, and, finding myself more at ease without them and gaining a little bit of strength, I decided to follow my own prescription and risk my all. It had been nineteen months that this quaternary fever had been my constant companion.[50]

And so, one day around two o'clock in the afternoon, which was when the fever generally began to rise, I prepared myself for her visit by eating a good salad with a nice plate of curdled milk. I drank at least two bottles of Bordeaux wine. On top of that, I smoked three or four pipes of tobacco, and when I felt that the fever was about to hit me, I went to bed, periodically swallowing large mouthfuls of eau-de-vie. You might say that I did as the good father Noah did, but that saint was ignorant of the power of the liquor made from the juice of the plant that he himself had planted, whereas I did it consciously and on purpose as a reception for my companion the fever.[51] The fever had had no fear of the water; she was more concerned about the wine and eau-de-vie. There soon followed a furious combat in my body, between the fever and everything that I had ingested, that forced me to throw up everything and more until I was vomiting blood, and to further punish me, she hit me even harder for an entire forty-eight hours. I believe that I reached a truce with her, because at the end of that time, she left once and for all, and I have never had her again. Is that not a fine remedy? Anyone who finds it suitable is welcome to try it, but although it did not kill me, I [135] will not dare answer for others who try. So at last the fever left me, leaving behind a body very thin and deprived of all strength. But little by little, with good food, I was entirely cured. But this only preserved me for other battles more cruel than those I had fought against that fever.

50. This recurrent fever is presumably malaria, dating back to his illness in Lorient; see above, original manuscript [89–92].

51. See Genesis 9:20–21. Dumont personifies the fever as a woman, since the word *la fièvre* in French is feminine.

Chapter Four

QUARRELS IN NEW ORLEANS;

BATTLES AT NATCHEZ

OCTOBER 1722-AUGUST 1724

No sooner was I fully recovered than I went to see M. Le Blond de la Tour to report to him on my duties, for he was both the royal lieutenant and the director of the concessions of the minister and his illustrious associates. I say "concessions," plural, because there were three that had then begun to be established: ours at Yazoo; another at Natchez, one league distant from Fort Rosalie at a place called Terre Blanche, which had been founded by the Clairacs, as I explained above; the third at an Indian village called Chaouachas, five leagues downstream from the capital on the left bank; and, if one includes Le Petit Desert, that would make four. As I was paying my respects to M. Le Blond de la Tour, I asked him to give me an order to have the Company of the Indies pay the one year's service that was owed me, amounting to the sum of 480 livres. He replied that it was no longer to him that I should address myself to obtain such orders—it was to the commandant of the colony, and if I truly was owed for this service, I could seek payment by making a request to the Superior Council.[1] So I drew up a petition and presented it as he had told me to, explaining what was owed to me as well as the loss of my clothing and linen that I had suffered while in their service under M. de la Harpe on his voyage of exploration along the Arkansas River. But in recompense for my [136] service and as a salary for my troubles, the councillors, together with the commandant and the royal lieutenant, wrote at the bottom of my petition this reply: "The council has demoted the petitioner and orders him to report to the com-

---

1. See above, original manuscript [108], for more about the four concessions of the Le Blanc / Belle-Isle partnership. A list of salaries for officers in Louisiana dated September 28, 1726, confirms Dumont's annual salary as a "lieutenant réformé," or half-pay lieutenant, at 480 livres; see *FFLa*, I, 226. The Superior Council of Louisiana had been created as an advisory body to the governor and commissaire ordonnateur of the colony but came to function as a court and a de facto legislative body. See Jerry A. Micelle, "From Law Court to Local Government: Metamorphosis of the Superior Council of French Louisiana," *Louisiana History*, IX (1968), 85–107; Shannon Lee Dawdy, *Building the Devil's Empire: French Colonial New Orleans* (Chicago, 2008), 194–196.

pany of the Sr. de Richebourg as a cadet." This was the subterfuge of the commandant of the colony as well as the payback from the Sr. de la Tour for what he had read in the letter addressed to me from the minister, which had been intercepted by the director.[2] They no doubt believed I was going to obey them, but they miscalculated, for I forced them to see that it was not they who had made me an officer and that they had no right to take away my commission. But as I had explained how I had lost my clothing in their service, they did add at the bottom of the petition—perhaps in an effort to recompense me a little—that I need only address myself to the Sr. Bonnaud, the warehouse keeper, who would provide me with the uniform of a cadet, including the rifle and belt.

I believe my reader can well imagine that I, an officer of the king, honored to serve him as a half-pay lieutenant, did not fulfill these orders and that, satisfied by their reply and their good intentions for me, I walked back to my dwelling at my landlord's, ruminating along the way over what weapon I might use to force them to see the light. I was far away from France, from her courts of justice and my dear protectors. I was embroiled in a dispute with the commandant of the colony and with his royal lieutenant, both of whom were against me. This was enough to cause all my friends to abandon me, even the officers, who should have supported me and taken my plight to heart, insofar [137] as they were in the same boat and might foresee how the same thing could happen to them. But as truth always prevails, and having performed my duty like an honest man, even if I had some quarrel with these two men apart from my duties, this did not merit an affront such as they were trying to impose on me. Therefore, I armed myself with forbearance, and that afternoon, a soldier was sent to me from the Sr. Pailloux, major general, with orders to go speak with him. I asked the soldier who had given him this order. When he told me it was from the major, I said, "Very well, go tell him that when he sends someone fit to speak to me in my quality as an officer, I will come." He went back to deliver this message. Soon after came the sergeant on duty. I was then resting on my bed. I told him to go say to the major that I sent my regrets, but having arisen very early that morning, I needed to take an afternoon nap, and after that, I would have the honor of replying to his orders. Such was the first volley of their attack and the response to their summons.

I waited for a good hour and a half before going. At last, I reported. He asked me whether I had picked up the clothing the council had supplied for

2. See above, original manuscript [99, 102]. The director (and royal lieutenant) is Le Blond de la Tour.

me and stated that when the guard was mustered at four o'clock that afternoon, he was going to enroll me as a cadet in the first company. I replied to him: When an officer is demoted from his command over some troops, he is never ordered to serve in that same regiment, whether as a cadet or a soldier; and also, even though he was a major, I would not recognize him any more than the two commandants who had given him these orders, since they were not the ones who had made me [138] what I was, and they could not force me to do what they demanded of me. If my service was no longer required in this country, they could send me back to France. "Ah," said the Sr. Pailloux, "you are needed here, and you will not go home as you would wish. But," he continued, "come with me to see M. de la Tour."

I went there, where I found a large group waiting for the royal lieutenant to awake from his siesta so as to speak with him. As soon as we arrived, however, the major went into his room alone, woke him up, and told him that he had brought me. M. de la Tour no doubt remembered the exchange that we had had not long before, because he emerged from his room in his dressing gown, walked up to me, and said, "So, sir, you do not wish to take what you have been offered?"

I asked him, If he, as a royal lieutenant and commander of the engineers' brigade, were demoted to a simple officer, would he accept it willingly? He told me, "That could happen."

"You may have a heart so base, but mine is not like that," I said to him.

Then M. de la Tour, speaking to the major, told him in these exact words: "Take this scoundrel to prison."

I could not tolerate those words, and putting my hand on my sword, I drew it out of its scabbard and was about to run him through. He recoiled so suddenly that he fell to the ground. I was seized, but while being taken away, I said to him that such words were insulting to an honest man, which he was only in name, and that if I went to prison on his account, I would not come out when he wanted me to. But I was [139] taken there.[3]

It was a place they called "Pailloux's Box." It was a large square built, not out of bricks or lumber, but of huge beams some two feet thick, which were laid one atop another and secured on the outside by stout iron bars. Here I was to be detained, and my tongue could not restrain itself from hurling invectives against councillors and commanders such as these. At the end of four or five hours, I was brought the rations and the pay of a soldier, which I refused. I was paying for room and board at my landlady's, and she had

3. Dumont here and on the previous page uses the term "honeste homme." See Introduction, above.

not chased me out. At sunset, orders came regarding the prisoners, but, as I expected, I was not among those to be released. I would have to sleep there, and I leave it to you to imagine whether I was able to sleep at all, even though I had several comrades there with me. The next day, word was sent to me that if I wanted to return to duty at the rank of cadet, I would be released from prison. I rejected these propositions. Night came, and I was told to leave. I asked by whose order, and was told:

"On behalf of M. de la Tour."

I said, "Close the door of the prison. I will never leave on his orders, only on those of the commandant or of the council."

That night, I slept as if in my bed, seeing that if I was still a prisoner there, it was on my own volition. To be brief, I stayed there six days. During the night between the sixth and the seventh, a sergeant came to make an inspection of the prison. It might have been half past eleven. As he [140] entered, he began to say that he had information that we prisoners were going to try to escape. He then went to check on those in irons. We were all lying down on the floor. I had been given a mattress. I was thus the king of the prison, although I was the most recent arrival and would have to either pay my entrance fee or undergo the diamond dance. In short, everything was going smoothly.[4]

When the sergeant had finished his inspection of one side of the prison, he came to the other, and, astonished to see me in such a place, said to me, "What are you doing here, sir?" I asked him from what land had he come, that he did not know who I was.

"I arrived this morning from Mobile and went on guard duty this afternoon. I was told to watch over the prisoners, who were going to try to escape, but no one mentioned you, and so I did not know that you were among those detained." He spoke to me of one thing and another, and then, all of a sudden, "Parbleu! All is quiet. Let's drink a dram." He pulled out of his pocket a nice, big bottle, and we set about emptying it, having given a small shot to each prisoner and to the soldiers of his squad. They only drank a single shot, but we had two, the sergeant and I, and then we repeated the round several times, to the point where I felt the need to relieve myself.

I said, "Father Sans Souci," for this was his name, "I'm going to go two steps over there, to do what you cannot do for me, and I'll be right back."

"Go ahead," he said. "I'll wait for you."

4. Dumont's phrase "subir la dance du diamant," or, literally, "submit to the dance of the diamond," is an obscure expression that likely refers to an initiation dance or mock sword-fight with other prisoners.

I had no sooner gone out than he [141] closed the door. When I returned, he didn't want to open if for me, saying that he would never be blamed for it and that I would be better able to see to my affairs on the outside than from within. Thus, as you see, I had my liberty in spite of myself. I followed him to the guardhouse, where he returned my sword, and on the way back to my landlord's, I encountered two drunken soldiers involved in a fistfight. I called for the guard and consigned them to the same prison, pending new orders. They were not released until after I had sent a sergeant with a request for their pardon to the commandant, who, upon my request, granted them their liberty. I arrived back home, where they were not expecting me at that hour. They believed that I had escaped from the prison, but I enlightened them by explaining the manner of my release.

At last, I found myself on the outside. I had no food except what I could obtain on credit. I was owed money, but no one wanted to pay me, even as they tried to keep me alive by offering me the rations of a soldier. What to do? Two days passed after my leaving Pailloux's Box, time to reflect and consider what course to take to continue my defense and bring my enemies to reason. And the third day, at about half past noon, I took my gun and the papers granting my commissions and went to the home of the commandant, who was then living at his country house, some four hundred paces distant from the first houses on the edge of the town, because the seat of government had not yet been built at that time.[5] Since then, this country house has become the site of [142] the mission of the Reverend Father Jesuits, the commandant of the colony having granted it to them on terms he concluded with them. So I went to this house and, when I arrived, propped my gun up against a large, handsome orange tree. There were two rows of these, forming an avenue. From there, I passed to the door of the dining room, where he was at table. As soon as he saw me, he stood up with his napkin folded over his arm, came to me, and asked what I wanted. After greeting him, I explained that hunger had forced the wolves to come out of the forest, that lacking the food that was due to me, I begged him to give me some on credit, not simply as an officer serving in this country but also as one appointed by His Majesty. I showed him my commisson papers. He took the time to read them, after which he returned them to me and said:

"Go, sir, and address yourself to M. de la Tour."

I replied that it was not the royal lieutenant who was in command here; he was.

5. See Figure 7, where Bienville's residence is no. 9, "gouvernement," in the legend.

"That's not what you were saying before. But anyway, go to him, because I do not want to get involved in your business."

Then I spoke up and said to him, "Well, sir, you will get involved tomorrow, because I am going to blow out the brains of your royal lieutenant." And, taking my gun, I left.

He sent his nephew running after me. I thought this was to disarm me, and there would have been a showdown between us. To avoid him, I doubled my pace and soon arrived at the room of M. de la Tour. But, fortunately for him—and for me—I did not find him there. The commandant's nephew entered a moment after I did and grabbed me by the arms:

"What are you going to do, sir?"

"Kill my enemy, who has reduced me to despair."

[143] "Present your case tomorrow and you shall get what you need, I assure you." He fired my gun into the air and then returned it to me. I returned home and did what he had told me; I presented myself the next day to the council, which granted me rations, but only for two weeks, whereas for more than three months I had been living entirely on credit. I accepted this anyway and took the fortnight as a respite from all my pains and troubles.[6]

As soon as these rations were gone, I went back and again demanded what was legitimately mine, but my appeal received no response. At the bottom of my petition was written simply: "NOTHING." Even at my landlady's, I was beginning to be treated, not as a lodger, but as a liability, a man who was fed only out of a sense of charity. To go and borrow money without knowing how to repay it did not seem to me the right thing to do. I was desperate. I knew not with what wood to make an arrow. There was only one [idea] that came into my head, and I did not let it escape me.

This was the plan: one day, when all of the councillors, the commandant, and the royal lieutenant were meeting in the council chambers, I stationed myself in between the house where the meetings were held and the house of M. de la Tour. I hid myself so as not be seen. I had had a note drawn up, in a fine hand, stating these terms: "The Sr. Bonnaud, warehouse clerk, will deliver to the Sr. (giving my name) one barrel of flour, one jug of eau-de-vie, and one hundred twenty pounds of lard, which I will charge to his account when he returns this note to me. Signed [144] at New Orleans, this day, and

6. The nephew was likely Gilles-Augustin Payen de Noyan. The Superior Council at this time included Bienville, Le Blond de la Tour, Brulé, Fazende, Perry, Guilhet, Masclary, and Fleuriau; see "Lists of Officials," *MPA*, II, 4–7.

year, etc."[7] When M. de la Tour was returning home alone, after the council meeting had finished, I came out, stood in front of him, and presented him the invoice, along with a pen. I said that he would have to sign these orders or I would run him through with my sword. This fine sir was so surprised that he did not hesitate for a second; he signed it and gave it back to me.

As it was not yet 11:30 in the morning, I went straight to the warehouse with six soldiers, and the clerk, when presented with the invoice, delivered to me the contents, which my men carried back to my residence with my landlord, who was most agreeably surprised. At his house, as at any other home where someone arrives carrying gifts, I was greeted most cordially as soon as I entered and had paid the soldiers. Thus, through my bravery, I won a laurel of victory and had food to eat while waiting patiently for the fine day that would bring me total victory. It has to be assumed that M. de la Tour was so startled and surprised that he gave me the time to collect this bounty, for it was barely one o'clock when he sent to the Sr. Bonnaud an order to seize the invoice and not fulfill it. But the deed was done.

As news of this event spread through the town, everyone judged it according to his own imagination, but some of those whom I encountered told me I had done the right thing. The officers said so themselves and added that this was what was necessary [145] to maintain the dignity of an officer. This was what they said to me, but perhaps they would have said otherwise if they had been questioned by those two men. But at least my landlady now looked upon me as someone who paid for his room and board, being such a horn of plenty for her house. I passed the time by drawing or by going out hunting or fishing. I was no longer regarded as an officer but as an individual obliged to live, against his will, in that country.

About this time, it so happened that the Natchez Indians killed some of our Frenchmen and attacked some others. A pirogue hurried down from the post that we had there, to alert the commandant of the colony and ask him for reinforcements. The general sent the Sr. Pailloux, a major, with a detachment of soldiers to bring these enemies to reason and punish them for their hostilities. He had with him at least a hundred men, well armed. But the Indians, having foreknowledge of the arrival of the convoy and knowing perfectly well why it was coming, came to offer the calumet to the major,

7. Dumont's index note reads "25 pots," a liquid measure roughly equal to 25 quarts. In the French text, he refers to one "ancre" of eau-de-vie, using slang for "bouteille d'encre," a black, glass, wide-bottomed wine or liquor bottle common in this period, of a design similar to an ink bottle so as not to spill on shipboard. In reproducing the note he drew up for Le Blond de la Tour, he suppresses the date as well as his name.

who granted them peace on the condition that, to pay for their misdeeds, they would deliver to him a quantity of fowls, which were duly supplied. And after such a grand victory, won without the loss of a single man, he returned to New Orleans triumphant and crowned with laurels, bringing with him more than six hundred feathered slaves, who were shared between the commandant and his general of infantry. This led people everywhere to say in private that the two men had gone to wage the poultry war.[8]

But a peace such as that will not last for long. [146] Barely two months had passed after his triumph when, one day, the Sr. Guenot, director of M. de Kolly's Saint Catherines concession (formerly owned by the commissioner M. Hubert) was returning there from Fort Rosalie, just one league distant, riding on a fine horse. As he was passing a ravine, five shots were fired at him, one of which struck him in the collarbone. Luckily for him, he did not fall off his horse and so arrived wounded at the concession, where there was a very skilled surgeon who treated his wound. Only the next day did those at the fort learn of this attack and provocation, as well as of one against a poor soldier who was living alongside the road to Saint Catherines. During this night, the Indians stole everything he had in his little house and, not content with this, removed his scalp and killed him.[9]

As soon as we learned of these cruel acts, there was great unrest among our Frenchmen, who at that time were few in number. To augment their

8. The conflicts of 1722 and 1723 are called by historians the Second and Third Natchez Wars, with the first taking place in 1716. Dumont did not take part in the skirmishes in the autumn of 1722, which he briefly describes here. Dumont refers sarcastically to the chickens exacted as payment at a conference held on November 6, 1722, between Pailloux and the Natchez war chief Serpent Piqué; see "Present Given to the Natchez and Speech Made to Them by Order of Bienville," *MPA*, III, 327–329. The most complete narrative of the conflict is "Relation de la guerre des Natchez avec les François," ANOM, 04DFC 31. See also James F. Barnett, Jr., *The Natchez Indians: A History to 1735* (Jackson, Miss., 2007), 84–95; Arnaud Balvay, *La révolte des Natchez* (Paris, 2008), 101–105; and Patricia Dillon Woods, *French-Indian Relations on the Southern Frontier, 1699–1762* (Ann Arbor, Mich., 1980), 73–75.

9. This poor soldier is identified as "la Rochelle" in *Mémoires historiques*, II, 95. The attack on Guenot took place in October 1722 and hence did not follow but preceded the so-called poultry war. There was some debate over whether Guenot had provoked it. As Bienville reported to the Superior Council in August 1723: "This village was continuing to disturb the concession of St. Catherine against which they have seemed to be particularly angry since Sieur Guenot put an Honored Man of this village in chains even before there was any quarrel between the French and the Indians" (*MPA*, III, 360). Dumont and Le Mascrier wrote: "The Sr. Guenote brought this misfortune upon himself, or at least it was suspected that he had been attacked only after having caused some offense to some of the Natchez Indians living in the Pomme village" (*Mémoires historiques*, II, 94). See also *HJEFL*, 157; Balvay, *La révolte des Natchez*, 95–101; and *Histoire de la Louisiane*, I, 182.

ranks, they rushed a pirogue down to the capital to tell the commandant that in spite of the peace cemented by so many chickens, delivered in bondage into his hands and those of the major, the Indians had nonetheless declared war again. So the commandant of the colony, seeing that people were mocking him, not only among his own people but among the Indians as well, resolved to go there himself, and while everything was being prepared for this . . . [147][10] I vanquished my enemies. For there arrived in the country two royal commissioners to weigh matters and bring justice to those whose pleas were well founded. You may be persuaded that there were many petitioners.

The same day they arrived in the town, I went to see the royal lieutenant. He told me that I had done well by standing up for my rights, that everything he had done was only to test me, that he forgave me for all that I had done to him, and that he was going to write up an order to the warehouse for some cloth and linen for clothing for me, adding that in my current state I was not fit to go present myself to the royal commissioners, Messieurs de la Chaise and du Saunoy. I replied that I was much obliged for the pardon he was granting me, that what I had done was only to defend myself—for, having truth on my side, I could not give in—and that I thanked him again for the offer he was making, but during the time when I was most in need, I had not been paid and had been relieved of my commission without an honorable discharge. I was counting on getting the salary befitting my rank, even though I had not held that rank for some time. To this, he said that it was not possible, because one could not be paid for a job one has not done, and given that I had not performed this service, it would do no good to repeat myself. I replied that it was not he who would decide this matter, but I would bring it to their excellencies, the commissioners. Thus I did not hide from him that I would appeal his decision.[11]

10. The ellipsis is in the original manuscript.

11. The royal commissioners arrived on April 17, 1723. They held jointly the post of commissaire ordonnateur, the head of administration and supply with powers equal to that of the governor and military commandant, Bienville. They were sent by the directors of the Company of the Indies to investigate Bienville's leadership and audit the books of his expenses, and they carried out orders to seize his property and papers as soon as they arrived. Jean Pérault replaced Saunoy, who died shortly after he arrived (*HLF*, V, 42–46). La Chaise wrote two lengthy reports to the directors of the Company in June and October (see *MPA*, II, 294–391), in which he details the corruption of Bienville and his officers as well as the plight of soldiers and subordinate officers who were not adequately fed, clothed, or housed. He complained that Pailloux was not performing his duties and owed eight thousand livres to the Company for supplies he had embezzled, and that soldiers were held in prison for months

Finally, at the [148] end of a week, at about ten-thirty in the morning, I went to greet the two envoys of the king. Addressing me by name, M. du Saunoy said that he was very pleased to find me at New Orleans and that he had brought me a letter from my brother. After some general conversation, he asked me, out of curiosity, whether I was pleased to be in that country. I told him yes, if only there were not so many injustices and if persons who acted with zeal and honor in performing their duties were not given so much pain and despair. In a few words, I recounted to him the treatment that I had been subjected to. I had the honor of sharing their table, where we spoke of diverse matters. When I was ready to retire after dinner, they told me that I ought to present them a petition to expose the mistreatment done to me. I did so the very next day—the day on which the honorable commissioners held their public audience. After having their secretary read aloud the contents of my request, they had him put at the bottom of it: "So heard by the council of the colony," so that when the response came, orders would be issued to whoever was responsible. It was then forwarded to the Superior Council.

Unfortunately, not everyone agreed. They kept my petition for five days. Officers were ordered to appear before the council, to urge it to rule against me, but none would agree to do so. Finally, the council simply wrote that they had ruled against me because I was living like a vagrant. [149] But I proved the contrary to the fair-minded commissioners, who had not yet breathed in the air and the fashions of the land. And so, the council, as well as the commandant of the colony and M. de la Tour, were all found culpable, and I was restored to my rank as officer and paid not only what was owed me and what I had so often asked for without being able to obtain but also the arrears due from the day of my demotion to the day of this judgment.

A few days after, M. du Saunoy fell ill with cholera, and in five more days, we lost him. On his death bed, he recommended me to M. de la Chaise, who has made me feel that he has not forgotten this recommendation ever since and from whom I have received benefits on many occasions. The arrival of these inspectors was thus a blessing from heaven that came to me in my sad state of misery, for by their wisdom, justice was meted out to those who deserved it, and they made me victorious.[12]

---

without being brought to trial. In this context, it is easy to understand why La Chaise was sympathetic to Dumont's complaints.

12. Saunoy, also spelled "Sauvoir" or "Sauvoy," died on August 7, 1723. See Bernard Diron d'Artaguiette, "Journal of Diron Dartaguiette," in Newton D. Mereness, ed. and trans., *Travels in the American Colonies* (New York, 1916), 89. The most important corroboration

All I had to do now was resume my service, but as it had been recorded that my post was at Yazoo, when I went to the commandant's residence, he ordered me to return to my garrison and gave me a pirogue as well as six soldiers to paddle it. He told me to prepare for my voyage and to let him know as soon as I was ready. I prepared as quickly as I could. At the same time, there were eight large boats with soldiers being outfitted to go to war against

---

of Dumont's account here comes from La Chaise, who wrote in his report to the directors of the Company of the Indies in September 1723:

> I can not refrain, Gentlemen, from speaking to you of the crying injustice that Mr. De Bienville is doing here to Sieur Du Mont de Montigny, a half-pay lieutenant. This young man is recommended by Mr. Le Blanc. He has his commission as a half-pay lieutenant at Port Louis. You sent him here on the same footing. Two years ago, he was sent up to the Yazoos on the concession of Mr. Le Blanc. He remained there, and after he had returned to New Orleans all naked like a poor wretch Mr. De Bienville refused him not only provisions but also stockings and shoes. He has however been forced to grant him a soldier's suit since we have been here, but as for provisions and salary he has never been willing to let him have any so that all the petitions that he has presented to the Council have always been answered by a refusal. He told him that if he wished to become a soldier, he would have rations given to him, but that he must not count on being in the number of the officers because he was slovenly. This young man replied to him that if his salary were paid to him regularly in merchandise as was done for the other officers, he would dress more neatly. Since he was not able to obtain any provisions he presented to us a petition against Mr. De Bienville which we referred to him and we asked him to tell us the reasons that he had for not giving provisions to this officer. He said that he was not under obligation to tell us, and having spoken to him about it by word of mouth, all that he could tell us was that he was a bad fellow and slovenly. We told him that that was not a strong enough reason to strip a man of his position, that he was more thrifty than the others, that he owed nothing to the Company, that on the contrary it was in debt to him and that that was an indication of his prudence, that we had brought from France a commission of ensign in the infantry for him and [we asked] for what reason he had not delivered it to him. He made us no other reply than that he was unworthy of it. That led us to ask the said Montigny what reason could have brought Mr. De Bienville's hatred upon him. He told us the same thing as that which is contained in his memorandum enclosed herewith, which I do not repeat. This young man aroused pity in everybody since he was obliged to beg his bread. Sieur Du Puy Planchard, adjutant major, took him home with him through charity while waiting for his account to be drawn up. I drew it up for him, and there is due to him thereby as a balance of salary until April 17, 1723, one hundred and forty and some odd livres, and since that time four months more have passed and Mr. De Bienville is quite unwilling to do him justice or to have him paid the amount due him on his account or for the four months that have passed since or to have provisions given to him. That, Gentlemen, is how this young man is treated.

MPA, II, 337–338. The French text, from ANF, AC, Correspondance générale, C13A, VII, 36–37, is printed in Marc de Villiers du Terrage's introduction to Dumont's "Poème," 278–279. Dumont's memorandum has not been located.

the Natchez Indians. When I was ready, I presented myself to obtain leave from the [150] commandant. He told me that I was to go upstream with the convoy.

We departed New Orleans the twelfth of October, with the eight boats and more than twenty pirogues. We were nearly two thousand persons, and we arrived on the eve of All Saints' Day at the Natchez post. Everyone disembarked, and we officers—including our general, who was the commandant himself—went to stay at the residence of M. Berneval, where we supped together. After supper was finished and all had risen from the table, we took four or five pieces of linen, white and rather sheer, and cut them into strips, such as one makes for tourniquets, about two yards in length and four inches wide. These were distributed to all of our Indian allies to tie around their arms so that we might recognize them, either in attack or defense. When the armbands had all been distributed, we divided into two parties. One took the main trail and arrived, about an hour after midnight, at the Saint Catherines concession, which was under the direction of the Sr. de Longraye since M. Guenot had descended to New Orleans to be treated for his wound. The other party went by a narrower path across some prairies and small valleys. When all were reunited and had passed the night well guarded, at daylight, we marched out against our enemies—not in the direction of the Grand village, but in the direction of the Jenzenaques and Grigras, who were accused, word had it, of being the rebels and murderers of the French.[13]

We set out, as I've said, to go [151] surprise them. We marched, if you can call it that, in single file along narrow paths, and after progressing nearly

13. Dumont might have erroneously added a zero to the number of troops. Other sources list from 364 to 400 troops (including 200 native Americans) for this campaign. See "Punition des Natchéz en 1723," BNF, MSS fr. 2550, 3–10; Antoine-Simone Le Page du Pratz, "Le Page du Pratz à sa mère, février 1724," Chicago History Museum; and *Mémoires historiques*, II, 99. Research by Villiers du Terrage confirms Dumont's appointment: "The Council of the Marine, in a document dated October 17, 1722, named Dumont as an ensign in the company of Berneval at Natchez, where the latter was commandant of Fort Rosalie" (ANF, Marine, B4 I.37, fol. 413, cited in "Poème," 279). This assignment represented a demotion from his previous commission, and one can understand why Dumont would have omitted this fact, given his story of proud defiance in the previous pages. Native allies of the French included "the Tunicas . . . and some Yazoo Indians, and a party of Choctaws commanded by Red Shoe" (*Mémoires historiques*, II, 100). The Natchez were divided into factions, with some villages (including the Grand village led by Serpent Piqué) supporting the French and other villages supporting the English, who sent trade and envoys overland from the Carolinas. See Karl G. Lorenz, "A Re-examination of Natchez Sociopolitical Complexity: A View from the Grand Village and Beyond," *Southeastern Archaeology*, XVI, no. 2 (Winter 1997), 97–112.

two leagues, we found a cabin that was fortified, or manured, by which I mean that the walls had been filled in with a mixture of mud and straw. Along these walls, there were holes at regular intervals to serve as loopholes. Near the door of this house were four Indian women who were pounding maize to make it into flour. As soon as they saw so many armed Frenchmen approaching, they went back inside the house, closing the door and yelling and crying out. The men who were inside jump for their guns. They, three in number, begin firing at us through the loopholes. We answer with the same, against the walls of the house, after surrounding it.

An order had been given to set it on fire. The Sr. Tisserant, who was one of the warehouse keepers, wanted to do this, and to this end, he put his gun into the thatched roof of the house, which was not very high, and pulled the trigger. But it did not catch fire, even though the straw that made up the roof was very dry. His gun split open, either because, as he pushed it in there, dirt got into the breech, or because it was overcharged. A soldier named Couturier, who wanted to capture some Indian women for slaves, seeing that we were not making any progress, resolved to either achieve victory or die and, setting a course straight toward the cabin, reached the door, which was made only of canes set lengthwise and lashed together, and grabbed it at the top with the intention of pulling it off and throwing it aside. But an Indian who was inside, [152] seeing the Frenchman, let off a gunshot right through the door, and the ball entered his right side and pierced his heart. But as he fell, Couturier did not let go of the door and pulled it off so that it covered him as he lay on the ground.

The Sr. Mesplet immediately rushes inside the house. The Indian who had just fired the shot, being unable to reload, took the gun by the barrel and swung it at the head of the Sr. Mesplet with the intention of killing him. But luckily he did not land the blow, only barely grazing his ear. Despite receiving this wound, Mesplet grabbed the Indian by the throat, disarmed him, and held on. While the two were struggling, the Sr. Tisserant entered the cabin with several soldiers, who killed the two other Indians who were there. The warehouse keeper Tisserant, however, did not divert himself by battling with these enemies but went to look under the beds, where he made himself the master of four Indian women, who henceforth became his slaves. We tied their arms behind their backs and placed them among the supplies in the train of the army. After taking this cabin, the Sr. Mesplet, who was wounded, who had been the first to enter the house, and who had seized an Indian without doing him any harm, hoped to keep him as his slave, but our commandant would never consent to it. He ordered that this Indian prisoner be killed by one of his [153] own slaves and promised the Sr. Mesplet that the next Indian woman who might be taken would be for him.[14]

After this exploit, we continued on our way through the forests, always along very narrow trails. We covered a good league and a half and arrived at the Apple village, where our army paused in the central plaza. We found no one there; all the Indians had retreated into the woods. As we talked with one another, we came to realize that if the Indians had any sense, they would be able to take a French scalp easily, for they had only to go cut off that of Couturier, whom we had left lying on the ground next to the cabin. Our commandant ordered me to go to that house with eighteen soldiers and a sergeant and to set fire to it after placing the body of our French country-man inside. He told me to set fire to everything I thought appropriate.[15]

I obeyed, and we set off in a group of twenty to retrace our steps. We left the path several times, however, guided by a habitant of the area, who led us to Indian houses so that we could set them on fire. We marched as a battal-ion in square array, or as close as we could, fearful of being surprised. For, to be honest, two Indians in a forest like this could have easily destroyed us by firing at us, one after the other. But happily for us, we found no one and soon arrived at the cabin. We put the corpse of [154] our Frenchman inside the house and set fire to it as I had been ordered, and we turned back to re-join the army, which, as soon as we arrived, began marching back along the same path by which we had just come. It is true that, inside the houses our detachment of twenty men had torched, we found cooked maize and baked pumpkins (a kind of squash), which the soldiers gathered up and ate.

During all this time, the others were still marching, and they arrived at about six in the evening back at the Saint Catherines concession. So it went—the first expedition of our army. We rested for two days without marching, no doubt so that the enemy might have the time to either build fortifications or retreat. On the third day, the army was divided in two, and the first party, in which I was included, went toward the Grigra and Jen-zenaques villages, and the other along the same route as in the first ex-pedition, with the goal, it was announced, of surrounding or catching the

14. This episode involving Tisserant, Mesplet, and the death of Couturier is also told in *Mémoires historiques*, II, 103–106, and in "La guerre des Natchez en 1723," ANF, AC, 04DFC 30, fol. 5–8. In that document, Dumont de Montigny is identified as an ensign who, in early October, reached the Tunica village after traveling upstream toward Yazoo with six soldiers. He was redirected to join the troops attacking the Natchez and took part in the battle de-scribed here, but it is dated October 22–23.

15. Dumont's role here is not mentioned in *Mémoires historiques*, II, 105–106.

Indians if they tried to flee. But they had done so already, all except a few boasters who wanted to show more courage than the others.[16]

We did not bring any of the thunder of war against the Grand village of the Natchez Indians, which had for its chief Serpent Piqué, and so, as one might well imagine, others of this nation who had belonged to the villages we had just attacked had all taken refuge in the Grand village, since it was protected from our blows. The result was that our group had hardly marched three leagues from the place we had left and arrived in one of the hamlets of the Grigras, where there were several cabins, only to find nobody in them. There was a temple, too, and we showed no respect for it. We set fire to it just [155] as to the houses.[17]

A French habitant who was very thirsty, as were many others in the army, set off to look for water but could not find any. While searching all around, however, he found an old Indian woman, more than a hundred years of age, with completely white hair and scarcely able to walk. He took her all the same and led her back to the army. Our general had him ask her, through the Sr. Papin, the interpreter, where there might be some water. She told him. And once we had slaked our thirst and rested, because this old woman was not able to follow the army, our commandant, rather than show respect for her age, had her killed and scalped.[18]

After this expedition, we continued on our route, looking for enemies who had fled. As well as our army of Frenchmen, we had with us some of the Tunica nation, which, although not the most numerous, holds the advantage of courage and stout hearts and still remains a friend of the French, since no other nation has yet been able to win them over. It is true that they were then commanded by a chief who, although a savage, had been baptized

16. Archaeological evidence indicates that the Jenzenaques and Grigra (or Gris) villages were about fifteen kilometers to the northwest of Fort Rosalie, farther up Saint Catherine Creek from the Saint Catherines concession. The Pomme, or Apple, village was nearer. See map in Ian W. Brown, "An Archaeological Study of Culture Contact and Change in the Natchez Bluffs Region," in Patricia K. Galloway, ed., *La Salle and His Legacy: Frenchmen and Indians in the Lower Mississippi Valley* (Jackson, Miss., 1982), 180. English-language scholarship commonly uses "Apple" as a translation for the village of the "Pomme," but original sources sometimes refer to it as the "village de la pomme blanche" (as in ANF, AC, 04DFC 31), and it may properly refer to a tuber, or potato *(pomme de terre).*

17. In the *Mémoires historiques,* II, 102, Serpent Piqué is mentioned earlier in the sequence of events as having come to Fort Rosalie to beg forgiveness and insist that only the hostile villages of Gris, Jenzenaques, and Pomme were to blame for the revolt. There is some variation in chronology given in *Mémoires historiques,* II, 102. See also the anonymous "Punition des Natchéz en 1723," BNF, MSS fr. 2550.

18. See *Mémoires historiques,* II, 106–107.

along with all his family. But in spite of his good example, he had not been able—not with advice, persuasion, counsel, or even orders—to convince his village to follow him in this righteous path.[19]

While we were marching along as I have described, a rumor suddenly began to spread that there was a fortified cabin in which at least 120 enemy Indians were holed up, resolved on either victory or death. On this news, we marched in the direction where this cabin was said to be. As soon as we saw a village or a house, the drummers would start to beat a rat-a-tat, as much to alert the soldiers and others [156] to be ready as to strike terror into the enemy, which, on this occasion, perhaps had a strong effect because even if they had been there, as people were claiming, as soon as our army appeared near the cabin, we found no Indians there. The chief of the Tunicas was courageously marching in the lead, and having reached the top of the mound or high place where the cabin was, he saw below the mound an enemy Indian who was also a chief, called Petit Soleil. I should say that each saw the other, for they both took aim and fired at the same moment. The shot of our Indian friend threw his enemy to the ground, stone dead, but he himself was hit by a ball that passed through his mouth without breaking his teeth, making a hole in his right cheek, then struck the breech of his gun, and slid along it, finally making a wound in his collarbone. He, too, fell to the ground from the blow.

The news of the wound sustained by the chief quickly spread through our army, particularly among his subjects, our Indian allies, who believed that their chief was dead and that they would all have to die as well, for among the Indians it is a law that if the chief of their detachment is killed, all the men in it must either perish on the spot or else take the life of the enemy chief to avenge that of their own leader. M. Manadé, our head surgeon, bandaged the Tunica chief, both the wound on his cheek and on his shoulder, where he also put a preliminary splint. A portable litter was quickly made for four men to carry on their shoulders. The wounded chief was [157] laid upon it and carried away, surrounded by the rest of the army. We walked very gingerly for fear of tiring him, and because we had come more than five leagues from the concession, we could not reach it that afternoon, and night overtook us along the way.

We were forced to spend the night in a prairie encircled by large, tall trees. Each company separated from the others, and each lit a fire. I was in the company of Captain Deliette, and at eleven or twelve o'clock, we heard,

19. This long-standing French ally was Cahura-Joligo. See Jeffrey P. Brain, George Roth, and Willem J. de Reuse, "Tunica, Biloxi, and Ofo," in *HNAI*, 587–588.

at about one rifle's range distance, more than thirty shots fired. We all believed that it was an enemy attack. We jumped for our guns, which were all stacked together, and walked out in that direction. The movement we made caused others to do the same, and we were on the verge of firing at one another, but the commandant of the army, who knew well the Indians' tactics (as I will explain elsewhere), told us each to return to our encampments, which were simply the places we were sleeping on the grass around the fire. We did not sleep well there, not least because we had nothing to eat, and hunger, as soldiers say, was gnawing at our guts. For, during this entire war, the soldiers scarcely had enough to sustain them; they were only issued a little husked rice that they heated up in water or a bit of oil. And even that, they had to buy at their own expense.

When daylight came, we set out again, and around six o'clock in the morning, we arrived at the concession. We were very tired. The injured Tunica chief was taken to the French fort, where special care was given to him. Our army did not reach the fort until the next day, when the habitants also returned to their homes. At Saint Catherines, there remained only one large detachment of [158] soldiers, well armed, in order to protect the concession from the attacks of the Indians. While we waited for new marching orders, the Great Chief of the Grand village came to ask for peace for his rebellious subjects. It was granted to him, on the condition, however, that he deliver to us, within two days, the heads of two men. One was Vieux Poil, chief of the Grigra villages, and the other was that of a free negro who had established himself among the Indians and was said to have shown them not only how to build fortifications but even how to conduct their war parties. The chief of the Grand village, named Serpent Piqué, promised this and followed through on his promise, for the two heads were delivered up, and so this war was ended and the peace granted.[20]

The next day, I received orders to return to my garrison with the six soldiers who had been assigned to me. One more had been added while I was in that place, and yet, as rations for my men, I was given just fifteen

20. Dumont refers to Serpent Piqué here and elsewhere as the "Grand Chef du Grand Village," although other sources on the Natchez, such as Le Page du Pratz, refer to him as "Chef de Guerre," or war chief, and as a brother of the "Grand Soleil," or "Great Sun." See John R. Swanton, *Indian Tribes of the Lower Mississippi Valley and Adjacent Coast of the Gulf of Mexico* (Washington, D.C., 1911), 139. On the peace terms, see the "Deliberations of the Council of War, 23 November 1723," *MPA*, III, 385–387; *Mémoires historiques*, II, 111–113; "La guerre des Natchez en 1723," ANF, AC, 04DFC 30; and "Punition des Natchéz en 1723," BNF, MSS fr. 2550, 3–10, which provides the names of three warriors as "Tchictchiounata capine Ouyon," "Natcoa," and "Outchita Yoova."

pounds of husked rice. It would take me at least nine days for the journey. Although I explained that this was not enough, I nonetheless had to take it and depart, for I was then under the orders of the commandant of the country, since the news had come of the death of M. Le Blond de la Tour, royal lieutenant, commander of the engineers' brigade, and director of the concessions of the ministers. But how, then, was I to sustain my detachment, or myself, for that matter? I truly did want to reach my garrison, and under normal circumstances, it would take only nine days to get there, but I spent thirty-two days in making the trip. For lack of food, I was forced to follow the Indians of the Yazoo village that is located one league from our post there. They were returning upstream, having come down to Natchez to [159] smoke the calumet with the Great Chief of the French. These men make five leagues the first day, after which they rest for six or seven days in the same place in order to go hunting, and so, after I gave a present to their chief of one yard of limbourg cloth, along with a little vermilion, they supplied us with meat.[21]

At the end of the month of December, I arrived at our concession, where I found M. Petit de Livilliers serving as commandant of the place because the Sr. de Graves had been recalled to New Orleans on the orders of M. de la Chaise, the royal commissioner, to respond to grievances that the soldiers of the concession had made against him and his monopoly. He could not defend himself. He was ordered to pay ten francs to each soldier (they were seventy in number), as well as a fine of ten ecus to the executioner after receiving a reprimand from the prosecutor. In spite of the dishonor he received then, one might say that it was a stroke of luck for this captain to find himself punished in this manner, because a short time after, there arrived in our capital a ship from France that carried an order that this captain be sent to the minister with his hands and feet bound. But because he had pleaded guilty and paid this fine, he was exempted from making the voyage under that penalty, and he made it as a simple passenger, paying for his passage. The Sr. de Livilliers was delighted to see me. We were friends to the end.[22]

21. Evidently, Dumont's garrison was still based at Yazoo, even though he had been assigned to Berneval's company at Natchez for the expedition in the autumn of 1723. Le Blond de la Tour died on October 14, 1723, from what La Chaise described as "a lingering illness of sorrow" in a report to the directors of the Company of the Indies (*MPA*, II, 373).

22. La Chaise wrote a condemnation of Graves in his report to the directors of the Company of the Indies (*MPA*, II, 336) immediately preceding his defense of Dumont; see also Antoine-Simone Le Page du Pratz, "Extrait d'une relation de voyage que M. le Page du Pratz a fait de la nouvelle Orléans au Natchez," 10, Chicago History Museum. François Fleuriau

Toward the end of March, as food was beginning to run low at our garrison, I was ordered to go with six soldiers to the Arkansas, sixty leagues north, as I've said, of our post. I went to try to buy some from the Indians. [160] It took me only ten days to get there, and the Sr. de la Boulaye, in three days, was able to find among the Indians 120 quarts of corn kernels and 300 pots of oil, which were loaded into my boat, and I arrived back in my garrison three days later carrying food for the soldiers, which was distributed to them.

Nothing new happened at the post. Everyone performed his duties faithfully. There was only one company of fifty soldiers, two sergeants, the commandant, and myself. We had no chaplains with us and simply said our prayers twice a day in the chapel. Life was happy and peaceful there. Each had a plot of land nearby to work on and planted whatever he pleased. Everything grew there. I remained in command of the large garden, where I grew some beautiful, large heads of lettuce. We had plenty of bear's grease, but no vinegar. How could we serve it? We were obliged to put sorrel leaves into our lettuce salads, but without vinegar to season these herbs, you can imagine the taste. Finally, I thought to take some of the water, or rather syrup, from an oak tree, which, after sitting out in the sun, gave us a very strong, good vinegar—for cold foods, at least, as putting such a thing in hot dishes causes it to lose its edge. As well as the garden, I had another arpent of land that I cultivated on my own time. Thus I passed the time, either drawing, writing, or working the soil, and every so often leading the maneuvers of our troops.

One day, it was only by the grace of heaven that I escaped from a grave peril. [161] That afternoon, toward sunset, I was out walking in the woods and reading a book, and while sitting near a ravine filled with canes, I saw a deer that was rooting about, looking for a place to make its bed. I withdrew, thinking that I could easily find it in the same spot the next morning. I decided to go back, and during supper, I could not prevent myself from saying to the Sr. de Livilliers that the next morning I would bring him a deer. He offered to come with me, and I thanked him, saying that it wasn't necessary. "I'll wager you," he said, "that you won't bring back anything." I bet ten ecus against him.

I could not sleep that night, and at the first light of dawn, having loaded my gun, drunk a dram (which is a shot of eau-de-vie), and eaten a piece of

---

was the *procureur du roi,* or chief prosecutor, for the colony at this time. The minister of the marine referred to was Jean-Frédéric Phélypeaux, comte de Maurepas.

bread, I went back to the spot where I had seen the animal the day before. I looked all over, but I did not find it. I did see, on a large tree, a plump eaglet. I was approaching little by little to get within range for a shot when an Indian, passing to one side of me, said, "Ichela, mongoula," which means, "There it is, my friend."

I replied, "Ÿama," or "Yes."

At this, I did not turn my head, my eyes being fixed on my prey, and when I was about to take aim, having raised my gun for the shot, the Indian, who was behind me, tried to strike a blow with a club made of wood—what we call a tomahawk. But instead of hitting me on the ear, luckily for me, he hit the breech of my gun, which by this force sent me falling to the ground. Then the Indian let out a cry known as the death cry, [162] and grabbing a butcher's knife, he put himself in position to take my scalp. But the cry that he made woke me up with a start, and grabbing him above the heel, I pulled him toward me, and with my right hand, I gave him a blow to the stomach, pushing him back. This made him fall over backward and gave me the time to get up and retrieve my gun (which, although it was cocked, had not gone off when it fell from my hands), and I fired it straight at his heart. With his own knife, I then took his scalp, and without waiting another moment, I quickly set out on the path back and reached the fort more dead than alive, bringing, instead of the deer, a scalp of a man that I knew only as my enemy.

After dinner, however, our commandant sent a man to fetch the chief of the Yazoo Indians, and having been shown the scalp, the chief told him that it was one of the Chis, of a group of fifteen or so that had been scouting the area around our fort, and that I was very lucky to have been attacked by only one. The next day, the Yazoo Indians came to give me a calumet congratulating me for my victory. My word—as long as I remained there, I no longer wanted to go hunting so early in the morning, and least of all alone. When we went hunting, there were seven or eight of us.[23]

Overall, not much happened during the time I was at this garrison, which was not a long time, because, even though I had performed my [163] duties as an officer with exactitude and even though M. de la Tour was dead, the commandant of the country was still quietly pursuing me. Toward the month of June, I received a letter by some *voyageurs* who were going to the Arkansas and who stopped off at our post to deliver it to me. The letter was

23. The Chickasaws, or "Chicaças," who inhabited what is now North and Central Mississippi, were the enemies of the French Louisiana colonists throughout most of the eighteenth century and were referred to as "Chis" for short.

even signed by the directors in France.[24] I bought a small pirogue from the Indians, loaded my trunk, many shallots that I had grown myself (there were at least three barrels of them), and twenty-odd pots of bear's grease that I had traded for from the Indians, and, having taken leave of the Sr. Petit de Livilliers, whom I was leaving alone at the post, I set off alone in my boat and floated down to Natchez, where I found M. Deliette, who was still the commandant there as well as director of the concession of the illustrious Belle-Isle. For, by then, my dear protector, the just and worthy minister (I refer to Mgr. Le Blanc), was dead.[25] When I had greeted M. Deliette and told him that I had received my letter of discharge and had shown it to him, he said to me, "This letter was certainly not intended for you, and there is some snake in the grass here."

He gave me lodging for three days, and he gave me many letters to carry, both for the commandant general and for M. de la Chaise, who, from royal commissioner, had become the ordonnateur of the Company of the Indies. There were also several letters for other officers and individuals. He also asked me to deliver as a present to the commissioner a live bear cub, as well as a large package of maidenhair fern, and to assist me in paddling my pirogue, he had [164] a young soldier embark with me. After giving the commandant my thanks and a warm farewell, I set off with my traveling assistant.[26]

We thus left Natchez and floated day and night to get ourselves to New Orleans. We passed by the Tunica Indian villages, and when we were out in the middle of the river, I was lying on top of the pile of baggage I had in the boat, covered with the bears' skins that held it down, and fell asleep. But

24. Apparently, Bienville's writings against Dumont had prevailed over La Chaise's efforts to protect him. The Company wrote to Bienville on October 21, 1723: "Being informed of the bad conduct of the Sr. Dumont de Montigny, half-pay lieutenant in the troops stationed in Louisiana, we order the Sr. de Bienville to demote the Sr. Dumont de Montigny, depriving him of his command and forbidding the troops from now on to recognize him as an officer" (ANF, AC, B, XLIII, 355, cited in "Poème," 279).

25. Dumont was in error here, as Claude Le Blanc died May 19, 1728. Deliette had replaced Berneval as commandant at Natchez in the interim, and in 1725, Deliette was appointed commandant at Illinois.

26. La Chaise had shared this appointment with Saunoy and did not actually hold it alone until July 11, 1725; see "Lists of Officials," *MPA*, II, 6. Dumont calls the herb "capillaire," which, in Europe, generally refers to the spleenwort, or maidenhair, fern. On two of his maps of Natchez, Dumont identified the spot, on the banks of the Mississippi, where "excelant Capilaire" could be found. See "Carte du fort Rozalie des Natchez françois," ANF, Cartes et plans, N III, no. 1² (Louisiane); "Fort Rozalie des Natchez eloigné de la N.lle Orleans de cent lieües" SHD, Château de Vincennes, État-Major, 7C 211.

either I rolled over or the pirogue started to tip to one side, for I fell into the river and found myself, for a second time, in that aquatic empire. This time there was no fisherman's line, for it happened right in the middle of the river, where there was a strong current.[27]

So I fell in, and while I was sinking to the bottom, or at least under the surface, the pirogue drifted away. The surprised soldier, who knew only how to paddle and not how to steer, could not give me any help. I was moving along with the force of the water, which swept me off and carried me toward a bend where the current is strongest. As I surfaced for the second time above the water, I found that my head came up between two branches of a tree that was drifting there, and with my arms spread out like a cross, I grabbed the two branches. With the help of God and his protection, I was able to get myself astride the large trunk of the tree. Holding on to its roots, I drifted down on top of it. My boat was farther downstream, and I began crying out to the soldier, called La Jeunesse, to try to paddle back upstream, so as to [165] let the tree pass in front of the pirogue. After he had done this, I told him to let the tree come up against the stern of the boat, calling to him to paddle first on one side, then on the other, as the tree approached. This he did, though with great difficulty, and I thus was able to reboard, leaving the tree that had served me as a vessel, much as the prophet Jonah, I have no doubt, bade farewell to the whale that had rescued him in the sea. Luckily for me, I was clad only in my shirt and a pair of light knickers, with no shoes on my feet. It was about the twenty-sixth of July, and it was very hot. This accident only seemed like a bath to me, although an involuntary one, and upon climbing back onto my boat, I was scarcely wet.

The next day, we at last arrived at Pointe Coupée, where a few farms were already getting started. I arrived at one belonging to a man named bonhomme Ducuir, who received me graciously and who appeared morti- fied at the accident that had happened to me. I stayed there the rest of that day until the thirtieth, when we left this place to continue our descent. The thirty-first, at four in the afternoon, when we were in the middle of the river, just within view of Baton Rouge (the concession of M. Diron d'Artaguiette), the sky darkened all of a sudden, and there rose up a furious wind that made the river appear like the ocean, with mountainous waves; we found ourselves in danger, my traveling associate and I, of both drinking from the same cup.

It was a hurricane.[28] We needed all the strength in the world just to

27. The first time he had fallen in the Mississippi was above, original manuscript [131].
28. Dumont uses the word "ouraguan," or "hurricane," although no other documents from

reach the shore on our left, facing downstream. When we came [166] near it, we had to throw ourselves into the water up to our shoulders and pull our boat, steadying it so that the waves would not throw it onto the land. But this could not be done without great effort. We reached a small eddy that seemed to have been made expressly to shelter us from these mountains of water. We set up our berre on shore, on a small elevation we found. Our pirogue being made fast to a large tree root, there fell from the sky a torrent of water, and we both placed ourselves under our cloth house, where we got soaked just as if we had not been covered at all. At about nine in the evening, the wind redoubled its force. I had tied the little bear cub to the branch of a tree with a thick rope, and although we were now on land, we were afraid of being crushed because trees were falling down all around us, making the earth shake and making us quite afraid. If I had died on that day, my years would have come out evenly, because it was my birthday, being that I was born on that date in the year 1696.

We were two voyagers, but in this weather, we were more like two devout hermits who spent all their time praying to God to preserve them from danger. We addressed ourselves to the Mother of Fishermen, singing amid these vast forests litanies in Her honor.[29] It was then that we came to the brink of being crushed, for we had barely time to leave our little cave under the tent and stand back, one of us on one side of it, one on the other, when the tree next to us began to bend, crack, and fall into the river. We could not see anything except by the glow of the lightning that flashed from time to time, [167] and I will admit in all sincerity that although I had twice fallen into the water, I had never felt so much fear as I did at that time. Perhaps it was also that, because I had been rescued after the accident in the water, the one that I faced now appeared to me all the more vivid, in imitation of Saint Paul the Apostle after his shipwreck, when he was bitten on the hand by a snake on the island of Malta, and the islanders believed that he must be a great sinner because God had preserved him at sea only to torment him on land. We looked upon ourselves in the same manner, since we had been endangered both at sea and on land.[30]

Finally, toward four in the morning, the weather calmed, and as night gave way to day, I approached the shore of the water where my pirogue was, and what did I find? It was sitting on the bottom, swamped with water. The

---

Louisiana could be found that report a hurricane on this date. A severe thunderstorm or tornado is more likely.

29. The Virgin Mary, referred to above as the "Queen of the Sea."

30. See Acts 28:1–6.

packages of maidenhair ferns, the shallots, the garlic, my chest with the letters inside, everything that I had, all was out of the boat, some of it on the bank, the rest floating on the water in the eddy. I had taken the precaution, when we reached the shore, of putting my jugs of oil on the height of the bluff or bank. I ought to have found them there, but no. The tree, which was a large bald cypress, had shaken the ground as it fell, broken the earth apart, and sent the boat sliding into the river, taking with it my jugs, except for two that were found under the water, caught among some tree roots there that had not been visible when we had first landed. What is more, our little bear, who, as I've said, had been entrusted to me to give as a gift, had been crushed [168] by a branch of the tree. We had to pull up our pirogue, empty it out, and, having collected all that Providence had left me with, I ripped off what I could of our tent cloth, a part of which was pinned under the trunk of the tree. I retrieved from the water a few of the shallots, garlic, and ferns and placed in the boat my two poor jugs of oil, and we set sail again. We did not forget our poor, crushed friend, for we needed something to fill our stomachs, which were not doing very well. We had only one piece of cornmeal biscuit, the rest having gone to feed the fish. For fear of losing the only sustenance we had, we ate him with the best appetite in the world, although we had not slept all night long.

It was at least eight in the morning when we embarked. We had only three-quarters of a league to go to reach Baton Rouge. We thought it best not to travel in the main channel but coasted along the edge of the river, where, from time to time, we stopped to retrieve some belongings that we found caught up in some of the willow trees growing in the water. I had the good fortune to find my chest, and we had a lot of trouble loading it into the boat because, although it was not large, it was very heavy, everything in it being soaked with water. Lifting it on board nearly caused our pirogue to capsize, that is, to turn upside down. Finally, we arrived at the concession, but what did we find there? The houses overturned, the storehouse broken up and destroyed, a large part of it in the [169] river, the pirogues that were still there swamped, and what is more, not a single habitant. They all had retreated into the prairies. We found only one house that was upright and had received no damage, and as you might well imagine, we entered it. We found some bread in the oven and some cooked pumpkin, which served to restore our strength for reloading what we could save from our shipwreck, both aquatic and terrestrial.

Toward one in the afternoon, the habitants of the concession returned. They were like ghosts, but after we had greeted one another, we rejoiced together that we still found ourselves among the living. I unloaded my chest, and after opening it, I found the packets of letters. But their addresses were washed off. Although I tried to dry them out, it was impossible to know to whom they were addressed—nothing was visible. I had no curiosity to open them. So I drew up a deposition in front of the habitants, who signed it, specifying the quantity of letters, after which I burned them, because I was quite aware that the commandant general and the royal commissioner dealt with one another only out of political necessity, and if I had the misfortune to deliver a letter intended for one to the other, it might cause me more grief than I would have in not delivering them at all.

I stayed seven days at this concession, not wanting to travel anymore in my boat, which had been the subject of so many accidents. When a large pirogue coming from the Arkansas landed at the post, we embarked in that and arrived all together on the eleventh of August. There was a vessel named the *Profond,* commanded by the Sr. Amelot, which was supposed to be departing immediately for France. [170] As I had been demoted and, in effect, discharged, I asked for passage on it. This was granted me, and after settling my debts and bidding farewell to my friends, I embarked on this ship on the eighteenth of August to return to my homeland and there enjoy more peace and happiness. But the decrees of heaven are quite different from the ideas of men, and the proverb is quite accurate that says, Whereas man proposes, God disposes.

There I was, on board a good ship to return to France; we were leaving New Orleans and floating down the river. We arrived at La Balize, which is a post that serves as a gateway to the river, built on a spot that is no more than a bundle of large trees—what's known in this land as a logjam—upon which M. Pauger, the royal engineer, had built a fort of stone and palisades, which is furnished with good cannons. I will describe it further elsewhere. Anyway, it is at the entrance of the river, to demonstrate, by raising the flag for vessels coming from France, that this is French territory, and also to serve as a defense if necessary, should an enemy try to enter the river. On the twenty-fifth of August (the king's name day), after saluting the post with five cannon-shots, we set sail with fond hopes of seeing our homeland once more. But we would not enjoy that comfort this time, least of all myself.[31]

31. August 25 is Saint Louis's Day, for Saint Louis of France (1226–1270).

Chapter Five

PASCAGOULA; NATCHEZ:

AUGUST 1724-SEPTEMBER 1729

[171] So we departed, as I just indicated, on the twenty-fifth of August, the Feast of Saint Louis.[1] We had the best weather in the world going through the Bahamas Channel. For three days running, it seemed that we were lucky and that all was going as we wished. It even appeared as if no vessel had ever made such quick progress as ours. But alas, we were mistaken. The sixth of September, we were struck by a gust of wind so furious that it broke our mainmast in two. This meant that the Sr. Amelot was obliged to declare the ship disabled, and after holding a council, he determined that we would return to New Biloxi to get a new mast made. We had with us as passengers—along with myself—M. Delorme, who had been the director for the Company in New Orleans, M. Fleuriau, the chief crown prosecutor, and many others. Most significant, however, in terms of an expert on ocean voyages, was Master Drouard, a famous builder of royal vessels, who was not shy about saying: first, that the broken mast could only have happened because of some malfeasance; and second, that although it was broken, it would make more sense to jury-rig it so as to make it capable of carrying us to France, and that it was not necessary to return; he said he would stake his reputation on this. But all this did not change a thing. We reversed course and arrived on the fourteenth of the month at New Biloxi, where there were then only fifteen men in the garrison, commanded by M. le chevalier de Louboëy, as well as some habitants and warehouse keepers. All the passengers disembarked and were obliged to nourish themselves at their own expense in this place. We stayed there until the twenty-second, when we prepared to set sail again for the port we had hoped to reach. We had good weather and good wind. We were navigating across the aquatic empire, [172] and it appeared as though the god Neptune was favoring our voyage.[2]

---

1. Index note: "1723," although these events actually took place in 1724.

2. Delorme submitted a petition to the Superior Council on August 18, asking permission to take a young African servant with him back to France, so the *Profond* did not leave until after that date; see "Minutes of the Superior Council of Louisiana," *MPA*, III, 422.

However, around the fifteenth of October, we began to be surprised that we had not yet spied land, either on the side toward Cabo San Antonio or the shore near Havana or Matanzas, or that of Florida. We asked the Sr. Amelot where he believed we might be, but he did not want to give us any answer. Everyone was talking of the possibility that we had passed the cape and gone through the channel during the night and that we must be close to the Azores bank. We had been sailing with good winds and making good progress, and on the thirty-first of October, at daybreak, we spied land. But the closer we approached, the less we recognized it. Finally, we saw, to our great disappointment, that we were at Ship Island, two leagues from New Biloxi, where we had set out on the twenty-second of the previous month.[3]

A boat came out to meet us. We took this opportunity, the passengers of the captain's table, including myself, who were all weary of the sea, to put our chests into the boat and leave the ship, making a vow never to board it again. We set sail and on the third of November found ourselves back in New Orleans. Of all the passengers, it was only M. Delorme who did not want to leave the ship. But it has since become known that it was for his profit that we had taken this promenade around the sea, that he had forced the men of the Superior Council, along with myself and the others, to turn back as we had done. Into that vessel, the *Profond*, had been shipped for France many ingots of silver, taken from the mines of Illinois, five hundred leagues from the capital. These were the first produced by the Sr. Renaud, chief of the miners, who, by virtue [173] of his labor, had made these ingots, which were supposed to go to France but which never arrived, as I will explain in what follows. Since they were in the *Profond*, they were taken out, and instead of the ship's going straight to France, as it should have, it was forced to go to La Caye Saint-Louis. This had, by then, become the depot of the Company for resupplying ships coming from France to Louisiana, replacing the previous stopover, which had formerly been made in Cap François, Saint-Domingue. There was a ship named the *Bellone* then being outfitted for France, and Monsieur the commandant of the country was supposed to sail in it.[4]

3. The "Minutes of the Superior Council of Louisiana" for November 10, 1724, mention that the council received a letter from the Sieur Amelot, dated November 5, from Ship Island, explaining that the *Profond* had returned after thirty-nine days of contrary winds, during which time it had been driven near Cabo Catoche, at the tip of the Yucatán Peninsula. There is no mention in the minutes of a dismasting—only that the ship returned because of a shortage of provisions and the illness of the crew. See *MPA,* III, 444; *HLF,* V, 34.

4. Philippe Renault (or Renaud, as Dumont spells it) developed a mine along the Meramec River, just south of the Missouri River, that produced lead and a small amount of silver.

The Sr. Amelot thus set out once again for his destination. This time, he was not so slow in reaching the channel; before he could pass through it, however, he put in at Havana, saying that his supply of water was leaking into the bilge—but it was really to retrieve M. Delorme's treasure of piastres, which was lodged with a Spanish banker. And after taking on water in the form of silver, he set sail again, went back through the channel, and arrived at La Caye Saint-Louis, where he stayed almost three months. After that, he departed, but rather than going to some French port, he put ashore in Ireland in order to conceal the knowledge of the piastres that he was carrying and that he returned to the Sr. Delorme, who paid him as promised. The other passengers continued on to France at their own expense. For this affair, which must have become known, the Sr. Amelot was relieved of his duties. I saw him later in that country, for he returned there in 1733, hoping to find protection and support from the Sr. Delorme, who was also returning there but who was not so fortunate as to arrive, for he died a few days before reaching land. My reader may well understand, by what I have just related, that there is a lot of deceit in the world and that men think little of harming their neighbors [174] when it is a matter of adding to their wealth.[5]

But let us come back to our story. I found myself, upon my return, alone in that country, without a job or a skill to earn my living and with very little money to support myself.[6] How, then, was I to survive? I can say truthfully that if I had gone to live among the Indians, I would have learned from them what charity means, for although they are not Christians, charity is better practiced among those barbarians than it is in the centers of religion. Ultimately, I did not do this. The great God, who reigns over all, preserved

---

His efforts were not profitable, however; see *HLF,* V, 441–445. In 1724, there was a dispute between Bienville and La Chaise over why Bienville did not set sail for France more promptly after his recall became official in April; see "Minutes of the Superior Council of Louisiana," *MPA,* III, 454–456.

5. La Caye Saint-Louis, or simply "La Caye," was located on the north coast of Saint-Domingue, present-day Haïti. Delorme was director of the Company of the Indies in Louisiana until the royal commissioners removed him in 1723 and accused him of corruption and malfeasance. The "Minutes of the Superior Council of Louisiana" for November 10 and 14 (*MPA,* III, 444–445) confirm that "three boxes of piastres and silver bullion" from the *Profond* were transferred to the *Bellone* for shipment to France and that the *Profond* then sailed to La Caye. There is no confirmation that the *Profond* landed in Ireland, but the story of Delorme and the *Profond* suggests that silver was more likely acquired through illicit trade with Mexico than from mines in the Illinois country; see *HLF,* V, 131.

6. A list of officers from September 1724 includes Dumont at the rank of half-pay lieutenant, assigned to Natchez; see *FFLa,* I, 160–162, and below, original manuscript [183].

me from famine and from the shame of being destitute. I had offered my services in France to M. François Dugué, a habitant on the Bayou Saint John, who was supposed to make the crossing in the *Profond* with me and had likewise returned with me. I had helped put his affairs in order before leaving and thereby earned his respect and friendship. We were, in a sense, like one person, although two, and when we arrived at the Bayou Saint John, one league from New Orleans, he did not want to let me go. Since he had his farm and houses in that place, he not only gave me a room there but offered me his table and his purse, asking only that I manage his farm, his expenses, and his debts and accounts. In a word, from an officer commissioned by His Majesty, an officer of the Company and the concessions, and even a beneficiary of the Company, I now became the secretary, the confidant, and the manager of a private farm. What change is man not subject to in his pilgrimages on this earth?

I very much enjoyed gardening and engaged in this activity whenever I had spare time. I managed the slaves, and as he owned some boats that went on daily trips carrying supplies to the city, [175] and as they were not always paid every time for their sales, I wrote up the names of those who owed. He quickly perceived the advantage of knowing how to write, an art of which he was ignorant, as well as reading. But with some goodwill on his part and with my persistence to prove to him that the favor he was doing me was not expended upon an ingrate, I taught him in four months not only how to read and write but also the four operations of arithmetic. This is how I passed my time.

Toward the month of November,[7] I was asked by the Sr. Delagarde to come to his concession, which was at Pascagoula, not only to put his affairs and accounts in order but also to design some projects that he wanted to build. The Sr. Dugué suggested me to him. As I wanted to be of service to this concessionaire, and as I had only briefly passed through this place and wanted to see the country, I accepted his offer of employment. We embarked in the Sr. Delagarde's boat, which was at New Orleans. The Sr. baron d'Hombourg, captain and commander of a Swiss regiment, went with me. Having been discharged and not wanting to go over to France because he hoped to be reappointed, he was going to that concession to wait for further news. So the two of us departed with a woman who was going to Biloxi to join her husband. We had for boatmen some negroes of the concession and, for captain, a Frenchman. We crossed Lac Saint-Louis, formerly known as Pontchartrain. It is very dangerous in certain winds. After crossing it, we

7. Index note: "1724."

reached the shore of the mainland, but just as we were pulling in, we were hit by a sharp wind from the north that reversed our course, and we went aground on a sandbank facing [176] the mainland and right next to Round Island. We were forced to go into the canoe and put ashore on this island, where we stayed for two weeks, without much food and sustaining ourselves only on oysters and raccoons and a few times on the meat of wild pigs, which are numerous there. We would have expired if not for the freshwater that we were lucky to find there.[8]

Finally, at the end of fifteen days, the wind changed. From the northerly that had been blowing, it shifted around to the south, which caused the waters in the sea to surge slightly toward the coast, giving us enough to make our boat float free. We embarked as quickly as we could, and taking advantage of the favorable wind, we quickly reached land on the New Biloxi side. No sooner had we arrived than the wind became contrary again. We had to set the anchor. We went ashore and we started a fire, for it was cold. It was the twenty-third of December. We slept on the sand around the flame. During the night, the baron proposed that I go with him by land to New Biloxi to get some food for our crew, who had none, although they had many barrels of flour from France that were being carried to the concession. I was more than willing to make the trip.

There were still a good two and a half leagues to go. We left at daybreak with his young negro, who carried a flagon filled with eau-de-vie. We followed right along the oceanfront. We saw nothing of note until, toward the end, we came to a large cougar sitting like a cat on its rear end and looking at us.[9] I had with me a little dog that followed me around. As soon as he perceived the cougar, he ran toward it. [177] We then had a kind of theater, as this ferocious animal, seeing such a small creature as the dog in front of him, did not at all become angry toward it, and for more than a quarter of an hour, they played together, making great leaps on top of one another, the cougar slapping him with soft paws just as a cat does. They lay down, hugged each other, rolled around in the sand, and even played dead a few

8. Dumont's "Map of the Pascagoula River," BNF, Ge DD–2987 (8818 B), includes a detailed inset portrait of Delagarde's plantation. Round Island, directly off the mouth of the Pascagoula River, is shown on that map and also on one of Dumont's manuscript maps in the Delisle sketchbooks, also entitled "Map of the Pascagoula River" (ANF, Cartes et plans, 6 JJ 75, collection Delisle, pièce 262). Lac Saint-Louis is today called Lake Pontchartrain and is actually a brackish bay.

9. Dumont calls this cat a "tigre." It was probably a Florida panther (*Puma concolor coryi*), a subspecies that once ranged the Gulf Coast though today is nearly extinct in its last remaining habitat in the Florida Everglades.

times. One might say that the furious, ferocious, and wild beast appeared to us to have all the honor and civility of a member of the royal house of its nation. After much playing on the shore, the animal went into the woods and the dog followed behind him. The first climbed up a large pine tree using its claws and stretched out on one of the branches, and from there was making faces at the little dog, which by its barking down below was no doubt imploring him to descend. Then I approached the tree and, disregarding the Sr. Baron, took aim and fired, bringing the cougar down as quickly as he had climbed up. He was no sooner on the ground than the little dog approached, no doubt to play some more, and the cougar grabbed him with his paws and tore him to pieces. This was the death of the cougar and of my poor little dog. Not having the strength to carry it, I left the corpse there.

A soldier from the garrison at New Biloxi who had gone hunting to get something for the feast of midnight Mass, having heard the noise of the gunshot I had fired, came toward the sound. I recognized him, and we ran toward him. We told him of our disaster. He took out of his backpack a large piece of bread and gave it to me. I broke it into three parts: one for the baron, another for the negro, and the third part for me. We gave him [178] two large drams to drink. I asked him whether he had killed anything yet. He told me no, he hadn't found anything. I retraced my steps and made him a present of the cougar. I left him there to set to work upon it and rejoined the Sr. Baron, and it seemed to us that the morsel of bread we had eaten was a heavenly bread for us, as it gave us so much strength that if someone had been able to see us after we ate it, he would have said that we flew rather than walked.

It was close to noon when we arrived at New Biloxi. We went to salute M. le chevalier de Louboëy, the commandant, who, when he learned of the situation our boat was in, sent a detachment of six soldiers to bring some food to our crew and to give them help. As for us, we dined at the commandant's residence, and for as long as we were in this place, we took our meals there. We slept in the home of the warehouse keeper, a very brave lad who, though he had come over with me in the *Portefaix* as a simple soldier, had by his intelligence and good judgment been found worthy of that employment. His name was the Sr. de la Salle. We stayed there until the Feast of the Holy Innocents, when, after renting a pirogue for ten livres a month and loading it with provisions, we embarked, together with four negroes that we had taken from the boat, and we set sail on the short trip to Pascagoula. We passed across the bay of Old Biloxi, leaving Goat Island on our right.[10]

10. The Feast of Holy Innocents took place on December 28.

[179] At about five in the evening, we saw the entrance to this river. There are three entrances that then converge into a single stem, but this comes more than two leagues from the entrance, which is filled with tiny islands. As soon as we saw it, then, our hope was to go in and proceed upstream, but our desires were frustrated. All of a sudden, there arose a wind from the northwest so furious that, although we tried to row against it to find shelter in the mouth of the river, we found ourselves on the verge of sinking to the bottom. Our boat was filling up with water, and we were forced to reverse course. Even so, more than half a barrel of water came into the boat as we performed this maneuver. But once we were under sail with the wind behind us, we reached open water and passed by Round Island, a good two leagues away from the mouth of the Pascagoula. We then made our way behind the island, in the lee of the large trees that blocked the wind, and landed. We stayed on the island two days, and when the wind had changed, we embarked again; and after four hours' passage on the liquid element, we reached the landing at the home of the Sr. Graveline, where we spent the night. The next day, we ascended the river one and a half leagues, after which we found a place known as the portage. We unloaded and went overland to reach the concession, walking partly through the forests and partly across prairies for about a league and a half, whereas if we had gone by river, it would have required us [180] to cover at least fourteen leagues. I have made a map of the area, and thus I can well attest to this.[11]

I was welcomed as the manager of this concession. Not only did I put its accounts in order, but I oversaw the building of two lumber mills for making planks, for which I had previously built a model out of wood, and these two mills, with two saws in each, have since brought handsome profits to that concession. While I was there, the vessel named the *Bellone* was being outfitted. The ingots that had been taken out of the *Profond* were put into it. One might say that this ship was the rich storehouse of all profits from the beginning of the settlement up until this time, the ship which was supposed to be the first to have the glory of bringing the fruits of revenue from that

11. "More than half a barrel of water": Dumont uses the term *barrique*, which is a barrel (usually of wine) measuring between 200 and 250 liters. Quite likely, the map Dumont refers to here is the "Map of the Pascagoula River," BNF. It is signed by Dumont, and a note on the front reads: "On the back of this map is a manuscript note which explains that this document was sent to Paris with a letter from M. de la Chaise," and gives the date the ship sailed as October 30, 1726. The note itself is not visible because the map has been backed with linen by the conservators. Dumont's route described here can be traced on the map. The Graveline plantation is marked by the letter *E*, and he then went upstream to the portage *(H)*, passing overland to La Garde's plantation *(K)*.

province, not only the precious ingots but also tobacco, pelts, oil, lumber, etc.; in a word, a treasure for France. It was in the roadstead by Dauphin Island, ready to depart. The commandant general had come to Dauphin Island with his brother to return to France in the *Bellone* and had left in New Orleans, to command the country in his absence, the Sr. de Boisbriant, who had come down from Illinois. But a tragic accident prevented their wishes from being fulfilled, for amid the finest weather, without wind nor storm, at six o'clock in the morning, the ship was seen sinking beneath the water. The shallop and dinghy had just left its side to go [181] to Dauphin Island to fetch these two gentlemen to bring them on board before setting sail.[12]

They were loading up a few chests they had with them and were just about to go aboard when, two by two, the cannons of the *Bellone* were heard, asking for help. As the vessel was filling up with water and sinking into the sea, every live body was trying to save himself by climbing up the masts to the level of the lookouts or into the highest shrouds of the rigging. The dinghy and the shallop of the ship as well as another boat came to rescue everyone. The only ones lost were a father, who, in trying to save his son, had fallen into the sea and was drowned along with him, and another man who was too weighed down with piastres. The remainder were saved, but not the ship nor any of the wealth that it was carrying, which became buried in the shifting sands of the bottom, covering them so quickly that we were never able to recover the silver ingots nor anything else that had sunk to the bottom. Hence, the general of the country was forced to return to the capital and take up the helm of his command once again. Some months after this accident, a ship called the *Gironde* was ready to return to France, and the first commandant of the country for the Company embarked in it and was lucky enough to reach France without any difficulties or delays. But when he arrived at Court to give a report of his conduct to the king, his [182] reception was not the best. We had as commandant M. the chevalier de Boisbriant, a man filled with goodness and justice and a worthy commander, who made himself liked and respected not only by the populace but also by the soldiers.[13]

12. Bienville's removal as governor of the colony was intended to be temporary, as a suspension from his duties in order to answer charges in Paris, and indeed he returned to power in 1733; see *HLF*, V, 3–37. The *Bellone* sank while at anchor off of Dauphin Island on April 1, 1725; see Jean-Baptiste Le Moyne de Bienville to the duc d'Orléans, *MPA*, III, 494; *Mémoires historiques*, II, 114–117.

13. Bienville left New Orleans in June on board the *Gironde* and arrived at Lorient on August 20, 1725; see Bienville to the duc d'Orléans, *MPA*, III, 494. He wrote a lengthy "Mémoire

When the Sr. Delagarde arrived from New Orleans at his concession on the Pascagoula, I gave him an account of my management during his absence. He was so pleased with my conduct that in addition to a complete suit of clothing, which I had long needed and which he gave me as a gift, I received out of his generosity five hundred livres. He was now in residence at his concession, and things were coming along well, and as he was sending to New Orleans a boat loaded with tobacco and finished planks of lumber, I took advantage of this occasion to return and see my friends. In just under three days, I arrived at the home of the Sr. Dugué, my loyal friend, who received me with open arms and gave me back my room. So I stayed there and was fed as I had been before. The next day after my arrival at his house, I went to New Orleans and paid a visit to M. Dupuis, who was the adjutant major for the troops of the Company. He asked me to stay for lunch, an invitation that I accepted eagerly, along with two other new officers whom I did not know. He told them over dinner about my misfortunes. He seemed, from the way he spoke, to sympathize with my plight. But when lunch was finished and I had thanked him [183] and was passing by the main warehouse of the Company, I encountered the Sr. l'Estivant de la Perrière, who had previously been the warehouse keeper at the Yazoo concession and who, since then, had become bookkeeper for the Company. When he saw me, he came up to me, speaking all the courtesies, and then asked me what I was doing. After I told him, he replied to me, "Listen, you must keep a secret and never reveal to anyone the secret I am about to tell you, even when you are asked to."

When I promised him, he said, "You should know that your commission has not been annulled and that M. Brulé, the councillor and commissioner, includes you every month in the review of the ranks, and that rather than the forty livres that you were being paid before, the orders are that you should have sixty. So you should go right now and present your request to M. Boisbriant, and he will surely give you justice."

I thanked my friend and returned for the night to Dugué's house on the Bayou Saint John. The next morning, I told him how I had dreamed that the commandant, who had departed for France, had come to me in a dream that night to inform me that I had not been demoted, and had advised me

sur la Louisiane," addressed to the king, defending his leadership of the colony; a translation is in *MPA*, III, 499–539. The directors of the Company of the Indies were not convinced, but after the Natchez revolt in 1729 and the retrocession of the colony to the crown in 1731, Bienville regained favor as the man believed to be best able to conduct Indian policy; see *HLF*, V, 35–37.

to continue in my service as an officer. In short, I said to my friend that because I had had this dream, I was going to go present a petition to the new commandant. I wrote one up, and on the following day, I went by horseback to the morning audience of M. de Boisbriant. I saluted him and presented him with my document. And to support it, I had had a letter written up by a young man who wrote in a good hand, as if this letter had been addressed and mailed to me by my relatives. As soon as the commandant had read my request, he asked me who it was who had told me that I had not lost my commission. [184] I showed him the letter and told him that I had not shown it to him earlier only because I was at Pascagoula, where boats were not easy to find. He immediately sent for Commissioner Brulé, asking him to bring the log of the staff reviews from the previous April. While his aide was off looking for him, M. de Boisbriant sent me into another room, and when the commissioner arrived and gave him the log book, the just and fair-minded commandant began to read it out loud, beginning with the officers. But when he came to my name, he asked the commissioner who this officer was, and which post he was at. The Sr. Brulé admitted that his predecessor did not want me to be an officer and that I should be at Pascagoula.[14]

"But then who has been drawing his salary for him?" said M. de Boisbriant.

"It has been held in the treasury for the time being," answered Brulé.

"Well then, Monsieur," the commandant replied, "the man who was here before me did as he wished, and now that it is I who command, I know how to do things as they ought to be done. This officer is not at Pascagoula."

He called for me to come in.

"Here he is," he said. "Pay this man," pointing to me, "what he is owed for the time since he was put down as being deprived of his commission. And you, sir, when you are paid, prepare to go to the post where I'm going to send you."

I thanked the commandant and went to receive from the Sr. Bru, the treasurer, the sum of 880 livres for nineteen months. So it was that after suffering for a long time, I had the good fortune to see myself once again an officer, and all owing to a tip from a friend.[15]

14. La Chaise had ordered that Dumont receive back pay up through April 1723; see original manuscript [149], and Jacques de la Chaise to the directors of the Company of the Indies, *MPA*, II, 338.

15. If this exchange occurred in the summer of 1725, the nineteen months might date back to April 1724 rather than April 1723. A list of officers drawn up in September 1726 shows Dumont at a salary of 480 livres per year, as Dumont himself stated above; see *FFLa*, I, 226; original manuscript [135]. The reason for this one-year gap could be that his time spent in

[185] While I was preparing to return to duty and buying linens and clothing so as to be ready to go receive the order from M. de Boisbriant, that commandant was relieved by M. de Périer, who came from France to take command of the country. Since the beginning of our settlements along the beautiful Saint Louis River, known by the Indian name Barbancha, which means "serpentine," there had only been about a dozen posts built that were worth anything. Already they were being deprived of manpower and of help from the negro slaves, who, although they had arrived in the country on several different ships, were being delivered only to men and women who had connections. During the time when the first commandant was in power, they had been awarded only to the Canadians, because they were the compatriots of that first commandant, and even the habitants at Natchez had been completely forgotten in this distribution, although there were a few who did get some. They were given to those at Arkansas, however. Our new general, Périer, did not act in this manner. As soon as he arrived, we suddenly saw the country flourishing. He brought with him abundance, justice, generosity, and good works for everyone. He was always ready to provide services and assistance to the habitant rather than make trouble for him. Everything changed, and these habitants would have been happy and might still be today, if they had all been able to keep their lands. For as soon as he arrived, there began to be disputes about whom the farms belonged to. The poor who had been deprived up until now saw themselves in a position to make some progress. Some received two negroes, men and women; [186] others got as many as four. And what is more, to those who had not had food, M. Périer lent supplies from the storehouses of the Company, to be repaid from the next harvest. A barrel of unhusked rice that up until now had cost ten francs in paper money was sold for only forty sols, and likewise for other local products.[16]

Pascagoula and at Bayou Saint John was excluded when his back pay was calculated. Another document in the colonial archives partly confirms Dumont's account here, although it describes one year of salary being paid in advance rather than for arrears: "11 June 1725: On the request presented by the Sieur Dumont de Montigny, lieutenant reformé, in which he askes for one year advance on his pay so as to put himself in a position to return to his post, the Council grants him one year's advance on his pay to begin on the 1st of July, provided that he ascends to the post at Natchez, because [if he does not] he will not be paid again from that time until one year's hence, to which he signs this document to confirm his assent. Signed Boisbriant, de la Chaise, Brulé, Perry and Fleuriau, and Dumont de Montigny" (ANF, AC, Correspondance générale, C13A, VIII, 280, and a duplicate at IX, 151). Dumont's chronology in this section of the memoir can be confusing. For example, the next page refers to the appointment of Périer as governor, which did not occur until a year later.

16. Périer was commissioned as the new commandant general in August 1726. He de-

A few days after his arrival in the capital, I went to him to pay my respects. He asked me who I was. I told him not only that but also of the deceits that had been practiced on me by the first commandant and the justice of the second toward my case. M. Périer told me that I would have to go to serve at Natchez, and so, after taking leave of him, I set about preparing for this voyage. Six days later, I received correspondence and orders to take up to Natchez. It was again in a pirogue that I was to travel. I had five boatmen, one of whom was a younger son of a good family who was also a cadet in the troops of the Company. This younger son was called the Sr. de Bonnafaux. Departing New Orleans, we traveled for a week as best we could along the river, paddling from point to point. It is very rare to see voyageurs going upstream along the outside of the river bends because of the current. In addition, there are nearly always snags of dead trees caught up on one another, which one has to paddle around with great effort, taking care that the force of the water doesn't grab the bow of your boat and force it broadside to the current, [187] which is called being knocked down and can send you downriver in spite of yourself, losing more than a league of progress. And if you allow yourself to be knocked down into these snags, you run the risk of filling your boat with water and being forced down under them, so you must have good foresight and take precautions when making such voyages. I steered our boat, and after a week, as I've said, I arrived at Pointe Coupée, which by then had grown in inhabitants. I stayed at the home of the bonhomme Ducuir, where I made him a generous return of the help that he had given me.[17] We stayed there two days, after which we went on our way and four days later reached the portages at the Tunicas. This is a place where, when the river is swelled with water above its banks, it flows over the land, which provides a much shorter route to reach the Indian village. If you take this route, instead of following the usual course of the river, which is sixteen leagues, you only have to travel two leagues. We resolved, therefore, to shorten our trip. We entered this passage, but it was not by paddling that we proceeded. There was no clear route, and we followed our instincts, pulling

parted Lorient December 1, 1726, and arrived in Louisiana March 15, 1727. Dumont's complaints about Bienville and praise for Périer are a frequent refrain in his "Poème," such as in these lines: "Périer, the Great Caesar, arrived from France itself and was given the power held by Bienville. He was to put everything right and by his actions to bring our enemies to reason" ("Poème," 332). Marcel Giraud, in the most comprehensive history of the Louisiana colony in this period, praises the efforts Périer made in the first two years of his administration to reduce corruption, maintain public order, and promote the development of the concessions; see *HLF*, V, 101–103.

17. See above, original manuscript [165].

on branches and passing through the trees wherever an opening appeared. The rudder of the pirogue was taken out, since some of the branches might strike against the boat as they passed under it. This is how one has to navigate in such situations.[18]

After we had made a good league and a half through this water, or rather [188] through this forest, pulling from branch to branch, we found ourselves in a spot where many others, less experienced than we were, would have been at a *plus ultra*—that is to say, they might have been forced to turn around and retrace their path. Why? Because we came to a large, fat tree trunk that had fallen across the passage not long earlier, blocking it. What to do? Either we had to return or cut through the tree, which could not have been done in fewer than three or four days. But no, we made it through, and this is how.

We unloaded everything that was in our boat and set it atop the trunk of the tree, after which we passed the bowline of the boat under the tree and filled the hull with water. A man standing toward the bow forced it beneath the surface, below the level of the tree, and we thus pulled the entire boat under. Once on the other side, we bailed it out, reloaded, and got back in to continue on our way. This is how, in spite of such obstacles, which may block a passage in the smaller rivers and bayous, one can get through. It's true that this cannot be done without a great deal of effort, but once one has succeeded, the trouble vanishes and one is content. So we passed this barrier, and after three quarters of an hour, we reached the Tunica village, where the chief, a Christian, although an Indian, received me graciously and served me supper in the French fashion. He was completely healed from the wound he had received in his right collarbone during the first war under our first commandant, who was there in person, as I have described above.[19] I slept in the village at the home of a Frenchman who had settled there and who was doing very well in trade, since he was the only Frenchman in the place. [189] He obtained from the Indians all that he wanted in exchange for the supplies he sold and for which he made a nice profit for himself by going down to New Orleans to resell what he had, such as poultry, corn, oil, pelts, etc.

18. Contemporary maps confirm that the Mississippi had formed a meander at the Tunica village and was close to cutting a direct channel through the peninsula. See, for example, Baron de Crenay, "Carte de partie de la Louisiane qui comprend le cours du Mississipy," ANOM, 04DFC 1A.

19. On the chief of the Tunicas, see above, original manuscript [156], and *Mémoires historiques*, II, 110.

I stayed two and half days at the Tunicas, after which we departed, and on the fourth day, we reached Natchez, which, under the protection of our new commandant (I refer to M. Périer), was beginning to revive and flourish. Many new habitants had taken up lands all around, even some of the Germans. Along the path from the post to Saint Catherines, as well as on that toward Terre Blanche, one saw new farms being laid out and built everywhere. And this was not the only such place, for from La Balize at the entrance of the river up to Baton Rouge, a distance of seventy-two leagues, things were quickly getting established, and if this had continued, we would have one day seen viable overland roads. It was a beautiful sight to see how the Natchez post was beginning to blossom under the Sr. Broutin, the commandant, who also had the job of manager of the Terre Blanche concession.[20]

I had no sooner arrived at this post than the commandant returned to his concession and left me to preside in his absence over the fort and its dependencies. Whenever something delicate came up, I dispatched a soldier from my garrison with a letter explaining what was happening. Then, either the Sr. Broutin returned to the post to attend to it, or he sent me orders that I promptly carried out. Although all the troubles that I had suffered up to [190] this point could never be erased from my memory, I believed at that time that they were behind me and that I was going to be lucky enough to enjoy some peace and tranquillity. But there are vicissitudes in this world, and the life of man here below is bizarre and subject to so many reversals that one cannot trust in the appearance of tranquillity even if, at its outset, it seems likely to last forever. Alas, we so often deceive ourselves. Still, I did enjoy peace for the moment.

I commanded over two officers. One was a lieutenant named Sr. de Cazeneuve, a young man blessed with intelligence and good conduct. He had a good farm and some negroes, men and women. The sublieutenant was the Sr. Massé, who was married but who had only begun to put together a farm. I lived in the fort and made my own meals there. But I was tired of living alone in this manner. The Sr. Frédérique, a German, who was married, was the chief surgeon for the post. His wife had just had a baby, and I was chosen as godfather. I held the infant over the baptismal font along with a very wealthy habitante who was also the godmother to the Sr. de Cazeneuve. A few days after the ceremony, I asked the husband of my co-godparent to take me in as a boarder. He was happy to oblige, and so I slept in the fort

20. See *Mémoires historiques*, II, 117–118.

and went to take my meals at his house. But when winter came, this was too inconvenient for me, and so I became a boarder both for lodging and meals.

While I was serving as the deputy commandant, it so happened that we came to the brink of a war against the Natchez Indians, who were living in a [191] large village one league away from the French fort and right between the Saint Catherines and Terre Blanche concessions. This arose out of an act that is well recognized in that country as a declaration of war. But owing to the genius of the Sr. Broutin, war did not come about, even though the Indians ended up paying the price. Here's what happened.[21]

At the Terre Blanche concession, there were many horses, and one of these animals, having been put out to graze in the forest where it could find some shelter from the heat of the sun, was attacked by some Indians, who not only cut off its tail but also gave it a blow with a tomahawk in its left side. This action is looked upon in the same way as taking the scalp of a man. Fortunately, the horse was found in this state by a soldier who was out hunting and returned with the news. The horse was located near the spot where he had seen it, and it was only with some difficulty that it was brought back to the concession, where a skilled farrier bandaged the wound. It healed perfectly. But at the moment the horse was found, the Sr. Broutin, the director of the settlement, sent the interpreter to the Grand village of the Indians, to ask their chief, named Serpent Piqué, to come speak with him. He came with some members of his court, that is, with some honored men, who are, one might say, like his officers.[22] M. Broutin showed the chief the way that

21. On Dumont's maps of Natchez, a large "Village Sauvage" is shown midway between the Terre Blanche and Saint Catherines concessions, near the present-day location of the Grand Village of the Natchez Indians historical site on the right bank of Saint Catherine Creek, although Dumont and other mapmakers locate it variously on the right, left, or both banks of the creek (labeled "Rivierre Blanche" by Dumont in Figure 9).

22. Dumont uses the word "considerez" for the officers who serve Serpent Piqué, and Le Page du Pratz used the same word in his description of the Natchez caste system (*Histoire de la Louisiane*, II, 393–397). Translators have often used the word "honored men." The complexities of this caste and kinship structure and the rules of descent aroused a debate among anthropologists over what they called the "Natchez Paradox." See C. W. M. Hart, "A Reconsideration of the Natchez Social Structure," *American Anthropologist*, XLV (1943), 379–386; Elisabeth Tooker, "Natchez Social Organization: Fact or Anthropological Folklore?" *Ethnohistory*, X (1963), 358–372; J. L. Fischer, "Solutions for the Natchez Paradox," *Ethnology*, III (1964), 53–65; Jeffrey P. Brain, "The Natchez 'Paradox,'" ibid., X (1971), 215–222; Douglas R. White, George P. Murdock, and Richard Scaglion, "Natchez Class and Rank Reconsidered," ibid., 369–388; Patricia Kay Galloway and Jason Baird Jackson, "Natchez and Neighboring Groups," *HNAI*, 598–615. Recent interpretations conclude that the status of "considerez" was acquired through service to the chiefs or Suns rather than strictly by lineage; see Arnaud Balvay, *La révolte des Natchez* (Paris, 2008), 86–89. Dumont elaborates further on the negotia-

the horse had been treated, asked him if his subjects were tired of being friends of the French, and said that if they no longer wanted peace, he need only say so. The chief replied that he disclaimed any involvement in the incident, that he was always ready to stand behind such an act if it was the work of his nation, but that this time, it was [192] more probably done by the Tioux, another nation to the south of his, a league and a half away from Natchez, on the right as one departs from the fort. In a word, Serpent Piqué did not give an adequate explanation and went away from Sr. Broutin's residence very angry and in a pique, and had no sooner arrived back at his village than he called an assembly of his warriors.

As soon as our commandant learned of this maneuver, he ordered the troops of the concession to take up arms and load the cannons and catapults, and he sent me an order to be on guard and to watch for a surprise attack from the Indians. I loaded a cannon and ordered it fired right away as a signal to the French settlers and habitants to come to the fort.[23] They all came. I let them know what was happening. They returned to their homes, sent their slaves and their women and children to the fort, closed up the doors of their houses, and stood ready inside. The next morning, the Indians, having slept on it and come to their senses, no longer wanted a war. Their chief, with a party, came to the concession to offer the calumet to the Sr. Broutin, asking that they remain friends. But the commandant, thinking of his well-being and the interests of his concession, gave the chief to understand that he wanted nothing more than to be friends, but the act, whoever was responsible for it, was not at all that of a friend, and the concession must not lose the horse that had cost it so much; and so, to compensate for this crime, it would be necessary for all the Indians—that is, the Natchez as well as the Tioux—to each give the concession a basket of corn. It takes only two such baskets to [193] make a barrel, or, to be exact, a barrel holding one hundred twenty quarts. The chief agreed to this, and both the Indian nations supplied it, one basketful for each Indian. So my reader can judge from this how well the horse was paid for, having brought the price of more than four hundred barrels of corn worth ten livres each, and the horse

tions with Serpent Piqué and identifies the chief of the Tioux as Bamboche (*Mémoires historiques*, II, 119–122). Dumont's residence with Roussin was near the Tioux village.

23. Dumont writes "bourgois et habitants françois," which I have translated as "settlers and habitants." The term "bourgeois," literally, a town or city dweller, at this time connoted those of a status in between peasants and nobles, and in the Louisiana context referred to those of a somewhat higher status than the simple farmers called *habitants*. In the following pages, Dumont also uses the term as a pseudonym for Jean Roussin, his host or landlord.

itself, which healed from its wound, continued to work at the concession. When the chief had given his word for this payment, the Sr. Broutin agreed to receive the calumet.

At ten o'clock on that morning, I did not know at my fort what was happening at the concession. We saw a large party of armed Indians, a cannon's shot away but coming straight toward us. I quickly ordered the general signal for the troops as well as the residents to be armed, as much to alert those who might still be in their homes or at other places as to strike fear among the Indians, not knowing what their plan was. I knew, however, that the Indians do not march thus in formation and are not so bold as to come and attack in the open. Finally, so as to know their intentions, since the Sr. Broutin had not informed me of anything, I ordered that a cannonball be fired and that they should find one that had holes in it. As soon as the shot was fired and went whistling over their heads, it made them throw themselves on the ground and let out cries and shrieks, like men who believed they would not live to see another day. They were lying on the ground like corpses. Having nevertheless recovered from their shock, they lifted up the calumet into the air and showed a letter that they had brought me from the Sr. Broutin. Seeing this, we allowed them to advance and even to come into the fort, where they gave me [194] the letter. I read it and saw the conditions according to which they had made peace. This goes to show that when one maintains, as we did, a defensive readiness, the Indians hardly dare to attack and generally strike their blows only by surprise. Everything returned to normal, and on the next day, we did not foresee what would come of this affair.[24]

Finally, toward the month of August,[25] M. Dutisné, who was a Canadian and captain in the Company of the Indies, was sent to command this post. M. Broutin thus became merely the director of the Terre Blanche concession. This new captain did not remain commandant for long, but in his short time in this job, he ordered me to go make a palisaded fort in the Grand village of our Indian friends and to design it after the French fashion. I tried to dissuade him, explaining that this would give them a rod with which to beat us, but alas, I was the unheralded prophet, as we shall soon

24. In the *Mémoires historiques,* Dumont does not intimidate the Natchez by firing the cannon. Rather, Broutin insists, "It was not sufficient to make peace with him, if the same was not done with his Lieutenant who commanded at the Fort . . . which led the Indians to come to Fort Rosalie, where I hosted the same Calumet, the entire garrison being armed for as long as the ceremony continued" (*Mémoires historiques,* II, 122).

25. Index note: "1727."

see. In any case, I had to obey, and so I laid out a fort with four bastions, similar to the one at the Yazoos, only much larger.[26]

Toward the end of October, the Sr. Merveilleux, captain of the Swiss regiment of Karrer, came to relieve M. Dutisné, who went to the Illinois country, four hundred leagues upstream of this post. The Sr. Merveilleux did not have a long tenure at this post, either. In the month of February,[27] the Sr. Chepart, a captain, came to relieve him. He was a Basque who believed himself to be a descendant of our kings. He had no sooner become the master here than the officers stopped doing their duty. Orders were followed only as a matter of form by the soldiers and the sergeants; there were no rules, no discipline; everyone did as he pleased. The officers just drew [195] their salaries and thought only of their own plantations. As for me, who did not have one, I continued to live with my landlady, where I passed my time either drawing or fishing or farming the land, where I was growing tobacco.

M. Cazeneuve, the lieutenant commander of the post, fell ill, and before he died, he named as the heir of his property, movable and immovable, his godson, the son of my hostess. Sr. Chepart, who believed that he, himself, was the master of all the habitants and that there was no one who would dare oppose his orders or desires, one day sent two of his men to a patch of green peas to pick two large baskets without asking permission of those to whom the peas belonged nor even letting them know that he wanted some, which would not have been denied him. It was, in fact, the home of the habitant with whom I was living. When he sent his men, we were at Mass. But on returning, the farmer and his wife, seeing that someone was pillaging the pea patch, asked:

"On whose orders?"

They replied, "From the commandant."

My hosts, without discussion, immediately seized what by all right belonged to them. Sr. Chepart became very angry with them and with me on their behalf.

A few days later, my landlord and I were at the Saint Catherines concession, at the home of the Sr. de Longraye, who was the manager there, to buy a horse and a pregnant heifer. Three or four of the latter animals were brought out, but my landlord was not at all satisfied with them. So the Sr.

26. This small palisade appears on Figure 9 and on Dumont's other detailed maps of Natchez: "Carte du fort Rozalie des Natchez françois," ANF, Cartes et plans, N III, no. 1^2 (Louisiane); and "Fort Rozalie des Natchez," SHD, Château de Vincennes, État-Major, 7C 211.

27. Index note: "1728."

de Longraye said to him, "There are some more in the woods that we could bring in. When they have arrived, I will let you know, and you can come and choose one that you want, but without having previously seen it. It will [196] cost you, for it and the horse, 380 livres worth of tobacco, payable at the fall harvest, at the rate of five sous per pound of tobacco."[28]

The sale was concluded in the presence of the farrier of the concession and another habitant, a toast of wine was drunk, and the bill was drawn up and signed by witnesses, of whom I was one. After all this was done, we returned to our house, leading the horse, who was not gelded. Some days after that, the Sr. de Longraye ran into my landlord and told him straightaway, "You know that your heifer is dead."

"But I hadn't chosen one yet," he told him. "So how could it be dead?"

"Ah," said de Longraye, "the one that you saw was yours; you shall have no other. You have to pay me for that one."

On that, they went their separate ways. My landlord told me of this. I told him there was no use fretting about it, but he should be prepared to prove it to the Sr. de Longraye by showing him that it was settled in the bill of sale, even if the clause about the choice had not been fully specified — only that the director had sold to the habitant a horse and a pregnant heifer. He trusted me and went to summon the Sr. de Longraye before the Sr. Chepart, who, as commandant, was also judge. This was simply the prey giving himself up to the enemy. But the prey nonetheless had to come and submit to the commandant's judgment. The witnesses to the sale were summoned, and I was among them. But when we appeared to testify, the Sr. de Longraye rejected me, saying that since I lived in the household I was partial. I was stung to the quick by such a [197] compliment, and knowing that the facts of the matter were in favor of my landlord, and even convinced that he could not lose in court, I replied that, no longer being a witness, I would take the case, just as Daniel had taken that of Susannah.[29]

Six weeks passed before the trial, during which time the Sr. de Longraye gave away presents, meals, dances, and entertainment in order to win over the good graces of a judge who preferred amusing himself to rendering any

28. The large Saint Catherines concession was established by Marc-Antoine Hubert, director general of the Company of the Indies, and then sold in 1721 to Jean-Daniel Kolly, one of a few concessionaires who continued to invest in the Louisiana colony even after the Mississippi Bubble had burst.

29. An allusion to the Book of Susannah in the Apocrypha. The beautiful Susannah is victim of an attempted rape by two elderly judges. When she rebuffs them, they accuse her of adultery and testify against her in court. Daniel cross-examines the judges, exposes inconsistencies between the testimonies of the two, and thereby saves Susannah.

justice. And it is only too certain that he violated protocol in this case and that he should have been dismissed and even demoted and prosecuted.[30] But there was no one else who could be judge, since he was the commandant. The affair went along in this way, in spite of the rights and the veracity of the bourgeois. When the day of the verdict in the case arrived, he lost. His wife, who was present for this iniquity, could not keep from speaking out. She said to the Sr. de Longraye that he was acting like a scoundrel and that the judge had been paid off, and thereupon, she left the commandant's room, where the verdict had been read. He not only condemned the bourgeois to pay for the heifer in question, plus interest, damages and court costs, but also condemned his wife to make reparations for the honor of the Sr. de Longraye in the presence of ten settlers, who were to accompany her to Saint Catherines to plead for his pardon and forgiveness.

I had no sooner learned of these two judgments than I declared my opposition to both, and I called upon Caesar, that is to say, the celebrated Solomon of Louisiana. I believe my reader understands me: the courageous, just, and equitable Périer, commandant general and chair of the Superior Council of New Orleans. I believed I did no wrong, as I saw myself compelled by conscience, [198] although an officer, to present myself as a lawyer to protect oppressed innocence, just as in ancient times Daniel did for Susannah, and also in imitating Caesar, as it is recounted in the histories how he served now in the senate, now at the head of the armies of the Romans. Therefore, I notified the victorious parties in that place that I was appealing their verdict to the Superior Council.

I worked on this case like a real attorney. I made a brief in which I laid bare, primo, the facts of the case, secundo, the false assertions of the opposing side. Even if I granted to the opposing party, just for the sake of argument, that the heifer had been chosen and marked (which it had, in fact, not been), then it would have been necessary to prove that it was dead and to have called upon the buyer, who was only a league away, to come verify its death. And even if the buyer had been one hundred leagues distant, it would have been necessary for the seller to draw up an affidavit and then to preserve the hide as evidence. But he had done none of these things and merely said it was dead. In fact, a rumor was going around that he had sold it for a higher price to a habitant at Yazoo, who had taken it to that post in a boat. I demonstrated also, in this brief, that it was not at all honorable for the Sr.

---

30. Dumont may be alluding here to the *Ordonnance criminelle*, ratified in August 1670 by the Parlement de Paris, where his father and brothers practiced law. This decree established criminal procedure in France, including standards for the competence of judges.

de Longraye to see a woman coming to make reparation for his honor as he had asked, that it was unheard of for a man to ask for such satisfactions. Finally, I described the presents that had been received, the meals given—in a word, I spared nothing of the crookedness on the part of both the winning party and the judge.

The bourgeois, my host, went down to New Orleans to carry this [199] and at the same time to present himself to the council on behalf of his son, as the sole beneficiary of the will and testament of the late Sr. de Cazeneuve. He had no sooner arrived at the capital than he presented the brief, which was copied and forwarded to the Sr. Kolly, who had arrived from France not long before to come see for himself the state of his concession at Saint Catherines. When he, along with all the councillors, and even Messieurs Salmon and Périer, had read this brief, the commandant and his intendant called a meeting of the council, which examined this affair and rendered a judgment quite different from that given at Natchez. The Sr. de Longraye now found himself ordered not only to deliver up another heifer, with her calf, but also was ordered to pay costs, expenses, damages, and interest. The equitable judge, by this same verdict, prohibited the reparation of honor and gave an order to the director at Saint Catherines that when he might next see the wife of that habitant, he should greet her, and she should greet him. Thus the case was concluded.[31]

The bourgeois being in New Orleans, the Sr. de Longraye was further ordered to pay him expenses for each day not only on the trip down but also on the return. But the bourgeois did not leave as soon as he had won his case. He showed the council the will and testament of the deceased in favor of his godson, the son of the bourgeois. He was appointed by the council and recognized as the trustee of the estate of the deceased on behalf of his son. Moreover, he made it known that he had caught the Sr. Chepart using his authority to take from [200] the bailiff of that place forty-two promissary

31. The records of the Superior Council provide details on the outcome of the case involving Cazeneuve's will but only an incomplete reference to the judgment in the suit with de Longraye over the heifer: "17 July 1728: Petition to Obtain Legacy. Jean Roussin and his wife, settlers at Natchez, moved to gain possession of the property which the late officer Cazeneuve willed to their son Jean-Baptiste Roussin when he should be of age; his parents meanwhile to enjoy the usufruct. Executor, Major Desnoyers, restricts himself to settling debts. Let Council order full execution, and grant possession to J. R. and his wife, who offer to give due security for payment of debts concerned. Attorney General approves on given condition." Then, months later, following entries for December 1728, appears a record with the date torn off: "Judgement Rendered in Suit of: Deslongrais vs. Roussin." See "Records of the Superior Council of Louisiana," *LHQ*, IV (1921), 492, 507.

notes listed in the inventory, ordering them burned so as to escape from a debt of three thousand livres that he owed to the late officer for money he had borrowed. M. Périer gave the bourgeois letters and orders to Sr. Chepart, and one for me, complimenting me on my suit and asking me to look after the affairs of this inheritance. I had already been asked to do so by my landlady and co-godparent, and I had even begun examining the will, or, rather, the inventory.

The bourgeois was no sooner back at Natchez than he delivered the letters of the commandant general to the residence of the Sr. Chepart, who was not at home. The habitant then went home, but when the commanding officer of the post returned to his home and read the letters, which doubtless contained some reprimands, he went into such a fury against the bourgeois that he sent a sergeant to summon him immediately. When he arrived in the presence of Sr. Chepart, that officer said to him, "So it's you, sir, who dares to lodge a complaint against me," and immediately struck him with a cane. But the bourgeois, finding himself so abused, grabbed the commandant by the arms, who called out to the guard to take the bourgeois and put him in irons and declared his intention to have him flogged as if he were a soldier. I made an appeal to Sr. Chepart about this injustice, warning that the settlers could well rise up against him, which would cause trouble for him. But rather than listen to me, he has me seized by the guard and [201] orders that the bourgeois be taken out of the irons and me put there in his place, with orders not to allow me to speak to anyone, nor to write, nor receive any messages. As there was no prison, it was on a cot in the guardroom that I was placed with the irons on my feet. It was even forbidden me to have my mattress brought to sleep on; I was to sleep on bare boards. When food was brought to me, the soup, meat, or bread was examined to make sure no note was concealed in it.

Two days after I was thus put in irons, worse than a prisoner accused of treason, the Sr. Desnoyers, who, from his initial rank as a sergeant on the Yazoo concession, had become the director at the Natchez concession called Terre Blanche, came to see me. Having been sent by the Sr. Chepart, that officer told me the commandant had made it clear to him that there was only one way that I might be released from the irons, if I so wished, which was to have the bailiff of the post draw up a letter that I would sign, which would declare that, having examined all of the papers concerning the estate of the late Sr. Cazeneuve, I had found in them all the items listed in the inventory, and that if there were forty-two notes missing, it was I who had torn them up, as being of no value. As such a proposal was met with silence, I stayed in irons.

It was in the month of November, at the end of the month, that the Sr. Bailly came to the post to serve as judge. I would have expected that he was going to dispense [202] justice, but he did not know, or pretended not to know, that I had been detained for the truth and took no notice of the affair. I had acquired a residence near the Tioux village, adjacent to the one owned by my landlady and co-godparent, who had purchased it from the Indians of that same nation when they abandoned their villages and went to live elsewhere. However, the bourgeois for whom I was held in the irons had rented out, or at least was trying to rent out, the house that he had at Natchez in order to shelter himself from the wrath of the Sr. Chepart, and so, while he continued to live at Natchez, his negroes and his slaves worked building houses at Tioux.

Toward the middle of December, Mme. Massé, wife of the sublieutenant of the post, was asked to be the godmother of the son of a habitant. She chose as godfather the Sr. Chepart, and for the baptismal feast, she got the commandant to release me from irons, so long as I remained under arrest within the fort. So it was that after two months' detention, as I have described, I found myself at least partly free, able to walk around within the fort, without, however, being allowed to write, since no one would agree to carry my letters, for fear of provoking the wrath of the commandant of the post.

The Day of the Kings in the year 1729,[32] I was summoned to see the Sr. De———eage,[33] who had been an officer and who from this rank had let himself slip and become drill sergeant of the troops of the garrison, which consisted of just thirty [203] men, of whom only twenty remained in Fort Rosalie. The fort, composed of palisades that were for the most part rotten, was open on nearly all sides. The ten other soldiers had been dispatched to Terre Blanche to guard the concession commanded by the Sr. Desnoyers, who had Madame his wife and two daughters with him. I was asked by this sergeant to celebrate the kings with him. Given that this is a joyous holiday, I accepted this honor with pleasure. It was in the lodgings of the officer that we were to dine. We sat down at table. Wine, eau-de-vie, and ——— flowed freely.[34] A marvelous feast it was. But I was thinking more of my freedom than of entertainment. I let them all get deep in their cups, and when I saw

32. Index note: "1729." The Feast of the Kings, or Epiphany, is January 6.

33. The name is illegible in the original manuscript and does not appear to be "Desnoyers."

34. Another word here, probably a third type of beverage, is illegible in the original manuscript.

that they were—by "they," I mean the sergeant and soldiers and guards, who had been relieving one another from time to time to come in and get a drink—as soon as I saw that they were almost drunk, I left the room, pretending to go out to answer the call of nature, and passing through the palisade, I crept away until I reached the home of my landlord, who received me heartily. Fearing the fury of Sr. Chepart, however, he told me not to stay for long in his house, and when I stepped out, I spied a detachment coming to search for me. I had gone scarcely a dozen paces. They banged at the door of my bourgeois, who, pretending to have been awakened, asked what they wanted. They named me, and he replied that he had not seen me.[35]

I was not armed,[36] so when an idea came to me to remedy this, I acted upon it immediately. Another man in my place, seeing the detachment, would have run away, but [204] not I. I walked up to the sergeant and three soldiers who were with him and said to them:

"Who the devil are you searching for? Don't you see that my intention is not to escape? I was feeling ill up against the walls of the fort, as I was drunk. But here I am. Don't let on that you know anything. Does the commandant know I am absent?"

"No," the sergeant replied.

"Well then, send your three men back to the fort. I'll go back with you, and if Sr. Chepart hears about this from some snitch, you will tell him that because we were out of linen, you took me to my landlord's home to look for some, on my honor as an officer."

He believed me and sent back his detachment. We lingered a little while chatting and then set out on our march. Because the ordnance gun from the guardhouse was very heavy, I had hidden it in the grass, and my plan was, when we passed by it, not to allow myself to be put back in the cage. So as soon as I was near the gun, I knelt down and seized it, cocked it, and aimed at the sergeant, saying to him: "Throw down your arms, or I'll kill you."

"Alas," he replied, "do you want to get me cashiered?"

"Cashiered or not, put your gun on the ground."

The poor sergeant, trembling with fear, obeyed, and ran back toward the fort, unarmed and without me. I threw the ordnance gun into my landlord's yard, took the sergeant's gun, which was loaded and a much better gun for me, and escaped into a canebrake in a ravine.

It was rather cold. Luckily for me, someone had set fire to the large, half-

---

35. On Desnoyers, see *Mémoires historiques*, II, 126.

36. Dumont placed here a footnote: "Having only the guard's ordnance gun, very heavy and not loaded."

rotten trees there. The fire was still smoldering, and I made good use of this, both to warm myself and, from time to time, [205] to light my pipe. As my reader might imagine, I was on the lookout all night, without closing my eyes. At the break of day, the Sr. Chepart ordered a cannon fired. The habitants, at this shot, gathered at the fort, as it was the signal to summon them. Standing there, they had no idea what was going on. Then the commandant came out, ordered a drumroll, and finally, in a loud voice, declared: "On behalf of the king and of me, your commandant, it is enjoined on all men, upon pain of insubordination, to expel from your houses the Sr. (giving my name), and in case you see him, to seize him. And if he refuses to stop, shoot him."

Thus my life was put at his mercy. But whoever God looks after is well protected. Each man went home after this decree, which would never have been followed by any of those habitants, as they loved and treasured me, although I cannot say the same for all the habitants in general. The few who were zealous and servile flatterers might have followed it. He also ordered all those who had pirogues or boats to pull them well out of the water, so that I would not be able to make my escape by that means. That order, at least, was promptly carried out.

In my hideout in the canebrake, I knew nothing of all this. But as I was resolved to leave this post and go down to New Orleans, I left the place where I was and reached the side of the house that served as a chapel, where the Capuchin priest who was our chaplain lived. Next to this house was another: that of a settler named Villeneuve, a Gascon. Once there, I called to him through the window. As soon as he saw me, he said, "Ah, you must flee, sir, there is an order out to shoot you, and if anyone should see me speaking to you, I will spend a month in irons."

I told him, "I have no bread."

He replied, "I'm going to go out and close the door. Climb in the window [206] and take what you want."[37]

I gladly took two loaves of cornbread, ran away with them, and went to hide in the woods. It was already about ten o'clock in the morning. I holed up like a fox in my den, watching those who went past on their way to or from the landing and all the while looking for a way to get close enough to try to get into a boat myself. As I was hiding there, the bailiff came. Whether he was actually searching for me or not, he appeared to be gathering the

37. Villeneuve's house is identified on Dumont's map, "Carte du fort Rozalie des Natchez" (ANF, Cartes et plans, N III, no. 1² [Louisiane]). The chapel and chaplain's house nearby appear in Figure 9.

little canes that have their joints close together, the ones used to make the pretty cane baskets that we call "badines." These come from the roots of the mother plant, which grows very tall and of which the seed can, in time of need, be used to make a bread, stew, or gruel.[38] In so searching, the bailiff found me. He told me that there was a detachment of eight men with a sergeant out looking for me but that I was in a good place, that they would never find me, and that I could remain there in safety. I begged him to keep my secret. He promised to do so, embraced me, and told me he wished with all his heart that I might make it to New Orleans without danger. Finally, he left.

But making a promise and keeping it are two different things. I should have mistrusted him, but his promise made me neglect prudence. It was, in fact, he who, in his capacity as notary, had held the probate papers of which he had given me the inventory. But it was also he who had delivered the forty-two promissary notes from the same estate into the hands of Sr. Chepart. Therefore, to pay me back for taking the side of [207] wronged innocence, as soon as he got back to the fort, he revealed where I was. A detachment of eight armed men came and surrounded me, although with a good distance between each man. Because they were moving through the forest and canebrake, I heard their noise, and in trying to save myself, I almost fell into their ambush. I barely had time to turn around and jump, like a frightened deer, into a ravine some twenty-five or twenty-six feet deep, landing on the sand. As I threw myself off the edge, four shots were fired at me, of which one ball passed through the folds of my ordnance uniform, on the left side. The other gunshots missed me. I had the good luck not to injure myself in falling. Immediately, I withdrew to another hiding place.

Finally, noonday sounded, and I returned to my initial refuge, where I picked up my two loaves and turned my clothes inside out, which, instead of the original white, now appeared blue. Carrying my things, I made it to the river's edge, but I saw that it would be impossible to put any of the pirogues into the water. However, God was looking after me, because a habitant who was working in the cypress woods stripping logs, at half a league from the fort and on the other side of the river, having heard the noise of the cannon firing that morning and not knowing the reason for this signal, believed that something had happened. He crossed over the river alone in a small pirogue and arrived at the landing, where, having tied his boat to a picket at the edge of the water, he climbed up the bluff to go to the fort. Although he moved

---

38. Dumont refers to this cane flour in the natural history section below, original manuscript [415].

quickly, because the path was curved, he had not yet reached the top of the mountain when I hurried to seize his pirogue, into which I threw my gun, [208] my two loaves of bread, and a blanket that my hostess had given me. I jumped in after I had untied it and pushed into the current. Thus I escaped a place where my life was insecure, to say the least.

It was the seventh of January, 1729, at three o'clock in the afternoon and with hard paddling, that I reached the middle of the river.[39] Letting myself drift down at the speed of the current, I was three leagues from Natchez when I encountered a pirogue going upstream. It was an ally of Sr. Chepart, who was returning from New Orleans. As soon as he saw me, although from some distance, he asked me what news there was from the fort and why they had fired the cannon at dawn. I told him that it was for me, to wish me a safe journey. We soon separated, with the current carrying me along and him ascending the river by the force of oars. But he had no sooner arrived at the commandant's residence than he told him that he had seen me in a pirogue. Twelve men, with the sublieutenant from the post, were sent to embark in a flatboat to try to arrest me or capsize my vessel, for they knew that if I saw behind me some soldiers in a boat, I would no doubt put ashore and try to hide in the woods, and they would have been content to recover my boat and abandon me in the forest. But He who had provided for me in time of need by offering the vessel that I had taken—I refer to God Himself—was opposed to the embarkation of this party of thirteen persons, because He sent [209] a deluge of rain that lasted more than two hours, which held up everything at Natchez, while I was exempted from this inundation.

Toward six o'clock in the evening, having made seven leagues, I spotted on a sandbank a place where there were some cabins made of rushes. I had been past here before, and I had never seen any such houses constructed. Though it was not easy, I was able to reach the site by paddling. I recognized that it was a chief of the Illinois nation, from five hundred leagues upstream of the capital, who was descending with a small party of his men, women, and children, to come offer the calumet to M. Périer, our second Solomon, just as in olden times the Queen of Sheba did for the first prince and king of that name.[40] This chief recognized me from seeing me in irons at Natchez. He spoke French passably. All those who were with him were Christians, a result of the charity of the Very Reverend Jesuit Fathers, who, by their tireless prayers and zeal for religion, had converted this nation. When I told

39. Index note (partly cut off): ". . . with paddle strokes." Dumont was glossing *pagaille,* a word not yet commonly used in France.
40. See 2 Chronicles 9.

him of my escape, he told me that I must stay with him and that he would defend me against all. I made him a present of my gun and blanket, and at the break of dawn, I embarked in his boats, of which there were five. I left my own tied to a good picket. Just before we set out, I was amazed to see the women folding up their shelters, just as one would a tapestry, and loading the houses into the pirogues.

No sooner had we gained the midstream than they tied all the boats together, such that [210] one would have said it was a large bridge across the water, which traveled without any impulse other than that of the water's flow. We could move from one boat to another as we wished. At noon, we reached the village of the Tunicas, which we passed without stopping. Five leagues before Pointe Coupée, we encountered a boat tied up in a cove. We put ashore next to it, and, after climbing up the small bluff, we found that it was a Jesuit Father, who was heading up to the Illinois. He recognized the Indians from there. We dined together. I told him of my disaster. He sympathized over it but told me that God would acknowledge my troubles and what I had done, because I had acted only according to religion and truth. We stayed the night there. The next morning, he said Mass, at which the young Indians served as acolytes, and three Indian women took communion. After it was over and the Reverend Father had said grace, we breakfasted together on some fine meat pie and each had two good drams of eau-de-vie, after which we parted—he to go up to Natchez and we descending to Point Coupée, where we arrived around eleven in the morning.[41]

On either side of the river, there were many farms and habitants, among whom I went begging. One gave me a loaf of bread, another, two, and others, some tobacco or some salted meat. In a word, I gathered there provisions to make a long voyage. But as I was with my Indians, I shared my alms with them, which we stored in our [211] boats. At four in the afternoon, we left this place and continued downstream for three days, except the nights, when we did not drift, for fear of falling onto a logjam or onto some large trees or sawyers, which often stick out of the middle of the channel and are constantly swaying, even though they are held by their roots to the bottom fifteen or twenty feet down. River men call these sorts of trees "jug breakers."

41. On the Jesuit missionary activity during this period, see Charles Edwards O'Neill, *Church and State in French Colonial Louisiana: Policy and Politics to 1732* (New Haven, Conn., 1966), 160–164; and Jean Delanglez, *The French Jesuits in Lower Louisiana, 1700–1763* (Washington, D.C., 1935), 249–256. It has not been possible to identify this missionary or the Illinois chief.

Finally, we arrived at the capital on January 19, where I went to find a lodging. Having found one, I went to pay my respects to our general, M. Périer, who was astonished to see me and asked me by whose order I had come down. I explained to him in a few words my reasons. He said that he had not heard any news of this but that for abandoning my post without leave, he would put me under house arrest. I obeyed and went back to my landlord's. But happily for me, I was not there for long, since a habitant from Natchez arrived in the capital two hours after I did. Because our general had heard me complain of the Sr. Chepart, he had the habitant come to him and asked him whether what I had told him was true. The habitant told him that I was absolutely right and that M. Chepart had treated me unjustly. The day following my arrival and my arrest, I was ordered released. I went to thank M. Périer, who told me not to stray far, because Sr. Chepart would soon be in town to account for [212][42] his conduct. Indeed, he arrived on the twelfth of February, and on the fourteenth, we were both notified to report to the council chambers, where I entered my pleas against the Sr. Chepart, who offered only the weakest arguments in his defense. He received a very severe reprimand and yet nonetheless was sent back to his post. Alas, I could not refrain from prophesying by saying, "If you send Chepart back to Natchez, Messieurs, there will be either a rebellion of the habitants or some other great catastrophe."[43]

And so Sr. Chepart, during his sojourn in New Orleans, got provisions for his post and obtained negroes to build a farm. As for me, M. Périer advised me to build one ten leagues from the capital, downstream on the left bank, the same side as La Balize. I was given, at the distribution of the negros, one man and one woman.[44] But the woman died on me two months later, in the

42. Figure 8, "The Author's Farm on the River," was located at this spot in the original manuscript.

43. See *Mémoires historiques,* II, 127, which recounts very briefly the story of "a lieutenant in the garrison" at Fort Rosalie who incurred Chepart's wrath, escaped to New Orleans, and then forced the commandant to come defend himself in front of the Superior Council. A footnote reveals that this lieutenant "is the author himself." The records of the Superior Council make no mention of this judgment.

44. These slaves might have been from the *Galatée,* which arrived from Gorée, Senegal, on January 18, 1729. It had departed with four hundred slaves but had put ashore forty-five at La Caye Saint-Louis in Saint-Domingue, and twenty-five to thirty slaves died of scurvy within the first ten days after landfall in Louisiana; see Etienne Périer and Jacques de la Chaise to the directors of the Company of the Indies, *MPA,* II, 620. Dumont does not mention that Périer arranged for his discharge from the military, but he appears as a lieutenant (resigned) on a list of officers in Louisiana dated April 1, 1730 (*FFLa,* I, 187).

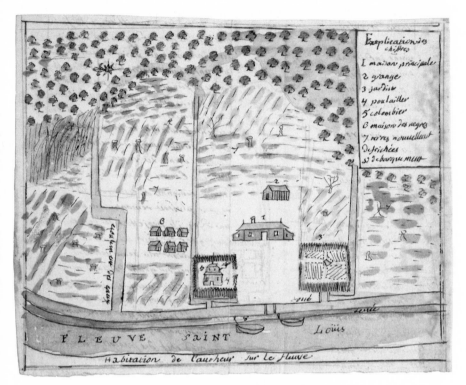

Explications des chiffres
I maison principale
2 grange
3 jardin
4 poulailler
5 colombier
6 maison des negres
7 terres nouvellement défrichées
8 debarquement

FLEUVE SAINT Louis

Habitation de l'autheur sur le fleuve

Figure 8. *The Author's Farm on the River.* VAULT oversize Ayer
MS 257, map no. 8. Courtesy The Newberry Library, Chicago

hands of a surgeon named Brosset, who opened up her body and found that
she had been infected with scurvy and was in no state to arrive at a cure, her
liver being entirely rotted. He gave me a certificate attesting that she should
have been sold at auction rather than delivered as healthy and valuable. But
still I had to pay the one thousand livres. So I found myself reduced to one
negro and an old laborer, whom I hired. I cleared my land, built a house,
planted, and at the harvest, barely reaped what I had sown. The land was
not good.

Toward September, I left that plot of land and started over again on a
new farm a league and a half farther upstream, toward New Orleans, still
on the same [213] side of the river. I began anew to clear the land; I built
another house and a small barn and a storehouse, enclosed by a palisade of
cypress logs, as well as the cabin for my slave. The upper part of the barn
served as a dovecote, the lower, as a chicken coop. I made an oven using a
mixture of mud and straw, as well as a rather spacious garden. M. Périer

had ordered that I be paid what I was due at Natchez, as well as a year's advance on my wages, and with this sum, I purchased all that I needed for my first farm: tools, a pirogue, spirits, and flour. I was also excused from duty, upon the justification that I needed time to establish my farm. This is what I found myself reduced to.

Plate 1. *Map of Cap François (Gulf of Mexico).* VAULT oversize Ayer
MS 257, map no. 1. Courtesy The Newberry Library, Chicago

Plate 2. *Plan of the Fort at Yazoo, Concession of M. Le Duc de Belle-Isle and His Partners, Destroyed in 1729.* VAULT oversize Ayer MS 257, map no. 6. Courtesy The Newberry Library, Chicago

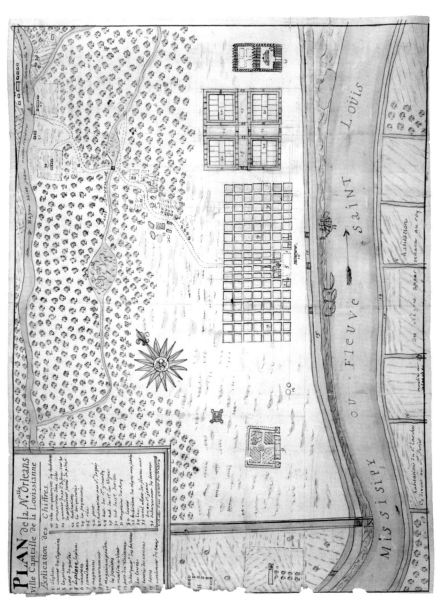

Plate 3. *Plan of New Orleans, Capital City of Louisiana.* VAULT oversize Ayer MS 257, map no. 7. Courtesy The Newberry Library, Chicago

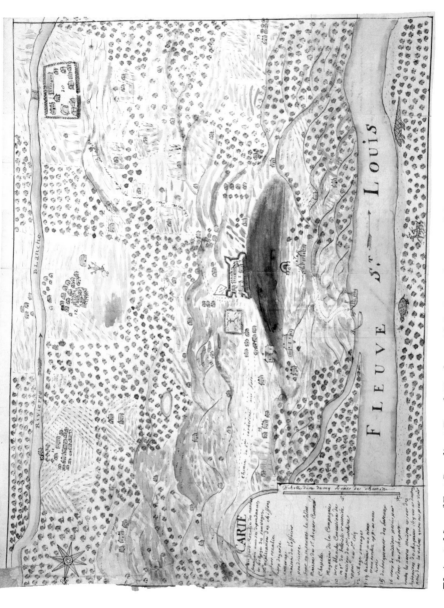

Plate 4. *Map of Fort Rosalie at French Natchez, with Its Dependencies and the Village of the Indians.* VAULT oversize Ayer MS 257, map no. 9. Courtesy The Newberry Library, Chicago

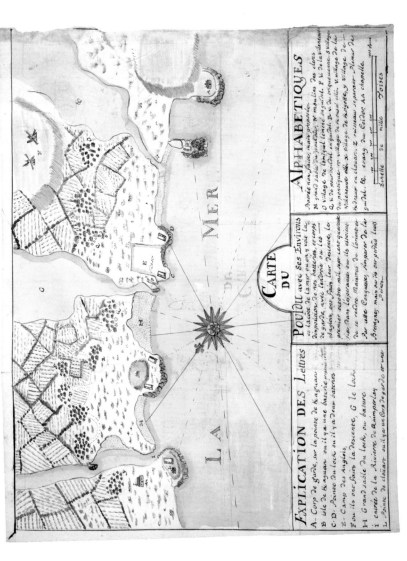

Plate 5. *Map of Polduc and Environs and the Coast of the Sea Where One Sees the Arrangement of Our Batteries and Corps of Guards, as well as the Place Where the English Landed on the First of October 1746, in the Hope of Making Themselves Masters of Lorient and, by This Conquest, Seizing Brittany; but Where Their Attempt Was Foiled.* VAULT oversize Ayer MS 257, map no. 12. Courtesy The Newberry Library, Chicago

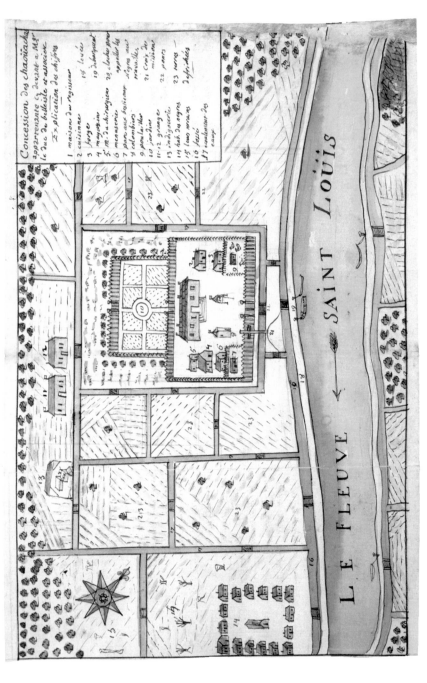

Plate 6. *The Chaouachas Concession, Formerly Belonging to Monseigneur le Duc de Belle-Isle and Partners.* VAULT oversize Ayer MS 257, map no. 13. Courtesy The Newberry Library, Chicago

(top) **Plate 7.** *Indian with His Former Weapons; Indian Dancing; Indian Tattooed.*
VAULT oversize Ayer MS 257, figure no. 2. Courtesy The Newberry Library, Chicago

(bottom) **Plate 8.** *Indian Woman Chief; Indian Woman; Young Woman.* VAULT
oversize Ayer MS 257, figure no. 4. Courtesy The Newberry Library, Chicago

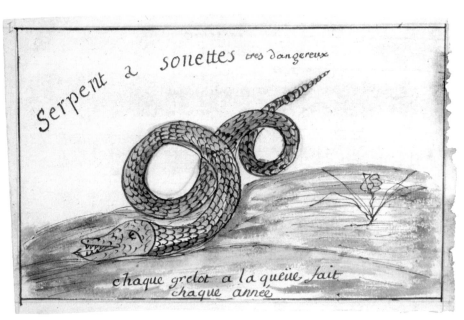

(*top*) **Plate 9.** *Crocodile, or Cayman, Watching Its Eggs.* VAULT oversize Ayer MS 257, figure no. 8. Courtesy The Newberry Library, Chicago

(*bottom*) **Plate 10.** *Rattlesnake, Very Dangerous, Each Rattle on the Tail Marking One Year of Life.* VAULT oversize Ayer MS 257, figure no. 9. Courtesy The Newberry Library, Chicago

Chapter Six

THE NATCHEZ REVOLT

AUTUMN 1728-SUMMER 1735

Let my reader return to the story of the Sr. de Chepart: he had no sooner returned to Natchez than, believing himself a king, he planned to build a magnificent estate. And, so that it would not cost him too much and to have a nice plot of land, he cast his gaze on the fields belonging to the Grand village of the Indians. He sent an order through his interpreter to be read to the Great Chief, a relative of the one of the Pomme village who had been beheaded on the order of the first commandant, since the Serpent Piqué was dead by this time. He told the interpreter to say that the Great Chief of the French—meaning M. Périer—wanted his land to build large storehouses there and that he and all the Indians, as subjects of M. Périer, would have to abandon their homes and go find another place to live. And, to make it clear [214] that it was by the order of M. Périer that he was taking this land, he had a missionary cross planted in the fields of the Grand village.[1]

Never had the lands of the Indians been so brazenly confiscated. Up until then, if one had built on the Indians' lands, either the Indians themselves had granted the land so as to gain the friendship and protection of the

1. According to the *Mémoires historiques*, II, 130–132, Chepart demanded land both in the Pomme village and in the Grand village, whereas other accounts mention only the Pomme village; see [Antoine-Simone Le Page du Pratz], "Suite du Mémoire sur la Louisiane," *Journal œconomique* (December 1752), 119–149, esp. 141; *Histoire de la Louisiane*, III, 232–233; and the account of the revolt by the Sr. de Laye, "Relation du massacre des françois aux Natchez et de la guerre contre ces sauvages, 1er juin 1730," ANF, AC, 04DFC 38, 58. The Grand village had been a close ally of the French, but the Pomme village had been consistently hostile to the French. The interpreter mentioned was Papin, according to *Mémoires historiques*, II, 131. The "chef de la Pomme" is Vieux Poil, whose head Bienville had demanded at the end of the 1723 conflict. See *Mémoires historiques*, II, 113, 129; above, original manuscript [158], and below [215]. For more on Serpent Piqué, who died in June 1725, see Gordon M. Sayre, "Natchez Ethnohistory Revisited: New Manuscript Sources from Le Page du Pratz and Dumont de Montigny," *Louisiana History*, L (2009), 407–431. Chepart's cross is identified by the number 16 on Figure 9. This cross does not appear on the map in *Mémoires historiques* nor on Dumont's other manuscript maps of Natchez.

French for themselves and their habitations, or else those who had settled on the Indian lands had paid them in advance with trade goods. What's more, these Indian inhabitants called Natchez were friends of the French, hunting for them, trading each year some of their poultry, grain, and oil, and working for the French as willing servants (for pay, that is). It was these Indians who carried the wood and water, cleared the lands, and even rowed like galley slaves in the boats up and down the river. They not only hunted for the French, as I have said, but also fished. They did all this of their own free will. The Indian women sold bread, corn meal, and pots and plates that they made with great skill, as well as hiring themselves out to make beds and to unmake them. They ground the corn into flour. The landlord with whom I stayed at Natchez and for whom I had argued in court had withdrawn to his new place at Tioux, which, before becoming his farm, had been the village of a nation carrying that name. He had negotiated for the plot and paid in good, valuable merchandise, and the Tioux Indians [215] had abandoned their lands to him. This habitant and his wife, who had served as godmother alongside me, were living at their new home, removed from the wrath of M. de Chepart, who wanted only to annoy them—to nip at them, as we say.[2] They had rented out to others the farm they had in Natchez. All seemed peaceful, and everyone was beginning to prosper.

The Indians tried to explain that the lands M. de Chepart wanted to take had always belonged to them and that the bones of their ancestors were held there in their temple, but the more they protested, the more he threatened to set fire to the temple. Finally, the Indians seemed resigned to moving away but could not do so immediately. It would take at least two moons longer, they said, to be able to prepare their new home. The Sr. de Chepart granted them this time, but on the condition that they pay a large sum in poultry, grain, and pots of oil, as well as pelts, as interest for the delay that he was allowing them. All this was promised, but we will soon see the effect both of the promise and of his barbaric behavior toward these Indians, who were our friends and were so numerous.[3]

Alas, such ultimatums and conditions, so contrary to the basic rights of mankind, awoke the spirit of the late chief of the Pomme, who had not yet

2. On Chepart's harrassment of Jean Roussin, see above, original manuscript [195].
3. Dumont also explains in the *Mémoires historiques*, II, 131, that the village was the site where "the ashes of their ancestors were resting." If the village were to relocate, these ashes would have to be exhumed and interred in a new temple. See André Pénicaut, *Fleur de Lys and Calumet: Being the Pénicaut Narrative of French Adventure in Louisiana*, ed. and trans. Richebourg Gaillard McWilliams (Tuscaloosa, Ala., 1988), 91.

been avenged. The Indians—the Natchez, I mean—sent envoys to all the other Indians, to the Choctaws, to the Chickasaws, asking them for help. And among themselves, they resolved to strike back at all the French posts and declared that this [216] blow would occur on the third of December of that same year, which is to say, in two moons, or sixty days. And as they have neither calendars nor almanacs among them, they delivered to the chief of each nation a quantity of little sticks like matches, one for each day, to indicate the date for their barbaric attack. While they waited for the explosion, the days passed, and the Natchez had no intention of vacating their land. Alas, if God had not come to our rescue, all the French posts would have ended up in the same state as the one commanded by the Sr. de Chepart. But God is just, and He abandoned only this one post because its chief had raised himself to such a height of pride that he no longer listened to anyone. He threatened the Indians with extermination. He mistreated the habitants, disdained the officers, and punished the soldiers unjustly and arbitrarily. He ignored his duty and thought only of lining his own pockets and of building the plantation of his fantasies that would cost him next to nothing. In his deeds, he was imitating Belshazzar, king of Babylon, who, by his pride, attracted the wrath of God, ending in his own condemnation and the loss of his kingdom. This was, in essence, the fate of the Sr. de Chepart, as we shall see shortly, for he saw himself in his post as more powerful than the king. But the French Fort Rosalie was porous on all sides. [217] It was no more than a palisade of old and rotten logs, manned by a very small garrison of soldiers who scarcely went through the motions of performing their duties.[4]

Every morning, when the sun appeared above the horizon, all the chiefs of the allied nations, as well as that of the Natchez Indians, went to their

4. This technique of counting days by an equal number of sticks was a common practice among southeastern native Americans; see Gordon M. Sayre, *The Indian Chief as Tragic Hero: Native Resistance and the Literatures of America, from Moctezuma to Tecumseh* (Chapel Hill, N.C., 2005), 253–260. The earliest known reference to the practice in French Louisiana is in a 1724 narrative by Franquet de Chaville (Georges Musset, ed., "Le voyage en Louisiane de Franquet de Chaville, 1720–1724," *Journal de la Société des américanistes de Paris*, N.S., IV [1903], 98–141, esp. 128). No archival or published reports of the Natchez Massacre before Dumont's "Poème" mention the use of these *buchettes*, or token sticks, to count the days leading up to the attack, but the story was repeated and embellished in subsequent accounts; see "Poème," 323; *Mémoires historiques*, II, 135; Le Page du Pratz, "Suite du Mémoire sur la Louisiane," *Journal œconomique* (December 1752), 143; and *Histoire de la Louisiane*, III, 241–250. Dumont equates Chepart with Belshazzar by alluding to Daniel 5–8, where the Babylonian king orders a great feast, drinks wine, and is confronted by the prophetic writing on the wall, which Daniel interprets as foretelling the fall of his regime. Dumont also implies a comparison between Daniel and himself.

temples, where each day they threw one of the matchsticks, or little pieces of wood, into the fire. It was upon the last day that they were to strike the blow. There are grounds to believe that the attack would have been general, falling upon many other posts, such as at Mobile, Yazoo, Alabama, Biloxi, Pascagoula, Arkansas, Bayagoula, Natchez, etc., and many other places. But God protected them, and He intervened in a very simple way. For, one day, the Natchez chief, who had a young son, went to the temple, and took his son with him that morning to throw into the fire one of the matchsticks, upon which rested, so to speak, the lives of all of the Frenchmen living at that post. After throwing in one, he turned and began to walk away. The young boy, wishing to imitate his father, threw in four more without being noticed.[5]

Finally, the fatal count of matchsticks approached its end; two days before the final stick, it so happened that a flatboat came to the French post at Natchez, filled with a cargo of valuable merchandise not only to supply the garrison but also to trade and sell to the habitants and the Indians. M. Kolly, with his son, who had come from France to inspect their concession at Saint Catherines, arrived in this boat, and as soon as they set foot on shore, they mounted two horses to go on to their concession. It was the twenty-eighth [218] of November, 1729. Everything was tranquil, or so it appeared. M. Chepart set out with the Sr. Bailly, the judge and commissary, who, as I have said above, had arrived in the month of January to replace M. La Loire des Ursins. The latter, having lost his job, stayed at the post to establish a farm alongside the main path to Saint Catherines.[6] These two men—that is, the commandant of the post and the judge—along with the warehouse keeper called Ricard and a French merchant who had come to trade at the post, after dinner went on horseback to go visit the Grand village of the Indians. They had their negro slaves carry along a supply of eau-de-vie, and wine and bread, as well as some trade goods to give the Indians.

5. Although the uprising occurred only at Natchez, at Yazoo, and at Tunica, the French, in their surprise and fear, imagined a conspiracy of many tribes. See Etienne Périer to comte de Maurepas, *MPA*, IV, 31–43; and the account by Jesuit Father Mathurin Le Petit, "Lettre du Père le Petit, missionary, to Father d'Avaugour, Procurer of North American Missions," in *JR*, LXVIII, 161. See also below, original manuscript [229]. The romantic story of stolen counting sticks as an explanation for why the Natchez attacked without coordination from their allies first appears in Dumont's "Poème" (324) and again in *Mémoires historiques*, II, 166–167. Le Page du Pratz attributes the theft, not to a young boy, but to Bras Piqué, the female Great Sun who was sympathetic toward the French; see Le Page du Pratz, "Suite du Mémoire sur la Louisiane," *Journal œconomique* (February 1753), 94–132, esp. 98; and *Histoire de la Louisiane*, III, 253.

6. Dumont identified the "habitation de Mr. la loire des urzins" in the lower left corner of the map of Natchez in the "Poème," 316.

When they arrived at the land where he was going to make his habitation, he described the plans for them: where his house was going to be, his garden, his storehouses. After this, they went to the village, which was only fifty paces away. They were well received there by the Indians and by their chief and began to drink and smoke and trade boasts together, after which they chose Indian women with whom to spend the night in debaucheries, combining the worship of Bacchus with that of Venus. In a word, the night passed in pleasure and celebrations.

Around four o'clock in the morning, the four of them left the village for the fort, to go bed and sleep off the fatigues that they had undergone, not only from the horseback ride but from what they [219] had done in the empires of Cytherea and Bacchus. While they were en route from the village to the French fort, some of the Indian women, who were maintained by certain Frenchmen in the capacity of mistresses, could no longer conceal the plans the Indians had to kill all of the French on that appointed day, the twenty-ninth of the month. Friends may be found anywhere; the interpreter learned the news, as well as the sublieutenant M. Massé, two or three other habitants, and some soldiers in the garrison. No sooner had M. Chepart arrived at his residence than they came to inform him that today the Indians would rise up against the French.

Did he open his ears to these warnings? Not at all. He flew into a rage, fulminating against these prophets, abusing them for disturbing the public peace, and calling them traitors and lazy cowards unworthy of any protection. "I have just come from the Indian village," he said, "and all is more tranquil than ever. Our Indian friends," he added, "have only good manners and good intentions toward us. You will be put in irons, you, the interpreter, and you, habitants, and you, M. Massé, who ought to show greater courage and fortitude than the others. I'm placing you under arrest, and this evening, you shall feel what happens when you deceive me." This is how he received the warnings that were given to him. If a single cannon shot had been fired, with powder alone, to sound a general alarm, it would have prevented the storm that followed. But no, no, he threw himself on his bed to go search, perhaps, for some great common sense and reason, but it was too late. M. Bailly, the commissary, went to bed and fell into a [220] sleep from which he would never awaken in this world, as we shall see shortly.

It was eight o'clock in the morning, the eve of Saint Andrew's of the Arts, when all of the Indians left their villages to come execute their plans.[7] At the same hour, the commandant of the Yazoo post, the Sr. Ducouder, arrived at

7. The Feast of Saint Andrew of the Arts occurs on November 30.

Natchez, to look around there. He could not speak to the Sr. de Chepart, as he was still in bed. He retired to the home of Villeneuve, the habitant who had been so kind as to give me two loaves of bread at his place, as I said earlier. His boat remained tied up alongside the flatboat, from which the supplies had already begun to be unloaded and organized for transport to the main warehouse. At around nine o'clock in the morning, the Indians arrived at the French post. The fatal matchsticks were all gone. There were many Indians dispersing in all directions—to the two concessions of Terre Blanche and Saint Catherines, to the Tioux, and, in fact, to the home of each habitant. These parties were larger or smaller, so that, where a dwelling housed only a man and a woman and a few children, three Indians were sent, and so on with the other targets. And they were under orders not to strike, that is, not to kill anyone until the signal that they had agreed upon was given. What is more, Indians who were known to each household as friends and comrades went to certain French dwellings, and since they did not all have guns, the Frenchman himself [221] supplied the weapons that would help to kill him. The Indian who needed a weapon would say to the familiar Frenchman, "My friend, loan me your gun, I will bring you a deer or a bear, for I just saw one very close to here, and I will kill it for you." The Frenchman, too kind and too credulous, lent it to him. Other such ruses were also employed.

Finally, the Indian chief who had hosted M. Chepart at supper the night before, accompanied by thirty Indian men and by some younger people carrying poultry, corn, and deerskins, appeared in front of the fort, singing and carrying the famous calumet, which is a ceremonial pipe with a stem at least two feet long, decorated with feathers and porcupine quills, and is the general symbol of peace among all the Indian nations. By showing this well-known symbol, they were able to advance right up to the residence of the commandant at about nine-thirty, who awakens at the noise of the beating drums and the songs they sing and who opens his door. The esteemed calumet enters, followed by the great quantities of riches that were supposed to be presented as gifts to this great and proud tyrant, who was puffed up with his glory and pretense. He gave immediate orders that those who had been held in irons and under arrest should be set free to come and see whether the Indians are our enemies, they who sing, orate, offer the pipe, and raise the captain of the French to the highest level of honor by the titles that they give him. He makes the most of his moment, examining the fowl to see if they are large, if the cocks will be good to castrate, if the pelts are fine and saleable. So much wealth, such a fine present! [222] But you, you fool, will never enjoy it, for here is the price and the reward for your folly.

As the chief was giving the calumet to the commandant, who was beside himself with joy and who had only one soldier as a sentinel at his door, a party of fifteen Indian men set off well armed and went down to the riverbank, where the flatboat was being unloaded. They began to fire at the boat's captain, whom they killed, and on the Frenchmen who were working there, without missing any of them. The firing of these shots was the signal for the others. And then the death blow falls on all the habitants, in their own homes, where they suspected nothing and were not armed. The commandant's sentinel is massacred at the door, and the same is done to the soldiers, both those who were on duty and those in their barracks without powder or lead. The Sr. de Bailly receives the death blow in his sleep and never wakes up. The Sr. de Chepart is still alive, sees the butchery going on around him, and hears the gunfire on every side. He stands up, but like a fool, rather than grab a pistol or rifle so as to sell his life dearly to those who wished to take it, he does nothing of the sort. He takes a whistle that he was in the habit of using to summon soldiers from the fort, and, believing that they were ready to come help him, he goes out of his house in his bathrobe, into the garden, blowing on the whistle to call to duty the soldiers who are no longer there. Before his eyes, the Sr. Ducouder, who had a fine head of hair, has his throat cut and his scalp removed. In a word, he hears [223] only blows, sees only blood, and he is still alive, as if God had wanted to make him see that he deserved more than one death, by watching or bearing witness to those for whom he was the cause of death. Finally, when it was no longer necessary that he live, since there are no longer any living Frenchmen around him and he cannot see those being massacred farther away, he was ordered seized. But who will kill him? None of the Indians who surround him want to do it, each saying that it was a disgrace for him to kill such a man, a man regarded and treated as a dog, for this was how they referred to him. Would he have to be left alive? No, no, he is unworthy of that, even as he is unworthy of a glorious death. So the Great Chief of the village ordered the chief stinkard, who is what we would call an executioner, that he should be killed, which was done in his own garden.

One might well say to me that I'm making this up and ask whether I was there to see the events of which I speak. No, certainly not, I wasn't there. But since the Indians bore their rage only toward the men, the French women explained how it was carried out. And although in the massacre the Indians spared the women and the children, there were nonetheless some women killed as they tried to defend their husbands, even one woman who was in labor. The savages, in their fury, tore the innocent infant from the womb, from the entrails of its mother, and then killed her. She would not have needed any further assistance to find her own death—not after the torments that they had just made her suffer. No, one cannot express [224] in writing the degree of barbarity that the Indians achieved on that day. Of all the garrison of the fort, only a single soldier escaped, by hiding himself in an oven that sat at the base of the bluff below Fort Rosalie, where, seeing the massacre of his companions, he hid until nightfall. Under cover of darkness, he emerged, reached the forest, and went to Tunica by land.[8]

At Terre Blanche, the concession of Mgr. de Belle-Isle, the Sr. Desnoyers, manager of this fine plantation, was killed in front of his wife and his children. They were taken prisoner, and the soldiers' throats were cut. And at the Saint Catherines concession, the Sr. Kolly and his son, who had arrived only the day before, were also massacred, as were the Sr. de Longraye and all his French laborers and habitants. The Sr. Massé, who was leaving his detention in the officers' chamber in the fort and trying to return to his home, received the fatal blow just as he placed his foot on the threshold of his house. The Sr. de la Loire des Ursins—who, with a Natchez Indian woman, had had a son whom he named Rosalie, after the French fort—hearing the gunshots on all sides and not seeing any Indians coming toward his house, believed that the drum was being beaten for all men to return to the fort, for, in fact, the noise of the drum was the signal used by the French. But no, it wasn't our man drumming this time; it was one of the Indians. This former judge, a man of great intelligence and merit, who deserved more luck than he had, seized his arms, mounted his horse, [225][9] and galloped toward the fort. But what bloody spectacle was offered up for his eyes? The soldiers killed, scalps stripped off their heads, and their naked bodies strewn about here and there. So he quickly turned his eyes and his horse back toward his farm to defend his life along with that of his son and his slaves and servants. But he had not gone thirty or forty paces when the Indians let loose a volley of gunshots, from which he received a deadly blow and fell from his horse, without life or feeling.[10]

8. In the published version, Dumont and / or Le Mascrier wrote that Dumont had left Natchez for New Orleans the day before the attack, when, in fact, he had left in January, some ten months earlier; see *Mémoires historiques*, II, 154; and above, original manuscript [208–211]. Dumont's source for his account of the Natchez uprising was likely his wife, Marie; see below, original manuscipt [231]. On the soldier who hid in the oven, see *Mémoires historiques*, II, 149.

9. Figure 9, the map of Natchez, was located at this spot in the original manuscript.

10. The death of Loire des Ursins and the subsequent heroic defense of his house by eight French men and women is related in *Mémoires historiques*, II, 146–148; and by Périer in his account of the revolt sent to the minister of the marine, the comte de Maurepas, *MPA*, I, 62.

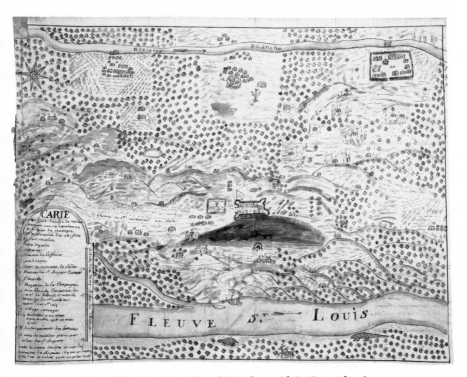

Figure 9. *Map of Fort Rosalie at French Natchez, with Its Dependencies and the Village of the Indians.* VAULT oversize Ayer MS 257, map no. 9. Courtesy The Newberry Library, Chicago

In a word, in fewer than two hours, there were more than fifteen hundred people killed, massacred.[11] It would require as many quills as there were

Marcel Giraud cites this passage in support of his claim that sexual relations between the French and the Natchez precipitated the massacre; see *HLF*, V, 392.

11. This is more than four times the number of victims recorded, but such exaggerations were common. Dumont states in a similar passage in his published account, "In less than a half hour there perished more than seven hundred" (*Mémoires historiques*, II, 144); and Le Page gave the same figure (*Histoire de la Louisiane*, III, 258). Jean-Bernard Bossu later wrote that more than two thousand were killed; see Bossu, *Nouveaux voyages aux Indes occidentales* . . . , ed. Phillippe Jacquin (1768; rpt., Paris, 1980), 60. The most reliable count is by Father Philibert, who compiled for Périer a census of 235 victims; see *MPA*, I, 122–126; and *FFLa*, II, 141–143. The anonymous narrative known as the Rheims manuscript reports that twenty European men and five or six Africans escaped the massacre and carried the news to New Orleans on December 2; see Winston De Ville, ed. and trans., *Massacre at Natchez in 1729: The Rheims Manuscript* (Ville Platte, La., 2003). The Caillot manuscript tells of the initial arrival of a boat of refugees, although it does not give the exact date, and states that twenty-one French habitants of Natchez escaped the massacre; see "Relation du voyage de la

people killed to be able to describe the butchery and record the excesses of cruelty by which the Indians carried out their vengeance, killing each victim by one means or another. My landlady and her husband had come early that morning from their farm at the Tioux village to Natchez. The husband met his death, and his wife was taken as a slave at Natchez, whereas his negroes, his children, and his belongings were seized by other Indians' hands. These savages spared no one who fell into their hands or within range of their weapons, except for two Frenchmen kept alive as slaves. One was a tailor, who was needed to make alterations in the clothing of the French to adjust it to their sizes; the other was a carter, who was needed to carry all the loot of the French settlers back to their village in his cart.[12]

There were two French habitants who were arriving at the Terre Blanche concession when they saw [226] that the soldiers and workers were being slaughtered. They were not so foolish as to approach further and hid themselves in the canes in a ravine. They stayed there until eight o'clock in the evening, when they emerged to go to the French fort, where they did not imagine that the same tragedy had just occurred. Not daring, however, to risk themselves on the main path, they passed through the forests, braving the thorns that grow out of the stems of the greenbrier plant as well as the wild animals, and arrived at the main warehouse of the Company. One of the Frenchmen, named Postillon, peered through the keyhole and thought he saw some French people. For, as it was raining a little, the Indians had gone inside the houses, and others into the warehouse, to rest after the great struggle and mayhem they had been through that day in ridding themselves of so many Frenchmen. Once inside, they dressed themselves in the French fashion, except for breeches. That is to say, they wore stockings without shoes, and shirts, vests or coats, and hats. And so Postillon went on in. But imagine his surprise. He would very much have liked to be outside again, but the door was shut after he entered, and as the Indians were regaling themselves drinking wine and eau-de-vie, they offered him something to drink. He drank as they did, but after this charitable reception, the Indians chopped off his head on the butcher's block.

His companion, who had watched this tragic scene through the keyhole,

---

Louisiane, ou Nouvelle France, fait par le Sr. Caillot en l'année 1730," MS, 146, The Historic New Orleans Collection.

12. Father Philibert listed "Jean Roussin, and his child" among those killed; see *MPA*, I, 123. For the two men spared by the Natchez, see *Histoire de la Louisiane*, III, 260–261; and *Mémoires historiques*, II, 155–156, 188, where the carter is named Mayeux, and the tailor, Le Beau.

fled quickly from the site, and after thirty or forty paces, he heard fluent French being spoken inside a house on his left. He opened the door and rushed in, and he saw a veritable [227] seraglio of women and children of both sexes who were being held there as slaves, and a single Indian who was guarding them. As soon as they saw him, they cried out, "Oh, what have you come here for, my dear countryman, run away or you are dead! All the other Frenchmen have been killed!"

So, taking a knife in his hand, he stabbed the guard in the gut and escaped from the house. From the top of a bluff some fifty or sixty paces away, he hurled himself into the ravine, just as I had done eleven months earlier, and the same good fortune that had protected me protected him also, for he did not hurt himself. The wounded guard called for help, and others came running, but the lucky Frenchman had reached the riverbank and had passed by the flatboat without being seen by the Indians who were in it, amusing themselves with the wine and eau-de-vie. Having passed that spot, he arrived at the house of a man named Rousseau, a master potter, who, at the time, was in the capital.[13] He went in and found some Indians there. It was some Yazoos who had come to offer the calumet to the Natchez, who had not told them of the evil plan they had just carried out upon the French. The Yazoos then, seeing this poor refugee, gave him food and warmed him up, for it was cold outside. What's more, they furnished him with food for three or four days and even a pirogue, and launched it into the river, so that he made his escape. This was a great act of charity from a barbarous nation. The Yazoos had not [228] yet offered the calumet to the Natchez, but a few days later, after they had done so, they returned upstream to their villages, where, when they arrived the next morning, they slaughtered the entire French garrison, which had no commandant. They believed he was at Natchez. They spared only one woman as a slave, who suffered many pains and torments and was on the brink of being burned but had the good fortune to return to New Orleans.[14]

Two leagues upstream from Natchez, on the left as one ascends the river,

13. Rousseau's residence is shown on the anonymous sketch map "Carte particulière des Natchez . . ." (SHD, Château de Vincennes, receuil 68, no. 60). In the *Mémoires historiques*, II, 150–152, the companion of Postillon is named Louette.

14. In the *Mémoires historiques*, it is Ricard, not Louette, who takes refuge at Rousseau's house and is assisted by the Yazoos, who are not yet aware of the massacre. This event contradicts the assertion above, original manuscript [217], that the Natchez had conspired to attack simultaneously with many other tribes, including the Yazoos. Moreover, it is Ricard who is the first to reach New Orleans to inform Périer of the uprising; see *Mémoires historiques*, II, 149–150, 160–161.

there was a work camp led by a M. Charpentier, who cut lumber out of a cypress forest to use in construction. One French habitant from Natchez saved his life by swimming across the river and made it to this work camp to bring news of the murders at the post as well as at the two concessions. When the workers and their master heard this, they killed two Indians of that cruel nation, who were working for pay as hunters and fishermen and helpers on the site. They then embarked in a large boat to go as fast as they could to the capital. As the boat reached the middle of the river opposite the flatboat, two volleys of more than twenty shots each were unleashed by the Indians, but luckily no one was hurt, except for a few holes in the side of the boat. Floating day and night without stopping once, the boat brought the news of the horrific disaster that had struck the French post at Natchez. [229] No one wanted to believe it at first, but one day, one poor, fortunate refugee came in, and the next day, two more. The Sr. Ricard, the warehouse keeper at Natchez, was one; he had been unloading the goods from the flatboat, and at the first shot that the Natchez fired as their signal, he saved himself by swimming out in the river.[15]

A few days before those of us in the capital learned of this cruel catastrophe, there came a party of six hundred Choctaws from the other side of Lac Saint-Louis, with the intention of coming into New Orleans, supposedly to offer the calumet to M. Périer. But, as this plan was also set for the third of December, they might have been planning to do the same to the capital that the Natchez Indians had done to the French post there. But our great general did not want to allow so many Indians to enter the city, and he ordered them to be told that he would permit only the chiefs and a few of their men to come. But when they saw their hopes thwarted, they would not consent to this and returned the way they had come. If M. Périer had been trying to enrich himself, as so many others were, he would not have refused to entertain so many men offering the calumet, as they would certainly have brought many valuable presents. But he was more concerned for his people than for himself.[16] And when he had learned of what had happened to the

15. The identity of this *charpentier*, or carpenter, by his name or his work, is confused in various sources. In *Mémoires historiques,* Dumont writes: "Some other French crossed the river . . . to a cypress forest where a master carpenter named Couillard worked" (II, 153, 170–171). See also the anonymous "Relation de la Louisianne," VAULT Ayer MS 530, chap. 4, Newberry Library, Chicago; and *MPA,* I, 54, 61–62, 65.

16. Lac Saint-Louis is Lake Pontchartrain, as Dumont noted above, original manuscript [175]. The *Mémoires historiques* is more definitive about the sequence of dates, stating, "The first of December they arrived, 600 in number, within sight of New Orleans" (II, 167). Mod-

French post at Natchez and that women and children were in slavery, he ordered the Sr. de Louboëy, his royal lieutenant, to go there with four hundred men to bring the Indians, who were now enemies, to justice. But before sending them off, Périer sent a Canadian named the Sr. de Léry to the Choctaws to ask them for [230] help. And to ensure that they would not decline, some presents of trade goods were taken to them, for, in general, Indians are very greedy. As soon as the Sr. de Léry arrived among the Choctaws and the latter had learned the reason for his trip and the request that he was making for them to go to war for us, they were astonished that the Natchez had struck their blow earlier than the date agreed upon, and they realized that this was the reason they had been prohibited from crossing Lac Saint-Louis. They willingly joined our side against the Natchez and promised that they would go with the Sr. de Léry to wipe out those cruel enemies.[17]

---

ern historians have generally followed Dumont, Le Page du Pratz, and Périer in asserting that the Natchez had conspired with many other tribes to attack the French at many settlements on the same day. See, for example, Kathleen DuVal, "Interconnectedness and Diversity in 'French Louisiana,'" in Gregory A. Waselkov, Peter H. Wood, and Tom Hatley, eds., *Powhatan's Mantle: Indians in the Colonial Southeast*, rev. ed. (Lincoln, Neb., 2006), 144. Périer had a strong motive to portray the Natchez revolt as less damaging than it might have been had the conspiracy with the Choctaws not been thwarted. Less accessible archival sources, written by less biased sources, reveal that the massive pan-tribal conspiracy was a myth. The sharpest witness is Jean-Baptiste de Laye, who dismissed the idea that the Choctaws were part of a conspiracy to attack on that day: "Many want to believe that this conspiracy was widespread and instigated by the English and that the Choctaw wanted to strike New Orleans at the same time as the Natchez attacked, but that the latter struck too early"; in fact, "the Natchez kept the plan very secret, they did not want to communicate it to any other nation for fear of being betrayed" ("Relation du massacre des françois aux Natchez," 66–67). I am grateful to Arnaud Balvay for sharing his transcription of this text with me. Balvay's own account is in *La révolte des Natchez* (Paris, 2008), 129–149.

17. It is puzzling that Dumont calls the leader of the expedition "de Léry," since other sources agree that it was Jean-Paul Le Sueur who led the Choctaw allies against the Natchez starting on January 1, 1730; see Charles E. O'Neill, ed., *Charlevoix's Louisiana: Selections from the History and the Journal* (Baton Rouge, La., 1977), 99–100; John R. Swanton, *Indian Tribes of the Lower Mississippi Valley and Adjacent Coast of the Gulf of Mexico* (Washington, D.C., 1911), 235; Patricia Dillon Woods, *French-Indian Relations on the Southern Frontier, 1699–1762* (Ann Arbor, Mich., 1980), 97; and Balvay, *La révolte des Natchez*, 138. The name is also given as "de Lery" in *Mémoires historiques*, II, 171. No Le Sueur is mentioned in the manuscript memoir. Jean-Paul was the son of Pierre-Charles Le Sueur, an in-law of d'Iberville's who had explored the length of Mississippi in 1700 and made the first detailed map of the river. "De Léry" was a nickname of Joseph Chauvin (see "Abstract of Testimony Taken by Mr. d'Artaguette against Mr. de Bienville, Feb. 24–27, 1708," *MPA*, III, 81). Another Sr. de Léry to whom Dumont may refer was Gaspard-Joseph Chaussegros de Léry, fils, son of a famous officer and explorer and himself an officer who played a key role in the First Chickasaw War (see Bienville's narrative of that war in *MPA*, I, 297–310, which also mentions Le

Let us leave the Choctaw Indians for a moment, preparing to go to war, as well as M. le chevalier de Louboëy with his little army, and return to the Natchez Indians, to see how they conducted themselves after the murders they committed.

They were—the party of 150 men, I mean—attacking the house of M. de la Loire des Ursins, in which there were only four people: his son Rosalie, one negro man and one Indian slave, and his wife, who defended themselves so well during the entire afternoon on the day of the massacre that they killed and injured several Indians and had the good fortune to escape capture. This goes to show that the Indians only strike using deception. That night, when the rain forced the Indians to take cover inside the houses, as I said, these four brave defenders made their escape.

[231] The next day, Saint Andrew's Day, the Indians put the carter to work moving things from the French fort to their own fort, the one that I had designed for them: first, the powder, shot, and cannonballs, and then, on the following days, all the belongings of the Frenchmen. Each woman was at the home of her master, that is, the men who had captured them. My landlady was with an Indian man, along with her children and part of her wealth, but her slaves fell into the hands of a female chief, who is, as they say, like an empress, since her authority over the nation is absolute. She had my landlady brought to her home with her children, and it calmed her fears to find herself reunited with her three children. The female chief liked her very much. The negro slaves became free, you might say, and the French-women, slaves. It was the latter who ground the corn, made the bread, heated the kettles, and had to go look for water and for corn in the fields. In a word, they were reduced to the utmost extremes of slavery. What's more, when an Indian master of a French woman happened to die, either from wounds or from illness, the French woman slave was strangled so as to go serve him in the afterlife.[18]

Sueur). It is possible that Dumont confused Le Sueur and one of the two Lérys, as all three were involved in the 1736 war against the Chickasaws, in which Dumont fought.

18. Dumont uses the word *esclave*, or "slave," rather than *captif*, or "captive," for all the prisoners taken in the uprising, including the African slaves of the French. We have used "captive" for clarity regarding the subsequent negotiations for the release of the French women and children. In eighteenth-century Louisiana, the legal status of freedom and servitude was a more significant determinant of social status than race; see Shannon Lee Dawdy, *Building the Devil's Empire: French Colonial New Orleans* (Chicago, 2008), 139. The *Sacramental Records of the Roman Catholic Church of the Archdiocese of New Orleans, 1718-1750* (ed. Earl C. Woods and Charles E. Nolan, I, *1718-1750* [New Orleans, 1987], 230) lists a Jean-Charles Roussin as having died July 28, 1733, aged six years. A child is listed along with Jean Roussin as among the victims of the massacre (*MPA*, I, 123). The identity of the third and

Mme. Massé, wife of the sublieutenant who had been killed as he entered his house after being released from detention, was sick and incapacitated. The Indians gave her a universal medicine to cure all her ills; they shot her full of arrows at close range. They did the same thing to many others. Notwithstanding these amusements that they enjoyed together, they did not fail to transport all the merchandise of the French post to their villages. What is more, they used the two Frenchmen they had kept [232] with them as a means of decoying unfortunate travelers who, coming downstream from Arkansas or Illinois, or even from a nearby place where they had just gone hunting, were passing in front of the quay of the fort in their boats. The two Frenchmen cried out for them to come to shore, and the travelers knew nothing of the loss of the post. So they came in, and the Indians pounced on them, killing them and seizing their goods. They even took one of these men and led him in triumph back to their village, where, after the ceremonies customary in this nation, which I will describe below, they burned him on the square frame.[19]

One month from the day of the attack that they made on the Sr. de Chepart and others, the Natchez sent the French women slaves from their villages back to Fort Rosalie to bring from the flatboat cheeses, pepper, and anything else they wanted. But as soon as they arrived at the place where the fort was, they found along the path the corpses of many Frenchmen stacked like sardines, without any sort of grave, and who were not yet putrid, since it had been quite cold. The Indians, certain that they would not go unpunished for their actions, kept themselves well fortified but nonetheless considered themselves fortunate to have protected their lands, their temples, and their homes by ridding themselves of the Sr. de Chepart. It is true that they lamented many of the Frenchmen who had been killed along with him, and when some of the French women slaves asked them why they had acted against everyone, when they could just as well have killed only the Sr. de Chepart, they replied that when a chief of a band was killed, [233] his people had to die also.

---

possible fourth child (if three survived the massacre) is uncertain, for Dumont does not mention any stepchildren after he marries Marie Baron Roussin. The Natchez practice of mortuary sacrifice was the focus of intense interest for French observers; see original manuscript, below [382–384]. Dumont, in his published account, states, "A child of one of the Indians having died, they took the child of a French woman and strangled it, to go, as they said, keep company with the other child in the land of the spirits" (Mémoires historiques, II, 159).

19. The Mémoires historiques specifies that the tailor Le Beau was forced to serve as a decoy to lure French boats off the river and also goes into details of the execution of one victim, Le Hou, a warehouse keeper at Yazoo (II, 156–158).

The Sr. de Louboëy left near the end of January[20] with four or five hundred men to go to Natchez.[21] The Sr. de Bessan was his adjutant major. When they arrived at the Tunica village, twenty leagues short of their destination, they unloaded all of their boats, and the soldiers, following their commander's orders, set about building a palisade to protect themselves from any surprise attacks by the Indians while they waited for confirmation that the Choctaw Indians had arrived with the Sr. de Léry as promised. But as he wanted to know what the enemy was doing in the meantime, the commander ordered the drummer to sound a muster call and asked for volunteers to go on a reconnaissance mission. His call was answered by the Sr. Mesplet, two habitants who had escaped from Natchez, and a drummer, who together gathered the necessary provisions and set off in a small pirogue. After three days' journey, they arrived at the small river that flows past the Terre Blanche concession, and, leaving their boat and taking their arms and ammunition, they went to the concession, and then, proceeding under the cover of the forests, they advanced from there to the Grand village of the Indians. They planned only to find some women prisoners and tell them to be patient, that help would soon arrive to release them from slavery. But they were not so lucky as to find any. So they retreated into a canebrake in a ravine half a league from the village. There, they were discovered by an enemy party that tried to capture them. With much gunfire, they valiantly defended themselves. One, the bravest of the four, was killed; his name was Navarre. After his death, the [234] others threw down their arms and surrendered. They were led in triumph to the village and presented to the Great Chief, who demanded in a loud voice why they had come so armed into his lands and whether it was to declare war against him.[22]

The Sr. Mesplet responded that such was not the intention of the French chief, that they had been sent to find out whether he wanted to be a friend

20. Index note: "1730."

21. Compare the report of Diron d'Artaguiette, who wrote that Louboëy left New Orleans on December 18 but lingered for twenty-eight days at Tunica before continuing upstream to Natchez (Diron d'Artaguiette to Maurepas, *MPA*, I, 77).

22. This small river is Saint Catherine Creek, although today it does not flow into the Mississippi at the same point as it did in the eighteenth century. In the *Mémoires historiques*, the five members of Mesplet's reconnaissance mission are "Mesplet, Navarre, a soldier and habitant at Natchez, who had married a girl of that nation, the Sieur de Saint Amand, and two drummers," and they prepare for their dangerous mission by drinking excessively (II, 173–174). Le Page du Pratz also recounts the story, with many colorful details, in *Histoire de la Louisiane*, II, 269–270; see also de Laye, "Relation du massacre des françois aux Natchez," 18–23.

of the French, and that, if he did, he need only say so. The chief therefore believed that the French feared him and that this was why they were asking for his friendship. So he ordered Mme. Desnoyers, who was his captive, to write a letter to the Sr. de Louboëy and to state that if Louboëy wanted to be his friend, he would release the French women, but Louboëy would have to send him a certain number of yards of limbourg cloth or other trade goods for each slave. This woman wrote the letter, listing these proposals and adding an account of the Indians' state of mind. When she had finished it, the Great Chief gave it to the drummer with instructions to take it to the Sr. de Louboëy and to bring back his reply as soon as possible. As you might imagine, he did not tarry but ran off as fast as he could, leaving his two comrades prisoners. They had as much liberty as the other captives but were watched so closely that they could never escape.[23]

At the end of a week, the chief had not seen his ambassador return, for when the letter was received at Tunica and the demands of this impertinent chief became known, our men did not feel that he deserved a response but that we should simply attack. This chief, I say, when he did not see [235] the drummer or any other messenger return, flew into such a rage that he summoned the Sr. Mesplet and his companion and condemned them to death. They were stripped of their clothes and left stark naked, their skin smeared all over with black. They were each given a switch to hold, and they became toys for the bannerets, that is, the children and youths, who made them run back and forth while periodically firing blank shots of powder at their bare flesh. While they diverted themselves with the prisoners, two square frames were set up on the plaza facing the temple, close to the spot where the missionary cross that had been planted there so rudely still stood. The victims, worn out from so much running, scarcely had the strength to walk or even stand up. They had to be dragged to the squares, where their hands were tied to the top crossbar, and their feet rested on the bottom crossbar without being attached. The savages then began to burn them little by little, carefully, a bit on one side, a bit on the other, after removing their scalps. Such was the death of those two poor Frenchmen, who lost their lives only for allowing themselves to be captured and taken to the Natchez village.[24]

23. Le Petit lists the quantities of powder, balls, tools, food, other trade goods, and slaves demanded by the Natchez as ransom for the prisoners; see "Lettre du Père le Petit," *JR*, LXVIII, 190. The bearer of this message was named Legrandeur, according to de Laye, "Relation du massacre des françois aux Natchez," 20.

24. Dumont juxtaposes the Natchez "cadre," or square torture frame, shown in Figure 18, with the equivalent instrument of torture in Judeo-Christian tradition, the cross. *Mémoires*

Toward the beginning of January 1730, the Natchez set fire to all the houses of the French, both around the fort and at the two concessions.

At the beginning of the month of February, the Choctaws, to the number of seven or eight hundred men, arrived with the Sr. de Léry in the territory of the Indian enemies. [236] They divided into two groups, one going toward the main fort of the Natchez Indians and the other toward the house of the female chief, where my landlady was with her children and two other Frenchwomen, who, as soon as they saw the Choctaws around the house, cried out to them to come closer, telling them that there were no Indians there to guard them. Indeed, the Indians, with the female chief, had holed up in the fort of the Grand village and had left their slaves in the house, being pressed for time when they fled and not daring to risk going back after them. So the Choctaws came in unopposed and seized the French women, who thought themselves lucky to have fallen into the hands of those who came in the name of the French. But they were merely changing to a different nation, for they were, in fact, worse off among the Choctaws than they had been among the killers of their husbands. The Choctaws pillaged everything that was in the house of the female chief. They found there an elderly Natchez woman, ripped off her scalp, laid her across a pile of old dry canes, and burned her.[25]

The first party of Choctaws had run off to surround the large fort and were periodically firing their guns into it. Finally, toward sundown, the two groups of Choctaws rejoined one another and retreated toward the Saint Catherines concession. The wife of the interpreter the Sr. Poulain, who had been killed on the day of the massacre—this woman, who was pregnant—got shot in the thigh. She had to suffer this wound and bandage it herself, as there was no surgeon. The Frenchmen reached this concession where the Choctaws had claimed their space [237] and pitched their camp, and all night long, we were firing into the air, an Indian custom that I will explain

---

historiques, II, 178, and Histoire de la Louisiane, II, 279–280, both celebrate Mesplet as a martyr who endured the torments with admirable fortitude. See also Figure 54 in "Poème," 403, and the account of this Natchez custom below, original manuscript [376–377].

25. Dumont reports in his published version, "In February 1730, the Choctaws, numbering around sixteen hundred men, arrived at Natchez, accompanied by the Sieur de Léry" (Mémoires historiques, II, 181). Le Petit, however, wrote, "Seven hundred Tchactas mustered, and conducted by Monsieur le Sueur, marched toward the Natchez"; see "Lettre du Père le Petit," JR, LXVIII, 187. Other sources differ on the date, but Charlevoix, like Le Petit, gives January 27 as the date that Le Sueur arrived; see O'Neill, ed., Charlevoix's Louisiana, 100. Neither source offers what Dumont does here: an account of the Natchez perspective.

below. The next day, we went out searching for some enemies to scalp, but there were no supplies to take.[26]

The Sr. de Louboëy, having learned that the Choctaws had arrived at Natchez, set off with his little army—which had grown a bit larger from the Tunica warriors, who joined after encouragement from their Catholic chief—and arrived four days later at the quay formerly used by the French, to find the settlement destroyed and deserted, without a single house left standing.[27] They saw only the signs of a fire and some spots that were still stained by French blood. It was a frightful spectacle that inspired only horror and vengeance. Nonetheless, they stepped ashore and began carrying the powder, cannons, tents, provisions, and all that was necessary to begin a siege up to the top of the bluff. Marching up and down, they came to establish themselves in front of the fort, into which the enemy had withdrawn. By this time, the enemy had gathered inside the fort not only the French slaves but all the negro men and women as well. When they saw the French soldiers, they let loose all kinds of cries and howlings. As our men brought up the cannon, they filled up gabions to begin building protection for a battery. Trenches were sketched out and preparations laid for a siege. The enemies defended themselves vigorously by firing a cannon, or rather ordering some of the negroes who had formerly been our slaves to fire it at us. But as they were not trained in this process, it was, not the cannonballs that gave us trouble, but rather gunfire from Indians who were shooting at us. For, when [238] they get someone in their sights, they do not miss the target.

It so happened that one day, early in the morning, an enemy Indian left his fort and came out onto the field between the two armies to plant a flag that they had taken from the French, as if to say in defiance that no man among us would be brave enough to come and take it. But one young soldier, stung to the quick by this insult, set off running in plain sight of the two armies, reached the flag, and grabbed it. More than four hundred shots were fired at him, but he was not hit, although eight balls went through the flag itself, which he presented to the Sr. de Louboëy, who promoted him to sergeant major on the spot. Later, a sergeant named Brinville, who had been assigned to the battery of cannons, took fuses and some grenades and, ac-

---

26. For plans of this siege, see the "Plan des deux forts des Natchez assiegez au mois de Fevrier 1730 par les Français Tchachtas Tonicas Colapissas . . . ," BNF, Département des estampes et de la photographie, XXI, fol. t. 3; and "Relation de la Louisianne," 69.

27. According to Diron d'Artaguiette, Louboëy arrived at Natchez on February 8; see *MPA*, I, 78.

companied by two other Frenchmen, sneaked up under cover of darkness to the base of the enemy's palisade with the aim of throwing the grenades over the wall. When he got there, he found he had not had the foresight to bring any flint and steel with him, and as he was unable to do anything without them, one man came back to ask the Sr. de Louboëy for some, but he [Louboëy] forbade them to throw anything over the wall for fear of killing the French captives. Thus they had to return without accomplishing any of their plans. The trenches were slowly coming along. The Choctaws were mere spectators to the maneuvers that our troops were undertaking, and one day, when the battery of cannon had been moved a little closer, the same Brinville decided to make a show of defiance toward the enemy. In between two of the cannons, he lowered [239] his drawers and displayed his fair derrière to the Indians, crying out, "Here's my white flag!" But he quickly paid the price for his bravado, as he received a ball just below his anus, which laid him on the ground and, a moment later, took his life. This goes to show that such acts of bravery are not in good form and are always harmful to those who perform them. He was a good young man with a bright future, but this proved to be his last act.[28]

I would never finish if I had to describe all the sorties, retreats, and volleys from one side and the other, up to the point when the French began to worry that they would not be able to force the enemy out. God, however, who had withdrawn His hand of vengeance from those French who had escaped the initial massacre, now struck fear into our enemies, and the Great Chief of the Natchez called for Mme. Desnoyers and asked her whether the French wanted to grant him peace. She promised him that if she were allowed to leave the fort and go speak with the Sr. de Louboëy, a peace could be made. Then our men saw a flag raised above the enemy fort and, a moment later, a woman coming out. Like Pallas Athena, she crossed the field that separated the two parties and came to the tent of M. de Louboëy. She spoke, asking for peace on the part of the Indians.[29] This she was granted,

28. *Mémoires historiques*, II, 185, and *Histoire de la Louisiane*, II, 288 both recount this story of Brinville, but only here and in "Poème," 325, is the nature of his injury detailed.

29. Madame Desnoyers's embassy is mentioned by Diron d'Artaguiette (*MPA*, I, 78) and by Charlevoix, but Le Page differs. He claims that the messenger was Ette-Actal, a Natchez stinkard and trickster who never appears in Dumont's accounts. See *Histoire de la Louisiane*, II, 290–292. Ette-Actal also appears in the anonymous "Relation de ce qui s'est passé de plus remarquable sur le massacre . . . ," in VAULT Ayer MS 293, IV, 386–393; and de Laye, "Relation du massacre des françois aux Natchez," 50–56, although the latter two texts spell the name "Tactale."

on the condition that the Indians surrender the French captives. This was proposed to the Natchez; they accepted, and a truce was declared. Immediately, the poor women and habitantes were seen emerging from slavery. No sooner were the women free than we formed the intention to attack the Indians the next day. During the rest of the day, the Indians brought out some presents for the Sr. de Louboëy; some of them even approached our trenches to kiss the hands of the French soldiers. [240] That night, each man retired to his tent, and although a close watch was kept, with our sentinels all around, the entire Natchez nation took advantage of the darkness to abandon their fort and escape into the forest. The Choctaws, although they claimed to be our friends, only surrendered the captives that they were holding after they were given trade goods, and they held on to the negroes in the absence of such payments.[30]

The next morning, just as our men hoped to exact our vengeance on the enemy, they were surprised to find that the enemy had abandoned its fort.[31] They took vengeance on the fort itself, reducing it to ashes, and after that, our army fell back to the spot where our former Fort Rosalie had stood. The French women with their children, and even the tailor and the carter, who now found themselves free, were loaded into a large boat to return to the capital, where, upon arrival, they were lodged in the hospital. Each was alloted ten ecus worth of credit at the storehouse, since most of the women were clad in little more than rags, particularly those who had fallen into the hands of the Choctaws, who had robbed them worse than had the killers of their husbands, their actual enemies. The ten ecus given to these poor women were not, however, a loss for the Company, for its manager made them repay later.

For, although the Royal [241] Company of the Indies withdrew from that country on account of the loss of funds that it claimed to have suffered at the Natchez post, in fact the poor survivors, after losing all that they

---

30. This line only hints at the difficulties and embarrassments the French faced in trying to purchase their women, children, and slaves from the Choctaws, who were angry at the poor conduct of the siege by the French and the failure to gain captives and loot from the Natchez. See Joseph Christophe de Lusser to Maurepas, *MPA*, I, 105–109; *Mémoires historiques*, II, 189; and *Histoire de la Louisiane*, II, 293–295.

31. Under cover of darkness on February 25–27, 1730, the Natchez abandoned their forts and fled across the Mississippi, taking much of the loot and slaves with them. Le Page du Pratz and others blamed Louboëy for allowing the enemy to escape. See *Histoire de la Louisiane*, II, 292; James F. Barnett, Jr., *The Natchez Indians: A History to 1735* (Jackson, Miss., 2007), 116–117; Woods, *French-Indian Relations on the Southern Frontier*, 99.

owned—both their belongings and real property—are still paying the Company every day all the debts they owed that predated the massacre.[32] And I can say in all fairness, for it is the truth, that it was the Company itself that had caused the loss of the post and the ruin of these poor habitants: first, by putting the post under the command of a man with no brains; second, by putting in it a garrison of only twenty men; and third, by dreaming only of building grand forts and training engineers and employing them only for building great structures to bring themselves profit rather than thinking about fortifying each place in a manner that would protect it from the surprises and deceptions of the Indians. And how can the Company have the audacity to say that it had suffered losses, since the widows, orphans, and other refugees had lost their farms and belongings, their livestock, slaves, clothing, linens, and all their crops, and no one was exempt from paying the debts they owed to the Company? For the Company claimed to have lost, when in fact it was enriching itself under the cover of this great loss by withdrawing from the country and not sending any more ships to help the people whom it had hired and brought over to establish its operations there. But what should console all the habitants of this New World is that our great, invincible, charitable monarch, Louis XV, took them under his protection. I hope my reader will excuse me for this careful and equitable reflection, for although I was in New Orleans at the time, God so deemed that I would suffer some of the same effects. [242] But let us return to our story.

After this victory (if chasing one's enemies out of a place that they abandoned on their own is a victory), the Sr. de Louboëy returned to New Orleans, leaving at the post a strong garrison under the command of the Sr. le baron de Crenay, a captain, and the vigilant eye of the adjutant major the Sr. de Bessan, who, out of his own native genius, had built a very handsome terraced fort on the same site as the old one, and in the fort built barracks, guardhouses, and storehouses. And for roofing to cover these buildings, he sent out a detachment of fifteen men, commanded by the young man who, through the feat of capturing the flag, had advanced his rank from soldier to sergeant. Among the fifteen men, there was also the soldier who had saved himself by hiding in the oven, as I've already described. They went to a cypress forest to strip bark from the trees to cover these buildings. This place is at least a league away from the fort. For three days already, they had been working there, but on the fourth day, they were surprised by

32. The order of retrocession of the colony from the Company of the Indies to the crown was signed January 23, 1731. The crown agreed to pay the Company seven hundred livres for each African slave; see *HLF*, V, 433.

a party of the Indians with whom a truce had been concluded, who massacred them and took their scalps. And the same soldier who had escaped the first time had the same luck again, by hiding in a hole in the trunk of a dead tree. The next day, he returned alone to the fort to announce this sad news. It was only with great difficulty that the fort was finally finished. The Indians made several efforts to surprise and take the fort, but because it was commanded by men of courage and intelligence like Mssrs. de Crenay and de Bessan, the Indians who came in were killed and massacred, [243] and a sense of tranquillity was soon restored. The savages retreated from their lands, crossed over the great river, and established themselves along a smaller stream called the Black River, which flows into the one coming from Natchitoches.[33]

In New Orleans, our altars were all adorned in black, and we saw nothing but the smoke of the censors burning for peace for those poor victims' souls. Most of the widows of the dead habitants remarried after their periods of mourning. As for myself, I had built a farm that, little by little, was beginning to produce something but was lacking in the most important thing, which is the labor of negroes, for at the time I had only one. Since my fellow godparent was a widow, I proposed to her myself and my farm. She accepted, and with the permission of M. Périer, we were married. As I had been her guest and had never been able to pay her for her generosity toward me, I saw no better way to satisfy this debt than by offering myself as her spouse.[34]

33. See above, original manuscript [238], for the man who captured the flag, whom Le Page names "le petit parisien," and original manuscript [224] for the man who hid in the oven. Le Page du Pratz also writes of this ill-fated party; see *Histoire de la Louisiane*, III, 299–300. This new Natchez fort was located near Sicily Island in modern Concordia Parish, Louisiana, between the Mississippi River and the Red River (on which the French post of Natchitoches was located, much farther upstream).

34. The marriage certificate is in the register of Saint Louis Parish of New Orleans, page 199, dated April 19, 1730. The ceremony was performed under the authority of Père Raphaël de Luxembourg, a Capuchin priest and the vicar general under the bishop in Quebec. Dumont's wife is identified as "Marie Baron daughter of Jacques Baron bourgeois of Morin, and Marie Le Gras, her father and mother, and widow of the Jean Roussin deceased at Natchez." Of many French towns including the name "Morin," it is not possible to identify Marie's father's home. Another clue to Dumont's life at this time is in the records of the Superior Council of Louisiana from the meeting of April 6, 1730, where the council heard a "Petition to Evict. Dumont Demonsigny [sic] complains that Nicolas Dartet alias Francoeur has occupied petitioner's town house for a year gratis, and even tries to expel the owner when he comes to town and seeks lodgment. Let Nicolas be cited instrumentally to eviction." An entry for April 22 confirms a decision in Dumont's favor in the suit, with Francoeur being evicted ("Records of the Superior Council of Louisiana," *LHQ*, IV [1921], 518, 521). Because

At about this time, there came to Tunica a party of fifty or sixty Natchez Indians to offer the calumet to their Great Chief, who asked M. Périer if he should accept it. The commandant general allowed him to do so but gave him an order that, during the calumet ceremony, he should attack the enemies. But alas, the Natchez anticipated this attack, and at the break of day, they assassinated the chief and took his scalp. It should be said in his praise that he was a very good Christian, although an Indian, and a brave and skilled warrior. There were two Frenchmen killed in this attack and their wives taken as slaves, and twelve or fifteen Indians from this village were massacred. After this stunning blow, the Natchez retreated to their new [244] village.[35]

The Indians had found a way to win over our negro slaves and convince them to murder us and make themselves masters of all. This plot was discovered, and M. Périer had its leaders, two negro men and one negro woman, burned, to make an example of them for the other slaves. He took an even wiser action when he learned that this conspiracy had been fomented by the Indians from the region around the capital: he sent word to the negroes on the Chaouacha concession, belonging to Mgr. le maréchal de Belle-Isle and his illustrious partners, that if they wanted to show him their fealty to their master, they must go attack the Indians who were their neighbors. And sure enough, these negroes, along with the neighboring habitants, carried out this mission. They went to the village and killed eight or nine Indian men, as well as some women, with the result that the negroes became the enemies of the Indians, who no longer trusted them. This action restrained the fury of those savages, whereas up until then, they thought only of making surprise attacks, murders, and assassinations throughout the land.[36]

The Sr. Périer de Salvert, the brother of our commandant general, arrived

---

Dumont writes of living on farms downstream of New Orleans during this period and does not mention purchasing a house in New Orleans, it is likely that this townhouse was a property that belonged to his new wife.

35. Le Page also mourns the Tunica chief Cahura-Joligo; see *Histoire de la Louisiane*, III, 301–302; and Périer to Maurepas, *MPA*, IV, 103.

36. Le Page du Pratz writes in detail of this slave revolt, which he claims he foiled by spying on the plotters, then capturing eight of them and interrogating each separately; see *Histoire de la Louisiane*, III, 304–317. Gwendolyn Midlo Hall notes that no other sources give Le Page such a key role as he claimed; see Hall, *Africans in Colonial Louisiana: The Development of Afro-Creole Culture in the Eighteenth Century* (Baton Rouge, La., 1992), 107. Périer was forthright about his Machiavellian tactics in the massacre of the Chaouachas. He wanted to prevent alliances between natives and Africans, as had occurred at Natchez; see Périer to Maurepas, *MPA*, I, 71. Philibert Ory, the comptroller general in the finance ministry in Paris, rebuked him for this atrocity; see Périer to Ory, *MPA*, IV, 47–48.

from France with some soldiers of the marines. They had no sooner arrived than M. Périer brought together not only the troops of the garrison but also the townspeople and habitants, and having assembled an army, he ordered supplies prepared, all that was needed for combat or for a siege. He was like a real Caesar. The Sr. de Salvert, with his troops, was there as well, [245] and boats and pirogues were lined up on the river ready to go seek out the enemy in their new abode. After ascending to a point five leagues beyond Tunica, one leaves the Saint Louis River and enters the Natchitoches River, which, on the right hand as one goes upstream, meets the Black River. They entered there, and not knowing exactly where the enemy was and uncertain of the way, they advanced only with great caution, for fear of a surprise. But one day, having halted all the boats and gone ashore to allow the men to eat, a habitant who was prowling around the area found a young Indian whom he led back to our general. M. Périer gave him food to eat and promised that he would spare his life and take good care of him if he would guide us to the village. He promised he would, and after ordering all to make ready, each man with his gun and his rucksack, Périer leads the march through the forests, on paths then unknown to the French, silently following the young Indian. In less than three quarters of an hour, the cabins and fort that the Natchez Indians had built appear through the leaves of the trees. A halt is called, and marching in one body, flags waving in the wind, leaving behind all the gear that might weigh down a soldier, the drums beat and the army emerges from the forest to approach within one and a half musket shots of the enemy fort.[37]

Imagine their surprise in seeing the French come from so far to find them in a secret place where they believed themselves safe from any surprise. What a shock it was! Yet in spite of all that, they shut themselves up in their fort with [246] their women, their sons and daughters, and their belongings. As they thus shut themselves in, our army attacked them. After this maneuver was complete, M. Périer gave them a harangue, telling them to surrender. But following his speech, they began firing at us, and our men fired back at them. One of our men was injured. The remainder of the army was occupied in digging a trench that they planned to extend right under

37. The Black River, or Rivière Noire, as it was called in the eighteenth century, is now known as the Red River and the lower part of the Ouachita River. See original manuscript [243]. The campaign took place in January 1731. For more lengthy accounts of this battle, see *Histoire de la Louisiane*, III, 321–327, and O'Neill, ed., *Charlevoix's Louisiana*, 113–124. Also see "Plan du fort des sauvages Natchez, bloqué par les françois le 20 janvier 1731 et détruit le 25 du dit mois," BNF, Estampes, XXI, fol. t. 3.

the walls of their fort to plant mines there. But this was abandoned, because on the third day, the enemy began to run out of water. They lowered their flags and asked to capitulate. As it is said by the Indians, they "laid down their arms" and surrendered. But as the sun had set and night was closing in, the parley was put off until the next day. The darkness was very thick that night, and it was also raining. A band of more than two hundred Indians took advantage of the darkness and escaped.[38] The next morning, the others were captured. Our men marched them out of their fort, bound each one, and led them, thus restrained and under close guard, into the boats. There were more women, girls, and boys than men. They numbered 342. The soldiers ransacked their houses and set fire to them and reduced the fort to ashes, after which Mssrs. Périer and de Salvert returned in glory to New Orleans, along with all the army. As soon as they arrived in the capital, the slaves were put in prison, and some days after that, they were loaded onto a ship that took them to Cap François, where they were sold just like negroes to serve [247] as slaves to the habitants of that island. And the Company of the Indies, which had lost so much, or so it claimed, no doubt claimed all the money from the sales as compensation.[39]

When those in France learned of the massacre that had occurred at the Natchez post and the dangers faced by the other French persons who were in the country, what do you think they did to help? The king was told that this disaster must have happened because the first commandant, the Sr. de Bienville, was no longer in the country and that if he were sent back there, he could put a stop to these troubles. And so he was named to the post. He boasted that he would quickly put everything right. He was offered more troops, for which he was grateful. His grand promise came to no effect, as we shall see in the remainder of these memoirs. At last, he departed from France, leaving behind a wealth of promises. Without remarking on all the details of his voyage, we'll just say that as soon as he arrived at La Balize, he sent the Sr. de Macarty, an officer who had come with him, to New Orleans to tell M. Périer that he no longer held the command in the country.[40] He finally arrives in New Orleans, where the air resounded with cries of joy and delight, inspired by rumors stirred up by the party of the former gen-

38. The Natchez leaders Saint Cosme and the chief of the Farine, or Flour, village were among those who escaped.

39. Charlevoix gives the number of prisoners taken to New Orleans as 40 male warriors and 387 women and children (O'Neill, ed., *Charlevoix's Louisiana*, 120), most of whom were sold in Saint-Domingue as slaves.

40. Index note: "1732."

eral, which is to say, by the Canadians. So here he is, with his government restored. He will continue to succor the habitant, favor the officer, and help establish peace and tranquillity throughout the land. A true Alexander the Great.[41]

But alas, all too soon, everyone began to appreciate what we had just lost in [248] the generous, illustrious, and fair-minded Périer. Justice, love, and charity characterized his rule; he was a brave and generous commandant. As soon as he was taken away from us, everything began to collapse. Farms were abandoned for lack of the support that he had provided, all the more so because this new (and former) commandant thought only of returning the country to its former peace and tranquillity, and acted as if it were too large and difficult a task to support and assist the habitants. But whatever the difficulties might be, he did not even try. He spent a year and a half relaxing, no doubt recovering from the strain of his voyage and taking stock of his opportunities for making a stunning coup by which he hoped to impose peace and bring all the Indians to heel. He therefore accepted many calumets from the Choctaws, the Biloxis, the Mobiliens, etc., knowing that, according to these Indians (among whom he had been raised and educated), the Natchez had found refuge among the Chickasaw nation. Before this, they had attempted a surprise attack on the garrison at Natchitoches, commanded by the Sr. Saint Denis, who had answered them very well, killing several of their warriors, and so they had retreated from this engagement toward the Chickasaws.[42]

At the end of the year 1734,[43] the present general sent a Frenchman to that nation, who, as soon as he arrived, asked the Chickasaws' chief for the heads of the Natchez, saying that otherwise we were going to declare war on

41. Bienville arrived in New Orleans in late February 1733. This is one of two places in the original manuscript where Dumont writes Bienville's full name. The allusion to Alexander seems an unlikely choice, given the intended contrast with Périer, "le César." The point, presumably, is that the goal of "bringing peace" or "reestablishing peace" was the wrong one, insofar as the Natchez and Chickasaws had not yet been punished, and the habitants did not have confidence in their own security. These events also begin the second canto of Dumont's "Poème," and this narrative, down to original manuscript [274], follows closely that in the "Poème" and in *Mémoires historiques*, II, 210–231. Unlike in the narrative of the 1729–1731 war against the Natchez, the "Poème" provides more detail on some of the events of the Chickasaw campaign than the prose manuscript does.

42. The Natchez attacked Natchitoches in October 1731. Juchereau de Saint Denis and his Indian allies defended the post, and he claimed to have captured or killed eighty-two of the enemy, including the chief of the Flour (Farine) village; see Périer to Maurepas, *MPA*, IV, 105.

43. Index note: "1734."

them. But because the Chickasaws had promised them safe refuge and even permitted the Natchez to live among and intermarry with them, the French envoy [249] could not obtain what the general demanded. And so the war continued, and to try to bring it to an end and subdue these nations, the general ordered that pirogues and boats be built and outfitted, which was carried out during all of the following year.[44]

Toward the middle of that year,[45] he ordered Sr. de Blanc, a captain, to go up to Illinois with four boats, of which one was filled with powder for the garrison at that post, where there was a fort, and the three others filled with merchandise. He gave this captain a letter for the commandant at Illinois, who was the Sr. Diron d'Artaguiette, the brother of the Sr. Diron, then the royal lieutenant at Mobile. In this letter, he explained that he wanted to exterminate our Indian enemies, referring to the Natchez and the Chickasaws, and that the Sr. d'Artaguiette must take the men of his garrison—both soldiers and habitants—and a party of Indian allies and proceed with them into the Chickasaw territory, where, on the tenth of May of the following year, he would rendezvous with the French army from the capital. When these four boats were ready, the soldiers of the detachment embarked in them with the Sr. de Blanc and left for Illinois. After covering two hundred leagues and arriving at the French post and settlement at Arkansas without having found so much as a cat to whip along the way (as the saying goes), the captain had hardly arrived at the post when, fearing the Indians would attack him during the rest of the trip, he ordered that all the powder be unloaded from the boat and put into the warehouse of that post, giving as his reason that he needed to see whether the route was safe before he exposed his cargo to such a risk. After placing the powder in [250] safety, he left the post and continued safely to his destination at Illinois without making any encounters or seeing any signs of Indians during the entire three-hundred-league journey.

As soon as he arrived at the settlement, on the third day after his arrival, he sent the best boat, commanded by the son of the Sr. Dutisné, a second lieutenant, with twelve soldiers, to go get the powder they had left behind. They departed, went to Arkansas, loaded the powder in their boat, and departed again. They had covered half the distance when, while on shore cooking their kettle, they were attacked by a very large party of Chickasaws,

---

44. The French envoy was likely Diron d'Artaguiette or the Sr. Benoît de St. Clair; see Diron d'Artaguiette to Maurepas, *MPA*, IV, 135–138; Jean-Baptiste Le Moyne de Bienville to Maurepas, ibid., I, 254–260.

45. Index note: "1735."

who killed all of them save the Sr. Dutisnet, whom they kept as a slave. They took all the powder, the guns, and some other merchandise, removed the scalps of the soldiers, and chopped the boat into pieces. Some days later, a habitant coming down from Illinois learned of this incident, and when he reported the news to the commandant general, the latter embarked in his canoe to the Bayou Saint John and proceeded directly, by sail and by paddle, to the fort at Mobile. This is another post, thirty leagues from Dauphin Island. The fort at this place is magnificent, built entirely of brick, with four bastions, and well fortified. One hundred men inside it with enough food could endure a siege by the Indians almost as long as the Trojans did against the Greeks. The Chevalier Diron was the commandant there.

When, at last, our general had arrived, he called for the chief of the Choctaws, [251] gave him some merchandise as a present, and by his largesse was able to secure the chief's promise to provide some of his subjects to escort us and come with us to make war on the Chickasaws.[46] While the general was at Mobile, the pirogues and boats were brought to the port in New Orleans as well as to the Bayou Saint John. After he had obtained this promise from the Great Chief of the Choctaws, he returned to his capital and had the drummer muster up all the soldiers, habitants, and townspeople. When all were assembled on the Place d'Armes, which is very large and attractive, he chose those who would make up his army, and the managers of concessions who could not come along each supplied in his stead two negroes, since this campaign was for the protection of the entire population. Let us leave them to prepare and to load up what is needed for such an essential project as that, and let us just say that . . .

46. Dumont does not identify this Choctaw leader by name, but Bienville, in his letters (e.g., Bienville to Maurepas, *MPA*, I, 276–294), refers to a "Grand Chef" as well as to Alabamon Mingo and Red Shoe, two chiefs who had long relations with the French.

Chapter Seven

LIFE IN NEW ORLEANS;
THE FIRST CHICKASAW WAR
SEPTEMBER 1732-JUNE 1737

As for me, I was with my companion at my second farm, where I made a rather good harvest of tobacco, cotton, and produce, since my wife had retrieved her male and female slaves from the hands of the Choctaws. When they refused to restore the slaves to the Company of the Indies unless paid for them in trade goods, the Company did so, and then also made payment to the owners of the slaves. Although she had kept the negroes working for her at her farm in order to make a double profit, it took a good deal of trouble to get them back to our property.[1]

Toward the month of September, 1732, I wanted to go to La Balize to sell my tobacco, which I had rolled into bundles called carrots, in order to obtain other merchandise. I took one of my neighbors along to accompany me. We each had our pirogue. I arrived at the post and made a pretty good sale of my little crop of tobacco, and after we left and had traveled some four leagues, we [252] entered a bayou, or little river. After covering another league and a half, we entered into some lakes of salt water, where we took in many beautiful oysters—enough to fill both our pirogues. Then we went ashore, set our negroes to opening the oysters, and packed and sealed them in ten or twelve jugs, each holding at least eight or ten quarts, after which we loaded up on oysters in their shells with the intention of carrying them to New Orleans and selling them. We paddled back up the bayou and arrived at the Saint Louis River, which we took back up toward my farm, where a great misfortune had occurred. And one misfortune is some-

---

1. The crown agreed to pay the Company seven hundred livres for each slave when it took over the colony in 1731. Marie Baron Dumont appears to have avoided the exploitation that Dumont accused the Company of the Indies of perpetrating against the colonists. See above, original manuscript [240–241]. The census of Louisiana in 1731 recorded "Le sieur Montigny" living on a farm along the Mississippi River below New Orleans, along with his wife, three children (of whom one might have been their newborn daughter, Marie-Françoise), two adult African slaves, and one child slave. See Charles R. Maduell, Jr., ed. and trans., *The Census Tables for the French Colony of Louisiana from 1699 through 1732* (Baltimore, 1972), 114.

times followed by another, as I experienced on this occasion. We had almost arrived at the port, being only three leagues away, and had put ashore to spend the night, as is the custom of all voyagers who ascend the Saint Louis or other rivers in canoes or pirogues, and often even for those traveling at sea. In the morning, when I wanted to embark, I was quite surprised to find my pirogue sunk to the bottom of the river. All of what little I had amassed by the sweat and fatigue of my body was lost, having either floated away or sunk to the bottom of the river, for we were then on a bend where the water is at its deepest. It was only with great difficulty that we retrieved my boat from where it was resting and emptied it of water. My neighbor left first to get to New Orleans as soon as he could, to be able to earn something from the oysters in the shell that filled his pirogue.

I myself did not arrive at my farm until about three in the afternoon, where I found [253] all the cabins of my negroes, with their clothes and belongings, burned by a fire, as well as my barn filled with unhusked rice, and next to that, a little study where I had my papers, my commissions, my writings. Everything was completely burned. My wife and two negro women she had with her just barely prevented the house where we were living from suffering the same fate, but by spreading water all around the house, they were able to save it. My wife and I had had a daughter a year earlier, and my wife was about ready to give birth again. What to do in this sad situation? I had nothing for my slaves to eat, since, in the granary in my house, I had only thirty quarts of rice and a few barrels of corn. Luckily, the potatoes had not yet been dug up from the ground. So I went to New Orleans to see whether the commandant would be willing to make me a loan of some quarts of rice from the royal plantation so that I might be able to continue to develop my lands and sustain my household. But the commandant was no longer that friend of the people, the courageous and charitable Périer. The man I saw would not hear my plea, would not listen to me at all, and even pretended not to recognize me. I told him I was an officer. He told me that he did not know me as one and that I would have to return home and make the best of it. I was therefore forced to abandon my farm, just as many others were doing, and to sell one of my negroes and buy a house and a lot in the capital. I thus changed from a country dweller to a resident of the city. I had no sooner moved in than the commandant ordered me to report for a [254] review of the guard in the status of a soldier of the militia, but I opposed this strongly and with justice on my side, and he could not force me.[2]

2. Dumont's daughter, Marie-Françoise, was baptized November 28, 1731, and his son, Jean-François, was baptized January 2, 1733. Antoine-Simone Le Page du Pratz was the

By the end of the month of February,[3] the companies had been formed and selected to pack up and go to war against the Chickasaws, who supported and took the side of the Natchez. Not wanting to get a reputation for staying at home like a coward while so many other honest men went to war, I voluntarily signed up as a cadet in the company of New Orleans militia under the Sr. Saint Martin, a former warehouse keeper who had retired to live off his wealth, and we embarked in a boat from the Bayou Saint John to report to Mobile, which was the rendezvous point for the entire army.[4] We arrived there on March 7, along with almost all the others. We stayed for the remainder of that month, preparing what was needed for our voyage. Twenty-two large boats, fully loaded, and more than forty pirogues filled with troops, soldiers, civil militia, habitants, and negroes left the fort on the first of April, Easter Sunday, and we made just three leagues that day, ascending the river from Mobile. Our commandant general arrived there last, and as soon as he did, he gave orders laying out the route and the manner for travel on this river, based on his long experience at war. In the morning, at the first light of day, when the drumroll sounded, the men were to strike their tents. Each tent had seven or eight men in it, who each drew one unit of rations. We were at least a thousand to twelve hundred men, and it was a fine sight to see us all encamped or along the river as we rowed upstream [255] one behind the other, both pirogues and flatboats.[5]

---

manager of the royal plantation after the retrocession of the colony to the crown in 1731. It had formerly belonged to the Company of the Indies. See *Histoire de la Louisiane*, III, 222–229.

3. Index note: "1736."

4. Dumont agreed to fight in the militia as a cadet under Lieutenant Saint Martin, even though he had formerly been a sublieutenant in the troops of the marines posted in Louisiana. This is the first of the two expeditions that Bienville organized to attack the Chickasaws. Since the destruction of Fort Rosalie at Natchez, the movement of essential supply boats up and down the Mississippi to the Illinois country had become endangered by raids that were attributed to Chickasaws. Bienville's initial goal was to exterminate the Natchez who had taken refuge among that nation. For a time in 1734–1735, Bienville hoped that he might persuade the Chickasaws themselves to deny such refuge or even to attack the Natchez. But Bienville then came to fear that the English were courting the Chickasaws for an alliance and might arrange a peace between the Choctaws and the Chickasaws or even persuade the former to attack the French, in spite of the Choctaws' long-standing support for the French. See Jean-Baptiste Le Moyne de Bienville and Etienne Gatien Salmon to Maurepas, *MPA*, I, 274–276; Patricia Dillon Woods, *French-Indian Relations on the Southern Frontier, 1699–1762* (Ann Arbor, Mich., 1980), 119; Kathleen Duval, "Interconnectedness and Diversity in 'French Louisiana,'" in Gregory A. Waselkov, Peter H. Wood, and Tom Hatley, eds., *Powhatan's Mantle: Indians in the Colonial Southeast*, rev. ed. (Lincoln, Neb., 2006), 148–152.

5. According to an anonymous "Narrative of the War against the Chickasaws," there

Two hours after departing, the convoy was halted to take some time for breakfast and a smoke and then resumed its course until around noon, when we searched for a good place and pulled over to the shore. Everyone went ashore except the sentinels assigned to each boat. One man went looking for wood to heat the kettle; another went to walk around and gather, in lieu of vegetables, wild ginger leaves, some small wild onions, and the stems of grapevines that were just beginning to sprout. This is what we had to do in these immense forests, inhabited only by wild animals, with no human dwellings. When the kettle was ready, we dined as quickly as we could and then returned to the boats. One boat always went a half league ahead of the others to serve as a vanguard, and, although they should not have been firing guns, they sometimes shot and killed bears, deer, buffalo or turkeys, even squirrels. At sunset, or rather a half hour before sunset, this first boat looked for a good spot to camp. Once the spot had been found, the engineer laid out the camp, and when the other boats arrived, each group pitched its tent. We ate dinner and went to bed, and during the night, sentinels were posted all around, both among the boats and in the depths of the forests.

Finally, on April 22, we arrived at Tombigbee. This is a place that had been chosen as a depot, and a fort was going to be built there, a wooden palisade made entirely of cedar wood: red, white, and multicolored. The fort was going to be erected on a rise, at the end of which was a handsome [256] and spacious plain on which we pitched our tents. Our soldiers built, on the right side of the camp, several ovens in which bread was baked for the sustenance of the army, which was rather tired of eating only biscuits made from a mixture of half rice flour and half wheat flour from France and was surviving on husked rice, beans, swamp beans (or peas), and salt meat.[6]

---

gathered at Mobile "nine French companies of thirty men each; one Swiss company of one hundred men; thirty-five French officers . . . two militia companies and one volunteer company to the number of one hundred and fifty men and eight officers. . . . There were also in addition one hundred and forty negroes, of whom there was formed a company of fifty men of those people commanded by free negroes" (*MPA*, I, 316).

6. Fort Tombecbé, or Tombigbee, was located near modern Epes, Alabama, on the Tombigbee River, though the site is now submerged beneath Demopolis Lake. According to Dumont's "Poème" and *Mémoires*, the army arrived on April 20, and the latter claims that the fort had been built by soldiers sent "nine months earlier"; see "Poème," 339; *Mémoires historiques*, II, 215. Other sources credit Jean-Christophe de Lusser with building the fort; see "Narrative of the War against the Chickasaws," *MPA*, I, 316. For a map, see Ignace-François Broutin, "Plan du fort de Tombecbé tel qu'il etoit au mois de mars 1737," ANOM, F3, 290, 10. Dumont's "Poème" and other sources differ on the length of the journey from Mobile, from twenty-three to thirty-nine days. On the ovens, see "Poème," 340; and Bienville to comte de Maurepas, *MPA*, I, 299.

When we arrived at that post, we met a detachment of sixty men, forty French and twenty Swiss, commanded by the Sr. de Lusser, who was their captain, with the Lieutenant Dutisnet, who had been rescued from his slavery among the Chickasaws.[7] There was also a tent that served as a guardhouse, in which four prisoners were held in irons—a sergeant, a French soldier, and two Swiss—accused of conspiring to kill their captain and seize their lieutenant and deliver him up to the Chickasaws, along with the entire Tombigbee post. And so, a week after our arrival, a council of war was held where they were condemned to have their heads broken (since no executioner was present). This sentence was carried out, more to give an example to the soldiers who were carrying arms than as a punishment for a crime that had been concocted under the influence of the fruit of the vine and revealed by a man drunk on the same beverage, who renounced it the next day, blaming it on the drink. But as the proverb says, "He who wishes to kill his dog claims that the dog is rabid." So these four soldiers had their heads smashed in, and when they were to be buried, it was necessary to carve out a grave [257][8] in the rock, for although it was a pretty prairie where we were camped, there were only four inches of soil on top of it. Beneath that was rock and stone, although it was a stone soft enough that the Indian women ground it up to make very fine jugs or pots, and the name "Tombecbé" that is given to this place signifies, in the Choctaw language, "land of pottery."[9]

The first day of May, we were still in that place, and we erected a maypole in front of the general's and the officers' tents. We had continuous rain with sleet and snow for more than a week. The Choctaw Indians came to offer the calumet to our general, and they received from him a large quantity of presents to encourage them to come along and accompany us in our great

7. On Dutisnet, see above, original manuscript [250], and *Mémoires historiques*, II, 216. This captivity should not be confused with the amusing story of how Claude-Charles Dutisné, father of this man, had escaped captivity among Indians years earlier, recounted by Le Page du Pratz in his *Histoire de la Louisiane*, II, 297–306; and by Marc-Antoine Caillot in "Relation du voyage de la Louisiane, ou Nouvelle France, fait par le Sr. Caillot en l'année 1730," MS, 126–128, The Historic New Orleans Collection.

8. Figure 10, "Encampment of the Army at Tombigbee," was originally located at this spot in the manuscript.

9. The difficulty in burying the executed soldiers expresses both the qualities of the soil and Dumont's sympathy for these men. The *Mémoires historiques* does not express such sympathy for the accused, who are identified as "one Frenchman, two Swiss, and a sergeant" (II, 216). Bienville wrote of how "I assembled the council of war and we sentenced to death a sergeant and a soldier of the company of Lusser guilty of conspiracy against the lives of the officers of the post and for plotting desertion" (Bienville to Maurepas, *MPA*, I, 301). The Swiss regiment might have had its own separate council of war.

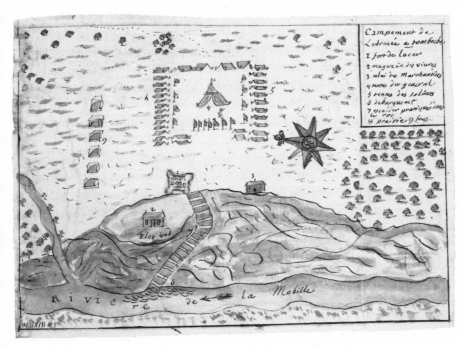

Figure 10. *Encampment of the Army at Tombigbee.* VAULT oversize
Ayer MS 257, map no. 10. Courtesy The Newberry Library, Chicago

enterprise that, according to the zealous declarations of everyone in the
army, was going to completely exterminate the enemy. Already, men were
planning to capture lots of slaves, and the officers were even bidding for
them in advance from the soldiers, giving out money in return for a promise not to grant the slaves to others. A great presumption, and soon we shall
see how well it succeeded.[10]

Finally, on the fifth of May, the signal was given. The tents were taken
down and stored in the boats, and we left that place. The Choctaws, to the
number of more than five or six hundred, were going overland to protect our
flank.[11] It was forbidden to fire a gun, not even a single shot. At about three

10. This cold weather seems unlikely at this time of year. Bienville wrote of rains but no
snow or ice storms; see Bienville to Maurepas, *MPA*, I, 295, 299.

11. In his published book, Dumont mentioned "a place where the river divides into two
forks, making a kind of Y. It is called *Tibia*" (*Mémoires historiques*, II, 217). This corresponds
to the fork in the river on the map "Plan du fort de la Mobile" (Figure 45), in "Poème," 341.
The spot is not shown, however, on Figure 10, "Encampment of the Army at Tombigbee" in
the prose manuscript. Dumont does not write here of the negotiations for Choctaw assis-

o'clock in the afternoon, the third day after we set out upriver, the sound of a gun startled us and set the convoy on alert. Every man grabbed his weapon and was therefore forced to let go of the oars; the boats were no longer being steered, and they drifted down into one another. It was the greatest confusion you could imagine. We believed that we had been not only [258] discovered by the enemy but also attacked. In fact, it was nothing. It was an Indian, who, not knowing of the strict ban against shooting, had fired at a deer and killed it.[12]

After this, the oars were taken up again, but out of fear of an actual attack, as we continued our voyage, half of the soldiers in each flatboat and pirogue kept their weapons ready for use, if needed. We passed by the base of some steep rocks, which was a very dangerous move for us because ten men on top of the rocks would have been able to damage or even destroy us without firing a single shot, using only stones, pushing them off the top into the river as we passed through the danger zone beneath the cliff. But our enemies were thinking only of meeting us face to face. The Choctaws, who, as I've said, were going with some Frenchmen by land alongside the river to protect our flank, had been forced to move inland away from the riverbank to avoid the dangers and precipices of these rocks. In the end, we were lucky to pass by the rocks without incident and reached the river landing closest to the enemy's territory. This was the twenty-fourth of May. We unloaded, set up the tents, and that same day began making the pilings or palisades for a fort in order to protect our belongings, our boats and pirogues, and for the sick and injured men. We went to sleep, without forgetting to place sentinels all around. The Choctaws, our friends and auxiliaries, had arrived there a day before us.

The next morning, the twenty-fifth of the month, after breakfast, the army was issued powder to fill the bulls' horns that served as containers. Some of these hold as much as three pounds of powder. They were also issued balls and rations for four days. At last, with tents struck, knapsacks

---

tance in the attack on the Chickasaws, but "Poème," 343, includes a harangue by a Choctaw leader who was likely either Alabamon Mingo or Red Shoe. Bienville writes of how he was dependent upon a third, unnamed Choctaw Great Chief, and upon Red Shoe, who led the Choctaw warriors and guided the French to the village of Ackia, even though the latter preferred to attack another village, Chukafalaya. Bienville had to make certain promises to Red Shoe in return. See Bienville to Maurepas, *MPA*, I, 300–305.

12. See "Poème," 342; and *Mémoires historiques*, II, 217. The BNF, Arsenal and Library of Congress manuscripts of "Poème" differ in describing this event, one of the rare points where Dumont did such a revision, but both tell the story at greater length than this passage does.

on shoulders, [259] kettle lifted, we set out on our route through the forests where there was no path, where no party had passed before us. The army marched in two columns, each man following in line one right behind another, the flags folded, the drummers carrying their instruments on their backs. All walked in silence, with the Choctaws on our two flanks. There were seven or eight leagues to go to reach the enemy village, and there was, among us, only one Frenchman who had come over this path several times before to sell merchandise to the Chickasaws. He was the guide for the entire army. He went ahead and marked the path for us. After we made five or six leagues by these narrow trails, the sun was starting to set, and a halt was called, each company arranged in separate groups. We ate supper in the forest, making only one small fire to light the pipes of the smokers, and we went to sleep on the natural bed offered by our common mother, that is, on the grass and even the dirt. It was not with complete tranquillity that we slept, however, for in the moonlight, at about ten o'clock that night, four Frenchmen were sent out by our general to reconnoiter. Whether they carried out the orders they were given or not, they came back two hours after midnight and said that they had found a party of seven or eight Indians in a ravine filled with canes, who had seen them, and that they had not hazarded to fire upon them since they had not received orders to do so.

The next morning, the twenty-sixth of the said month, at first light, the army resumed its march in silence, as on the previous day. Our general was between the two columns, mounted on a horse that the Choctaws had brought [260] just for him. After marching for a good league, we found ourselves at a small river over which there was no bridge. It was necessary to cross it, and, having found a ford, we waded through water up to the waist. All this caused us not a little difficulty and delay. After all had passed through, we traversed a canebrake, and after that, we entered a prairie, in the middle of which we saw the arrangement of the houses, temple, and fort of the Indians. This brought joy to the troops, who already believed themselves victorious and that no Indian would be able to resist them.

At this point, the army reorganized into one large battalion, flags flying, drums beating, and fifes playing. Our Choctaw Indians had no sooner seen the fort, situated on an eminence, than they separated and began running toward the enemy Indians, letting out cries and fearsome shrieks and trying to find their balls so they could fire their guns and bring down some of them. As for us, we were marching at a good pace, but this did not prevent us from gathering along the way big handfuls of strawberries with which the prairie was then completely covered. "Let us eat the strawberries," we said to ourselves. "We will eat the plum after."[13] Everyone was laughing in the expectation that we were soon going to be the masters of all the Indian villages. We advanced all the while. The intention of our general was, first of all, to unite his army with that of the Sr. d'Artaguiette, who, according to his orders, should have arrived and from whom we had still not heard any news. But then our chaplain, the Reverend Father Baudoin, a Jesuit, told him that the village we were looking at was only an outlying settlement of [261] separatists and that there would still be time to go join with the army from Illinois after we had taken this fort and village, in which we would find food for our army and which could also serve as our storehouse and staging ground. So he believed, and as soon as we arrived within two musket-shots of the enemy fort, a halt was called in a small valley bordered on one side by a creek and on the other by a small wood. Those hauling their loads had no sooner reached the place than they were ordered to put down their knapsacks, and, without pitching any tents, without even being given time to catch their breath or take any food, our general ordered the selection of a large detachment, at least nine hundred men, and commanded them to go take the fort, which we saw was flying an English flag.[14]

13. This was the Chickasaw village of Ackia, whose location has been placed by historians near Cotton Gin Port and the modern town of Amory, or in Tupelo, some thirty kilometers to the northwest of Amory. Both towns are in East-Central Mississippi. See Jack D. Elliot and Mary Ann Wells, *Cotton Gin Port: A Frontier Settlement on the Upper Tombigbee* (Jackson, Miss., 2003); James R. Atkinson, "The Ackia and Ogula Tchekota Village Locations in 1736 during the French-Chickasaw War," *Mississippi Archaeology*, XX (1985), 53–72. The hill, or butte, appears both in Figure 11 and the corresponding map in the "Poème," 346 (Figure 46). See also *Mémoires historiques*, II, 219–220. As Dumont explains below, there were three or four villages next to each other. This scene was particularly appropriate for the mock-heroic register of the "Poème," 345, and in *Mémoires historiques*, II, 219, where Dumont wrote: "Our soldiers, like those of Gideon, gathered handfuls of strawberries as we passed across this prairie," a reference to Judges 7, where Gideon's three hundred chosen troops defeat the Midianites. There are no strawberries in the biblical story, however, and Dumont's expression referring to the plum is obscure, unless it foreshadows the outcome of the war and might be translated "eat crow after."

14. Here begins Dumont's account of what became the most controversial aspect of Bienville's leadership in the First Chickasaw War. In the winter of 1735–1736, when Bienville was planning the expedition for February, he wrote to Pierre d'Artaguiette at Illinois with instructions to organize an attack on the Chickasaws from the northwest: "I had made an appointment with him for the tenth or the fifteenth of March at the Prud'homme Bluffs which are only four days march from the Chickasaws" (Bienville to Maurepas, *MPA*, I, 294). D'Artaguiette set out from Fort de Chartres with a force of 114 Frenchmen and 325 Indians. Because Bienville was delayed by low water, lack of food and munitions, and bad weather, he wrote again to d'Artaguiette, saying he would not arrive until the end of April, but d'Artaguiette attacked the Chickasaw village of Red Grass on March 24 and was captured. Bienville believed

And sure enough, when we approached the fort, we saw fifteen men of that nation who no doubt had come to this village to trade merchandise with the Chickasaws and who had put their trade goods and their proceeds into the fort as a protection against any insults. Instead of calling to them by the sound of the drums and asking them whether they were taking the side of our enemies, no such thing; the order was given to fall upon and seize the fort, which, although raised up on an eminence, was at one end of a wide and spacious platform. It was built of enormous stout pilings covered on the outside with thick planks, above which there was another terrace. Along the palisade, there were small openings that served as loopholes, or [262] crenellations. Within the fort on either side, there were, in the corners of the palisade, two strong houses with mud and straw walls at least a foot and a half thick, as well as similar holes for shooting at whoever might attack.

The detachment where I was, in the company led by Sr. Saint Martin, who marched with us, was assigned its orders and began to set out from the place where the captain had received them. We did not receive a benediction from our chaplain, which we did not demand and he did not propose. The grenadiers' company marched in the van, and the Sr. Saint Pierre, its lieutenant, was like a lion roaring with anger as he was the first to reach the plaza in front of the enemies' fort and to enter the first cabin, the door of which was open. He found there two Indians who were smoking a pipe and who apparently did not believe that we were going to come attack them so soon. They were holding a council or making plans, but the sight of our officer surprised them. They attempted to run for safety, but one of them paid with his life for coming there. The other reached the fort quickly.[15]

Meanwhile, our detachment was still advancing toward the fort, flags flying in the wind, crying out, "Vive la France!" The Swiss soldiers were following after the grenadiers, then came the troops of the Company, then the habitants and militia. As we climbed up the butte, a soldier of the Company, named Tisbé, was killed. We reached the top, and as soon as all had gathered there, we began to set fire to the cabins on our left and right atop the butte. They were reduced to ashes by means of rockets [263][16] with

---

that the Chickasaws also captured his letter with the plans for his expedition or learned of it from the captives; see "Narrative of the War against the Chickasaws," MPA, I, 324. Baudoin is not mentioned in Mémoires historiques. Bienville also wrote of an English flag and some Englishmen in the fort; see Bienville to Maurepas, MPA, I, 305.

15. In Dumont's poem, Baudoin does pronounce a benediction upon the troops, although only in the Arsenal copy is it quoted; see "Poème," 347.

16. Figure 11, "Encampment of the French Army," was originally located at this spot in the manuscript. It resembles the top part of Dumont's map in the "Poème," 346 (Figure 46).

combustible materials in them. We approached closer still, and the habitants, myself among them, divided into two parties, one to the left and the other to the right of the enlisted troops, with the goal of reaching the pilings of the fort and setting fire to them. But in spite of our strong efforts, in the midst of our march, the Sr. Juzan, adjutant major, suddenly stopped us and forced us to retrace our steps. This maneuver slowed our enthusiasm. No doubt he only did this so that the regular soldiers would have the glory of being the first to breach the walls of the fort. But the gunfire from the Englishmen and the Indians had already killed or wounded a few of their men, as well as of ours—some in the feet, some in the arms—and this restrained, or rather warned, them not to expose themselves so much, for we were all more or less in the open. The Swiss advanced and retreated three times, and the French troops arranged themselves in a column, taking cover behind a round cabin that had not been burned and that served as a retrenchment.

As the Sr. Juzan saw that the Swiss were retreating, he came up on their left flank close to where I was to encourage them to advance. But as he was trying to get them to put their hearts in it, as the saying goes, a shot fired from one of the stronghouses hit him between the shoulders. He staggered but did not fall. When he realized he was wounded, he redoubled his entreaties toward the Swiss, saying, "My friends, I am wounded. I'm going to return to camp, but before I die, at least let me learn that you have vanquished our enemies, and I will die contented." And he did die as soon as he arrived at camp. It was not long before at Mobile that he [264] had married, and he left his wife pregnant. The Sr. de Lusser, captain commandant of Tombigbee, was also wounded and carried to camp, where he died. He said that he forgave his enemy because he was convinced that the ball that had hit him was not fired by the Indians but by one of the garrison's soldiers, who had avenged the death of his comrades who had had their heads smashed in, as I described above. One habitant who was a boat captain was also killed but could not return to camp, whereas the sergeant of the grena-

---

The two maps are quite similar, as both emphasize the butte upon which the Chickasaw fort was built. A "ravine des cannes" running across the "Poème" map is not shown in Figure 11. Two maps by Alexandre de Batz obtained from the Alabama leader Pacana and dated Sept. 7, 1737, show the area's geography from a Chickasaw perspective. One of these, reproduced in *MPA*, IV, 155, shows a "path of M. Dartaguiette" coming from the north toward the Ogoula Tchetoka village, and the "path of the second party of Frenchmen" coming from the south or southwest toward "Apeony where the latter group of French attacked." This village is adjacent to "Aekya," or Ackia. Compare also Broutin's "Plan a l'estime ou scituation des trois villages Chicachas" (ANOM, 04DFC 49c).

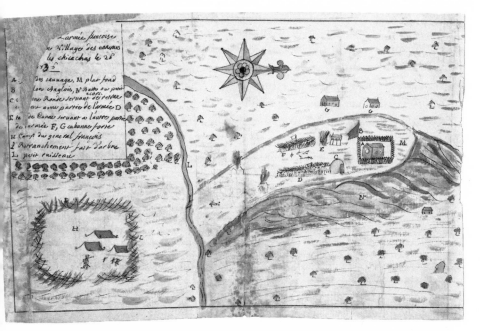

Figure 11. *Encampment of the French Army (at the Chickasaws)*. VAULT oversize
Ayer MS 257, map no. 11. Courtesy The Newberry Library, Chicago

diers and his captain, the Sr. Renaut, were wounded in the thigh and fell
and had to be carried back behind the front lines.[17]

So in a word, those who attacked the fort all got what was coming to
them, and even a little more. For, since the soldiers were lined up, as I've
described, behind the round cabin, anyone who stuck his foot out a little
more than his neighbor received a shot in the ankle. And the Sr. Grondel—
a lieutenant in the Swiss regiment and the son of Grondel, the half-pay
lieutenant for the Alsatian garrison at Port-Louis—this lieutenant, I say,
in trying to encourage his company to follow his lead rather than retreat
as they were doing, had set off running, along with the Sr. de Saint Pierre,
to attack the walls of the fort, yelling, "Follow me, my friends!" The latter
did not receive any wounds, even though his weapons, the brim of his hat,
and the folds of his uniform were riddled with more than a dozen holes.
But the former, the Swiss lieutenant, I mean, received two shots to his body
out of four that brought him to the ground, and he was not able to rejoin

17. Dumont's point here is that the militia helped the troops, but the troops did not re-
ciprocate. The sergeant of the grenadiers serving under Renaut d'Hauterive (Renaud) might
have been named de Velle; see the anonymous "Narrative," *MPA*, I, 319.

the army. He dragged himself [265] as best he could into a cabin that was nearby. M. Dupart, captain of the Swiss regiment, sent one of his soldiers to fetch him, which he did in the face of much gunfire. He carried his officer on his shoulders, much as Aeneas carried his father, Anchises, away from the walls of Troy. But there was this difference between the two: the latter was protected by a cloud that hid him from his enemies, whereas the Swiss soldier did not have this advantage when he carried his officer, and they were both hit by a single shot; that is to say, the ball hit the calf of the lieutenant, passed through his leg, and entered between the shoulders into the body of the valiant and generous soldier. It took several men to carry the two of them back to camp.[18]

As for me, I sought out an *antichon*, which is a house built upon four posts, with no enclosure or foundation, which one enters by climbing a ladder. I was there with the idea of firing at a loophole on the wall of the enemy fort from which constant fire had been coming. I wanted to try to hit the Indian behind it, but as I was aiming at him, a soldier asked me to step aside, saying he would not miss. As his gun was already loaded, I stepped back, gave him my place, and stood next to him. But just then, a ball entered the antichon through the bundles of canes that made up its roof; a gunshot was fired from two and a half feet above his head. The ball pierced his heart and came out at his knee. As I was right next to him, the sound rendered me deaf for nearly a quarter of an hour. I pushed the barrel of my gun up through the canes and I fired. The Indian who was up there quickly jumped down from the roof to escape, but some Swiss soldiers fired at him and made him plow the dirt with his nose. While I was reloading my gun, I was hit by a ball that passed [266] through the tail of my vest, through my shirt in two places, stripped off the button from my breeches, and made me fall to the ground. But this was a very lucky shot for me, as it did not at all hurt me. As I got up, I was more embarrassed than hurt, for I held in one hand my gun and in my other hand my breeches and in this state ran to rejoin

18. For more on this battle, see Bienville to Maurepas, *MPA*, I, 305–306; Jean-Marie Shea, ed., *Journal de la guerre du Micissippi contre les Chicachas, en 1739 et finie en 1740* . . . (New York, 1859); and *Mémoires historiques*, II, 222–223. All list Juzan, Lusser, Renaut d'Hauterive, de Noyan, and Grondel, among others, as having been killed in the battle, but they do not mention Dupart. In the Arsenal copy of "Poème," 349, the speech of Juzan is longer. None of the other sources mentions that Lusser believed he had been shot by one of his own men. For the allusion to Anchises, see the latter part of book 2 of Virgil's *Aeneid*. The cloud was created by Venus, who had mated with Anchises to bear Aeneas, and appeared to the latter to urge him to rescue his father.

the Swiss soldiers, where I found the broken-off end of a bayonet to use as a button.[19]

The Swiss were deployed along a straight line, as were the troops of the Company, but had for cover only a pile of long, thick canes, such as were plentiful around there. The captain of the Swiss was in a pigsty, as if it were a little fort surrounded by palisades. As for our men, it was like a slaughterhouse: 37 men had been killed and 117 wounded, some in the feet, others in the thigh, arms, stomach, or shot through the body, the hand, etc. The Sr. de Noyan, who was then the commandant of the detachment, had given a wounded soldier one of those small bottles of spirits, the kind covered with woven basket-canes, that we called a pistol. The soldier had drunk some of it and then given the pistol back to the captain, who was going to put it in the pocket of his breeches, when a ball came that broke the bottle in half and penetrated the thigh of the commandant, who, having fallen to the ground, received an initial treatment for his wound along with the wound itself, for the brandy entered the wound, which could only be good for it. He had to be carried to camp, where the general was sitting on a crate, no doubt praying to God to give him the victory. When the general, I say, saw his nephew thus injured, he sounded the signal for retreat. But how to retreat? The army had no more powder, having used it all firing at the walls of the enemy fort. If the Indians had known of the practice of making sorties, a mere twenty men would have found us [267] listless and would certainly have routed us. It was necessary to prepare a second detachment to rescue the first and to make our retreat possible.[20]

And so that is how our detachment was received by the Indians and the English. We returned to camp, where, at the time we left, not a single tent had been set up, but at our return, we found the general's tent as well as four others filled with wounded persons. It had been about ten o'clock when we had marched out against the enemy that morning, and it was three in the afternoon when we returned. We ate some food, which we badly needed,

19. *Antichon* is a Choctaw or Chickasaw word, defined as "little *antichons* or henhouses *[poulaillers]* with which the villages of the Chickasaws are all filled and where they gather in groups to defend the approaches of their forts" (Bienville and Salmon to Maurepas, *MPA*, I, 323). This mock-heroic episode is not in the "Poème" nor in the *Mémoires historiques*.

20. The anonymous "Narrative" states, "The said dead possibly amount to one hundred and twenty-five persons" (Bienville to Maurepas, *MPA*, I, 319). Bienville writes of 60 or 70 killed or wounded (*MPA*, I, 306); the *Mémoires historiques* gives 36 dead and at least 16 wounded (II, 223); and the "Poème," 37 dead and 107 wounded (349). This comic anecdote about the "pistol" of brandy is not in any other account of the battle.

but after that, we could not rest, for we had to fortify our position by felling trees and stacking them one atop another to make a barricade to protect ourselves from a surprise by the Indian enemies, who, in the face of this, did not try to do so.

While our army was occupied at this task, a party of six Indians from another Chickasaw village came to our camp, holding in the air both the calumet pipe and a letter that they were bringing to our general. He, adorned with the laurels he had just added to his previous ones, did not at all want to receive these envoys nor to know from where the letter came, and he immediately ordered our Indian allies to kill this party, which they did. But these envoys, seeing themselves betrayed and attacked contrary to the law of the calumet, defended themselves as best they could and tore up the letter but were forced to yield to the more numerous foes who massacred them. Night followed, and many sentinels were posted. We believed that finally we were going to enjoy a little rest.[21]

We were lying on the grass around [268] a fire, for it was cold. As we were trying to go to sleep and find in our slumbers some respite from our many rigors, we were all of a sudden surprised to see rockets in the air, set off by the order of our general either to cheer up the army, which was nearly over-come with sorrow, or else from a motive that we could not fathom, unless it might be to startle the Indians, who had never seen fire flying through the air like that. The army (by which I mean the regular soldiers, the Swiss, the militia, and also the negroes) could not stop themselves from joking to one another that it was in celebration of the victory they had just achieved. While our men shot off these fires of celebration, or rather of sadness, the Indian women in the village were beating on the great pot that they used as a drum, yelling insults and taunts at us in their songs, describing how ten of our men were worth less than one of theirs.

These mockeries of our spectacle continued for the entire night, but as the first light of dawn appeared, each man in the camp wanted only to at-

21. On the envoys and the letter, see original manuscript, below [274]; "Poème," 350; and *Mémoires historiques,* II, 224, which states only that "a party of Indians from another village . . . brought him a letter," not that the letter was from Pierre d'Artaguiette. Le Page asserts, "When the French saw them, they believed it was a party sent by Monsieur Dartaguiette" (*Histoire de la Louisiane,* III, 413), but Le Page had returned to France in 1734 and most likely copied this last chapter of his work from Dumont. Therefore, Marc de Villiers du Ter-rage believes Dumont invented this story; see his notes in "Poème," 350, 354. D'Artaguiette had been captured on March 24, and this version of events would require that the Chicka-saws kept their captive alive for two months. Other accounts suggest that he was killed during the attack in March or shortly afterward.

tack the enemy again and either conquer or die. Not only did we wish for it; we fully expected it. But as the day grew light enough to see objects, we perceived that the Indians, who no doubt had feared that the fire they saw flying through the air during the night would set fire to their fort, had now left the buildings uncovered. This redoubled our desire to attack the enemy, to make them feel the effects of our grenades, which, when we attacked the day before, had been useless; when we had [269] tried to throw them over the walls, they fell down from the roofs of the houses and exploded at our heels. Furthermore, we strongly wanted to return and avenge the insult that had been done to our poor warriors whose bodies, after being killed, had been left on the battlefield, where we could not remove them. The cruel and savage enemies had cut them into quarters and hung them up in the air so as to make us see the spectacle and to let us know that they would do, or wished to do, the same to us. During the night, a big pit had been dug on our side, in which the bodies of our dead were buried, and after they were covered with dirt, a fire was lit on top so as to conceal from the Indians the location of the grave and the bodies and thus prevent the savages from taking their scalps. During the night, we also made twenty-four stretchers with which to carry the most seriously wounded men and those who could not walk.[22]

Finally, at seven or eight o'clock in the morning, a cry went around that flags had been spotted flying in the wind, and people said that it was the army of M. d'Artaguiette. What an overflow of joy was felt in our army, for we hoped that with this reinforcement, we would have vengeance. Telescopes were brought out to see whether the rumor was true. But alas, this joy quickly dissipated, and our hopes vanished with the wind. For, in fact, it was nothing at all. The general signal was sounded and the soldiers ordered to pull up the tent stakes and place the casualties on the stretchers. And so, after making so fine a conquest over our enemies, after having come so far to find them, the order was given to march, not to go into battle against them, but instead to avoid them by returning to where we had disembarked.

[270] With drums beating and flags flying in the wind, we left the place that had been our camp, the army in the two columns marching at a measured pace, all the more so since the wounded were being carried by the strongest soldiers and negroes in the army and those who were only lightly injured or who, in spite of their wounds, were able to use their legs were marching with the rest. Filing out at nine in the morning, after marching

22. See "Narrative," *MPA*, I, 319, about the difficulties of retrieving the bodies of dead and wounded; and *Mémoires historiques*, II, 224, and "Poème," 351, about the Chickasaws' mutilating some of these bodies.

all day, the army only reached a point two leagues distant from where it had disembarked. We had to spend the night there, though we did not rest easily, for we had to be on the lookout for the enemy. In addition, the groaning and wailing of the wounded was heard all night, and every soldier was so seized with fear that at the slightest sound we heard, we believed the Chickasaws were coming after us. But by a blessing from heaven, the men of that tribe found themselves with the same fear, imagining that we had only left our camp as a decoy and to lure them out into the plain, and so, luckily, they did not come toward us. You can well imagine what kind of rest we had that night.

At the break of day, the march resumed, but when bearers were needed to carry the Swiss soldier who had rescued the Sr. Grondel from the enemy cabin where he had taken cover, no one volunteered, for with his height and girth, he was so heavy that he overwhelmed his porters. When the army had marched away and he was the last one left behind, a call to halt was passed up to the head of the column, and the surgeons were called together to examine his wound once more. They declared that based on their experience, his wound was fatal and [271] untreatable. This is why they condemned him to death. The Reverend Father Baudoin, chaplain of the army, came to him, heard his confession, and prepared him for a death that would be peaceful, but not natural; for once he had received his absolution, the poor, unfortunate, and brave soldier, in spite of his prayers and supplications that his head be broken, was buried alive in a hole and covered with dirt. This earth no doubt had greater charity than the general; it took away a life that had become worthless not only because of the man's wound but because of the cruelty and savagery of the commander. Such was the end of this poor Swiss soldier whose only recompense for saving the life of one of his officers was to lose his own and to earn, by his martyrdom, a happier life than the one he had known in this world.[23]

After he was buried, the army set off again and at ten or eleven o'clock arrived at the landing point. Once there, a break for lunch was called, and once that was over, everything was loaded as quickly as possible into the boats and pirogues. We left this place where staying longer could only lead to trouble, for as soon as we arrived there, the Choctaws, our friends and allies, began to grumble and try to pick a quarrel with us. Our general soothed this trouble with a gift of powder and balls and other trade goods. By nightfall of that day, the army found itself all assembled at a point five leagues down-

23. This story is not in *Mémoires historiques*. It is found in the Arsenal copy of Dumont de Montigny's "Poème," 352, but not in the Library of Congress copy.

stream from the landing and spent the night there. The next morning, each boat and pirogue was issued supplies: biscuit, rice, beans, and salt meat (although the last was now spoiled), so as to proceed to Tombigbee as quickly as possible.

So we floated downstream [272] without maintaining any order, each going along according to his own wishes but all sharing in the zeal to leave behind the land, or at least one spot in the land, that had been fatal to so many of our Frenchmen. Some arrived at Tombigbee earlier, some later, and it took nine days to reassemble the entire army. Our general arrived there last of all, much like a shepherd driving his flock to the manger arrives only after he has rounded up and driven in the last sheep who were lagging behind. Some of our wounded men died along the way, and they were buried without ceremony at the first spot where they could be put in the earth. When everyone had arrived at Tombigbee, we had some rest there, and food was again issued to each boat; in place of stale biscuit, there was bread and fresh biscuit, and then each went on to Mobile. As soon as we arrived, we learned that our vain boasting in front of the Chickasaws had led to the death of the Sr. d'Artaguiette, the captain commandant of Illinois, who, following the orders he had received from our general to go to the Chickasaw village by May 10 at the latest, had, in fact, been there then.

My reader may well recall, if he wishes to, that on that date we were not far beyond Tombigbee, having left on the fifth. As soon as the Sr. d'Artaguiette arrived at the Chickasaw fort, he made a camp there, and for ten days, there was no movement on his part nor on that of the Indians. He had with him only eighty Frenchmen and about three or four hundred of our Indian friends who had taken our side and come to help [273] avenge us. These Indian allies, frustrated to see themselves facing the enemy without engaging them in battle, began to grumble and to speak openly of how they were going to return home, saying that the great French general from across the salty water (by which they meant the ocean) would never arrive in this country. The Sr. d'Artaguiette, hearing these murmurs and complaints, called a council of war, and it was resolved that since they had no news from the general's army, they should simply attack the enemy to punish them for their bad faith and harsh words toward us and our allies. The drums sound, the troops kneel to receive from their chaplain the benediction and general absolution, and after that, they marched toward the enemy, all in formation with flags flying. But the enemies took fright, abandoning their fort to retreat to another one a half league away. Our troops thus pass by the abandoned fort and go to the second, where the enemy does the same thing, fleeing to a third. Our troops chase after them and kill several. But unfortunately, as the Sr. d'Artaguiette was getting ready to take the third fort and the enemies in it were about to abandon it to the victor, the commander was wounded in two places. When the Illinois Indians saw this, they believed that their leader was dead, took to their heels, and fled in many small groups along various paths, back to the landing point, where they started paddling up the river. The Sr. d'Artaguiette, forty soldiers, the chaplain, and two sergeants were thus abandoned to the mercy of the enemies, whose numbers continued to grow and who, when they saw only a small number facing them, surrounded the Frenchmen. At the end of the day, with no ammunition, the Sr. d'Artaguiette had to give himself up [274] prisoner, along with the forty men and the Jesuit chaplain. Contrary to the custom of the Indians, they were led into the fort without receiving any insults or beatings, since the Indians of the village saw them as the perfect ransom for making peace with us. It was with this goal that, knowing our great general was to attack one of their villages, they asked the Sr. d'Artaguiette to write asking for peace, and it was the party carrying this letter that was wiped out by the Choctaws on orders from the general. But not having read the letter and not knowing where the Illinois army was, we retreated as I've described, leaving behind the forty-one prisoners. But through the generosity and lenience of a Chickasaw who showed him the way, a sergeant from among the prisoners made his escape through the forest on a path that led toward Alabamon and the fort built there by the French. The sergeant reached that fort without incident, and then, from there, Mobile, where he told how, having run away from his liberator, he then retraced his steps and hid within sight of the village, where he had seen the forty victims burned, the Sr. d'Artaguiette among them, all together in the middle of the plaza. In this way, the Indians avenged themselves for the small number of wrongs that we had committed on their lands. Such was the death of the Sr. d'Artaguiette, who was a person filled with courage and nobility and a good Christian and who had a bright future. But he was unlucky, as were so many others. He and his men could well be called the forty martyrs of the New World.[24]

24. Dumont's chronology of these events increases Bienville's culpability for d'Artaguiette's captivity and death. Bienville, in his correspondence, claims that he postponed the rendezvous with d'Artaguiette to late April and that d'Artaguiette had arrived at the Prud'homme Bluffs on March 4 and attacked the Chickasaws on Palm Sunday, March 24; thus he was killed several weeks before Bienville, Dumont, and the army reached the Chickasaw villages. See Bienville to Maurepas, *MPA*, I, 312–313, 330. Dumont, in the *Mémoires historiques*, writes that d'Artaguiette, "having arrived at the Chickasaws on the ninth of May with fifteen hundred men, had camped there until the twentieth of the month" (*Mémoires historiques*, II, 229). In eulogizing the secular soldiers as martyrs, Dumont diverges sharply

[275] As for us, after staying for a while at Mobile, we embarked again and reached New Orleans. Each man went back home, counting himself lucky to have escaped and survived. Our general came home to his seat of government with the plan of returning another time to have his revenge on the Indians. We will see in what follows the progress and success of this plan. The rest of that year, nothing much happened, aside from learning of the continuing attacks made by our enemies. When they were able to find some of our men traveling, they did not spare them.[25]

About the month of March 1737,[26] there arrived at the capital a royal vessel called the *Somme*, commanded by the chevalier de Kerloret, coming from the department of Rochefort. As for me, I was living in New Orleans with my wife, who had had two children with me. We were living fairly well, although I now had no job. I did have two houses—one for us and the other for my slaves—and I had a large, spacious garden where I worked and from which I was selling vegetables. I also hired out five separate negroes to some men who were making bricks and tar over on the far side of Lac Saint-Louis. I rented them for fifteen or sixteen livres per month, in the money of that country, keeping only a single negro woman at home to make our rice bread. We raised turkeys, ducks, and chickens. We lived the life of city dwellers.

I was also known for my work on behalf of individuals drawing up petitions to be presented to the council, and I even served as their attorney, which did not at all please the councillors. Whenever a matter of some significance came into my hands—and I saw, in the first hearing of the council, [276] how the other side tried to tip the balance for the second hearing by challenging the case either upon the facts or the procedures—I cited to them the relevant ordinances, which so surprised them that, in the end, they could not rule contrary to law and justice and were forced to concur with my briefs. All this is to say that I saw myself on the verge of becoming a lawyer in this New World, and the council most assuredly did not want this. I was sent an ordinance signed by the Sr. Salmon (the commissaire ordon-

---

from François-Xavier de Charlevoix's *Histoire et description generale de la Nouvelle France*, which in 1747 was the only published account of these events. Charlevoix cast Father Sénat as a martyr who allowed himself to be captured so that he might minister to the other captives, and was later killed. But Bienville wrote that Sénat (who presumably is the chaplain Dumont refers to) was, along with Louis-Marie-Charles Dutisnet, among three survivors of the forty-four captives. See Bienville to Maurepas, *MPA*, I, 313; Charles E. O'Neill, ed., *Charlevoix's Louisiana: Selections from the History and the Journal* (Baton Rouge, La., 1977), 127.

25. See Chapter 8, below, for Dumont's account of the second French expedition against the Chickasaws, in 1739–1740, which was even less successful than the first one.

26. Index note: "1737."

nateur and judge) and all the councillors, prohibiting me from appearing again before the council as an advocate for other individuals. I obeyed this after a fashion, for I did not appear again in person, but this did not prevent me from working at home, and those for whom I was working transcribed what I had done in another's hand. The citations of council ordinances and precedents that I marshaled for them in my briefs made me well known. But nothing could be done to condemn me, since I was no longer seen in front of the council, and neither was my handwriting.[27]

At last, tired of living in a country like that, and my wife being home-sick, I decided to go back to France. I requested a passage, which I obtained only after many rejections, many visits, and many inconveniences. It was granted to me on the condition that I furnish the rations for my wife and my children on the royal vessel. As for me, I would be given a single ration, but I would have to pay all my debts, both to individuals as well as to the Company of the Indies, or rather to its agent—debts that, by all rights, were not owed, since [276][28] they had been contracted in the year of the fatal massacre and were supposed to have been repaid out of the tobacco harvest for that year (1729), of which all the habitants had been deprived by the fire that the Natchez Indians had set after murdering the habitants. I tried to explain this injustice, and I would have been able to win my case had I remained in the country, but the vessel was about to leave, and so I was obliged to pay all the same. The council said to me, "Pay now, and when you are back in France, you will make your case to the directors in person, who will take account of your losses."[29]

27. See Figure 21, the map of Dumont's New Orleans residence. The size of the garden and chicken coop confirms his claims here about the scale of his agricultural production, and that he worked it himself while hiring out his slaves attests to his skills. Renting out slaves for day labor was a common practice in early Louisiana, especially for widows and the lesser nobles. A large brick-making concern was located in New Orleans proper, in the neighbor-hood now known as Tremé, whereas several pitch-and-tar operations, including one run by a free woman of color, were located north of the city on the far side of Lake Pontchartrain. The Superior Council of Louisiana held judicial, administrative, and legislative functions in the colony and was the highest court of appeal in Louisiana. Lawyers were technically banned from the colony under the Code Noir of 1724; nonetheless, Dumont claims to have served in a similar capacity to that of his brothers and father in Paris.

28. Here and in a few other places, Dumont made an error in the pagination.

29. Dumont's appeal concerning one of these debts appears in the Records of the Su-perior Council of Louisiana: "Messieurs of the Superior Council of this province. Messieurs: It is an honor to represent to you, the subscriber, that his debt to the king on rice which he should have remitted to the store in 1735, when rice was worth one ecu per quart, should be acquitted by his labor and his troubles, for which he never demanded payment, as described in the attached certificate. Today he objects, as rice is now worth six francs. He pleads to

So, in the end, I had to pay. I sold my negroes for payment on the accounts of the Company, for a total of 1,500 livres in local currency. That left only my houses and land, which I sold for 400 livres of French currency, and having settled all this, I granted freedom to one of my female negroes, the nursemaid of my children. My accounts were signed by the council and a copy given to me; I was given approval for my passage, which was supposed to begin within three weeks. But because I had already sold and given up everything, we went to stay at the farm of one of our friends named the Sr. de Chavannes, two leagues away from New Orleans. We were welcomed there and treated very well, and the day that we were going to embark, he made us a present of a cow and a calf for our passage, which we brought on board the ship, as well as three dozen of my chickens and two dozen turkeys. For the remainder of our supplies (for the biscuit), I paid for my wife and my two children 70 livres in Spanish money. At last, after saying our farewells [277] to our friends and giving all the thanks we could to the generous Sr. de Chavannes, we embarked in the *Somme* on the twelfth of June, at about two in the afternoon. We floated down the river and were at La Balize on the fourteenth. Contrary winds detained us there until the twentieth, when we left, departing a country which, to speak frankly, was half abandoned, some of the habitants having retreated to the capital leaving lands uncultivated and others being exposed to the insults and depredations of the Indians. This, even as the general was nurturing his hopes and future plans to exterminate our enemies and had already written to France to send him more reinforcements.[30]

---

your justice, Messieurs, to acknowledge that if he had paid it back at that time, and he would not have done otherwise . . . [one line is illegible in the document] . . . the plaintiff has never worked by the day, and work at Bayou St. John is very different from that in the city, where the petitioner would be compelled to hire a negro at twenty sous a day. Thus, messieurs, he hopes that your justice in general will acquit the debt, by his pains and labors for the king. At New Orleans the 4 May 1737 ("Demontigny," Superior Council of Louisiana, *Proceedings*, no. 1737050404, Louisiana State Museum, Baton Rouge; translation from *LHQ*, V [1922], 399).

30. See *Histoire de la Louisiane*, III, 343, on slaves breastfeeding French children in the colony. According to Louisiana's Code Noir (1724), manumission required approval by the Superior Council, although, in practice, this appears to have been rarely done. No record exists of this manumission. Bienville and Salmon indeed wrote in February 1737 asking for supplies for another expedition against the Chickasaws; see *MPA*, I, 332–336.

Chapter Eight

RETURN TO FRANCE;
THE SECOND CHICKASAW WAR

JUNE 1737-SEPTEMBER 1746

[277] We set off in the *Somme* under full sail, and having a steady and favorable wind, we passed easily around Cabo San Antonio and through the Bahamas Channel. Leaving the English island of Bermuda to our left, we reached the Azores from the bank of Newfoundland. But just as we were approaching, we were hit by a furious gust of wind that tore our mainsail to shreds, as well as the mizzen sail. This wind was accompanied by a storm so fierce that we were on the verge of cutting away the mizzenmast. But in less than half an hour, the weather calmed, and we were able to regain control of the yards and to set new sails. On the fifteenth of August, we made a sighting of Belle-Isle, and early on the morning of the seventeenth, we arrived at Rochefort, guided by the experience of one of our sailors, who steered the ship right into the anchorage. It was nine o'clock. The customs [278] agents came aboard for their inspection, and around three o'clock in the afternoon, my wife and I went ashore with our two children. Having rented a furnished room, we stayed there for two weeks to recover from our sea voyage and to take the air, as people there say. Then we booked three seats on the coach to Blois. Without going into the details of our voyage, we arrived there in good health. In that town, we rented three post horses: one for our conductor, which also carried our trunk; one for my wife, with our son riding on the haunches; and the third for my daughter and me.

In this manner, we arrived at Vendôme, where we had the pleasure and diversion of doing, or rather helping with, the grape harvest in a vineyard owned by the man with whom we stayed. We departed from this place in the same manner and in three more days arrived at Le Mesnil-Thomas, birthplace of my wife. We found neither her father nor mother there; only her stepmother, who had remarried an inhabitant of that town. She did find—my wife did, that is—her godparents, very well-off people who welcomed us with many courtesies and great friendship. We were obliged to stay there longer than we had planned because the curate of the town had gone to Chartres, and we had to wait for his return (which was just twelve days later). When he returned, he graciously gave us the papers I asked him for: namely, copies of the certificates of my wife's baptism and of the deaths of her mother and father. Once we had received these, taken leave of her friends and relatives, and rented a covered wagon, which we all loaded into, we left behind [279] Le Mesnil-Thomas. We arrived on the tenth of November at Verneuil in Perche, where my wife's cousins were.[1]

We lodged at the sign of the Brass Pitcher. This inn was then filled with all sorts of people who gathered there at that date for the fair of Saint Martin, which goes on for nine days in that town.[2] As soon as our children were asleep, my wife could not resist her impatience to go to the home of one of her cousins, whom she loved most of all. We left our inn at about eight in the evening, and although it had been more than twenty years since she had been in this town, she walked straight to his house, where I knocked on the door. A moment later, this dear relative himself came and opened it. I said to him, after a polite greeting, that I was just passing through and did not want to miss the opportunity to give him news from one of his relatives who was in Louisiana, where I had just come from. He invited me in, as well as my wife. As soon as we had entered and were sitting with his family, which consisted of his wife, who was his second marriage, and an only daughter from his first marriage, he said to me that just that morning he had been re-reading a letter from his dear cousin. He asked after her health, how she was doing in that distant land, and whether she liked it there. All the while, he was staring straight at my wife. Whether it was the power of their common blood that moved him, or some sympathetic attachment, all of a sudden he jumped out of his chair and said, "Oh, Monsieur, you have played a nice trick on me, my cousin is right here!" and he hugged her tenderly. I leave you to imagine the joy that [280] we all felt. We left at about ten o'clock and went to bed, my wife and I, at our inn.

The next day had barely dawned when this kind cousin came to see us and offered to put us up at his house, which we accepted. We paid our bill at the inn and moved to his place, where we had the use of an apartment. That same day, we saw the rest of her relatives, who gave us just as many caresses. The whole time we were there we spent visiting in the homes of one or another of them. The genial cousin with whom we stayed is the Sr.

1. Le Mesnil-Thomas, about 35 km northwest of Chartres, is today little more than a crossroads, with a sixteenth-century church, a small municipal building, and eight or ten houses. But as late as the 1830s, it was a farming town with more than five hundred inhabitants. A search of the parish records from 1690–1705 did not turn up any entry for a baptism of Marie Baron. Verneuil, a larger town known today as Verneuil-sur-Avre, is located 25 km northwest of Le Mesnil-Thomas and 150 km west of Paris, in the region of Perche.

2. November 11 is the saint's day of Saint Martin of Tours.

Le Gras, of one of the oldest families in this little town, which, in days past, resisted several sieges and still has remnants of its old fortifications. As this relative has a house in the countryside a league away from town, we went there and tasted some of the new cider. All in all, we spent a most delightful time with her relatives, who would have gladly kept us longer, but after eleven days in the town, we took advantage of an opportunity to travel in a coach coming from a town called Aigle, which had three seats available. We paid for them, and after taking leave of our relatives, we departed and journeyed to Versailles and early the next morning reached Paris, my beloved hometown, which I had been away from for twenty-eight years.

I was, to say it again, no sooner arrived than I found myself lodgings, a well-furnished room in an inn. The next day, I went to see one of my brothers, who was married, but he had not yet returned from vacation. I saw my sister, who received me [281] with great kindness. I stayed for some time in Paris in this style, but seeing that I would have to be there for an extended period, I took an unfurnished room in the rue du Bout de Monde, and my wife and I wrapped ourselves in our rags, as they say. When his vacation was over some days later, I went to see my brother, who received me with true brotherly kindness and offered me his table, along with all my family.[3]

A few days after this, he introduced me to M. Michel de la Jonchère, who sat on all the councils of the king and was treasurer of the Military Order of Saint Louis. He also was so good as to present me to M. le duc et maréchal de Belle-Isle, who at that time was only lieutenant general of the king's armies. When these two gentlemen, as well as the late M. le maréchal d'Asfeld, learned that I had come from Louisiana, they asked me about the fine concession that they owned in that land. I described it to them with all sincerity and truth, and—so as to further satisfy them and bring them up to date with regard to this plantation, which is located near the Chaouachas, from which nation it has taken the name—I drew for them a plan of it, which they appeared to be pleased with, just as I was with the compensation that I received from their graces. And, in fact, I went every day to the home of M. de la Jonchère during the whole of the eighteen months that my wife and I stayed in Paris, and it is true that not once did I go there without receiving some token of his generosity toward me. It is not [282] only in Paris that he supported me from his purse but also in writing these memoirs, and he continues to do so.[4]

3. The rue du Bout de Monde is now the rue Léopold Bellan in the Second Arrondissement.

4. This plan would presumably be similar to Figure 13, which might be a copy of it. Curi-

Moreover, while I was in Paris, I went to pay my respects to the directors of the Company of the Indies. I presented them with a petition. M. de Fulvy questioned me about the country, and I answered him. Finally, he told me that he had read the reports and maps that I had sent from there and that he was mortified that I had had to stay on after the Company withdrew from the colony. He promised me his protection and offered to send me to the Indies in the service of the Company, which I said I would gladly accept. He told me to come back in a week; that the Company would by then have considered my appeals; that I had been wronged when I was forced to pay for my negroes in Louisiana; and that if I returned there, they would be restored to me. After this, I went away from the Company's headquarters with the hope of having a post with them. I returned again a week later to the headquarters in the rue de Saint Antoine. I asked to be announced and was taken into the personal office of M. Fulvy. After I had bowed to him and said that I had come in response to his request, he asked me whether I was not the brother of M. D——, the lawyer for the council, and when I replied yes, that I had that honor, he suddenly jumped up from his chair and said to me, "I'm furious with him. There is nothing I can do, there is no hope for you for help from me, because your brother just won a court case against the Company, on behalf of some Portuguese. He must be quite rich now, and so let him help you out."[5]

And so this is how I was rewarded by the illustrious and equitable Company for all the years of my youth spent in its service, for the long voyages I made at the mercy of the weather, to draw up the [283] plans for forts, to make maps and reports—in a word, for twelve years of service. One can see from this that the protection of such men is not a secure legacy. It is true that my brother was the attorney for the party opposed to the Company, but if only they had chosen to listen to him and believe him the first time that he had spoken of the case to M. de Fulvy, they would not have had the chagrin of losing it. For, after all, my brother had only done his duty in defending the truth, and I had done the same, and so I should not have been forced

---

ously, it was at this time, or shortly after, that the partners sold the Chaouachas concession. See Heloise H. Cruzat, ed. and trans., "Documents concerning Sale of Chaouachas Plantation in Louisiana, 1737–38," *LHQ*, VIII (1925), 589–646.

5. Dumont presumably refers here to his brother Pierre-Jean-Baptiste Dumont, fourth of the six Dumont brothers, who lived in the rue des Fossés-Montmartre, which today is the portion of the rue d'Aboukir between the Place des Victoires and the rue Montmartre. The rue du Bout de Monde, and the lodging the author rented during this period, was immediately adjacent to this street.

to carry the blame and bear the costs for a case they lost through their own fault.

Having knocked on the Company's door to try to obtain a post to support my family, seeing that all my efforts and service on their behalf were a lost cause for me, and knowing that I was still a half-pay lieutenant at Port-Louis—even though I had lost the papers for this commission in the Natchez Massacre because my trunk was still at the home of my landlady on that day, fatal to so many—I had recourse to the protection of Mgr. le maréchal de Belle-Isle. He arranged for a certificate verifying the commission to be drawn up by the Sr. Alexandre and signed by M. Dangervilliers, the minister of war, along with an order that I be paid the 240 livres due to me for each of the twenty years of my appointment as half-pay lieutenant in Louisiana. A short time later, I received an order to report to my garrison at Port-Louis in my rank as half-pay lieutenant. The partners in the Chaoua-chas concession again gave me some tokens of their generosity before I departed, saying to me that it was done to make my journey easier. [284] I received 100 livres from each of them, which made 400, because Mme. la marquise de Traisnel, being partnered with the three protectors (namely Mgrs. de Belle-Isle, d'Asfeld, and de la Jonchère), was eager to do her part.

I was able to obtain in Paris only three hundred livres, with which I bought clothing, consistent with regulations. I purchased what was needed most urgently and paid for three places in a carriage bound for Orléans. We departed Paris after taking leave of my protectors and asking for their continuing protection, which they promised me and of which I still enjoy the benefits every day. We bade farewell to my brother and my relatives and friends, of whom the most loyal and sincere is the Sr. Dumouchel [de Villainville], a fine gentleman whose uncle was the illustrious, just, and disinterested commissaire ordonnateur of Louisiana, the Sr. Hubert, who, at his death, had left to his brother the Sr. de Saint Memin instructions and memoirs regarding this New World, worthy of being brought to the attention of the ministers. So at last, we left Paris on the third of May and we did not arrive at Port-Louis until the twenty-second.[6] It was not that we stopped along the way; the contrary winds were the true cause, for from Orléans to Nantes, it took us twelve days in one of those small, covered boats that one rents for such voyages.

As soon as I was at my garrison, I went to pay my respects to the royal

6. Index note: "1739." Among the memoirs of Hubert, although not identified by his name, is the "Narrative of the Events after the Spaniards Recaptured Pensacola" (*MPA*, III, 242–254), cited above in Chapter 2.

lieutenant, the Sr. Burin de Ricquebourg, chevalier de Saint Louis and royal lieutenant and commandant during the absence of M. le marquis de Rothelin, who was the governor there but had not yet come. I presented him a letter of recommendation that [284][7] M. de la Jonchère had been so good as to write to the royal lieutenant. In it, he asked him to advance me a hundred livres, the balance of what those gentlemen had given me. Three days after my arrival in Port-Louis, M. le maréchal de Brancas arrived there as part of his tour of inspection in Brittany. He was greeted with a salute of cannonshots fired from the citadel. I had the honor of being presented to him after dinner by the royal lieutenant. When the maréchal learned my name, which he specifically recognized because of my dear father, he promised me his protection. The next morning, he left the garrison to continue his tour.

I went almost three months without receiving my back pay nor the confirmation of my new post. I had written about this to my illustrious protectors and especially to Mgr. le maréchal de Belle-Isle, who was so good to me that he did all he could to secure for me the eighteen years of back pay I was owed. He was so kind as to stipulate that I should get it, but the order that came was for twenty livres per month, pending approval by the commissioner, and in addition, there was another order that I be paid a lump sum of 240 livres out of the back pay I was owed. This was all I was paid.

There was, in the citadel, a militia major who was being detained on orders from the king. His name was the Sr. Blachère. I saw him frequently. He advised me one day that I should try to obtain the post of captain of the gates in the city, a post vacant ever since the death of the Sr. Boneton in 1736; the post remained unfilled because, for reasons I never learned, [285] he had not been replaced. I wrote to my protectors, and they requested this post from M. de Ricquebourg, who replied to them that he had promised it to the major of the fort and that he could not intervene in the matter, since to do so would decrease the payments going to the major; but if they thought it appropriate, they were welcome to try to obtain it for me. My request stalled at that point and made no progress. I had a family to support and only twenty livres per month and no lodging, since I had not been able to obtain a place with someone in the town as I had in 1720.[8] There was no room in the citadel, or so said the royal lieutenant, and I could not get a stipend from the king for my housing. When the major de la place was away

7. Dumont made errors in pagination in this part of the manuscript. Seven consecutive pages are numbered 284, 284, 285, 287, 286, 287, 288.

8. See original manuscript, above [79–80], where Dumont lodged with the widow "Le Sourd."

taking the waters in Dinan, the keeper of the artillery magazine suggested to me that I draw up a design for an ornament for the spacious garden that the major had in town. I gladly did so and also designed an ornament for the room he occupied at the citadel. And as a result, when the major returned and I went to pay my respects, he thanked me and promised me his protection. A few days later, he offered me his garden to plant or have planted, if I wanted, all for my profit, to help me, he said, to support my family. He let his former gardener go and gave me the keys.[9]

Thus I found myself the master of a large, spacious garden, just as our forefather Adam was long ago. I had all the garden at my disposal, but the fruit and a large, square plot of artichokes were reserved for the major. Since I very much enjoy gardening, this gave me the greatest pleasure in the [287] world. I had lodgings just across the street. Scarcely three weeks passed, however, before I was told that the major now regretted giving me his garden, and when he came that afternoon to see me, I passed on to him the news I had been given. But he told me that he was true to his word and that not only had he put me in his garden to support my family but also that I could do whatever I wanted there, that he gave it to me as my own. Holding his knight's cross as if to make a vow, he said, "Yes, on my word as a major, I am giving it to you for as long as you are here in Port-Louis. But when the king sees fit to send you elsewhere, I will be master of it and may give it to another." He again informed me that he wanted to have me in the post of captain of the gates. He had me write a letter to my dear protector de la Jonchère, and he wrote on the bottom of it a note to that personage, saying it was imperative that I have it and explaining what needed to be done to achieve this. He repeated his promise to me to look after my welfare. But all this was so that I would not aspire to any other work than in his garden, where he was very pleased with the plots that I had laid out, because in fact this letter was never sent to M. de la Jonchère. As well as his gardener, I was his factotum, for since he enjoyed the right to claim one faggot of firewood from each cartload that was brought through the gates of the town, he gave me the assignment of receiving this firewood and keeping accounts of it for him, as well as of the five sous that he received from the butchers for the

9. Dinan is a town on the north coast of Brittany, some 150 km northeast of Port-Louis. The major de la place who became Dumont's nemesis in Port-Louis is, in all likelihood, Simon de la Vergne de Villeneuve, captain of a regiment in the royal marines. A local historian of Port-Louis, Henri-François Buffet, confirms that he "managed a garden near the main gate, just behind the large bastion, as part of the royal dominions" (see Buffet, *Vie et société au Port-Louis des origines à Napoléon III* [Rennes, 1972], 32).

tax levied on each hooved animal that entered town. Alas, when every two weeks it was necessary to go collect this tax from the butchers, I endured [286] a torrent of insults and invective, all of it intended for the man who employed me.

Thus I passed my time agreeably, based upon the generosity of the major and upon what seemed to be his desire to increase the benefits of the promise he had made to me. I wrote verses in his praise, and if it had still been the fashion, as it was in ancient times, the beeches, oaks, and other trees would have each been emblazoned with the device or the name of this Maecenas. The smallest anxiety or discontent that I might feel gave him pain, and as for me, I responded by doing everything I could think of to show him that all he was doing for me was not done for an ingrate. This is how I passed the years 1740 and 1741.

Near the beginning of that year,[10] I learned, in a relation that had come from Quebec to the Reverend Jesuit Fathers, of how the commandant general of the country had avenged himself against the Chickasaws, our enemies, and how he had, in turn, found his comeuppance. As I already indicated above, he had written to France to ask for help, which had been granted to him, and three vessels were sent out under the command and orders of the Sr. le chevalier de Kerloret. The names of these three ships, I can give you: the *Somme,* the *Atlas,* and the *Charente,* which were well supplied with victuals, munitions of warfare, and many soldiers of the marines, all commanded by the Sr. de Nouailles, a young man of spirit and full of courage and valor. At last, these ships, together with a small [287] merchant vessel supplied by the Company, arrived safely in New Orleans, where the general of the country was waiting eagerly to go exterminate the Chickasaws, or so he put it. The flatboats and pirogues and all the other craft being ready, the soldiers and habitants all were vying with one another, wanting nothing more than to go after the enemy. When all was in order and the supplies for war and for sustenance were loaded, they left New Orleans, but not to go to Mobile along the route that we had taken via Tombigbee in the year 1736, for this was too difficult and too expensive. Instead, it was up the Saint Louis River, a distance of at least 360 leagues, which is only a short trip but which lasts many days. This does not deter the troops, however, for they are sure of victory. They attack the rapid current of the river with strong oarstrokes, meet the opposing winds head-on, and brave the rain and storms until they arrive at last at Fort de l'Entrepos, so named because it had been

10. Index note: "1741."

built next to a river that bore that name, under the command of the Sr. de Coustilhas, who had died there before the fort was even completed.[11]

There was, in that fort, a powder magazine and a casern and lodgings for the general, who had no sooner arrived there than he declared that the fort was too distant from the enemy. This is why he gave his order to reload all that he thought necessary, and rather than stay in this place, the army burned up its day of rest, as they say, and continued upstream for 120 more leagues, [288] still on the same river, stopping only when they reached the bluffs or low mountains along the Margot River. This was on the very day of the Feast of the Assumption of the Virgin, and this is why the fort that was built there was given that name. It was built entirely of palisades by the soldiers of the army. It had, like Fort Saint Francis, caserns, a magazine, and lodgings for the general, but as it was not large enough to hold the entire army, they encamped under tents in a pretty prairie that was near the fort and looked down upon it. Ovens were also built for the subsistence of the army.[12]

However, from mid-August until the month of February, there was no

11. Here Dumont narrates the history of the Second Chickasaw War of 1739–1740. He devoted most of the third canto of his "Poème" to the same events. He no doubt enjoyed the opportunity to describe a disastrous military failure by Bienville, who was relieved of his post as governor in October 1742. More than a million ecus were spent on the campaign, three times the annual budget for the Louisiana colony as a whole, and more than three thousand soldiers took part. Dumont's account here is not copied from any of the extant documents narrating the events of war, but given his mention of the Jesuits, it seems possible that the "relation" he refers to was the journal kept by Pierre Vitry; see Jean Delanglez, ed. and trans., "The Journal of Pierre Vitry, S.J.," Mid-America, XXVIII (1946), 23–59. Vitry did not return to Quebec or France, however; he died in Louisiana in 1749. The Somme arrived at La Balize on May 23, 1739, and at New Orleans on June 14. The Atlas reached La Balize on May 27; see Jean-Baptiste Le Moyne de Bienville and Etienne Gatien Salmon to comte de Maurepas, MPA, I, 400. Dumont implies that Bienville erred in choosing the Mississippi route over the Tombigbee route. The Chickasaw villages were located along the Yazoo River in the northern part of today's state of Mississippi; see Bienville and Salmon to Maurepas, MPA, I, 357–360, and Bienville to Maurepas, MPA, I, 389–395, in which Bienville explains his decision. A reconnaissance mission led by Duverger and some Arkansas guides in 1737 had determined that the Chickasaw fort was only twenty-five leagues from the confluence of the Saint Francis River with the Mississippi, which is why Coustilhas began to build a fort on that site (near modern Helena, Arkansas) before he died in November of 1738; but the true distance turned out to be closer to fifty leagues. Jadart de Beauchamp, the adjutant major at Mobile, however, wrote that the Tombigbee route was better; see Beauchamp to Maurepas, MPA, I, 438–441. See also the maps drawn by Alexandre de Batz in September 1737, reproduced in MPA, IV, 142, 154.

12. Fort Assumption was built near the confluence of the Wolf River and the Mississippi, in modern Memphis.

mention of going after the enemy. There were at least thirty leagues to travel to reach their village. How could the artillery necessary for a siege be transported there? Cannons, balls, mortar shells, and bombs had all been carried this far, yet now there was no road or practicable path. Hence it was necessary to make one, and so, through the immense forests, the soldiers struggled to fell trees, remove the branches, cut them up, and push them to either side of the path, which was eighteen to twenty feet wide. The route was surveyed by the two engineers, the Srs. Broutin and Duverger.

In addition, there were those from Illinois: the captain commandant, named M. de la Buissonnière, with his garrison and a party of habitants and even some Indians from the region, as well as the Iroquois, Nipissing, and Huron Indians from Canada, commanded by the Sr. de Céleron, a Quebec officer sent by M. de Beauharnois, [289] the governor general of all Canada. When all these nations arrived at the Illinois, those of that nation and all of the French garrison joined them and departed from the post. After two weeks on the march, they all reached Fort Assumption. To support the general's army, wagons and handcarts had been built. There was a large square, surrounded by tree trunks, in which were many cattle accustomed to the yoke, which had been purchased from the habitants in Illinois for the price of 200 livres apiece, and also horses purchased for 150 livres. It was an unwieldy army to say the least, one requiring great preparation before any movements.[13] Ten leagues of the route had already been cleared, and everyone wanted to receive the command to begin marching out toward the enemy, but their wishes were in vain. I leave you to imagine how contented this army might have been, as rations became so low that they were forced to eat horsemeat.

Finally, March came around, and there was still no thought of marching against the enemy. The Sr. de Nouailles, captain of the troops of the marines, made a case to our general that the season was too far advanced, that among his men, as well as among the ones in the general's convoy, more and more were falling ill each day, and that there was a risk of seeing the entire army perish from hunger and exposure. But our great, invincible gen-

---

13. The anonymous author of the "Journal of the War in Mississippi against the Chicachas," an officer in the regiment led by Nouailles, provides a more detailed list of the Indian warriors who arrived on October 11, 1739, from Canada with Céleron de Blainville; see Jean-Marie Shea, ed., *Journal de la guerre du Micissippi contre les Chicachas, en 1739 et finie en 1740* . . . (New York, 1859); this journal was translated by Fernand Claiborne and published in J. F. H. Claiborne, *Mississippi, as a Province, Territory, and State* . . . (Jackson, Miss., 1880), 64–85. He enumerates 162 Iroquois and lesser numbers from fourteen northeastern tribes, as well as four tribes from the Illinois region (see 41–43). See also "Poème," 367.

eral could not accept that anyone might be so forthright as to tell him what must be done; he replied that Nouailles need [290] only follow orders, that he would march against the enemy when he deemed it appropriate, and that if M. de Nouailles wanted to retreat with his company of soldiers, he could go ahead and do so.[14]

Neither at this fort nor in the vicinity was any attack mounted by the enemies. This was not the case with respect to our first convoy—on the Tombigbee side, I mean. There, a party of Chickasaws surprised one made up of eighteen Choctaws and killed them all.

At the end of the month of March, our general called the Sr. de Céleron to his quarters and, speaking to him in private, told him his idea: that Céleron should gather for duty the Indians that he had brought with him, as well as some volunteers from among his cadets, and go with this detachment toward the Chickasaw village. If the enemies came out and asked for peace, then he should promise it to them. This captain departed with the Indians who had come with him from Canada, and as soon as the army saw him go, they believed that orders would now be given for them to march. There was great rejoicing at this. The army waited impatiently for the drums signaling a movement to march, but they did not know the intention of their master, because when his deputy [Céleron] arrived in front of the enemy, drums beating and flags flying in the wind, he encamped in front of their fort. The Indians then believed that the entire army was going to arrive and lay waste to them, and so, without waiting to see masses of tents set up, they raised a white flag above [291] their fort and took the risk of sending some envoys to the captain to sue for peace and asked whether he would be willing to send one of his officers to their fort. And, in fact, his lieutenant, the Sr. de Saint Laurent, volunteered to go there with a young slave he had with him, and they set out. But he quickly saw that he had too hastily given himself up, for the Indian women were demanding his death and his head. In the end, the chiefs and the honored men ordered the envoy and his slave, who was exhorting him to death, to be detained, and after holding

14. The debate over the failure of the expedition is evident in the minutes of a council of war held in February 1740 (*MPA*, I, 428–431), in which Bienville laid out reasons why he ordered a retreat: rains had rendered the trail too muddy for travel, and many of the beasts of burden who might haul the cannons had died. The signatures of Nouailles, Gilles-Augustin Payen de Noyan, Charles Le Moyne de Longueuil, and Ignace-François Broutin were affixed. However, Broutin also wrote a letter to Salmon refuting Bienville's reasons as false (Broutin to Salmon, *MPA*, I, 431–433). See also Michael J. Foret, "The Failure of Administration: The Chickasaw Campaign of 1739–40," in Glenn R. Conrad, ed., *The French Experience in Louisiana* (Lafayette, La., 1995), 313–321.

council together, they entered the room where the prisoners were, held out the calumet, and smoked it with them, vowing that they would be eternal friends of the French.[15]

So, the Indians in general — that is to say, the Chickasaws and the Natchez together — left their forts to come present the calumet to the Sr. de Céleron, who received them like real friends and promised them a truce, on behalf of the great French general. And, indeed, he left the enemy lands and returned with his detachment and a large party of Chickasaws to Fort Assumption, with the ceremonial calumet and all its accoutrements. At first, the army believed that this was a group of captives taken from the enemy by our men, but when they all arrived before our invincible general and the army saw the calumet offered and received, they were astonished. I won't belabor my reader on this point but shall only say the peace was agreed [292] to by both sides, and all the cannons that had been carried to this place served only to fire powder into the air in celebration of the peace accord, which declared that all the Indians would henceforth regard the French as their brothers and that they would be friends with one another. Such were the conditions of the treaty concluded with vows on the part of the Indians. And of what use was Fort Assumption? None at all. There was no more need for it than for the one built on the Saint Francis River: the pavilions, caserns, bakeries, and magazines all were reduced to ashes.

So — after our general had, by his wisdom, courage, and force of arms, made good for our losses of 1736 and avenged, by the death of our enemies, the deaths of the Sr. d'Artaguiette and the other martyrs — no sooner, I say, had this second Scipio Americanus returned with his victorious army to New Orleans than, relying on a truce so lasting and permanent as what we had just sworn and agreed to with the Chickasaws and Natchez (our former mortal enemies now become friends), a boat filled with habitants from the Illinois departed the capital city to return to their homes.

A young woman from the Ursuline convent had taken passage on this boat. She was named La Potier and was going to Illinois to see her sister,

15. According to Gaspard-Joseph Chaussegros de Léry, who took part in this expedition and wrote a narrative of it (AC, F3, XXIV, 323–337), it included 201 French, 337 Canadian Indians, and 58 Choctaws, and they departed Fort Assumption on February 2, 1740. See also Delanglez, ed. and trans., "Journal of Pierre Vitry, S.J.," *Mid-America*, XXVIII (1946), 50. Céleron de Blainville, although commander of the expedition, left the fort after his troops did, owing to illness. Both Father Vitry's journal and the anonymous *Journal de la guerre du Micissippi* refer to this man as the Lieutenant Saint-Pierre, not Saint Laurent. For more on this confrontation, see the letters between Beauchamp and Salmon, *MPA*, I, 439–446; and Dumont's "Poème," 372.

who had married the wealthy storekeeper of the post, the Sr. Buchet. This girl was [293] then fourteen or fifteen years old. The boat left the city and rowed up the great river past Tunica and Natchez and reached the Arkansas, where, after stopping over at that village for three or four days to take on provisions for the remainder of their three-hundred-league journey, they reached a point twenty leagues beyond Fort Assumption (the place where it had stood, that is). There, counting their voyage as nearly completed, with only thirty or forty leagues to go by water, they were attacked by a party of Indians, who took this girl and tried to make her a slave and lead her back to their village. But by good fortune and the grace of God, the Indian who was guarding her strayed from her side in order to take part in the pillage, and she ran off into the forest and hid herself so well amid the undergrowth that she was able to escape and reach the Illinois settlement overland, living in the forest by eating herbs and the tips of vines. As for the others who were in the boat, they were all killed and scalped, their belongings and the merchandise seized, their boat broken up into pieces. It was this girl who brought to Illinois the tragic news of the acts of our friends the Chickasaws, who had sworn fealty to our general, who, though so well schooled in the ruses and deceits [294] of the Indians, was himself fooled.

Alas, if he had wanted to act when he was at Fort Assumption and had made the Indian enemies feel the courage and valor of Frenchmen when they are well commanded, the Indians would have been fearful and apprehensive thereafter. For they had never seen nor felt the effects of a cannonball nor ever seen a bomb in the air nor the chaos it creates when it hits. Yes, one single bomb fired on one single night into their fort would have been not only capable of making the Indians cry out in fright; it would have brought them to sue for peace under conditions that we could have dictated to them and would have at least included the payment of a good portion of the costs of the war. But our cannons were used only to show the Indians how they might make noise and create an entertaining spectacle.

So it was that the Indians made peace with the French, and I can assure you that when this news was made known to the general, he gave the opinion that neither the Chickasaws nor the Natchez had made this attack but some party of wanderers, perhaps from the Tioux or another Indian nation.[16] I am willing to believe him for the moment. But he will allow me

16. Although the manuscript says Bienville attributes the attack to the "Tioux," this may be a slip of Dumont's pen for "Sioux," as he wrote in the "Poème" (375–376). The Sioux were a large and powerful people but lived far away and would not likely have been in the area; the Tioux were a tiny group allied to the French, a band of Tunicas who lived just south of

to reply that if the Chickasaws, a very numerous nation feared by others, had felt what the French are capable of doing when commanded by a man of war, it would certainly have struck terror into the other nations, who see, on the contrary, [295] how the Frenchman is soft; they seek only to insult him, persuaded that the response to all their murders, assassinations, and piracies will be nothing but peace. But let him know (he being the general of that country), let him know what he should be aware of: that distrust toward Indians, as much as toward other enemies, is the mother of security, for since they have no law nor religion among them, one can never rely on their promises. But after all, this general was the master, and he did as he pleased. But I cannot stop myself from bemoaning the great expense that our grand and invincible monarch devoted to that country to try to restore security there, to reassure and assist the habitants and above all the voyageurs, who are the most at risk when they have to paddle up the river, since, when holding their oars, they cannot defend themselves from a surprise attack, which is the strategy most favored and most often employed by the barbarous Indian nations.

This description that I have just made is not based on what I have seen myself. It comes, as I have already stated, from what the Very Reverend Jesuit fathers gave me here in Port-Louis when they passed through to embark for Pondicherry.[17] Thus, if there were any errors in the account, I beseech my reader not to attribute them to me. But what is certain is that in spite of the three royal vessels sent from France to help those in that country, filled with men and munitions for war; in spite of the Canadians and Indians who came from Quebec, and Canada, and the Illinois country, as well as the Choctaws, all contributing to the numerous army that assembled in and [296] around Fort Assumption with an ardent desire to go fight and punish the enemy; in spite of all this, I say, nothing more was achieved from all that expense than to march around to the point of exhaustion, so as to go and grant a peace that proved to be more fatal than beneficial to the country.

I was not there, of course, since I was happily employed in the major's garden, where he came every day to proclaim to me his zealous desire to help me out and secure for me a tidy fortune. At about this time, the Sr. de la Bourdonnay came with his wife to Lorient to sail for the Indies. Our royal

---

Natchez where Dumont had lodged with the Roussin family. The Indian assailants were more likely from the Chickasaws, with whom Bienville had just made peace.

17. Pondicherry was a French colony on the southeast coast of India, established in 1683. When writing the manuscript, Dumont did not know he would one day live there himself.

lieutenant, the Sr. de Ricquebourg, offered me and my family the chance to sail with him, with a commission for me as an officer. He would provide whatever M. Bourdonnay asked for, for me, and our lieutenant and commandant himself made me the same proposition. I answered that this would please me very much, if the major would consent to it. But no, the major led me to believe that they wanted to take advantage of me and that he wanted me to owe no man other than him for what I might become someday. Based on this promise, I thanked the Sr. de Ricquebourg, and I stayed where I was, in expectation of a promotion from the generous major. I made countless prayers to heaven above for the health and well-being of my dear protector, and it is certain that if we were living in ancient times, one would have seen fatted calves smoking on the altars of my household gods as offerings to ensure his well-being.

I stayed put until the end of September,[18] when, with his permission and that of the royal lieutenant, I left to make a visit [297] to Paris, where I arrived on October 15, having made the journey on foot. As soon as I arrived there, I went to pay my respects to my generous and liberal protector M. de la Jonchère, who seemed very happy to see me again and without whose help I would have been destitute in the city. His liberal generosity toward me was renewed once again, beyond what it had been before. I spoke to him of the letter that the major had written to him to have me placed in the post of captain of the gates. He told me that he had never received it, but since I was in Paris, I could make my request in person. I did this by addressing a petition to M. de Breteuil, then the minister, detailing what I was owed for eighteen years of service as a half-pay lieutenant and how, as I was receiving only twenty livres per month with no housing, I could not support my family. I took my case to M. le maréchal de Brancas, who had promised me his protection, because at that time Mgr. le duc et maréchal de Belle-Isle was not in France. If he had been, I would not have had as much difficulty as I did in getting my requests fulfilled, as his greatness has always made me feel the effects of his protection and his generosity. So I then addressed myself to M. de Brancas, who gave me the benefit of his kindness, willingly accepting my petition and promising to lend his support to it. "While you are waiting," he told me, "for a satisfactory reply, please do come by for your meals for as long as you are in Paris." And several times, I took the liberty of doing this. I saw my brothers and sisters, who also took charge of similar petitions from me.[19]

18. Index note: "1741."

19. At this time, in late 1741 and early 1742, Belle-Isle was involved in battles in Prague as part of the War of the Austrian Succession.

[298] I wrote to my major about all that I was doing, and I told him that M. de Brancas was working to have me appointed to the post of captain of the gates. I have since learned that the forthright appeals I was making on my own behalf at Court had, in effect, turned him against me, and I still have the letter in which he told me that I should not have gone to Paris to ask for any such appointment; that I should be thinking of my family; that I should return as soon as possible; and that when the proper time came, he would ask for a post for me. I did not want to go against his orders, and I obeyed, but before I returned, I went to the Sr. Mouffe, the special treasurer at the war ministry, to ask for one month of my back pay. He said that he did not recognize me. I had recourse to the maréchal de Brancas, who gave me a certificate written in the following terms: "I understand the peculiar situation of the Sr. Du——, half-pay lieutenant at Port-Louis, who has just obtained the post of captain of the gates in that town. I authorize M. Mouffe to grant him enough to return to his garrison and to forward me a receipt."

Using this certificate, I received the money and left him my receipt, which was sent to Lorient to the treasurer so that he might make a deduction from my account. But the treasurer had no sooner received it than he showed it to the major, who, seeing that his aims had been thwarted, flew into such a state of rage against me that he vowed to destroy me. Nevertheless, I returned and regained my place under his wing; I left Paris on the sixteenth of January and arrived at my garrison on the day of [299] Mardi Gras, the sixth of February.

I had no sooner arrived than I went to pay my respects to my Maecenas, from whom I expected someday to receive my fortune. He seemed very happy to see me. I regained the possession of my garden, which my wife had arranged to be worked by others during my absence. I did all the spring planting. In a word, I arranged everything so as to secure, as they say, a good harvest. But there were no longer such frequent visits from the major, no zeal, but instead a sudden chill. He no longer tried to hide his abscess, which had now come to a head. His promises disappeared in smoke, and one day, he asked me why I had not received the appointment as captain of the gates. I replied that he had instructed me not to worry about getting that post, and I had obeyed him, and I was still waiting for him to fulfill his promise. He replied that I had done wrong and that whoever refuses an offer from the king loses. At last, the upshot of it all was that he asked me to return the keys to his garden, which was at that time filled with plantings, which appeared ready for harvest and might bring him some profit and which, in fact, he kept for himself. And so, in this modern age, I myself received the punishment that God meted out to our forefather whom he expelled from the terrestrial paradise. If I had to describe all the troubles and disappointments he has caused me since then, I would fill a volume fatter than the Montlery dictionary.[20]

I'll leave this aside and come to the point. Not being able to support my family in Port-Louis on nineteen livres and twelve sols per month, I addressed myself to the Sr. de Ricquebourg, who was still protecting me. He recommended that I [300] go over to Lorient and gave me reason to hope that I might have the post of lieutenant of the Invalides.[21] It was impossible for me to obtain the post of captain of the gates, because the major was opposed to it, and he had written to the minister, denouncing me. And so, with the permission of the royal lieutenant, I left Port-Louis on September 22, and I passed over to Lorient, where I had rented an apartment on two floors for twenty-four ecus per year, and there I waited impatiently for the post at the Invalides.

Not receiving any news, I took the liberty of writing to our illustrious minister, Seigneur d'Argenson, describing the state that I was reduced to and how, if His Grace had been influenced by the prayers of my protectors, I might hope to secure the post of captain of the gates. But no doubt the slanders that the major had applied to me prevented me from obtaining that good fortune, although they were false and beneath the dignity of a gentleman. I don't know whether the fair-minded minister took notice of my letter or the appeals of my family, but I know that through his goodness and his power and credit with His Majesty, he obtained from the king on the eleventh of October[22] the commission as captain of the gates, which he gave to the maréchal de Brancas, who forwarded it to the Sr. de Ricquebourg with a letter in which he explained that he had for a long time been proposing this commission for me.[23] The royal lieutenant received this on the eighth of November with an order to have me acknowledged and installed in the position, but since I was not then in Port-Louis, he called in the major de la place and gave him the commission to read. The major was not shy in reproaching the commandant for not keeping his word, saying that it was he who had been working to get me the appointment. But the royal lieuten-

20. Dumont no doubt is referring here to the *Grand dictionnaire historique* of Louis Moréri, of which some twenty editions were published between 1671 and 1759.

21. This was the landmark old soldiers' home in Paris, which was built beginning in the 1670s.

22. Index note: "1742."

23. The minister Dumont refers to here would be François Victor le Tonnelier de Breteuil, secretary of state for war from 1740 until 1743, referred to above, original manuscript [297].

ant replied that he had not meddled in this affair and would not meddle in it in the future. The royal lieutenant returned on the tenth to Lorient and called me into his [301] apartment, where he put in my hands the letter from M. le maréchal de Brancas. The commissioner of the army was there also, and when he saw that I had obtained this post, he advised me not to accept it, leading me to understand that this would displease someone in the army staff office and that I need only wait a little longer in Lorient. He gave me his word that soon he would arrange for me to have the lieutenancy in the Invalides. I thanked him on the spot for his good advice. I was dubious, however, of where it came from, and I told him that when the king wished to reward an officer, His Majesty always gave him the best available post.

Early the next morning, I crossed over from Lorient to Port-Louis and went to assume my post as captain of the gates. It was the royal lieutenant himself who performed the ceremony in front of several soldiers. I wanted to go pay my respects to the major de la place, but he did not want to receive me and said that he was ill. Thus I was installed as captain of the gates. My rank as half-pay lieutenant was annulled from this moment forward. I went for five months without receiving anything of my salary and was fortunate to find people who were willing to grant me credit for food. I asked permission from the Sr. Ricquebourg to be able to enjoy for my benefit some of the funds that gate captains enjoy, according to the ordinances and as outlined in the commission papers. He told me that, since he had promised the major not to get involved in this dispute, I would not be able to draw on these benefits as long as the major was opposed to it, absent an order from the court. I wrote to the minister about this, and I received, at the end of February, an order to receive twenty-five livres per month, or three hundred per year. But rather than getting this twenty-five livres, I was reduced to that which I had had previously as a half-pay lieutenant; the treasurer [302] withheld the balance, including my bonus of thirty-three livres a year, and thirty livres from the 10 percent tax, not to mention the fourth part per livre and the deposit.

And so I spent the years 1743 and 1744, without being able to obtain even the stipend for my lodging and forced to rent rooms in the town at my own expense. I had great difficulty in performing my duties, both in summer and winter. I was never able to obtain the order that I be granted the rights and emoluments of my post, and without the support of M. Ricquebourg and the periodic generosity of my dear protector, de la Jonchère, I would not even have been able to continue in my job. Finally, the maréchal et duc de Belle-Isle returned to my aid and to that of France, for the benefit of all.

I had the honor of complimenting him on his return, and he was so good as to thank me in a letter of September 28,[24] in which he promised to help me and to continue his protection. I cannot refrain from commenting here on the joy that this letter brought me, since I knew, from past experience, the generosity which His Excellency had bestowed upon me. I also knew that when he promised his good graces, one could await them and be sure of receiving them. It is often said that when the great make promises, it is like holy water from the Court, but this proverb or aphorism really is true in the case of the grand and illustrious maréchal. So I hoped that my labors and troubles would soon come to an end.

At the end of January, the Sr. de Ricquebourg, the royal lieutenant, fell ill, and in four days, he was taken from us. Imagine the predicament I then found myself in, to be at the mercy of a man who, in his letters and [301][25] in the reports he had filed on me, sought only to destroy me. I had the honor of writing of my plight to Mgr. le maréchal,[26] who informed me in his letter that he was extremely upset and that having known the late M. Ricquebourg for a long time, he hoped the man named to replace him might be someone known to him also, so that he could recommend me to him. Two or three days after the death of the commandant, the major tried to impose his authority upon me. He already regarded himself as the successor of the late royal lieutenant. In his mind, he believed that by going from house to house calling upon his godmothers, godfathers, and friends to put their seals on a petition addressed to the Court, he could prove that he was deserving of the position that had just become vacant. He imagined that such a request, coming from the townspeople to the king, could not be refused and that he was going to step into the post. He attempted to assume the powers of command ahead of time, in a manner that had nothing to do with military service.

Because the late royal lieutenant had allowed me to use a garden he had in the town, the major sent me an order, through the clerk of the office of the late Sr. de Ricquebourg, to hand over the key. And because the vegetables growing there belonged to me and were the product of my work, I did not immediately surrender the key upon his demand, as I first wanted to go collect what I needed, knowing well that if he had the key, he would take for his own profit whatever might be there, just as he had done with the first

24. Index note: "1745."

25. Here Dumont repeated the page numbers 301 and 302.

26. Dumont's index note has been cut off, but presumably it named Belle-Isle or gave the date of the letter.

garden. And while I was enjoying the opportunity to recover what belonged to me, the customhouse director came to ask to transfer the garden to the man who was its [302] possessor, by the stipulations of a lease, and was the notary of the place. He, knowing that the heirs of the late royal lieutenant did not wish to pay the taxes on it, had rented it to the director, who came with a document from the notary and asked me for the key. I gave it to him. The next day, the major again sent a demand for the key. I was not at home at the time and therefore was not able to give him a reply, and so he believed that I was disobeying his orders. What does he do? He sends two soldiers from the guards, armed, to seize me and bring me to him, and so these two deputies come to my home and ask my wife for me, who tells them that I was at Mass, for it was a Sunday. One soldier impertinently sits down on a chair in the house, and the other just outside, to wait for me, to arrest me either as I leave or when I return and try to enter.

I knew nothing of this little drama; I came home from the office of the commissaire ordonnateur of the marines at nine-thirty. The first sentinel who was at the door says nothing to me. I go in and find the second, which surprised me. I ask them openly what they want.

"Come speak to the major," is the response.

"That's enough," I say. "You may return."

"No, Monsieur, we have been ordered to take you there."

In spite of my surprise, I had to obey and go under their escort from the far end of the town to the citadel, through the crowds who were coming out of the Recollet church and others who were going in. I ask you to imagine the figure I cut, being dragged like a criminal who might be destined for the gallows. At last, with God's grace, I arrived at the major's and asked what he wanted from me:

"The key to the garden," he says in an imperious tone. [303] "I do not know what prevents me from sending you to the dungeon."

I replied to him that it was indeed in his power to do so, but as for the key, I had surrendered it, according to an order from the notary, which I showed him, to the customhouse director.

"I do not want him to have it. Go get it from him."

"But, sir," I said to him, "this did not merit my being dragged through the town by armed guards."

"I did not order that."

"But sir, they are standing there outside your door, waiting for me and for your orders."

"Send them back to their posts," he says, "and go bring me the key."

I made him understand that I could not get it back unless he gave me armed soldiers to compel the customs director to give it to me or to lead him back here, as I had been. The major, beside himself with rage so that he no longer knew what he was doing, says, "Take them, and bring me the key."

I had to obey, and I took the two of them with me and led them to the customhouse. I enter the building with them and ask for the director. He was at Mass, and so I tell the soldiers to wait there and, when he has arrived, to ask for the key to the garden or to tell him to come speak with the major. After I had left the citadel to carry out his orders, the major came to his senses and realized that he had only doubled his mistake by sending two armed guards to the customhouse director. He rushed to get dressed and left the citadel (although it was raining) and came to the Place de Notre Dame, where he saw me. He says to me, "Where is the key?"

"I did not find the director in, and I left the two soldiers there."

"Go back," he says. [304] "Tell the soldiers to return to their posts, and then come meet me at the notary's."

Having completed my mission, I proceed there as he asked. He strongly reprimanded the notary as well as me and insisted that he must have the key. The customhouse director, so as not to have any more trouble over this minor issue, let him have it, but wrote up a statement in strong terms declaring that neither the notary nor the director wanted the garden and that it was the local collector of tobacco taxes who was to have control of it. I was hoping to receive at least a little satisfaction from the major for the injustice that had been done me—a simple apology—but this would have been stooping too low for a major who would soon be named commandant and doubtless believed himself above the law. I waited from that Sunday until the following Friday, and when he was asked about it in meetings, he said of me, "He deserved that and much worse."

To whom would I then have recourse, if not to the justice and dignity of our incomparable minister, Mgr. le comte d'Argenson? I took the liberty of writing to him, but I still don't know whether this minister has seen fit to respond to my just plea.[27] Finally, I just swallowed my bitter pill, hoping and waiting to learn who would be named as the new royal lieutenant. I

27. It was most likely in 1742–1743 that Dumont wrote his "Poème," and he might have decided to dedicate the Arsenal copy to d'Argenson only after he became secretaire d'état à la guerre following the death of Breteuil in January 1743. During much of this period, Belle-Isle was leading French armies through Eastern Europe, and it seems likely that Dumont looked to d'Argenson and La Jonchère as his protectors, writing more regularly to them than to Belle-Isle. Here, in the prose manuscript dedicated to Belle-Isle, however, he writes little of these two years, from mid-1744 to mid-1746, and emphasizes instead how Belle-Isle protected and assisted him.

will not hide here the fact that I was making ardent prayers to heaven that the major would not be given the post, even if it would have meant that I, although unworthy, would have become major in his place. My prayers were answered. I had the pleasure of receiving a letter from the generous Mgr. le maréchal,[28] in which he indicated that he had every reason to hope that his repeated solicitations to the minister might succeed in [305] securing for me the rank of adjutant major, by means of which my situation would, in the future, not be so difficult as it had been up until now, since I would have a salary of seven hundred livres and a housing allowance of three hundred per year. Because on the address line of this letter from His Excellency were written the words "adjutant major" of this garrison, and his seal and crest were also imprinted below and were known to everyone, I was complimented on my new rank even before I opened and read the good news. The commissaire ordonnateur of the marines, to whom someone had spoken about this, also personally congratulated me. But, so as to be more certain whether the news was true, he says to me, laughing, "May I see it, sir, your letter?" I did not see how I could hide it from him, and so I gave it to him to read.

The major quickly learned the news, and it rekindled his desire to prevent me from advancing. He no doubt quickly prepared his own letters and sent them out, with the result that my commission did not materialize. I was an adjutant major–in–waiting, without being able to perform my duties. I said that my prayers had been answered. I say it again, because in a letter from Mgr. le maréchal,[29] I learned that the Sr. Deschamps had been named royal lieutenant, that he [the maréchal] had strongly recommended me to him, and that I could anticipate receiving from him all the assistance that would make me happy, aside from the fact that I would soon receive my commission as adjutant major. The new royal lieutenant had already left Paris to come join his garrison, and he had reached [306] Malestroit, where he was forced to make a stopover against his wishes, owing to an acute attack of gout that laid him up there. At last, however, we had the pleasure of receiving him. He arrived at the garrison on the third of June. It was a Sunday. I had the honor of going to pay my respects to him on that same day. The major was with him. He, the royal lieutenant, spoke to me of Mgr. le maréchal de Belle-Isle, and a few days after his arrival, I explained to him

28. Index note: "of the 9th of March 1746." "Maréchal" presumably refers to Belle-Isle, the only man mentioned in the memoir who held this rank, the highest in the French military, at this time.

29. Dumont's index note is cut off again but presumably gave the date of this letter.

my sad situation. He sympathized with me and told me, and also told my daughter, that we were invited to come every week on Fridays and Saturdays to eat at his table. After this, he wrote to the maréchal in my favor.[30]

But even with all this, my commission did not appear. This surprised him and myself even more so, given that we had no idea what might be holding it up. At that time, I was still living in town. The new royal lieutenant wanted to begin helping me and to find me lodgings in the citadel, but there was no space. Luckily, however, a lieutenant at the Invalides, who had obtained permission from the court to get married, asked for permission to reside in the town. Our royal lieutenant granted his request, and as soon as he had vacated the room, which was on the twenty-ninth of September, he told me to take the key and to come live there, pending the availability of a more substantial house that was to be ready in the next fortnight—the house where I am living right now with all my belongings. But no sooner had I moved into the room of that officer than we had a run-in with the English. Here is my account of it.

---

30. Malestroit, in the *département* of Morbihan, is about forty kilometers northwest of Vannes in Brittany.

Chapter Nine

THE ENGLISH ATTACK BRITTANY

SEPTEMBER-OCTOBER 1746

[307] By the fifteenth of September, the coastal guards had retired to their homes, and the English, who must have been told that the seashore would not be guarded, decided to make an attack upon Brittany. For
this expedition, they gathered a fleet of fifty-six sail, of which twelve were
warships of the line—one was a vessel of 110 cannon, the others fewer—with
bomb galliots and transport vessels as well, and departed England with this
goal.[1]

On the twenty-sixth and twenty-seventh, some boat captains and fishermen gave an alert that they had spied the enemy fleet off the Iles de Glénan,
coming toward our coasts.[2]

On the twenty-eighth, M. de Clairambault, *commissaire général* and
ordonnateur of the marines, received a letter from Mgr. le comte de Maurepas, telling him that the English might well attempt an attack on Brittany.
Preparations began that same day, and several coastal guards were sent to
each position. A marine lieutenant was sent to Talut, a fort located on the
coast of the mainland, and a captain of the marines was sent with his men
to the fort at Locqueltas. Talut had eight cannons, and Locqueltas, sixteen.[3]

---

1. Rear Admiral H. W. Richmond's account is the best source on the history of this British
attack on Brittany. He lists fourteen naval vessels attacking the Lorient area, under the com-
mand of Richard Lestock; see H. W. Richmond, *The Navy in the War of 1739–48*, 3 vols.
(Cambridge, 1920), III, 41. The invasion of Brittany occurred while much of the French navy's
fleet was occupied in an ill-fated expedition to retake the fort of Louisbourg, on Cape Breton
Island, Canada, which had been captured by British and New England forces in June 1745.
See James Pritchard, *Anatomy of a Naval Disaster: The 1746 French Naval Expedition to
North America* (Kingston, Ont., 1995).

2. The Iles de Glénan are group of small, uninhabited islands some thirty kilometers to
the west of Le Pouldu and twenty kilometers to the south of Concarneau.

3. Pointe du Talut is eight kilometers west of Port-Louis. About four kilometers west is
Locqueltas, which Dumont spells "Lokxestas," using the Breton subscript "x" (this usually
corresponds to an "-er" sound, but not in this case). These two forts were positioned to attack
the British on land or sea as they approached Port-Louis and Lorient.

On the thirtieth, the enemy fleet was sighted as it approached, under full sail, the coast near Le Pouldu.[4] This place is about two and a half leagues from Port-Louis, and from Lorient, about two. Overlooking the spot where they were trying to land was a battery with two cannons. A large number of peasants and coastal guards were sent there, supported by M. le marquis de l'Hôpital with 150 dragoons from his regiment.[5] [308] The enemy anchored in a place that, in certain winds, is very risky and exposed. The next morning, the first of October, one could tell from the cannon shots they were firing that they wanted to land, and indeed they did, accomplishing their goal with a brilliant maneuver, landing two divisions while protecting them with more than six hundred cannon shots. The vanguard consisted of more than 2,500 men, and the rear guard, even more. They had earlier attempted a landing at the mouth of the Quimperlé River, but there they were pushed back, and so shifted to the site at Le Pouldu. The two cannons in the battery there were fired at the enemy, as well as some gunfire from our men, but at the first death on our side, all the coastal guards and peasants turned around; seeing that the dragoons were not going to charge the enemy, either, all the peasants took flight. M. le marquis de l'Hôpital tried to rally them, but it proved impossible, and so he retreated with his men (the dragoons, I mean) toward the town of Lorient, as quickly and safely as he could. Thus the enemies landed without serious opposition and took control of the area. If the reports of the first two deserters can be believed, they were heard to say that in this landing, the enemies lost forty-seven men.[6]

You can well imagine that as soon as word spread that the English had

4. Corrected for the eleven-day difference between the Julian calendar, used in Britain before 1751, and the Gregorian calendar, used in France, Dumont's dates match those from the British military archives as reported by Richmond.

5. Figure 12, "Map of Polduc and Environs," was orginally located at this spot in the manuscript. It shows the coast of Brittany along the Anse du Pouldu, from the town of Le Pouldu in the northwest to the Pointe du Courégan in the southeast, eight or nine kilometers in extent. Dumont's letter G, "le lock," is the Etang du Loc'h, a small lake that has since been mostly drained. The English landing point was on the Plage du Loch, next to this, and the encampment, E, is on a small cliff to the southeast of it.

6. Other sources do not mention an earlier landing being repelled, and the mouth of the river that flows through the town of Quimperlé, today called the rivière de Laïta, is right between Le Pouldu and the beach where the British did land. In any event, this section of the coast was exposed to onshore winds from the west and south; hence the British had to land their troops quickly so they could sail their ships on to anchor in the Bay of Quiberon, wait for the forces to take Lorient, and march overland to meet them; see Richmond, *Navy in the War of 1739–48*, III, 28–29. Richmond writes of two detachments of six hundred and of one thousand men who were put ashore.

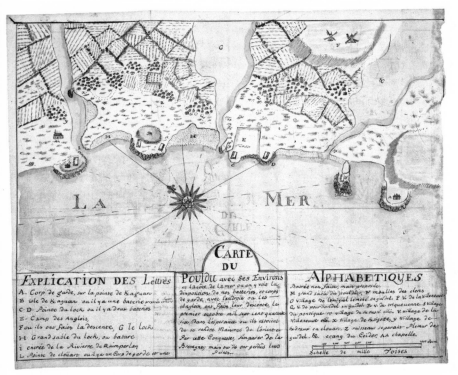

Figure 12. *Map of Polduc and Environs and the Coast of the Sea Where One Sees the Arrangement of Our Batteries and Corps of Guards, as well as the Place Where the English Landed on the First of October 1746, in the Hope of Making Themselves Masters of Lorient and, by This Conquest, Seizing Brittany; but Where Their Attempt Was Foiled.* VAULT oversize Ayer MS 257, map no. 12. Courtesy The Newberry Library, Chicago

come ashore, fear overcame the peasants and other people of the country-side, and they abandoned their homes, villages, and lands. This fear seized not only those people, who had little experience with war, but it also over-took the captain of the marines, in the fort [309] at Locqueltas, who, see-ing that the greater part of the men he had under him were abandoning the post, believed that he was doomed. He sent an express to his lieutenant at Talut ordering him to spike the cannons, but that officer did not immedi-ately carry it out. As for the captain, he did do it, and then abandoned his fort to return to Port-Louis, as if the enemy had actually forced him to take this action. It was quite simple for him to do this, because, before going, he had had a master locksmith make some steel pins for him. I leave it to you to imagine the shock that our royal lieutenant found himself in when he learned that the sixteen cannons that were in that fort for the purpose of preventing ships from entering the harbor of Port-Louis had been rendered useless. He sent for some skilled blacksmiths to make the necessary tools to try to unspike them, and while this was being done, the lieutenant at Talut sent a soldier with a letter addressed to the commandant of the marines, to ask him whether he should obey the order he had received from his captain to spike the cannons. This commandant, unaware of the smiths' working on tools to unspike the cannons at Locqueltas and not wanting to share his plans with M. Deschamps, gave the order in writing to his lieutenant to do the same thing to the eight cannons there, and so he did, some thirty hours after the first were spiked.

The third, which was a Monday, the workers were sent with two hundred armed men, and the same captain also went. The men of Vulcan's forge worked so skillfully that after just one day and one night, they were able to unspike twelve of the sixteen cannons. On Tuesday, a fog developed at daybreak [310] that wet the cannons and the soldiers' guns, so the captain, without alerting the commandant to what he was going to do and without hoisting the French flag over his fort, let off a volley of fire from all his musketeers and a salute from the twelve cannons, which led us all to assume that he had seen the enemy and that he was being attacked. Our citadel fired off two rounds from twenty-four–pound cannons, of which one ball reached the fort of Locqueltas and grazed one of our men, carrying away his uniform, vest, and shirt and even burning his flesh. When the truth was learned, the captain was ordered to come back to Port-Louis, and because this action demonstrated that his fear was not yet dispelled, his lieutenant, the Sr. de Saint Pierre—a young man with a heart filled with courage and valor—remained there to command the fort instead. As soon as the captain reached the citadel, he was discharged and retired from the service, which was a loss to the marines all the same, for, in fact, he was just recovering from an illness and was still convalescent when he was chosen to go command that fort. It might be said, in his defense, that he was not yet in full command of his faculties, since this officer had earned the Croix de Saint Louis by his exploits and voyages at sea and earlier service in the marines and had never before fled in the face of the enemy.

On this same day, a shallop appeared at the break of day in the waters off Kernével.[7] It was a local [311] fisherman, but his shallop was mistaken for an enemy boat that had come to make soundings in the ship channel. The boat was hailed, but the owner inside it did not hear, and so a gunshot was

7. Kernével is just northeast of Larmor, facing the citadel of Port-Louis across the narrow entrance to Lorient harbor.

fired to call him to come alongside the commanding ship of the king's fleet. He still did not obey. The master cannoneer on that vessel was then ordered to fire a single cannonball. He tried to obey and loaded the cannon, but whether it had already been loaded or whether, in his rush to follow orders, he put in a split ball and did not adjust the measure of powder accordingly, when he put the flame to the touchhole, the cannon burst, ripping off his head and his arm. By some miracle, this explosion injured only two other men, one a drummer in the marines, who was hit in the eye and lost his sight, and the other a soldier, who was lightly wounded in the arm.

On the first, second, and third [of October], the enemy advanced overland, reaching as far as Ploemeur. Everyone in that parish had fled, leaving behind wine and spirits for the enemies, who also gathered bulls, cows, and horses as they went—in short, everything they found useful. On the same day, the third of the month, the major of Port-Louis was sent to Lorient to command there in the absence of M. de Flechier, who, although appointed by the king, had not yet arrived.

The fourth of the month, at about seven-thirty in the morning, the Sr. Sinclair, general of the English forces, sent a young officer named Barbot with a drummer to Lorient. They were brought in blindfolded, as is the custom, to the council of war, and once there, the officer presented [312] a letter from his general, which read as follows:

Having landed near the port of Lorient with a party of my forces on behalf of my master, the king of Great Britain, and having determined, at close range, that Lorient is not at all fortified and could not withstand a siege for long, I send you this letter, sir, so that you might send me by your messenger the keys of the city. If not, I will burn the town and take all its inhabitants and run them through with the sword.

After reading this letter, rather than pass it on to our royal lieutenant, commandant of Port-Louis as well as Lorient, the city council instead met privately and concluded that they had to negotiate a surrender. The officer and the drummer were sent back, along with one of our officers, with a request to the Sr. Sinclair for a twenty-four-hour cease-fire, which he granted.[8]

On this same day, the fourth of the month—Saint Francis's Day—three deserters from the enemy were led from Lorient over to Port-Louis. They declared themselves to be of the Fitzjames regiment and to have been cap-

8. Dumont rendered the name of James Sinclair, commander of the English forces in the invasion of Brittany, as the "Sr. de Sainte Claire."

tured in the affair of the Pretender in Scotland. They were sent back to their regiment.[9]

I have forgotten to say that from the moment the enemy landed on our shores, our royal lieutenant had sent out runners to all quarters asking for assistance, whether in men or supplies, and there arrived in Port-Louis more than 6,000 men, although no more than 1,200 of them were armed, the others carrying only pitchforks, pikes, or staffs.

While the council at Lorient was putting together its proposal for a surrender, in the citadel at Port-Louis we were putting the cannons into their embrasures and withdrawing from the powder house [313] more than 120,000 livres' worth of powder in order to place it farther away from the fire. Others were arming most of the militia, and I have to say that the armaments keeper, the Sr. Desnoyers—an intelligent man and gifted draftsman with a knowledge of mathematics—was saddled with many troubles and headaches. Others were filling the cisterns with water, for they had, until now, been completely empty. There was no shortage of tasks at the citadel, such as setting up large, wooden screens to girdle, or mask, the magazines and the doors to the underground bunkers, so as to protect them from being hit by shells. All this work was going on in the citadel, as well as the preparation of explosive devices to try to hold back the enemy, in case he should try to sail through the channel that passes in front of the citadel. These rockets were created out of the genius of the Sr. Perinet d'Orval, a man quite experienced in the art of explosives.

In the town of Port-Louis, there was likewise plenty of work being done, under the able leadership of the Sr. l'Allemand, who is now the ensign of the port, with a commission from the king for this region. He was working to increase the thickness of the walls of the town, which were built simply of stones stacked atop one another, work that dated from long ago. He had wide, grassy terraces constructed behind the walls and had the embrasures

9. October 4 is the saint's day of Saint Francis of Assisi. In 1745, when so much of the British military was occupied on the continent or in the colonies, Charles Edward Stuart, the Scottish pretender to the English throne, saw an opportunity to foment an uprising in Scotland, and his French supporters were willing to help. He sailed from Saint-Nazaire in mid-July on a merchant ship called the *Doutelle*, or *Du Teillay*, escorted by the warship *Elisabeth*. Although the *Elisabeth* was met and attacked, the *Du Teillay* made it through and landed on the Isle of Barra on August 3. The Jacobite uprising that followed scored its biggest victory at the Battle of Prestonpans on October 2. During the autumn of 1745, Britain was on the defensive, but Frederick the Great's victory in Prussia, concluded in the Treaty of Dresden, and then the retreat of the Jacobites in January 1746 turned the tide in their favor. The men Dumont mentions were among the prisoners taken in the Jacobite war who were impressed into the British navy.

of the cannons placed on their carriages, something that perhaps had never been seen in our lifetimes. In the center of the town, the bakers were working on making bread. In a word, everyone had a task to look after, to work on to the point of exhaustion—everyone, that is, who had stayed in the town. [314] Although there were plenty of men who had their hearts in the right place and were fit to bear muskets and bring fire upon an enemy, there were also some who had abandoned their houses and decamped, taking away their families and their wealth. As for women, there were also many of them, but I won't cast blame on the weaker sex; it is the others who deserve the laurels for cowardice, who deserve the scorn of our ancestors and of our poets who have ridiculed such behavior as unworthy of manly hearts.

Let us return now to what is happening in Lorient. The council being assembled, an officer was assigned to go to the English general along with a subdelegate from Mgr. the intendant, who was ready to offer 2,500,000 livres and free access to the town on the following conditions:

That the town and its inhabitants, as well as the Company of the Indies, would retain all their rights and privileges;
That nothing would be done to harm the honor nor the belongings of the inhabitants;
That the Sr. Sinclair would be allowed to stay as long as he saw fit;
That Lorient would be a neutral city.

This fine proposition was nonetheless rejected, and the general sent the reply that he wanted everything at his discretion.[10] And when M. Deschamps, our royal lieutenant, learned of this proposal, made without his knowledge and without his orders, I don't know what he thought, but I do know that he immediately sent the Sr. de l'Abbé Doyers, a gentleman of courage and intelligence and an officer in the marines, to the council at Lorient with a letter written more or less in these terms: [315]

That Brittany was a province more dear to the king than his recent conquests in Flanders; that it was well worth defending; and that he had never seen a city so well equipped as Lorient was—with cannons,

---

10. Richmond summarizes the French proposal as follows: "The regular troops should be allowed to withdraw with arms, horses, baggage and all honours of war, and the militia to disperse to the villages to which they belonged; while in addition the agents of the East India Company demanded that their warehouses and shipping should be untouched" (*Navy in the War of 1739–48*, III, 30). He makes no mention of the 2,500,000 livres, however.

mortars, munitions, and supplies for war and for sustenance, and with more than 25,000 men—surrender without firing a single shot; that if they did surrender, they would be disobeying the king, his master and theirs; and that they would never recover their honor or reputation.

When the council had read this letter and the delegate had returned to report that the English general wanted everything at his discretion, a sense of honor returned to the hearts of those on the council, which now decided to defend the city. All of this took place during the cease-fire on the fifth of the month. Lorient had six batteries ready to fire and three mortars that had been set up by orders from the Sr. Duvelaër, the senior director of the Company of the Indies. One could say in praise of him that he had spared nothing of his intelligence and effort to put the town of Lorient in a position not only to defend itself but also to prevent the enemy from realizing its goal of burning down the city. For the director had the foresight to order that both water and piles of manure be placed in the streets, ready to put out fires, and although he had been rebuffed when he appeared before the council, one might say that he deserved more than any of them to be a member of that body. But for some reason—I'm not sure why—he retired from the council, as did M. de Montaran and also the Sr. Perrault, mayor of the city of Lorient.

Thus I say that the town was ready, but the Sr. Sinclair [316] was not, just yet. Taking advantage of the cease-fire that he had been asked for and had agreed to, he sent his soldiers to their ships to bring back four thirteen-pound cannons and one mortar, and having found a small bank and trench about an eighth of a league from Lorient, which a landowner had himself dug out in order to protect his field from roaming livestock, the enemy built embrasures in it, filling it in at these spots so as to make platforms. The enemy ordered the cannons set up on these and the mortar placed in the bottom of the trench. And on the sixth, which was a Thursday, at two in the afternoon, the enemy began to attack Lorient with cannon, shells, flaming oil, and even a few red-hot cannonballs. They fired off four volleys without any reply from Lorient. Terror had seized the council, which had ordered the fuses extinguished and did not even give the order to fire. Nonetheless, the master cannoneers in the port, seeing that they were being attacked in full force, relit the fuses and fired without permission, and with this, the defenders responded to the attack. The fighting continued on both sides for the rest of the day, but when night fell, hostilities were suspended.

During the night, M. Deschamps, our royal lieutenant, ordered the assembly of nearly 1,500 men, Breton militiamen under the command of M. Depenhoüet, to go out on reconnaissance and try to distract the enemy by marching past them, with orders not to fire except as a last resort. In case of necessity, they should retreat to Larmor, within the range of the cannons in the citadel and those at Locqueltas. These 1,500 men were supported by cavalry from the local mounted police. They departed [317] in good order and marched toward the enemy, but as soon as they reached the village of La Croix de Ploemeur, along the road from Lorient, some in the rear guard, believing that the enemies were upon them, began firing on those in the van. Some were killed, and in the chaos, others were trampled by the horses of the mounted police, whereas still others took flight and broke apart their guns, or simply dropped them, in order to be able to run faster. Others threw themselves down on the ground. In a word, it was a complete rout. Fear gripped the men, one group of which fled to Lorient, another to Port-Louis, and the remainder to Larmor. One may judge by this the quality of troops we had.

Meanwhile, at Lorient, there was a sortie that succeeded somewhat better, as the detachment fired three rounds upon the enemy. Some English were killed, and there was only one overly rash soldier on our side who was killed before the detachment returned to the town in good order.

That day, the sixth of the month, the major of Port-Louis returned from Lorient in the morning, having been relieved by the Sr. de Volvire, commanding general of the province of Brittany and *maréchal de camp* of the royal armies, a man respectable in his own right who had received recognition from the king for his bravery. He would surely be able to restore courage to the hearts of those who were lacking it. On Friday, the seventh of the month, at about seven-thirty in the morning, the enemy resumed the offensive, and Lorient its defense. Around ten o'clock, our royal lieutenant wrote to the Sr. de Volvire, who was now chief of the council at Lorient, proposing that Volvire send out a strong party from Lorient during the night, that the royal lieutenant would do the same from his town (so as to catch the enemy in a cross- [318] fire), and that if Volvire agreed with this plan, he should send a reply. The Sr. de Volvire did so, saying that if the plan was still on, the royal lieutenant should fire a flare into the air above the citadel, which he did at noon the same day. And so the royal lieutenant caused a large armed force to be sent across on boats to the Kernével side, where they were joined by three hundred more troops from the fort at Locqueltas, under Messieurs Penhoüet and Bidard, for a total that might have approached three thousand men. They organized their ranks and awaited the order and the signal to march. Everyone was eager to begin.

While these men were being organized at Kernével, the fighting continued on both sides. The battery at Lorient was particularly active, unleashing heavy fire on the enemy. Toward eleven o'clock in the morning, a shell fired from Lorient struck the enemy's battery, killing or disabling many soldiers and mortally wounding the Sr. La Garde, major general of the English forces. The soldiers carried him away on an armchair, as if it were a stretcher, as far as Ploemeur, where he died shortly after arriving, and they buried him in the orchard of the rectory. When the rector returned after the battle, he said that the pits of his privies were filled with dead bodies. The nephew of the Sr. Sinclair was sliced in two by a cannonball. But since their batteries were toppled, they were unable to fire a single shot for more than two hours, and having retreated more than sixty *toises* behind the trenches, they could only let off a weak fire, and their shells, bullets, and flaming oil could barely reach the walls [319] of the town.

As for us, we were one league distant from this battle. It seemed to us that Lorient was a town that, although afraid of the enemy at first sight, had now, we said, shown a taste for the discipline of Mars and was defending itself well; it seemed to us that it would succeed. Nonetheless, in the end, the advice of the marquis de l'Hôpital and of Heudicourt, which was to surrender at discretion, prevailed. The Sr. de Volvire, who was the head of the council and thus the man who had to approve this decision—rather than defend his city and the interests of his king, I say, rather than take the advice of men experienced in warfare or (if he might choose to ignore their wisdom or if he had no such experts around him) follow the advice of the mayor and the leading men of the town—did nothing of the sort. He allowed himself to be governed and led by the youth. After hearing their advice, he allowed himself to be persuaded and concluded that it would be best to surrender the city at discretion, even though there hadn't even been ten men killed, not a single house burned down nor even razed to the ground. He had to surrender. There is no way of predicting what might have happened if the defense had continued in this manner. An officer under l'Hôpital even offered to go at the head of a hundred soldiers from his regiment and attack the enemy, but M. le marquis himself was opposed to the idea and refused his offer. The officer then went to the Sr. de Volvire to ask him for an equal number of volunteers, which was granted him in the form of a signed order, but after he left to execute his plan, he found that obstacles had been put in his way, insofar as the decision to surrender the city [320] unconditionally had already been made.

Once this decision was final, it was sent to our royal lieutenant, informing him that as they were marching out of the town to surrender it, they would fire a flare into the air, between two cannon shots. During this evening of the seventh of October, M. Deschamps, our royal lieutenant, sent out small parties from time to time to reconnoiter. Whether the enemy had learned of the movements of our forces at Kernével and Locqueltas and Larmor, about to march toward them (which I'm sure they had), or whether they feared being surrounded and cut off from communication, in any case, once the continual fire from the batteries of Lorient had ceased, they began to dismantle their camp and retreat toward Le Pouldu—or, rather, to the place where they had landed. But before retreating completely, they lit huge fires in their camp, at their batteries, and also near the castle in Keroman, and at about eight-thirty they fired into the air a large flare, which must have been a signal to their ships of their retreat. They also set fire to two large barrels of powder that they had near their trenches, and this made such a loud noise and powerful explosion that it shook the earth and rattled the windows in the citadel and in the town of Port-Louis.[11]

When our royal lieutenant had learned of the decision made by the council at Lorient to surrender at discretion, he sent the Sr. Langat, his secretary, to go to Lorient to carry his message and try to rouse some courage into the guts of those who showed none, and who, you might say, had lost all signs of life. The secretary arrived and spoke to the council very strongly and with passion and wit, but it was too late. The flare had been fired into the air between the two cannon shots, and the [321] marquis de l'Hôpital had marched out the gates with a detachment of one hundred men to go surrender the city at discretion. He carried with him a capitulation signed by the entire council of Lorient, on which were listed these articles to present and try to obtain from the Sr. Sinclair. To wit:

1) That the king's troops be allowed to leave the city with full honors of war;

2) That the inhabitants not be in any way pillaged or mistreated;

3) That only the warehouses of the Company of the Indies be fair game for seizure, at discretion.

One can well imagine the consternation that prevailed in Port-Louis when this signal flare was fired off. For it is certain that in spite of the brav-

11. "The army decamped from before l'Orient after dark [on September 25 / October 6] and arrived at the coast at 3 a.m. where with all needful precautions, covered by sloops and armed vessels, the soldiers were put silently back on board." L'Hôpital decided to surrender later that day, September 26 / October 7. Sinclair wrote, according to Richmond, "With respect to the difficulty of the enterprise the whole resulted from the ignorance of those who have nothing of the Engineer but the name and the pay" (*Navy in the War of 1739–48*, III, 31).

ery of our royal lieutenant, we would not have been able to hold out for more than forty-eight hours. It is unlikely we could have lasted even that long, since there was almost no water in the cisterns (which, although they had been filled, had leaked) and no food. We had only 280 disabled soldiers, who were respectable more for their service to His Majesty in their youth or by past acts of bravery and venerable more for their wounds or great age than for their current abilities or fitness to survive an attack. The best that can be said of them is that they were all willing to fight. But God, who controls the destinies of all things here on earth, had dispelled our fear and dispersed the enemy, for, while l'Hôpital was marching out with drums beating the signal for surrender, an officer in Lorient was posting an ordinance from [322] the council of war prohibiting any of the inhabitants, townspeople, or armed men from firing a gun, under penalty of death. What kind of outrage must this have caused? After all, here was a city given up to a handful of people, in spite of the will of its mayor, who had not been consulted at all since he was not trusted by the council; a city rendered to the enemy in spite of the fact that its residents, like the soldiers, wanted nothing more than to go out and attack the enemy and could have defended the city themselves using its ninety-six cannons and three mortars. So, on one side of the city, an order was being posted to not fire any guns while, on the other side, drummers were beating the signal for everyone to take up their arms. If, by some chance, an Englishman had approached and tried to enter the city, a horrendous slaughter would have ensued, because the inhabitants were resolved to fire not only on the enemy but also on the cavalry and dragoons of our forces. But God, who knew the goodwill in the hearts of the men who had not been given the permission to march out to battle, restored peace through His power. For, as l'Hôpital advances, probably pleased with his plans, and arrived at the trenches of the enemy, what good fortune, or rather what miracle, occurred? He found no one to surrender the city to or even to speak with. Thus the marquis de l'Hôpital achieved the goal he had set for himself, but his expectations were thwarted by the grace of heaven. He found, in the trenches of the enemy, only the four cannons, now spiked; the mortar; and a cassock, or uniform, of a cannoneer, hanging from a tree alongside a dead veal calf.[12]

Not [323] finding, as I said, anyone in the camp, he returned with his one

12. Richmond writes that l'Hôpital found "Four spiked guns, a mortar and a furnace for heating shot [that] were all that remained of the invading army" (ibid.). He says nothing, however, of the second articles of capitulation, the death of Sinclair's nephew and of Joseph de la Garde, or the explosions of powder.

hundred men to the city to report this news. Several others were curious and went out to see the reality of the situation for themselves. However, at the same time, the marquis de l'Hôpital, declaring an intention to run after the enemy, took all the post horses to go announce to the king the flight, or, rather, the rout of the enemy, who, by the courage of his dragoons, had been forced to retreat. In exchange for this fine tale, His Majesty made the marquis a chevalier de Saint Louis, and the Sr. de Volvire was made lieutenant general, and our royal lieutenant, a brigadier. But I will say, without flattery and without supposing any obligation on his part for what I might put here in writing, the last of the three, our commandant, alone merited all the rewards bestowed upon the other two. One can imagine, based on this, that only luck lies behind who is rewarded and who is forgotten.

So the enemy flees during the night of the seventh to return to their vessels, still preoccupied with their fears of being surrounded. Those in Lorient do not dare pursue them, fearing that this might be a feint by the enemy to set up an ambush. However, men of courage again present themselves and ask for permission to go out in pursuit, but the council does not share their view and cannot back their resolve. For an enemy that is fleeing, they say, one should build a golden bridge. Those are your words, Messieurs leaders of Lorient. But this is not the view of our royal lieutenant, for, when the Sr. Langat, his secretary, arrived at half-past midnight [324] bringing news of the enemy's unexpected retreat (we were gathered in the council chamber to plan our defense, certain that after the surrender of Lorient we would soon have the gun at our heads); when, I say, he had spoken, our royal lieutenant complains of being held back and unable to make an attack and of not having any men of spirit or courage. The Sr. de Fonfay, lieutenant general of the artillery, volunteers, and the royal lieutenant takes up his offer and gives him a written order to go put himself at the head of whatever troops he finds suitable from among those now on the Kernével and Larmor side. Fonfay leaves the citadel to find a boat and crosses over to where the troops were assembled, as I've already said. He describes his plan and displays his orders. The first detachment that he finds tells him that they are very tired and cannot march. The second replies that they are dying of hunger and have no more strength. At last, he comes to a third, where the captain in command offers to follow him wherever he believes necessary for the good of the service and has his troops ready to march in good order. Fonfay encourages them, explaining that only one quick strike is needed to drive back the enemy and put them to rout. All march out in double time, full of zeal, but as soon as they spy the enemy, they dissolve and turn tail. Thus the Sr. de Fonfay, being a man cut out for victory, came back with the glory of volunteering for a mission, of going out to perform it, but not of winning the victory that might have gone with it.

The English, not the least bit worried, loaded up their ships methodically, without being disturbed by their enemy. It was only the [325] strong southwest wind that was causing them trouble. We, for our part, were hoping to see their ships driven aground on the coast. But by their skillful management, they lost only one shallop out of the whole fleet. Before embarking, they had burned fifteen villages or hamlets and killed a great number of livestock, which they left lying on the ground, taking others on board either slaughtered or alive. And on the twelfth of the month, they raised anchor and set sail for the Quiberon peninsula. As the wind was a bit too close on its bow, one ship of their fleet was not able to clear the point of the Ile de Groix and had to come through the Courreaux, the usual passage our ships take between the mainland and that island. It anchored in the roadstead for the night from Wednesday to Thursday. But the next morning, it was spotted from the island, and the islanders fired several cannonballs at it without causing much damage. The ship responded with its own, and, still under sail, it coasted along the length of the island, regained a clear wind, and then slowly disappeared, heading for its rendezvous.

The royal vessel named the *Ardent*, of sixty guns, with all its crew ill and in their bunks, was returning from the fleet of M. le duc d'Enville, and its captain put in on October 10 at Belle-Isle, where M. de Saint Cernin, the royal governor there, provided him with 110 sailors to help manage the ship and try to sail to Brest. But on the eleventh, he encountered two large English vessels that wanted to make a prize of his ship. He battled them for more than three hours and was able to get free, while killing many men among their crew, and would himself have [326] made prizes of those ships had not two other enemy vessels come to the aid of the first two. The contest not being equal, the captain of the French royal vessel did not wish to yield, preferring instead to run his ship aground on the tip of Quiberon, where the officers fortunately got ashore. There were some sailors in his crew who drowned and some of the ill who got ashore, but there remained on board about sixty of the ill and the most debilitated.[13]

13. According to Richmond, there were three English ships, the *Exeter*, the *Tavistock*, and the *Poole*, that engaged the *Ardent* in a four-hour battle. The French ship was driven aground on the southwest point of the peninsula, near the modern city of Quiberon, where "most of her crew got ashore" in the midst of a strong gale; see ibid., 32. In this storm, four of the English ships anchored in Quiberon Bay, with nine hundred men aboard, were lost. The *Ardent* was one of the ships of d'Enville's squadron that had set out to retake Louisbourg; see Pritchard, *Anatomy of a Naval Disaster*, 148–150.

On the fourteenth of the said month, all of the enemy fleet lay at anchor off Quiberon. The fifteenth, the Sr. Sinclair sent an officer to demand of the Sr. de Penneverte at Auray that he be allowed to go ashore with his troops, threatening that if even one of his men were killed, he would set fire to everything and shed much blood. After he delivered this ultimatum, at about eight or nine in the morning the enemies came ashore and made themselves masters of the peninsula without firing a single cannon, for there were very few French troops there. The English found there twenty cannon, which were not in a state to be fired, because the batteries had not been built. There were many finished stones, some barrels of lime, and more than three thousand livres' worth of tools and materials belonging to a contractor named the Sr. Robinet, who had not yet begun the work of building the platforms. The enemy moved in, set up camp, and made trenches, which gave the appearance that they wanted to spend the winter there and wait for reinforcements they expected to have. Among the little hamlets of this peninsula, those that the English soldiers wished to stay in were not burned, but the others were. The Sr. Sinclair wrote to our royal lieutenant [327] a very polite letter inviting him to send a naval commissioner to come retrieve the sick Frenchmen who had been in the *Ardent,* after paying him a ransom. The Sr. Bouris, a young company scribe, went there, and he was well received by the general, who turned over the men to him.

The nineteenth of the month, the enemy seized two tiny islands named Houat and Höedic, on which there might have been fifty men, an officer, and some sergeants. They were taken as prisoners of war. The Sr. Sinclair thought that he would get a ransom for them. And so he sent the demand to the Sr. de Saint Cernin, governor of Belle-Isle, who sent back the reply that those who had been put on those islets were not good soldiers, and so he could take them back to England with him if he wanted to. But the English, after forcing them to work on their ships, returned them to Quiberon on the condition that they not fight again for a year and a day.[14]

The enemy fleet sailed back and forth, threatening to make landings at any moment, which caused us to make frequent movements and to send powder and balls to places where it was believed they were needed. The enemy, seeing without a doubt that they could not set foot on the mainland, sailed from Quiberon out to Belle-Isle, where, we learned, General Sinclair had sent an officer to demand of the Sr. de Saint Cernin that he must surrender the citadel and all the island within twenty-four hours. But the gov-

14. These two islands, of which Houat, the larger, is fewer than five kilometers long, are situated about ten and twenty kilometers southeast of the end of the Quiberon peninsula.

ernor had responded to this envoy that he would only give him the time to return to his ship.

[328] Hardly had the English cleared out of the anchorage off of Le Pouldu to go to Quiberon, as I've said, which was on the eleventh and twelfth, than a sense of tranquillity replaced fatigues and anxieties and gave us a chance to take a deep breath. At this point, everyone told what he had seen and learned. I was telling my version when I received a letter from Mgr. le maréchal de Belle-Isle, in which he indicated that I would do him a service—in the place of M. Deschamps, who had no lack of tasks right then—by making known to him all the details of what I might know about what had happened in our neighborhood and in the region. It need not be doubted for a moment that I obeyed; to think otherwise would be to harbor an unfair assumption about me and make me guilty of ingratitude. I sent His Excellency an initial narrative, shorter than the one in these memoirs, but just as accurate and truthful.[15]

Since our commandant, M. Deschamps—amid the fatigues and worries that afflicted him—knew that the enemies before him were about to attack Lorient, he being the only one who, by his experience in warfare, his intelligence, and his courage, carried the weight of this war, and having no one around him to assist him (since the major was at Lorient), he selected three people in his city to carry his orders or to have them executed. The first of these three people was the Sr. de la Motte, an interpreter of languages and the major of the town militia, an intelligent young man who knew his duties well. The second was the Sr. Calvé, previously an officer [329] in the Company of the Indies. These two men were like the aides-de-camp to a general. And the third? It was I who had this honor. I was the captain of the gates, and I performed the functions of an adjutant major and an errand boy. My zeal and my pains have been rewarded, as well as those of the two others, by the generosity of our commandant and general, who, exhausted to the extreme by sleepless nights, the responsibilities of his work, and his worries in commanding and steering all by himself the wheel of this important enterprise, could not avoid falling dangerously ill. We saw him on the verge of being taken away from us, of being lost forever. Each man carried grief in

---

15. In January 1747, the maréchal de Belle-Isle led the successful French defense of Provence against the Austrians and British, driving them back across the southern Alps into Italy. Deschamps, Rothelin, and other officers would have been understandably nervous about having Dumont, a subordinate, writing for Belle-Isle a narrative of the inglorious defense of Brittany.

his heart, and the prayers addressed to the Lord, having reached this Master of Destinies, preserved his life. God answered his servants.

But while he was laid low by illness, the major de la place took control of things. One day, when I was leaving the citadel to go into town, he wanted to come in, and on the bridge that led from the half-moon to the approaches of the castle, he was on horseback and encountered me. He said, addressing me by name and with no sense of honor, "When it was M. Deschamps who commanded, you performed the functions of an adjutant major, but now I forbid you from doing so. Go back to just opening and closing the gates." I made a low bow to him, and I quickly went along on my way. I was not yet so fortunate as to have received my commission as adjutant major, and so in obeying him, I cannot be blamed, but still, it was a real insult, spoken in front of three or four passersby. What could I do? I could do nothing except [330] write to our fair-minded minister. But I was not so fortunate as to be heard as I was on other occasions, even though I had always possessed a gift for making myself credible in the face of all that was said and written against me. The weaker party is most often held at fault, however unjustly.

On the twentieth of the month, Alexandre d'Orléans, marquis de Rothelin, maréchal de camp of the royal armies and governor of this city and of Lorient, Quimperlé, Hennebont, and their dependencies, arrived in this town for the first time since he had been appointed governor. M. the major de la place met him and, at his entrance, presented him the keys of the city, a ceremony at which I was also present, of course. The cannons of the city and the citadel announced his arrival with a salute. The militia and the troops stood in review in rows along either side of the route to the house where he was staying, which was that of the customhouse director, the Sr. Benier, because the citadel was too small to have any lodgings suitable for such a dignitary, and our royal lieutenant was still sick. And so the entrance of the governor was honored with all necessary pomp, and I can say without boasting that the noise of the cannons reached as far as Quiberon, and the enemy having thus learned of the arrival of this governor, on the twenty-eighth of the month, the entire English fleet set sail and left the coasts of Brittany to return to England, with nothing better than the fish that they had caught and eaten.

Chapter Ten

FINANCIAL DIFFICULTIES;
IMPRISONMENT 1746-1747

[331] So as I was saying, our governor having arrived, he settled in at the home of M. Benier, who was a conniving person—one who, although rewarded with a post, did not show any more wit than was absolutely necessary to perform the duties of his commission. It was decisive, I say, that the marquis de Rothelin was staying with him. First of all, the director was alone in the house, for although he was married, he had sent his wife to stay with one of her uncles in Burgundy, for reasons that they had agreed to and of which I don't know the details. And so it was sufficient that Benier was able to spend the evenings alone with the governor to enable the former to find a way to win the latter over and make him believe that everything he told him about one person or another was the truth.

While M. Deschamps, the royal lieutenant, brigadier of the royal armies, and our commandant, was convalescing after his illness, one evening the commissaire ordonnateur of the marines and some of the officers of the garrison came to see him and submitted some complaints about me: namely, that I had been so insolent as to write up a report, without his permission, on the operations that had been carried out in the recent battle. Our royal lieutenant told his secretary to ask me to come speak with him, but the secretary, believing that I was going to be entrapped, advised me to stay at home rather than appear there and told me he would say that I was not at home when he called for me. But as soon as he told me what was happening, I grabbed my sword and went as ordered. I go into [332] the room, where a large group has gathered. I salute them, and, speaking to the commandant, I asked him what he wanted of me.

He says to me: "Did you, Monsieur, write to the minister with an account of the war?"[1]

---

1. Here and throughout this chapter, the "minister" is Marc-Pierre de Voyer de Paulmy, comte d'Argenson, who was appointed minister of war (the post was known as *secrétaire d'état à la guerre* during the ancien régime) in January 1743 and to whom Dumont dedicated the Arsenal manuscript of his poem. Dumont here denies writing to d'Argenson because

I answered that no, I had not received such an order from His Excellency.

Then the commissaire of the marines spoke up: "You did nonetheless write and send one, in which you were not very circumspect in what you said about our unit. You know, Monsieur, that when we put things down in writing, we must be politic, and that it is not always good to speak the truth."

I replied that in telling the truth, one was not a liar.

"So you did, in fact, send one?" he says.

If I had wanted to, I could have declined to answer him, but since I had indeed written the truth, I told him that it was to Mgr. le maréchal de Belle-Isle.

"Ah, so it was to him," he says; "and why, sir, did you write? You could be put under arrest for that, at the least."

I said to him that if our royal lieutenant ordered it, I was ready to obey, but then, to silence them, and as I became a bit more heated on seeing that they were accusing me unjustly, I said to the commissaire of the marines:

"Monsieur, when I wrote, and whenever I write again, I will not ask for your permission, as I have only one person who commands my obedience."

And then I showed them the letter from the maréchal de Belle-Isle. They read it and quickly became contrite, like foxes trapped in a snare. They retire, not having been able to get me punished as they had wanted. But I don't doubt for a moment that they are all in league together [333] to destroy me in the estimation of our governor, as we will see in what follows.

Sometime after the arrival of M. de Rothelin, I went to pay him my respects and to present to him, along with my commission as captain of the gates, a report in which I explained all my outstanding debts here in Port-Louis: it stated that since I was being paid only eighteen livres per month and was receiving none of the benefits that came with my commission, those which all the gate captains appointed by His Majesty enjoyed, I owed three years' rent to the man who had leased me his house; that my predecessor had received a full three hundred livres a year in order to pay this expense; that I expected I would obtain the effects of his presence and his justice; and that he would surely protect me in remembrance of my dear father, who had always faithfully served his family. But I was frustrated in my expectations, because the only response I got during this initial visit was that he declared: Why had I been so forward as to ask the Court for a post without

_____

he had instead sent his account of the battle to Belle-Isle. The prose memoir dedicated to Belle-Isle seems to minimize his devotion to d'Argenson during the mid-1740s, even though d'Argenson might have been Dumont's primary protector during that period.

his permission; whether I was not aware that he was the governor of this city; and that I did not deserve his protection and so should address myself to those who had agreed to provide it. I fell from the clouds like Icarus, but I have not drowned in the sea.

His Serene Highness Mgr. le duc de Penthièvre arrived here and made his entry with the usual ceremonies: the local militia, the soldiers of the garrison in full dress, and the full salvo of cannons; nothing was spared. As soon as he disembarked (for he had come over from Lorient by boat), M. le marquis [334] de Rothelin presented him with the keys to the city. This prince, very respectable for his virtues, had hardly set foot in town when he went straight to the Church of Notre Dame, where he attended Mass. You may be sure that the church was filled with people, as were the streets when he left there to go visit our governor. People were crying, shouting, "Long live the king!" After dinner, the prince made his inspection of the city, which is to say he examined the fortifications. Then, that evening, he came to see our royal lieutenant, who was still ill. Finally, the next morning, he left, having slept only one night in the house of the commissaire of the marines.[2]

I received, on the ninth of December, my commission as an adjutant major, which was sent to me directly from my dear protector de la Jonchère. I went to present it to M. Deschamps, who told me to go show it to the governor. I did so, and he read it. He was still lodging at the home of the Sr. Benier, who, through the influence and protection of M. le marquis de Rothelin, has become not only our customhouse director but the deputy tax farmer for the province. The governor resided in his large house, given that he was waiting for Madame Benier, his wife. I went there to present my commission as adjutant major. While he was busy writing, and because the major de la place had entered the room, the governor said, "Here is a commission as adjutant major for this gentleman, please have it approved," and he gave it back to me. However, a few days later, he did not shy away from telling me that he was on the point of denying it, because I had sought out the promotion without his orders and permission.

I was thus received on the sixth of December,[3] and because the commis-

2. The church of Notre Dame in Port-Louis, located on the Place de Notre Dame, was first built in 1660–1670, designed by the architect and entrepreneur Le Hagre. It burned down after being struck by lightning in 1918 and was rebuilt, with only the facade remaining from the original structure. It was the primary church of the town, and the town council met there until the Hôtel de Ville was built.

3. Index note: "1746." It seems likely that Dumont made an error in these two dates, for the events of the sixth of December could not have taken place after those of the ninth.

sion papers specify all the rights and privileges, I [335] believed, as I still believe now, that I was owed and had the right to receive a third of the fees collected at the gates, according to the ordinances of His Majesty with regard to all adjutant majors. I did not wish to make this demand, however, without going and securing some kind of permission from the major de la place. I went to his home that morning to report on an order that he had asked me to carry out. It was very cold outside. He told me to take a seat and warm myself. When seated, I say to him:

"Monsieur, am I not entitled to have a third of the fees from those who enter the town?"

"No," he replies.

"But the regulations grant it to me, and my commission specifies it."

"Be that as it may," he says, "you don't deserve it."

"It is not you who gives it to me. It is the king."

"Haven't you written against me?"

I replied to him that I had only written when he had made affronts against me that I did not in any way deserve, and that since he was not ready to grant them to me willingly, I would obtain my rights nonetheless.

"Do as you wish," he says. "But you shall never have them."

The next day, since it was Saturday, market day, there were many more cartloads of firewood coming in to be sold in the square, and I ordered a sergeant of the guards to take, from the faggots that were set aside for the major de la place, the third that, according to law, belonged to me and to put them in the guardhouse, without giving any to anyone except by my orders. The sergeant obeyed. There were eleven faggots for my share. The man who usually came to collect them on behalf of the major, not seeing a pile as large as he expected from the number of carts that had entered, asked the sergeant, who replied,

"These are for the major, [336] and these are for the adjutant major."

This was enough to send him straight off to tell the major, who gave an order that the sergeant of the guard would have to surrender the faggots. But the sergeant replied that I had forbidden him from giving them to anyone except me. So he sent for the staff sergeant, who told him to his face that the firewood by rights belonged to me, that he had been in many different garrisons, and it had always been done this way. What does he do? The major gets dressed right away. The weather was atrocious. He would not have left his rooms even to serve the king, should that have been asked of him, but this is for his own profit. He goes out and runs to the governor's residence, to explain to him what he had learned and what he wants done.

So one of the town's leading men was entrusted with carrying out an order to summon me to speak to M. le marquis. I did so. The major had left, and when I entered the room, the marquis says,

"I find you rather bold to be giving such orders without my permission. I don't know what is preventing me from sending you to rot in a dungeon."

I tell him, honestly and respectfully, that I did not deserve that, and that I did not even know what I had done wrong.

"What? Then why are you seizing faggots at the gate?"

"Because, Monsieur, the king grants me by his regulations a third of the revenue, and so those faggots belong to me."

"But I do not want to you have them, so go return them."

I tell him that I would not surrender them without an order from the Court.

"And I agree. If an order comes that says you must have them, you will be compensated for those you have not been able to claim, but until then, obey my orders, or I will make you feel what it means to disobey me."

I was thus forced to yield, and I have still not managed to obtain such an order, although in fact and by all standards of fairness, there is really no [337] need to have one, because the regulations of His Majesty define our rights and our laws.

So it was that once again the major triumphed, and as I have no doubt that he spread the word to M. le marquis that I was a drunkard and was applying this label to me in reports to the Court, he plotted to set a trap for me to become guilty of just this sin. I was not expecting this, but I was trapped, and it was the only time that this occurred since M. de Rothelin had come to serve as governor. Anyone else would likewise have fallen for it. Here is what really happened:

One day, a lieutenant of the royal regiment invites me to dinner, with great urgency. I cannot refuse him, and it was, in fact, an honor to me, so I accept. Now, this lieutenant was from the same hometown as the major de la place, and a friend of his. He was a young man, but cut an impressive figure. The two of us leave the citadel together to go to his inn. At the gate in the outer wall, we find the major, who says to his young friend, in front of me:

"Would you like to come to dinner with me?"

"I am much obliged, Monsieur, but I am having our adjutant major over for dinner."

"That's good."

I then spoke up and said to the major de la place, "Shall I come later to get your orders, Monsieur?"

"No, it's no trouble; I will summon the guard. Go and have a good time."

We continue on our way, we arrive at the place where he dined, and more than an hour passed before we sat down at the table. We eat, we drink, and at dessert, each is given a bottle, only mine contains half wine and half eau-de-vie. When I began drinking it, I found the wine to be stronger than usual.

The lieutenant said to me, "Isn't it strong stuff?"

"Yes," I replied.

[338] "That's the way it's supposed to be," he told me; "it won't do you any harm. Watch how I drink it," he said. But his was not mixed.

So we drank, I along with all the others, but this strange force came over me all of a sudden. By then, more than three hours had passed. A soldier comes to inform me that the guard is not posted and that the soldiers are crying out. My zeal for duty overcomes me, and I run to a place where frankly I should not have shown my face. I enter, however, and when stopped, I ask to have a word with the marquis. He looks at me and says, "You are in no state to receive him." I persist in my demands, but he raises more objections against them. At last the major appears, takes over for the guard, and tells me to follow him. I obey, and he leads me into the citadel, gives the order to mount the guards, and then tells me to give myself up for arrest. I did deserve this punishment, but nonetheless I believed that my fault lay in my attention to the duty of mounting the guard. I was held in prison for six days, until New Year's Day, when, through his generosity, our governor allowed himself to be persuaded by the appeals of my son, on whose behalf he granted me a pardon. I went to thank him. He said that he was forgiving me this one time but that it must not happen again. I promised and even said to him that if it happened again, rather than punish me, he should demote me. I have kept my word, and since that moment, I have never failed to perform my two jobs every day: that of captain of the gates and that of adjutant major. The major himself only rarely is present in the citadel to witness the changing of the guard, if only because he is dining at the table of our governor. And I cannot omit pointing out that when this major has a grudge against someone, he abandons his religion, his duty, and even the regulations of the king. Here's another [339] example:

The first lieutenant of the fourth company of disabled veterans, of the five companies posted here, was an officer who had served His Majesty for more than sixty years. He was a fine gentleman from a good family, who had resided in the veterans' home for twenty years, yet had not been able to overcome the antipathy of his captain, who spoke ill of him to the major, and this was enough to bring down the major's hatred on this lieutenant, even though the poor man could proudly and justly claim to have never neglected his duties in this garrison in any way. Still, this officer felt the wrath and torments the major imposed upon those to whom he was not friendly. It's also true to say that when he was off-duty, this lieutenant had the weakness of drinking a bit too much, but never to the point of foolishness or belligerence. Nonetheless, his captain had confined him to barracks and reduced his pay to five sous per day, saying that was all he needed, although he was owed for more than three months of his lodging by the administrative commissioner. When I was in charge of the accounts, at a time when the major was absent, I asked the royal lieutenant to grant a pardon to this officer, so as to relieve some of the others in his company, who were fatigued by performing his duties. This was granted. The officer thus was freed from his punishment and confinement, where he had spent more than two months straight, and he resumed performing his duties. This pardon no doubt shocked the major, but he waited for the right moment to take his revenge.

The second time that this officer mounted the guard at the head of his company on the Place de Notre Dame, where the assembly and parade took place, the major de la place at the last minute wanted to have two young women run the gauntlet, one through the soldiers of the Swiss regiment of Witmer [340] and the other through the soldiers of the marines. This punishment was to be performed at the site of the town whipping post. You can well imagine that there was a large crowd gathered, of all stations and all ranks mixed together. Before this spectacle was to begin, the major told me to go fetch the sentence from the governor's residence and then to go tell the lieutenant and his men to begin marching so as to put themselves in front of the Swiss, who were already whipping their girl, and then to be ready to march onward as one united company. I obeyed, went to fetch the paper, and returned to the Place de Notre Dame, where I gave the order to the lieutenant to march in with his men. The company marches in formation, with drums beating, and comes into the position on the square that I myself had indicated to them. Upon arriving there, I ordered a quarter turn. The lieutenant halted, holding his pike a bit too low, and just then the spectators moved back, and a man in the crowd turned, catching in his face the pike of this officer, who was looking at his troops. The officer felt that his pike had touched something, but neither he nor I saw the man at all.

As luck would have it, an associate of the major was there and ushered away this man, who was indeed bleeding a bit from the wound that he had given himself. This accomplice, I say, then presented him to the major, saying:

"Look, Monsieur le major, at what was done by officer so-and-so who commands the guards."

The major, who was on horseback, came to the head of the company at the moment it was going to march away, and addressing the lieutenant, says:

"Look, you've done it again."

The officer, completely surprised, says to him, "But Monsieur, am I drunk now?"

"No, but you have injured this man here."

"I did not even see him," he says.

"Go surrender your pike to that officer there, and give yourself up for arrest, or you will not escape so easily this time."

[341] The lieutenant obeyed, but before going to the place he had been ordered to go to, he tried to go make his case to M. le marquis de Rothelin, the governor. The major, catching sight of him, spurred his horse to gallop ahead and stop him, crying out to the soldiers who were marching along to break their formation and seize him by the badge of office that was still around his neck as well as by his belt. They led the officer like a criminal to his barracks, where he remained for more than two months, not as a prisoner, as the major had ordered, but in confinement nonetheless. The royal lieutenant was able to secure this for him, but the major still did all he could to convince the royal lieutenant of the officer's crime. And he would still be under arrest if the major, together with the captain of the lieutenant's company, had not written a letter justifying their sentence to M. de la Courneuve, governor of the veterans' home, who wrote back asking for the officer to be released, if only to lock him up in the home in punishment for an accident that had not been his fault.

These are the instincts of brotherly charity of the man in control in this place. But his word carried weight, and the weak are always the victims. If, however, such acts as these had come to the attention of our just and incomparable minister, I cannot believe that this officer would have been thus exposed to the hatred of those who bear a grudge against him.

Let us return to the landlord, to whom I owed rent for the house that I had been living in for three years and who finally brought a complaint about me to M. le marquis de Rothelin. The marquis ordered me to come speak with him, and I complied. He told me that I would have to pay this man. I replied that I was still owed the stipend for my lodgings, that as soon as that was paid, I would settle the debt.

"Give him an IOU regardless."

I replied that since everyone knew the situation, [342] I did not have to do so, and that I had even written of this problem to the minister.

He told the landlord that as soon as the commissioner arrived, "I'll see to it that you are paid."

So I had recourse to His Serene Highness Mgr. le duc de Penthièvre, who was then presiding over the Estates in Rennes. I took the liberty of sending him a petition in which I asked him for my stipend for three years of room and board that was due to me from the administrative paymaster, in my capacity as captain of the gates of his city of Port-Louis. This prince sent it on to our governor, who promptly told me that he had already forbidden me from writing to the maréchal de Belle-Isle, to the minister, or to anyone else, unless I first showed him my letters. He demanded to know why I had written to His Highness without permission, since I well knew that he could lock me up for good in a deep dungeon. I replied to him that since he did not care to show me justice, I had to plead my case elsewhere.

"But look what happened to your latest petition," he said. "The duc de Penthièvre forwarded it to me. If you had shown it to me first, I would have been able to support it, but now you will never have a penny to pay for your lodgings."

With this fine promise and threat, I left, but I was still not discouraged. I wrote again in February[4] to His Highness, who, at last, was so good as to hear my plea, and I had the honor of receiving a letter from this prince dated March 9, in which His Serene Highness indicated that he had ordered that I be paid the sum of 900 livres, which was owed to me for my lodgings in my capacity as captain of the gates. It was not long after this good news, the result of the justice of this amiable prince, that I received from the administrative paymaster the approval for payment of this sum, and although our governor had had no hand in it, [344][5] I believed it was my duty to go thank him anyway.

The news spread through the town that I was going to receive 900 livres for my lodgings, and the Sr. Benier, now deputy tax farmer as well as customhouse director, let it be known to M. le marquis de Rothelin that I owed one of his clerks the sum of 1,077 livres and a few sous and that I should be required to give an account of what I owed.[6] The governor came to find our royal lieutenant, M. Deschamps, and recounted what the deputy tax farmer had said to him. I was summoned and asked whether

4. Index note: "27 February."
5. Dumont skipped the number 343 in his pagination.
6. This clerk is Maur de Tronquidy; see original manuscript [346] and [351], below.

I truly owed this sum. I told them that no, this was about a letter of exchange that I had given to this clerk, when he was my neighbor as a habitant in Louisiana, in order to obtain some money from my brother; that I did not owe him this sum, but in truth, I might owe him 200 livres in the currency of that country; that he had only taken on this letter of exchange as a favor to me; and that, while in Louisiana, he had never been in a position to lend me that sum of money. Those are the sorts of things I was told when I went to collect what was owed me, 810 livres, after a 10 percent fee was deducted. I was also told that there was an order to withhold 100 livres against a debt that I owed. I had to fight the battle again. But since 100 livres in French money was worth at least 900 livres in Louisiana card money, and I did not even owe that, I took the liberty of writing to the minister, who forwarded my letter to M. de Viarms, the intendant at Rennes.[7] This gentleman referred it to his deputy at Lorient to adjudicate between the parties. But it didn't stop there, for the deputy came over from Lorient to Port-Louis and brought my [345] letter to our governor, who was angry that I had exposed his clever designs. One night, when I was finished shutting the gates and was going to report to him on my duties, he received me as if I were the lowest of men. The Sr. Benier was there and said to him in my presence, as well as that of a virtuous woman who was also there, that I was slanderous in my writings, that I was here as a spy of M. de Belle-Isle, and that without the protection of the maréchal and without the support of M. Deschamps, I would not have even one crust of bread to put in my mouth. If it had been suitable to draw my sword against this man and fight a duel to the death, I would have gladly done so, but I scorned such an act because he was no more than a clerk. I told him, however, what I had written. "I want to see your letter," said the marquis de Rothelin. I promised to let him do so.

I left there in a state of high dudgeon, having been unjustly attacked. For what? Simply for defending my rights and my livelihood. Did I deserve to be treated so? I drafted a letter addressed to Mgr. de Belle-Isle, and showed it to M. le marquis de Rothelin, who read it and said to me, "Is this how you are writing?" He tore it to pieces and threw it in the fire. "Go away. I will write to him." So I withdrew, and I went to make a second copy, and sent it to my dear protector, His Excellency, who can still deliver me justice in this affair, since he received it before he departed to take command of the army in Provence.

7. In Louisiana, as in Quebec, a shortage of specie forced authorities to issue informal currency, such as playing cards.

Four or five days later, I went to receive my orders at the governor's residence, as I did every day. When he had given me them, and I was on my way out, he called me back and said to me:

"I do not forbid you from writing to whomever you wish, but do not mention me at all in your writings, whether favorably or unfavorably."

"I have never written against you and I will not do so."

"Continue to perform your duties as you are doing. I am content, and you shall soon feel the effects of my protection."

I made a low bow to him, thanked him for his goodness, and he added,

"I am [346] too good a friend of M. de Belle-Isle, who protects you, to do harm to you."

I then went away, pleased with his promise. The Sr. Benier, however, was still pushing the case of his clerk, who caused me to be sent notice by the court in Hennebont that we were involved in a lawsuit.

I believed, at the time, that as I was performing my duties scrupulously, I was soon going to enjoy some peace, and since I would now feel the protection of Monsieur le marquis, I believed myself the happiest of mortals. But it was not to be. The governor immediately wrote a letter against me to the minister, and I received a letter from Paris dated the sixteenth of June saying that in his letter to the minister, the marquis complains strongly about my irregular conduct; that often, I drink wine or spirits and am in no condition to appear before him; that, in a word, he requests respectfully that I be removed from his presence and sent to a post in the administration of M. de Belle-Isle, that is, in the region of Metz. In this letter, I was advised to prepare myself for this move. The accusation against me being false, it has not been difficult for me to find a credible and eloquent defender who sees me every day—indeed, almost every minute—and who has written to the minister with a contrary report. So I remained quiet for a few days, awaiting his departure at the end of June to go live at Hennebont, two leagues away from this town. The marquis, knowing that I had been informed of what he had written to the minister regarding my conduct and having spoken about it to M. de Sulpont—a chevalier de Saint Louis and a young man filled with courage and spirit, always ready to do a favor—the latter must have told him how I was going to react, for the marquis asked me what I had to say about a certain letter from M. d'Argenson. I replied to him that I was quite surprised that after [347] promising me his protection, he had written against me to the minister. I told him this in front of a large company that had been given the honor of dining with him and were, at that moment, about to take their coffee. As soon as I had said this, the marquis de Rothelin, taken aback, said to me, "I have my reasons, and when I write against the conduct of an officer, I write what I wish, and I do not have to answer to anyone for my actions." How was one to respond to that? I bowed to him once again, thanked him for his generosity and for his efforts to remember me and to have me known at Court. I then retired and went off, as I did every night, to see to the changing of the guard.

At the end of June, he left town. One could justly say that this separation of only two leagues brought joy to the hearts of the town's leaders, residents, officers, common folk, and perhaps to me more than anyone else, since at least he would no longer see me drinking. If, in his report that he had given to the minister, he had put me down as mad, instead of as drunk, I should be able to say that he had partly spoken the truth, because all that I was seeing happen every day that he lived in this city, the seat of his government, was truly driving me mad.

So he left this town to take command of a small garrison a quarter of a league outside Hennebont, and it was in the town of that name that he made his residence. I now believed myself, as I've said, to be sheltered from his influence. I congratulated myself on my good fortune, believing that I was now going to enjoy peace and persuaded that the minister would pay more attention [348] to a letter from a protector who was a longtime resident of this garrison than to a governor who was only doing the rounds, so to speak, determining what he might be able to take for himself, since this had been (as I said above) the first grand entrance and visit to Port-Louis that he had made since he was named governor.

But I was not born under a lucky star; my life is merely a tapestry of pain, troubles, and misfortunes; and whenever I get my head above water for a breath of air, it is only to give me the strength to survive a new storm that throws another wave down upon my head. This is what I am experiencing now as I write these lines.

By the time the governor departed, he had provided ample fodder for poets (of which there are a good number here, including at least one woman, the wife of a council member); these poets, I say, have composed some verses upon the conduct of his administration. The author is anonymous, and because I have written some verses in praise of our royal lieutenant, who richly deserved them, when the author of these other verses, which spoke the truth and expressed the wishes held in the hearts of many, did not come forward, that was enough. The governor held a grudge against me and saw a way to make me the target of his vengeance, and so, on the twenty-first of July, I was placed under arrest, and only after four months and three days was I released by order of M. de Coëtlogon, maréchal of the royal armies and commandant general of His Majesty's forces in Brittany.[8]

You need not doubt for an instant the joy I [349] felt at the moment I regained my liberty and at the order from M. Deschamps, our royal lieutenant, who asked me continue in my role as his adjutant major.

However, I have nothing of the lucre of office, since my commissions are still not finalized (I refer to the the latter appointment, for, in the case of the former, it is stipulated in the ordinances of our kings, collected in the book of the Sr. Briquet, that I am to receive a third of the revenue). I have not collected anything in my status as captain of the gates during the three years that I have been performing that duty. I continue to fulfill it, however, as well as that of adjutant major, and have nothing to show for it. But in any case, I now see myself as overwhelmed by miseries, just like Robinson Crusoe. He was alone. This was, for him, a comfort, whereas in my case, I am not alone in my unhappiness, having a wife and a son and a daughter, who, as one might well imagine, feel themselves the misery of an unfortunate parent—unfortunate, I say, not owing to his own actions but because fortune runs against him. The only thing that can console him is his hope that one day, the Court will decide to cast some sign of its goodness upon him and give him the justice and the rights that are his due. But this time cannot arrive without the continued protection of Mgr. de Belle-Isle, maréchal de France, a person who does not allow himself to be won over by the discourses of common flattery.

I continue my [350] service and am still the pack mule in the service of the staff officers. I have just learned, by a letter written to me from Paris, that M. de la Jonchère had the pleasure of seeing M. de Rothelin at an audience held by Mgr. d'Argenson at the Hôtel des Invalides; that the treasurer of the Order of Saint Louis spoke to the governor in my favor; and that M. le marquis gave him to understand that he was granting me his protection, but he wanted me to be reassigned out of his government and suggested that I be given a commission as a half-pay lieutenant in Metz.[9] I have already held this rank for twenty-seven years, and I believe that in having the good fortune to advance from this rank to adjutant major, I should not

8. While he was in jail for these four months, from July to November 1747, Dumont lost his appointment as captain of the gates, for, according to Buffet, he was replaced in 1747 by Jacques-François-Arnauld Dessuslepont, Sr. du Pin; see Henri-François Buffet, *Vie et société au Port-Louis des origines à Napoléon III* (Rennes, 1972), 33.

9. Belle-Isle, among his many other titles, was head of the government at Metz until 1753, so Rothelin apparently tried to prevail upon Belle-Isle to get Dumont reassigned there.

drop back down. I was named to the post I hold by the king, after all, and I have never been delinquent in my service. On the contrary, without lucre, without sinecure, without emolument, I have fulfilled my duty. And because I do not please the governor, owing to the influence of the major, whom I annoy, is it any wonder I complain, and should I be held at fault for this? The Court is too fair-minded to be won over by such simple accusations, and the better [351] a state listens to its dissenters, the better His Majesty's service is fulfilled. As for me, I will continue to cry out, *Fiat voluntas tua, Domine, et non mea.*[10] Alas, I must have been born under a star fatal to my fortune. But as it is said that the wheel of that goddess keeps turning, I hope against hope that it might someday turn in my favor and stop there, so that I might be able to enjoy some relief from my labors and torments. In spite of this glimmer of hope, I still find or see so many enemies working against me that I am close to losing all hope, unless a god looks after me. I know two such gods: one is the foremost of all beings, who has given me strength to endure and survive thus far all my labors and torments; the other is in the person of the illustrious and incomparable duc et maréchal of the great empire of France, the just Fouquet de Belle-Isle, who, by his goodness, has enabled me to obtain the rank of adjutant major in this garrison and upon whom I rest all my hopes.

I have indicated how a clerk in the office of the Sr. Benier brought a lawsuit against me in the jurisdiction of Hennebont, demanding of me the sum of 1,100 livres in French money, which I do not owe him at all, for I received from him only two hundred and some livres in the money of the country. Nonetheless, during the time [352] I was held in prison, this suit was brought to trial, and although I could not defend myself, I was still found guilty. But because this is contrary to the basic laws of justice, I have appealed to the parlement.[11]

My son, who had sailed as a gentleman volunteer on the *Philibert* (a vessel of the Company of the Indies), after six months in prison in England, arrived in Saint-Malo and, while coming to rejoin me, fell dangerously ill at a place called Matignon, four leagues from that port. He has been within a whisker of death. What's more, rescuing him has cost me 132 livres and 10 sous. I mention this to show that misery always falls on the poorest, for

10. "May your will be done, Lord, and not mine."

11. A judgment dated November 3, 1747, was recorded in the seneschal court in Hennebont in a case between Maur de Tronquidy and "Jean-Baptiste-François Dumont de Montigny," granting the former's claim and ordering Dumont to pay court costs (ADM, B 2660, fol. 2v).

with only 18 livres per month, all that I have, where would I be without the help of God, who never abandons His own? My only consolation, for the time being, is that the Company, in recognition of the voyages that my son has made in its service, has just named him a supernumerary officer on one of its ships, the *Hercule*, which will depart this spring for a destination to be determined. As for me, I continue my service with zeal and precision and wait hopefully for my post to be finalized. Once it is official, I look forward to peace and rest, which is what I am wishing for the year 1748 until the end of my days, which will arrive according to the will of the Master of the World and the immutable law of nature.[12]

12. The *Philibert* was armed in Lorient for a voyage to Ile de France (modern Mauritius) on March 28, 1747, but was captured by the British along with seven other ships near Cape Ortegal, Spain, on May 14, 1747. The *Hercule* was armed at Lorient on January 9, 1748, for a voyage to Ile de France under Captain Nicolas Fremery, and returned in July 1749. See "Les armements au long cours de la deuxième Compagnie des Indes," nos. 1446, 1458, 1483, 1573, SHD, Lorient. Matignon is about 20 km west of Saint-Malo and 150 km northeast of Port-Louis.

Chapter Eleven

ETHNOGRAPHY

[353] As I have promised to speak generally of the lands where I was and to explain to my reader the wealth and opportunities that might be had there, I shall now follow through and set down in writing some things about the province of Louisiana, the manners of the Indians, their religions, their dances, their customs; then I shall describe the French settlements, what they do in that country, their trade, their explorations, and, in a word, the truth about everything.

The province of Louisiana, at first known by the name of Mississippi, is a land located in the island of North America, extending from latitudes 18° to 50° north. Without stopping to repeat what I have already said about the three initial settlements of the French at Dauphin Island and at Old and New Biloxi, I will tarry only to speak of the mouth of the river called Saint Louis, known under the Indian name of Barbancha. It is one of the most beautiful rivers in existence, being more than 600 leagues in length, twisting this way and that, and without these bends, it would be impossible to ascend, given its rapid and impetuous current. It is, at some points, more than a league and a half in width and never less than three-quarters of a league, very deep in the middle, with water excellent to drink and a tidewater that extends for more than 130 leagues.[1] Its mouth is at 29°, and to reach it from France, one must make a long voyage, beginning by passing Cape Finisterre and the mountains of the Canary Islands, then proceeding to either Cap François de Saint-Domingue or La Caye Saint-Louis. [354] At Le Cap or La Caye, take on the water and supplies you will need to continue your route, and after leaving either of those two spots, you advance to

1. The Mississippi is today measured at 3,780 km, but its course has been straightened and shortened by dams and dredges. Likewise, the extent of tidewater in Dumont's time cannot be compared with modern conditions. Zadock Cramer's *Navigator*, compiled around 1800 and reprinted in many editions, indicated that tidewater extended to New Orleans, 108 miles upstream, and so Dumont's 130 leagues, or 600–700 km—a point just below Natchez—is inaccurate.

the island of Cuba, which will be on your right as you run along the coast. This island belongs to the Spanish. You leave to the left Jamaica, which is an island belonging to the English. Avoiding both Grand and Little Cayman Islands, you come upon Cabo San Antonio, and setting a course toward the northwest, you come to Ship and Chandaleur Islands; after that, you reach the mouth of the Saint Louis River. You anchor, or—to make myself understood to one who is not at all knowledgeable in nautical terms—you let the anchor fall to the floor of the sea so as to stop the ship, after which you fire off a cannon loaded only with powder so as to call out the coast pilot to come on board and steer the ship into the waters of the river. This bar is very difficult, and it is unfortunate that funds have not been made available to improve it, because the larger ships cannot enter at all, as there is only eighteen to twenty feet of water during the highest tides. Once past that, you come face to face with the first French post, which was built by the ingenious engineer M. Pauger and named La Balize, where there is a fine fort with palisades, caserns, magazines, a chapel, barracks for officers, and a forge, all built on pilings and armed with plenty of cannons properly placed to defend the entrance of the river from the enemy.[2]

Once you have entered the river, for seven or eight leagues upstream on either side, you see no trees but only large canes and bushes. It is true that [355][3] one league up on the right facing upstream, there is a single tree on the riverbank, called the bottle tree because some travelers hung a bottle from this tree and others found it there, and so the tree came to have that name. Another league farther up, you come upon another tree called Picard's gallows, after a soldier of that name who was heard to say that if he were condemned to be hanged, he would choose that tree for the noose, and that is how those two trees got their names.[4]

After eight or nine leagues, you reach the forests, which are so thick and so high that they prevent any progress by sail. To move upstream, it is abso-

2. Construction of the fort at La Balize began in 1722. Thirty years later, the outlet of the river at the southeastern pass had moved seven kilometers away, and the foundations of the fort on the island had begun to subside. It was replaced with a floating fort still in use into the nineteenth century. This, in turn, was replaced by Pilottown, situated a short distance upstream on the main branch. See Kenneth J. Banks, *Chasing Empire across the Sea: Communications and the State in the French Atlantic, 1713–1763* (Montreal, 2002), 86; and Samuel Wilson, Jr., "Early Aids to Navigation at the Mouth of the Mississippi River," in Jean M. Farnsworth and Ann M. Masson, eds., *The Architecture of Colonial Louisiana: Collected Essays of Samuel Wilson, Jr., F.A.I.A.* (Lafayette, La., 1987), 24–40.

3. Figure 13, "The Chaouachas Concession," was originally located at this spot in the manuscript.

4. These stories are also in *Mémoires historiques*, I, 5.

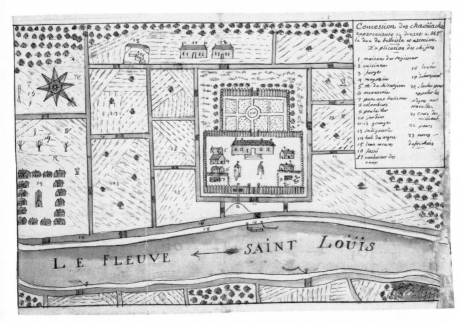

Figure 13. *The Chaouachas Concession, Formerly Belonging to Monseigneur le Duc de Belle-Isle and Partners.* VAULT oversize Ayer MS 257, map no. 13. Courtesy The Newberry Library, Chicago

lutely necessary to winch the boat. This is rough and unpleasant work, especially for the stomach, and sometimes it takes six weeks to cover the thirty-two leagues from La Balize to the capital.[5] After twenty-eight leagues, you see the Chaouachas, which is the finest of all the concessions in the country. It belongs to Mgr. le duc et maréchal de Belle-Isle and his partners, the late maréchal d'Asfeld, the late Mgr. Le Blanc, minister of war, and M. de la Jonchère, treasurer of the Order of the Grand Croix de Saint Louis. One might say that this concession is very rich, with more than 120 negro men and women, a fine manor house and outbuildings, a storehouse, forge, workshop, indigo works, wharf, a fine courtyard, livestock, cabins for the laborers and the negroes, and a manager to look after it all. In my time, this was the Sr. Rougeau, who had married Mme Desnoyers, widow of the officer who was killed at Terre Blanche, another concession belonging to the same

5. Marcel Giraud confirms that "merely crossing the bar might take fifteen days . . . and ascending the river to New Orleans sometimes took a month or more" (*HLF*, V, 339). In *Mémoires historiques*, I, 6, Dumont stated the distance to New Orleans as being twenty-nine leagues.

founders, in the massacre by the Natchez in 1729.[6] These two plantations are worthy of their wealthy founders. In earlier times, this place [356] was a village of Indians known under the name of Chaouachas, who, in exchange for trade goods or loot, abandoned this place and retired to a place farther inland. From this concession to New Orleans, it is at least six leagues, and to get there, one must pass English Turn. This is so named because, before the French had established themselves in this land, the English wanted to settle there and so sailed up to this spot on the river, which appeared to them to be only a great wide lake, so that, believing it a lake, they made up their minds to retrace their steps, or rather, turn their boat around and sail back to find the route that they had been following up the river. And from this came the name "English Turn." One might well say of them the words in the Psalm of David, *Oculos habent et non videbunt*.[7] So after you have gone around the bend in this place, which is easily done on the right-hand side if going upstream in a pirogue (although, if in a ship, you must make many tacks to pass through, or, to better explain it, the ship must turn through the full circle of the compass), having finally passed through there and continued five leagues beyond it, you arrive at New Orleans, which is currently the French capital in that country. I will not make a further description, having done so above, where I explained that it is not at all fortified, that

6. The deed of sale for the Le Blanc / Belle-Isle concessions in 1737–1738 confirms that "Sieur Rougeot, who is now the manager of the Chouachas plantation, and that by the account to be settled with him the vendors are found to owe him some salary, the said purchasers will retain him in their service at least until the payment of the first year of the principal falls due." See Heloise H. Cruzat, trans., "Documents concerning Sale of Chaouachas Plantation in Louisiana, 1737–38," *LHQ*, VIII (1925), 597.

7. Dumont neglects to mention that the Chaouacha village, numbering thirty adult male warriors, had been wiped out in an attack undertaken by African slaves on orders from Governor Périer in December 1729. See Philibert Ory to Etienne Périer, *MPA*, IV, 47–48. The village was located on the left bank of the Mississippi, in the northern end of present-day Plaquemines Parish. This area is underwater now. It was in September 1699 that an English ship ventured up the Mississippi. This had been sent out by Daniel Coxe, who later published *A Description of the English Province of Carolana, by the Spaniards Call'd Florida, and by the French La Louisiane* (London, 1722). The expedition was turned back by the French under Bienville, who claimed to have established a fortification there at the "English turn." In omitting this information, Dumont evidently did not wish to show Bienville successfully defending the French colony. See Pierre-François-Xavier de Charlevoix, *History and General Description of New France*, in Charles E. O'Neill, ed., *Charlevoix's Louisiana: Selections from the* History *and the* Journal (Baton Rouge, La., 1977), 10; and André Pénicaut, *Fleur de Lys and Calumet: Being the Pénicaut Narrative of French Adventure in Louisiana*, ed. and trans. Richebourg Gaillard McWilliams (Tuscaloosa, Ala., 1988), 30. The line from Psalm 115, verse 5, translates as "They have eyes, yet cannot see." A marginal note here is partly cut off and might have provided the reference for this verse.

the Sr. de Salmon is the commissaire ordonnateur and the chief judge along with the six councillors, that it is the former who governs the city and its inhabitants, and that it is under his orders that merchandise is delivered to the warehouses.[8]

Before any Frenchman had been in these lands, they were [357] inhabited, as they still are today, by various Indian nations, which are spread about, more or less distant from one another. Each nation has its own particular customs and even its own language. I will not speak of all of them but limit myself to the customs of the Natchez and Arkansas, among whom I have spent the most time. However, one can extend one's understanding from the part to the whole.[9]

The Indians live in the prairies or in the midst of the forests, and even on the shore of the sea. Some of the former have no permanent dwellings and so are called itinerant Indians, but others have fine villages situated in the prairies, such as the Chickasaws, Choctaws, Alabamons, etc.[10] Still others are in the forests, such as the Arkansas, the Mobiliens, the Pascagoulas, and the Chaouachas. Finally, still others are on the rivers and lakes, such as the Tunicas, the Chitimachas, the Yazoos, the Illinois, the Natchitoches, etc.

As for the Natchez, they were settled one hundred leagues from the capital in a wide and beautiful plain one league back from the river. All the Indians in general are ruddy in complexion and, indeed, all over their bodies, nearly like the Bohemians who come to France. But the former have no beards, indeed, no hair on their bodies at all nor even any hair on their heads, except on a small part, like a toupée, or one or two locks growing on one side of their heads or the other, depending on the nation. It is by these that one can distinguish them from each another. I say that they have no

8. For the previous description of New Orleans, see above, original manuscript [132–134]. Early plans of New Orleans called for fortifications, and some early maps showed them, even though they had not been not built. Levees and drainage canals were a more immediate priority. See Shannon Lee Dawdy, *Building the Devil's Empire: French Colonial New Orleans* (Chicago, 2008), 86–96. Salmon had actually been replaced as commissaire ordonnateur by Le Normant in 1744 and died in France the following year. See the list of colonial officials in *MPA*, II, 6.

9. In literary accounts and in the eyes of most Frenchmen, the Natchez were the most fascinating of Louisiana's indigenous peoples. Previous ethnographies by Louisiana colonists, which also emphasized the Natchez, included those by Paul Du Ru, André Pénicaut, Jacques Gravier, and Charlevoix, although only Charlevoix's had been published before 1747. Moreover, the population of hundreds of French colonists and approximately five thousand Natchez in the 1720s exceeded that of New Orleans itself. See Dawdy, *Building the Devil's Empire*, 79.

10. Index note: "Natchez, etc."

Figure 14. *An Indian Hunting.* VAULT oversize Ayer MS 257, figure no. 1. Courtesy The Newberry Library, Chicago

hair because, from their youngest years, they pull it out, and then rub in a certain liquor or juice of an herb that prevents it from growing back. As for the women, they also have no hair except on their heads, but there they have a great deal, very long and black in color, all the more so since they rub it with a kind of [358][11] dirt that gives it this color. The girls, when they are very young, have hair that is chestnut or blond, but as they grow older, it turns black.

In earlier times, the Indians had only bows and arrows for weapons. The children use these in their youth up to the age of fifteen or sixteen and are known as bannerets. They are very skilled with these bows. But the men are equally so with guns, which nearly all of them own, the French and the English having provided them in exchange for their trade goods such as poultry, grain, etc., and I can assure my reader that they can land a ball wherever they aim. It is also true that in the hunt, they never miss when they

11. Figure 14, "An Indian Hunting," was originally located at this spot in the manuscript.

fire at an animal. Why? It is because patience is the very foundation of their hunting strategy. For whether they are out to kill deer or buffalo or bear, or even ducks, geese, or cranes, they approach their prey carrying the head of a deer with its skin and horns attached. This lightweight disguise they hold in front of them, and when the live animal looks at them, they move with all the manners of a deer. They pretend to lick their flanks or to graze or look about to the right or left. So when the living animal resumes grazing, that is the moment when they approach it, and when I say "approach," they truly come so close that they could place a hand on the animal. But instead, they shoot a fatal blow into the shoulder of their prey and bring it down.

The hides of the deer or buffalo, they clean and tan in their own manner, which is to say, they first submerge them in water until the hair falls off, and then make small holes all around the edge of the skin like the eyelets on a corset. They pass a cord [359] through these and fasten them to a square frame made in the same manner as the one on which they burn their captives. This frame is always set up in the shade. They then rub the hide with the brains of a deer that they have cooked, a supply of which they carefully maintain. This marrow greases the skin. They do not have the crescent-shaped scrapers used by tanners in France but instead use a piece of flint attached to a large wooden handle, and holding this firmly, they scrape the hide, making it soft and much whiter. From both buffalo and deer skins, they make superb rugs, and the former are used to cover their beds. And the side that has no hair, or, rather, no wool, they bleach and then draw designs or figures on it to suit their fancy, for they do not have the same notions of painting as do other nations in Europe. They draw buffalos, birds, deer, or whatever comes into their heads, as well as the figures of their imagination, all in red, black, and yellow, and they trade these to the French, who use them as blankets. On the other side remains the wool of the buffalo. When they travel, they carry two of these, which are not decorated or painted, and use them as a bedroll. In hot weather, they lie on the side that has no hair. When it is cold, on the other hand, they lie between the two woolly pelts.

From the deerskins, the French make very nice breeches, and the Indians make *mitasses*, which are like stockings that are not sewn up.[12] They also make shoes, or, rather, slippers or moccasins, for walking and to protect from thorns. But in that case, they tan the leather in a different [360][13] way

12. *Mitasse* is a native American word that entered colonial French. See the glossary by Patrick Griolet, *Mots de Louisiane: Etude lexicale d'une francophonie* (Gothenburg, 1986).

13. Figure 15, "Indian with His Former Weapons . . ." was originally located at this spot in the manuscript.

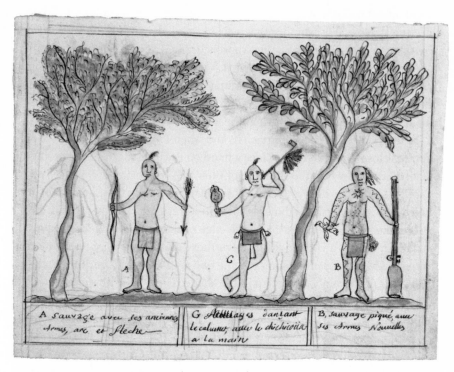

Figure 15. *Indian with His Former Weapons; Indian Dancing; Indian Tattooed.*
VAULT oversize Ayer MS 257, figure no. 2. Courtesy The Newberry Library, Chicago

so that when it gets wet, it does not become stiff. Here is the method, which is quite unusual:

Once you have one or two deerskins bleached and treated, and you wish to make a coat or pants or shoes in the Indian style, you need to make a large hole in the ground a foot and a half deep, one foot wide, but rounded on the bottom, like the bottom of an egg. Put in hot coals or light a fire in it. You throw onto the fire some cow or buffalo manure or some wet, rotten wood, so as to make it smoke. Then you cover the hole with two curving sticks to form a cross, and on these, you place your deerskin. Seal up the perimeter with earth, close up any bullet holes in the hide, and leave it there to absorb the smoke, which penetrates into the leather. When you have done this to one side, you need to do it again to the other side. Then wash it and let it dry. The smoked hide is called *boucanné*. The leather takes on a pretty, yellow color, like chamois, and it will never become stiff or brittle but remain always soft like gloves.

In each village, there is a chief who rules, but among the Natchez, he has absolute authority. When he speaks, one must obey absolutely. Even when it might come to taking the life of one of the leading men of the village, the victim is certain to allow his head to be cut off without objection and without ceremony. The chief is, in addition to this, the master of all the village. He has several wives, as many as he [361] wants, as well as several slaves and several *loués,* a term that refers to his domestic servants in life and in death, who, whenever he speaks, answer by howling six times, like dogs.[14] The Indians in past times generally wore only simple animal skins on their bodies, as in paintings of Saint John the Baptist in the desert. But today, it is not the same. They have clothing, although not our shirts, vests, and pants; I have seen only two who wore clothes of that fashion: the two chiefs, one of the Natchez and the other of the Tunicas.[15] As for the others, they wear shirts without stockings or vests, or even a shirt alone, and they never cover their heads. Instead of pants, they wear a loincloth one ell in length and a quarter as wide, which passes between the legs and hides their nudity, coming up in the front and the back, where each end passes through a belt they have around their bodies, and folds back down in front and in back. There are loincloths of two colors, blue and red, and it is from limbourg cloth that they make these.

Smoking tobacco is their delight. When they smoke, they take in ten or twelve mouthfuls of smoke, which they swallow. After it goes into their bodies, they do not let it float out again, as the French do. Then, after they take the pipe away from their mouths, they force the smoke out, one puff after another. The smoking ceremony is called a *calumet.* The tube through which one draws the smoke is two or three feet long, decorated with porcupine quills of various colors, and from the midpoint of the tube hang fourteen or fifteen long swan's feathers, also colored either white or red, with small, rattling eagle's claws [362][16] attached to each end of the feathers. Regardless of these decorations, at the end of the tube is a pipe of red or black

14. The despotic authority of the Natchez Suns, or *soleils,* was remarked upon by all the French ethnographers, for it contrasted with the egalitarian social structures of many other North American peoples. The number of exclamatory yells followers made to show their loyalty to a soleil was an oft-cited instance of this power. See original manuscript [363], below; *Histoire de la Louisiane,* II, 370; and *Mémoires historiques,* I, 176, where Dumont states, "They yell out nine times to salute him." The word "loués" translates from French as "rented," or "contracted for," but likely was a Mobilien or Natchez word, as it was used specifically with reference to the Indians of Louisiana. It was spelled "allouez" by some French writers, for example, Pierre-François-Xavier de Charlevoix, *Journal d'un voyage fait par ordre du roi dans l'Amérique septentrionale,* ed. Pierre Berthiaume, 2 vols. (Montreal, 1994), 805.

15. This refers to Serpent Piqué and to Cohura-Joligo, the chief of the Tunicas.

16. Figure 16, "Musical Instruments," was originally located at this spot in the manuscript.

stone, one or the other, according to their whims. I've forgotten to say that the feathers are arranged in a fan-shaped circle, like a turkey's tail, and that they will send a party of their ambassadors sometimes as far as five hundred leagues, though usually less, to present the calumet. The ceremony is always accompanied by presents, and when they have arrived in a village and they want to present the calumet to a chief, the envoys are dressed up like real harlequins in their best outfits, most often with rattles hanging all around them and occasionally small bells, with feathers on their heads and their faces painted red, which is none other than our cinnabar or vermilion. Others might have their faces half red and half black. Still others might simply have stripes on their faces, of red, white, black, and yellow. Finally, others will be smeared with bluish dirt. In a word, they put on real masquerades or carnival dances. They walk all together in rhythm, dancing and holding the calumet aloft, keeping time with arm gestures, with their bodies and their feet, following the sound of one who beats on a drum, which is merely an earthen pot covered with a deerskin spread over the top and held tight with a cord. They thus arrive dancing and singing in front of the foreign chief.[17]

So then the tobacco is placed in the ceremonial calumet pipe, and it is presented to [363] the mouth of him who is to be honored, who lights the tobacco by drawing upon the pipe while one of the presenters holds the flame above the bowl. And once he has drawn in five or six mouthfuls, the calumet is taken from him and passed along from mouth to mouth among those who are present and seated next to the chief. While the calumet is thus being passed from one to another, the speaker pays his respects and announces the subject that has brought him to the village, whether it is to ask him for help or to simply ask for the continuation of his friendship and that the two villages might be as brothers and friends. At each phrase or each pause, the chief who is being honored expresses his thanks with the sound "houis, houis," spoken from deep down in his belly. When this oration, or harangue, is finished, the chief is presented with his gifts: perhaps tanned deerskins; skins filled with oil; guns; shirts; glass beads; vermilion;

17. Compare this account, continuing to original manuscript [365], below, with *Mémoires historiques*, I, 189–195, a chapter titled "The Calumet Ceremony: What It Is." In that chapter, Dumont does not emphasize the meal served to the ambassadors as he does here. For a modern anthropological study of the ceremony, see Ian W. Brown, "The Calumet Ceremony in the Southeast and Its Archaeological Manifestations," *American Antiquity*, LIX (1989), 311–331.

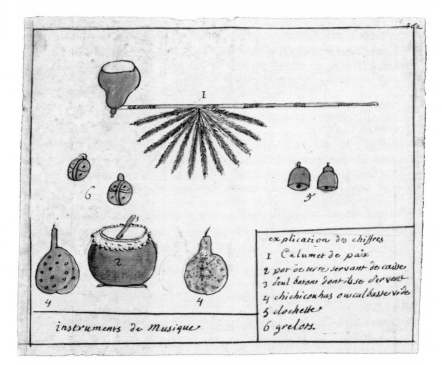

Figure 16. *Musical Instruments.* VAULT oversize Ayer MS 257, figure no. 3. Courtesy The Newberry Library, Chicago

knives; or sometimes even slaves. When the ceremony is complete, the chief who has received these presents brings out a meal, often of *sagamité*, which is a gruel made from husked maize, or corn, cooked in water, to which is added some of the oil that the Indians extract by heating the flesh of a wild animal called bear. This oil is nearly as white as lard, never congeals, and is just as good as olive oil or even better. I do believe, however, [364] that in cold lands it can coagulate, and when it does, it becomes mealy. The French eat it on salads and also use it as they would butter, for making soups or for frying vegetables. It does not impart any unpleasant taste, and even when it is congealed, it can be eaten spread on bread, like butter.

So the host offers, as I've said, a dish of sagamité to these so-called ambassadors. The one large dish made of wood (for it is rare among them to use clay dishes) typically contains just one spoon called a *micouene*. It is made from a bull's horn cut in half lengthwise and polished; it is so fine, one can even see the light of day through it. The handle of this micouene is carved according to their fancy. But in any case, there is only one, even if twenty or thirty are eating together. The chief takes a spoonful of the saga-mité, puts it to his mouth, takes only as much as he wishes, and then puts the rest back in the dish, and the others each do the same. This is how they eat: communally, which is to say, like real pigs. Another may take the saga-mité between his thumb and four fingers. If there is any cooked meat or other things such as fish, they each take a large chunk of it. They gnaw on it, then put it back onto the plate. They show no repugnance for one another. It is rare to see the women eating with the men, however, for even within the household, the wife gives food to her husband, [365] the master of the house, to eat all alone, and I can state that I have only seen men with men and women with women.

The calumet, as it is carried and presented in ceremonies, is the symbol of peace among all these savage nations, and perhaps only the Natchez have ever violated it, in the massacre that they committed on the French at that post and on the Tunicas and their Christian chief, as I have described.[18] But perhaps there is a lesson to be learned here, that caution is the mother of security and that one must be distrustful of the Indians because it must be understood that they are thieves, traitors, and scoundrels, and when they come into the home of a French farmer to bring him poultry or other goods to trade, he has to watch their hands and their feet.

The Natchez formerly had in their village a temple that in ancient times had been, according to what they say, covered in gold; that is, with woven mats of the color of gold, beautifully worked. But in my time, either from the wear of age or from some damage, these were only simple mats. It is in this temple that they inter their chiefs after death. They maintained inside the temple a sacred perpetual fire and had, for this purpose, several guard-ians to bring wood and look after the fire, and if, through their negligence, it happened that the fire burned out, then all the guardians, their wives, and their children would pay for this error with their lives. To be able to relight this fire, they would have to go more than twelve hundred leagues away to declare war on the Taensas, another Indian nation that has and preserves a similar fire. It is true, however, that [366] if this party of Natchez, while en route to declare war on that nation and take their fire, might, during the voyage, find that a lightning storm had struck at some place and set it on fire; then it was permitted to take this fire as a gift from the heavens, and their voyage and intention was considered to be fulfilled by the aid and pro-

18. Compare *Mémoires historiques*, I, 190: "The sad experience that our Frenchmen have had . . . proves that the Indians often violate this symbol of peace."

tection of their gods. One might speculate, from what I have just described, that they have had some knowledge of the sacred and perpetual fire of the vestals in the time of ancient Rome.[19]

But one might ask me, What is their god who assists them in this manner? I reply to that question by saying that it is the god they choose themselves. Some worship the sun, others the moon, some the snake, the alligator, etc., according to their wishes. And when one speaks to them of our God, infinitely good, who created all things, they reply that they know him also, as a "mingo, coustiné la hoüa," which is to say, a Great Chief blessed with a powerful spirit, and moreover that this is goodness itself, which cannot do evil. But they then add that there is also another divinity who is great and who has a powerful spirit, as well, but uses it to do evil, who is forever trying to injure them in their bodies and their possessions, whether in hunting or fishing or even in war, and that because he is evil, it is to him that they must pray, so that he does not do them any harm. From this, one can judge what blindness they are trapped in, these people for whom the god they worship and respect takes the form of a snake, crawfish, or turtles, etc. The god they thus adore is the demon tyrant who afflicts our souls and who, [367] in order to maintain his sway over their poor souls, gives them the power he has, since the *alexis*, who are like the doctors among them, and the *jongleurs*, who are like magicians, practice their art of divination so well that, among other things, they will, for a few trade goods, make water come when the weather is locked in drought. They can also make the rains cease and bring fair weather. This is no fable of my invention, as you must have already read in this memoir that this happened at Yazoo, the former concession of the illustrious and invincible Fouquet, duc de Belle-Isle, maréchal

19. This passage seems to be based upon a jumble of sources. In *Histoire de la Louisiane*, II, 337–341, Le Page du Pratz recounted a story told to him by the Natchez temple guardian about how a previous temple guardian had allowed the sacred fire to burn out and had relit it with profane fire. A pestilence followed, until the guardian admitted his fault to the Sun and restored the sacred fire. Dumont writes "Tença s" in the manuscript and appears to refer to the tribe whose name has come to be spelled "Taënsa." However, that tribe lived only about one hundred kilometers upstream from Natchez on the Mississippi. In a description of the temple and sacred fire published in the *Mercure de France* during the Mississippi Bubble period, and apparently based on Pierre Le Moyne d'Iberville's explorations of 1699–1700, the Taënsas are said to have a temple and sacred fire like the Natchez, and the temple is said to have been destroyed by lightning. See Richebourg Gaillard McWilliams, ed. and trans., *Iberville's Gulf Journals* (Tuscaloosa, Ala., 1981), 128–130; *Mercure de France*, February 1718, 138–140. The missionary Du Poisson wrote instead that the Natchez tradition stipulated that the sacred fire could be relit from the fire of the Tunica nation; see Jeffrey P. Brain, George Roth, and Willem J. de Reuse, "Tunica, Biloxi, and Ofo," in *HNAI*, 591.

de France. And this they did nearly every year, either on behalf of travelers or for themselves.[20]

The temple guardians who maintain the sacred fire observe among themselves certain fast days, as do the other Indians. On these days, they neither eat nor drink, so long as the sun is shining on their lands. It is easy to tell whether they are keeping this fast, once one is a little bit informed of their customs, for everyone who is keeping the fast has his face all black like a real negro, having blackened it with charcoal. When they have this on, you can give them the best food in the world to eat, and they will not even look at it but will simply say to you, *"Alouta la houa,"* or "I am full."[21]

When an Indian comes to the home of a French habitant, he is generally given a piece of bread, which they call by the word *pasca*. Then the Indian sits down, either on the floor cross-legged, like a tailor, or on a chair. He will break this piece [368] of bread into four little parts and throw each toward one of the four corners of the world, making the form of a cross. The Indians' alexis, or, as I've already said, their doctors, cure illnesses strictly by means of simple herbs or from the juices of herbs and roots. They never use lancets to bleed their patients, but when they do want to draw blood, they use a small piece of flint that they make, and with it, saw at the skin back and forth. Then they suck at this place, and with their mouth thus pump out the blood. If, by some accident or a gunshot, one has an arm or a leg broken, it is certain that they will not be able to set it or heal it. So, after having a fine meal and bidding farewell to his friends and relatives, the person is strangled and sent to join the dead. This ensures that one never sees

20. Although a few French learned to speak the Natchez language, the colonists more often used the Mobilien trade jargon, as in the words quoted here. "Mingo" was a Choctaw word for "chief," and "coustiné" is defined by Le Page as "spirit" in the "vulgar language" of Mobilien. See *Histoire de la Louisiane*, II, 326. Dumont quoted the Yazoo shaman using the word "Minguo" for "spirit" in *Mémoires historiques*, I, 165–166. In sum, Dumont's occasional transcriptions of native languages suggest that his own fluency in those tongues was limited and influenced by Mobilien. See Patricia Galloway, *Practicing Ethnohistory: Mining Archives, Hearing Testimony, Constructing Narrative* (Lincoln, Neb., 2006), 224–225; Charles D. Van Tuyl and Willard Walker, eds., *The Natchez: Annotated Translations from Antoine Simon Le Page du Pratz's* Histoire de la Louisiane *and a Short English-Natchez Dictionary* (Oklahoma City, 1979). *Alexis* was not used by other French colonial writers aside from Jean-Bernard Bossu but might have been a Choctaw and / or Mobilien word for "shaman" or "medicine man" that passed into French usage in Louisiana. *Jongleur,* used in France for jugglers, minstrels, or carnival entertainers, had been applied to native spiritual leaders elsewhere in French America. *Mémoires historiques*, I, chap. xxi, is titled "Of the Alexis, or Jongleurs." For the story about the Yazoo medicine man who controlled the weather, see *Mémoires historiques*, I, 174–175, and original manuscript, above [128].

21. On the fast days, see *Mémoires historiques*, I, 158.

Figure 17. *Indian Woman Chief; Indian Woman; Young Woman.* VAULT oversize Ayer MS 257, figure no. 4. Courtesy The Newberry Library, Chicago

any cripples among them. They believe that when they are dead, they go to a land filled with fine buffalo, where game for hunting is abundant. I mention hunting because, among all the Indian nations, hunting is their true vocation, of which they never tire and which they will not abandon. Neither rain nor wind nor cold nor storm can keep them from this exercise. Thus, when they are at home, if an Indian finds himself short of meat, he goes out, and when he has killed a buffalo or deer, if it's the first, he will take only the tongue, carry it back to his house, and throw it at the feet of his [369][22] wife, who goes out with her children or others to fetch the buffalo and carry it back in quarters. But how can she find the place? This appears to be almost impossible. But it is not, because the Indian, as he returns to his house, breaks off at regular distances small pieces from the branches of shrubs or small trees, and by this clue, he marks the route for his wife while he is walking back to the house. If another Indian passes by the place and

22. Figure 17, a drawing of three Indian women, with no title, was originally located at this spot in the manuscript.

sees the dead buffalo, he will not touch it at all, since he knows it does not belong to him, and among themselves, they never steal at all.

I've already spoken of the dress of the Indian man, but not of that of the woman. I said that the Indian had a loincloth made from a quarter ell of limbourg cloth. The female sex does not use this but, instead, a little skirt that they call by the name *alconand*.[23] This is a half ell of red or blue limbourg that she wraps around her body, without sewing it into a dress, and it only comes down to the knees. They will also have another ell of limbourg that they attach at either end, put over their head, and thus cover a part of their body. The flesh of their body is tattooed with various designs. Some will have a series of dots; others, snakes or suns. The Indian men, the chief and the honored men who are like their officers, will also be tattooed. The tattoos that they make on their bodies are done in this way:

They take seven or eight needles; the finest points are best. [370] They lay them out along a small, flat stick. Then they dissolve cinnabar or vermilion in water, or perhaps charcoal of willow wood that has been finely ground. There are even some who use gunpowder, but this causes an itchy rash in the flesh or on the skin. They draw upon the skin the design that they wish to inscribe. If it is red, they use the vermilion; if it is black, the charcoal or gunpowder. Then they dip each needle into either of these two colors and lightly prick the skin with them, as quickly as possible. The color enters into the holes made by the needles and incorporates itself into the flesh, marking the design. This lasts for life, although I myself, having had a Croix de Saint Louis tattooed on my left arm when I was young, found the secret to erase it. At the time, it nearly cost me my arm, but nonetheless I did succeed and removed it, although there remain a few lines, almost imperceptible. This is how I did it: with the needles, as I have described above, I re-tattooed the outline of the design upon myself using the milk of a woman who was nursing a boy. This caused a most violent fever that lasted for eight or nine days. My arm became swollen with palpitating lumps that became scaly, but at the end of nine days, this subsided, and the skin flaked off like wheat germ, leaving behind a fresh, new skin with the design nearly entirely effaced. [371] Ordinarily, all those who have themselves tattooed get the fever. But in any case, among these nations, it is only the warriors and men of valor, and even the wives of chiefs and honored men, who are thus tattooed.[24]

23. See original manuscript [372], below, and *Mémoires historiques*, I, 138, which says that this garment is restricted to young virgins.

24. In his published book, Dumont claimed that the tattoo, or *piquage*, "never wears off; one carries it to the grave" (*Mémoires historiques*, I, 140) and did not include a method by

I have said that the Great Chief had several wives and even as many as he wished. The others have only one until separated by death, at which time they take another. Although I have also said or made it understood that he was like an absolute ruler of the Indians and of the village, he is himself subordinate to a female chief, who has more power and authority than he does. This woman is not his wife; she is like an empress, and her husband, for his part, has no authority at all nor any rank in the nation and is looked upon as a stinkard, which is to say, a man of the vulgar people. It was this man who killed the Sr. de Chepart in his garden.[25] He is regarded in the nation as the lowest of all, and if the empress happened to die, her husband would go with her into the grave. In the event that he dies before she does, she has the right to take another spouse, for these men are husbands in name only, and she can, during her life, choose any one or several men whom she wants to sleep with. The reason for this is because it is this woman from whom the kings and the chiefs of the nation are descended, and on the contrary, the children of the Great Chief himself have no right to succeed him to this position; they rejoin the general population. One can see from this that the Salic law is not in fashion among them, that the eldest son and successor to the place of value must be born from the woman of the lineage, for the child who [372] comes out of her womb is truly her son, and on the other hand, the children who might be born to the wives of the chief in power cannot, with any certainty, be linked to him as their father. For, when I was there, one had only to make a present of a bottle of spirits, and one could easily obtain one of his wives or, indeed, whichever woman of the village one might

---

which a tattoo could be removed. Jean-Bernard Bossu described a different method for removing tattoos, in a passage that may be a satire upon Dumont. In his *Nouveaux voyages aux Indes occidentales* . . . (Paris, 1768), Bossu claims that while among the Arkansas, he met "an Indian who, although he had never done anything outstanding in defense of his tribe, decided to have himself tattooed with one of those marks of distinction . . . so that he could marry one of the prettiest girls of the tribe." Bossu compares this faux brave to a French officer he knew who, in 1749, stole a Croix de Saint Louis so as to impress the mother of a young lady. He then removes the Arkansas man's tattoo: "I applied some cantharides to the tattoo on his chest and then added plantain leaves, which formed blisters or tumors." See Bossu, *Travels in the Interior of North America, 1751-1762*, trans. Seymour Feiler (Norman, Okla., 1962), 95–97. On tattoos as symbols of military valor among natives in Louisiana, see also *Mercure de France*, February 1718, 124; and original manuscript [375], below.

25. For the killing of Chepart, see above, original manuscript [223]. Compare to *Mémoires historiques*, II, 146: "They regarded him as a dog, unworthy of being killed by a brave man, and they called for the chief stinkard, who brained him with a blow from a club." *Histoire de la Louisiane*, III, 255–256, also indicates that it was a stinkard who was assigned the task of killing Chepart but not that it was the husband of the female Sun.

ask him for. He promptly gave the order to his wife or to a girl, and she came to spend the night with the Frenchman, who, to pay her for her favors, gave to his mistress of one night one or two handfuls of vermilion.

There were even some Indian women who came to offer themselves to the soldiers or habitants, to the officers and the sergeants, and this at a very cheap rate. But if you paid them a little more generously, such as with an alconand that cost eight livres at the king's storehouse, then the Indian woman served as your wife and your slave all at once.[26] She looked after the cooking, made the flour and the bread, both fluffed up the bed and helped to flatten it. Others hire themselves out for one or two days like field slaves to pound the corn and make flour from it, and this for very little, perhaps a handful of salt, a yard of ribbon, or an assortment of green, blue, red, white, or black beads such as on a rosary. In spite of this liberty, there can be seen among them some girls who are quite well made and who are still virgins. How can they be recognized? It is that, instead of the alconand that the others wear around their waists, these have a belt made of buffalo fur, which is more like wool than [373] fur, made into a braid, from which hang a number of cords, at the ends of which are attached the hind claws of the birds that in this country are called eaglets. One might well raise the objection that any girl, by wearing this, might be able to pass herself off as a virgin, but I reply to this objection that it is not an honor among that sex to wear these birds. The sooner she gives them up, the sooner she is ready to offer her services to the republic.

The Indian women spend their time at their housework. They make the jugs and pots from clay, plates and bowls that are pretty and very well made. And how do they do this, as mere amateurs who do not use a wheel? They make large coils from a fine clay that is mixed with pounded shells, and when they have enough of them ready for completing the piece that they wish to make, they lay them out in a circle and continue in a spiraling line, or volute, beginning at the bottom, or base, of the vessel and continuing to lay the clay coils one atop another, polishing and flattening them equally all around. When they have made their pieces, they let them dry out in the shade, after which they put them in the fire, which makes them red, from the power of this element. This fire is made in their fire pits, which are not like our fireplaces but are in the middle of their houses or cabins, or else the fire is built in the open air, across from the house. Around their houses, there are no windows, just perhaps some holes, but these only rarely unless

26. Dumont's index note is partly cut off, but the words "the one... to say... months" are legible.

it is a fortified dwelling built to withstand an enemy, in which case these holes [374] serve as loopholes. The doors of their houses are very low, and a person must bend down to pass through them. They are built this way for their greater convenience, however, particularly during the warmer season, when there are midges, or gnats—known as *cousins* in France—and mosquitoes, a type of small, almost invisible fly, both of which bite and suck the blood and cause a bad itch. The small fire that they build in their houses and the smoke it makes prevent these insects from entering, because the smoke, once it rises to the top of the house, then descends to the level of the top of the door and flows out with enough force and volume to block any entrance by these enemies of exposed flesh. One cannot remain standing in these houses. As soon as one enters, one must sit down on the ground or on a bed, for there are no chairs or couches or stools. Their beds are made simply of four forked sticks placed in the ground, upon which there are two cross members, and on those are placed canes close together, lashed to another cane running across. On this mat, they might put a blanket they have obtained by trade with some Frenchman, or they might place on top robes made from the skins of buffalo to cover themselves; instead of a straw-tick mattress, there will be some bearskins tanned on one side and with the fur on the other side. One might say that the name "savage" suits them very well and that they have learned nothing of what one reads about civility in Pibrac. They are intelligent, however, and they put their wits to use when they need to.[27]

[375] I have explained that it was only the chiefs and their wives and the men of quality who could be tattooed, either on their buttocks, legs, arms, thighs, or faces. This restriction is real, but nonetheless, a stinkard, if he is not the spouse of a female chief or empress, can achieve the honor of being tattooed if he makes himself renowned. The tattoo is the badge of honor among the warriors, just as we have among us the military Croix de Saint

27. Compare Dumont's article "Poterie des peuples de la Louisiane, par M.D.M.———," in *Journal œconomique* (November 1752), 133–135; and *Mémoires historiques*, I, 154–155. Dumont's detailed knowledge of Natchez pottery techniques supports the findings of archaeologists who believe that some tableware found at French sites in Louisiana was not imported but was made by native potters for the French. See Ian W. Brown, "An Archaeological Study of Culture Contact and Change in the Natchez Bluffs Region," in Patricia K. Galloway, ed., *La Salle and His Legacy: Frenchmen and Indians in the Lower Mississippi Valley* (Jackson, Miss., 1982), 176–193. On the design and furnishings of the Indians' houses, compare *Mémoires historiques*, I, 142–145. The reference for civility is to Guy du Faur, Seigneur de Pibrac (1529–1584), whose *Les quatrains: Les plaisirs de la vie rustique* appeared in many editions during the seventeenth century.

Louis. Thus even the lowest of the common people can achieve this, and how better to distinguish oneself in war than by bringing back a scalp taken from the enemy, even if it is taken in an ambush, the most common method used by these nations? The lock of hair cut off with the skin attached is called a scalp, and when a village is at war with another, they will go as many as ten or twelve days to seek out and surprise a party that is unsuspecting and kill and pillage it. I say ten to twelve days without eating, and how can they go such a long time without eating, one might ask? They definitely can, but in order not to have pains in the stomach for lack of food, they tie a large, tight belt made of leather or wool around their waists to the point where their stomach is folded in half, and they say that this torture prevents them from feeling hungry. But they do loosen it from time to time. If, in a surprise attack or in combat, they take a live prisoner, whether a man or woman, this adds doubly to their renown. They lead the prisoner in triumph back toward their village, and just [376][28] before arriving at the village, they send ahead one or two messengers with the news that they will soon be there. Then the bannerets, or boys, of the village, the girls and the infants and the women, all come gather around to congratulate the victors upon their conquests, at which point they all return to the village dancing and singing.

The prisoners are led into the plaza in front of the temples, and if they are not to be kept as slaves, a council is assembled in the home of the chief, and there they are condemned to be burned. To signify this, each victim is given a stick to carry. Their clothing is removed, leaving them as naked as your palm, and their body and face are all blackened. They remain tied up during this entire ceremony. The square frame is set up in the plaza, and when this is ready, they go fetch the poor victims. They are untied from the post and made to run from one side of the plaza to the other while periodic shots are fired at them, the guns charged with blank powder and nearly touching their bare flesh. This is how their victims provide them with amusement. When the mob tires of this, the prisoners are led up to the frames, and the moment when they arrive, there is the last opportunity for a female chief to come spare one of their lives by offering a ransom in merchandise (for this power is reserved to them, in which case the prisoner becomes her personal slave). When it appears that no such buyer will come forward, then they begin to remove the scalps from the victims' heads. Then their two arms are tied to each end of the top beam of the square, and their feet rest

28. Figure 18, "Method and Representation of a Square Frame on Which the Indians Burn Their Enslaved Prisoners with Small Fires," was originally located at this spot in the manuscript.

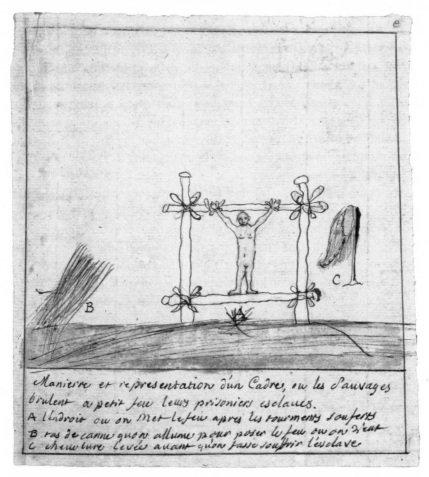

Figure 18. *Method and Representation of a Square Frame on Which the Indians Burn Their Enslaved Prisoners with Small Fires.* VAULT oversize Ayer MS 257, figure no. 5. Courtesy The Newberry Library, Chicago

on the lower one without being tied to it, and then more than twenty or thirty Indians holding [377] dried canes flaming at one end burn the victims, first on one side, then on the other, or perhaps first on an arm, then a buttock, all the while taunting them with a thousand insults and raillery. And if, during this barbecue, he should cry out[29] or shed a tear, this fault is among all the nations accounted as a weakness, and rather than continue the torture, it is halted so that the victim might be given something to eat to restore his strength, after which it will begin again in earnest. I've seen

29. Index note: "They resemble stoics."

Indian men and women burned without shedding a single tear. On the contrary, they call out with more taunts and insults for their torturers, either to show their courage or perhaps to make them accelerate the process. This is so true that when these poor victims are dead, their suffering complete, one who had not cried any tears is recognized in everyone's esteem as a great warrior, whereas, on the other hand, he who has wept is nothing but a weak woman. I have seen also a young woman, no more than fifteen or sixteen years old and rather pretty, endure this torment of fire for more than four hours straight and die all roasted, without shedding a tear nor even complaining of the pain of the fire.

When the Indians are in the midst of inflicting these torments upon their enemy, in the fury they feel at seeing the victim defy them, they sometimes are not content to merely burn his body but also cut off his flesh and gnash it between their teeth. This must be what has prompted some to say that they are cannibals and that they eat men. But this occurs only in the fury of their anger and wrath. Still, I do know that there is one such nation in this vast and spacious continent, who are called the [378] Attakappas, which in truth signifies "man-eaters," because *attaque* means "man" in their language, and *appa* means "to eat." And, in fact, the Sr. Delisle, the major of New Orleans, was taken captive by this nation, along with another officer. The latter was eaten because he was rather plump, but the first was very slim. They kept him alive, and he found his way into the hearts of this nation, where, after some years residing among them, he became chief of a village and very well respected, having learned their language, and he had the good fortune to be able to carry the calumet to M. Périer, then commandant, as if he were a real Indian. When an interpreter was called upon to translate his words, the Sr. Blanpain being absent, much was the surprise to discover that the leader of the party knew how to speak our language. He made himself known and remained among us to become major of the capital, where he has even married a well-to-do woman and has retained the alliance of that nation with the French, since he gave them some presents of merchandise to reward them for not eating him.[30]

---

30. Dumont misidentifies as "Delisle" François Simars de Belleisle, who was, in fact, adjutant major of New Orleans from 1735–1740. He and his plump companion, Alain, were among four or five men cast away on the Texas coast in 1719. *Mémoires historiques*, I, 250–258, recounts the story, without giving Belleisle's name or the misnomer "Delisle." Le Page du Pratz recounted the story in *Histoire de la Louisiane*, II, 232–240, where he gives the same etymology as Dumont does for the tribal name he spells "Atac-Apas." Bossu again retold it, with many romantic embellishments, in his 1768 *Nouveaux voyages aux Indes occidentales;* see *Travels in the Interior of North America*, trans. Feiler, 186–191. According to at least

This officer, as well as his comrade, embarked on a vessel bound from France for Louisiana, but the ship was never able to find its port nor even the proper landfall. On its first attempt, it was forced to turn around in the Bahamas strait and put in again at Cap François, where, after taking on the necessary supplies, it returned toward Louisiana, but the second attempt was no more successful, for [379] it came ashore too far west, toward Saint Bernard's Bay. The two officers, weary of being stuck on board for so long, prevailed upon the captain to grant their wish to be put ashore with some hardtack biscuit and a little eau-de-vie, in the hope that they might find the French settlement. They were, I swear, 240 leagues away, but still they went ashore and said farewell to all on the ship, which raised anchor and set sail for France without having found the French settlement, which was then at New Biloxi. The ship arrived in the port of Lorient just as I was leaving there in 1721. After two or three days, the two officers made themselves known to the Attakappa Indians owing to the gunshots they fired into the forests, either in trying to kill something to eat or just to call for help. Those Indians did not yet have any guns but came out armed with their bows and arrows and found the two Frenchmen, surprising them while they were asleep and leading them back to their own village, where the one officer, owing to his plumpness, became their meal. The Sr. Delisle was spared because he was thin. This is the honest truth, confirmed by those who were in Louisiana at the time. The king rewarded him for his trials and travails with the military Croix de Saint Louis, and I believe that he is still alive.[31]

Although the Indians might go out with the intention of surprising and killing the enemy or taking someone's scalp, this is not to say that they always find a way to succeed. They might, in fact, spend two or three weeks lying hidden someplace, waiting for [380] a chance to strike a good blow. But if, in spite of their hopes, they do not find such an opportunity, then before returning home, they strip the bark off of a tree and paint one side black and the other red. This signifies that their war party has come to make

---

one source, a De Lisle was among five men in this party and the second to die; see Charles Gayarré, *The History of Louisiana*, vol. I, *The French Domination* (New York, 1854), 274. Dumont evidently remembered this tale poorly or did not want to give credit to his nemesis, for it was Bienville, not Périer, who was commandant in February 1721 when Belleisle reached Natchitoches and his sojourn with the Attakappas ended.

31. Today, Saint Bernard's Bay is known as Galveston Bay. The ship that put Belleisle and others ashore was the *Maréchal d'Estrées*, which, after a tortuous, two-year voyage, arrived and was disarmed at Lorient on January 9, 1721; see "Les armements au long cours de la deuxième Compagnie des Indes (1713–1773)," no.154, SHD, Lorient. This was when Dumont was about to sail for Louisiana for the second time; see above, original manuscript [93].

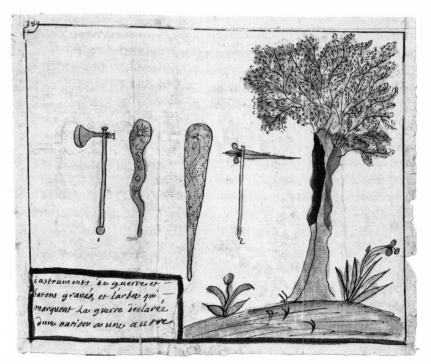

Figure 19. *Instruments of War and Engraved Sticks, and the Tree That Shows That War Is Declared by One Nation to Another.* VAULT oversize Ayer MS 257, figure no. 6. Courtesy The Newberry Library, Chicago

an attack at that place, where they did not succeed, but the inhabitants of the village are now at war, and the war party will come again soon. And if, on the other hand, they do strike a blow and take a scalp or capture some prisoners, they throw down, upon the field of battle where the action was done, some wooden clubs they have made and inscribed with the god of their own village, so as to indicate what nation has thus declared war. In fact, the same design is carved on this club as in the tattoo that the leader of the war party has inscribed on his body. It was by symbols such as these that we learned from the Yazoos that it was the Chickasaws who had declared war on us when they attacked Sergeant Riter, his wife, and his son, as I said before.[32]

32. These two paragraphs explain Figure 19, "Instruments of War," which was originally located at this spot in the manuscript. It also corresponds to a passage in the *Mémoires historiques,* I, 184–185, which has no illustration but describes some of the symbols of the Indian nations: "A sun, for example, for the Natchez, a crawfish for the Houmas, a crocodile for the Bayagoulas, etc., or what the chief of their party carries on his belly. These marks are their

So it is that the Indians declare war—that is to say, they most often do so by stealth, and hence, if two parties from enemy nations should by chance run across each other in the immense forests, they never fight a formal battle but instead must try to find a means of tricking or trapping one another. This is why, during the dark of night, wherever they are, they periodically fire blank powder from their guns to make [381] known to the enemy that they are on their guard, and the enemy does the same in its camp. And if, in a surprise attack or other encounter, the defense is effective, the winners not only take the scalps from the enemy dead; they also take them from the men of their own village who have been killed or seriously wounded with a broken arm or leg. They then quickly finish off such casualties by taking at once their scalps and their lives simply to ensure that the enemy nation will not have the glory of taking the scalp themselves, which shows the contempt they have for life.

I knew at Yazoo a chief of a village of that Indian nation who was ill for a long time with a slow fever, and seeing that he would not be able to recover his health in spite of all he or his alexi could do, he told his wife and his daughter to go find certain herbs that he named for them. As soon as they were outside the house, he took a pistol, loaded it with three balls, and fired it at his head, to cure himself of so tiresome an illness. Is this not the true remedy for all such ills?

As I have explained how hunting is the Indian men's singular craft, pastime, and occupation, I will say that the Indian women have as theirs the cultivation of the soil, sowing and planting all that is useful in their household, and that [382] the men do not get involved in this at all. And while their wives stay to look after the house, the men, as they go hunting, take with them a kind of second Ganymede, who is useful to them when love arouses urges contrary to the craft of hunting. This Indian wears an alconand like the women, has hair like theirs, has altogether the appearance of a woman, and in the village is looked upon as the chief of the women. When he returns to his house, he is permitted, during the three days of the full moon, to go to see the wives of the men with whom he has had relations, so as to return at least some of what had been lent to him during the hunting trip and thus to relieve, in part, the jealousy that the women might have on

---

heraldry." Compare the illustrations of native hieroglyphics and heraldry in Louis-Armand de Lom d'Arce, baron de Lahontan, *Nouveaux voyages de Mr. le baron de Lahontan, dans l'Amerique septentrionale,* in Réal Ouellet and Alain Beaulieu, eds., *Œuvres completes* (Montreal, 1990), I, 726–729. For the Sergeant Riter story, see above, original manuscript [122–125].

his account. During the rest of the lunar cycle, he is regarded as female and works alongside the women.[33]

It was the custom among the Natchez that when the Great Chief died away from the village, he was always brought back there. Many of his subjects went to accompany him on his voyage into the afterlife, sometimes as many as 300 or 400 people. But because the French are too good and have so strongly opposed this practice on two such occasions, there have been no more than 150 such victims.[34]

Here is how the ceremony was done. As soon as the Great Chief died, his corpse is dressed in his finest clothing, just as if he were alive, and he is laid out upon his bed. He continues to be [383] given food to eat and a pipe to smoke, just as if he were alive and speaking, for nine days. While he is lying in state on this bed, women with young infants at their breast come to offer him their innocents, whom they suffocate and throw down before him as sacrificial victims. And during all these days, his friends and relatives come to see him and congratulate him for making the right decision, to ask him a thousand questions and wish him the best for his long voyage. During all these comings and goings, his servants and wives are taking part in the festivities and not showing any kind of sadness or dread, which defies any-

33. In Greek mythology, Ganymede was the son of Tros (or Laomedon), king of Troy. Because of his unusual beauty, he was carried off either by the gods, disguised as an eagle, or, according to a Cretan account, by Minos, to serve as cupbearer. Compare *Mémoires historiques*, I, 247–249, although there Dumont does not mention the custom connected with the phases of the moon or menstrual cycles. Dumont's account of these transgendered Indians is consistent with the berdache phenomenon described in many early French accounts. See Raymond E. Hauser, "The Berdache and the Illinois Indian Tribe during the Last Half of the Seventeenth Century," *Ethnohistory*, XXXVII (1990), 45–65.

34. The mortuary sacrifices practiced by the Natchez following the death of important Suns was the most sensational element of French ethnographic accounts of the tribe. As for the two occasions when the French intervened to oppose these sacrifices, one was following the death of Serpent Piqué in 1725, narrated at length in *Mémoires historiques*, I, 208–239, which resembles the account here down to original manuscript [386]. The second might be the death of the female Sun in 1704, told by Pénicaut, or the death of a male Sun in 1700, told by Gravier and du Ru: see Pénicaut, *Fleur de Lys and Calumet*, 92–96; Jacques Gravier, "Relation or Journal of the Voyage of Father Gravier, of the Society of Jesus, in 1700, from the Country of the Illinois to the Mouth of the Mississipi River," *JR*, LXV, 139–141; Paul du Ru, "Journal d'un voyage fait avec Mr. d'Iberville de la rade de Bilocchis dans le haut du Mississipi avec un detail de tous ce qui sest fait depuis ce temps jusquau depart du vaisseau par le R. P. Du Ru Jesuite," VAULT Ayer MS 262, 37–39, Newberry Library, Chicago. In any case, the number 150 is an exaggeration, as on those occasions, only 7 to 15 people were sacrificed. Dumont himself wrote that there were 13 victims following Serpent Piqué's death; see *Mémoires historiques*, I, 237.

thing one would expect to see or describe, since I believe that they must feel this dread even as they comport themselves in such a manner, given that most of them are in the prime of life and that now they know the hour and the moment at which they will die. At the temple, a large grave is prepared, deep and spacious enough to be able to hold, as if in one grand vessel, all the corpses that are destined to accompany their chief into the land of the dead. When the day of the ceremony has at last arrived, those who must die arrive in the village plaza at dawn, dressed in all their best finery, their faces *mattachés*—which means "painted with colors"—and striking poses just like harlequins. They bow toward the four corners of the earth as if to bid them a final farewell. Then the corpse of the chief is taken up on a litter, and four of the Indian leaders or honored men of the village carry it on their shoulders, though, rather than take it straight to the temple, they turn back and forth so as to take the longest possible route.[35] Along this path, [384] women continue to throw, at the feet of the pallbearers, their suckling infants, who are crushed. Those who thus sacrifice their own blood are regarded henceforth as persons of merit and distinction. The other victims, at the sound of the drum, rattles, maracas, and jingle bells, and of the cries and wails of the populace, march in step, jumping and striking a thousand different poses, some of them indecent, around the chief's litter.[36]

35. See the description and illustration of this procession in *Histoire de la Louisiane*, III, 55–56. It is significant that Dumont's published book shifted from the generalized ethnographic account of mortuary sacrifice given here to a specific narrative about the death of Serpent Piqué and his funeral during the first five days of June 1725; see *Mémoires historiques*, I, 208–231. The manuscript memoir reveals that Dumont was not at Natchez at that time, and the narrative in the *Mémoires historiques* opens by crediting an anonymous source: "I will make use here of a narrative sent to me by a Frenchman who in 1725 was a witness to these ceremonies" (I, 208). The two manuscripts of Dumont's "Poème" (407–409, and in the LOC manuscript 125–127) begin as the memoir does here, including the claim that up to four hundred people could be sacrificed. But the Arsenal copy adds, "At the death of their chief, whom I saw buried / Fifty-three at least were put to death" (407). Hence it is uncertain exactly whose funerary sacrifices Dumont witnessed. See Gordon M. Sayre, "Natchez Ethnohistory Revisited: New Manuscript Sources from Le Page du Pratz and Dumont de Montigny," *Louisiana History*, L (2009), 423–428.

36. According to Le Page du Pratz, those whose relatives were sacrificed were rewarded with a promotion to the next higher caste in the Natchez hierarchy; see *Histoire de la Louisiane*, III, 45. The French original here reads "considerez du village," equivalent to the "gens de valeur," above, original manuscript [375], and "les grands considérés," below, original manuscript [390]. This was the third of the four ranks: *soleils, nobles, considerés,* and *puants,* translated by John R. Swanton and most other anthropologists as Suns, Nobles, Honoreds, and Stinkards (*Indian Tribes of the Lower Mississippi Valley and Adjacent Coast of the Gulf of Mexico* [Washington, D.C., 1911], 107). See also original manuscript [191], above.

And now, at last, in spite of all the detours, the body of the Great Chief arrives at the temple and is set down in front of the grave, or, rather, catacomb. All the servants of the chief, his wives, and even his friends who are sacrificing themselves voluntarily so as to never abandon him, are seated in a row facing the temple on the grass or the bare earth. The alexis, or medicine men, as well as the jongleurs, come out of the temple and begin a speech, complimenting them on their joy in going to keep the company of their good chief. After this is finished, they give each of the victims three large balls, like pills of medicine, which are, in fact, tobacco ground up finely into a powder mixed with the juice of an herb that is a subtle poison, and all the patients swallow them in unison. No sooner have they swallowed these than a deerskin stripped of its fur is put over their heads and then secured around the neck with a cord as thick as your little finger. Then the victims' relatives, fathers, mothers, and even their children, each according to their rank and degree of kinship, stand on either side to pull the cord. At the same time, there is one who pushes with his knees upon the stomach of the victim, or on the breasts, in the case of women or [385] girls. So this is the practice of the festivals and ceremonies by which all these poor souls are sent to accompany the soul of the chief and to serve him in the other life, just as they have served him in this one. In the grave or catacomb, one group of servants is placed at the bottom, the chief on top of them, his wives at his sides or even on top of him, and then the infants who have been strangled and crushed are placed on top of that, along with the remaining servants and those who have sacrificed themselves voluntarily. They do not forget to place, near the chief's head, his kettle, his guns, and the rest of his belongings, including his smoking bag with its tobacco pipe, tinder, and several gunflints, so that in case he is in need of light in that distant land, they will be able to start a fire. Although this sacrifice ceremony is like an inviolate law among the Natchez nation, and every time the chief dies such a funeral is performed, this does not prevent the spectators from letting out pitiful cries and wails when the cords are about to strangle the poor victims.

Other nations do not use the same ceremony, and when the chief dies, his corpse is displayed for only four or five days, after which, with cries and wails, he is interred all by himself, and for three months, the widows, children, relatives, and even the friends of the chief come in the night to stand on the tomb of the deceased and weep for him.

Still others do not even put the corpse in the ground; instead, after five or six days of display, a casket is built of hard wood and raised up on four posts next to the chief's cabin or house and the corpse of the deceased placed in it. The joints of the casket are sealed with [386] a mixture of ashes and pitch. Next to this casket are placed his guns, pipe, and some of his wealth, whereas on the other side is put the corpse of his dog. This casket has a peaked lid and is covered either with saw palmetto leaves or tree bark, so as to prevent the rain from falling in it.

There are yet others who neither bury nor in any way preserve the body of their dead chief. After the days of display are completed, they take the corpse of the chief and place it on a square frame, and there it is smoked over an open fire until it becomes as dry as a stick. By this time, he is a like a skeleton and is displayed in the temple standing on his feet, supported from behind by a stout rod, and he remains there until his successor comes to take his place, which he willingly relinquishes. After having been so long on his feet, he is placed prone upon the corpses of the ancestors in the back of the temple, where they all repose together.[37]

I would never finish if I had to describe all the different ways of burying the chiefs or the kings of each particular nation. This is enough said, I believe, about death, and from sadness let us move on to dance and entertainment.

These nations have no violins, basses, flutes, nor oboes among them. All their music consists only of the melodies they intone with their words while slapping their bellies with their hands as if to keep time. For instruments, the Indians have only the drum, such as I have already described above, on which they beat just as our army drummers do, except that whereas the latter have a pair of drumsticks, the Indians have [387] only one. And when they beat upon this drum, it is in the cadence of the song they are singing, and one might say that all follow in time with that. As well as that fine instrument, they also have the *chichicoühas*. These are nothing but medium-sized, hollow gourds pierced with small holes in a design according to their fancy and then filled with large pebbles, and while dancing and marching, they shake these like children's toys and by their noise make a melodious concert, according to their fashion.[38]

Toward the end of July, the last month before the new harvest that ordinarily comes in August, the Natchez Indians hold a kind of fair and celebration for the tribe. In French, it is called the sacred silo. This is what it is.[39]

---

37. The peoples using this custom are the Pascagoulas and Biloxis, according to *Mémoires historiques*, II, 240, where a similar description follows.

38. The chichicoühas are a local version of the rattles known as maracas, a word that entered Portuguese and English from the Tupi language of Brazil.

39. Corn harvest festivals were common among Southeastern Indians. Dumont refers to it using the name of the receptacle in which the food was stored: "la tonne de valeur." On the peculiar meaning of *valeur* in Natchez ethnography, see Gordon M. Sayre, *The Indian Chief*

When those in that nation have completed their harvests, they are each responsible for bringing one basket of grain, beans, potatoes, or squash. These baskets are of such a size that only two of them fill up a barrel containing 120 quarts. They bring all this to a large container made like a tower, wide, tall, and spacious, and covered so that the rain cannot penetrate it. Each carries his basket and other provisions that are stored in this container, which is erected about a league distant from the village so as to protect it from fire. There are guardians who look after it both day and night until the end of the following year, as if it were a large storehouse of provisions. One would not dare touch it without the permission of the Great Chief and the guardians, whose lives depend on its protection.

[388] The Great Chief informs his subjects of the date of the festival or celebration some days in advance, so as to give them time to prepare everything. A party of Indians clears a path from the village to the silo as straight as they can make it, removing all the bushes and brush so that not so much as one piece of straw remains. This is like a grand avenue, only even wider, being some forty to fifty feet wide. At the site of the silo, cabins are built out of tree boughs, one of them especially grand and square, which will serve as the palace, the residence, and throne of the chief.[40]

At first light, all the Indian men are ready, and the women with the women. The chief then emerges from his home dressed in all his most handsome and magnificent finery, with a plumed hat bordered with a ribbon.[41] For, as I've said, the chief of the Natchez and that of the Tunicas are the only

---

as Tragic Hero: Native Resistance and the Literatures of America, from Moctezuma to Tecumseh (Chapel Hill, N.C., 2005), 222–224. The corresponding chapter, "Of the Tonne de Valeur: Description of This Festival," in Mémoires historiques, I, 195–208, specifies that it lasted for one week and identifies the Natchez Sun who presided as Serpent Piqué. The word tonne in modern French is a metric ton, one thousand kilograms. In the eighteenth century, it was a variant of tonneau, a measure used in shipping and trade that was, depending on region, close to the same weight as the metric ton. Rather than the archaic "tun," I've chosen "silo," which matches its shape.

40. Le Page du Pratz, in his calendar of the thirteen moons of the Natchez year, indicates that the third moon, in May, was the "Festival of the Small Corn," and the seventh, in September, was "The Festival of Corn or of la Tonne" (Histoire de la Louisiane, II, 361–363), of which his description is similar to Dumont's here. Dumont places this festival in July, but because, on original manuscript [397], below, he mentions the festival of small corn separately, it would appear that this festival corresponds to the one in Le Page's seventh month. Gravier also mentions two harvest festivals in June and in November, a calendar that might have been adjusted for the climate in Illinois. See "Relation or Journal of the Voyage of Father Gravier," in JR, LXV, 145; and Swanton, Indian Tribes of the Lower Mississippi Valley, 122.

41. The French reads "galon faux," or fake ribbon, suggesting that it is an imitation of ribbons that indicated rank on French military uniforms.

ones whom I have seen outfitted with French clothing and hats. The chief thus comes out of his house holding his pipe in his hand and with the wing of a swan to use as a fan. He does not go to the silo on foot nor on horseback. He is not carried there, either, and yet, nonetheless, he does reach the spot. Here is how it is done. The chief lies down on a litter covered with a very fine cloth. His pipe is lit for him. Then the litter is raised above the heads of the Indians, who arrange themselves in a straight row of four or five and pass him overhead from hand to hand, as in a game [389] of leapfrog. Each man, after passing him ahead, then leaves his spot and runs quickly to put himself at the head of the line once more to move the chief again, until they reach the site of the silo. One might well say that this is a new method of post riding, for myself and several officers were on horseback, and we could barely keep up with them. It is true that we had to descend into the bottom of some ravines with our horses and then climb out the other side again, whereas he went only halfway to the bottom and passed over to the opposite side more quickly than we did, using his airborne route. While he travels in this manner, gunshots are fired off from time to time as a sign of rejoicing. And if, by some misfortune, the chief were allowed to fall, I can well assure you that this would cost the lives of more than one hundred of his subjects. But they are so agile that during the two years I saw this procession, there were no such accidents.

The chief at last arrives on the site, where there is a fine plaza. His litter is placed at the entrance to the tent that has been prepared and decorated with boughs laced with flowers. When the chief has arrived, he sits cross-legged, like a tailor. His wives are also there at his sides. Then he is brought his ceremonial pipe to smoke, the famous calumet. Every word he speaks draws howls in response. After he has smoked, more than four hundred plates of food are brought and set on the ground in front of him and in his tent, all sorts of dishes including sagamité, gruel, broth, biscuits made from cold flour, roasted corn, roast or barbecued alligator, fish, tortoise; in short, all the different things prepared according to the custom of the nation. He chooses what he wants, and it is set aside. He then makes [390] a speech to all those present, after which all the dishes are distributed among those assembled, more or less according to the different bands to which they belong. These bands are dispersed here and there around the plaza united by their friendship or kinship to the chief. As for me, along with the Sr. Broutin, who was the commandant at Natchez as well as the administrator of the Terre Blanche concession, we found ourselves at a festival or assembly such as this during the term of the Great Chief named the Serpent Piqué. And sure enough, he had a serpent tattooed on his body, which began at the corner of his mouth on the left side and made a tour of his body, descending from there toward his stomach and encircling his waist, winding up at the ankle of his right leg. This chief was a good friend of the French, and he did not lose anything from this allegiance, for not only was he often invited to dinner; everyone also gave him presents. We dined with him that day in his tent, or ceremonial palace, in the French manner, seated at a table covered with fine dishes: fricasséed chicken and other roast meats that he had had killed. It is true that we had taken the precaution of bringing him a large and fine paté, with bottles, or rather flagons, of wine and eau-de-vie, as well as bread. There was a table set for nine, all men: five Frenchmen, the Great Chief, and three of his honored men.[42]

After we had dined well, drunk, laughed, and risen from the table, the Great Chief with a single word called together all his warriors and addressed them with a speech like this: "What? Are you not ashamed of yourselves, not having thought to go hunting for these French chiefs who have [391] come to see you and honor you with their presence? You are like dogs who think only of yourselves and not of others, who imagined that they had great wit, but who in fact had none at all." In a word, he stung them to the quick and so strongly inspired them that, to satisfy their chief, they left immediately in groups of fifteen, twenty, and some of thirty, more or less, dividing among themselves the territory of lakes, woods, and cypress swamps.[43]

They were gone for more than three hours and at the end of that time were all assembled in the same spot, where we suddenly heard their cries

42. Based on Dumont's account, it seems that in the 1720s, the Natchez of the Grand village under the leadership of Serpent Piqué adapted their corn festivals to create a role for the French. In his published book, Dumont wrote that his description of the festival is based upon "one year when the French commandant of the Natchez post attended this celebration with several officers from the garrison" (*Mémoires historiques*, I, 196). The manuscipt memoir reveals that Dumont was at Natchez in late July during the years 1724, 1727, and 1728, although, in 1724, he left in time to be at Baton Rouge during the storm that struck on his birthday, July 31; see original manuscript, above [166] and below [397]. Dumont thus enjoyed the honor of being among the officers hosted at the festival when Ignace-François Broutin was commandant in 1727. But according to *Mémoires historiques*, I, 208, Serpent Piqué died in June 1725. A possible solution to this contradiction is that Dumont used "serpent piqué," not as the name of a specific Natchez Sun, but as a title accorded the Sun of the Grand village, which carried the right to wear the tattoo described here. Serpent Piqué would therefore be the best-known Sun by this title—the one Le Page du Pratz refers to as his friend, who died in 1725 or possibly even earlier (see *Histoire de la Louisiane*, I, xv)—whereas another man might have taken the title and hosted the corn festival in subsequent years. Dumont recalls meeting this Serpent Piqué in 1727; see above, original manuscript [191].

43. See *Mémoires historiques*, I, 200; no such speech is quoted.

once again. We would have bet among ourselves that they could not have brought back very much. We were then smoking and chatting with the chief, and at this cry, the chief arose, had the table and chairs cleared away, and asked us to sit at the entrance of his tent. After he had given the order to one of his servants to reply to these cries three separate times, we saw more than six hundred Indians, lined up one behind the other, coming in dancing and singing and marching in rhythm, carrying to the chief all that they had been able to find during the short period they were away. They threw it all at his feet: tortoises, birds, fish, crawfish, some seven or eight deer (already cut into quarters), and five or six bears. There was not one of them who did not offer something, all of which would now be passed on by the servants to the Great Chief for the Frenchmen to eat for supper. After this, their chief expressed his satisfaction, and having given his orders to one of his honored men, we all of a sudden saw a movement. The women lined up on one side along with the elders, the girls, [392] and young boys and bannerets, and then there appeared in front of the chief two separate teams of more than 150 men each. The two groups were equal in number. I estimate 150, and thus there is only 1 out of 300 who wins the prize. But that makes 149 who help him to win it. Occasionally, it is the weakest member of the team who takes the prize, which consists of an ell of limbourg cloth or a gun, whatever the chief chooses. This time, it was an ell of limbourg.

There are, as I have said, two separate teams. They arrange themselves in the middle of a large plain, and there are two goals, one at either end of the plain. These will be either a tree, if one is found there, or else a bow with one end stuck into the ground. The distance between these two goals is quite long, about a quarter of a league. The teams are in the middle. The chief comes out carrying in his hand a rather large ball, stuffed with ashes and covered with a skin. He throws it into the air, straight above the heads of one of the teams, and it then falls into the hand of one member of that party, who throws it in the direction of the goal they are aiming at. Then everyone runs as hard as he can to catch it. But the one who first gets it does not keep it long, for everyone else jumps on him and tackles him. They tear the ball out of one another's hands, and occasionally the ball disappears and might seem to be lost but then suddenly reappears. Just when it seems to be over, that is, when the ball nears the goal sought by one team, it is grabbed by the opposing team and thrown back toward the other goal, for, if a player allows the ball to get into the hands of one of his opponents, the latter will start it in the opposite direction. Sometimes, as they run, they do not [393] pick up the ball up but push it with their feet. They fight so hard at this game that there are many hard blows landed and received between the goals. In the end, however, there is one who becomes the winner: he who, by his skill or by his strength or both together, has the good luck to throw the ball into the goal. He who succeeds in striking the goal with the ball wins the prize, which he receives from the chief, and he becomes the leader of the group of 149 who helped him, although each was trying to get the prize for himself. This kind of game is also played in Brittany; it is called *soule*.[44]

After the prize is awarded, there are some Indians who contest with one another for money or trade goods at a ball game played on a clear pitch without any brush, trees, or even grass. Instead of each having his own ball, however, as in France, they have only one, which serves as the *cochonnet*, and instead of the other balls, there is a long stick, about two inches thick and twelve to fifteen feet long. The ball and the stick are thrown both at the same time, and while the sticks fly through the air, the ball rolls along the ground, then bounces over one and slides along another until it comes to rest against one of the wooden sticks, which have a hook at the end, and he whose stick this is wins the point over all the others, and he adds it to his total. It is often necessary to get five or six points to win the game. But because there are often forty players [394] and only one who wins, a game can sometimes last all day long.[45]

They also have a kind of wrestling, just as the Bretons do. But whereas the latter try to throw their opponent on his back by grasping his body with strong arms or attempting to trip him with a blow to the leg, the Indians don't do that. They grasp one another around the middle of the body and try

44. On the Natchez ball game, compare *Mémoires historiques*, I, 201, and a comment in a footnote in Dumont's epic poem: "According to the classical authors, the Bretons, especially those in Morbihan, brought to this game a determination perhaps even greater than that of the Indians. Frequently players were killed" ("Poème," 411n). As a no-holds-barred ball game contested by teams of unlimited size, Breton soule indeed resembled the Natchez game Dumont describes.

45. Dumont describes the Natchez "jeu de boule" in the context of the French *petanque*. In this game, the cochonnet is the smaller ball toward which players toss their large metal balls, in an effort to be closer to it than their rivals. In the *Mémoires historiques*, this game is called "la Crosse. . . . The game is played to *Pocolé*, that is, to ten" (I, 202–203). Modern lacrosse involves sticks resembling those described here, but it is a team sport more like soule than petanque. The "jeu de boule" resembles a ball game known as *chunkey*, played by many native American peoples of the Southeast and still played by Natchez in Oklahoma studied by Swanton in the early nineteenth century. It involved throwing a stone or ball at a target mounted atop a tall pole that stood in the middle of a square known as a "chunkey yard." See Patricia Galloway and Jason Baird Jackson, "Natchez and Neighboring Groups," *HNAI*, 612.

to make their adversary lose ground, and when they have managed to do so, they make him lose his breath by stifling him against their stomach. At that point, they lower him to the ground, where he sometimes slowly comes to, and the other man has won the wager or the prize.

But while all this is carried on by the Indian men for their amusement, the women are sitting in a circle, where they sing songs and beat on the drum. I can certify that they do not have any traditional or customary songs. The song is composed on the spot and according to the melody they choose to set it to. It might be praises for the chief, it might be a reproach that one is making toward another, or it might be advice that one wants to give; whatever comes to mind at that moment.

As night was near and the sun was going down, plates of food were again served as in the morning. The chief took only the one that had crawfish and another featuring new corn. The dishes were then distributed to the populace. We supped with the chief, quite lavishly, from more than twenty different dishes. The Sr. Broutin had sent to the Terre Blanche concession for [395] eight jugs of wine and four of eau-de-vie. After dinner, when the daylight was gone and night had spread through the place, the celebration became even grander. Bundles of dried canes four yards in diameter and twenty feet in height were ignited. The canes are broken off at one end right at a joint and, when lit, give light like a torch, and there were at least a hundred of these spread about.

Next to the chief's tent, facing it at a distance of twenty paces, there is a wooden pole set in the ground, eight or nine feet high, to which the famous calumet is attached. The men and women make a half circle around it in several ranks, one behind the other. They beat on the drum and sing. From time to time, a warrior or hero or even a young banneret comes out to the pole and pretends to try to attack it, shouting all the while. At these moments, the drumming and singing cease, and the Indian says in his language, "Listen, everyone, to what I have done," and he recounts what he has done in his life: his loves, his achievements, his attacks and tricks and surprises, whether he has feared being captured or killed, whatever he wishes to tell of. And at each pause or after each phrase in his speech, the crowd replies with a lively "homs, homs," gallantly repeated, which means, "That is good, that is true, that is well done." When he is finished, he throws down at the base of the pole a shirt, a knife, a packet of vermilion, or something like that, and withdraws into the crowd. The drumming and singing begin again, and another appears, always with the same ceremony. The Frenchmen come out as well. Those who know the Indian language speak it and,

[396] in their harangues, pronounced more lies than truths. But it was all accepted. Some other Frenchmen who did not know a single word of their languages also came out and spoke a string of absurdities, to which they responded with the same "homs, homs." So long as presents are thrown at the pole, whatever they say is good, and that is the way they pass their time in these amusements.

I say "amusements and celebrations" with respect to the elders and the women, but for the young people, this night is not the same for them; it is, instead, a time for libertine pleasures. Everything is permitted. The girls go around alone or in pairs, strutting out across the prairies, looking for their lovers—at least, those who are so fortunate as to have lovers. The others try their luck, and each is allowed to choose whichever partner he or she wishes. During this festival, there are many who lose their virginity, and this is something accepted according to their customs. The Frenchman, the Indian, everyone mingles together on this day: so long as, after he has satisfied his pleasures, either in conversation with a girl or in another sort of amusement that I will not name for fear of offending chaste ears; so long, I say, as one gives the girl a handful or two of vermilion or a little mirror worth a few pennies or a few bracelets, she is perfectly happy and will thank you kindly for it.

No one goes to bed on this night. If, on the other hand, sleep should overcome you, there is the soft grass where you can rest if you find you need it. In any event, this celebration and its games last as long as there is food remaining in the silo, and as soon as that is finished, the party [397] is also finished, and each one, including the chief himself, quietly retires to his cabin.

In the time of Serpent Piqué, the Indians took six days to eat what there was in the sacred silo. We were only able to stay for the first two days. This was enough for us to learn of the celebrations that take place on that occasion. One can only say that each country has its own fashion or custom, that the Indians in general are happy in their land, that with a little wealth they believe themselves rich, that they have no need for formality [politesse], and that whatever they do, they do in freedom.

There are other festivals during which the amusements I have just described are commonly permitted, such as that of the small corn that takes place in springtime, the name coming from a species of Indian corn with a small kernel. It can be planted in the ground, grow, and ripen in six weeks' time.

In autumn, they also have the festival of the *ollogolle* and the *chipicholle*, a very small grain resembling millet, which they gather from the wild grass that grows on the banks of the river and which they prepare much as the Bretons do their black wheat and millet.[46]

One could well say that they use everything, even the acorns of the forest trees from which they make bread, as well as from walnuts. The same goes for the fruit of the persimmon, which resembles the medlars of France, except for the difference that their fruit first emerges as a golden yellow, and when it is quite ripe, they mash it and make loaves that they dry and roast and even trade to the French. One would say from looking at it that it was a spice bread. It is astringent and good for dysentery and bloody stool.

[398] If I had to, I could explain all the plants and fruits that they use for food and as cures for illnesses. However, their most important remedy is the sweatbath. They did not use this cure, however, when they had the greatest need for it: when, one year, smallpox was brought over on a French ship (yes, I say it was brought over, because the Indians had never seen it before), they were almost all stricken with it, and as they believed it was a swelling or cyst under the skin, rather than sweat themselves as they usually would, they bathed in the river. There were a great number who died. They practice medicine more as a theory than as a science or an art, and our Frenchmen have in several instances sought them out for help. There are some of us who owe our lives to them for the cure of wounds or from an illness called *gros lots* that they treat very successfully, as they also do dropsy and apoplexy.

The Natchez Indians truly loved the French, as my reader may have already come to understand from what I have told him. But in spite of this friendship, they massacred us, and it is a great shame and a great loss that this powerful and numerous nation has gone into exile among the Chickasaws. For, first of all, we have more enemies on our hands, whereas if the alliance had been maintained, I can assure you that yes, they alone would have helped us to destroy all the others. If they had, those that remained, the several nations all joining [399] together, would never have equaled in numbers the Natchez such as they were before the massacre. And I can even say that it was all the fault of a single man, who has deprived us of these good and generous Indians who loved the French and wanted nothing more than to help us with everything and trade with us for all kinds of

---

46. According to Dumont's description, this is most likely a plant in the goosefoot family, *Chenopodium spp.*, which includes South American quinoa and may correspond to Le Page du Pratz's eleventh moon of the Natchez calendar, that of "farine froide," or cold flour; see *Histoire de la Louisiane*, II, 382.

goods.[47] But that time is past, and we can only languish at the post and fort at Natchez, bemoaning the loss of this fine nation. We have still the Choctaws, but this nation is distant from us and will only act on our behalf if we pay them generously, in the absence of which they are ready to revolt; whereas the Natchez marched out to defend us simply out of the friendship they had for the French. But alas, discord had to inject its venom and divide us from one another.

Enough said about the Natchez; let us return now to some of the other nations, who each are small in population. They have been our allies, and why? Because we are their neighbors and because we have greater strength than they do, they cower at our feet, trade with us, go hunting for us, and appear to be our friends. But in the bottom of their hearts, I can assure you, they feel differently. What makes them appear to support us is the authority that we have over them to enforce our mastery, much as one sees a group of schoolboys commanded and managed by a schoolmaster. Everyone in the class wishes him far away, and it is only the superior power he has over them [400] that keeps the lid on and prevents them from acting as they would like to. It is the same with our Indian friends, who, being so close to us as they are, fear us, but when farther away, fear us no more.

There is a difference, however, between the Indians here and those in Illinois. By the good advice and wise counsel of the illustrious, charitable, and virtuous priests of the Company of Jesus, who have formed a community at that post, they have—through their preaching in the language of that nation, which they have learned, and their good example—they have, I say, done so well that they have gathered the greater part of that nation to the bosom of our mother the church and Christianized and baptized them, so that they now form with us a single society and assembly in Jesus Christ. And through the advantage of being Christian, the Illinois have acquired that of joining in the sacrament of marriage with some of the French and Canadians, making a single people under a single God.[48] But it must be said that between New Orleans and that post, some five hundred leagues distant, this is the only nation that has opened its eyes to the gospel, and that although it has taken part, I believe, in the virtues and gifts of Christianity, it has not inherited the courage and valor of the French, since it was this same nation that, in the affair of the Chickasaws, took to their heels and

47. Clearly, he is referring to Chepart here.
48. The success of the missionaries in the Illinois country, in contrast to Louisiana, was also remarked upon by the Jesuit Father Louis Vivier in his 1750 "Letter from Father Vivier of the Society of Jesus, to Another Father of the Same Society," *JR*, LXIX, 201–227.

abandoned the Sr. d'Artaguiette, their commandant, to the wrath and furor of his enemies and ours.[49]

So there, in a few words, is an account of the Indians, their manners and religions and dances. Let us now turn to what our French people do in this colony . . . and . . . let us now speak of . . .

49. See above, original manuscript [260–262].

Chapter Twelve

NATURAL HISTORY AND
THE STORY OF JUCHEREAU
DE SAINT DENIS

[401] When the Company of the Indies, after sending so many people over to settle there, withdrew from the country, it left these people at the mercy of its enemies, for the Company might be held responsible for the sad misfortunes that have occurred in that land, or at least for not knowing how to choose officers for the command of its far-flung posts. They were clearly not chosen for their merit and experience but instead were proposed by friends won over by the shower of gold that fell into their hands. These friends might have been secretaries or clerks in the offices empowered to select the officers, which explains why the Company so easily granted its consent. Alas, this metal is the cause of so many failings; the sight of its golden hue renders inaccessible paths practicable, and thus persons who do not even know how to obey find themselves in command over others.

Those who are lucky enough to find themselves close to the capital, where there is less to fear from the enemy, have made their plantations succeed. The largest of these produce indigo, and the others, less wealthy, plant rice, corn, squash, beans, peas, etc., and sell the grain to those who have no such harvests.

In winter, it is not as difficult to survive as in the summer, because in the cold season there is an abundance of game of all sorts: geese, teals, ducks, bustards, swans, moorhens, deer, bear, and buffalo. There are large quantities of the first type, so much that there are some people who, with a single gunshot, have killed more than thirty geese, ducks, or even teals, as well as sea larks, which are excellent eating. A pound of buffalo is worth three sols, and a good, fresh hindquarter of deer, twenty to twenty-five sols. Aside from this abundance of game, the greens and small legumes are never more abundant than in this season. However . . .

[402] In summer, it is not the same. Then one can get by only with difficulty, living on salted or smoked meat or on bacon, and on fish, which are excellent in the river and lakes. There are many species: the carp, some of which are three to four feet long and more than eight inches in diameter; the gaspergou, which is the best of the river, is a fish that has scales edged

with red and a firm flesh; the brill is a fish without scales, but it can be cooked up into a fine fricassee or sometimes even a good soup. In the lakes and small rivers, such as in the Bayou Saint John, one league from New Orleans, there are some small fish that can be caught with pins or hooks sewn into a net. These are called *patassas,* and in the lakes or bays, there is also a fish called the choupique. All these varieties are freshwater fish. At New Orleans, as in the surrounding area, there is no lack of crawfish, such a great quantity that in the early days of the settlement, people caught them even in their houses. Nowadays, crawfish are still found in any water hole, and straight out of the water they are red, like those in France when they are cooked. Saltwater fish are also abundant in the capital, although, in the summer, one cannot go out to seine for them because of the heat of the sun, which is so strong that it often causes severe headaches and even death to some who have been exposed to its rays. There are some in particular who feel its impact on their skin, most of all the French voyageurs, who, when obliged to paddle the flatboats or pirogues, strip naked like the Indians and thus are exposed to the sun. Exposure often causes a fever, and after nine days, their skin peels off in strips.[1]

[403] What is extraordinary is that every seven years, there come windstorms so powerful that they are capable of toppling the best-built houses. Even the largest and best-rooted trees are thrown to the ground. Birds, unable to fly, fall to the ground or onto the seashore, and it would be easy to kill them with a stick at these times if you had a mind to. But people fear for their lives—fear being either crushed inside their own houses or drowned, for with these storms, which last for two or three days, there very often comes a deluge of water. Woe to whoever is in a flatboat or pirogue, because he finds himself at the mercy of the wind and the storm, and all the more so

1. "La carpe": There are no native carp in the lower Mississippi, so Dumont is probably referring to one of three freshwater catfish species common in Louisiana (*Ictalurus punctatus, Ictalurus furcatus,* or *Pylodictis olivaris*). See *Mémoires historiques,* I, 94–102, for a similar description of Louisiana fish. Dumont included in his "Poème," Figures 50 and 52, illustrations of three fish, labeled "casse burgot," "grondin chouxpique," and "barbue." In Acadian French and regional American English, the name of the first has become *gaspergou,* and Le Page du Pratz called this fish *Le Casse-Burgo* (*Histoire de la Louisiane,* II, 151–163). It is the native *Sciaenops ocellatus,* the red drum, or redfish, still sought after by Louisiana *chefs de cuisine.* The names "patassas" and "the choupique," spelled "pataças" and "le choupic" in the manuscript, are still used in Louisiana French today. The former is from the Choctaw name meaning "flat fish" and is one of several Louisiana species of sunfish in the family *Cetrarchidae.* The latter is Choctaw for "mud fish," the native species *Amia calva,* and is known as "bowfin" in American English. Thanks to Shannon Lee Dawdy for sharing her expertise on Louisiana fish and cuisine.

if he is on the Mississippi, which becomes like a tempestuous ocean. These are the travelers most at risk. They cannot ride out the storm because the river makes a turn every half league, and so the winds will not allow a boat to hold a course down the middle of the channel. They are at the mercy of the weather, even if they can put ashore, as sometimes occurs, on a large sandbank in the middle of the river, where they would at least be safe from the trees that fall down all around. But one can only hope to find these sandbanks when the river is low, that is, from the twenty-fourth of June, feast day of Saint John the Baptist, to the twenty-fifth of March, Annunciation Day. For, on [the latter] day, the water begins to rise, as I have explained in its proper place.[2]

Although I advance the claim that it is only every seven years that the hurricanes come, this does not, however, prevent strong windstorms from being felt in other years.

Our French people who have settled in New Orleans or have moved [404] there because, for fear of an Indian attack, they could not remain on their farms, spend their time working in their gardens and support themselves by selling their produce. And if they are lucky enough to have negro slaves, they rent them out to others by the month. The going rate is twelve to fifteen francs.

Other Frenchmen will be cloth merchants, drapers, etc. Still others are wholesalers of wine, eau-de-vie, or beer brought from France, although one can make excellent beer in that country with corn, since hops grow abundantly there in the woods. Finally, some are keepers of dining halls, bakeries, or taverns. In short, everyone makes a business as best he can to support himself.

In my time, it was M. de Salmon who was the commissaire ordonnateur, or rather the intendant, who, by his laws and ordinances, keeps everything in good order. The king's warehouse is to the French what the sacred silo is to the Natchez Indians, for whoever needs the smallest article of merchandise and wants to have it at a better price than offered by the other merchants, can address himself to M. Salmon in a memo in which he asks for such and such thing that he wants.[3] It is true that there will never be as much as he would like to be able to buy, but it is certain that a little will always be made available so long as the intendant signs the memo. Then he

2. See original manuscript, above [132], where Dumont mentioned the annual floodwaters on the Mississippi.

3. Salmon was commissaire ordonnateur from May 1731; see *MPA*, II, 6. On the sacred silo of the Natchez, see above, original manuscript [387].

goes to present the memo to the warehouse keeper, who sets the price of the merchandise and parcels out a quantity corresponding to a given sum. Then the individual goes to the treasurer to pay for it. The treasurer then puts his receipt below the [405] seal of the intendant, and thus having paid, one can afterward go receive delivery at the warehouse. The money of the country is of three types: that of France, which trades on the same footing as in France; that of Spain, where one piastre is valued at five livres and the smaller coins in proportion; and thirdly, there is card money—playing cards—except these are all white without any impression of hearts or clubs, etc. That money circulates at the same rate as the piastres, which is to say, there are picayunes worth six sous, three pence, Dutch pennies at twelve and a half sous, and the double, twenty-five sous. There are also piastres; in fact, there are cards of five livres, ten livres, fifteen, twenty, twenty-five, fifty, one hundred, and one thousand livres. This is the actual currency of the country. Nobody can refuse it; it is how business is done and how people not only subsist but buy and sell goods.[4]

But when you want to go over to France and all your wealth is in card money, you are greatly disadvantaged, since the cards no longer have value there. You need to have friends, or, if the treasurer himself is your friend, he can give you letters of exchange for France. But this is rare. The merchants who come to the country and sell their wares and obtain card money have the right to exchange it, but the simple habitant does not. He wants to leave the country, where he has fattened himself a little, and in effect, he has to imitate the weasel in Aesop's fables, who, having entered a granary through a hole, so fattened himself by eating that he could not get back out. To escape, he had to wait until he was roughly the same size he had been before.[5] It's the same situation; you have to exchange your money. If you are rich on

4. Dumont's "des picaillons" is one of the earliest known references to what became later in Louisiana French *picayune*, meaning "a little something extra." Dumont's characterization of the colony's being poor in French currency is verified in many sources, and the use of playing cards for currency was also practiced in Quebec; see above, original manuscript [12–14].
5. Dumont refers to Aesop's fables but likely knew the story as "La Belette entrée dans un grenier," or "The Weasel in the Granary," in the verse fables of Jean de la Fontaine, book 3, fable 17. One popular English version is titled "The Swollen Fox": "A Fox, very much famished, seeing some bread and meat left by shepherds in the hollow of an oak, crept into the hole and made a hearty meal. When he finished, he was so full that he was not able to get out, and began to groan and lament very sadly. Another Fox passing by, heard his cries, and coming up, inquired the cause of his complaining. On learning what had happened, he said to him, 'Ah, you will have to remain there, my friend, until you become such as you were when you crept in, and then you will easily get out.'" See George Fowler Townsend, ed. and trans., *Three Hundred Aesop's Fables* (London, 1867), 100.

paper, you have to discount your assets to allow for this exchange. As for myself, I was forced [406] to do the same, as I paid as much as forty livres in card money for one ecu, or six French francs. Piastres are proportionally worth thirty or thirty-five livres each, and there are some people in that capital city who engage in this exchange as their only business, although surreptitiously, and will even provide silver specie. When I say this is surreptitious, I will add that the man who gives you the pleasure of providing you an exchange at this rate is regarded as someone who is doing you a great service, as a favor.

The merchants who come from France cannot refuse the card money, but they sell you their merchandise at a corresponding rate, although this does not seem at all fair, given that, for them, the treasury cannot refuse to exchange their money, which is paid to them in the form of letters of exchange on France. However, when they actually return home, they are generally not paid the full sum, and they have to wait sometimes seven to eight months or even a year for their payment. Therefore, in the capital city, as in Mobile, it is a great fortune for a man if he can have piastres or French coin, since he often can exchange them at a rate of seven or eight to one.

However, in the upper country, such as at Arkansas, Natchitoches, Illinois, and other places, good quality trade goods, or even wine and eau-de-vie, are much more valued than all the piastres in the world. A simple, plain shirt such as is used in the Indian trade will change hands for twenty or thirty livres apiece, whereas in the capital, it would not cost more than two or, at most, two livres, fifteen sous. The bottle of eau-de-vie that sells retail in New Orleans for forty sous is sold in those places for as much as eighty. [407][6] It is true, however, that you will not be paid that sum in cash, but in fine pelts, in oil, in flour, in French wheat, in hams, or even in bars of silver, if you like it. Below Illinois, at other posts, it will be in Indian corn, in poultry, in deerskins (tanned or untanned), in blankets of buffalo or other skins, even bear. And from this, one can well imagine that those who have such merchandise, when they are lucky enough to get it to the capital, can quickly sell their cargo for the currency of the country at these prices. And there are other Frenchmen who, late in the summer, set out in groups to go spend the autumn and even the winter in the forests two hundred, three hundred, even four hundred leagues upstream from the capital, where they kill many buffalo and bears. From the former, they remove all the bones and salt the meat in large pirogues that they build for themselves wherever they are, which is generally close to a river where they can launch their craft. It is

6. Figure 20, "Wild Buffalo," was originally located at this spot in the manuscript.

Figure 20. *Wild Buffalo.* VAULT oversize Ayer MS 257, figure no. 7.
Courtesy The Newberry Library, Chicago

from the trees called cottonwoods or aspens that they make these pirogues, which are as long as fifty or sixty feet and six to seven feet in width.[7] In building these pirogues, they try to have enough space to salt their meat on board. They save the fat separately. From the second kind of animal—from the bears, that is—they take the oil, saving the skins of all the animals they kill, and toward the end of March or beginning of April, they return to New Orleans to sell their salt meat. In this manner, each tries to earn his living as best he can.

If the Sr. Périer had remained in that country until now, it would be a very

7. The trees here are "liar ou tremble." John Francis McDermott identifies "liard amère" as "a Canadian name for the narrow-leaved Cottonwood," corresponding to *Populus deltoides, Populus hetereophylla,* or *Populus trichocarpa,* common in the area. He also glosses "tremble, tremblier" as quaking aspen *(Populus tremuloides),* but this species is rare in the Mississippi valley. See McDermott, *A Glossary of Mississippi Valley French, 1673–1850* (St. Louis, Mo., 1941), 93. Either would seem ill suited for dugout canoes, which were more often made from bald cypress. See *Histoire de la Louisiane,* II, 32–34; and *Mémoires historiques,* I, 62, which indicates that "un liar ou un cipre," a cottonwood or a cypress, is chosen for a new pirogue.

different place. There would certainly be practical overland routes instead of always having to travel on water by boat to go from one post to another. From my first farm to Cannes [408] Brûlées, there are only eleven leagues that are at all passable by land.[8] This road was established in the time of the generous and valiant Périer, and since he has departed and many have been forced to abandon their farms, it is certain that the trees, grass, and brush have regrown and this path is no longer practicable. It is certain, I say, that there are many places one can no longer get to. Happy are the poor farmers who, in the time of that commandant, had obtained the negroes that they were contracted to receive from the Company of the Indies, because since the Company withdrew from the country (since 1730, that is), its accounts have been managed by an agent who, as soon as he got the job, began to enrich himself. With the authority in his hands, he attacked the poor farmers, ruined them, to be honest, and put them in a position where they could not pay for their negroes because they had been driven from their homes and their lands by the effects of the war. He claimed the slaves from them and sent them to his own plantation to put them to work there, until he could resell them for the highest price he could get, crediting the Company of the Indies only at the rate of five hundred livres each. If the Company sent a fair-minded commissioner, and he listened to the complaints of those involved and made an accounting of how many of the confiscated negroes have been resold, I bet it would show that he earned profits of more than 150 percent.[9]

I have explained how this agent imposed himself upon the poor, ruined farmers of Natchez and not upon the lords of the land, who are, for the most part, Canadians who have become wealthy under the protection and support of their commandant and countryman. This is the honest truth, although they cannot in good faith call themselves opulent, [409][10] because they had to repay the Company for their negroes.

Thus it is that our Frenchmen in this colony work and are reduced to misery, being obliged or forced to take refuge in the capital, unable to continue to develop the farms where they would have been able not only to

8. Dumont presumably is referring to his farm at Chaouachas, although it would be more than eleven leagues from there to Cannes Brûlées.

9. It's not clear who was the corrupt agent Dumont is alluding to, for the commissaire ordonnateur from 1731 to 1744 was Salmon, referred to respectfully above in original manuscript [404], and in 1730–1731 it was La Chaise, one of Dumont's key allies. It may be Arnaud Bonnaud, Bienville's secretary.

10. Figure 21, "Home of the Author in New Orleans," was originally located at this spot in the manuscript.

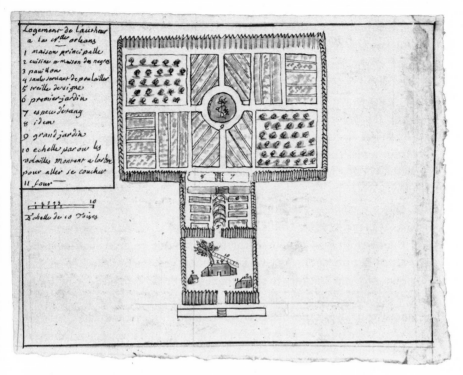

Figure 21. *Home of the Author in New Orleans.* VAULT oversize Ayer
MS 257, map no. 14. Courtesy The Newberry Library, Chicago

repay the Company but also support themselves and gain some measure of
happiness.

In the time that the Company of the Indies controlled that land—by
which I mean from the mouth of the river to the Illinois—it was forbidden to raise grapes, to plant wheat or barley or flax for linen, the Company
having reserved to itself the right to import these commodities, even though
grapevines would have grown very well there, especially at the Natchez post,
which nature seems to have made expressly for this plant, because there are
fine little valleys with hillsides facing the sun. One could imagine that the
wine would be excellent in the capital, where I had my house and a large,
spacious garden, where, right by the entrance, I had planted muscat vines
that grew along a trellis twelve or fourteen feet long, which I would have
(had I remained in the country) expanded many times over, since I could
thereby have enjoyed our natural right of trade, no longer being subjected
to the orders of the Company because the country found itself under the
control of His Majesty.

So I had this arbor that produced excellent grapes, which were nearly ripe in the month of June, for it is in that month that one harvests grapes there. There was one vine that hung close to the ground, and one day, when the door of the garden had not been shut, my son (who was very young) entered it and, seeing these grapes, which no doubt appeared tasty to him, began [410] to eat them. Then he tried to harvest the entire bunch but broke off the branch. After supper, when I entered the garden, I saw this vine broken. I took my knife and trimmed it back, as in springtime, leaving only three buds. The plant grew back beautifully and, in less than a month, reached the same height as the others, refilling the empty spot in the bed. The leaves were not as dark as the older ones, but that was the only differ- ence. When the vines reached the height of five feet, I let them go as they wished. At the end of that trellis, I had another of hops. When my name day came, on the fourth of October—the feast of Saint Francis, that is—I did not want to put my negroes to work on the soil, and I asked them to cut the hop flowers for me. In order to show them how this was to be done, without going to the far end of the trellis, I began with a few plants that had become interlaced with the grapevines, and I was happily surprised when I found three nice, large bunches of grapes that were ripe and had grown from the branch cut back in the month of June. This can lead my reader to imagine how vines can be harvested twice a year there, which other individuals in the country have also demonstrated since I did and thus found to be true.

The tobacco plant can be cultivated and grown very well there and gives as many as three harvests a year. The same with indigo. There are many people in Europe who may believe, when they see indigo, that it is a type of blue rock or crystal taken from a mine. Here I will have to disprove that belief by providing a description of this plant and the manner of making indigo, or, rather, extracting it.

The indigo plant comes from a small seed, shaped like a very small, elon- gated, round cylinder, cut off square at the ends. You take a field well worked with a hoe and make [411] rows from one end to the other, at least six inches apart. You plant the seeds in these as evenly as you can (which is always the best) or make small holes in the earth with a hoe and put the seeds in these. It is toward the end of March that this planting is done. From the seed sprouts a little bush, or rather a grass, which, as it grows, forms deli- cate little branches to which are attached the leaves, which grow as densely packed as those of the boxwood but strongly serrated and less thick. If the soil in the field is good, the plant will reach a height of about two and a half feet. In order to know whether it is ripe and good for cutting, you have to go into the field before the sun rises, gather several branches in your hands, and if you hear them pop as you squeeze and break them, then the plant is ready to be cut and to produce the indigo so sought after not only in France but everywhere else in the world.

Before cutting the plant, find a spot for what is called an *indigoterie*. In this place, you build three basins, one above the other. The highest of the three must be the largest. It is called the fermenter. It has to be well sealed so that no water leaks out. At the bottom of this basin, on the side nearest the one below it, there is a large hole, so that the water from the fermenter flows into the second, which is usually square. On either side of this are set up four to six "candleholders," which are forked sticks, and attached to each of these are long poles, connected by iron pins that pass through holes in the ends of the fork and through a hole in the pole, so that one has a kind of lever. At the ends of these long poles, which extend over the middle of the [412] basin (called the battery), there are things like buckets without bottoms. On the right or left side of this basin are three holes, one near the bottom of the battery and the others six inches and a foot above it. There's also a hole in the bottom through which the contents can fall into the third basin, much smaller than the two others, which is called the *diablotin*.[11]

When your three basins are thus prepared, and the sun has dried the dew off of the leaves and the ground, you go out with a knife and cut the plant off as close to the ground as you can, setting aside the best stalks for the seeds, as I paid thirty-two livres per pound for seed. When you have cut enough to fill the top basin, you bundle them into faggots, carry them to the fermenter, and arrange them inside it. When it is loaded up to within three inches of the top, you fill it with water and put planks on top so that the leaves are forced below the surface of the water. In the very hot weather of June, July, and August, it will not require more than three hours for this plant or herb to ferment in the water. Then you pull the plug from this first basin and let the water flow into the second. Once it is in there, it is from this water that the indigo will be derived. This liquid is similar to that seen in certain swamps, which has rotted in the sun and appears green, blue, and yellow.

The negroes organize themselves in groups of three or four at these long sticks that I have described, at the ends of which are the buckets without bottoms, and they plunge the buckets into the water, then lift them up and let them fall again. This movement is repeated over and over, the faster the better, [413] so that they beat the water and agitate it to the point where you

11. Compare this description with that in Denis Diderot and Jean le Rond d'Alembert, "Indigo," in *Encyclopédie; ou, Dictionnaire raisonné des sciences, des arts, et des métiers . . .*, 17 vols. (Paris, 1751–1772), VIII, 679–681, http://encyclopedie.uchicago.edu.

would say the basin is boiling like a kettle over a fire. It builds up a thick and heavy white foam, and if this is not dissolved and gotten rid of, all the water in the basin will evaporate or fall over the edge. But when you see that the foam is building up, you pour into the basin some fish oil and spread it around with a feather. As soon as you do this, the foam disappears. When the water has been well beaten for two and a half or three hours, you stop the agitating and let the water rest, and you will see in it what look like shiny little glowing pinheads the color of gold, which slowly fall toward the bottom.

After some time—perhaps half an hour—you open the topmost of the three holes on the side of the basin and allow all the water that appears to be clear to flow out. But if it seems a bit murky, you quickly replug the hole and let the water settle some more. In short, you proceed to open each of the three holes, draining off what is clear and reserving what is muddy. Finally, you drain out the thick substance into the diablotin, the third and smallest of the basins. Then you bring some sacks made of coarse fabric, like the ones that children use to carry their books when they go to school, or like a night bonnet or headdress with a drawstring on it instead of a ribbon. You put the mud in these and attach the sacks to some hooks or wooden pegs in a wall, so that the pure water can drip out of the sack. When no more water comes out, you turn the sack upside down and, with a wooden knife, scrape out the thick substance, which at this point looks completely black, and put it into some little boxes something like drawers [414] containing slabs of the indigo about six inches wide and one and a half inches thick. You put them out in the sun, which, with its rays, dries out the mud and makes cracks in it, as in the baked, dry ground in the summer. Then you take a mason's trowel and knead this matter until it forms one solid block. It can be cut with a steel wire attached at its ends to two pieces of wood, such as is done to cut soap, and thus the indigo is formed into small pieces, the stones of it that you see in France and elsewhere. This is where indigo comes from and how it is made. There are two types, the cultivated and the wild, and mixing them together produces indigo of the color of a pigeon's throat. There is a bastard indigo that grows in that country along the Mississippi, but it is not used at all.

The habitants live on bread made from rice or corn, which is the kind that is called Turkish wheat. However, in that country, there are two sorts of it. One is good for making flour, and the other is for making gruel, or sagamité. But whether of rice or corn, the bread is made in nearly the same way. The rice has to be husked, but for the corn, this is not needed. Then you soak either of the two grains from sundown until sunrise the next morning in some water that is a little warm. The following day, the negro men or women pour out the grain onto a table to drain, after which they pound it in wooden mortars. The many blows from the pestle reduce it to flour, which they pass through fine sieves made from slivers of cane, the work of Indian women of the country, which they have brought to the height of perfection. But because this flour, particularly the rice flour, is coarse like sand between the fingers and cannot by itself hold the form of a loaf, it has to be mixed [415] as it cooks with husked rice. When the latter is well cooked and, as they say, like gruel, you pour it into the rice flour, which dries or thickens it, and then put yeast in to make it rise. You must not stir it as one does with dough in France, but when the oven is hot, you take a pot and pass a long stick through the handle. Then you put a little water into the pot and then some of this thinned dough. You put some tree leaves on top of the dough, and you put this pot into the oven, turning it upside down. The heat of the fire strikes it immediately and prevents it from spreading out, thus forming a loaf of bread, which is very good and excellent to eat, especially when it is fresh and soaked in broth. The bread made from corn is done in the same way, but put in half rice flour or half corn and half French flour, and you will have excellent bread.[12]

In a time of great famine, there were some negroes in that country who fed themselves on the seeds of cane and made a very good porridge from it. The grain from this plant resembles the oats in France. Birds and especially bears and squirrels are very fond of it.[13]

About these latter animals, there are two species. One is like ours in France, and the other is named the flying squirrel, for the reason that when it is high in a tree, it virtually flies to another tree, which may be twenty or thirty paces away or more. It has no wings to speak of, but attached to its front paws there is a skin that it uses like a wing and that catches the wind when the squirrel launches itself into the air. The skin is a little like the wings of a bat. [416] It is much smaller than the first type of squirrel and of a very pretty color and pleasing to the eye, and it makes the same gamboling games as the first type.[14]

12. Compare to *Mémoires historiques*, I, 28–34, a chapter entitled "Of Rice and Corn, and the Manner of Making Bread from Them," which offers a somewhat clearer set of instructions.

13. Most likely this is *Arundinaria gigantea*, a native species of bamboo ("giant cane") that once grew extensively throughout the southeastern American bottomlands, now uncommon.

14. These are the Carolina gray squirrel *(Sciurus carolinensis)* and the southern flying squirrel *(Glaucomys volans)*.

All this country is wooded, with different species. From the fort at Pensa-cola to the entrance of the Bayou Saint John, it is all pines and firs covering the land, as well as other brush.[15]

The first are good for the masts and yardarms of ships. From these also are made pitch and tar. It is not with the trees that are upright that one can make the most of this but, instead, from those that are found on the sand or in the dirt and have lain there for more than ten or twenty years.[16]

When you are lucky enough to find three or four of these fallen trees, you cut them into pieces and then split them into lengths with a hatchet and put them in a large heap or pile, and when you have enough for more than a hundred barrels of pitch, you have the negro slaves dig a pit, square in shape and a half foot deep and quite spacious, in which you can stack up the cord-wood in crosswise fashion to make a pyramid. From one side of this pit, you dig a trench of the same depth, called a *saignée*, leading to another, deeper pit large enough to contain forty or fifty barrels of tar, and from this, you dig another trench, which leads to another pit similar to the previous one, and so forth, until there are ten or twelve pits, all the same size.

When all this is ready, you set fire to the pyramid, and because all the wood is rich and oily and therefore flammable, as it burns, it allows this grease to fall into this first hole, which is directly under the pyramid. When it is full, this [417] grease or bitumen flows into the next pit by means of the trench and fills it up so that when this one is full, it flows into another, and so on with the rest. That is for tar, but what if you want to have pitch, which is worth twice as much as tar? Here is how it is made.

You throw into one of the tar pits three or four cannonballs that you have heated in a fire until they are red-hot. This sets the contents on fire, just as a pot filled with oil or butter would do if you put into it that devouring ele-ment. By this means, the water evaporates, and when you see that the oily matter has been sufficiently reduced, you need to extinguish the fire, but not with water, for, as this is its enemy, there would be a hellish result if you threw that in there. You need, for this task, to make a kind of trapdoor out of planks or beams that is larger than the pit and covered with turf, or a

15. The most common pines in preindustrial coastal Louisiana were the loblolly *(Pinus taeda)*, slash *(Pinus elliottii)*, shortleaf *(Pinus echinata)*, and especially longleaf *(Pinus palustris)* pines. There are no native firs, so Dumont may be referring to the spruce pine *(Pinus glabra)*.

16. Compare to *Mémoires historiques*, I, 66–69, a chapter entitled "Of Tar, the Manner of Making It, and of Making Pitch," and Dumont's article on the topic in *Journal œconomique* (April 1752), 60–65.

mixture of grass and earth. The negroes set this platform over the hole and then, with scraps of moss or grass, they cut off the air. Thus the fire is extinguished, and the bitumen that is in the pit is pitch. A well-made pyramid of well-conditioned wood will be four or five days in burning and furnish more than three hundred barrels of tar. The longer the trees have lain on the ground, the more resinous they are.

From the Bayou Saint John north to Illinois, there are trees of many types, different from those found on that bayou. There are wild olive trees that carry olives, although they are small. There is a member of the council who was from Provence and introduced some from his home into that new land, and they were not bad at all.

There are many oaks, from which are cut the shingles that are used to cover houses instead of slate. They are also used for staves for barrels and tuns, [418] which can be cut to whatever length and width one wants. At the beginning of our settlement, the houses were covered, not with shingles, but only with cypress bark or palmetto leaves.

I promised my reader to explain in what season the bark is stripped, and I now must make good on my word.

The cypress is a large tree, very straight, and it is rare to see any fork in the trunk, from the base right up to the head; although I have seen a few that do have some, this is very rare. From this tree, one can make a beautiful pirogue in one piece. One can make planks, beams, palisades—in short, anything you want. There are some that are very large, even enormous, both in their circumference and height. At the concession of the late M. Diron d'Artaguiette at Baton Rouge, there was one that I can say is still there and is nine spans of the arms around and more than one hundred feet high at its tip, and may be fifteen feet in diameter. One could, from this tree, not only make a pirogue but, at the least, one very fine ship and two or three pirogues. The director of this concession promised three hundred livres to any man who would like to try to cut it down, so long as he could guarantee success. Owing to this last clause, no one wanted to take the challenge, and the tree remained standing.

It is from these same trees that the bark is taken. This is done when the sap rises in springtime or in the month of August. The trees are felled, and when they are on the ground, measurements of four and a half feet square are marked off and the bark cut. Then, with a wooden tool, the bark is detached from the trunk, and it lifts off easily. From a single tree, one can get two hundred [419] and sometimes three hundred or more bark squares, depending on the size marked off. They are arranged one atop another in a pile so that they do not roll up in the sun. Once they are well dried, there is no more risk of this. Two hundred such bark sheets are sufficient to cover a good-sized house.

The other kind of covering is made from palmetto, which is a plant with a leaf that sticks out of the earth like a folding fan. As the plant grows, it opens out, just as one opens the other kind of fan; from one side to the other, each fold of the leaf is linked together. Its texture resembles that of an iris, but it is much larger, wider, and thicker. Using leaves such as this, one can, by lashing them to two canes twenty to twenty-four feet long, cover a house. The two of its own fronds at either side of the leaf can be attached to the two canes. When you have enough of these prepared, you can cover the house. But on top of each of these pairs of long canes placed on the house, put other canes on top, like lattices, to prevent the wind from lifting up the leaves. When a house is covered in this manner, for the first few days, you can see the light outside coming through, but as soon as it has rained, the leaves spread out and plug up all these holes. This will last at least three or four years.[17]

Some time before the massacre by the Natchez, the French habitants had taken on the practice of covering the storage barns where they dried the tobacco. These were covered with straw thatch in the French fashion.

Ever since buildings in the capital have been constructed in superb designs of brick, or half brick and half timbers, these two kinds of coverings are not used but, instead, either shingles or flat or round tiles, which are fabricated right there in the country. It [420] is even possible to get slate, which would be readily available along the Arkansas River if peace prevailed in that area and the routes were open. Although this source is abundant, in the outlying farms, they continue to use the old-fashioned roofing techniques.

Around New Orleans and in New Biloxi, there is a tree that is rather large and very thick. Its leaves are similar to those of a French laurel, but a little smaller. After it flowers, it produces small, round balls on stems, rather like large pins and pinheads. You collect these and cook them in a large basin of water, periodically skimming off the oil that appears on the surface of the water as it heats, which you put into another container, on which you have placed a wooden crossmember with a string hanging perpendicular and tied to its midpoint. You continue to pour into the container what you take out of the large kettle, and when no more oil appears on the surface of the water, you allow the contents of the second vessel to congeal. There, you will find

17. See Le Page du Pratz's illustration of the "Latanier," in *Histoire de la Louisiane*, II, 48.

a fine loaf of green wax, as good as any in the world and ready to use as a candle. This wax is firm and hard and burns brightly.[18]

The soil in the country is excellent, very black and profitable for plantings, excepting, however, from the mouth of the Mississippi River to Pointe Coupée. Between these two places, it is nothing but a heavy and claylike soil, flooded every year for three months with the river's water, and it is with great difficulty that one can make it produce anything, unless it be rice, which has to be in the water to prosper.

[421] In the upper country, on the other hand, one can look forward to great pleasure and profits from land that produces on its own all kinds of fine herbs, both for wild animals and for man, both for eating and for treating illnesses—in a word, excellent herbs supplied with thousands and thousands of virtues and good qualities. There is hercules's allhead, chamomile, veronica, sanicle, plantain, greenbrier, sassafras, tarragon, tansy, roses, and St. John's wort, from the last of which people in that country draw an oil for cuts and wounds. And there are many others.[19]

In the forest as well as in the prairies, one finds sorrel, trefoil (a small sorrel excellent to the taste), watercress, onion, corn salad (or lamb's lettuce), purslane, and chervil.[20] All these grow wild. One sees, in season, strawberries, raspberries, and mulberries, from which excellent jams are made; and grapes of all kinds in the wild—white, black, blue, and another species large as cherries, although they grow no more than three or four in a bunch.

In autumn and winter, the earth is covered with mushrooms that are red underneath and white on top. In the forest, there are morels. On dry and rotten willows as well as on dried vines, there also grow mushrooms, which are excellent eating when they are well cooked and prepared; they remind one of sheep's strawberries.

When the canebrake has been burned and the canes are sprouting anew, you can gather them and cook them in water, then drain them and make a sauce as you would for asparagus. With your eyes closed, you could not say

18. Compare *Histoire de la Louisiane*, II, 36–40, which includes an illustration of the "cirier" and a somewhat different account of the process for making the wax. The plant is *Morella cerifera*, or *Myrica cerifera*. Both are known commonly as southern wax myrtle or southern bayberry.

19. The local or native American genera or species likely corresponding to these are, in order: *Heracleum maximum*, *Matricaria discoidea*, *Veronica spp.*, *Sanicula spp.*, *Plantago spp.*, *Smilax illinoensis*, *Sassafras albidum*, *Artemisia dracunculus*, unknown, *Oenothera spp.*, or *Rosa spp.*, and *Hypericum ascyron*.

20. In order, likely local equivalents are *Rumex spp.*, *Trifolium pratense*, *Rumex spp.*, *Arabis spp.*, *Chenopodium spp.*, *Portulaca spp.*, and *Chaerophyllum spp.*

whether it was asparagus. The difference is that, with asparagus, you eat the green part, whereas, [422] with this other kind, you eat the white part and throw out the green. In the upriver country, toward the Missouri and Osage Indians, it is all immense, beautiful prairies, and it is there that the wild animals congregate.

But this country that produces so many excellent herbs produces just as many excellent trees. There are live oaks, laurels, walnuts, lilacs, sycamores, cedars, and so on, and it is certain that four master carpenters, each paid six hundred livres per year, assisted by some negroes belonging to the crown, and supplied with the usual rations that are usually spent to do not much of anything, could, between 1730 and 1747, have—yes, I can guarantee that if they had set to it and been made to work, His Majesty could have seen in his ports in France more than forty new three-decked ships. The only costs for supplies from France would have been for the ropes and fittings for the ships, which could have been sent back carrying, in their holds, the lumber for more ships that could all have been constructed in His Majesty's ports in France. And I daresay that if the English have their eyes on that country, it is more for the advantage and the profits to be had from its forests than from mines of gold or silver, lead, copper, or iron, in the heart of the mountains. One cannot, for a single moment, doubt what I have reported here, given all the examples I have cited. But the lack of zeal, lack of manpower, and the absence of security for people exposed as they are to the savagery, deceits, and surprises of the savages—all this I say, has meant that until now, men have not been able to be motivated to go tear these treasures out of the earth.

In addition to the trees I have described above, there are Spanish laurels, acacias, and a tree called the *noli me tangere*, [423] since, from its base to its tip, it is nothing but stiff, sharp spines some three inches in length. There is also a tree called the pecan, which carries as its fruit pecans that are as thick as a finger and as long as an olive. The shell is shaped like that of the filbert, soft enough to break with one's teeth, and it contains a nut that is pleasant to eat, as does another tree called the pawpaw, which has an equally good fruit. There are wild apple trees, too.[21] In short, if I had to name all the many

21. The first plant Dumont mentions here could be the Spanish laurel or bay laurel (*Laurus nobilis*), but both were introduced from the Mediterranean region. The second may be a reference to hackberries (*Celtis spp.*). The "don't touch me" tree could be the native toothache tree, or hercules club (*Aralia spinosa*, or *Zanthoxylum clava-herculis*), or, based on an illustration in *Histoire de la Louisiane*, II, 46, it may be the passion thorn or bearded creeper. The native pecan tree is *Carya illinoinensis*. The pawpaw, or "l'asminier" (*Asimina spp.*), is illustrated both in *Mémoires historiques*, I, 54, and in *Histoire de la Louisiane*, II, 20.

kinds of trees that one sees and finds in that immense country, I would never be done. Suffice it to say that every hundred leagues or so, you see different kinds of forests or trees—not that one no longer sees any of the trees seen earlier, but rather, one finds new trees that establish a contrast; each particular climate creates a different forest than the others. What is certain is that willows and aspens are seen all along the Mississippi River on both sides, on the points of land around which the river abounds with all kinds of fish: those that I have already spoken of but also the trout and tench and pickerel and another fish that is called the armed fish because it has three rows of teeth. Where this fish is found, it is rare to find others, for they flee it as their enemy. And yet it can occasionally be caught on a line if you attach, next to the hook, a brass chain of two yards or more in length. When it is on shore, its scales cannot be stripped off, even with a blow from a hatchet; you have to put it on hot coals, such as is done with a tortoise, in order to eat its flesh. These are sometimes eaten, as is the cayman or alligator, which is an amphibious fish—that is, both aquatic and terrestrial. There are some that are monstrous, at least fifteen or twenty feet in length. They have, in truth, the shape and appearance of a lizard, but whereas [424] the lizard, with its small size, is not at all unpleasant, by contrast, this creature with its massive size is terrifying.[22]

Its body is armored, as it were, with thick, strong scales, to the point where, if hit by a ball fired with the force of powder from a gun, it will not injure him at all, and the ball even bounces off. It is very hard to wound unless it is hit in the eye. When it is, it comes out onto land, since it would lose all its blood if it remained in the water. But when out of the water, it is quite easy to kill it with a blow from a club, the more so because its body is long, and, when it wants to turn around, its tail, which is extremely long, has to turn with its head in one motion. It is highly carnivorous. A poor soldier from the Bayou Saint John, at a post near the entrance of the bayou where there is only a small corps of guards, was sleeping on the ground in the shade of a tree, and one of these animals caught him by the foot and

22. There were no true trout or tench in lower Mississippi waters. Dumont may be referring to species of the brackish water sea trout or to varieties of sucker fish with similar body types. The third fish, "Brochet amerique," is likely the grass pickerel *(Esox americanus)*. The fourth is the remarkable alligator gar *(Atractosteus spatula)*, one of several species of gars in Louisiana waters. The alligator species present in Louisiana is *Alligator mississippiensis;* Dumont's estimation of their length is not unreasonable for older males in the colonial period. The spelling here is "crocodrille," close to the medieval French *cocodrille*, which was carried over into Louisiana French. *Mémoires historiques*, I, 103–107, spells the name "crocodile" and expands on the tale of the soldier who was eaten by one.

dragged him to the bottom of the water, where the poor, unfortunate man was eaten as he drowned. The alligator could easily pull this soldier in, since they truly are strong enough to carry off a buffalo drinking water at the edge of a river.

When the French voyageurs are coming down from the upstream country in a pirogue or flatboat loaded with meat, they have to cover it carefully, for when they come ashore in the daytime to cook their meals, which they do not do often, the alligator, who is naturally selective and hungry only at night, would climb into the boat, not to enjoy the meat there, but to throw it into the water so that he could then go find it again to feast on it.

These animals, although they have four legs and are monstrous, do not multiply their species by breeding little ones but instead make a large quantity of eggs that they lay on the shore of [425][23] a lake or bayou or on a snag or logjam. They will lay as many as 120. The shell of these eggs is, not at all hard, but soft, like those that certain chickens also will lay when they are very fat. These animals do not sit on their eggs but leave them in the rays of the sun, which, by its warmth, makes them grow. The male as well as the female stand guard near their pile of eggs and, in fact, keep such a sharp eye on them that when they are thus fixated, it is truly the case that they will allow themselves to be clubbed or even burned without running away or moving at all. This is what leads the Indians to say that they hatch their eggs with their eyes. When their little ones have poked through the skin that confines them and they begin to wriggle out, they go toward the water that is nearest to them and jump in. But because they are still dragging their shell behind them, they do not sink into the water right away but remain on the surface, as a cork floats on the liquid element. Thus the fish can feast on them, and the carnivorous birds, such as the gulls, herons, terns, pelicans, spoonbills, and even eaglets will also eat them, so that if, out of a hundred, two survive, that is a lot. After all, if every one of them reached maturity, it would not be possible to travel in safety. And, in fact, there are many more of these animals in the remote lakes, for God, who governs all things, has removed them from the sight of men, as is true of other animals that are harmful to us, such as the rattlesnake. Yes, I must say, and will not be silent about it, that land is very good, the soil excellent, and the air not at all bad or unhealthy.[24]

23. Figure 22, "Crocodile, or, Cayman," and Figure 23, "Rattlesnake," were originally located at this spot in the manuscript.

24. See the illustrations of the pelican, or *grand gosier* ("big throat"), and the spoonbill, or *spatule* ("spatula"), in *Histoire de la Louisiane*, II, 98, 113.

So let us return to the subject of how the colony that we had begun to establish in its current form in that country, between 1718 and the present, sadly has not grown but has, I will say it, gradually declined. Why? For not being well managed [426] or governed. Those who have had the power in their hands have thought only of how to enrich themselves without thinking of how to put the colony on a sound footing. And why is that? Because, having been sent there only temporarily, what one leader tried to begin to do, the next who came after tried to improve upon by doing nothing. Yes, I cannot stop myself from repeating it again, and will say it forevermore, that if the Sr. Périer had remained in that country—great God, you know it—the country would be in a condition to survive without the aid of France, and the Indians would have felt what a Frenchman can do when he is commanded by a true warrior such as Périer. They would not have gained the upper hand over us, and I speak, not of the first time, but also the second and third times, as they have done since the Natchez Massacre. And again, why is this? It is not difficult for my reader to discern the reason after I have given him the narrative of all that has happened in the province of Louisiana, which would be a very fine province if we had known how to profit from the advantages that it contains, not simply in one place, but throughout. And I say it again: If there had been men free from self-interest, dedicated to the settlement of such a country, all for the glory of our invincible monarch, the growth of our nation, and the profit of its people, then (without speaking ill of Peru) the country would lack none of Peru's advantages: the trees, plants, mines, animals, the rocks, stones, and soil itself, the lakes, water, everything together adds up to a mine filled with immense treasures, capable of enriching a kingdom and making other nations envious and, not the least important, making its inhabitants happy in their new homes. This is how advantageous Louisiana would be if it had been settled properly. And yet one can only say truthfully that in its current state, it is pitiable, and that [427] it is like a beautiful flower exposed to the sun, which, for lack of water and nourishment, slowly shrivels and, unless it receives help, runs the risk of dying altogether.

There is reason to believe that if the Indians have turned against us, it is from our treating them too gently—having, as it were, given in to them too much rather than stood up to them—and that they have become accustomed to getting whatever they've seen fit to ask for, so long as they put their hands together to beseech us. In truth, the generosity of the Frenchman has been his undoing. If we have been or are now at risk every day of having our men killed and of being insulted by the Indians, it is because all the recognition for the good works we have done for them disappears as soon as the

(top) **Figure 22.** *Crocodile, or Cayman, Watching Its Eggs.* VAULT oversize Ayer MS 257, figure no. 8. Courtesy The Newberry Library, Chicago

(bottom) **Figure 23.** *Rattlesnake, Very Dangerous, Each Rattle on the Tail Marking One Year of Life.* VAULT oversize Ayer MS 257, figure no. 9. Courtesy The Newberry Library, Chicago

supply of gifts stops. All at once, from the friends they were, they become our enemies, and if we had known how to wean them little by little, the French people in that country would enjoy a stability that they currently have none of.

What makes it worse is that the English, who are not far away from us and who, as everyone knows, are much given to shipbuilding, would love to be in possession of a land that produces such magnificent and excellent trees. One can presume it is they who have acted surreptitiously to arouse the Indians, not to openly declare war against us, but to destroy us little by little. And if our invincible monarch, in his concern for his people, decided to send special commissioners to this country—men who would have the authority to examine what has happened there, merely from 1730 to the present, and who would be ready to listen to the poor as well as to the rich— how many abuses, how many wasted expenditures they would find! How many injustices inflicted and imposed upon the widow and the orphan! [428] How much cronyism—I will dare to say it—how much treason and deceit, and even impieties and abuses of the sacraments, in a land that by now is close to expiring or destroying itself for the lack of a sound mind, a popular, just, and disinterested leader.

If I dare again to give some advice, it is that the commandant of such a country should not spend more than four years in control of the helm. In this short span of time, he would try to attract the gratitude of the people, to make himself loved rather than feared, although he must not by any means forswear severity when it is absolutely necessary. Finally, at the end of this term, he would return and report to His Majesty's ministers, who, informed of what was needed in the country, would lend their aid and would help it regain its luster. He would, at the same time, give an account of his own conduct, which would redound to his own glory, as did that of the unbiased Périer. But no, the man who was sent to replace him knew all too well how to seize the tiller and hold on to it. He had never learned how to obey and still less how to lead, unless it was from the practices of the Indians, among whom he had spent his childhood and from whom he learned how to make use of the arts of treachery instead of the courage and valor of the French. My reader may object that what I am putting forth here is to repay him in some way for his actions in my case. No, no—I say it for the public good and at risk to my own life; if he had acted like Caesar and as a good and impartial commandant, my pen, which only writes the truth and which now comes [429] to the end, would be inclined to publish my support for him. And, as I have proclaimed that he learned only treason from the Indians, I refer my dear reader to the old proverb that says, "Tell me whose company you keep; I will tell you who you are." In a word, he betrayed me, or he tried to do so. How would he have done otherwise, given that he behaved the same way toward his own kinsmen? And to confirm the truth of what I am saying, I must tell, in a few words, of the sufferings and tribulations that he imposed upon the Sr. de Saint Denis, chevalier de Saint Louis, commandant of the fort at Natchitoches, and a man of great intelligence and courage, both dignified and prudent. The passage of time cannot erase the memory of such a great individual.[25]

He was, in fact, the cousin of the governor and a native of the same land, a Canadian. He was assigned to travel from Quebec overland to Dauphin Island, in the time of the Sr. Crozat, when there were yet very few Frenchmen there. The Sr. Saint Denis came in the capacity of a cadet. I cannot confirm it, but I believe that he was an ensign. The Sr. Lamothe Cadillac was then the commandant on the island, but he died there soon after, and the king named another commandant, who never had the chance to take command, as he died on the voyage over.[26] When the ship arrived at that island, which then found itself with no leader, the Canadians, who outnumbered the French, chose with a unanimous voice the Sr. Le Moyne de Bienville as their commandant because he was the brother of the famous d'Iberville, so well known in America. They sent a petition to the king, asking His Majesty to approve of their choice, which the king [430] granted them, with the result that the Sr. de Bienville came out from among the Choctaw Indians, where he had been learning their language and customs, and arrived to

25. Dumont had already devoted the last section of his "Poème" to an account of the heroic career of Louis Juchereau de Saint Denis, and there, too, his aim was to criticize Bienville by a comparison with his cousin; see "Poème," 425–433. The *Mémoires historiques* included only a brief reference to Saint Denis (II, 65–66), but Le Page du Pratz wrote a more comprehensive account in the *Journal œconomique* ([November 1752], 157–164, and [December 1752], 119–130), and then placed the story at the very beginning of *Histoire de la Louisiane*, I, 11–24. The other significant contemporary account of the Saint Denis story is by André Pénicaut, *Fleur de Lys and Calumet: Being the Pénicaut Narrative of French Adventure in Louisiana*, ed. and trans. Richebourg Gaillard McWilliams (Tuscaloosa, Ala., 1988), 183–203, 220–227. An essential study of Saint Denis's life and legend in colonial Louisiana texts is in Germain Joseph Bienvenu, "Another America, Another Literature: Narratives from Louisiana's Colonial Experience" (Ph.D. diss., Louisiana State University, 1995), 224–270. For a biography of Saint Denis, see Ross Phares, *Cavalier in the Wilderness: The Story of the Explorer and Trader Louis Juchereau de St Denis* (Baton Rouge, La., 1952).

26. Saint Denis was born in Quebec in 1676, might have been educated in Paris, and first traveled to Louisiana with d'Iberville's second voyage in 1699. He did not travel overland from Quebec to Louisiana. The short-lived commandant appears to be the Sr. de l'Epinay, governor of Louisiana from 1717–1718, after Cadillac and before Bienville. But, in fact, he lived until 1721.

take command of the island, which, even as it passed out of the hands of M. Crozat into those of the Company of the Indies, remained under the command of the Sr. de Bienville. However, before the Company was able to send its men there, the presence of the Sr. Saint Denis proved so irritating to the commandant that he sought only to pick quarrels with him, to the point of treating him as the lowest of men.

This is painful to any man who has courage and nobility in his blood, and the result was that the Sr. Saint Denis, seeing himself mistreated, determined that he would never achieve anything by staying on the island, even if he had been a true Cato and that any good deeds he did would be regarded by his cousin as evil acts. So he left the island and withdrew among the Indians, traveling from tribe to tribe, where, with his noble spirit and all that he had learned from his relatives, he attracted from among those barbarians only their best qualities. That is to say, he learned several different languages—above all, the one that serves as mother tongue, for, in a country so vast and wide as that, filled with so many different nations, there is truly one language which is spoken throughout, in addition to the national languages, much as Latin is among us. He eventually reached the Illinois, where he stayed for at least six months, that is to say, the length of the winter, for in that place, the winters are harsh and the river freezes over. From there, he went to the Missouris' country, where he [431] lived for several years and became recognized as one of their chiefs. From that nation, he went to the Osages and, in a word, as far as Mexico, where he learned the Spanish language perfectly.[27]

Because, in those areas of Mexico, the supervision of the populace operates efficiently and the man of whom I'm speaking was a stranger, he was no doubt taken straight to the governor, who asked him who he was, where he had come from, and to whom he belonged. The Sr. Saint Denis, being a man of truth, did not wish to tell a lie and admitted that he was a French Canadian, come from Massacre Island, where his relative was the commandant.

27. The Mobilien trade language, derived from the Chickasaw, Choctaw, and Alabama languages, served as a lingua franca for trade in the Southeast, used both by natives and French colonists. The Osage are a Siouan-speaking tribe who, at the time of French colonization, lived in southern Missouri and northern Arkansas. The Missouris are another group of Siouan-speakers whose territory at the time was in the center of the present state of Missouri. However, other accounts of Saint Denis's journey maintain that he traveled up the Red River to Nacogdoches and across modern Texas to the Rio Grande. He might have explored Missouri earlier in his career, but he did not take such a northern route to Mexico. Moreover, Le Page and Pénicaut maintain that Saint Denis made two trips to Mexico City rather than just one.

We were not then at war with Spain, and so, after his deposition was taken down, he was given free rein to go where he wished, whether to Veracruz or to Santa Fe.

Then the governor of the place wrote a letter to the commandant at Massacre Island to find out whether the Sr. Saint Denis was known to him.

As soon as this man learned that his cousin was in Mexico, he resolved to be rid of him, and to bring his plan to fruition, he wrote to the governor appointed by the king of Spain for Mexico, that the deposition of the Sr. Saint Denis was false, that he did not know this man at all, unless possibly he was a spy whom he had heard talk of. This letter reached the governor of Mexico, who had the stranger arrested and put in prison, where he was allowed to bring only his innocence.

In every country, there are found some good souls and some charitable people, and such people not only assisted the prisoner from their wallets; they spoke about him to their governor, who had written to the commandant at Massacre Island to ask what he should do with this spy. The commandant wrote a letter in which he suggested to the Spanish general that he could [432] put the spy to death. When this letter was written, he gave it to an Indian to carry. After traversing the immense forests and vast prairies, this Indian arrives at the town where the Sr. Saint Denis was being held prisoner, and since he was a Missouri, he wanted to see his chief before going to the Mexican governor's residence. He enters the prison and goes straight to carry his message to the Sr. Saint Denis, who was surprised to see him there and asked him why he had left his village or what discontent there might be.

At this, the Indian told him that he had been sent by the French chief (as he called the commandant at Massacre Island) to carry a letter to the chief of Mexico. He showed it to him; the prisoner took it, opens it, and sees his death sentence. He tells this to the Indian, who is at once ashamed and infuriated to be carrying a letter that orders the demise of his good chief Saint Denis, and asks whether there is anything he can do to save his life. Then the prisoner, whom God had placed under his divine protection, said to the Indian that if he wanted, he could secure his freedom, which he agreed to do. So the Sr. Saint Denis created another letter to the governor, and after sealing the wax with the same signet, which he possessed, he gave the letter to the Indian while keeping the real one. The joyous Indian leaves the prison and runs to the governor's residence, all out of breath, as if he came from far away, and asks to speak with him. Once in his presence, he puts the letter in his hands. The governor opens it, reads it, and immediately issues an order to go release from the prison the Sr. Saint Denis to be brought to speak to him, which was done.[28]

[433] When the prisoner was in the presence of the governor, the Spanish grandee said to him, "Do not blame me for what you have suffered in the prison; look at the letter from your commandant, who you say is your cousin. It is by his order that you were made prisoner. You now have left prison, but on the condition that you promise me to stay in the city awaiting new orders."

The Sr. Saint Denis gave him his word and stayed in the city, where, with his noble bearing, his genial and happy physiognomy, he made many friends and in fact fell passionately in love with a beautiful and pleasing young Spanish girl, rich in wealth and honor. He even asked her father for her hand in marriage. She was promised to him once he enjoyed his full liberty again.[29] The Indian who had brought the fatal letter was sent back with one from the governor of Mexico to the commandant at Massacre Island, who, when he saw the Indian who had carried his letter, was trembling with joy at the thought of having got rid of his relative of whom he was so jealous. This letter would confirm that his cousin's days were over. He opens it, but imagine his surprise to see that his cousin is still alive! He cannot understand how such a thing could happen. The more he tries to think about it, the less he can understand it. He fulminates and works himself into a rage, perhaps accusing the governor of Mexico of being an ignoramus and of not comprehending what he had told him in his last letter. But he could not himself understand the will of God, who, in his justice, governs and reigns over all. What nonetheless consoles him somewhat is to learn that the man is still a prisoner in the city and that he thus can still quickly have him killed. So he writes again to the governor of Mexico that, according to the order he has received from the king, his master, as soon as [434] the governor has received this letter, Saint Denis is to be put back in prison and put to death, and that when this execution has been done, to let him know so that, as he says, he can pass along the news to His Majesty.

This fatal letter arrives in Mexico, but the Indian who managed to rescue

28. Dumont's story of the interception of letters from Bienville to the Mexican governor seems to be his own invention, another of his creative slanders against his enemy. It is also included in his "Poème."

29. Saint Denis's wife's name was Emanuela Sanchez de Navarro, but Pénicaut named her Maria and identified her as a daughter of Don Pedro de Vilesca. Le Page du Pratz identified her as the granddaughter of Diego Ramon, governor of the presidio of San Juan Bautista, modern Piedras Negras, Mexico, on the Rio Grande.

the Sr. Saint Denis from prison also found a way to rescue him from death. For the victim himself, walking in the street, recognized the Indian, who was surprised to see the Sr. Saint Denis still in the city, and said to him, "My chief, what are you doing here? You are dead! Here is another letter." Saint Denis led the Indian into his room, opened the letter, read it, and replaced it in its envelope, which he resealed and returned to the Indian and asked him to promise not to carry it to the governor for six more days. The Indian, having so promised, was generously paid by the Sr. Saint Denis, who, without sharing his plan with anyone, without even saying farewell to his lady, donned a disguise and fled the city as quickly as he could, fleeing the rage of a kinsman who could not live content as long as his cousin remained alive.

But where did he seek refuge? Not in any sovereign realm, but in the woods, vales, and prairies, without any weapon save a single staff in his hand and carrying with him neither food nor supplies. Providence was his only resource. For three days, he kept ahead of whatever pursuit might have been sent after him. On the fourth day, toward nine in the morning, he saw, in his path, a Spaniard mounted and armed like Saint George, who might have been searching for our fugitive or might not have known about him at all. The Sr. Saint Denis bowed to him and asked for alms. As the man made a motion to give this to him, putting his hand inside his cloak, our fugitive landed a blow with his staff on the back of his head, which caused [435] the knight to fall off his horse onto the ground. Our pretend beggar quickly grabbed the saddle and jumped onto it, leaving the man who wanted to do him an act of charity to wait for someone else who would show him such charity.

Thus mounted, I will leave you to imagine how, supplied with a strong steed, he set a pace twice as fast as he would have been able to make on foot. The first few days of his flight, he survived on the sprouts of canes, watercress, and chervil. But when he reached the prairies, where there were flocks of goats, lambs, and sheep overseen by shepherds, he went after them like a fox in the night, carrying away several of these animals, skinning them and smoking the meat on a grill. While he did this, his equine companion grazed on fresh grass. Our traveler completed his fine meal and continued on his route, where, after four hundred leagues, he at last arrived at the Missouris, who were overjoyed to see him after such a long absence. They had believed him to be dead. They regarded him as their chief, and after staying some time with them, he gathered a party of two hundred men and went with them to Illinois, where they built pirogues and floated down the river, surviving solely by hunting, and arrived at the site of the capital, which at that time was occupied only by a few river boatmen. They continued by portaging their pirogues into the Bayou Saint John and, embarking them there, went on to Massacre Island, where we were then setting sail with the squadron led by the Sr. de Champmeslin to go take Pensacola.

Our traveler, dressed as an Indian, like his escort, had no sooner learned that we were setting out against the enemies of the king than his desire to be of use and to distinguish himself led him to depart Massacre Island with his companions and cross over to the Pensacola peninsula, [436] where he went ashore and continued overland to join the land forces commanded by his kinsman. When the latter recognized him, so tender were his caresses, such pleasure he displayed in embracing his dear cousin once again, that the soldiers believed he did love him. Such tears of joy he shed at seeing his cousin after such a long absence, after believing him to be dead from some illness or from the rigors of travel. In short, he appeared at the moment to be opening his heart to him; yes, for the moment, but in the depths of his heart, in his secret self, what was he thinking when he saw in front of him a man whom he had condemned to death? Who could have saved him from death? This was something he could neither guess nor know. And he could only assume that his cousin knew nothing of his own designs, and this is what preserved his calm temper.

When we had captured Pensacola, as I have described in its place, and everything was complete, the Sr. Saint Denis had a secret meeting with the chief of the squadron and let him know exactly how his kinsman's hatred had caused him so many sorrows and difficulties, assuring Champmeslin that all he was saying was the honest truth. This was supported by the letters that he put in the hands of the Sr. Champmeslin, who, once he had examined each of them with an unbiased eye, saw that, indeed, everything the Sr. Saint Denis was telling him was only too true. He took him under his protection and promised to make sure the king learned of his innocence. He also advised him to withdraw to someplace where he could escape the continuing treachery of his cousin and assured him that before a year passed, he would enjoy the fruits of this promise.

[437] M. de Champmeslin returned, as I have said, to France and told the king of the innocence of this oppressed subject, who by then had retreated to Old Biloxi, before we had even imagined the settlement that we later built there. But later, when the Sr. de Valdeterre did go there, he invited the Sr. Saint Denis to his table. And when I returned in the ship called the *Portefaix*, I had the pleasure of seeing the commandant of Massacre Island, the cousin of Saint Denis, being forced by an order from the king to put the Croix de Saint Louis on the lapel of the man whose death he had plotted. Alas, how God's designs are hidden! Who would have believed that a man

who had been abandoned, who had been tarnished with such a damaging portrayal at Court, would end up being so honored with the favors of such a great king! But this cannot erase the fact that a series of lies, calumnies, and falsehoods were perpetrated to destroy a man because the commandant took umbrage against him.

Alas, how happy I would be if, like the Sr. Saint Denis, I might have the good fortune to find, on the one hand, a judge so impartial as the Sr. de Champmeslin was on this occasion and, on the other hand, a protector such as him, who can, after carefully examining my conduct, see that it is not at all like that of my enemies. But what am I saying about "enemies?" I don't believe I have any except for the major de la place here, who sees that, in spite of him and his designs, I have secured a post, and this gives him umbrage. He made his false report against me [438] to the Court and had so spoken to M. le marquis de Rothelin, who, seeing the candor and devotion on the face of a major who had served for so long in the garrison, believed what he was saying against me. Why? Simply because he did not believe that a man in such a position as he was could lie to him. However, the major is charitable, giving only what he has freely, and could easily say much more, going out of his way to prove the animosity he has toward me, and no doubt is making himself known to the reader or readers of these memoirs that he seeks only to destroy me, and that is the honest truth.

I ask, therefore (and let us leave aside the hatred and envy that drives him to try to undo me), I ask if a poor officer such as I am—with a wife and two children to support, with no means except what His Majesty pays me for my job, from which three hundred livres per month I actually receive only eighteen livres, nineteen sous, and three deniers, that is, about one-tenth, including the fee of four deniers per livre and my receipt—I ask if it is not true that since he is so generous, he would want to show it, for it seems to me that he should want to help and assist a poor officer such as myself. But no, I am forced to try to extricate myself from this poverty and misery by appealing to Mgr. le maréchal Belle-Isle, who, out of his consideration for my family, has obtained for me the post of adjutant major. This [439] only heightens the major's animosity toward me and further inflames his desire to undo me and destroy me altogether. This is why he made it known to M. le marquis de Rothelin that I had come to this garrison only through the influence of the maréchal de Belle-Isle, who, when he could not think of anything for me in Paris, made me a lieutenant at Port-Louis, and from that, a captain of the gates and adjutant major. But what he did not understand, or pretended not to, was that since 1720, I had been a half-pay lieutenant in this garrison, at a time when he was only a mere half-pay captain in the royal marines. He had had the good fortune to find a major who was generous toward him, who made him what he is. And I have found an illustrious protector in the person of our great duc et maréchal de Belle-Isle. I hope that in his goodness, he will make it known to our inimitable minister the comte d'Argenson that my conduct has been quite different from what might have been suggested and reported by this major, so charitable toward his neighbor, a major who was so devout in his campaign that he took the trouble to defame an officer not only for his character but also for his performance in his duties.

I would be content if, after suffering so many trials and travails, I could live in peace. This is what I expect and hope for from the goodness and greatness of my generous protector.

Let us return to our story. After the Sr. Saint Denis had received the Croix de Saint Louis, another order specified that a separate letter from the king was to be opened, and when this was done, one saw that His Majesty was not only giving the Croix de Saint Louis and an annuity to the Sr. de Saint Denis [440] but also naming him commandant of the post at Natchitoches, without having to take or receive any orders from the general of the colony. He was to be independent and was to receive his orders only from the king or his minister, such that one could say there were now two commandants general in the country, though it would have been a much happier country if the newer commandant had been the only one. After this, the Sr. de Saint Denis, having gathered the supplies and troops needed for his post, left New Biloxi, where we were then based, and took up his post at Natchitoches, where he ordered the construction of a fort with palisades, caserns, and barracks. He then sent an Indian to Mexico with a letter asking for his betrothed, who came in a caravan to the fort, where she married the man who had run so many risks in New Spain.[30]

I will not stop to describe the joy of these two persons at finding themselves united again after such a long separation. I will only say that the Sr. Saint Denis was a man of valor, courage, and intelligence, who knew how to command and how to make himself obeyed. He was beloved not only by the habitants but also by the Indians, as he spoke their languages well, which is a very important asset among those nations. He was a father toward the soldiers, their judge and their protector, and France would have been happy if the entire colony had been so lucky as to have him for its commandant. The first Canadian who held that post ruined everything and left the place

30. The Company of the Indies also granted Saint Denis special dispensation to trade with the Spanish and a 5 percent commission on the revenue from it.

looking like a withered plant, ready to [441] perish; and the second, in two years of service, what changes would he not have been able to effect? But His Majesty did not see fit to do otherwise, and now God has taken the Sr. Saint Denis from this earth.[31]

I have learned, since I left that country, that the king had recalled the first Canadian and had handed over the leadership of the people there to the son of M. de Vaudreuil. I do not doubt for a moment that his command is far better than that of his compatriot, who had learned all he knew from the Choctaw Indians, whereas the new commandant learned from his father, who was governor of Quebec at the time I was there. He was a good commandant, impartial and replete with a thousand virtues, and I can't imagine but that his son has inherited these important traits. I hope that the country will soon feel the benefit of them; this is my prayer and my desire. I leave everything to the will of God, who reigns over all, and I will say *fiat voluntas Dei,* as well as that of His Majesty and his ministers, who, distant as they are from this charming country, believe that everything they are told about this faraway land is true, that the colony there is flourishing with abundant settlements and forts, with indigo, pelts, tobacco, rice, etc. Alas, there are few who speak the truth: *verba volant sed scripta manent.*[32]

All that I have put forward up until now—what I have written, what I have brought to light—is completely sincere. If someone might object that I have composed these memoirs out of a desire to write and make myself known, let him [442] know, and I implore him to believe, that this is not my intent nor my pretension. My name is fairly well known already on account of my dear father, and if I should remain in obscurity, I would be more worthy to be there than to try to raise myself up by lying. No, my intention has been to describe the injustice, the treason, the corruption, and the massive expenditures that have been made and are still being made in a country that is new and far away from France, where France has spent great sums and which has not made a return on this investment. Why? Thanks to the errors of those who have been sent to that country, who thought only of enriching themselves while forgetting their duties and, I will say, even their own protectors, the men who had sponsored them and (to put it frankly)

31. Louis Juchereau de Saint Denis died June 11, 1744, and was buried in Natchitoches, Louisiana.

32. *Fiat voluntas Dei:* "God's will be done." *Verba volant sed scripta manent:* "Spoken words fly away; written words remain." Pierre de Rigaud de Vaudreuil de Cavagnial, son of Philippe de Rigaud de Vaudreuil, governor of New France during Dumont's time in Quebec, was named governor of Louisiana in 1742 and arrived in New Orleans in May 1743.

made them what they were and what they still are at present. Alas, alas, great God, you alone know how many injustices are committed in that country, how many thefts. It would be good, even if it came a little late, to send over royal commissioners who could call a *chambre de justice*. How many heads might roll! But I'm getting carried away with my zeal. Is it my place to give such advice? No, no.

After having written the truth, I submit it all to the will of a God, to whom I owe thousands and thousands of thanks for not leaving me to perish amid the numerous and perilous dangers that I have faced and that my reader must by now have seen. And [443] as my feeble voice is not by itself enough to thank Him, I will cry out with the holy prophet, *Laudate Dominum omnes gentes, laudate eum omnes populi.*[33]

33. "Oh praise the Lord, all ye nations, praise him, all ye peoples": Pss. 116:1. The "prophet" is David.

APPENDIX 1 [Title page]

Memoir[1]
of L—— D——, Engineering Officer, Containing the Events That Have Occurred in Louisiana from 1715 to the Present, as well as Remarks on the Manners, Customs, and Strengths of Various Native Peoples in North America, and Its Productions

1. This title appears on the recto of the first leaf of the manuscript. The paper of the three leaves used for the title and preface differs from that of the manuscript, and those leaves are written in a different hand. See the "Translator's Note" in the front matter.

APPENDIX 2 Preface[2]

In writing these memoirs, it has never been my intention to gain rewards for myself and still less to immortalize my name. I have had no other goal than to seek an honest occupation and to offer to my protectors not only an account of my conduct but also some details of events that took place in the land known until recently as the Mississippi, where we wished to establish a colony. Some have called it the New World, even though this land is not newly discovered, being claimed in parts by several different nations:

> In the north, there is Quebec, the capital city of the French.
> In another part, New York and Virginia, belonging to the English.
> In the south, New Mexico or New Spain, belonging to the Spaniards.

The center of this isle, however, is occupied only by the Indians, and it is this part that was chosen for the establishment of a colony in 1715 under the aegis and the name of the royal Company of the Indies. M. de Crozat granted to the Company an isle called Massacre Island, where he had, at the time, a small post, a refuge for ships returning from the trading that he was doing in Mexico.[3]

It was then that this company began to send people to this isle. It became, as you will see in reading these memoirs, a kind of Noah's Ark, where were gathered persons of all ages, all ranks, and both sexes to take possession of the mainland, a beautiful country, and to form some settlements known as concessions. Most of these began well enough but collapsed soon after. There were only a few that were able to sustain themselves, and only thanks to the wealth of their founders, such as M. le duc de Belle-Isle, Mme la marquise de Traisnel, M. de la Jonchère, and the treasurer.[4]

One may ask why I got mixed up in what happened in this land. I have explained myself here at the start of this preface. I would also declare that I have written this to show how, when one is far from one's homeland, from the king and his ministers, one is utterly at the mercy of commanders, who, holding all power in their hands, act with impunity and abuse this power, acting like despots over the places where they command. Hence, I yearned for my homeland and the protection of its laws. But as we shall see, with the help of God, by virtue of the patience He gives to those whom He does not abandon, one can outlast one's enemies.

[iiir] My separation from my homeland for such a long span of time, the changes in

2. This preface begins on the recto of the second leaf of the manuscript and continues on the verso of that leaf and the recto of the third.

3. Here the unknown author of the preface reveals that Antoine Crozat was violating the terms of the trade monopoly by trading with the Spanish colonies around the Gulf of Mexico.

4. This presumably refers to the marquis d'Asfeld, although La Jonchère was treasurer of the Royal and Military Order of the Croix de Saint Louis and treasurer of defense.

language, the voyages and travels I have made, should earn me some indulgence for all the errors and mistakes that fill this memoir. If such is granted, it would be by virtue of the truths I bring to light as much with respect to the lands of Louisiana as with respect to myself. Travelers now and in the future will only confirm what I have advanced. Let the Supreme Being, after so many trials, grant me a favorable wind and a tranquil peace in the heart of my country.

APPENDIX 3 List of the Names of Nations Known to the Author That Are Found in the Island of North America[5]

Les Alli Bamons	peu nombreux
Les Mobiliens	peu nombreux
Les Paskagoulas	peu nombreux
Les Appalaches	peu nombreux
Les Billoky	peu nombreux
Les Chicachas	très nombreux
Les Chactas	très nombreux
Les Natches	très nombreux
Les Chaoüachas	peu nombreux
Les Attaquappas	peu nombreux
Les Tenças	peu nombreux
Les Bayagoula	peu nombreux
Les Tonicas	peu nombreux
Les Naguitoches	peu nombreux
Les Sioux	peu nombreux
Les Yeukenais	peu nombreux
Les Gris	peu nombreux
Les Cheraquis	peu nombreux
Les Illinois	assez nombreux
Les Iroquois	assez nombreux
[illegible; page cut off]	assez nombreux
Suite [verso]	
Les Epissingles	peu nombreux
Les Missouris	assez nombreux
Les Osages	assez nombreux
Les Yachoux	peu nombreux
Les Poux	peu nombreux
Les Chetimachas	peu nombreux
Les Renards	peu nombreux
Les Arcanzas	très nombreux

There are also many other nations that are not known to the author and do not have villages or fixed places of residence, being only wandering Indians moving here or there, although in substantial numbers.

5. The list remains untranslated, with names spelled as in the original. "Peu nombreux" means "few in number"; "assez nombreux," "fairly numerous"; and "très nombreux," "very numerous."

APPENDIX 4 Table[6]

A

1st attack of the French on the Natchez Indians 151

2nd attack 237

3rd attack 246

4th attack 262

[arbre] tree producing wax 420

Arkansas Indians, 200 leagues from the capital of the French 119

Alabamons, French post 140 leagues from Mobile 274

assassin punished 16

Attakappas Indian nation 378

arrival of the author at Port-Louis 285

B

baptism of the sailors 42

Baton Rouge concession of M. d'Artaguiette 110

Balize, French post at the entrance of the Saint Louis River 354

Biloxi, Old 69

Biloxi, New 105

C

[calle] keelhauling, naval punishment 9

cook, part of the crew of a vessel 32

Cap François, Saint-Domingue 45

Cuba, island of the Spaniards 48

Chaouacha concession of the duc de Belle-Isle 355

[commissaires] royal commissioners 147

chief of the Tunicas, a Christian 152

D

[disette] famine of the French 103

[decouverte] voyage of discovery to go look for a topaz rock 117

d'Artaguiette, his martyrdom 274

[Détour des Anglais] the English Turn 356

[De l'isle] Simars de Bellisle, his story 378

declaration of war of the Indians 37[5]

[descente des Anglais] invasion of Brittany by the English 30[8]

E

[ecors] bluff, or mountain 145

[escadre] English squadron 48

[escadre] idem 30[7]

embarrassment of the author 16[1]

[espece] type of fair or diversion 28[0]

F

[forban] a new pirate [7]

[fleuve] Saint Louis River 10[2]

Fort Rosalie at Natchez, French post 1[___]

[fort] entrepot at Saint Francis 28[7*bis*]

Fort of the Assumption [288]

[feu sacré] sacred fire of the Indians 36[5]

G

[glacé] frostbite, how to cure [2]2

---

6. The page numbers refer to the pagination in the original manuscript. Where necessary to preserve the alphabetical sequence, the original French word appears in brackets. Some of the page numbers were cut off when the manuscript was trimmed, and I have tried to fill in correct page numbers where they are missing.

A BIOGRAPHICAL DICTIONARY
OF THE PERSONS NAMED IN DUMONT'S
MANUSCRIPT MEMOIR

Dumont mentioned, in his memoir, nearly 250 individuals by name or title, and research by the editorial team has been able to identify more than two-thirds of these people in other archival and scholarly sources. They are listed below. Names not included here have been omitted because no further information could be found beyond what Dumont provides or because a nickname or ambiguous spellings of a name make it impossible to positively identify the person. Each entry begins in boldface with a standard spelling as used in the text of the translation, although in some cases it is not a spelling used consistently in other sources. Following this is a list of variant spellings, if any, that Dumont uses in the manuscript.

Some of the people listed here were prominent in France or in the French colonies and are included in major biographical dictionaries such as the bilingual *Dictionnaire biographique du Canada / Dictionary of Canadian Biography*, online at biographi.ca, and the still incomplete *Dictionnaire de biographique française, sous la direction de J. Balteau* . . . (Paris, 1933–). For these prominent individuals, the entries here are brief and concentrate on the period and events covered by Dumont's memoirs, 1715–1747, and on the titles or jobs held by that individual, the places where he or she lived, and the dates of passage to and from America.

Sources for entries on the lesser-known individuals include passenger lists from the 1719–1722 period and censuses and lists of officers in Louisiana from 1718 to 1731, many of which have been translated and published in the *LHQ* and in Glenn R. Conrad's two-volume *First Families of Louisiana (FFLa). A Dictionary of Louisiana Biography*, also edited by Conrad, is another important reference. The reader will notice how many of these people died in the Natchez Massacre, as confirmed by the list compiled by Father Philibert in 1730 (reprinted in *FFLa*, II, 141–143, and in *MPA*, I, 122–126). The most important source, however, has been Carl Brasseaux's CD-ROM publication *France's Forgotten Legion: Service Records of French Military and Administrative Personnel Stationed in the Mississippi Valley and Gulf Coast Region, 1699–1769 (FFL)*, which contains entries for thousands of individuals who served in Louisiana, including roughly half of those whom Dumont mentions, and cites extensive sources in the French archives. Brasseaux organized his CD-ROM, not in a single alphabetical list, but in six parts: administrators and governors, officers, noncommissioned officers, cadets, soldiers, and finally support staff (such as engineers, interpreters, and surgeons). Because of this structure, it can be time-consuming to locate an individual, and some have multiple entries, such as for service both as an officer and an administrator. As an aid to researchers, the entries below provide references to the corresponding entries for each individual found in the *FFL* CD-ROM. The first of the three numbers corresponds to the six parts, the second to the chapters within that part, and the third to a page number. If the name differs from what Dumont used, the name of the entry is also included. Other sources that have been essential for the compilation of the biographical dictionary include the summary of the records of the Superior Council of Louisiana published in *LHQ*, II–V, the *MPA*, the *HNAI*, Dumont's own *Mémoires historiques*, Marcel Giraud's *HLF*, and Shannon Dawdy's database of New Orleans property owners, printed as Appendix C in "La Ville Sauvage: 'Enlightened' Colonialism and Creole Improvisation in New Orleans, 1699–1769" (Ph.D. diss., University of Michigan, 2003).

Amelot, d'
Captain of the *Profond*, which sailed from New Orleans in 1723 with Delorme. He later became a pilot at La Balize in 1732.

Andriot, Nicolas (died in 1722)
Sailed to Louisiana with Dumont as a sublieutenant on the *Marie* in 1719. Commissioned as lieutenant in 1720. Performed the duties of major at Biloxi and at Dauphin Island. Died at Old Biloxi. [*FFL*, 2:1:4]

Argenson [d'Argenson], Marc-Pierre de Voyer de Paulmy, comte de Weil (1696–1764)
A magistrate at the court at Châtelet in 1717 and appointed lieutenant general of the police in Paris in 1720. He was close to Belle-Isle and became one of Dumont's most important protectors, probably owing to connections with Dumont's father and brothers in the legal profession. He became a secretary of state for defense in 1743, and while he was in this capacity, Dumont wrote him letters from Port-Louis asking for an appointment. To him, Dumont dedicated the copy of his poem that is held today at the Bibliothèque de l'Arsenal in Paris, a library founded by Argenson's nephew, Antoine-René.

Artaguiette [Dartaguette], Jean-Baptiste Martin d' (1683–after 1747)
Shared, with Nicolas de la Salle, the post of commissaire ordonnateur of Louisiana from 1708 to 1711, when he returned to France and was named a director of the Company of the Indies. [*FFL*, "d'Artaguiette Diron," 1:1:23–24]

Artaguiette [Dartaguiette d'Itouralde], Pierre d' (died in 1736)
Younger brother of Bernard Diron d'Artaguiette and of Martin d'Artaguiette, he arrived with them in 1707 as a cadet. He went to Illinois in 1718 as a captain. After courageous service in combat against the Natchez in 1730, he was named commander of the fort that replaced Fort Rosalie there. In 1732, he was a major at New Orleans and in 1733 returned to Illinois. He was awarded the Croix de Saint Louis in 1735 but died in the ill-fated expedition against the Chickasaws, in which he was ordered to lead a detachment from the Illinois country that arrived weeks before French troops reached the Chickasaw villages from the south. [*FFL*, 2:2:11–14]

Asfeld [Dasfeld, Asphel, Dasphel], Claude François Bidal, marquis d' (1665–1743)

Appointed maréchal de camp in 1702 and awarded the Croix de Saint Louis in 1703 for service in the War of the Spanish Succession. In 1715, he joined the council of war and then the Council of the Marine and became commander of the Order of Knights of Saint Louis. His most significant role in the military was as director of fortifications. He became a marquis in July 1719 and a maréchal de France in 1734. With Belle-Isle, La Jonchère, and Le Blanc, he invested in several concessions under Law's scheme.

Bailly, Charles (died in 1729)

Embarked on the *Mutine* bound for Louisiana from Lorient in November 1719. He had his wife, Marguerite, with him. Served as a director for the Company of the Indies at Natchez in 1727–1729, where he was killed in the revolt. [*FFL*, 1:1:2]

Baldic [Baldy], Theodore (died in 1737)

Listed as a surgeon for the Company of the Indies in 1727. Served at Yazoo and elsewhere. In a census of farms and concessions along the Mississippi River in 1731, his land lies "below Chapitoulas," he is not married, and he employs one servant and ten African slaves. Shortly after his death in January 1737, his succession was recorded before the Superior Council, and his plantation on the Mississippi, near Bienville's lands, was put up for auction. [*FFL*, "Balduc," 6:2:2]

Baron, Marie

Born at Le Mesnil-Thomas (Eure-et-Loir) around 1700, she arrived on the *Mutine* in 1719 as one of the young women forcibly transported from Paris. Her daughter Marie-Louise Baron is recorded as dying at Biloxi on March 28, 1722. Later in the 1720s, Marie lived near Natchez with her husband Jean Roussin. She was captured by the Natchez in the revolt but was ransomed after the siege later that winter. She married Dumont in New Orleans on April 19, 1730.

Baudoin, R. Père Michel, S.J. (1691–1692; 1766–1768)

Born in Quebec, he sailed to Louisiana around 1728 and lived for eighteen years as a missionary among the Choctaw Indians, where he helped to maintain their close allegiance to the French. He served as a chaplain during the First Chickasaw War (1736). In 1749, he became superior of Jesuit missions, and then, in 1750, grand vicar of Louisiana, which was still administered through the Bishop of Quebec, as well as director of the Ursuline convent in New Orleans. He remained in the colony even after the Jesuits were expelled from Louisiana in the 1750s.

Beauharnois de la Boische, Charles, marquis de (1671–1749)

Governor of New France from 1726 to 1747, he led wars against the Fox Indians in the western Great Lakes region and began the offensives against the English in North America during the War of the Austrian Succession. He was a cousin of Jean-Frédéric Phélypeaux, comte de Maurepas, minister of the marine from 1723–1749.

Bégon de la Picardière, Michel, fils (1667–1747)

Although he was named intendant of New France in 1710, he did not sail for Quebec until 1712, where he served until 1726. During his first few years in Quebec, he enriched himself by buying up card money for less than its face value.

Belle-Isle [Belisle, Bellile], Charles-Louis-Auguste Fouquet, duc de (1684–1761)

The principle sponsor and protector of Dumont, who dedicated his prose memoir to him. With his partners Le Blanc, La Jonchère, and d'Asfeld, he invested in the colonization scheme of John Law. He was also implicated along with La Jonchère and Le Blanc in financial improprieties and imprisoned in the Bastille in 1724–1725, but he recovered his reputation and was named maréchal de France, the nation's highest military rank, in 1741. During the War of the Austrian Succession, he invaded Prague, only to be forced to retreat in the winter of 1742–1743. In August 1744, he was captured in Germany and held in England for a year. When the English forces attacked Lorient in 1746, he was leading French troops in Italy.

Bénard de la Harpe, Jean-Baptiste (1683–1765)

Born at Saint-Malo, he arrived in Louisiana in 1718 and, in the following five years, became an important explorer. His first expedition, from December 1718 to November 1719 up the Red River, established a post among the "Nassonites," or Caddo Indians, and continued overland into present-day Oklahoma, seeking a route to the Spanish colony of Santa Fe. The second expedition, from August to December 1721, was undertaken with Simars de Belleisle to search for survivors of the lost ship *Maréchal d'Estrées*. Dumont took part in the third expedition, from February to April 1722, on the Arkansas River. Bénard de la Harpe returned to France on the *Alexandre* in 1723. He was the author of several maps and of narratives of his voyages (BNF, MSS fr. 8989). A manuscript first published in 1831 under his name was based on a manuscript that is likely the work of Jean de Beaurain but based on Bénard de la Harpe's writings. [*FFL*, 2:1:22]

Berneval [Barnaval]

Sailed for Louisiana on the *Victoire* in 1718 as a lieutenant. Served as captain commandant of the Natchez post in 1721, when Dumont arrived there. He sided with Bienville in a dispute with Hubert and the officers of the Saint Catherines concession. Accused of malfeasance and dismissed in 1724, he returned to France the next year. According to Giraud, he "was accused of having sacrificed the Company's interests by estimating too low a price for the domain of Terre Blanche, which had been sold to the Le Blanc–Belle-Isle concessions. He was dismissed and banned from ever returning to the service" (*HLF*, V, 52–53). [*FFL*, 2:1:27]

Bessan, Arnaud de

Served in Louisiana 1728–1733 and possibly as late as 1737. Bessan is listed an ensign in 1728 and 1730 and as an adjutant major under Louboëy in the Natchez war of 1729–1731. He then appears as an adjutant major at New Orleans in 1731–1733. [*FFL*, 2:1:33–34]

Bienville, Jean-Baptiste Le Moyne de (1680–1767)

Born in Montreal, he was commandant and governor of the Louisiana colony for three separate periods: 1701–1713, 1718–1724 (sharing the post with his brother Sérigny in 1717–1718), and 1733–1743. A son of Charles Le Moyne de Longueuil et de Châteauguay and Catherine Thierry, he took part in naval expeditions in Canada led by his older brother d'Iberville and traveled with him on the first voyage to the mouth of the Mississippi River in 1699. He led an expedition against the Natchez in 1716 and was awarded the Croix de Saint Louis in 1717. Dumont reports the events of his command from 1719 until 1724, when he was replaced as governor due to the inquiry of royal commissioners La Chaise and Saunoy. After the Natchez massacre, Périer's leadership was discredited, and in the summer of 1732, the king reappointed Bienville as governor. [*FFL*, 1:4:15–26]

Bizard [Bisarre, Bizaire, Bizarre], Louis Hector

A Canadian from a Swiss family, he served in the Great Lakes region before obtaining a commission in Louisiana. He arrived on the *Dromadaire* in 1720. As a captain of a company in the Le Blanc concession, he replaced La Boulaye in April 1721 as commandant of Fort Saint-Pierre at Yazoo. Named captain in 1722, he was discharged in 1723, and Dumont reports that he died in that year. [*FFL* ("Bissard" and "Bizart" are likely the same man), 2:1:36]

Blanc [Leblanc], César de (1683–1763)

Sailed to Louisiana aboard the *Aurore* in 1719 and became captain of infantry in 1720. He was listed on a census as living at Biloxi in January 1721. Bienville appointed him a captain in 1734, and he served in Illinois and then as commandant of Natchitoches from 1746, following the death of Juchereau de Saint Denis, his father-in-law, until shortly before his own death. [*FFL*, 2:2:16–18]

Blancheron

This likely was the family name of a wigmaker who, on the census of 1726, is identified by the given name François Dizier (or Didier?), living in the rue Bourbon in New Orleans along with his wife, two children, one servant, and four other Frenchmen, who apparently were boarders. It seems that Dumont was a boarder in his household several years earlier.

Boisbriant [Boisbriand, Bois Brillant], Pierre Sidrac Dugué de, chevalier de (1675–1736)

A cousin of the Le Moyne family, he was born in Montreal, came to Louisiana with d'Iberville in 1699, and remained, occupying a number of positions: at a Company of the West post at Wabash from 1713–1717, as commandant of Mobile in 1717–1718, and then as commandant of Illinois, in 1719–1723, where he built Fort de Chartres. During a leave in Paris in 1717, he received a commission as royal lieutenant of Louisiana as well as a seat on the Superior Council. He served as governor and commandant of the colony from 1724–1727 during a hiatus between Bienville and Périer. He refused to cooperate with La Chaise, who helped to force his recall. Once back in France in 1728, he was demoted and banned from royal service. [*FFL*, 1:4:6–9]

Bonnaud, Arnaud

Secretary to Governor Bienville, warehouse manager at New Orleans, and, later, administrator for all the Louisiana concessions of Le Blanc and Belle-Isle. He came to Louisiana in 1717 as a scribe and helped to clear the concession at Bayagoulas called Le Buisson, one of the most prosperous in the colony. [*FFL*, 1:1:13–14]

Bourgmont [Bourgmond], Etienne Véniard de (c. 1675–1734)

A noted explorer of the Arkansas and Missouri Rivers and author of two memoirs and several maps based on his explorations. He sailed to Canada in 1695, possibly as a forced transportee. In 1706, he replaced Cadillac as commandant of Fort Pontchartrain at Detroit. He left that post after less than a year, however, and lived among the Indians. In 1712, he reemerged at Mobile with a plan to secure an alliance with France of several native nations along the Missouri River. He made another expedition up the Missouri for this purpose in 1714 and participated in the battles for Pensacola in 1719. He then sailed for France along with a son born to a Missouri Indian woman and, in 1720, he encountered Dumont at Lorient. Upon his arrival in France, he was given a commission as captain and awarded the Croix de Saint Louis and the title of commandant of Missouri, with the expectation that he would establish a post on the Missouri River for the Company of the Indies. He returned to America and succeeded in building Fort d'Orléans, some 450 km from the mouth of the river near the present-day town of Carrollton, Missouri, where archaeologists have located remains of the fort. He returned to France in 1725; at first, he was to embark on the *Bellone*, and after it sank, he sailed on the *Gironde*. With him traveled a delegation of Indians, and all were feted at Fontainebleau by the duc de Bourbon. Bourgmont was presented to the king, who elevated him to the noble rank of *écuyer*. The memoirs of his explorations were first published in *Histoire de la Louisiane*, III, 141–221. [*FFL*, "Véniard de Bourgmont," 2:6:59–60]

Brancas, Louis, marquis de (died in 1750)

A military leader since 1690, he was France's ambassador to Spain in 1713 and in that capacity participated in the Treaty of Utrecht with Spain, Savoy, Portugal, and Holland. He was reappointed as ambassador to Spain in 1727. In 1738, he became commandant of Brittany, and in 1741, a maréchal de camp.

Breteuil [Bretiville], François Victor le Tonnelier de (1686–1743)

Appointed in 1721 as *prévôt* and master of ceremonies to the king, he served a first stint as minister of war, from 1723–1726, when he was replaced by Claude Le Blanc. But in 1740, he returned to that post after the death of Dangervilliers and thus was minister of war during France's involvement in the War of the Austrian Succession.

Brosset, Michel

Arrived in Louisiana on the *Duchesse de Noailles* in 1718, then on the *Seine* on a second voyage in 1720. He is listed as a surgeon and a resident of New Orleans from 1726–1732. His name also appears as the godfather in a baptism in 1753.

Broutin [Brontin], Ignace-François (died in 1751)

An engineer, cartographer, and surveyor, he arrived in Louisiana on the *Alexandre* in 1720 with a commission as a half-pay captain in the troops of the Le Blanc / Belle-Isle concessions. He served as commandant at Fort Rosalie in 1726–1727, where (Dumont writes) Broutin delegated many responsibilities to Dumont. As engineer, Broutin replaced Pauger and thus was responsible for repairing the fortifications at Natchez as well as for several projects around New Orleans. He is further known for his remarkably accurate building plans and maps of Natchez and other regions. His son Ignace also served as an engineer in the colony. [*FFL*, 5:1:6–9]

Bru [Brut], Louis

He was appointed chief commissary for the Company of the Indies at New Orleans in 1723 by La Chaise and the third ranking member of the Superior Council in 1726. Later, he was acting chief commissary at Mobile.

Brulé [Bruslé], Antoine-Philippe

A Parisian, he was the chief judge of the Superior Council of Louisiana and the *conseil de la régie* from 1722–1731. He was linked by marriage to the head prosecutor Fleuriau. Named general director for the Company of the Indies in Louisiana in 1730, he succeeded his close ally La Chaise. [*FFL*, 1:3:4]

Buchet [Buchette], Joseph (died after 1759)

A wealthy habitant and warehouse manager in Illinois, first at Kaskaskia and then at Fort de Chartres. He later served as acting chief commissary and as judge in the Illinois country from 1748 to 1760. [*FFL*, 1:1:14–15]

Buissonnière, Alphonse (died in 1740)

Listed as a half-pay lieutenant at Natchez in 1730, he was soon promoted to captain and then to major. Served as a major at Illinois from 1734 to 1736 and earned the praise of Bienville and of Beauchamp, the adjutant major at Mobile. He survived the Second Chickasaw War but died at Illinois in December 1740. [*FFL*, 2:1:56]

Cahura-Joligo (died in 1731)

The Tunicas were living on the Yazoo River when two missionary priests of the Quebec Seminary, François de Montigny and Antoine Davion, arrived in 1702 and earned the friendship of their leader, Cahura-Joligo. The missionaries were expelled around 1703 but later returned. When the French fought a brief war with the Natchez in 1716, the Tunica assisted French soldiers and officers, including the memoirist André Pénicaut. As Dumont reports, the "Chef des Tonicas" was a loyal ally of the French all through the 1720s. In the aftermath of the Natchez uprising in 1729, however, a group of refugee Natchez attacked the Tunica village and killed him.

Carpeau de Montigny [Carpot de Montigny]

Commissioned sublieutenant in 1719 and as a captain in 1720, with these comments next to his name: "He is at Pensacola. He has a drinking problem but promises to correct it." (*FFLa*, I, 142) He returned to France in 1723 with his uncle, Bénard de la Harpe. [*FFL*, 2:1:60]

Cavagnial
See Vaudreuil de Cavagnial

Cazeneuve, M. de (died in 1728)
Listed as an ensign in 1720 and as lieutenant at Natchez under Berneval in 1721 and under Merveilleux in 1727–1728. [*FFL*, 2:61]

Céleron de Blainville [Céloron de Blainville], Pierre Joseph (1693–1759)
Born at Montreal, commissioned as a lieutenant in 1731, he was commandant of the fort at Michilimackinac when Bienville launched the Second Chickasaw War. He led a detachment of some two hundred Canadians and three hundred native Americans to join this failed offensive. Afterward, he was transferred to Detroit and awarded the Croix de Saint Louis in 1741. Between 1750 and 1753, he led expeditions into the Ohio valley to consolidate the allegiance of native nations against the English. [*FFL*, 2:1:61–62]

Chamilly, François-Jacques Bouton, comte de (1663–1722)
Nephew of a more famous maréchal de France, Noël Bouton de Chamilly, he rose to the ranks of maréchal de camp in 1702 and then lieutenant general, as well as governor of La Rochelle, in 1704.

Champmeslin [Chamelain, Chamelin], Desnos de
Commandant of the French fleet that sailed to attack the Spanish at Pensacola in 1719, he was also chosen as commandant of a planned expedition to attack Havana in 1723. [*FFL*, 2:1:66]

Chateaugué [Chateauguay], Antoine Le Moyne de (1683–1747)
A brother of d'Iberville and Bienville, he arrived in Louisiana in 1703 as a captain and was involved in illicit commerce with Havana and New Spain. He received a commission as a second royal lieutenant in 1718 and commanded Fort Pensacola while it was under French control. He was awarded the Croix de Saint Louis in 1721, returned to France in 1726, and later served in Martinique and Cayenne. Later in life, he was governor of Ile Royale (Cape Breton Island) and died at Rochefort. [*FFL*, 1:4:26–28]

Chavannes [Chavanne], Jean-Baptiste de
Sailed with Dumont on the *Marie* in 1719, having been sent to the colonies under a lettre de cachet. He rose to be secretary of the Superior Council of Louisiana and to the conseil de la régie from 1723–1729 but was recalled to France by orders of Périer in 1729. Nonetheless, he appears to have stayed in Louisiana, married Marie-Thérèze Fichou in New Orleans in 1730, and lived on a farm just upstream of the city during the 1730s. [*FFL*, 1:3:8]

Chepart [Detchéparre, Etchepar, Chepare, Chepar]
    He arrived in Louisiana on the *Duc de Noailles* in 1719 as a lieutenant, but his given name is unknown. Dumont reported that he was of Basque origin. He was promoted to captain in 1723 and wounded at Natchez in a duel with Jean-François Pasquier. In 1728, he was named commandant of Fort Rosalie at Natchez. Broutin, Dumont, Le Page du Pratz, and others blamed him for provoking the catastrophic Natchez attacks of 1729, which cost Chepart his life. [*FFL*, "de Chépart," 2:2:24–25]

Clairambault, Charles-Alexis
    Commissaire ordonnateur of the navy at Port-Louis from 1742–1761.

Coëtlogon, Louis-Emmanuel, comte de (born in 1709)
    Commissioned as a half-pay lieutenant in 1720 and as captain of a company in 1722 (at age thirteen), he led a distinguished military career in the War of the Austrian succession, part of it under Belle-Isle at Prague and then in Brittany, where, in 1746, he commanded at Lorient and Port-Louis in the absence of Governor Rothelin.

Couillard
    In the *Mémoires historiques*, this is the name of the carpenter (charpentier) who was logging cypress trees along the Mississippi opposite Natchez at the time of the revolt. Périer wrote that he was one of the first two people to bring news of the massacre to New Orleans.

Coustilhas [Coustillars], Jacques de (died in 1738 or 1739)
    Came to Louisiana on the *Union* in 1719 as a sublieutenant and in 1720 advanced to lieutenant. In the 1720s, he owned a farm on the left bank of the Mississippi just below New Orleans. Served as captain and commandant of the Natchez post in 1732–1733 and participated in the First Chickasaw War as well as the Second, when he assisted in the construction of Fort de l'Entrepos. Following his death, the Superior Council heard protracted disputes over his debts and estate. [*FFL*, 2:1:84–85]

Couturier, Louis
    Listed among soldiers serving the Company of the West who embarked on the *Victoire* in 1718. [*FFL*, 4:2:69]

Crenay [Crenet], Henri de Poilvilain, baron de (died in 1736)
    A captain under Louboëy, royal lieutenant at Mobile from 1730, and commandant of the post at the Alabamons in 1732–1733. He drew a fine manuscript map of Louisiana. [*FFL*, "de Crenay," 2:2:24–25]

Crozat [Croisac, Croizac], Antoine
    Born into a family of merchants in Toulouse, he became a very wealthy financier and patron of the arts. In 1712, the king granted him a fifteen-year monopoly for trade with Louisiana but ended it in 1717, when it was turned over to Law and the Company of the Indies.

Dangervilliers [d'Angervilliers], Nicolas Prosper Bauyn (died in 1740)
Served as French minister of war from 1728 to 1740.

Delagarde
Came to Louisiana on the *Gironde* in 1720 and served as a warehouse keeper and manager of the concession at Pascagoula, owned by Chaumont. A New Orleans census of 1727 indicated that he also owned a residence on Chartres Street. [*FFL,* "La Garde," 1:1:51]

Deliette [de Liette], Pierre Charles (died in 1729)
A brother of Charles-Henri Joseph de Liette, he was from an Italian family and a cousin of Henri and Alphonse Tonty. He was commandant in the Illinois country from 1704 to 1718 and was commissioned as a lieutenant in 1718 and a captain in 1720, but then resigned and returned to Montreal. During his time in Illinois, he wrote the "Mémoire de De Gannes" preserved as part of a large, four-volume manuscript held at the Newberry Library (Ayer MS 293, III, 264–362). It was published in *Illinois Historical Collections,* XXIII (Springfield, Ill., 1934), 302–395. Later, he served briefly as commandant at Natchez in 1723 and returned to Illinois in 1725 until his death. [*FFL,* "Desliettes," 2:2:54]

Delisle
See Simars de Belleisle

Delorme (died in 1729)
He came to Louisiana on the *Alexandre* in 1720 and was a director of the Company of the Indies until December 1722. As Dumont indicates, he was dismissed from his post due to accusations of corruption and smuggling. Nevertheless, the Company appointed him to a new commission in 1729, but he died at Saint-Domingue on the way back to Louisiana. [*FFL,* 1:1:28–29, 1:3:11]

Deschamps, Charles-Etienne
Royal lieutenant at Port-Louis from 1746 to 1752, replacing Ricquebourg.

Deslos
A Canadian and a cousin of Bienville, he participated with Dumont in the establishment of Old Biloxi in 1719 under Valdeterre. In a 1721 census, he is listed as living in the region of Chaouachas and the English Turn, with no wife or children but one Indian and six African slaves. In a 1726 census, he is residing in the same location as owner of seventy arpents of cultivated land, as well as nine Indian and thirty African slaves.

Desnoyers [de Noyers, Denoyers], Laurent (died in 1729)
A second sergeant at Yazoo in 1722, then adjutant major and manager of the Terre Blanche concession at Natchez at the time of the revolt. [*FFL,* 2:2:55]

Desnoyers, Madame

The wife of Laurent Desnoyers, she spoke the Natchez and/or Mobilien language well, and following the Natchez revolt, she served as an interpreter during the siege of 1730. After the death of her first husband, she married one Sieur Joye, nicknamed Rougeau, or Roujot.

Diron d'Artaguiette [d'Artaguette], Bernard

Younger brother of Martin d'Artaguiette, they arrived in Louisiana together on the *Renommé* in 1707. He was appointed lieutenant in 1716 and captain in 1717 and became a concessionaire at Baton Rouge. He was a director of the Company of the Indies at La Rochelle when Dumont sailed from that port in 1718. From 1728–1738, he was commandant at Mobile, and then he quarrelled with Bienville over policy toward the Chickasaws and relocated to Saint-Domingue. His narrative of his voyage up the Mississippi to Natchez was published in translation in 1916 ("Journal of Diron d'Artaguiette, Inspector General of Louisiana, 1722–1723," in Newton D. Mereness, ed., *Travels in the American Colonies* [New York, 1916], 15–92). [*FFL*, 2:2:71–74]

Drouard, Sieur

Employed by the Company of the Indies as a carpenter, 1728. [*FFL*, 6:2:36]

Ducouder [Ducoud, Decoder, Ducauder]

He was commissioned as a lieutenant in 1720 and was commandant at Yazoo in 1729 when he was killed in the Natchez revolt. His brother Pierre-Laurent was a second lieutenant in 1736 when he was captured by the Chickasaws. [*FFL*, "Docoder," 2:2:74]

Ducuir

He was listed in 1722 and 1731 as a habitant at Pointe Coupée on the Mississippi.

Dufour

Captain of a Company of the Indies vessel, the *Portefaix*, armed at Lorient on February 22, 1721, and destined for Louisiana.

Dufresne [Dufreine, du Freine], Bertrand

Director of John Law's concession near the mouth of the Arkansas River beginning in March 1722, when he arrived there with Bénard de la Harpe and Dumont. He voyaged to Louisiana on the *Venus* from Lorient in 1721, attached to the Mezières concession. He appears on a list of Company of the Indies employees in March 1724, at the Arkansas post.

Dugué, François

A Canadian who arrived in Louisiana in 1708. In a 1721 census, he is listed as a habitant at Bayou Saint John, where he owned three African and three Indian slaves.

Dumanoir [Du Manoir], Jean-Baptiste Faucon

Manager of the Saint Catherines concession at Natchez in the 1720s. In 1720, he embarked on the *Saint André*, bound for Louisiana from Lorient, listed as an officer and as the director of the concession of Mssrs. Deucher and Coëtlogon. Upon arrival, he became the resident director of the Saint Catherines concession, later owned by Kolly, with more than one hundred arpents of land.

Dumont, Jean-François, Geneviève, Marie-Anne-Françoise, Pierre-Jean-Baptiste

See "The Dumont Family," above.

Dumont de Montigny, Jean-François-Benjamin

The author is included in *FFL*, 2:2:90.

Dumouchel de Villainville, Claude

A nephew of Marc-Antoine Hubert, he came to Louisiana in 1716 as ensign and became a captain in 1719. He replaced Valdeterre as captain of a company in 1720. He was reproved by Périer for cowardice during the Natchez war of 1730. [*FFL*, 2:2:91]

Dupart, Jean-Baptiste (died c. 1742–1744)

Captain in a Swiss regiment, he also held a commission as a lieutenant from Rochefort in 1722. He took part in the First Chickasaw War and died at New Orleans. [*FFL*, 2:2:92–93]

Dupuis

Listed as an ensign in 1722, he rose to the rank of adjutant major for troops of the Company of the Indies by 1727. [Possibly the father among the father and son who appear under "Dupuy Planchard," *FFL*, 2:2:96–97]

Dusablon

A soldier listed in a 1726 census as a resident of Illinois, married and owning five arpents of land.

Dutisné, Claude-Charles (died in 1730)

Born in about 1690 in Paris, he came to Quebec in 1705 with a commission as an ensign. In 1708, he married Marie-Anne Gaultier de Gaudarville, who brought him the title of Seigneur de Gaudarville from her first husband and left it to him when she died in 1711. He remarried two years later, and his second wife accompanied him when he was assigned to the post at Kaskaskia in Illinois. In addition to service at Wabash and Kaskaskia, he helped to establish Fort Rosalie at Natchez in 1716 and served as commandant there from 1723–1726. According to a letter by Father Raphaël de Luxembourg, who claimed that Dumont had written him with the information, Dutisné was homosexual. He escaped the Natchez Massacre because he had been assigned to command Fort de Chartres in the Illinois country in 1729, but he died shortly afterward from wounds sustained in an attack by Fox (Renard) Indians.

Dutisnet [du Tisné, Dutissenet], Louis-Marie-Charles (died in 1736)

The son of Claude-Charles and his first wife, he served in Illinois for some years and led a convoy from the Missouri River country to Fort de Chartres in 1725. Married the widow of one Girardot in 1731 and was chosen to accompany Pierre Groston de Saint-Ange to Missouri in 1734. In March 1736, he was part of the expedition of Pierre d'Artaguiette against the Chickasaws, where he lost his life. [*FFL*, 2:2:103]

Duverger, Bernard (died in 1766)

A native of Béarn in southwestern France, he came to Louisiana in 1720 and was commissioned as an engineer and half-pay lieutenant in 1724. Served at that rank in the siege of the Natchez in 1730. Took leave in France in 1730–1733 and, on his return, was commissioned as a captain and engineer. With Broutin, he surveyed routes for French troops to approach the Chickasaw villages in the Second Chickasaw War and was held partly responsible for the failure of that campaign. Nonetheless, he remained in the colony, working at La Balize and elsewhere, and was appointed chief engineer in 1752 and awarded the Croix de Saint Louis. [*FFL*, "de Vergés," 6:1:11–15]

Enville [Anville], Jean-Baptiste-Louis-Frédéric de la Rochefoucauld de Roye, duc d' (1704–1746)

In spite of scant experience at sea, his aristocratic pedigree and the influence of Maurepas (minister of the marine) earned d'Enville an appointment as lieutenant general of the navy in 1745. The following year, he was placed in command of a large expedition to recapture the fortified city of Louisbourg, and, with it, the rest of Acadia, from the English. Storms, illness, and all-around misfortune led to the deaths of more than two thousand troops as well as d'Enville himself.

Estivant de la Perrière [Lestievant de la Perriere]

Warehouse keeper at the Yazoo post in 1722 and, later, at the Company of the Indies warehouse in New Biloxi. Possibly the same as Estienne de la Perrière, who served as an engineer at New Orleans in 1719.

Femme Chef, of the Natchez

The Natchez had a matrilineal, exogamous kinship structure under which the husband of the *femme soleille*, or female Sun (chief), was from the lowest caste—the stinkards—but their son was in line to be the future male Sun, or Great Chief, as Dumont calls him. Dumont wrote that his own future wife, Marie Baron, was held prisoner by the female chief during the winter of 1729–1730. However, Le Page du Pratz, whose account of the 1729 massacre agrees with Dumont's in other respects, identified the femme soleille as Bras Piqué, whom he knew at Natchez and spoke with in New Orleans when she was captured by the French in 1730. He even claimed that the Grand Soleil at the time of the revolt was her son by a French father. Dumont does not give any proper name for the *femme chef*, so it is impossible to know whether the two authors referred to the same woman.

Feret [Ferret], Charles

Captain of the Company of the Indies vessel *Les Deux Frères,* armed at La Rochelle on July 22, 1720, with the initial destination of Lorient.

Fleuriau, François (died in 1752)

The son of a prosecutor in Rennes, he became a magistrate at parlement and then, in 1723, was named crown prosecutor for Louisiana. He was also a member of the Superior Council, but he quarreled with La Chaise. He married and lived in the colony until his death.

Frédérique

A surgeon at Natchez from 1726 to 1728. His house appears on Dumont's map of the area ("Carte du fort Rozalie des Natchez françois," ANF, Cartes et plans, N III, no. 1² [Louisiane]). He moved to Illinois in 1732.

Fulvy

A director of the Company of the Indies from 1734. Dumont encountered him in Paris after Dumont returned from Louisiana.

Girardy, Joseph

A habitant at Bayou Saint John just outside New Orleans, he is listed in a 1721 census as having a wife and two children, and owning ten African and two Indian slaves.

Graveline, Jean-Baptiste Baudreau dit

A Canadian who came to Louisiana in the colony's early days and established himself on Dauphin Island, then at Pascagoula, where he had a large concession. He was later one of the first habitants on the Bayou Saint John. In 1726, the Superior Council granted him a large concession there, and he supervised work to make the bayou navigable for larger boats.

Graves [Grave, de Graves]

Captain of a company in the troops of the Le Blanc / Belle-Isle concessions, in which Dumont was a lieutenant, during the voyage to Yazoo in 1721. In 1723, he abandoned his post at Yazoo to become a manager of the Le Blanc / Belle-Isle concession at Natchez. He was accused of selling Company of the Indies merchandise for his own personal profit. [*FFL,* "Graves," 2:3:30, and "Desgraves," 2:2:53]

Grondel, Jean-Philippe Goujon de (1714–1807)

Born in Saverne in Alsace of Swiss parents in 1714, he came to Louisiana in 1732 along with his father, who was also an officer in Karrer's Swiss regiment. He was celebrated in the colony for his gaiety, his duels, and his daring. As Dumont writes, he was seriously wounded in the 1736 Chickasaw war, but contrary to Dumont's report, it appears Grondel did not die of these wounds. He was made captain in 1750 and awarded the Croix de Saint Louis. He married a daughter of the elder Dutisné. In the 1760s, he quarreled with then-governor Kerloret and returned to France; Kerloret pursued the grudge and had him imprisoned in the Bastille, but he was quickly exonerated. Toward the end of his long life, he was a strong supporter of Napoleon Bonaparte. [*FFL*, "Goujon de Gondel," 2:3:25–29]

Guenot de Tréfontaine [Guenaut], Pierre (died in 1723)
 Along with his brother, Guenot was an investor in Law's scheme and came to Louisiana in 1717 on the *Paon* or the *Duclos*. In 1719, they were clearing a plantation in Chopitoulas. After selling that concession, he became a deputy director of the Saint Catherines concession at Natchez, where he supervised the planting of tobacco. In October 1722, he was wounded in a Natchez attack in a forest between Fort Rosalie and the concession, and he died a few months later at New Orleans. According to both Bienville and Dumont, he had provoked this attack by imprisoning one of the Natchez Suns.

Heudicourt, Gœuri Sublet, marquis d'
 The marquis who, alongside l'Hôpital, advocated the surrender of Lorient was likely Gœuri Sublet, comte d'Heudicourt and then, after 1737, marquis d'Heudicourt.

Hombourg [Domsbourg], Jean-Frédéric, baron d'
 An Alsatian who commanded one of the Swiss regiments deployed in Louisiana in the 1720s.

Hôpital, marquis de l'
 Commander of a regiment of dragoons, he organized the defense of Lorient in 1746.

Hubert, Marc-Antoine
 Commissaire ordonnateur of Louisiana in 1716, he became, after the end of Crozat's control of the colony, the director general under the Company of the West and then commissaire ordonnateur once again in 1718–1720. In 1719, he decided to take up residence at Natchez, where Bienville and Le Gac had granted him a concession, later known as Saint Catherines. In 1720, he sold this property to Kolly, and Le Page du Pratz brokered the sale. He returned to France in 1722, penniless, and requested a pension from the Company of the Indies. [*FFL*, 1:1:50]

Iberville, Pierre Le Moyne d' (1661–1706)
 The third son of Charles Le Moyne de Longueuil et de Châteauguay and Catherine Thierry, d'Iberville earned fame for leading naval expeditions against the English in Hudson Bay and Newfoundland. In 1698–1699, he led an expedition to locate the mouth of the Mississippi River and constructed a fort at Biloxi, leaving behind a garrison led by his younger brother Bienville. On a second voyage in 1700, he established a temporary fort on the Mississippi River, and a third expedition in 1701 led

to the founding of Mobile. He left Louisiana for the last time in 1702 but was active in the defense of France's Caribbean colonies until his death at Havana, Cuba. [*FFL*, 1:4:30–33]

Japy [Jaspie]

Elie Jaspie is listed as captain of the *Marie*, a Company of the Indies ship armed at La Rochelle on May 15, 1719, bound for Louisiana.

Joly Coeur, Louis Colet dit

A sergeant responsible for a fire that destroyed eleven houses at Old Biloxi in the winter of 1720–1721. A 1727 New Orleans census lists a woman named "Colier" and a sergeant called "Jollycoeur" living together in the rue Clairemont with two children.

Juchereau de Saint Denis, Louis (1676–1744)

Born in Quebec, he accompanied d'Iberville on his second voyage to Louisiana. From 1700 to 1712, he explored the basins of the Red and Ouachita Rivers, and in 1713, Lamothe Cadillac, then governor of Louisiana, put him in charge of an expedition that established a post at the site of modern Natchitoches, Louisiana. From there, he continued to the Spanish garrison of San Juan Bautista (today's Piedras Negras, Mexico). Dumont recounted the story of his imprisonment in Mexico City at the end of the memoir, as did Le Page du Pratz (*Histoire de la Louisiane*, I, 1–24) and Pénicaut (*Fleur de Lys and Calumet*, 146–153, 183–203, 220–227). During the battles with the Spanish in 1719, he was active in the defense of Mobile and the retaking of Pensacola. After some of the Natchez fled to the Natchitoches area in 1730, his garrison attacked and dispersed them. He continued to live at the Natchitoches post until his death. [*FFL*, 2:3:58–61]

Juif, Jean-Claude (died in 1723)

In spite of his name, which means "the Jew," he was a Catholic chaplain for the LeBlanc / Belle-Isle concession at Yazoo. He sailed to Louisiana with Le Blond de la Tour and soldiers on the *Dromadaire* in 1720.

Juzan, Gabriel de (died in 1736)

A half-pay lieutenant under Périer, he mounted an expedition up the Ouachita River in 1732–1733 to track down refugee Natchez. He served as an adjutant major at Mobile and at Dauphin Island in 1734 and under Noyan in the First Chickasaw War. In Dumont's epic poem, he is mortally wounded in this war but gives a rousing speech to inspire Dumont and other troops. In June 1736, the Superior Council assigned a tutor to his son Pierre. [*FFL*, 2:3:63–64]

Kerloret [Kerlorec], chevalier de

The man Dumont mentions is, not Louis Billouart de Kerlérec, governor of Louisiana in 1752–1763, but a commandant of troops who sailed to Louisiana on the *Atlas* in 1739 to participate in the Second Chickasaw War. [*FFL*, 2:3:65]

Kolly, Jean-Daniel (died in 1729)
Director of the Saint Catherines concession at Natchez, which he purchased from Hubert in 1721. Kolly invested a large sum of money in John Law's scheme but was one of only a few concessionaires to travel to Louisiana to attempt to recoup his losses. As Dumont reports, he and his son were both killed in the Natchez revolt.

La Boulaye (died in 1732)
Obtained a commission as a sublieutenant in 1720, replacing Andriot. He traveled to the Arkansas River in 1721 to establish a concession, which Dumont visited in February 1722. Promoted to lieutenant in 1730, he was discharged in the year of his death. [FFL, 2:4:2–3]

La Chaise, Jacques de (1675–1730)
Nephew of the confessor of Louis XIV, Père La Chaise, for whom the famous cemetery in Paris is named, he was chosen by the Council of the Marine in 1722 to go to Louisiana together with Saunoy to audit the finances of the Company of the Indies. He arrived in April 1723 and served on the Superior Council and conseil de la régie. He died in New Orleans, and his son continued to serve in various influential positions in Louisiana. [FFL, "de la Chaise," 1:1:26]

La Corne de Chaptes, Jean-Louis de (1666–1732)
A major at Trois-Rivières in 1714 and at Quebec in 1716, he became royal lieutenant at Montreal in 1726.

La France, Jacques Joignier dit
According to a 1716 census of Quebec, he ran an inn in the Upper Town, on the rue de Buade.

La Galissonnière, Roland Barrin de
The father of Roland-Michel Barrin de la Galissonnière (1693–1756), who was commandant general of New France during the 1740s.

La Garde, Joseph de
Major de la place in Lorient and Port-Louis in the 1720s.

La Jeunesse (died in 1729)
Father Philibert's list of the victims of the Natchez uprising includes "Pierre Billy, dit La Jeunesse," likely the man who traveled with Dumont.

La Jonchère, Gérard-Michel de (1675–1750)
Rich financier and partner with Belle-Isle, d'Asfeld, and Le Blanc in several concessions in Louisiana. In 1711, he was appointed *trésorier de l'extraordinaire des guerres*, a post empowered to collect reparations from defeated enemies and called "extraordinary" inasmuch as it operated outside the ministry of finance. A commis-

sion appointed to investigate his finances found that he had used the post to enrich himself, and in 1723, he was arrested, ordered to repay more than one million livres, and banned from holding financial appointments. For two years, he was imprisoned in the Bastille, where he nonetheless enjoyed his own furniture and library, wrote a journal, and maintained correspondence. He later held the post of treasurer of the Royal and Military Order of Saint Louis.

La Pointe, Joseph Simon dit

A Canadian habitant who, after the end of Crozat's administration of the Louisiana colony, built a house on the Pascagoula River, which is identified on the maps Dumont drew of that region ("Carte de la riviere de Pascagoula . . . ," BNF, Ge DD 2987, and "Carte de la riverre des Pascagoulas . . . ," ANF, Cartes et plans, 6 JJ 75, collection Delisle, pièce 262).

La Salle, Pierre de

A native of Carcassonne, Dumont wrote that La Salle sailed over with him on the *Portefaix* as a simple soldier, but he quickly rose to be a warehouse keeper at New Biloxi. He appears in a March 8, 1724, list of employees of the Company of the Indies in Louisiana as being at Biloxi and receiving a salary of six hundred livres. His death and burial were registered at New Orleans December 9, 1728, at about fifty-six years of age. [*FFL*, 1:1:57]

Lavigne

A habitant at Bayou Saint John. His residence is indicated on one of Dumont's maps of the New Orleans area ("Carte de la province de la Louisiane," SHD, Château de Vincennes, receuil 68, no. 74).

Law, John (1671–1729)

Born in Edinburgh, he came to France in 1715 to offer his services to the regent Philippe d'Orléans after the death of Louis XIV. The French national debt was enormous, and Law was given authority to create a national bank and issue currency that would replace the gold coin in circulation. In 1717, he obtained, for a twenty-five-year term, the monopoly privileges of the Company of the West formerly held by Antoine Crozat, with the understanding that he would settle the Louisiana colony with at least six thousand Europeans and three thousand African slaves and thus provide a buffer against Spanish and English influence in the region. Capitalization for this enterprise was set at two hundred thousand shares paying 4 percent dividends. The operation enabled Law to retire sixty million livres of state debt. The shares in his company rose quickly, creating the so-called Mississippi Bubble, inflated by promotional tracts that created an image of Louisiana as a paradise with abundant mineral wealth. However, in the autumn of 1720, the scheme collapsed, along with the South Sea Bubble, which burst at the same time in England. An economic depression spread across Europe; Law fled France and died in Venice.

Le Blanc

A "Jacques White, dit Le Blanc" purchased a house in Port-Louis in 1735, at 15 rue des Dames.

Le Blanc, Louis-Claude (1669–1728)

Son of Louis Le Blanc, intendant of Normandy, he was named to the council of war in 1716 and assumed the post of minister of war upon the dissolution of the polysynodie system in 1718. He entered into partnership with Belle-Isle and La Jonchère to invest in concessions in Louisiana under Law's scheme in 1719. When La Jonchère was accused of financial corruption in 1723, Le Blanc was implicated and forced to resign. He was imprisoned for several months in the Bastille, but then acquitted. He served again as minister of war from 1726 until his death.

Le Blond de la Tour, Louis-Pierre (died in 1723)

An engineer who drew several fine maps of the colony, he arrived in Louisiana in 1714 and served as a lieutenant in Alabama in 1716. He quarreled with Governor Cadillac and returned to France, only to make a second voyage on the *Dromadaire,* along with one or two of his brothers. He led the troops assigned to the concessions of Le Blanc / Belle-Isle, in which Dumont served. As chief engineer in the colony in 1721, he supervised the planning of New Orleans. Died on board the *Bellonne* before the ship set sail for France. [*FFL,* 1:3:19, 2:4:25–27, and "Boispinel de Latour," his brother, 6:1:5–6]

LeBrun, François

A priest and professor of hydrography and mathematics at the Séminaire de Québec in the 1710s.

Le Gac, Charles

Arrived at Dauphin Island in 1718 as director in the colony for the Company of the Indies. As he writes in a memoir translated and published in 1970, he managed the Company during a difficult period, when hundreds of settlers arrived only to be left unsupported after the collapse of Law's financial scheme. [*FFL,* 1:1:60]

Léry [De Lery, Deléry] and Le Sueur

Dumont errs, both in the manuscript memoir [original pages 229–230] and in the *Mémoires historiques* (II, 171), in giving the name Léry to the officer who led the first expedition to retaliate against the Natchez in January and February 1730. That officer was actually Jean-Paul Le Sueur, a son of Pierre-Charles Le Sueur, who had voyaged the length of the Mississippi River in 1700 and who made the first accurate map of the river. Pierre-Charles's wife, the mother of Jean-Paul, was a cousin of Bienville. Léry, or Deléry, was an officer who played a key role in the First Chickasaw War, according to Bienville's narrative of that war, which also mentions Jean-Paul Le Sueur. For more, see Chapter 6, n. 17, below. [*FFL,* "De Léry," 2:2:34–36; and "Chauvin de Léry, 2:1:69–71. The two entries are nearly identical and must refer to one man.]

Loire des Ursins [la Loire des Urzins, La Loire], Antoine de la (died in 1729)
Another victim of the massacre, he had previously been the clerk of the Company of the Indies at Illinois, was serving at Natchez as Company clerk and as judge, and apparently had fathered children with his Natchez wife. According to Broutin and Diron d'Artaguiette, he had warned Chepart and even Périer of the danger of a revolt. [*FFL,* "Antoine de la Loire des Ursins," 1:1:28; "Marc-Antoine de la Loire des Ursins," 1:1:54–55; and "De la Loire des Ursins," 1:3:10, though it is not clear that these are three separate individuals]

Longraye [de Longraye, Delongray, des Longrais] (died in 1729)
Director of the Saint Catherines concession at Natchez following the attack on Pierre Guenot in October 1722 that set off a skirmish between the French and Natchez. Killed in the Natchez Massacre.

Louboëy [Loubois], Henri, chevalier de (died in 1749)
Served as an officer in France beginning in 1690 or 1691 and was sent to Louisiana in 1716. In 1721, he was listed as a captain and commander at Biloxi. In 1723, he was listed as the captain of a company at Mobile. In 1729, he received a commission as major of New Orleans. Led the first expedition against the Natchez following the uprising, December 1729–February 1730, and directed the siege of the Natchez forts. In 1731, he is listed as chevalier de Louboëy, royal lieutenant at New Orleans. On leave in France in 1735, he returned to Louisiana in 1737 and in 1740 was assigned to Mobile, where he died at an advanced age. [*FFL,* 2:4:46–51]

Lusser [Lucer], Joseph Christophe de (died in 1736)
Commissioned as an ensign in 1718, as lieutenant in 1720, and as captain in 1730. Périer ordered him to go to the Choctaws in 1730 to recruit warriors for an expedition against the Natchez. Served as captain commandant at Tombigbee in 1735 and was killed in the attack on Ackia. [*FFL,* 2:4:54–55]

Macarty de Mactigue, Jean-Jacques (c. 1706–1764)
Born in France of Irish parents and might have come to Louisiana in 1720 or as late as 1732. Listed as a musketeer, promoted to adjutant major in 1732, to captain in 1735, awarded the Croix de Saint Louis in 1750, and finally became royal lieutenant at New Orleans in 1759. During several return visits to France, he served as recruiter of soldiers to go to Louisiana. [*FFL,* 2:5:3–7]

Manadé (died in 1737 or 1738)
A surgeon at New Orleans, 1724–1728, and subsequently chief surgeon there. Manadé appears in the 1726 census as being married and owning forty arpents of land. [*FFL,* 6:2:19]

Mansillière [Mancelière], Jean Gravé de la
Captain of the Company of the Indies ship *Union,* which sailed from La Rochelle to Louisiana in 1719. Dumont mentions him again as commanding the *Venus* on its

voyage from Lorient in 1721, but he was instead listed as a passenger on that ship and an administrator of the Mezières concession. He immediately returned to France on the same ship. Nonetheless, a Mansillière is included in the 1732 census as a landowner in New Orleans.

Massé [Macé], Sieur de (died in 1729)
A close ally of Bienville and enemy of Périer. A lieutenant to Chepart at Natchez, where he and his wife were killed in the uprising. His eight-year-old son, who witnessed the killings, survived, was raised by Louboëy, and went on to a military career in the colony. [*FFL*, 2:5:17]

Maur de Tronquidy
Archives in Brittany have revealed that this was the name of M. Benier's clerk who was involved in a lawsuit with Dumont in 1747 concerning a debt that the latter had supposedly entered into while the two men were living in New Orleans. He came to Louisina on the *Gironde* in 1720 and was serving as an inspector in 1723. In 1727, he sold two lots and a house in New Orleans.

Merveilleux, François-Louis de
Came to Louisiana on the *Mutine* in 1720 as a captain in the Swiss Karrer regiment, organized by his older brother. The family name was "von Wunderlich" in German. His younger brother Jean-Pierre was a soldier in the regiment. In 1727, he was named commandant of the Natchez post, but after only a few months, he was replaced by Chepart. After the Natchez revolt, he was sent to warn residents along the Mississippi River. He returned to France in 1733–1734. Certain historians believe he is the author of the anonymous "Relation de la Lousiane" (VAULT Ayer MS 530, Newberry Library) as well as a short manuscript account of the Natchez revolt, held in Rheims. [*FFL*, 2:5:30–31]

Mesplet (died in 1730)
Listed as a native of Pau and among the victims of the Natchez Massacre, although he was actually killed in January 1730 when he volunteered to scout Natchez positions and try to release captives. His estate included 1,163 lbs. of tobacco, nine deerskins, tools, glassware, and a copy of a book described as "'Voyage to the South Sea' with prints." [*FFL*, "Misplet," 6:1:55]

Mezières [Mesierre, Mexierre, Mezierre], Louis Christophe or Claude Mauguet
This family was one of the major investors in Louisiana concessions under John Law's system and was related by marriage to Juchereau de Saint Denis. Dumont does not refer to any specific member of the family.

Miragouin
A Canadian and one of the first habitants on Dauphin Island. A neighboring island close to Mobile Bay was named after him, as well as a bayou in the Atchafalaya Basin.

Navarre (died in 1729–1730)

An officer who embarked on the *Profond* in 1720, bound for Louisiana from La Rochelle. He appears in a 1727 census as a surgeon at Mobile for the Company of the Indies. Dumont, in *Mémoires historiques*, II, 173–175, and Le Page du Pratz, in *Histoire de la Louisiane*, II, 266–267, both wrote that he spoke the Natchez language well and had a Natchez mate who helped him survive the initial revolt; but he subsequently died, along with Mesplet, in a sortie against the Natchez in 1730. [*FFL*, 6:2:20]

Nouailles [Nouailles d'Aymé]

Arrived from France in June 1739, as commandant of troops sent for the second war against the Chickasaws. He appears to have avoided any punishment for the failure of his expedition. [*FFL*, 2:5:50–51]

Noyan, Gilles-Augustin Payen de (died in 1751)

A lieutenant who arrived in Louisiana on the *Victoire* in 1718 and participated in the battles for Pensacola. A nephew of Bienville, he advanced the interests of his uncle during Périer's command of the colony. Married Jeanne Faucon Dumanoir in New Orleans on May 1, 1735. As commander of a detachment during the First Chickasaw War, he was wounded at Ackia in 1736. Received the Croix de Saint Louis in October 1736. Also served in the Second Chickasaw War and reached the rank of adjutant major and, finally, royal lieutenant by the time of his death in New Orleans, where he owned many properties. [*FFL*, "Payen de Noyan," 2:5:54–59]

Pailloux [Payou, Payon], Jacques Barbazon de

A native of the Cévennes and originally a Protestant. Served as major general of Louisiana, where he arrived in 1707, and led the construction of the first Fort Rosalie at Natchez in 1716–1717. In November 1722, Bienville named him to lead an expedition against the Natchez Indians, and he was involved in the battles in the fall of 1723 as well, though this led to his being punished and demoted. He returned to France in 1724. [*FFL*, "Barbazant de Pailloux," 2:1:10–11]

Papin (died in 1729)

Interpreter at Natchez, killed in the uprising there. Arrived in Louisiana on the *Chameau* in 1720, listed as an edge-tool maker employed at the concession of Dartagnan. A René Papin is listed in a census of 1726 as living at the concession of Le Page du Pratz in Natchez, with a wife and two children. [*FFL*, 6:1:27]

Pauger, Adrien (died in 1726)

Chief engineer for the Louisiana colony, he arrived in 1721 and helped to plan New Orleans as well as designed the first fort of La Balize at the outlet of the Mississippi River. He served on the Superior Council of Louisiana, received the Croix de Saint Louis, and was buried in New Orleans. [*FFL*, 6:1:20–21]

Penthièvre, Louis Jean Marie de Bourbon, duc de (1725–1793)

His full title was duc de Penthièvre, d'Aumale, de Rambouillet et de Gisors. Born at Rambouillet, he was the only son of Louis Alexandre de Bourbon (1678–1737), comte de Toulouse, duc de Penthièvre (a son of Louis XIV and of Madame de Montespan), and Marie Victoire de Noailles. He succeeded his father in the titles of Admiral of France and governor of Brittany in December 1737.

Périer, Etienne (1690–1755)

Born in Le Havre, he began his military career in the gardes de la marine in Brest in 1717. Later, he commanded a ship for the Company of the Indies. He was appointed commandant general of Louisiana in 1726 and arrived in March 1727 to replace Bienville. He requested for himself, and received, the Croix de Saint Louis. He responded to news of the Natchez Massacre by ordering African slaves and native allies to destroy the Chaouachas village just below New Orleans. With his brother, he led the attack on the Natchez at Sicily Island in modern Concordia Parish, Louisiana, in December of 1730. Was recalled to France in 1732 and resumed service as a ship's captain out of Brest until his death. [*FFL*, 1:4:37–38]

Périer de Salvert, Antoine

Brother of Etienne Périer, he was serving in Senegal before being sent to Louisiana in 1730–1732 to assist in the retaliations following the Natchez Massacre. After his time in Louisiana, he continued his service in the navy and rose to the rank of *chef d'escadre*. [*FFL*, 2:5:67]

Perrault, Etienne

Mayor of the city of Lorient from September 12, 1736, to March 11, 1762.

Perrier (died in 1718)

Named chief engineer of Louisiana in 1718 by the Company of the Indies and embarked on the *Victoire*. He died en route. [*FFL*, 6:1:22]

Petit de Livilliers [de Petit-Leuilliers], Charles (c. 1702–1738)

Baptised at Boucherville, Quebec, where his father was an officer in the marines. In 1720, he was commissioned as a sublieutenant and then a lieutenant, along with Dumont, in the troops assigned to the Le Blanc / Belle-Isle concessions. He appears in the census of 1724 at a habitation on the Mississippi in the German Coast area, listed as M. Petit de Livilliers, aged twenty-two, an officer from Canada, with a son, five negroes, and two Indians. He married Louise de Malbec, or Malbeque, at New Orleans in 1726. In 1736, he took part in the disastrous expedition of Pierre d'Artaguiette against the Chickasaw Indians. Killed in a duel with Macarty de Mactigue. [*FFL*, 2:5:67–68]

Petit Soleil (died in 1723)

A Natchez Sun, war chief of the Pomme village; also, he was a brother of Serpent Piqué and of the Great Sun of the Grand village. In the First Natchez War of 1716,

Bienville detained the three men as hostages, until Petit Soleil was sent off to kill and deliver up to Bienville the heads of three men said to be responsible for deaths of five Frenchmen. Petit Soleil was later identified by Bienville as one of the instigators of the 1723 conflict with French colonists. Whereas Dumont reports that he was killed by the Tunica chief Cahura-Joligo, the anonymous manuscript "Punishment of the Natchez in 1723" (BNF, MSS fr. 2550, 3–10) reports simply that he was one of two Natchez leaders killed next to the temple in the Pomme village or the Noyers (Jenzenaques) village in late October of that year.

Plessis
    Treasurer at Quebec, possibly Jean-Louis Plessy dit Bélair, a tanner and merchant born in Montreal in 1678.

Postillon (died in 1729)
    In Philibert's list of victims of the Natchez Massacre, he is identified as a soldier and a native of Abbeville. His wife survived and married an Aubergiste, an innkeeper (or a man who bore that as a name) from Avignon.

Poulain, Gabriel (died in 1729)
    Interpreter of Indian languages. A native of Paris, he is listed in a 1726 census with a wife, three "engages," and eight arpents of land. Killed in the Natchez uprising.

Poulain, Mme de
    Wife of the interpreter, she was wounded in the Natchez uprising but survived. She later married a man named Vandome.

Renault [Renaud], Philippe
    A surveyor and director of mines in the Illinois country from 1726 to the early 1730s. [FFL, 1:2:15]

Renaut d'Hauterive [Renaud] (c. 1696–1741)
    Came to Louisiana in 1720 on the Aventurier. Served as captain commandant at Yazoo and at Natchitoches in 1722–1724 but then returned to New Orleans. Fought in the battles against the Natchez in 1730. After returning to France for a leave in the early 1730s, he later served as a captain of grenadiers in the First Chickasaw War in 1736 and was wounded at Ackia. Recommended for the Croix de Saint Louis. Died at Saint Jean-Baptiste on the Mississippi River's German Coast. [FFL, 2:6:7–9]

Requiem
    Charles Requient, a locksmith or metalworker from Poitiers, is in a list of workers for the Company who embarked on the Dauphiné in 1719, bound for Louisiana from La Rochelle. The wife of a man named Requiem appears on a list of those who died at Old Fort Biloxi between 1720 and 1723. She died on January 14, 1721. [FFL, 6:2:55]

Ricard

Dumont reports that the Sieur Ricard was one who escaped the Natchez Massacre and brought news to New Orleans (*Mémoires historiques*, II, 149, 170). It may be his widow and child Richard who are included on Philibert's list of those killed in the Massacre.

Richebourg, Louis Poncereau de Chavagne de

Came to Louisiana in May 1713 as a half-pay captain, became a captain in 1714, and was part of Bienville's circle of trusted officers during a time when Bienville was opposed by Governor Cadillac. In 1716, Bienville sent him to Natchez, where he dealt with the first violent conflict with that tribe and helped establish the post there, events he detailed in his manuscript "Mémoire sur la première guerre des Natchez." Given the Croix de Saint Louis in 1717, he was named a captain of a company of soldiers under Chateaugué and fought under him in the battles for Pensacola in 1719. He accompanied Jean-Gaston, chevalier des Grieux, and Jérémie de Meschin to Havana with the prisoners taken in the first French attack on Pensacola, only to be imprisoned there himself. After he was ransomed, he was appointed royal lieutenant at New Orleans in 1722 but did not wish to serve there under Pailloux. Departed for France on the *Saint-André* in 1722, but that ship was also detained at Havana. Might have returned in 1723, for Giraud claims that he was captain of a company into which Bienville tried to put Dumont when he was broken in rank (*HLF*, IV, 365). [*FFL*, "Chavagne de Richebourg," 2:1:71–72]

Ricquebourg [Ricquebour], Sieur François Burin de (1674–1746)

Royal lieutenant and commandant at Port-Louis from 1722–1746. He was born in Ruis in Picardy and died in the citadel of Port-Louis.

Rigby [Ricqueby, Ricbic], Edouard (died in 1720)

A Scots Jacobite who fled to France and became an officer in the royal marines. John Law appointed him as a director of the Company of the Indies and as manager of the port of Lorient in 1719, and secured for him an appointment as royal lieutenant. He became involved in the fast-growing shipbuilding industry in Lorient and facilitated the emigration of poor German peasants who, just before the collapse of Law's scheme, were camping in the vicinity of the city in numbers as high as four thousand. He was recalled to Paris in November 1720, accused of corruption, and imprisoned in the Bastille, where he died.

Riter [Ritter], Henry (died in 1722)

He arrived in Louisiana on the *Eléphant* in 1720 and served as a sergeant at Yazoo. The story of how Chickasaws attacked his family's home was told by Dumont in the memoir and in the *Mémoires historiques* (II, 85–90), by Le Page in the *Histoire de la Louisiane* (II, 272–290), and by Beaurain in the *HJEFL* (330). [*FFL*, 3:2:81]

Rothelin [Rothelieu], Alexandre d'Orléans, marquis de

Louis XV appointed him as the military governor of Port-Louis on November 10, 1731. He later rose to maréchal de camp in 1734 and lieutenant general in 1748.

Roussin, Jean dit "le bourgeois"

As a habitant at Natchez, he is listed on a 1726 census with two children and no slaves. Although Dumont conceals Roussin's name, Dumont lived in his household near the Tioux village south of Natchez and became the second husband of Roussin's widow, Marie Baron. Roussin is listed, with one son, among the victims of the Natchez Massacre.

Saint Denis, Sieur Denis
  See Juchereau de Saint Denis

Sainte Claire
  See Sinclair

Saint Laurent, Jean-Baptiste Laurent de Montbrun (died in 1748)

A Canadian, he traveled from Illinois to Ackia as a volunteer during the First Chickasaw War. Later, he replaced Léry as leader of an expedition up the Yazoo River in 1738, served in the 1739 Chickasaw campaign, and reached the rank of half-pay lieutenant. [*FFL*, "Laurent de Montbrun" 2:4:18–19]

Saint Martin

Warehouse keeper at Dauphin Island in 1719 and a lieutenant in the militia during the First Chickasaw War in 1736. He was appointed acting commissary at Mobile in 1737. [*FFL*, 1:2:20]

Saint-Vallier [Saint Valier, Saint Valiers], Jean-Baptiste de la Croix de Chevrières de (1653–1727)

Appointed Bishop of Quebec following Mgr. François-Xavier de Montmorency-Laval and arrived in the colony in 1685. During the 1690s, he quarreled with his predecessor as bishop as well as with Governor Frontenac and with the Jesuits. But he also helped found the hospital in Quebec and continued to serve as bishop until his death.

Salmon [Salmont], Etienne Gatien (died in 1745)

Commissaire ordonnateur of the Louisiana colony and chair of the Superior Council there, beginning in 1731. Reprimanded by the ministry of the marine for mismanagement of the Chickasaw campaign of 1739–1740. Feuded with Bienville and Vaudreuil and left his post to return to France in 1744. [*FFL*, 1:2:20–23]

Saugeon [Saugon, Saujon], Cézard-Louis Campet, chevalier de

Commander of the *Deux Frères* and of the convoy including the *Achille*, *Mercure*, and *Content*, which departed Brest on November 22, 1719, to attack the Spanish at Pensacola. [*FFL*, 2:6:26]

Saunoy [Sauvoir, Sauvoy, du Sauvoir, de Saunoy] (died in 1723)
   One of the two royal commissioners sent to Louisiana in 1722, along with La Chaise. He died shortly after arriving in New Orleans. [*FFL*, "Sauvoy," 1:2:23]

Sérigny et de Loire, Joseph le Moyne de (1668–1734)
   Sixth son of Charles Le Moyne de Longueuil et de Châteauguay and Catherine Thierry, he entered service in the French navy at Rochefort in 1686. He saw combat in the Iroquois country, in Hudson Bay, and in the Caribbean, and first came to Louisiana in 1718 as co-commandant along with his brother Bienville. Dumont describes his role in the battles for Pensacola in 1719–1720, after which he was awarded the Croix de Saint Louis. He returned to France in 1723 and was appointed governor of Rochefort, where he died. [*FFL*, 1:4:29–30, and 2:6:33]

Serpent Piqué
   Natchez Sun, war chief of the Grand village, ally of the French, and arguably the most intriguing Natchez individual in the French history of the region. Dumont wrote at length in the *Mémoires historiques* of the funeral ceremonies following his death on June 1, 1725, and yet the manuscript memoir indicates that he was not in Natchez then and that he met with a living Serpent Piqué after that date. Based upon his description of the tattoo that was the source of the name "Serpent Piqué," it is likely that the name went with the office of war chief of that Natchez village.

Simars de Belleisle, François (died in 1763)
   Born at Fontenay-le-Comte, he received a commission as sublieutenant and embarked on the *Maréchal d'Estrées* from La Rochelle on August, 14, 1719. The ship went aground on the coast of Texas, and a pestilence broke out on board. He went ashore with four other men to try to reach a French post. They were captured by the Attakappas, a nation reputed to be cannibals. When Belleisle finally reached French Louisiana, he set down his adventures in a document first published by Margry, VI, 320–347, and translated into English by Henri Folmer in "De Bellisle on the Texas Coast," *Southwestern Historical Quarterly*, XLIV (1940), 204–231. Because of his knowledge of this swampy coastal region, he took part in a 1721 expedition under Bénard de la Harpe. He later was wounded in the wars against the Natchez in 1730 and again in the First Chickasaw War of 1736. He received the Croix de Saint Louis in 1752 but subsequently quarreled with Governor Kerlérec and was stripped of his rank. Returned to France in 1762 and died in Paris. [*FFL*, "Scimars de Bellile," 2:6:29–33]

Sinclair [Sainte Claire], James (1688–1762)
   Member of a noble Scots family, he was commissioned an ensign in 1694 at age six and became a captain in the Royal Scots by 1708. He rose through the ranks and was general of the British forces in Flanders during the War of the Austrian Succession in 1745. His career did not suffer very much from the failed siege of Lorient; he was defended by the philosopher David Hume, who later served as his secretary.

Tisserant [Tisserand], Louis

Arrived in Louisiana in 1720 and served as a warehouse keeper at Natchez and Biloxi. In a 1731 census, Tisserant is listed as being married, having five children and one servant and owning thirty-three African slaves. In a 1732 census of New Orleans, he is listed as a homeowner, though not as a resident on his land. [*FFL*, 2:6:42–43]

Tonty, Alphonse de (1685–1727)

Younger brother of Henri de Tonty (d. 1704); together, the two accompanied Robert Cavalier de La Salle. Alphonse was born in 1685 to Lorenzo de Tonty, Baron de Paludy, and Isabelle de Liette (or di Lietto, in Italian), and died at Detroit on November 10, 1727. He served as commandant of the French forts at Michilimackinac, Frontenac, and Pontchartrain (Détroit).

Traisnel [Trenelle, Grenelle], Louise-Madeleine, marquise de

Daughter and heir to French minister of war Claude Le Blanc. Upon her father's death in 1728, she became one of the associates in the partnership that owned several concessions in Louisiana, along with Belle-Isle, La Jonchère, and d'Asfeld.

Tunicas, Chef des

See Cahura-Joligo

Valdeterre, Prosper Drouot de

Traveled to Louisiana with Dumont on the *Marie* in 1719 and served as commandant of Biloxi in 1720. Sérigny wrote in a report that Valdeterre was always drunk and making speeches against the government. [*FFL*, "Druout de Valdeterre," 2:2:80]

Vauban, Sébastien Le Prestre de (1633–1707)

The most famous military architect in French history, designer of many citadels and forts during the reign of Louis XIV, who appointed him maréchal de France.

Vaudreuil [Vaudreuille], Philippe de Rigaud, marquis de (1643–1725)

Born in 1643, he came to Quebec in 1687 and served as governor general of New France from 1703 until his death. He was granted permission to return to France following the death of Louis XIV in 1715 but was back in Quebec in 1716, during the time of Dumont's sojourn there. He died at Quebec in 1725. His son, François-Pierre de Rigaud de Vaudreuil, later served as governor of Louisiana.

Vaudreuil de Cavagnial [Cavagnolle], Pierre de Rigaud, marquis de (1698–1778)

The fourth son of Philippe de Rigaud de Vaudreuil, Pierre began his military career as an ensign in the troops of the gardes de la marine at age ten and in 1711 was promoted to lieutenant. Two years later, his father sent him to deliver an annual report to the Court in Paris. He returned to Quebec in 1715 as a captain. In 1743, he was chosen as governor of Louisiana, replacing Bienville. He stayed until 1753, when he returned to Quebec as governor general of New France. He signed the capitulation of Montreal in 1760.

Vergne de Villeneuve, Simon de la (born 1722)

Dumont conceals his name, referring to him by his title as major de la place of Port-Louis, a rank signifying an administrator of a garrison. He was a captain in the regiment of the royal marines that played a key role in the French defense during the siege of Lorient in 1746. Henri-François Buffet, the historian of Port-Louis, confirmed that he "managed a large garden near the main gate, inside the main bastion, part of the royal domain" (Buffet, *Vie et société au Port-Louis des origines à Napoléon III* [Rennes, 1972], 32).

Vieux Poil

Natchez Sun, either of the Gris village or the Pomme village, who was killed in 1723, and his head delivered up to the French by Serpent Piqué. His name translates as "Old Hair." Both Dumont and Le Page wrote that the 1729 revolt was, to some extent, inspired by revenge for the death of Vieux Poil. For his part, Vieux Poil was said to have instigated the 1723 attacks to avenge the execution of his relative Le Barbu, war chief of the Jenzenaques, or Noyers, village, which Bienville demanded in 1716.

Villeneuve, M. de

A "Ville Neuve" is included on Philibert's list of victims of the Natchez Massacre with the note that he was a Gascon and that his wife and one child were also killed. His house is identified on one of Dumont's maps of Natchez ("Fort Rozalie des Natchez eloigné de la N.lle Orleans de cent lieüeues," SHD, Château de Vincennes, État-Major, 7C 211).

Volvire, Joseph-Philippe, Seigneur de Bois de la Roche de

A lieutenant general at Lorient during the War of the Austrian Succession.

INDEX

367; wrestling of, 366–367. *See also* Calumet; Native American nations; Pottery; *individual nations*

Natural history, 16, 42, 372–392

Navarre (surgeon), 242, 434

Navigation: and piracy, 31; Dumont's knowledge of, 66; and maelstrom, 87; in Cap François, 100; in Biloxi, 125; and entering Mississippi River, 334–335, 374

Newberry Library, 7, 59

New Biloxi, 115, 116n, 139, 141, 144–145, *146*, 196, 200–201. *See also* Biloxi; Old Biloxi

Newfoundland, 74, 80, 88, 97

New Mexico colony, 18

New Orleans: founding of, 21; maps of, 39, 41; gender ratio of, 54–55; description of, 167–169, *169*, 336–337; assembly of militia in, 255; economy of, 374–376

Nouailles (soldier), 285, 287–288, 434

Noyan, Gilles-Augustin Payen de, 269, 434

Old Biloxi, 115, 116n, 117, 120, *121*, 124–125, 139

Orléans, 282

Orléans, Philippe, duc d', 3

Pailloux, Jacques Barbazon de, 172–173, 177, 434

Papin (interpreter), 185, 227, 434

Paris, 40–41, 43, 52–53, 59, 68, 129, 280–283, 292–293

Pascagoula, 39, 199, 202, 204–205

Pascal (pilot), 153

Patronage and patrons, 4, 64, 292–296, 319–320, 329, 406

Pauger, Adrien, 38, 155n, 195, 334, 434

Penhoüet, M., 309

Pénicaut, André, 109n, 228n, 336n, 358n

Penneverte, Sieur de, 315

Pensacola, 21, 104–108, 110–115, *111*, 145; battles at, 26n, 31, 33, 102–115, 399

Penthièvre, Louis Jean Marie de Bourbon, duc de, 320, 326, 435

Périer, Etienne: in "Etablissement de la province de la Louisiane," 8; and favoring of Dumont, 27, 217, 225–226; as governor, 66, 206, 391; as "Solomon of Louisiana," 215, 222; and Chepart, 224, 227; and response to Natchez uprising, 238–239; and massacre of Chaouachas, 250; and attacks on Natchez at Sicily Island, 251–252; replacement of, by Bienville, 252–253, 257; and reception of Simars de Belleisle, 354; improvement of roads by, 377–378; final praises of, 401, 435

Périer de Salvert, Antoine, 251–252, 435

Perinet d'Orval, Sieur, 306

Perrault, Etienne, 308, 435

Perrier (engineer), 40, 93, 108, 435

Peru, 71, 95, 391

Pesron, Bernard, 55

Petit de Livilliers, Charles, 151, 188–191, 435

Petit Soleil, 186, 435

Philibert, Father, 54, 235n

Philip V (king of Spain), 111

Picaresque novel, 24–28

Picart, Bernard, 14–15

Picbrac, Guy du Faur, Seigneur de, 351

Pipes and smoking, 78, 141, 145, 170, 263, 265, 341–342, 360, 363

Pirates and piracy, 31, 75, 103n, 138

Pirogues, 142, 167, 206–207, 221–223, 254, 376–377

Plessis (treasurer), 77, 436

Ploemeur, 305, 310

Pointe Coupée, 152, 192, 207, 223

Pomme village of Natchez, 227n

Pondicherry, 15, 55–56, 291

Pontchartrain, Louis Phélypeaux de, 19

Port-Louis, 33, 40n, 53, 55, 67, 127, 133–134, 282, 291, 294, 305–307, 311–312

Postillon (soldier), 236, 436

Pottery, 12, 37, 260, 350

Poulain, Gabriel, 166–167, 436

Shamans and medicine men, 38, 85–86, 164–165, 345–346

Shipbuilding, 388, 393. *See also* Pirogues

Ship Island, 125, 139, 334

Ships and vessels: *Profond,* 17n, 195–199, 202; *Charente,* 23, 133–134, 138, 285; *Mutine,* 54, 125–126; *Achille,* 55; *Auguste,* 55; *Bourbon,* 55; *Hercule,* 55, 100–102, 107–113, 332; *Paix,* 55; *Victoire,* 73–74, 77; *Astrée,* 74, 77; *Cheval Marin,* 86, 90, 92; *Eléphant,* 86; *Providence,* 86–87; *Marie,* 95, 100–103, 107, 110; *Union,* 95, 100–102, 110; *Mars,* 100–103, 107; *Triton,* 101, 110; *Venus,* 101, 145–146; *Maréchal de Villars,* 104n; *Philippe,* 104n, 110; *Comte de Toulouse,* 104n; *Grand Diable,* 106–108, 113–114; *Neptune,* 111; *Deux Frères,* 125–126; *Portefaix,* 137–138, 144, 201, 399; *Saône,* 137n; *Duc de Noailles,* 145; *Afriquain,* 147n; *Duc de Maine,* 147n; *Bellone,* 197, 202–203; *Gironde,* 203; *Somme,* 275, 277–278, 285; *Atlas,* 285; *Ardent,* 314–315; *Philibert,* 331

Shipwrecks and castaways, 74, 139–141, 200

Silhouette, Etienne de, 6n

Silver and mines, 17, 18, 197–198, 203, 388

Simars de Belleisle, François, 354–355, 439

Sinclair, James, 305–312, 315, 439

Slaves and slavery: Europeans enslaved by native Americans, 67, 236–237, 240, 246–247; native Americans enslaved by Europeans, 67, 119, 148, 183, 252, 260; Europeans enslaved by Europeans, 113–114

—enslaved Africans: trade of, 21, 23–24; first, in Louisiana colony, 23, 147; with Natchez against French, 36, 240, 250; and agriculture, 44, 381, 383; and social structure, 67; at Cap François, 101; at Pascagoula, 199; distribution of, by Company, 206; of Dumont, 224–225,

249, 275–277; conspiracy by, 250; rates for renting out, 374

Smollet, Tobias, 25n

Smuggling. *See* Crime and lawlessness

Soyez, François, 122n

Spanish, 101–108. *See also* Mexico (New Spain)

Storms, 88, 102, 139–140, 163, 192–195, 260, 278, 373

Stuart, Charles Edward, 306

Sulpont, M. de, 328

Superior Council of Louisiana, 66, 171, 180, 197, 215, 249n, 276

Superior Council of Quebec, 79

Swanton, John R., 7n, 187, 359, 366n

Swiss regiments, 199, 266–269, 324

Tar and pitch, 142, 384–385

Tattoos, 348

Terre Blanche concession, 22, 41, 152, 171, 209–210, 212, 217, 218, 232, 236, 242, 335, 416, 423

Tioux village, 211, 218

Tisbé (soldier), 265

Tisserant, Louis, 183, 440

Tobacco. *See* Agriculture; Pipes and smoking

Tombigbee, 259–260, *261,* 273

Tonty, Alphonse de, 167, 440

Tortures and floggings, 83, 243, 324, 352–354, *353*

Traisnel, Louise-Madeleine, marquise de, 282, 406, 440

Treaty of Aix-la-Chapelle, 12

Treaty of Utrecht, 21

Trees: bald cypress, 123, 385–386; of Arkansas, 156; as landmarks on Mississippi River, 334; pine, 384; olive, 385; oak, 385, palmetto, 386; wax myrtle or bayberry, 386–387; other species, 388–389

Trois-Rivières, 79

Tunica nation, 208, 243

Tunicas, Chef des. *See* Cahura-Joligo

Twain, Mark (Samuel Clemens), 5